Contemporary
Social Work

Donald Brieland
University of Illinois

Lela B. Costin
University of Illinois

Charles R. Atherton
University of Alabama

And Contributors

Contemporary Social Work:

An Introduction to Social Work and Social Welfare

McGraw-Hill Book Company
New York St. Louis San Francisco Auckland Düsseldorf
Johannesburg Kuala Lumpur London Mexico Montreal New Delhi
Panama Paris São Paulo Singapore Sydney Tokyo Toronto

Acknowledgments

The following publishers have given special permission to reprint selections or extensive quotation: The American Association for the Advancement of Science; The Brookings Institution; Columbia University Press; Council on Social Work Education; Curtis Books; Farrar, Strauss & Giroux; The Family Service Association of America; The Free Press; Grove Press; Holt, Rinehart and Winston, Inc.; Houghton Mifflin Company; Jossey-Bass, Inc.; National Association of Social Workers; Pocket Books, Inc.; Time-Life Books; The University of North Carolina Press; and John Wiley & Sons, Inc.

Library of Congress Cataloging in Publication Data

Brieland, Donald, date
  Contemporary social work.

  Bibliography: p.
  1. Social service—United States—Addresses, essays, lectures. I. Costin, Lela B., joint author.
II. Atherton, Charles R., joint author. III. Title.
HV91.B69   362'.973   74-13505
ISBN 0-07-007765-7

Contemporary Social Work:
An Introduction to Social Work
and Social Welfare

34567890KPKP798765

This book was set in Optima by Black Dot, Inc.
The editors were Lyle Linder, Janis M. Yates, and John M. Morriss;
the cover design and part opening drawings were done by Anne Canevari Green;
the production supervisor was Judi Frey.
The technical drawings were done by Vantage Art, Inc.
Kingsport Press, Inc., was printer and binder.

Contents

List of contributors

During the writing of this book the authors were members of the faculty of the Jane Addams School of Social Work at the University of Illinois, Urbana-Champaign.

Donald Brieland is a former director of the Illinois Department of Children and Family Services. His interests include public administration, family law, and social work education.

Lela B. Costin is a specialist in school social work and child welfare. She developed a special project concerned with the development of school social workers to emphasize systems change.

Charles R. Atherton recently joined the faculty of the School of Social Work of the University of Alabama. He teaches courses in research and program evaluation.

Richard J. Anderson is a former administrator in special education. He now teaches courses in social work at the University of Georgia.

Nancy Weinberg Asher specializes in vocational rehabilitation and is a member of an interdisciplinary team to provide education for day care workers.

Estie Bomzer holds a graduate degree in counseling and served as adviser to students in the Bachelor of Social Work (B.S.W.) program.

Ruppert Downing is director of a university community outreach project and teaches courses on minorities.

Gerald L. Euster is now at the University of South Carolina. He is especially interested in group work in hospital settings and in research on aging.

Marilyn Flynn is involved in teaching and research on social insurance and the economics of income maintenance.

Ketayun H. Gould teaches courses and conducts research on population and sexuality.

Mark P. Hale is Director of the School of Social Work. He has special interests in international social welfare and social work education.

Ellen Handler teaches courses in social policy and corrections and conducts research on correctional programs.

Charles H. Henderson teaches courses in community work and minorities, is Associate Director, Dean of Students, and a member of the Urbana Human Relations Commission.

Frank Itzin teaches social treatment and serves as director of field instruction. He is also concerned with social welfare in England.

Bok-Lim Kim teaches social treatment and conducts research and seminars on Asian-American problems.

Arnold Panitch is a specialist in community work and continuing education. He is now a member of the faculty at Boise State University, Idaho.

Gary Shaffer developed the field instruction program for the B.S.W. program curriculum and is especially interested in manpower.

Merlin Taber is Associate Director of the Jane Addams School. His research includes projects on aging, mental health, and public policy.

Ione Dugger Vargus was director of the pupil personnel project and served as consultant to community projects for minorities. She is now Associate Dean at Temple University.

Anthony J. Vattano teaches social treatment and specializes in mental health, family therapy, and special uses of groups.

Shirley H. Wattenberg teaches social treatment and an interdisciplinary course on health delivery and is especially interested in social work in the health professions.

About this book

Contemporary Social Work provides a comprehensive introduction to the field. Major topics include the context society provides, the way agencies are financed and operated, the major problem areas that make social work necessary, the methods of social work, the people it serves, and its workforce and educational systems.

The book is written by twenty specialists expressly for social work students and edited to a common style for continuity and coherence. Each author conducted the class sessions in which his material was used for four semesters preceding publication. Over four hundred undergraduates used two preliminary editions and supplied their comments and suggestions on standard forms as well as in class. We gratefully acknowledge the many ideas contributed.

Individual chapters were also used in a variety of graduate courses. Doctoral candidates requested the book as a basis for review for comprehensive examinations and agencies used portions of it for staff development and volunteer training.

Contemporary Social Work has a practice focus, a problem focus, and a management focus. It provides comprehensive content for a semester course meeting three or four hours per week. With additional assignments and use of the suggested projects it serves well for a full year. For a one-quarter course, topics can be used selectively. Its coverage encourages module course organization, but provides much more material of interest to the student than would a customized selection of chapters.

The sections as presented establish an immediate linkage with information from other social science courses. Some instructors, however, prefer to begin with the methods of social work and others with social work careers. Faculty members will find the material easy to use regardless of the topical order they choose to follow.

The instructor's manual is also comprehensive. It summarizes the class testing experience on each topic and provides extensive suggestions for each chapter for the teacher who is new to social work education.

We acknowledge the fine cooperation of our colleagues who contributed chapters; the McGraw-Hill Book Company, in encouraging the class testing; Muriel LaRue, who used the second test edition at Kennedy-King College in Chicago; the secretarial staff at Jane Addams School of Social Work, which produced various teaching materials; and Judy Birch, who typed the final manuscript and provided some of the cartoons. We recognize with gratitude the continuing interest and support of Mark P. Hale, Director of the Jane Addams School of Social Work, and the help and patience of our families in this complex project.

Donald Brieland
Lela B. Costin
Charles R. Atherton

Contemporary
Social Work

Part One

Social Services and Social Welfare Organizations

Helping people with serious problems and improving social conditions that contribute to them are the business of social work. The problems social workers are expected to deal with have their roots in society and in people's responses to it. Both society and social welfare organizations contribute to effective service. What opportunities must society provide to its citizens? What major social welfare organizations and programs are available and how do they operate?

Since the functioning of society determines the type and volume of demand placed on social welfare organizations, this book begins with societal issues that are familiar, but in this context they will be analyzed for their impact on social welfare.

To the person needing help who may have no knowledge of resources and little confidence to seek them out, social services may be obscured by jargon and delays, rules and red tape. The first step in obtaining social work help is to understand the maze.

Specifically, this section deals with:

Opportunities for life and health, adequate housing and a secure environment, and a fair deal for consumers

A close look at social service programs and comparisons with provisions in other countries

What problems of society are of special interest to you?
What organizations can deal effectively with them?

Chapter 1

Social Work
and Society

What are the social worker's dual roles?
What opportunities in society affect social work?
Why do political and economic issues affect housing?
How does transportation enlarge the lifespace?
Do governmental jurisdictions create confusion?

Social workers are expected to help people experience increased satisfaction and function more adequately. At the same time the social worker has a strong interest in improving society and social institutions. Social workers have had considerable success in their helping efforts, but unlike Jane Addams and other pioneers in social action, they have come to spend most of their time *treating* people—helping individuals and families to cope with society.

Now social workers give increasing attention to social institutions as targets for change. Community work seeks to improve the well-being of neighborhoods, and social workers serving individuals have become advocates as well as helpers, seeking new services, new policies, and new legislation.

Social work in the schools illustrates the dual emphasis on personal problem solving and social change and will be the topic of a later chapter in this book. Traditionally the school social worker's time was spent with individual children to help them with learning and behavior problems. It gradually became evident that children with similar problems could often be helped efficiently in group sessions. However, social workers took little responsibility for helping to change a school system.

Now the leaders in school social work are analyzing curricula and recommending changes. They are helping to modify attendance policies and school rules. They act as advocates for groups of students and for individuals. They develop flexible work-study plans for high school students and review placement policies for special classes to be sure that children are not mislabeled mentally retarded. Social workers are also in the forefront in more controversial and costly changes, including open classrooms and free alternative schools to supplement traditional settings. Schools have rediscovered the need for community support and the value of the community as an educational resource. Such efforts have much greater permanence than a role that involves only working with the child directly.

In addition to education, what other institutions and systems provide opportunities for our citizens and dominate the societal context of social work? The framework for our discussion will be the opportunities that society must offer for life and health, employment and financial self-sufficiency, effective consumership, transportation and mobility, and governmental responsiveness to special needs. All are strongly influenced by economics and politics.

We must avoid the temptation to limit our concerns to urban society. The social problems of large numbers of people in limited space are highly visible, and their frustrations can be dramatically expressed, but at the same time smaller cities and rural areas have similar limitations of opportunities and social problems—problems that often lead people to move to a large city to try to improve their situation.

OPPORTUNITIES FOR LIFE AND HEALTH

Environmental quality related to life and health is particularly relevant to two areas—maternal and infant mortality and opportunities for older people in our society. Both involve social work intervention. The questions raised by Daniel Schorr[1] in *Don't Get Sick in America* still trouble our citizens:

> . . . why the world's wealthiest nation is far from being the healthiest; why the cost keeps zooming more than twice as fast as other consumer costs, taking a bigger and bigger bite out of our Gross National Product (from 4.5 to 6.8 percent in twenty years); why, for more than $63 billion a year, the American public is not getting anything like adequate health care; and why in America a baby's chance for surviving its first month is worse than in fourteen other countries, its mother's chance of surviving delivery worse than in seventeen other countries.

Maternal and Child Health

Maternal mortality, miscarriages, stillbirths, and deaths in early infancy are far too common. Regardless of one's view on population control, family planning, and abortion, crises attendant to birth have no defenders. These problems involve not only medical management techniques during pregnancy and childbirth but antecedent health and nutritional status. The correlation of maternal and child health problems with poverty is well known.

One of the major roles for social workers has been facilitating services for pregnant women—especially younger unmarried girls, a group characterized by high risk. Family income levels to assure adequate living standards before and during pregnancy and medical care throughout pregnancy are required. Educational programs on human reproduction are essential to reduce the number of unwanted pregnancies and to assure that women take the initiative to seek medical care soon after they become pregnant.

Needs of the Aged

For the aged, economic and psychological status needs are interwoven with needs for medical services. A sense of worth is closely related to a sense of health and well-being. It has been easier to add years to life than life to the years. It is tragic when older people deny themselves medical care because of cost or lack of motivation. It is more tragic when relatively healthy older people get the message from society that they really have nothing to live for.

Access and Cost

Social workers have had two special concerns about health services—getting the patient to the care and finding the means to meet the cost. Urban and rural areas have parallel problems concerning accessibility of service. When doctors leave the ghettoes, family care is given through hospital emergency rooms—the least efficient and most expensive way to do it. In the country, people may have to drive fifty miles to a doctor who will not live in a small town—especially if it has no hospital.

High costs and lack of an adequate insurance system deter medical care for rural and city people alike and discourage both the poor and the middle-class groups from seeking the care they need. We will return to the issues of health care in Chapter 7 and population and family planning in Chapter 8.

EMPLOYMENT AND SELF-SUFFICIENCY

Employment is a major element in creating opportunities in a society. Not only is an income necessary to meet basic needs, but work is fundamental to identity. People usually identify themselves first by what they do. Social workers are very much involved with the labor market. When there is a demand for labor, they can help people get jobs; when the demand is lacking, even the highly motivated applicant may be unsuccessful.

Unemployment Rates

As Figure 1-1 indicates, the unemployment rate based on those working and those seeking work fluctuates from time to time but averages about 5 percent. What proportion of the 5 percent would have to find jobs for us to have full employment is difficult to determine. There will always be some people in the process of moving from job to job and others who are unemployable. Unexpected events like the energy crisis may have a sudden depressing effect on

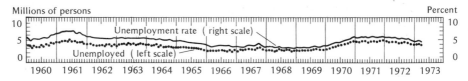

Figure 1-1   Rate of unemployment 1960–1973. *(Source: Chart prepared by U.S. Bureau of the Census. Data from U.S. Bureau of Labor Statistics.)*[2]

employment. Paradoxically, a substantial improvement in the labor market often results in a temporary increase in unemployment, because more people begin to seek work at that time.

For particular groups the 5 percent figure can be multiplied several times. Urban adolescents from minority groups and female heads of households who have no previous work experience are two examples. Skilled workers also face critical employment needs when a large industry has major contracts canceled and its plants close. Increasing relocation of industries from the center city to the suburbs works to the disadvantage of employees who cannot move with the industry, and it may involve total loss of employee pension benefits.

Economic conditions which produce more jobs are the primary remedy for unemployment. As the result of labor shortages, at least until the energy crisis, European industries were willing to hire more people with special employment problems—the young and inexperienced, the handicapped, and those who require retraining because of technological advancement. These are the groups of primary interest to social workers.

Work as the Answer to Welfare

A strong emphasis on work as a solution to social welfare problems has been part of our heritage. Able-bodied people who receive "relief" have always been suspect. Social workers tend to feel that there is often too much coercion for people to go to work, but at least to enforce a work policy the jobs have to be available. If people train for a certain role and then cannot find a job, they are often worse off than they were before.

Unless we develop more jobs in the private sector, full employment will be achieved only by making the government the employer of last resort. This is a question of primary interest to social workers who work with the poor. Can we afford such a policy? Can we not afford it?

Job Satisfaction   The social worker is also interested in job satisfaction. To get accurate data on this question requires careful research. Strauss[3] has observed that statements of job satisfaction cannot always be taken at face value. When a worker says that he's got a pretty good job and the interviewer asks what makes it a "good" job, the employee may reply, "Don't get me wrong. I didn't say it is a good job. It's an OK job—about as good a job as a guy like me might expect. The foreman leaves me alone and it pays well. But I would never call it a good job. It doesn't amount to much, but it's not bad."

Social workers also soon find that unlike people in the professions, many others never expect much satisfaction from their jobs. We also talk about the importance of advancement, but for many people the only realistic advancement is more pay for the same kind of work.

EFFICIENT CONSUMERSHIP

After health and work we need to look at the business community and the practices that affect the way people spend their incomes. How can society help the citizen to buy wisely? Is food clean and wholesome, or is it contaminated? Are manufactured products hazardous to health? Can a child strangle himself because the slats in a crib are placed too far apart? Seven slats are cheaper than eight.

Are products advertised honestly, or are claims exaggerated? Are advertised products actually available, or are the ads a come-on for higher-priced items? Are products packaged and priced without deception? Do repair shops do work that is not necessary? Do they charge for work that is not done or overcharge for parts?

What credit terms are offered? Is the interest rate stated clearly? Is a sales contract available in the customer's own language? In case of default what are the conditions of repossession?

Consumer Protection

Agencies at the federal, state, and local levels try to protect the consumer. The Federal Food and Drug Administration is responsible for standards for food and medicine, and advertising claims are the concern of the Federal Trade Commission. Recent statutes cover such subjects as toy safety, flammability of fabrics, and truth in packaging and lending. Many states have consumer fraud programs sponsored by the Office of the Attorney General. Better Business Bureaus supported by the businesses in local communities collect and process complaints from consumers.

The Poor as Consumers The poor are ideal candidates for consumer problems. They have limited freedom to shop and compare and often have no credit rating to obtain low-cost bank loans. Conditional sales contracts are their only alternative. They may have to buy used appliances that wear out before payments are completed. Articles partially paid for may be stolen. The poor cannot buy food in quantity or take advantage of sales because of lack of money, transportation, or storage space.

Caplovitz discusses a special kind of merchandising directed toward the poor:[4]

> Characteristic of the comparatively traditional and personal form of the low-income economy is the important role played in it by the door-to-door credit salesman, the customer peddler. The study of merchants found that these peddlers are not necessarily competitors of the store-owners. Almost all merchants make use of peddlers in the great competition for customers. The merchants tend to regard peddlers as necessary evils who add greatly to the final cost of purchases. But they need them because in their view, customers are too ignorant, frightened, or lazy to come to the store themselves. Thus, the merchants' apparent contempt for the peddler does not bar them from employing outdoor salesmen (or "canvassers," as they

describe the peddlers who work for one store or another). Even the merchants who are themselves reluctant to hire canvassers find they must do so in order to meet the competition. The peddler's main function for the merchant then is getting the customer to the store and, if he will not come, getting the store to the customer. But this is not his only function.

Much more than the storekeeper, the peddler operates on the basis of a personal relationship with the customer. By going to the customer's home, he gets to know the entire family; he sees the condition of the home, and he comes to know the family's habits and wants. From this vantage point he is better able than the merchant to evaluate the customer as a credit risk. Since many of the merchant's potential customers lack the standard credentials of credit, such as having a permanent job, the merchant needs some other basis for discriminating between good and bad risks. If the peddler, who has come to know the family, is ready to vouch for the customer, the merchant will be ready to make the transaction. In short, the peddler acts as a fiduciary agent, a Dun and Bradstreet for the poor, telling the merchant which family is likely to meet its obligations and which is not.

How the Social Worker Helps Consumers

The social worker is often asked to help families rebudget to pay their debts and to meet their basic daily living expenses. He or she often has to act as advocate in disputes with dealers or small-loan companies and as the conduit to legal aid services when a court suit becomes necessary. The social worker must have the help of more adequate consumer legislation and of business groups that will police their members to eliminate practices that make the poor pay more.

SOUND HOUSING IN A SAFE NEIGHBORHOOD

Living in a neighborhood implies a series of conditions that may expand opportunities or constrict them. Aaron illustrates the pervasive effect of location on the resident:[5]

> When a homeowner or renter chooses a house or apartment, he purchases not only housing services, but also a wide range of goods and services—public schools, stores, parks, public transportation, neighbors, and other amenities. Though they cost him nothing beyond the price of housing and attendant property taxes, his satisfaction—indeed his welfare—depends on these conditions as much as on his housing. He does not express in the marketplace his demand for housing but for the entire package. Statistics on housing expenditures really measure the value placed by residents on housing and residential services.
>
> The residents of poor neighborhoods are victims of high prices, inferior merchandise, high interest rates, and aggressive and deceptive sales practices. They pay for the cost of doing business where pilferage and default risks are above average. Costs are averaged over all customers so that reliable households suffer from living where high cost customers are particularly numerous. Such extra costs of living are among costs of residential services that affect the price people will pay for housing services. Another social cost that varies by neighborhood is the probability of crime. The major market response the individual can make to differences in crime rates is to alter the price he is willing to pay for housing.

Poverty Means Fewer Options   One of the major characteristics of poverty is that it restricts options. The poor are generally effectively prevented from owning their own homes. The choice of paying more to get into a better neighborhood as identified by Aaron is not realistic for the poor.

Common Housing Problems

We are all familiar with the problems of older structures—poor sanitation, faulty wiring, rats, inadequate provisions for garbage, and lead paint that threatens children's lives. Housing problems are perceived as urban, but we find the same conditions in rural slums. They are more scattered and therefore less obvious. Varying definitions of substandard housing make it difficult to determine our progress on housing programs. For purposes of classification the type of plumbing has been more important than the general condition of the house.

The economics of slum ownership cannot be ignored. Converting large units to smaller ones to get more rent, spending as little as possible for maintenance and repairs, and finally abandoning the building when the property reaches an advanced stage of disrepair are common details in a familiar story. When the property is abandoned, residents may try to stay there without heat or light until fire or thieves turn them into the street.

Violations of housing regulations often involve long legal battles followed by token fines. Inspectors may accept pay-offs. Tenants cannot complain too much or they will face eviction. The next place may be even worse. It is little wonder that dramatic presentations about poverty often begin with housing conditions.

A Mother Speaks from Experience

During the early years of raising my family I lived with my mother, but it was too crowded and I finally had to find a place of my own. The only place I could find was a four room apartment across the street. With ten children we were cramped, but that was not the worst problem. The water pipes were always breaking, and this meant no water, and leaks. The floor round the commode was rotted from the water, it leaked so often. One time I had just gotten up when the ceiling plaster fell down all over the bed. Another time the mantelpiece fell over into the front room, all in one piece. If my baby had been there it most likely would have killed her. That is when I began to feel that I just had to move. I had asked the rent lady to fix these things, all along. She always said she would, if I gave her the rent, but she never did.

Finally, I told her I was not going to pay the rent any more. She threatened to call the High Constable. So, we both went down to the agency [Social Service Bureau] to complain about each other. My social worker talked to the landlady first, then to me. My social worker said I should pay the rent, but she would try to find a better place for me and my family. She must have called the health department because an inspector came out and condemned the house. This meant I had to move in 30 days.

I got a lot of help looking for a place, both from my social worker and from the Neighborhood Center operated by STOP [OEO]. But people just do not like to rent to families with a lot of kids. Even if the houses are big—6 or 7 rooms—they don't want large families.

Finally, I found the house I'm in now. It's a whole house. I told the landlord that I had only six children and he rented it to me.

He wanted two months' rent in advance, and a security deposit—$140 all together. That was the biggest problem. I borrowed $100 from my mother, and the agency gave me the rest. I paid them back out of my next check.

I moved last December and have not had too many problems since then. One or two things have gone wrong, but the landlord fixed them. My biggest problems now are utilities and furniture. But, at least I have a house, and as long as I pay my rent I guess I won't have any problems now. If I do, my social worker is ready to help me with them.

I have been asked—what would those on welfare like to see done to help them with housing problems? The main ones are:

1   For the city to enforce the minimum code for good housing.

2   Require that landlords keep houses fixed up—the repairs.

3   Owners should inspect their property more often than once a year, and should inspect inside as well as outside.

4   The welfare department should help with the security deposit in emergencies and allow us over the maximum for rent and utilities.

All of these things would help us in having a decent place to live and in which to raise our children.

A Right to a Decent Home.[6]

Public Housing: A Disappointing Solution

Public housing was supposed to be the ideal answer for urban society. Slums could be replaced by new dwelling units that would be clean and safe. With public funding, housing could be made available at low cost. First, massive slum clearance was tried, then spot renewal, in which sound structures were not replaced. Unfortunately the solutions have not been simple or successful. There has not been enough public housing, and it has not been cheap to build. In order to safeguard the property, management philosophies in successful projects have been conservative. No one wants people destroying property. Income ceilings forced people to move when they began to improve their earning power. Also public housing has been largely racially segregated, in fact if not by policy. With these constraints, as one would predict, public housing has worked better for the aged than for families with children.

High-rise projects in the largest cities have developed large concentrations of multiproblem families characterized by fear and isolation resulting from high rates of crime and vandalism. Some of these projects that promised potential progress have been virtually deserted and are being torn down.

The Federal Housing Authority has served middle-class home buyers, and newer programs for subsidies to rent or purchase dwelling units have been very limited.

Roles of Social Workers in Housing

Social workers have helped organize tenant unions. They have sometimes been able to get the help of legal aid to enforce fair housing laws. They have assisted in resettlement of residents while new housing was being built, but the original residents seldom moved back. They couldn't afford to. In some public housing projects, social workers offer a range of services including job counseling and day care, but as policy makers in housing they have had little involvement.

Urban Crime

Crime has been mentioned already as a special problem. While the stress has been on crime in the streets, stealing and other crimes against property are much more frequent. Strangers avoid the slums because of fear of violence, but most crimes are perpetrated by residents against residents. As a result urban life involves increasing uneasiness. Calls for more street lighting and added police protection are heard more clearly. Better locks and other individual security measures require the means to meet the added expense and the confidence that they will be effective.

Effect on Home Visits   In some cities possible physical danger has affected the practice of social work. Whereas the standard procedure used to involve regular home visits and first-hand consideration of the environment, workers no longer visit clients in some neighborhoods because of crime and harassment. Thus social services are provided in the worker's office, where he may remain more detached and remote. The current energy crisis serves to restrict home visits even more.

TRANSPORTATION AND MOBILITY

People have become increasingly mobile. Management personnel expect frequent transfers in order to advance. Members of the armed forces move after each tour of duty. Most people move several times for better jobs or better living conditions. Their quest often takes them across the country. Such states as California, Arizona, and Florida have been especially popular.

Mobility and the Social Services

Mobility has resulted in strong pressures on the social services. To control costs, states tried to increase legal residency requirements for eligibility. Social workers opposed this policy because it created many hardships. Residence requirements were outlawed in 1969 for assistance programs that received federal support.[7] As a result, the federal government is being urged to bear the full cost of financial assistance.

Private agencies may also operate under geographical limitations. United Fund contributions usually have to be spent for people who are in the area where the monies are raised. If the agency is to help "outsiders," it must do so with other funds.

Only one social agency has problems associated with travel as its specialized concern. The Travelers' Aid Society provides a range of short-term emergency services to newcomers and to those who are stranded before they reach their destinations. It receives the help of such agencies as the Salvation Army to meet needs for food and lodging.

Mobility is a special problem for migrant farm and food-processing workers.

This group includes some of the most deprived members of our society. Their transiency gives them little opportunity to exercise their claim to services.

Transportation Increases Opportunities

Efficient transportation enlarges a person's lifespace. The family car has become the symbol of mobility and prestige. Boulding considers the attachment to the automobile and its relation to the energy crisis:[8]

> The automobile, especially, is remarkably addictive. I have described it as a suit of armor with 200 horses inside, big enough to make love in. It is not surprising that it is popular. It turns its driver into a knight with the mobility of the aristocrat and perhaps some of his other vices. The pedestrian and the person who rides public transportation are, by comparison, peasants looking up with almost inevitable envy at the knights riding by in their mechanical steeds. Once having tasted the delights of a society in which almost everyone can be a knight, it is hard to go back to being peasants. I suspect, therefore, that there will be very strong technological pressures to preserve the automobile in some form, even if we have to go to nuclear fusion for the ultimate source of power and to liquid hydrogen for the gasoline substitute. The alternative would seem to be a society of contented peasants, each cultivating his own little garden and riding to work on the bus, or even on an electric streetcar. Somehow this outcome seems less plausible than a desperate attempt to find new sources of energy to sustain our knightly mobility.

Many people who have poor housing make up for it with their car. In crowded cities, however, the family car is too expensive and inefficient for use to get to work. Also, many young people can't afford a car, and many old people have vision and hearing problems so they cannot drive. Traffic conditions make even public buses less than ideal in our large cities. Unrestricted routes above and below the traffic are needed for efficiency. Metropolitan transit systems are affected by rising costs and inadequate subsidies, resulting in higher fares. Fare increases mean fewer riders, and fares go still higher. Fortunately some cities now offer very low fares to older people for transportation in non–rush hours.

New mass transit systems are very costly and have been characterized by long construction delays in San Francisco and Washington, D.C. The Los Angeles system is still in the planning stage.

The relocation of plants and offices to the suburbs and the outskirts of our cities creates new needs. Rush-hour schedules are still directed toward the central city. People who do not want to move or cannot do so may be forced to seek a new job downtown, where opportunities are decreasing.

Transportation and the Social Services

Local transportation is also important to the delivery of social services. Services such as day care must be accessible to make it possible for a mother to work. Ideally, decentralized neighborhood offices are established for basic services, but use of more specialized resources still requires considerable travel. In many cities, the Red Cross provides a motor pool to offer transportation for some types of services.

Efficient mass transit services are important for employment and for educational and leisure-time programs, and especially for those served by social agencies.

RESPONSIVE GOVERNMENTAL STRUCTURES

Governmental agencies usually play the key roles in providing human services. They are responsible for voter registration, land use and housing codes, police and fire protection, schools, parks, libraries, water supply, street lighting, garbage and sewage disposal, air and water pollution control, mosquito abatement, public health and control of contagious diseases, operation of passenger trains and airports, jails and prisons, ambulance service, and dozens of other services. On the other hand, some services that are publicly operated in other countries are privately managed here—telephone and electrical service, and more recently the mails.

Political Structures: Overlap and Confusion

With federal, state, county, city, and district, borough, or township programs, plus dozens of special agencies such as regional planning bodies, school, sewage, and fire districts that cross political boundaries, even the intelligent long-term resident often does not know where to go for help. In New York City, for example, many agencies are responsible for various problems related to housing. Problems with water involve at least five different agencies, according to Purcell and Specht.[9] If there is no water, you are to call the Health Department. If the supply is inadequate, the call goes to the Department of Water Supply. Small leaks are to be reported to the Buildings Department, but large leaks to the Department of Water Supply. "No hot water" is the responsibility of the Buildings Department. If water overflows from an apartment above, call the Police Department; but water coming up through a sewer inlet is a problem for the Sanitation Department. Any tenant who isn't confused simply doesn't understand the situation.

Information and Referral Services   Short of governmental reorganization, several means are used to reduce confusion. Some cities have a municipal information service to direct people to the appropriate service. A few have ombudsmen who will also act as advocates to represent citizens to further their requests or complaints. Antipoverty programs developed many neighborhood information services and also provided community agents to represent residents of a neighborhood. Welfare Councils often sponsor community referral services. Most services are available during business hours and do not provide around-the-clock coverage. With all these sources of information, however, it is still necessary for social workers in direct service roles to learn the maze of agencies and services to help guide people through it.

Consolidation   A more fundamental approach to overlapping political bodies and boards is the development of metropolitan government, in which cities and suburbs are combined into a single governmental unit. Both Dade County (Miami), Florida, and Toronto have moved in this direction.

Attitudes of Staff Finally, responsiveness depends upon the attitudes and motivations of staff members and the bureaucratic rules under which they operate. Even when people find the right agency, employees may express little interest in their complaints or requests. Some agencies make people register only at certain times and then sit and wait for hours until they can be seen. With the demands for accountability the multiple forms required by social agencies make them seem quite unresponsive. An application for service or registering a complaint may take too much time to make it worthwhile.

THE POWER TO DECIDE

Most citizens—and especially the poor—have regarded themselves as the passive recipients of services from society that other people feel they should have. Maximum feasible participation in community decision making and governance is encouraged to overcome this passivity, but too often it results in no transfer of power. Community advisory boards function as shadow cabinets that can only recommend changes. Power comes from being able to make binding decisions, control financial resources, and carry direct responsibility for operating community programs.

Example of "Power to the People"

Bromley Heath is one of the older housing projects in Boston with accommodations for 5,000 people. It experienced all the familiar problems—dilapidation, decay, and crime. Demolition was seriously considered. Late in 1972, the management of the project was turned over to the residents. Jobs in the project became available, and morale improved. New programs for education and recreation were organized by the tenants. Vacant apartments were rehabilitated, and new residents came in. Tenants spent many hours in volunteer work in maintenance and beautification. Participation in governance is gradually growing, although long-term residents have to be convinced that their wishes really can affect policies.

NEED FOR A SOCIAL WELFARE SYSTEM

Almost everyone has a stake in social welfare. Four million college students have low-interest government loans. Other young men and women get educational benefits because of military service. Over 5 million war veterans receive hospital care and pension benefits. Eight million blue-collar, white-collar, and professional workers collect benefits because they are out of work. Thirty million people receive social security checks, and virtually all who are employed pay social security taxes. Thirty-three million people get care through Medicare or Medicaid. About 25 million children eat a low-cost or free school lunch, and 13 million heads of families use food stamps. Unless you are unique, you have been a recipient of some form of social welfare service.

Who Uses Social Work

Although most people participate in the social welfare system at some point, they don't ordinarily see a social worker. One can grow up eating federally supported school lunches, attend a publicly or privately supported college, receive unemployment benefits, be compensated for on-the-job accidents, and retire to receive the benefits of social security and Medicare without ever consulting a social worker.

For many people who are unable to cope with crucial problems, social work is needed. The child who requires protection because of parental neglect, the adult with no work skills or no money, the delinquent group who sees crimes as the alternative to boredom, the sick, the mentally ill, the elderly with little meaning in their lives, the powerless neighborhood—all are central concerns of social work.

Informal Charity Is Not Enough

Many people would like to see their fellow citizens get the help they need, but informally. If Jack Brown needs money, his parents send him a check and advise him to be more careful with his cash in the future—he gets help. When Dick Jones has a run of hard luck, the local druggist who forgets about his medicine bill is helping informally. Civic club members volunteer their time to work with groups of "underprivileged" kids. Tom Smith, a lawyer, gives time to a neighborhood council to negotiate grievances with City Hall. The informal social service network involves family, relatives, friends, and others who offer assistance when they can.

Personal ties are important for informal service. In a highly mobile and urban society such personalized bonds are looser and less dependable. Also, the group that is enthusiastic about working with delinquents may turn next year to recycling glass and paper. Professional people cannot donate enough time consistently to community self-help organizations. Ongoing basic services cannot be wholly entrusted to the spontaneous goodwill of well-intentioned busy people. The informal helper can only do so much, since he or she has a living to make and other duties to perform. Needs are so great that adequate, effective volunteer effort is simply not available. Nor can all services be provided through private contributions, because in hard times contributions shrink just when they are most needed. The informal social welfare process is also obscure and inaccessible. Although numerous informal social services exist, their total impact remains small, fragmented, and highly variable.

The Formal Social Welfare Network   Social work is found in organizations with a specific charge from the community for a designated function. Community schools are mandated to educate children; the Lions Club is not, although it may choose to participate. Public assistance programs must provide support in some form for the poor; friends of the impoverished family need not. Eligibility requirements for services or assistance are spelled out by law or regulations subject to community review.

The demands on social agencies run the range of human problems. People need money, jobs, better skills as parents, emotional support, group services, and neighborhood and community action to solve common problems. Sometimes, people need simple advice; more often it is social or psychological treatment. Sometimes they need help to organize to achieve group and community goals.

People may seek services from the formal network on their own initiative or may be referred by someone else. Patients, probationers, or truants may be required by some public authority to deal with the social worker.

The formal network in which social work is offered is complex and often frustrating, but is the major source of help because it has the financial capability. Over the whole country, the formal social welfare network recruits and employs a quarter of a million people in social work tasks. Our next topic concerns public agencies—the largest components in the formal network.

Donald Brieland
Charles R. Atherton

KEY TERMS

advocate
gross national product
unemployment rate
employer of last resort

conditional sales contracts
substandard housing
ombudsman

FOR DISCUSSION

1 What opportunities must society provide?
2 Why have social workers had little effect on public policies?
3 Why are schools particularly important to an adequate society? Why should school social workers be concerned with system change?
4 Why have other countries a better record for infant and maternal mortality?
5 How do you think value systems of social workers and businessmen differ?
6 What are the objections to the government as employer of last resort?
7 Can creating new towns solve environmental problems?
8 Identify the needs of migrant workers. Should they settle permanently?
9 Why do street crimes get more attention than crimes against property? How do high crime rates affect residents' behavior?
10 Can housing-related services come from one united city department?
11 Must maximum feasible participation include the power to make and enforce decisions?

PROJECTS

1 Bring in examples designed to provide consumer education. Include such magazines as *Consumer Reports, Consumers' Digest,* and *Money.* Obtain other materials from the local public welfare office, banks, and supermarkets. Analyze the types of problems considered and the primary audience for whom the materials are designed.
2 Visit the local housing authority. Find out what governmental counseling and financial services are available to aid people in purchasing or renting housing. Make a chart of the programs and their eligibility requirements.
3 Get a map of your metropolitan area showing public transportation provisions. Locate the offices of the major social services. Report on their accessibility. What improvements would you suggest?
4 Choose several practical environmental problems, such as inadequate heat or possible danger of lead poisoning. Play the role of a tenant. Use the telephone to seek information from governmental agencies. Record the responses and evaluate the interest and adequacy of service provided.

5 Choose a major issue of public social welfare policy before your state legislature. Find out what efforts social work groups are making to influence opinions. Include major public agencies, the National Association of Social Workers, the state welfare association, the local welfare council, and other similar organizations. Summarize your findings.

FOR FURTHER STUDY

John E. Bebout and Harry C. Bradmeier, "American Cities as Social Systems," *Journal of the American Institute of Planners*, vol. 29, 1963, pp. 64–76.

Ramsey Clark, *Crime in America*, Simon and Schuster, New York, 1970.

Donald E. Gatch, "Malnutrition and Federal Food Service Programs," *Hunger in South Carolina*, in Paul E. Weinberger, *Perspectives on Social Welfare*, Macmillan, New York, 1974, pp. 967–971.

Wilfred Owen, *The Metropolitan Transportation Problem*, Brookings, Washington, D.C., 1966.

David M. Smith, *The Geography of Social Well-Being in the United States*, McGraw-Hill, New York, 1973.

The Commerce Clearinghouse of Chicago offers subscription services that provide current information on consumerism and on consumer product safety.

Chapter 2

Public Social Services

Why are public agencies the mainstays of social welfare?
Why do fifty states have fifty patterns of service?
What is the role of the federal government?
How are public agencies organized?
Why do some groups get special preference?

Some people visualize public agencies as composed of employees tied to their chairs by red tape. This view, however, obscures the scope and power of public programs. These programs carry the major responsibility for social welfare, produce the most significant volume of services, and involve the greatest accountability. Public agencies employ large numbers of people with varying levels of education and types of skills. The federal government alone spends over $100 billion each year for social welfare.[1]

A study of public agencies will also give insight into an important segment of American values and political processes. Adequacy, accessibility, and cost of services have become major themes. The public agency is the target for pressure from many quarters including taxpayers' groups, the National Association of Social Workers, and recipients of financial services who formed the National Welfare Rights Organization.

Because of the uneven distribution of private services, in many parts of the country public agencies constitute the only resources for special needs. Both the quantity and quality of public services vary, but they have clear legal responsibility to provide programs. Taxpayers have come to demand services, and now they often back up demands with legal action. Parents of the mentally retarded are but one group that has scored impressive successes in its campaigns for more and better services that emphasize the right to both education and treatment.

PUBLIC AGENCIES AS BUREAUCRACIES

Elaborate structures are characteristic of our society. A high degree of specialization is found in business, industry, and government. Bureaucracies are not automatically bad. They try to keep differentiated functions efficient and productive.

We usually think of governmental agencies as the most typical bureaucracies characterized by rules to maintain control. These organizations are created by legal authority that defines their character and specifies their jurisdiction. Administration of them is intended to be objective and formal, subject to clear rules and regulations. A bureaucracy is a hierarchy; therefore it reminds one of a pyramid. Personnel are selected for their positions according to merit and consider themselves permanent. Each job requires specialization and expertise. If complex activities are to be carried on effectively, bureaucratic organizations are indispensable. As a movement grows, it will proclaim a specialization, evolve a structure, and hire permanent employees; then it has the major characteristics of a bureaucracy. Even antiestablishment organizations become bureaucratic.

Criticisms of Bureaucracies

While bureaucracies are necessary to modern life, they have a negative side. Clients of social welfare bureaucracies, for example, protest that huge, impersonal organizations are inflexible and unresponsive. Controls seem to be im-

Drawing by Lorenz; © 1971 The New Yorker Magazine, Inc.

"Be patient. When your time comes, we'll call you."

posed over more and more aspects of personal life, so that people become only numbers or cases. Not only can the large bureaucracy usurp choices that belong to the individual, but the individual may lose awareness of the possibility of choice.

One consequence of bureaucratic monopoly is individual alienation from social institutions. When people feel powerless to influence their surroundings in any real way, a sense of estrangement sets in. Life may seem meaningless. The individual may surrender his own values and purposes. Making social welfare bureaucracies humane is one of the major challenges for social workers.

Peter Blau[2] believes that bureaucracies have the capacity to change:

> Bureaucracies are not such rigid structures as is popularly assumed. Their organization does not remain fixed according to the formal blueprint, but always evolves into new forms. Conditions change, problems arise, and, in the course of coping with them, the members of the organization establish new procedures and often transfer their social relationship, thereby modifying the structure.

Blau emphasizes that operations must further the attainment of the organization's objectives. The administrative problem is how to bring this about.

WHAT IS A PUBLIC SOCIAL AGENCY?

Public agencies are authorized by law, operated by governmental units, and supported from tax revenues. While most of them are financed, administered, and operated by the state, they are also run by counties or by larger towns or cities. Some townships also administer general assistance payments for persons who are not able to qualify for a federally aided program.

Funding When agencies are operated by local jurisdictions, substantial funds often come from the state, and the state usually prescribes the rules. States in turn generally follow federal guidelines for programs eligible for partial funding from Washington.

Purposes Most public agencies were established to provide services to individuals rather than to groups. However, programs for children and adults also include recreation and developing skill on a group basis. Out-patient and residential mental health facilities have found groups effective. Correctional programs also use them for implementing self-governance and developing internal controls.

Neighborhood Agencies

The antipoverty and model cities programs have resulted in public agencies taking more active roles in neighborhood development. Board members of model cities programs were elected from the communities. Electors often included all residents over the age of sixteen. Publicly sponsored community organization programs have a major problem—the political establishment has operated the social institutions most in need of social change. Even lead poisoning and rat control programs have been played down because they implied possible criticism of the establishment in power. Conflicts between community legal services and their parent governmental organizations have also been intense.

SERVICES OF PUBLIC AGENCIES

Programs for the Poor   Public social agencies provide money to the poor. They try to find jobs for the unemployed and training for those who lack skills. They also administer programs to provide social insurance for those who are employed—benefits that can be collected as the result of disability or retirement or by survivors in the event of death.

Programs for Families and Children   Public social agencies provide a range of protective services for children, including foster care and adoption. They may also offer institutional services. They work with the courts to deal with neglected children and with those having serious behavior problems, including delinquency. Public agencies counsel parents and provide homemaker service and day care. They do not always operate all services directly, sometimes buying them from other agencies—public or private.

Cooperation with the Courts   Public agencies also cooperate closely with the courts in serving mental patients and adult offenders. They try to serve both groups in their home communities, although a substantial number will require institutional care away from home. They also serve the disabled and the handicapped. They may pay for surgery and other medical services and provide training for independent living or for productive work. Public assistance provisions have included special programs for the aged, the disabled, the blind, as well as dependent children. Since 1973, financial assistance grants to the aged, the disabled, and the blind are provided directly by the federal government through the social security program.

Except for continuing financial aid programs and the prison system, all these services may also be offered under private auspices—either through nonprofit agencies or proprietary agencies established to make a profit, especially nursing homes for the aged and day care centers for children.

ELIGIBILITY FOR PUBLIC PROGRAMS

Eligibility is a complex issue. Public agencies offer a variety of educational and consultative services free of charge. In general, however, they operate with the philosophy that persons who can afford to pay should do so. Agencies are more likely to charge for day care and residential services than for counseling or other out-patient programs.

The Means Test   Public assistance payments are granted to families or individuals below a certain income level. Their income, savings, or real estate holdings as determined by a means test may make people ineligible for financial grants.

Fees Based on Income   Families with a wide range of income receive services from rehabilitation and crippled children's programs. Fees are assessed according to income. Mental health services are offered to people who feel they need them and to those who present a danger to society. People are not ordinarily charged for correctional services but relatives of patients in public mental hospitals are often held responsible for payments for care.

AUTHORITY OF PUBLIC AGENCIES

Most federal participation in welfare programs stems from the authority of four words in the Constitution: *promote the general welfare.* The federal government does not force a state to provide programs. American public welfare programs for the most part require authorization from each legislature.

The Power of Rule-making

The power and discretion of a public agency are more significantly contained in its rule-making and policy-making functions than in the initial legislation. Rule-making power can be used to limit or extend services. Consider one example of the importance of rule-making powers.

An Unfair Rule   Federal guidelines specify that children over eighteen are ineligible for benefits from Aid to Families with Dependent Children unless they remain in school. In its rules one state department of public aid held that the term "school" included technical or trade schools but not colleges. As a result college students from AFDC families filed suit. In 1971 in *Townsend v. Swank*[3] the Supreme Court held the rule to be invalid and ended the discrimination.

Townsend v. Swank was a *class action,* since it was filed on behalf of all AFDC recipients attending college. A similar case in another state involved a recipient who wanted to enter a professional nursing education program, but training support had been offered only on the condition that she become a licensed practical nurse.

Purchases from Other Agencies

Public agencies operate their own programs and are also authorized to purchase care and service from private organizations or individuals. As a result private agencies receive large amounts of tax monies. The largest expenditures go to doctors and hospitals. Departments of welfare provide funds under Medicaid. Vocational rehabilitation and crippled children's programs are also large users of medical services. Purchase of care arrangements between public and voluntary social agencies will be discussed more fully at the end of this chapter, since payments provide the basis for a relationship between public and voluntary agencies.

Licensing

Public agencies are given the authority to license programs operated under private auspices. A public agency is expected to meet licensing requirements even though it does not license itself. Protection of those served by the facility is the primary purpose of licensing. Standards for fire and safety are more easily developed than enforceable standards for good programs. Rules can specify the level of education of a teacher or a nurse, but they tend to avoid specifying desired personality characteristics or behaviors.

Agencies providing such services as adoption, institutions of all sizes, group homes operated by agencies, and private homes that regularly care for other people's children full-time or part of the day must be licensed. Departments of health license mental health facilities. Welfare departments approve children's institutions and agencies, adoptive and foster family homes, and day care homes and centers. Out-patient counseling programs usually are not licensed.

Licensing may present major problems. Many day care centers are organized on a profit-making basis with little money for alteration of facilities or for expansion of staff. Unrealistic standards may put centers out of business and drive people to use alternatives that are more dangerous.

Although the legal purpose of licensing is to provide protection, public agencies also use the licensing relationship to help facilities improve their programs. The public sees licensing as policing, but opportunities for consultation are often considered more important by social workers.

Licensing standards are expected to be equitable. Review and appeal procedures must be provided to ensure fair treatment. Controversy arises especially when licensing requirements increase costs for programs operated for profit.

Other Investigatory Powers

Public agencies also have a variety of other investigatory powers. Perhaps the most interesting example concerns alleged child abuse or neglect. Investigatory powers are often shared by the welfare department, the police, and the courts, and may involve a clash of philosophies. The agency may feel that the police are aggressive or punitive. The courts may seem to minimize serious situations by supporting the rights of parents. The agency may be seen as either too permissive or too prone to remove a child from his home. In serious situations that require legal action, social workers must become familiar with rules of evidence and prepare testimony so that conclusions follow from facts rather than from vague feelings or impressions.

Problems of Investigation and Authority   Social workers who prefer to work with highly motivated people actively seeking help often have difficulty accepting investigatory and authoritative roles. Not only do they have to gain access to families that are reported for neglect or abuse, but they have to find ways to work with them. Hostility is not limited, however, to those people who receive service unwillingly. Persons that seek service are also often critical and uncooperative.

SERVICES SINCE THE 1930s

The depression of the thirties provided the stimulus for public services as we know them today. Widespread poverty could not be dealt with by the limited private and local public services that heretofore had carried the load. Especially in the western half of the country, the depression provided the first clear need for organized social services for intact families whose only disability was sudden and dramatic poverty.

The philosophical issues of colonial times are still the philosophical issues of today. How much responsibility should the government take for the poor? What investigatory powers should agencies have? Should eligibility for services be tied to residence? Should everyone be required to work who possibly can? Should benefit levels for the poor ever be allowed to exceed prevailing levels of earned income?

THE SOCIAL SECURITY ACT

Framework for Cooperation

Following the emergency relief programs of the early thirties, the Social Security Act was passed in 1935. Federal participation in welfare programs has grown rapidly since 1937, when old-age insurance provisions of the act were declared constitutional by the Supreme Court.

Modified by frequent amendments, the act has provided the framework for federal-state cooperation for major public services except mental health and corrections. The power has come largely from the federal government's authority to set standards as a condition to receive federal funds.

Social Insurance and Financial Assistance   The original legislation created a social insurance system involving a payroll tax from employers and employees, provided unemployment compensation for a specified time while a worker looked for a new job, and established three categories of persons entitled to financial assistance—the needy aged, the needy blind, and dependent children. In 1950 aid to the needy disabled was added. In 1960 AFDC benefits were broadened so states could choose to include families in which the father was unemployed, and in 1960 and 1965 provisions provided payments for medical services to the aged and then for medically indigent people. In 1974, assistance programs for the aged, the blind, and the disabled were transferred from the states to the federal government.

Some needy persons are not covered for welfare payments under the provisions of the Social Security Act. Single individuals who are not aged, blind, or disabled, married couples without children, and families that are underemployed must depend on general assistance. Support, standards, and practices vary widely, since these programs do not receive federal funds. In some places, general assistance brings to mind the ancient English system of poor relief, with a political figure serving as overseer of the poor.

Grants to the States   From the outset the Social Security Act made *formula grants* available to the states for maternal and child health, child welfare, vocational rehabilitation, and crippled children's services. Formulas to determine the size of grants are complicated, involving the population and wealth of the state and its rural or urban character. Grants were made to extend services to rural areas and later, to urban ghettoes, to improve staff competence and to promote services that had a high priority. Agencies and individuals may also apply for federal research and demonstration grants for special projects to develop and test innovations.

Current Federal Agencies Until recently the U.S. Children's Bureau was responsible for child welfare and crippled children's grants as well as those for maternal and child health. The Department of Health, Education, and Welfare now provides public assistance, vocational rehabilitation, and child welfare funds through the Social and Rehabilitation Service. Grants for crippled children and maternal and child health come through the Health Services and Mental Health Administration.

The Community Mental Health Act of 1963 appropriated federal funds for community mental health planning and facilities. The creation of the Law Enforcement Assistance Administration in 1968 in the Department of Justice provided grants to states for police, departments of corrections, and other law enforcement agencies.

REVENUE SHARING

Federal Revenue Sharing authorized in a bill signed in October 1972 has caused changes in the federal financing of social services, with annual authorizations of from $5.3 to 6.5 billion over five years. Its purpose is to provide money and return discretion in decision making to states and local governments. There are no restrictions on state expenditures and few on local capital projects. Bricks and mortar are always very popular. Operating expenses may be covered by shared funds in eight categories—public safety, environmental protection, public transportation, health, recreation, libraries, social services for the poor and the aged, and fiscal administration.

The law also places a ceiling of $2,500,000 on matching grants to states for social services. The implication is that any hardships can be met by using shared funds to pay additional costs. However, there is strong pressure to use the funds to reduce present tax burdens. Taxes may be reduced if programs in the eight categories are paid for by shared funds. Reductions are possible because fewer local dollars are required. The next development was special revenue sharing, intended to abolish earmarked federal grants and consolidate block grants with increased local discretion.

Meanwhile, revenue sharing is likely to direct attention of agencies to local governments. There is a widespread fear that agency programs will fare less well than they did with help from specific federal programs—even with their arbitrary and sometimes confusing guidelines.

COORDINATION AND STATES' RIGHTS

Since 1909, White House Conferences on children and youth have been held every ten years to promote common goals and joint planning. White House conferences have also been convened in recent years on education, nutrition, and aging. Many of their recommendations have affected federal and state legislation, but the principle of states' rights has led to a rather passive role for the federal government in coordinating services.

Recently the federal government has chosen rehabilitation as the unifying concept in preference to welfare. Now, consistent with a work emphasis, the Social and Rehabilitation Service has replaced the Welfare Administration and the Children's Bureau.

People often need more than one service. A confusing web of differing jurisdictions, requirements, and operating policies makes it easy to get lost in the system. Personnel from several agencies also may advocate very different solutions to the same problem.

Structure of State Agencies

Unfortunately the structure and interrelationships of agencies are hardly comparable in any two states, let alone across fifty. For broken families with the father and mother living miles apart, administrative problems are compounded by interstate differences. The federal pattern of health, education, and welfare in a single department is not followed in any state. Because of the historical emphasis on local financing and control of the common schools, education is administered separately.

The Human Services Institute classified state structures in July, 1974. Fifteen jurisdictions were "integrated-comprehensive" with the agency providing at least three of the following programs: welfare/social services; health; mental health and/or mental retardation; employment; and corrections.* Thirteen were "integrative-coordinative"—the state's human resources department had broad authority for planning, staffing, budgeting, and training.† The remaining twenty-six were nonintegrated, although reorganization is planned in several. No state offered health, education, and welfare services in a single department.[4]

Administrative complications result from fiscal relationships among the agencies. As we have seen, purchase arrangements are not limited to public-voluntary combinations. Families receiving public assistance, for example, become the fiscal responsibility of that agency. When they receive other services, the public welfare department may be billed for the cost. Since there is federal participation in the financing of public assistance, this policy saves revenue for a state.

A Student Proposal

A group of students reviewed the organization of public agencies across the country. They found the familiar problems—gaps, overlap, little assurance that persons with a range of needs would get help quickly and effectively.[5] As a result they developed a model organization plan for state services (see Figure 2-1). The major innovation is the Division of Client Advocacy, intended to ensure that people obtain the services they need. Note also that Corrections are part of the Division of Rehabilitation.

Centralization versus Decentralization

How many state agencies should there be to provide effective service?

*Alaska, the District of Columbia, Georgia, Idaho, Iowa, Kentucky, Louisiana, Missouri, New Jersey, North Carolina, Oregon, South Dakota, Utah, Vermont, and Washington.
†Arkansas, California, Delaware, Florida, Kansas, Maine, Massachusetts, Minnesota, Nevada, New Hampshire, Pennsylvania, Virginia, Wisconsin, and Wyoming.

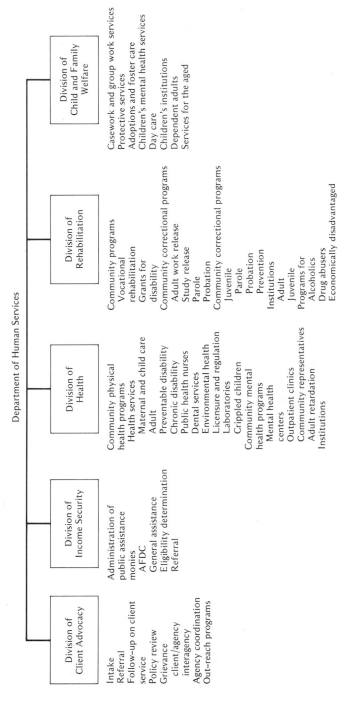

Department of Human Services

Division of Client Advocacy

Intake
Referral
Follow-up on client service
Policy review
Grievance
  client/agency
  interagency
Agency coordination
Out-reach programs

Division of Income Security

Administration of public assistance monies
AFDC
General assistance
Eligibility determination
Referral

Division of Health

Community physical health programs
Health services
Maternal and child care
Adult
Preventable disability
Chronic disability
Public health nurses
Dental services
Environmental health
Licensure and regulation
Laboratories
Crippled children
Community mental health programs
Mental health centers
Outpatient clinics
Community representatives
Adult retardation
Institutions

Division of Rehabilitation

Community programs
Vocational rehabilitation
Grants for disability
Community correctional programs
Adult work release
Study release
Parole
Probation
Community correctional programs
Juvenile
  Parole
  Probation
  Prevention
Institutions
  Adult
  Juvenile
Programs for
Alcoholics
Drug abusers
Economically disadvantaged

Division of Child and Family Welfare

Casework and group work services
Protective services
Adoptions and foster care
Children's mental health services
Day care
Children's institutions
Dependent adults
Services for the aged

Figure 2-1 An organizational model for states' services.[2]

Many Small Units Providing services in a considerable number of independent specialized state agencies has some advantages: a specialist can be selected as executive; program advocacy can be specific and clear-cut; self-help groups can be enlisted for support; budgets appear smaller and cannot be reduced as easily by across-the-board cuts; small specific programs may reduce waste, accountability may be stricter, and the span of control may be smaller. The staff may also have easier direct access to the governor. Disadvantages are also evident: families with multiproblems have more difficulty obtaining the variety of services needed; interagency planning is made harder, and agencies may spend too much time in competition for support; management costs may be higher because of duplication in such supportive services as data processing and accounting.

A Few Large Units Consolidation of agencies is often preferred by management consultants so as to develop better control systems and greater efficiency. Salaries for top management can be higher in order to recruit more outstanding leaders; planning efforts involving several programs can be more successfully

Figure 2-2 The diamond of organizational change.

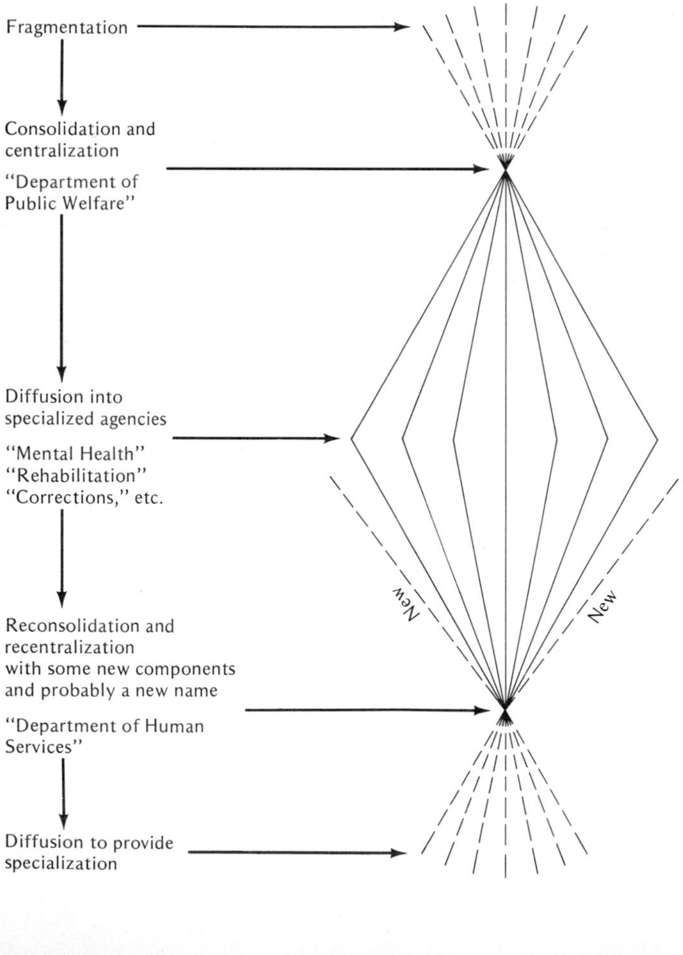

mandated; budgeting can be more responsive to the program goals of an administration in power. On the other side are dangers of concentration of power and competition among program divisions as much as among separate departments.

Dissatisfaction with the Status Quo   Most states tend to be dissatisfied with their current organizational patterns. When there are many public agencies, strong pressure builds up for consolidation. After consolidation, moves are made to break empires into smaller units. The trend is illustrated by the diamond-shaped diagram in Figure 2-2. Too often reorganization becomes a smokescreen used to delay innovations. The development of information systems and effective cooperative relationships are more important for the improvement of direct services.

Means of Coordination   Establishment of uniform areas, regions, or districts and the provision of basic services in the same building, however the agencies are organized, may achieve better service. A multiservice center can reduce the confusion created by differing geographical concepts and lead to the use of generalists who may represent several agencies. Agency autonomy and the need to be familiar with a variety of complicated and sometimes conflicting policies, however, impede cooperation. An ombudsman to receive and act on requests and complaints from any citizen may reduce inefficiency and buck-passing, but considering the passivity of many users of services, those that most need an ombudsman may be the last to find him.

The idea of advocacy discussed in the first chapter is especially attractive. Social workers serving individuals can also provide better coordination by acting as advocates for their clients to obtain needed resources from whatever source and to develop new services that are needed. Public agencies have been too timid about giving their workers sanction for such roles. Client organizations and self-help groups have often been able to apply pressures without social work help, but systems are often too formidable and impenetrable for their efforts to succeed.

Agencies are increasingly aware of the need for coordination of services, and some have demonstrated considerable success. As the final chapter on evaluating social services will indicate, emphasis on both efficiency and effectiveness may produce both better service and greater coordination.

PERSONNEL STANDARDS AND CIVIL SERVICE

A state department of personnel typically sets standards and handles personnel transactions for all departments. To get federal funds, direct services to clients must be provided by civil service personnel selected on merit. For most direct service positions, candidates take examinations that are objectively scored. For higher-level jobs, oral examinations may also be given. Training and experience and veteran status may also contribute to the final score. Selection is limited to the group scoring highest—often the top three applicants who would accept the position. After a probationary period, the employee is permanently certified for the position. Civil service is effective for initial selection but has not generally provided the rewards required to retain top employees. It has been more successful in protecting employees who may be mediocre. Civil service is often blamed for conservatism in public agencies. Since the system often includes nearly all employees below the level of director, a director may be unable to effect change unless new positions can be created. Since he cannot fire incumbents without cause, proliferation of personnel may result.

For some jobs, time-limited employment contracts may be preferable to permanent tenure. In house-parent positions in facilities for adolescents, for example, performance may be better with a group of young employees than with a permanent staff.

EXECUTIVE SELECTION: COMPETENCE AND POLITICS

In a public agency the director has to obtain the resources for the program and sanction new policies. While state laws may or may not spell out qualifications for a director, competence is essential. An interest in innovation and experimentation is also needed. Philosophies differ as to the type of education and experience required. In mental health, for example, to some the director must be an outstanding psychiatrist; to others he must be a layman. Those who favor the system of lay administration emphasize that psychiatrists should serve as medical officers, not as overall administrators. Furthermore nothing in his or her training prepares the psychiatrist for administrative tasks. The opposite view is that medical programs should be managed by physicians.

The law usually provides for selection of a department head either by the governor or by a board or commission. Both take into account political considerations.

Selection by the Governor   If the governor chooses the director, the system generally assures that the governor and the director can get along well and provides the opportunity to introduce new blood into the agency. The departmental budget, once agreed upon, becomes part of the governor's fiscal package, and he becomes its advocate. However, continuity of leadership may be broken with each new governor, and agency programs may become too politicized. An appointee in a professional area like mental health, however, may carry over from one administration to another. Some state statutes have tried to provide a director's term that does not coincide with that of the governor, so that the director may automatically carry over. This practice is in direct contradiction to the executive theory. It breaks down immediately if the governor requests the director's resignation.

Selection by a Commission   The contrasting system provides a board or commission made up of designated public officials and other citizens who hire the executive. It is designed to reduce direct political influence and to encourage "career service" regardless of administrations that come and go. Politics may still influence the initial choice, and extensive political activity is often necessary to get funds. Independence from the administration in power is usually an unrealistic expectation.

PUBLIC AGENCY BUDGETING

The process of preparing a budget differs somewhat from agency to agency and state to state, but usually past expenditures and existing programs are taken into account to establish baselines. Agencies have expected to get the same amount or a little more. New proposed programs have been put in supplementary budgets or given other special justification. Too much emphasis on the status quo can lead to the continuance of outmoded programs. This has led to interest in zero-based budgeting, in which each program—old or new—is considered as a "decision package." Established services compete with new ones for approval.

Especially in public assistance programs, costs have sometimes been routinely underestimated, with the realization that a deficiency bill will have to be introduced before the end of the fiscal period. This provides the illusion of lower costs. Increased personnel are often the most controversial item in the budget. Legislators associate personnel with needless expansion. Consequently most social agencies in the public sector have inadequate numbers of staff.

Advantages of Program Budgets Budgeting by gross *line items*—e.g., salaries, food, and transportation—is gradually giving way to *program* budgeting, in which costs are presented by major activities, rather than objects. Thus an agency must request one amount for out-patient clinic services, another for adoption, and another for recreational programs aimed at delinquency prevention. A program budget provides a way to show the true cost of a specific activity and is essential for zero-based budgeting.

Building a Budget Many agencies ask each regional or district director to determine his own projected costs. These proposals are used to determine the total budget request. An agency usually presents an optimum budget to be reviewed (and often reduced) by the administration and finally made a part of its fiscal package. The budget may also be studied by a special legislative budgetary control unit. Then an appropriation bill is drafted, testimony is presented at hearings before appropriations committees of both houses, and the bill is ultimately passed and signed by the governor. Obviously this process provides several opportunities for budgets to be cut. An administrator tries to revise his total budget at each stage. Wherever possible he will seek the discretion to apply any required cuts where they will be least harmful. Whether attempts are to be made to restore proposed cuts is often a decision of the administration rather than the prerogative of the agency executive.

Even with the signing of the appropriation bill, the agency is not home free. If revenues do not keep up with estimates, the administration may freeze expenditures to provide cost control—especially in the personnel category.

THE "PROFIT MOTIVE" IN PUBLIC AGENCIES

Business operations are relatively easy to understand, because a firm must already have or must create a market for its product and must ultimately make a profit which justifies continuing in business; on the other hand, public agencies have a larger market for their services than they can generally supply, and they are nonprofit by definition. What replaces the profit motive for them?

With the large market for their services, saving money is not the primary aim of the agency. Their goal, akin to the profit motive, is the establishment of public confidence that leads to a mandate to offer more and better service programs and to serve more people. For the agency that considers itself vital to a better society, these motivators are just as strong as profit.

With a look at the structure and organization of public services as background, the next issue concerns attitudes toward the various programs.

RELATIVE STATUS OF CLIENTELES

Some Are More Equal than Others

Understanding of the delivery systems for public services also requires recognition of special status and privileges accorded to the many self-help groups; for instance, parents' organizations on behalf of the mentally retarded, federations of the blind, and veterans' groups.

The Retarded Parents of the mentally retarded were mentioned earlier as being effective in extending and improving care and services for their children. Institutional programs have been improved—some of them dramatically. Many children are also now served in the community rather than in custodial facilities miles away. Such parents' groups usually have demanded neither administrative control nor staff positions in programs for retarded children.

The Blind As a group, the blind have successfully obtained special consideration. The group includes the visually handicapped (who have difficulty reading print) as well as those who are totally blind. The blind get talking books and record players mailed postage-free from the Library of Congress, and they receive an extra exemption on their federal income tax. Services for the blind are in a separate category in public assistance; they are usually offered in a separate bureau or in a different department from the rest of rehabilitation. This maintains high priority and guarantees jobs for blind persons at both professional and clerical levels. The deaf, whom most psychologists consider to have a more serious handicap, have had no comparable success, probably because their handicap is less evident.

War Veterans Veterans get preference on civil service examinations and in public employment agencies. They also staff the 20,000 positions of the Veterans Administration. Special benefits also include federal pensions for veterans and their dependents, a separate federal hospital system that treats illnesses both related and unrelated to their military service, and free burial and tombstones.

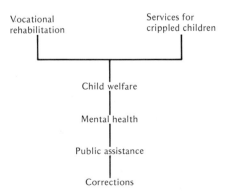

Vocational rehabilitation
Services for crippled children
Child welfare
Mental health
Public assistance
Corrections

Figure 2-2 Public acceptance of public services—A hierarchy.

A HIERARCHY OF PUBLIC AGENCIES

Public Acceptance and Support

Some public agency programs obviously have greater public acceptance than others. This section presents a speculative ordering intended to reflect American values. See whether you agree.

Vocational Rehabilitation and Services for Crippled Children These services are not widely known because of their specialized clientele and rather small volume of service, but the public has been supportive of efforts for the disabled and of the major medical services these agencies offer. Americans identify with an agency that tries to put people to work—the major goal of vocational rehabilitation. Budgets for services for the disabled are rarely controversial. Legislators sometimes say they support such programs in thankfulness for their own freedom from handicaps.

Child Welfare Children have been one of the major concerns of society, with our tradition of the state as parent with a clear interest in the welfare of the child. Both crippled children and those receiving child welfare services receive favorable interest—especially previous to adolescence. Child welfare services have generated goodwill through the publicity efforts of voluntary agencies that have offered adoption and foster care services. This goodwill has rubbed off on public child welfare programs, although foster care is generally misperceived as a service for orphans. Actually the vast majority of children in foster care are from broken homes. Adoption has had a particular appeal. Perhaps it captures the imagination of the American public because they see adoption as long-term altruism.

Mental Health The image of mental health services has improved. Short-term hospitalization and community-based services, along with successful use of drugs, have been helpful in maintaining the interest and responsibility of the patient's family. Many communities have conducted successful referenda to provide local tax funds for their own mental health clinics, indicating local support.

Services for the mentally retarded have improved but are still subject to the criticism of parent groups and others. Few public agencies have been able to offer the ratio of care personnel to patients required for good nutrition, sanitation, and other day-to-day care for the severely retarded.

Public Assistance "Welfare" has suffered from a widespread image of fraud and the fear that people will not want to work if they get used to being "on relief." People refuse to accept research indicating that most people receiving public assistance would prefer to work. The lack of available opportunities, rather than the attitude of the poor toward work, is the basic problem. That AFDC recipients rarely remain on the rolls permanently is also not understood.

Racism has also played a significant part in determining attitudes toward public assistance. Since Blacks make up a large proportion of the urban poor, it has been difficult to separate attitudes toward poverty from racism. This is apparent in discussions of illegitimacy. As an example of a double standard, sterilization is sometimes advocated to reduce public assistance costs, but it is considered undesirable for members of the middle class.

The Aid to Families with Dependent Children program generates opposition because recipients in many instances are still of child-bearing age and are perceived as employable. Providing AFDC benefits to intact families with unemployed fathers has also resulted in opposition. These benefits are available in only twenty-five states.[6] Welfare reform proposals suggest that negative feelings toward AFDC may be reduced if payments are made through a general program such as social security.

The attitudes of recipients toward public assistance are now also becoming more evident through welfare rights organizations. The size of grants, need of special funds for seasonal items such as winter clothing, and condescending treatment by staff members are examples of common problems. The great discretion of assistance staff in giving special allowances has resulted in proposals for flat grants that could be administered more easily and fairly.

Correctional Services Programs for offenders are at the bottom of the hierarchy. English and American criminal law tends to be punitive. Comparatively long sentences are standard procedure. Prisons tend to be both outmoded and overcrowded. Job discrimination against ex-convicts is commonplace and persists for years after release. Recently problems with "crime in the streets," riots in prisons, and exposés in the press have led to public support for improvements in the correctional system, but people are also increasingly afraid. Among juveniles, crimes like armed robbery—not car theft for joyrides—are becoming more typical. The public is particularly unsympathetic to growing crime and delinquency of suburban youth—"young people who have had every advantage."

If services are to be strongly supported, a better understanding of each one is essential. That college students are taking a greater interest in the development of an effective system of public assistance and reforms in corrections is a hopeful sign.

JOB OPPORTUNITIES IN PUBLIC AGENCIES

Improved public attitudes are essential to provide support for better public social service programs. Understanding the issues involved in public services affects your behavior as a citizen-taxpayer-voter. You may want to volunteer to help provide direct services or to interpret the program of the agency to the community. Perhaps you will be invited to serve on a public agency board to influence agency policy and to be an advocate for the program.

Public agencies may include several unique elements. A social worker can expect to give services without the protection of a waiting list and in most programs to deal with people who have economic as well as social problems. A worker may well have to represent authority to reluctant clients. Civil service rules will require a probationary period and convey tenure. Vacation and other fringe benefits may be somewhat less generous than in a voluntary agency, especially for new employees. Professional social workers in a public agency are likely to work with other personnel who have a wide range of education, including indigenous workers who have first-hand knowledge of the people being served. Since many public agencies are large, service workers may find it difficult to communicate through channels to top administrative personnel. The public agencies have the crucial problems and the major resources making employment both important and rewarding.

Malcolm X and the Welfare Department

. . . the state Welfare people kept after my mother. By now, she didn't make it any secret that she hated them, and didn't want them in her house. But they exerted their right to come, and I have many, many times reflected upon how, talking to us children, they began to plant the seeds of division in our minds. They would ask such things as who was smarter than the other. And they would ask me why I was "so different."

I think they felt that getting children into foster homes was a legitimate part of their function, and the result would be less troublesome, however they went about it.

And when my mother fought them, they went after her—first through me. I was the first target. I stole; that implied that I wasn't being taken care of by my mother.

All of us were mischievous at some time or another, I more so than any of the rest. Philbert and I kept a battle going. And this was just one of the dozen things that kept building up the pressure on my mother.

I'm not sure just how or when the idea was first dropped by the Welfare workers that our mother was losing her mind.

But I can distinctly remember hearing "crazy" applied to her by them when they learned that the Negro farmer who was in the next house down the road from us had offered to give us some butchered pork—a whole pig, maybe even two of them—and she had refused. We all heard them call my mother "crazy" to her face for refusing good meat. It meant nothing to them even when she explained that we had never eaten pork, that it was against her religion as a Seventh Day Adventist.

They were as vicious as vultures. They had no feelings, understanding, compassion, or respect for my mother. They told us, "She's crazy for refusing food." Right then was when our home, our unity, began to disintegrate. We were having a hard time, and I wasn't helping. But we could have made it, we could have stayed together. As bad as I was, as much trouble and worry as I caused my mother, I loved her.

The state people, we found out, had interviewed the Gohannas family, and the Gohannas' had said that they would take me into their home. My mother threw a fit, though, when she heard that—and the home wreckers took cover for a while.

Autobiography of Malcolm X.[7]

PURCHASE OF CARE AND SERVICE

In the next chapter we will consider voluntary agencies. The bridge between public and voluntary agencies is provided by purchase agreements. Public funds play an increasingly large part in agency budgets. Ninety percent of the funds of some private agencies come from governmental sources, but there are still a few agencies that will accept no governmental funds at all.

A Free Market   The purchase arrangement operates on a free market basis. The voluntary agency need not offer its services for pay, and the public agency may choose not to buy. The process gets a little more complicated, however, when a voluntary agency begins to serve a child and then expects the public agency to assume responsibility for payment, even though public agency person-

"A horse and rabbit partnership."

nel have never seen the child. Such arrangements are common in some states but are impossible in others.

Efficiency   Purchase makes sense in many ways. Specialized care and service are made available to the public agency at less cost than providing it directly. Existing facilities are used and duplication discouraged. At least traditionally, voluntary treatment services have been accorded higher quality than those offered by public programs.

Agency Support   Monetary advantages to the payees are obvious. Payments provide basic budget support that would be impossible to obtain through contributions alone. Agencies can use their facilities and staff members more efficiently because the volume of activities is increased.

Disadvantages of Purchase   Purchase of care may retard development of a public agency's specialized services, so that if a private resource is full or unresponsive, a needed program may be unavailable. The paying agency also may get strong pressure from payees to use services that may be inappropriate or ineffective. The cost of some services may be well beyond the reach of many public agencies. Residential treatment at an annual per capita cost of $15,000 or more may be impossible to finance.

Disadvantages to the voluntary agency include the tendency to become dependent upon referrals. Policies and programs may be dictated by the public agency. The agency that becomes a contractor for traditional services may continue to provide them without change. Innovations could be instituted more readily if parental payments and gifts could be the sole sources of current funds.

Certain costs are excluded from purchase of care agreements. Physical plant and depreciation often are not covered. In sectarian agencies, religious instruction and training costs are excluded. Parental payments, of course, are deducted.

After determining the items to be excluded, the public agency may pay the full remaining cost or only a portion thereof. Purchase-of-care agreements set the rates. If only care is provided, the cost may be low. If both casework and care are covered, costs will be higher. If intensive treatment is provided, rates will be further increased.

Cost Accounting   As public agencies have had to respond to demands for increased accountability, purchase agreements have placed greater emphasis on the use of uniform systems for calculating costs. In the past many agencies with several types of programs had no idea of specific costs. Their total expenditures were divided by the number of people served or the number of days of care given in order to get averages, but their bookkeeping systems were not designed for budgeting by programs. Uniform agency accounting standards related to purchase of care have been a stimulus for better business management.

These data have often led to conclusions about the relative *efficiency* of agencies. *Effectiveness*—improvement in the condition of persons served—is a more difficult area to measure. An indicator of efficiency would be the proportion of total time spent directly with clients. An indicator of effectiveness would be the degree of change in behavior resulting from services.

Problems of Change   Purchase agreements have other problems. Costs go up every year. Agencies consider that their rates based on past experience are already out of date. Also they may value their own services at a higher figure than does the agency controlling the purse strings. Sometimes agencies tool up for new programs but find that public agency needs or policies have changed. Then new services are not purchased, and the agency is worse off financially. Public agencies are also fickle. At times there is a strong emphasis on foster care. After a number of children flunk out of foster homes, institutional placement is rediscovered, but institutions are impersonal and costly. Then the agency may decide to remove the children and put them back in foster homes. Agencies also complain at times that personal dislike of a program by key public agency staff members may isolate the agency and cause it to "starve."

Other Frustrations   The public agency may find that the eligibility standards are not clear. One child is accepted—the next one with similar characteristics is not. The situation may be the result of lack of beds or of highly subjective criteria for admission. Delays often come in decision making because the voluntary agency insists on repeating the study and diagnostic process. This leads public agency staff to develop concerns about inferiority. The receiving agency may also summarily return the person to the public department for inadequate reasons. In short, purchase of care has elements of uneasiness for all participants; nevertheless, we are likely to see more of it.

Donald Brieland

KEY TERMS

bureaucracy	purchase of care	Social and Rehabilitation Service
means test	licensing standards	civil service
class action	formula grants	

FOR DISCUSSION

1 Why do public agencies have the greatest impact and carry the greatest responsibility for social services?

2   Although a local family service agency receives grants from a state department of mental health, why is it not a public agency?
3   What is a means test?
4   What were the issue and the findings in *Townsend v. Swank?*
5   What are the advantages of hiring indigenous workers?
6   Why have a Division of Client Advocacy in a Welfare Department?
7   Why have several specialized departments?
8   Why have larger, more centralized departments?
9   Describe the civil service system, including its shortcomings.
10 Differentiate between *program* and *object* budgets.
11 In social agencies, what replaces the profit motive?
12 What are the typical questions about working in a public agency?
13 Defend the use of public funds for purchase of care.
14 What are the problems with purchase of care?

PROJECTS

1   Study an annual report of a public agency. Ask an official of the agency at the policy-making level to visit the class and respond to questions that you have prepared and given to him in advance.
2   Identify the changes in organization of social services in your state over the past two decades. Compare structure and annual or biennial expenditures.
3   Debate the question: "Resolved, that the federal government should operate the AFDC program."
4   Devise and defend your own organizational chart for state social services.
5   If you have foreign students in your class, have them compare public agency programs in their country of origin with those in your state.
6   If you were responsible for a public agency's program, how would you measure the effectiveness of its services?
7   Read Stuart Dybeck, "Charity," *Commonwealth*, vol. 95, pp. 248–252. Compare it with the views of Malcolm X. How can agencies improve "The System" to meet needs and reduce resentment?

FOR FURTHER STUDY

Annual Directory, American Public Welfare Association, Washington, D.C. Includes the organizational structure of public social services in each state and the principal staff members. The APWA recently moved its offices to Washington.
Highlights, a news pamphlet of the Family Service Association of America, regularly discusses developments in voluntary agencies. *Child Welfare* serves a similar role for its field.
Bernice Madison, "The Welfare State: Some Unanswered Questions for the 1970's," *Social Service Review*, vol. 44, 1970, pp. 434–451.
Gordon Manser, "Implications of Purchase of Service for Voluntary Agencies," *Social Casework,* vol. 53, 1972, pp. 335–340.
Rufus E. Miles, *The Department of H.E.W.*, Praeger, New York, 1974.
Services for People. Report of the Task Force on the Organization of Social Services, U.S. Government Printing Office, March 1969.
Standard texts on federal, state, and local government will be helpful for readers interested in the details of public policy.
United States Government Organization Manual, Government Printing Office. Published annually.
Darrell J. Vorwaller, "The Voluntary Agency as a Vendor of Social Services," *Child Welfare,* vol. 51, 1972, pp. 436–446.

Chapter 3

Voluntary Social Services

How do agencies get prestige?
Are voluntary agencies losing their impact?
What private agencies make a profit?
How united is the United Way?

The voluntary agency is a nonprofit organization.[1] A charter issued by the state authorizes it to do business. The charter conveys no funds. It can be revoked for cause, but this rarely occurs. If it does, an appeal may be made through the courts. Usually the statement of purpose in the charter is very general. The broad goals expressed need to be translated into objectives and programs designed to meet the objectives. As a nonprofit corporation, the agency is usually required to issue minimal reports to the Secretary of State. In most states, any agency property used for commercial purposes will be taxed, but the agency is exempt from paying taxes on property used for program purposes and on supplies and equipment.

No single pattern typifies voluntary agencies. They differ too much in size, type, and program impact. Their variety reflects the free enterprise system in the human service area.

Staffing and Intake

Voluntary social service agencies are more likely than public agencies to be managed by professional social workers who have worked up to the post of director. Voluntary agencies rely mainly on professional staff with the master's degree, especially when they provide "treatment." The voluntary agency can regulate the amount of work by using waiting lists or by "closing intake"—not accepting applications. For many of its activities, the public agency does not have this option.

We have been using the term "voluntary" rather than "private" agencies. The general public often uses the term "private," but most social workers prefer "voluntary." Private sounds too exclusive and includes proprietary agencies organized for profit as well as nonprofit organizations. Furthermore, "private" may be confusing, since many voluntary agencies receive public funds either as grants or through purchase of services.

Some social workers would suggest distinguishing those agencies that do not employ considerable numbers of professional social workers from those that do. Neither the public nor local funding bodies make that particular distinction, however.

VOLUNTARY AGENCIES IN AMERICAN HISTORY

Voluntary agencies have a distinguished history. Their volunteer programs have given experience in direct service activities. Use of influential people on their boards has provided status for the agencies. Many citizens have also become familiar with agency programs through fund raising. Interest in a voluntary agency has often broadened people's understanding of the total range of human needs and made them advocates of policies favorable toward public human services programs. Public agencies have found that their cause is enhanced when leaders from the voluntary field lobby and testify on their behalf.

Until the nineteenth century, voluntary social welfare agencies were related to the churches or to nationality groups. In 1817 the New York Society for the Prevention of Pauperism was organized without religious or ethnic sponsorship. Many progressive proposals were made on behalf of the poor and were picked up later by other agencies.

The Association for Improving the Condition of the Poor was formed in 1843. It served individuals who could be "morally and physically elevated" and who were not served by other agencies, and it tried to reject all others. It gave relief and also concentrated on the improvement of housing and sanitary provisions. The first report on tenement housing led to the construction of a model tenement in 1855. Programs for mothers and children, vacation schools, and settlement houses were also provided. The association was merged with the New York Charity Organization Society in 1939 to form the Community Services Society, a group that continues to offer a varied program of social services. The general pattern set by the association was followed in other cities, but the agencies tended to emphasize relief and to have less success with other objectives. The Community Services Society was responsible for the development of a professional school of social work that is now a part of Columbia University.

The Charity Organization

The charity organization concept was imported from England to Buffalo in 1887 and spread to other cities. Its procedures resemble those of modern agencies in several ways. Cooperation of the various relief agencies was sought, and applicants were cleared through a central registry. Each family was investigated for eligibility, and home visits were made by volunteer "friendly visitors." These methods marked a great advance from some of the limited paternal efforts, provided the basis for community cooperation, and resulted in better coordination of helping resources.

The organizations were moving philosophically from moral failure and lack of individual motivation as the causes for poverty to consideration of a variety of conditions in society including housing, factory working conditions, and contagious diseases.

The Settlement House

The settlement house concept with services for new residents came from England to America with the opening of Neighborhood Guild in 1886 in New York, and Hull House in Chicago. Hull House also had a close tie with social work education in the establishment of what is now the School of Social Service Administration at the University of Chicago.

About the same time, agencies were developing for the care of children—some with romantic names like "New England Home for Little Wanderers." Names were often most explicit. There were homes for the *friendless*, hospitals for *incurables*, orphan *asylums*, and *psychopathic* hospitals. More recently, these names have been changed to provide a more positive image.

TYPES OF PRIVATE AGENCIES

Private agencies have many purposes. They may provide direct services in a city or county or district. Some are statewide. Some are national, but with varying degrees of local autonomy. Some provide no direct service but conduct public information programs or set standards for member agencies.

Many of the agencies were organized to provide assistance to the poor. Later, when public agencies took over financial aid, the private group offered family counseling as the core service. Marriage counseling, homemaker service, activities for the aged, family life education are all included in family service.

Programs designed to provide care for orphans have developed into broader child welfare programs offering institutional and family foster care, adoption, protective services, day care, and counseling for children in their own homes. Family agencies are often combined with children's agencies or with mental health centers.

Child guidance clinics were established to aid in the prevention and control of delinquency, but now they provide treatment for behavior problems primarily through casework with children and parents. Clinic services are frequently offered in a more comprehensive mental health center. These centers have added a planning function to develop a network of mental health services through public and private agencies.

A range of private institutions for the mentally ill, the retarded, and the disabled provide treatment and training. Many of the programs have vocational emphasis. Some provide transitional "halfway" services from restricted environments to the community.

Nonprofit hospitals and clinics receive some local charitable contributions for serving the poor. They also provide services for which other agencies are billed. They have received federal funds for plant expansion and equipment.

Many settlement houses which were originally developed for immigrants and other new urban residents have become community centers offering programs of socialization, treatment, education, and recreation. Both group work and casework are now principal methods in these agencies. Senior citizens' groups are often operated by settlement houses or by other agencies.

In addition, there are a range of youth-serving agencies—Boy Scouts, Girl Scouts, Campfire Girls, Boy's and Girl's Clubs, YM and YWCAs, YM and YWHAs. Big Brothers and Big Sisters have been oriented especially to the disadvantaged. In contrast, the 4-H program, operated by the extension service of the Department of Agriculture, is the only publicly sponsored national youth program. Recently 4-H has developed urban activities in ghetto areas.

Alcoholics Anonymous, Parents Without Partners, the Association for the Retarded, and Recovery—an association of former mental patients—illustrate the variety of self-help and parents' groups. These organizations differ in their policies toward the use of professional staff. Some welcome social workers; others prefer volunteer leadership. They ordinarily do not engage in extensive fund raising and may remain remote from other agencies.

Coordination of Agencies

The coordinator for social services agencies in local communities of any size has been a welfare council or council of social agencies that serves as a planning body. It may also be responsible for data gathering for the Community Fund or United Way. Welfare Councils should take positions on controversial community issues and develop plans for meeting critical needs. Councils may be satellites of the Fund and may represent only a segment of the health and welfare agencies, frequently excluding the public social welfare agencies and public education. Welfare councils often need more innovative plans, more power, and more funds to be effective, with comprehensive planning coalitions beginning at the neighborhood level.

Community councils and similar development organizations involve a wide range of coordination, planning, and service objectives. They often assist residents in obtaining housing and employment and in bettering the environment. They may get governmental grants for special projects and often carry on a lobbying function with city councils and other governmental units. The Economic Opportunity Act helped start urban progress centers to provide similar services. OEO programs have been incorporated as private agencies but are often quasi-public because of their political ties.

Community legal services recently have provided help to residents in consumer fraud cases, in debt counseling and credit reform, and in a host of class actions against state agencies, city departments, and other organizations. Most of these programs are now federally funded. Controversy has resulted because some legal services programs use federal funds to file suits against local governments.

A Partnership with Government

Let none of us who believe in the voluntary system delude ourselves. The mass thrust to move the poor from economic dependency to economic opportunity must be financed by government. The voluntary human care program is a major partner with government in our total objective to improve human performance in all walks of life and particularly for those who are most disadvantaged. As government and voluntary agencies work together, let us beware of easy solutions. We can legislate civil rights but not the elimination of prejudice. We can legislate law enforcement to protect us from irresponsible behavior but not the building of character. We can legislate the opportunity for economic achievement but not the incentive or the self discipline to grasp it. We may even try to legislate a great society, but we cannot legislate a great people. Only a great people can create a great society. Our voluntary welfare program should be judged in the future by its contribution to the creation of a society of great people.

Arthur H. Kruse.[2]

NATIONAL AGENCIES

National health agencies include the National Foundation (concentrating now primarily on birth defects), the American Mental Health Association, the American Cancer Society, the American Heart Association, and programs for many other diseases—tuberculosis and respiratory diseases, arthritis and rheumatism, muscular dystrophy, cerebral palsy, multiple sclerosis, and brain damage leading to perceptual handicaps. National associations emphasize research and study of these rather rare diseases. They usually operate drives outside the United Way. Some of the most important diseases in terms of incidence and social importance have not led to a specialized organization—German measles, responsible for great prenatal damage; gonorrhea, prevalent among young people; and stroke, a serious problem among older adults. National health organizations do not typically provide local medical services but issue educational materials, carry on research, and lobby for governmental funds. Some of the agencies have been criticized for high fund-raising and overhead costs.

The Red Cross is a long-established organization with special quasi-governmental status. At the local level it is especially concerned with disaster relief, hospital service programs, and provision of transportation for other agencies. In recent years, it has joined the United Way.

Other broad citizen groups have an interest in social work issues: the League of Women Voters frequently sponsors studies leading to legislative reform; the National Parent Teachers Association espouses the needs of the school-age child and legislation supporting education; there are a host of civil rights organizations, as well as the National Urban Coalition and Common Cause—groups with concerns for social betterment.

Accreditation and Standard Setting

Of particular interest to social workers are the national organizations with accreditation and standard-setting functions. The Family Service Association of America, the Child Welfare League of America, and the American Hospital Association study and evaluate agencies as a condition of continuing membership. Membership in the organization is associated with high standards of performance and protection of the public. Standards are higher than those of licensing bodies.

The American Public Welfare Association is made up of departments of welfare and individuals. This group has served as congressional spokesman for the state directors of welfare and for large city and county welfare organizations.

THE NATIONAL ASSOCIATION OF SOCIAL WORKERS

In social work the central membership organization has been the National Association of Social Workers, formed in 1956 from a number of more specialized groups. It offers individual memberships but not agency memberships. All professional social workers as well as social work students are eligible to join. It enforces a code of ethics. It sponsors the Academy of Certified Social Workers for persons who pass an examination after a mandatory period of social work practice. The association publishes the journal *Social Work*, sponsors regional institutes, and cooperates in the National Conference on Social Welfare. NASW also issues a periodic directory of social workers and produces a basic reference, the *Encyclopedia of Social Work*. It is active in lobbying and recently moved its principal office from New York to Washington. The association functions through chapters organized on a statewide or district basis, state councils, and some regional coalitions.

Problems of Funding

With rising costs many agencies and organizations report increasing financial problems. Those supported by dues have had to make substantial increases. High costs have generally reduced the impact of private agencies. Their funds buy less, and contributions from givers do not keep up with rising costs.

THE FINANCING OF PRIVATE AGENCIES

To supplement the unsolicited gifts they receive, private agencies appeal directly to the donor for unrestricted gifts to cover current expenses through mail appeals, solicitation by neighbors, benefits, and tag days. In addition, agencies receive bequests, income from investments, fees that users pay or another agency remits on their behalf, and less often, foundation or governmental grants.

Direct Mail Appeals   Fund raising by mail results in less than a 10 percent response. Such mailings may include an agency magazine or newsletter that recounts cases which have been served successfully. One of the more objectionable methods includes sending of unsolicited items for possible purchase. Appeals often attempt to link fund raising to altruistic impulses related to Christmas, Easter, Mother's Day, and other festive times. Direct appeals are considered important to remind the public of the agency and its work.

Neighbor-to-Neighbor Appeals   Personal friendships are used as the basis for appeals by most national health agencies. Housewives often give because they know that next time they may be the solicitor and their neighbor the donor.

Sales   Bake sales and rummage thrift shops, for example, are used for fund raising. Individuals may spend more time and effort preparing what is sold than the cash receipts justify, but if articles are donated and people contribute their time, the agency gains. Also, contributions in kind are tax deductible. The main byproduct is the development of a cohesive corps of volunteers who enjoy working together and who can aid the agency in a variety of other ways.

Solicitations   Tag days, poppy days, and "white cane" days require a large staff of volunteers to cover the main locations where people congregate. At least a minimum gift is expected, and the symbol obtained buys immunity from further solicitation.

Apart from the purpose and program of the agency, ethical questions about funding concern costs and benefits to a target group and to society. Efforts can involve high promotional expense that may border on fraud. Agencies often prefer independent rather than cooperative fund-raising efforts, because they involve minimum control from outside sources and no responsibility to share the proceeds.

Federated Financing   To overcome a rash of individual fund drives and to make possible"one-shot" fund raising, the system of federated financing was started. The system has had at least four different names. The Community Chest, the Community Fund, the United Fund, or now the United Way emphasizes *one* gift for *all*. The agencies submit their asking budgets to be analyzed. The total of approved askings often becomes the goal of the fund drive. Top officials and other employees are expected to contribute to the general goal by meeting the quota for their plan or business. This system includes provision for payroll deduction of gifts and has had the support of organized labor.

Fewer solicitations, lower fund-raising costs, and screening and approval of the programs of the agency by a citizen body are all advantages of the plan. Difficulties come in the restrictions placed on member agencies. Their programs are reviewed by the United Way Board. Approval must be obtained for new projects, substituting one program for another, or hiring additional staff. The United Way may be conservative about admitting new agencies into the system. More agencies mean more money must be raised, but competing fund drives damage the rationale. Therefore, agencies may constitute themselves as an elite and discourage fund raising by nonmembers.

"It's an Amalgamated Fund Appeal for the United Nations, the Democratic Party, Penn Central, Columbia University, the Catholic Church, Governor Rockefeller, and City Hall—to name a few."

Although some large United Way organizations provide only a portion of agency budgets and permit their members to have fund drives at other times of the year than during the general campaign, the more typical plan is to take over all solicitation and make up the deficits of its agencies. Except for user payments, payments from public agencies, investment income, and perhaps earmarked gifts, money comes from the United Way. This gives it great fiscal power.

Bequests and Annuities Bequests are still an important source of funds. Bequests may be worked out with an agency by a person long before he dies, or they may come as a complete surprise. Generally the agency prefers unrestricted bequests because of the strong need for funds for purposes that change from year to year. However, if the local United Way insists that undesignated bequests be used to meet current expenses and to reduce its asking budget, an agency may seek restricted bequests.

Large bequests for capital projects are one of the major ways to get new facilities. The interest of surviving family members may result in conflict between standards for a suitable memorial and agency program needs. The top priority may be a counseling program, but the family may insist on giving a residential center for children.

An annuity plan is used by some agencies—for example, the Salvation Army. A donor purchases an annuity. He receives monthly payments during his lifetime. At his death, the principal goes to the charitable organization. This method reduces the uncertainty of bequests because the arrangement is not revocable. Also, some agencies encourage interested persons to buy life insurance and to make the agency the beneficiary.

Endowment Funds   Investing large gifts and using the earnings is a preferred method of funding. Businessmen on the board, or a professional investment counselor, manage the investment portfolio. Large and long-established agencies often have substantial worth.

If agencies have difficulty in financing ongoing programs, pressure arises to use unrestricted endowment funds to meet current expenses. Unless these funds are replaced by new gifts, the agency may rapidly lose its investment income and must then depend on current contributions.

Payments for Services   Purchase by other agencies is an important source of funds. *Fees from users* contribute relatively less. The traditional idea that most private agencies were designed to provide free services for the poor has been modified with the development of services for groups at other income levels.

Foundations   By establishing a foundation, people of wealth have the chance to gain tax advantages and accumulate funds for useful purposes. Grants may be made on application from the agency or sometimes on an unsolicited basis. Foundation gifts may be small or large. They may involve considerable special negotiation. While some foundations are willing to pay the heat bill or to buy diapers, larger ones usually limit their grants to more innovative purposes. Foundation monies are regarded as venture capital for new time-limited projects. Foundation-sponsored programs often face a crisis toward the end of the grant if the program has not been gradually built into the regular budget of the agency. The result is often abandonment of worthwhile projects.

Foundations also have a special interest in research projects and frequently finance evaluations of programs. Voluntary as well as public agencies also seek research grants from federal programs.

THE BOARD OF TRUSTEES

The essence of voluntarism is nonprofit status, private funding, and control and accountability vested in a board of trustees. The board bears the legal responsibility for the program of the agency and for paying its bills.

Board Composition   To get a broad slice of community leadership, agency boards tend to be large. Often they meet but a few times a year, with the operation of the agency falling to the executive director. Specific policy responsibility is vested in an executive committee made up of the officers and a few board members. Sometimes people are nominated to agency boards in the hope that they will make large gifts, but such gifts are rare. Board members are likely to be chosen for their status in the community, their time and energy available to the agency as volunteers, or their expert knowledge in such areas as financial management, institutional operation, or adjunctory services. One board includes a leading stockbroker, a general contractor interested in plant maintenance, and the local superintendent of schools. Some board members do not attend many general board meetings but are willing to give time as consultants in their area of expertise. Such people may be of special value even though they seem inactive.

Leadership Training   Welfare councils and individual agencies often have leadership training sessions for new or prospective board members to make clear the purpose and functions of the board, its legal status, the committees that provide chances for specialization, and the functions and organizations of the agency staff.

Agency volunteers often become board members. This type of leadership training is usually effective because the volunteers have a good first-hand knowledge of the program and have already demonstrated their interest and commitment. With the increasing emphasis on the use of volunteers, a wider range of roles has emerged. They are no longer limited to menial tasks. They may work directly with the persons the agency serves, help in agency management, and conduct the agency public relations program.

Rotation   The board acts as a representative of the agency in the community. To gain influence it is desirable to have many advocates; therefore board memberships should be rotated. Former board members are expected to continue their loyalty, and their successors are expected to develop loyalty. Rotation also prevents long-term control by a very small group. For people who give outstanding service the category of honorary board member is often used.

How Boards Differ   The relationship between the board and the executive director can be quite different from one agency to another. In some agencies, the director works closely with the board and serves at its pleasure. In others, the board seems to work for the executive director and serve at his pleasure. Unfortunately for agency vitality, the board may become a rubber stamp.

Board membership is also the road to other kinds of public service. In some communities there is a hierarchy of agencies. People start on one board and move to another considered to have greater prestige. They may move from local boards to state boards, or to the United Way board, or its allocation committees. For the person interested in social services short of a career involvement, the board member role provides significant participation.

CHURCH SPONSORSHIP OF AGENCIES

Church wardens played a major role in the provision of care for the poor in England, but in the United States separation of church and state has made the church's efforts distinctly private. Churches developed institutions for orphans and for the aged in their congregations. They also collected alms for the poor and provided food, clothing, and shelter to the needy. Adoption and foster care were added later. Counseling was seen basically as pastoral advice, but clergy often found that problems required other expert help. This led to new counseling programs and to specialized family and children's agencies.

Jewish agencies have provided particularly significant leadership in the development of professional social work services. They have tended to provide the widest variety of services. With the concentration of Jews in certain neighborhoods, in addition to casework and financial assistance, settlement houses and community center services were developed. Aid to displaced persons and immigrants has particular importance. Although the agencies are not typically owned by a congregation, a major emphasis has been on Jewish education and culture. Until recently, many of the agencies have limited their services to Jews.

Catholic agencies provide social services in the various dioceses. They have advocated services for children that guarantee religious training in a Catholic institution or foster home. Concern about spiritual development led to a variety of institutional services. The agencies have tended to provide few services to non-Catholics.

Protestant welfare services provide a mixed picture over the country. A few communities have Protestant federations. Lutherans have organized their services into a separate federation in some communities. The agencies show the individualism of Protestant denominations and historically have been more willing to extend services outside their own membership group—perhaps because the criteria for membership are less clear-cut.

Lutheran agencies are likely to be church-owned. Other Protestant agencies tend to be church-related. This term generally means that churches are solicited for financial support but are not offered much real control of the program. A few also have social service organizations at the national or state level, but strong authority is not ordinarily exercised.

Management Trends   The most important tie between the churches and their agencies comes in funding. Church leaders also play dominant roles on the boards of the agencies.

Funding from church bodies is inadequate to meet the costs of agency operation. Both participation in federated funding and payments for services from public agencies have become characteristic for sectarian agencies. Increasing pressure to serve a wider community beyond their members has resulted in a reduction of church control. Merger of related church bodies has led to merger of sectarian agencies, especially within the Lutheran group.

Agencies are tending to become less sectarian. Their eligibility policies retain priority for their own members, but—especially in the case of Protestant agencies—the majority of persons served are often not members of the group sponsoring the agency. Jewish and Catholic agency eligibility policies differ from agency to agency.

Nonsectarian agencies are organized apart from religious sponsorship, but they often serve members of churches that sponsor sectarian agencies. To guarantee confidentiality some people would rather be served by a nonsectarian agency, especially if they are very active in their church. With scarce services such as the provision of infants for adoption, applicants may be involved with both sectarian and nonsectarian agencies—sometimes simultaneously.

In a few states, especially in the South, the separation of church and state is taken so seriously that sectarian institutions have been exempt from licensing. This clearly denies whatever protection licensing provides for sectarian services. Standards should be applied to sectarian and to nonsectarian agencies alike.

MERGERS OF VOLUNTARY AGENCIES

Mergers of agencies of equal strength are rare except as a consequence of the merger of church bodies. Most mergers in recent years have involved combinations of two weak programs or the assimilation of a weak program by a stronger one. The criterion for a merger should be whether the result is an increase in volume or quality service.

Strong agencies typically have been unwilling to surrender their independence through merger. In some cases United Funds insist on merger to reduce administrative costs and promote efficiency, but the result can be increased cost and no gain in efficiency. Merged agencies include family and children's services, family services and mental health, or child welfare and child protective programs, but mergers are most likely when two agencies have similar rather than complementary functions.

A Plea for Consolidation

I question whether or not the traditional organization and structuring of the voluntary social welfare field has the potential to be efficient and effective. This view grows out of what, I think, are the implications of the average size of the voluntary agency. Recently, in Chicago, we packaged 10 settlement houses with average budgets of $150,000 into one settlement house with a budget of one and one-half million. Instead of having 10 executives that were paid an average of ten to twelve thousand dollars a year, one man was hired and paid thirty. Instead of having 10 executive jobs, which, when you study them from a job study point of view, weren't executive jobs at all, we had one executive. The former had been part time janitors, part time accountants, part time group workers, and part time public relations directors. If you really looked at their jobs, only about 10% was being an executive. Nobody is so bright or able that they can do all those jobs. Furthermore, you can't get talent for that price to do a leadership job, that is going to do the things that the manager has to do by way of planning and leading.

We have come to a conclusion, that we need an agency which is large enough to organize a management capability which provides specialization and competence on the management level, so that we have a director whose job is full time management, a program director, a business and finance director, and a research and development person. Otherwise, we are not going to have the kind of leadership that can help hold up the head of the voluntary field in the face of the competition and pressure of government to do the total welfare job.

Arthur H. Kruse.[3]

PRIORITIES IN THE VOLUNTARY FIELD

Several communities have conducted priority studies to see whether support to an agency from the United Way should be increased or decreased. The following issues are important:

1 Services for the disadvantaged versus services for contributors and their families.
2 Shifts in governmental support. Strong support should not go to agencies that receive large payments from public sources. Hospitals and clinics are major examples.
3 Preventive versus custodial programs, with priority for the former.
4 Greater emphasis on services for minority groups, with control vested in the groups and agencies organized to serve a designated minority exclusively.
5 Charges for services, calculated on the basis of income, to release more contributed funds for services to low-income families.

Recommendations often tend to elicit hostility from existing agencies, and a power struggle leads to restudy. Priority studies have not always assured success in implementing the new priorities.

WORKS OF MERCY VERSUS SERVICES FOR OURSELVES

Students can learn a great deal about local social policy by studying the allocation of money. With the vast growth of public agencies and the increase in taxes for health, education, and welfare, the citizen-giver tends to show relatively less interest in supporting the private services designed for the poor and the disadvantaged and relatively more interest in those services that his friends and their children can use, such as the Boy Scouts, Girl Scouts, the YMCA and the YWCA. While these agencies have outreach programs for the poor, the bulk of their membership is middle-class. The organizations often make demands on the parents to become volunteer leaders—a hard system to institute successfully in many low-income neighborhoods. Also, these programs tend to have the support of very influential business leaders, so they are likely to have prominence in the community pecking order of agencies and in the United Way.

Social work has often been critical of recreation and character-building activities which are considered to have lower priority for public funds than services that concentrate their effort on the poor or provide treatment.

The question is: Should the users of group and recreational services pay the full cost whenever they can afford to do so, leaving charitable contributions for use for the disadvantaged? Thus far, the answer of citizen-givers has been to shift the services for the disadvantaged to the public sector and to continue to give a relatively high proportion of contributions to the services for the middle class.

THE VOICE OF THE RECIPIENT OF SERVICES

The National Welfare Rights Organization was created to represent the recipients of public welfare. Recipient leadership is hard to develop. Self-governance is an important technique to give institutional residents more of a voice in their own programs, but this may be window dressing with very little real power. Alumni groups made up of former patients or convicts have been formed, but the institutional graduate would prefer to forget mental illness and criminal conviction. Services for unmarried mothers or crippled children have the same limitation—the problems do not constitute an appropriate basis for grouping once the need for service has ended.

Use of former and present recipients on a board of directors is one way to get some feedback from users of a service, but the individuals are often highly selected and are in such a numerical minority that only tokenism results. Influence of consumers is not likely to grow until people regard services more as rights than privileges, and until recipient groups attract more powerful advocates from community leadership, including both contributors and legislators.

RACIAL AND ETHNIC AGENCIES

The avowed goal of both public and private agency policy has been to serve people in need without reference to race or ethnic origin. Agencies that receive public funds are covered under the Federal Civil Rights Act. Many states will not purchase services from agencies that have discriminatory practices. This issue has been considered largely in terms of adverse effects of white racism. But what of the agency that serves only Blacks or another minority? Black colleges and some black institutions may have no written policies against accepting Whites, but Whites just don't go there. In that case, the program may not be discriminatory in a legal sense. The new trend is to organize programs for Blacks, Chicanos, or American Indians (or as they prefer, native Americans), or to establish separate units for them within a larger agency program. We have such agencies as Afro-American Family Service, Martin Luther King Community Center, and many others. The Iowa Family and Children's Service in Des Moines recently opened a children's group home that serves only Blacks.

The rationale for separatism is clear. The services fill a need that arose because of racism. Proponents feel that it takes members of the group to fully understand the problem of their brothers and sisters. The agencies have a special appeal to minority givers. Some agencies have been able to get exceptions to the rules of the United Ways—both concerning segregation and the length of time required before an agency can qualify for grants.

All other things being equal, Blacks prefer black service givers.[4] They want competent service even more, regardless of race, but ideally they want both, simultaneously. No doubt private agency leaders find reverse segregation both troubling and difficult to implement. The only consistency in such instances may be inconsistency.

Public agencies often find that when a person wants to be served by a member of his own race, the request must be denied because of civil rights regulations. To grant the request is best, since we cannot relive the years that have led to polarization. At this stage in our development there is a place for special racial and ethnic programs. We may see a parallel with the situation in the traditional Jewish agencies. As conditions have changed, eligibility requirements have been broadened.

RESEARCH IN PRIVATE AGENCIES

The private agency has important freedoms that should promote the development of research and demonstration projects to advance knowledge and improve services. It can choose its own program objectives freely. The private agency may deny or extend services to applicants without elaborate explanation. It can choose to provide short-term help to large numbers or intensive service to a smaller group. It has the flexibility to experiment with costly methods without strong public criticism. It can drop programs that do not seem effective and replace them with new programs. Also it may have the prestige to get government grants more easily than the public agency.

One agency, the Community Services Society of New York, has made a sustained effort to produce basic studies concerning social welfare policies and programs. It was responsible for the development of the Hunt-Kogan Movement Scale[5] to evaluate changes in client functioning as a result of casework service and other important research. That more agencies did not use the scale suggests a common problem—the underutilization of available techniques for evaluation.

Voluntary agencies participate in special projects from time to time, but few carry on continuing research programs. Even successful demonstration projects are not always continued by sponsoring agencies—often because of cost or lack of commitment. So-called research departments often do little more than collect statistics. In spite of greater constraints, the most promising projects have come out of public agencies.

With the responsibility for large-volume services going to the public agencies, private agency leadership must be developed in research and demonstration efforts. Similar opportunities exist for participation in innovative manpower training projects in cooperation with schools of social work and other academic departments.

FEES FOR SERVICE

At the end of Chapter 2, we saw the importance of purchase of care and service from private agencies. Now we will look at fees for service—payments from individuals for the help they receive. Usually the agencies have a sliding fee scale related to net worth and annual income. The United Way may also insist that a fee policy be developed. Voluntary agencies indicate that fees make for a more businesslike procedure. Those who pay fees may also be asked to make gifts once service is terminated. Payments are also thought to increase the value of the service and to provide motivation for treatment.

The agency needs to have an accounting system capable of determining the costs of each program. The difficulties in the fees charged are illustrated in the case of adoption. Some agencies seem to base their fees more on the income of the applicants than on documented evidence of full cost. Most voluntary agencies charge fees to adoptive parents, whereas most public agencies do not. The few which purport to cover costs vary from less than $200 to more than $2,000. Fees are reduced or eliminated for lower-income families.

These questions relate to determining costs of adoptions: (1) Are only the costs of social workers included? (2) Are clerical and administrative costs apportioned? (3) Are all or part of the medical care costs for the unmarried mother included? (4) Are the costs of the service to unsuccessful applicants amortized and paid by successful applicants? (5) Are costs adjusted in terms of the service given? Ordinarily the amount of service required when a couple adopts a second child from the same agency will be substantially less. Original data gathering need not be repeated. Investigations of parental capacity are aided by the presence of the first child. Logically, the fee should be lower for such a placement.

Fees for service may discourage low-income families who either are not aware that fees are based on income or do not want to get "charity" after failing the agency's means test.

The reverse principle of fees is seen in both public and voluntary agencies in the new programs for subsidizing adoptions, with monthly payments for varying lengths of time to adoptive parents to cover costs of care. Subsidies are used for foster parents who wish to adopt a child but cannot afford to do so and for other low-income families—especially those who adopt children that are hard to place.

WORKING IN A VOLUNTARY AGENCY

Professional people who like the concept of altruism and prefer services supported by gifts rather than taxes may prefer to work in a voluntary agency. Fewer people may have to be served at a given time because the agency can more easily control the number of people accepted. There may be a greater stress on professionalism and less of an atmosphere of bureaucracy. Personnel policies are used instead of civil service rules, but there is less assurance of tenure unless the agency workers are covered by a union contract. Such coverage is not unusual but is becoming more common.

In some agencies, the staff is very conscious of fund-raising efforts and will have close relationships with board members. In large agencies, this is less true.

Rising costs are a threat to voluntary agencies, but fees for service, government grants, and increasing use of purchase of care have strengthened them. At the same time they have become less clearly the embodiment of traditional private charity.

Donald Brieland

KEY TERMS

charter	bequests
self-help groups	endowment funds
welfare council	board of trustees
community council	church (sectarian) agencies
United Way	nonsectarian agencies

FOR DISCUSSION

1 Why do voluntary agencies enjoy particular prestige?
2 Why would a protective services agency find it especially difficult to use a waiting list or to close intake?

3 Differentiate clearly between a public and a voluntary agency.
4 What private agencies "improve the condition of the poor"?
5 Discuss service programs of the private family agencies. Have they concentrated on the poor?
6 Explain the term "self-help group" and suggest examples.
7 What are major criticisms of national health agencies that solicit public funds?
8 Racism and poverty have been the two top priorities of NASW. What priorities would you suggest, and why?
9 Why do agencies use mail solicitations that raise little money?
10 Describe the rationale of the United Way. Why does it not include all private social agencies?
11 What is the effect of inflation on endowment fund income?
12 Evaluate rotating membership for a board of trustees.
13 Contrast sectarian and nonsectarian agencies.
14 Why is United Way support of some youth-serving agencies questioned?
15 Why don't more recipients of services participate on boards?
16 Explain the current interest in racially segregated agencies.

PROJECTS

1 Choose a member of your class as chairman. Organize a panel of voluntary agency executives to talk to your group. Choose a major issue and frame several questions to use as the basis for discussion. Possible topics are: meeting rising costs, problems of purchase of care, how boards of trustees function, and to what extent services to the poor should have priority.
2 Compare the financial statements in the annual report of several voluntary agencies to determine the source of funds. What proportion of income is derived from contributions, fees for service, purchase of care, endowments, foundation grants, and new bequests? How much do the agencies differ?
3 Organize a role play in which the chairman of the local Human Relations Commission discusses the organization of the board of a specific agency that has involved the same upper- and middle-class white membership for several years. Include a discussion of recruiting former clients as board members and of a rotation system that would result from limiting terms.
4 Find out the requirements for membership in the local United Way. Analyze the provisions in terms of needs for new services.
5 Study the periodicals *Social Work, Social Casework, Public Welfare,* and *Child Welfare.* Classify and compare the topics discussed in the last year.

FOR FURTHER STUDY

Alfred J. Kahn, *Social Policy and Social Services*, Random House, New York, 1973, pp. 101–109.
Ralph M. Kramer, "Ideology, Status and Power in Board-Executive Relationships," *Social Work*, vol. 10, October 1965, pp. 108–114.
Herman Levin, "Voluntary Organizations in Social Welfare," *The Social Work Encyclopedia*, National Association of Social Workers, 1971, pp. 1518–1525.

Chapter 4

Social Services
in Other Countries

Is the British health system a success?
How does France provide children's services?
Could we afford Sweden's welfare system?
Will the Common Market lead to new cooperation?

Americans generally know little about the social welfare systems of other countries, despite extensive travel throughout the world. Comparative study is useful to get new ideas and to avoid mistakes in the development of new programs.

Capitalistic industrial nations such as the United States and the countries of western Europe, industrialized communist nations of eastern Europe, and the developing nations that are primarily agrarian constitute three rather different groupings. To learn as much as we can for possible application to the United States, we will concentrate on western Europe.

Economic burdens and hazards will be classified to provide a framework to view social welfare programs. Illustrative programs from three countries—Great Britain, France, and Sweden—will be presented. Finally the European Economic Community (Common Market) and its importance for cooperative social planning will be discussed.

WORLD SOCIAL SECURITY AND WELFARE PROVISIONS

The average family needs to meet the economic burdens of adequate child care and to protect itself from such economic hazards as the death or disability of a wage earner, involuntary unemployment, illness, and loss of income in old age. Hazards bear particularly on low-income and poor families, but health problems can push otherwise economically independent families into poverty. In an economy where wages and salaries are the chief resources of the masses of people, systematic means must be provided to meet economic needs when wages cease.

CLASSIFICATION OF PROGRAMS

The United States Department of Health, Education, and Welfare identified social security systems in 125 nations throughout the world.[1] Five basic types of programs provide benefits or services. Work injuries resulted in some benefits in nearly all countries, but involuntary unemployment was included in provisions in less than one in three.

Program	American terminology	Number of countries
Work injuries	Workmen's compensation	122
Old age, retirement, disability, and death	Old-age, survivors', and disability insurance	101
Sickness and maternity care	Medicare, Medicaid	68
Family allowances and child care	————	63
Involuntary unemployment	Unemployment insurance	34

Obviously not all countries have a complete social security system, but the systems have certain common characteristics. They are all established by law. They generally include cash payments to replace lost income or provision of services such as health care or child care. They involve a mixture of approaches—social insurance, social assistance, and professional services.

Insurance   Social insurance is by far the most common approach to social security. More than three-fourths of the countries use some type of social insurance to meet presumptive need arising out of some threat to family income—disability and work accidents, retirement, or death. Benefits of a fixed and predictable amount tied to past earnings and contributions by wage earners and employers have had both political and economic appeal.

Assistance   Social assistance, known in the United States as welfare or public assistance, is considered less desirable than social insurance because of its means test, the suspicion of cheating, and the uncertain level of benefits. Social assistance is identified with our so-called "welfare mess." The average citizen does not understand how social assistance can provide economic security. Few countries rely on social assistance as the primary means of protecting citizens against absence of income; most use a combination of insurance benefits and assistance payments. In the United States, old-age insurance benefits are administered by the federal government and old age assistance by state and local governments, with increasing federal participation.

Personal Services   Finally, most systems provide institutional care and a variety of personal services given by medical and nursing personnel, child care workers, social workers, and rehabilitation workers.

The organization and administration of social security systems differ greatly. In some nations the administration is highly centralized. In others direction and management are dispersed among the local units of government. In some, private organizations share significantly in the provision of the benefits and services. In many foreign countries labor unions are more actively involved with social welfare systems than they are in the United States.

The adequacy of the systems to meet the social needs of their citizens is difficult to assess. To what extent is the population covered? How well do benefits meet people's needs? How efficient is planning and management? How acceptable are the programs to the people? What are the gaps in the system?

Selected aspects of program operation will now be summarized for England, France, and Sweden. Each of these countries has all five of the programs identified earlier in this chapter. The United Kingdom is selected primarily because of its health service. We provide only limited health care services—primarily for some of our aged citizens. Understanding the British health services may help us evaluate our health care delivery system.

France is chosen because of its provisions for child care. Here again, the United States lags behind other highly industrialized countries in providing for child care. Our deficiencies are particularly related to public welfare. Aid to Families with Dependent Children, a social assistance program for needy children and their families, has served to alienate groups of citizens and has singled out recipients as objects of scorn. The children aided often repeat the dependency pattern of their parents.

Sweden illustrates the range of social services that can be provided when a country is willing to tolerate a high rate of taxation.

SOCIAL SERVICES IN GREAT BRITAIN

The British have one of the most complete and highly developed social service systems in the world, with a history going back several hundred years.[2] The social security system is comprehensive and universal in its coverage of risks and persons. All employed persons over fifteen years of age contribute to the national insurance system and are covered by the programs. The system is administered through the Department of Health and Social Security with the cooperation of the

Department of Employment. Cash benefits are payable on retirement at age sixty-five for men and sixty for women; to survivors of a worker who dies before retirement or is killed in a work accident; when earnings are interrupted by unemployment, a work accident, or sickness; and for the expenses of childbirth. In addition families with more than one child get a family allowance. Benefits are chiefly flat-rate, but many are supplemented through special allowances based on need.

Complementing the cash benefits are the personal services of health care staff, child care workers, and other local authority personnel. Services are focused on the needs of four target groups in addition to the sick: mothers and young children, the elderly, the mentally disordered, and the physically handicapped.

THE NATIONAL HEALTH SERVICE

The year 1973 marked a quarter century of operation for the National Health Service in Britain. These basic principles have guided its development:

1 Health care should be available and free to all people irrespective of their means.
2 Care should be based on freedom of choice for both patient and doctor in arranging for and receiving medical services.
3 All medical services needed for health care should be included—the service should be comprehensive.
4 The service should be national in the sense that the same high quality of care should be available in every part of the country.
5 Doctors and other professionals working in the service should be assured full clinical freedom in their practice.
6 The service should be centered on the family doctor to provide the essential continuity of health care and to mobilize all services needed.
7 All services should be integrated and coordinated through rational planning for the development of the total program.
8 The system should encourage preventive medicine and early treatment.
9 The cost of the service should be spread over the whole citizenry and not levied primarily on the basis of need for medical care.
10 Citizens as well as professionals and civil servants should participate in the planning and direction of the service.

The National Health Service has not been entirely successful in meeting these standards. However, progress has been made on all of them.

Benefits The benefits provided by the NHS reflect the comprehensiveness of the program. The Service offers treatment of illness in the patient's home, the doctor's office, in hospitals, clinics, and health centers. Treatment includes care for acute and chronic illnesses, dental problems, ophthalmic needs, and mental illness and defects. A wide range of preventive and rehabilitative services are included, such as maternity and child welfare services, prenatal care, day nurseries, vaccination and immunization, home nursing, after-care services, homemaker services, and health visitors. Drugs, ambulances, and blood transfusions are also furnished.

Cost Both eligibility for care and cost to the patient are independent of contributions to national insurance. Services are generally free. Fees are charged for prescriptions, glasses, and dentures. The aged, expectant mothers, and children are exempted from payment. Only three out of five pay the standard fee (about 50 cents) for a prescription. An "amenity charge" is levied for such considerations as private hospital rooms when they are not necessary for medical reasons.

Availability The scope of service is practically universal. Approximately 97 percent of the population, 98 percent of the general practitioners, 94 percent of the dentists, almost all of the pharmacists, and a large majority of the medical specialists participate. Only a few very small hospitals are not part of the National Health Service.

Choice of Doctor The conditions of practice in the Service assure both the patient and doctor a wide degree of freedom. The patient is free to choose his own general practitioner. The doctor is free to refuse to add a particular person to his "panel" (official roster) of patients. Specialists who work out of the hospitals may combine a Service practice with a private practice. A patient may use a private general practitioner, whom he pays, but when he needs hospital care he can use the NHS. Many of the doctors have a mixture of NHS and private patients.

Compared with other industrialized countries the total cost of health care in the United Kingdom is relatively low. For example, in 1970 only 5.6 percent of Britain's national income was spent for health care, compared with 8.4 percent in the United States.[3] Four-fifths of the money for the Health Service comes from general funds, mainly income and excise taxes. Less than 10 percent is raised through the small flat-rate contribution from employed workers through the National Insurance Fund (comparable to our social security tax on employees). The worker pays only about 40 cents per week for the Health Service. Only about 5 percent is raised through fees.

Administration The organization and administration of the NHS is fairly complex and involves active participation by laymen. The system has been divided into three parts coordinated by the National Department of Health and Social Security. The General Medical Service includes general practitioners, ophthalmologists, dentists, and druggists. The Hospital Service includes medical specialists, hospital care, blood transfusions service, laboratory service, and research. The Local Health Authority Service includes home and after-care activities, ambulance service, visiting nurses, and other home aids, as well as general management of the few health centers which have been built.

The three parts of the NHS are under the control of more than 600 boards, councils, and committees, with 12,000 citizens serving as unpaid members. Another 5,000 citizens serve on the Regional and Teaching Hospital Boards and the Hospital Management Committees. Of the volunteers on the boards, one-fourth are doctors. Half the members of the Executive Councils of the General Medical Service are also doctors. One of the reorganization proposals is to unify these three services.

How Does the Patient Get Care?

Each of 134 Executive Councils of the General Medical Service publishes a list of doctors who provide general medical services in its area. The lists are usually displayed at post offices throughout the country. Anyone over age sixteen can choose a doctor from the list. If a person cannot find a doctor who can or will accept him, the Executive Council will help locate one.

To see the doctor one merely goes to the office and waits his or her turn or makes an appointment. Doctors must also treat anyone applying to them who needs treatment and is not on a doctor's panel or who is away from his place of residence temporarily. Patients too ill to go to the doctor's office can request a house call. The family doctors provide 90 percent of all care. They refer patients to specialists and hospitals. Except for emergency care, patients are not expected to seek out hospital care on their own.

AN ANALYSIS OF THE NATIONAL HEALTH SERVICE

The NHS shows how health services can be provided in a relatively large and highly industrialized society. More important as we consider proposals for an American health care program are the outcomes of Britain's experience. Both consumers and producers in the NHS generally support the system. They agree that the medical care, particularly for lower- and middle-income families, is better and more available than previously.

1 Public opinion polls have revealed that four-fifths of the people are "generally satisfied" and believe that they get their money's worth from the system.

2 Formal complaints made against doctors in the system have been few.

3 Only about 3 percent of the population have some form of private health insurance outside the NHS.

4 Both major political parties support the system.

5 The quality and amount of medical care have not deteriorated. On the contrary, all the indices of health such as life expectancy, maternal and child mortality rates, and general death rates show that Great Britain compares favorably with other countries. The volume of care and resources has generally outstripped population growth.

Other outcomes include a tight rein on costs, a better balance in the availability of resources throughout all regions, and systematic planning and development of health care resources.

Difficulties The Service has some problems. Complaints include long waits at times in doctors' offices; inability to obtain a choice of specialist for hospital care; long waiting lists for surgical procedures which are not critical (e.g., tonsillectomies); low pay and low status for general practitioners; slow development of new hospital facilities and updating and renovation of older units; some imbalance in medical resources between different areas of the country and different services; lack of coordination between the parts of the system; and an absence of an overall coordinated plan for the whole health program in a given area. Despite higher expenditure for medical care, the same complaints are charged against our system. Financing and cost of the Service have caused the greatest public debate. The doctors have also been critical of the small capital investment in hospitals and other medical facilities.

Recommendations   A recent study recommended the introduction of compulsory health insurance to pay the cost of general medical service, hospital care, dental care, and ophthalmic services.[4] The premiums would be determined by the cost of such services. The Department of Health would be expected to maintain control of price increases, but no mechanism for control is suggested in the study. The cost of expanding the physical resources for the health service and other aspects of the system would remain with central government and local authorities.

WHAT CAN WE LEARN FROM THE BRITISH?

Since 1948 the British have built a health service system which has resulted in a higher volume of care and better care for the mass of people. The service has provided a vehicle for a coordinated approach to problems and rational planning without completely socializing the health professions, bankrupting the nation, or subjugating the health care institutions to complete bureaucratic control. On the other hand the system still faces problems in financing and coordinating the parts, satisfying the general practitioners, and developing comprehensive coverage for some regions and localities.

The British have compiled an enviable record in their health care delivery system. Could their system be replicated here? The complexity of our present system, the different constraints, and the lack of developmental history would be serious obstacles. If replicating their system seems unlikely, the British experience does suggest principles for building a successful national health service—development of procedures for cost review and control, the need for regional and local planning and coordination of services, and the involvement of both professionals and laymen in policy development.

By comparison, public programs for health care in the United States are limited. Welfare recipients, the poor and the near poor, ghetto and rural residents, and the aged have the greatest unmet health needs. Rapidly increasing costs also place an excessive burden on the middle class.

As presently organized, there are pressures on health care facilities to increase costs and practically none to control them. The total organization is inefficient, irrational, and uncoordinated. It is characterized by lack of planning, proper monitoring, and accountability. In many areas there is a very serious shortage of health care personnel while in others there is useless duplication of facilities. Such conditions have led to a loss of confidence on the part of the public. As a result there is increasing interest in a public health care system. The British experience may provide useful guidelines for such a program.

CHILDREN'S SERVICE AND FAMILY ALLOWANCES

Lack of an adequate health service is the first great deficiency in American social security provisions. Absence of a national policy for children's services is the second. Services are now limited, disjointed, inadequately funded, and discriminatory. As a result millions of children live in poverty or near poverty. Many are doomed to the squalor, discrimination, and alienation of urban ghettoes and rural enclaves. They may grow up as a wasted human resource. They and their parents form the core welfare problem in this country. Present programs pit welfare clients, the working poor, and the mass of wage earners against each other.

CHILDREN'S ALLOWANCES AND SERVICES IN FRANCE

More than one-half of the countries of the world, including all the major nations of Europe, use family allowances in their child care system.

Children's allowances began in France with a system of voluntary benefits paid by employers. The system became compulsory in 1932 and now includes extensive professional services for children.

Administration The French programs are more decentralized in their administration than their English counterparts. They involve more than 100 governmental funds that collect contributions and disburse benefits to citizens in a given region or locale or in a particular employment group. The funds are subject to the general supervision of the national government. National laws establish and define the characteristics of the programs in terms of coverage, costs, benefits, and eligibility requirements. Boards are elected from the employers and employees related to the particular fund.

Benefits The cash benefits provided include:

1 Prenatal allowances during the period of pregnancy if the mother registers and undergoes three prenatal examinations.
2 A maternity grant upon the birth of a child.
3 A monthy allowance to families for each child after the first. The allowance is smaller for the second child than for each subsequent one. Amounts are also higher for children under age two and over age ten.
4 Allowances to families that are supported by a single salary and to mothers in incomplete families who stay home to care for their children. In 1972, a means test was imposed. "Single salary" benefit levels were increased, but 400,000 recipients became ineligible because the means test was applied.
5 Allowances for seriously handicapped children who need special educational treatment.
6 A rent or housing supplement to families based on need.
7 Three days' leave with pay for fathers on the occasion of the birth of each child.

Effect on Birth Rate The French family allowance benefits are available only to families who have two or more children. This provision is typical of a *pronatalist* approach—the hope that allowances would increase the birth rate. However, comparative data indicate that such allowances have not achieved the goal of larger birth rates. Birth rates vary similarly in industrialized countries regardless of the provision of the family allowance. Apparently people do not have children to get the allowance payment.

*"Family allowances
never attracted me."*

In-Kind Benefits   Social services for children and families complement the cash benefits. The family allowance offices manage infants' homes, nurseries, children's homes, maternity hospitals, rest homes for mothers and children, centers for young workers, family holiday settlements and homes, and social centers. The offices employ welfare workers and domestic science teachers. They train young women to be home help workers or mother's aides, teach home and child care, make grants to improve household equipment, and maintain rest and holiday camps.

The ninety-five Departments (districts) of France offer a service for the protection of the health of mothers and children. They provide compulsory prenuptial physical examinations, prenatal and postnatal examinations for mothers, and maintenance of a personal health record for all children under age six. They maintain day care centers, foster homes, and nurseries and employ medical social workers who provide health education. The Departments also maintain a child welfare service for child protection, foster care, and social counseling to parents regarding child care problems. Finally, a network of Family Associations —organizations of parents—serves an advocacy role in securing better child welfare and family services.

ANALYSIS OF THE FRENCH SYSTEM

Family allowances protect children in France by countering childhood poverty. In relation to average earnings the benefits are among the most adequate in the world. For families with two children, the cash monthly benefit totals about 10 percent of their earnings. The benefit for families with five children would amount to about 51 percent of these average earnings. For large families and for those earning less than average amounts, the children's allowance represents a substantial subsidy to provide an adequate standard of living for their children.

In our own program for dependent children, there is fear that if such payments are too large, the poor will be encouraged to have more children in order to get more welfare. The French expanded and strengthened their children's allowances after World War II, partly in the hope that more adequate payments would increase their lagging birth rate. However, their birth rate did not increase compared with that of countries having lower allowances or none at all.

Children's allowances alone will not eliminate poverty nor break the cycle of poverty. However, the French have demonstrated that cash benefits for child care coupled with health care, adequate housing, training in home management, social services to help parents with their child care problems, and protective services can strengthen a nation's families.

THE COSTS OF SOCIAL WELFARE

A third problem in the United States is the mounting cost of payments to public welfare clients. During 1971 and 1972, as the American economy slowed down and unemployment and inflation rose, the number of people seeking public aid increased sharply, and public assistance expenditures for the needy aged, disabled, and dependent children increased by more than $2 billion in one year. To meet this burden, some states had to curtail public services—education, recreation, street repairs, and garbage collection—creating a backlash against welfare services. Poor people were attacked as chiselers, deadbeats, and freeloaders.

In advanced economies, expenditures for the social system are among the largest elements in their public budgets. The United States now spends more for the human services than for any other purpose, including defense. How much of a nation's total product can be invested in its human resources without any adverse effect on the economy depends on economic conditions, social attitudes, and other competing demands within the economy.[5] This problem also bears directly on the balance between the private and the public sectors in a nation's economy and the maximum taxation that is possible without adversely affecting economic growth.

COMPREHENSIVE WELFARE SERVICES IN SWEDEN

Sweden has 8 million people and a per capita gross national product second only to our own as of 1970—$4,350 compared with $4,760 in the United States.[6] Sweden is often considered the prototype for a fully developed welfare state. Its social policy for families and children has as a major objective the provision for families of all the extra expense of having children.

Benefits Payments in the Swedish system for maternity and children's benefits are made to the mother. A tax-free children's allowance of about $300 per year is paid for each child under sixteen, irrespective of family income or the number of children. Free health supervision and inoculations up to school age are given in Child Welfare Centers and National Dental Service clinics. Later health supervision is assumed by the school. Children are also provided the same health care given to all other citizens—free hospital care; reimbursement of three-fourths of the cost of the doctor's medical treatment outside the hospital; most of the cost of out-patient services at hospitals and clinics; reimbursement for travel and part of the drug and dental services costs.

Prenatal and maternity care are provided free, including the costs of delivery and medical care in the hospital or maternity center. In addition the mother receives a cash maternity allowance. If she is employed, she receives a further allowance for any absences before and after the child's birth up to a total of 180 days. Such benefits vary depending on her income. The mother's job rights are protected during her absence should she desire to return to work.

Child Care   Sweden has also developed an extensive system of daily care for children of working mothers and counseling for parents regarding problems of children. Day nurseries, nursery schools, and after-school free-time centers serve about 25,000 children in Stockholm alone. There are long waiting lists for preschool services. These facilities are available to the entire group of working mothers. Fees are based on income. When facilities are inadequate to the demand, priority is given to the most needy families. Nurseries provide the children with hot meals, rest, and play and learning activities. Supplementing these facilities are locally approved "family day-nurseries" run by "day-mothers" in their own homes. The state pays a third of the costs. In addition "homemakers" and "childminders" are available in many localities through the child welfare authorities. The homemaker is prepared to assume the housekeeping and child care duties of the housewife. Childminders are responsible only for supervision and care of the children. Services of both are purchased on a sliding scale by the parents.

Foster family care and institutional care are also provided for children who cannot live in their own homes. Foster care is the preferred arrangement. Committees elected in every municipal area are responsible for enforcing the Child Welfare Act. They supervise foster placements and provide protective services and "preventive child welfare." They study child life in their districts and serve as advocates, guardians, interveners, and supervisors. They work in the interest of juvenile delinquents, children born out of wedlock, neglected and abused children, and children needing special institutional care.

A variety of "homes" provides for infants, unmarried mothers, children needing only temporary care, and children with behavioral or other problems which call for extended care.

Education   Education is free to all children and youth at practically all levels of instruction. Primary education is furnished through public schools which also provide all books and lunches. They likewise assume the supervisory health care provided by the child welfare centers for preschool children.

After age sixteen, when the children's allowances stop, youth who continue in school receive a grant. If they study outside their home district, they receive an additional travel or boarding allowance. Young people twenty years or over engaged in university study or advanced technical training can receive grants of 125 crowns per month, plus loans of up to 7,000 crowns per year for living expenses. The tuition is free. Higher education is not assured in all subjects. The numbers are limited in medicine and engineering and in such disciplines as psychology, chemistry, and physics.

Programs for the Elderly Social provisions for the elderly in Sweden reflect the same diversity and breadth as those for children and the family. Basic protection is provided through financial support programs, housing provisions, and personal care services. Support for the elderly is based on the National Pension Scheme. In addition, a National Supplementary Pension introduced in 1960 provides many elderly with an additional sum based on earnings before the age of 65. Together with the basic pension when the scheme is fully operative by 1990, it will provide two-thirds the average annual earnings during the fifteen highest years. Normal income of male industrial workers ranged from $5,670 to $6,300 per year in 1972. The supplementary pension scheme is financed by contributions from the employee and the employer. The basic pension is financed out of general revenues.

Half of all the pensioners are eligible for local authority housing allowances based on the retirement income of the individual and other conditions and needs. For many the allowance meets the actual housing costs. The general policy is to help older persons remain in their own home as long as possible. Local authorities help improve and modernize dwellings through interest-free loans. For those who cannot live entirely alone, flats are provided in institutional homes or spread throughout housing projects.

Home help services strengthen the individual's ability to live outside an institution. Home helpers assist with housekeeping duties, laundry, cooking, and the planning of meals. They run errands for the elderly and provide companionship for them. Meals-on-wheels also help keep older people in their homes. Finally day centers and such programs as pensioners' clubs, occupational and exercise activities, transportation, home delivery of library services, and good-neighbor services are offered. Numerous institutions that provide congregate living for the aged also offer the full range of services and activities that older people need.

Overall Costs In 1969 Sweden devoted 19 percent of its GNP to welfare services. Specific expenditures of GNP were: Health services, 8.3 percent; pensions (retirement, disability, and survivors), 6.6 percent; family and child welfare benefits, 3.0 percent; unemployment benefits, 10 percent; and all other programs, 0.5 percent.[7] The rise in expenditures from 14 percent of GNP in 1963 to 19 percent in 1969 is apparently due chiefly to reforms introduced in the pension programs.

Expenditures in the United States in fiscal 1969 for social welfare programs approximately comparable to those for Sweden totaled 8.3 percent of GNP, distributed as follows: Health, 2.6 percent; pensions (OASDI and public assistance for the aged and disabled), 4.9 percent; family and child welfare and aid to dependent children, 0.5 percent; unemployment, 0.3 percent; and all other programs, 0.1 percent.[8]

To a greater extent than other countries, our system is slanted in favor of retirement and disability payments for the total population. Health services are limited primarily to the aged and the poor. Family and child welfare are almost wholly restricted to the poor. Our expenditures are channeled to the protection of the middle- and higher-income groups against retirement and disability (social insurance), relegating poor families to the vicissitudes of welfare payments (public assistance), while the working poor (those fully employed but earning less than the poverty level) are generally ignored.

As might be anticipated, countries investing more in their human capital have higher tax rates and a higher proportion of their resources allocated to the public sector of their economy. In Sweden, in 1969, total taxes and fees for all purposes totaled almost 42 percent of the GNP, compared with 37 percent in France, 36 percent in West Germany and Great Britain, and 30 percent in the United States.[9] While many Swedes are unhappy about high taxes, no political party has advocated reducing health and welfare benefits. On the contrary, dental care benefits are being added.

As we try to improve our welfare system, we may be well advised to study the European experience. Welfare is an area where we have more to learn from others than we have skill to export.

SOCIAL ISSUES FACING THE EUROPEAN ECONOMIC COMMUNITY

The European Economic Community established in 1958 is the framework for economic cooperation in western Europe. Now the EEC has taken an interest in social problems as well. At the Paris summit meeting in October 1972, the heads of state "emphasized that they attached as much importance to the social field as to achievement of economic and monetary union."[10]

The EEC was established by six nations—Belgium, France, the Federal Republic of Germany, Luxembourg, Italy, and the Netherlands. In 1972, three others were admitted—Denmark, Ireland, and the United Kingdom.

The social problems summarized here are highlighted in the 1972 Social Report of the Community. Rapid growth in production leads to the need to recruit labor across national boundaries. Workers move among the member countries and also come from such nonmember nations as Spain, Greece, Yugoslavia, and Turkey, where there is a labor surplus. The workers' role in decisions affecting their own destiny, their political rights, and ultimate citizenship are major issues.

Concerns more directly related to welfare are the harmonization of social security benefits, since workers may have credits in several countries, housing problems brought on by increased labor demands from already overpopulated industrial areas, and wages and terms of employment.

Problems of readaptation, redevelopment, and reemployment led the EEC to establish a European Social Fund in May of 1972. Grants are given to projects to deal with changing economic and employment status and necessary vocational retraining. The fund also supports programs for handicapped workers.

Direct welfare concerns also include provision for children's education, employment opportunities for school leavers, child care opportunities and working conditions for women, and services for people who retire. Impressive developments are presented for each country in the social reports of the Community.

The most important step for cooperative planning is perhaps the development of a system of social indicators to provide data for the newly authorized Social Budget. As other nations join, we can expect that the impact of social recommendations of the EEC will be increased. The Community should eventually get the authority to enforce desired social policies.

Mark P. Hale

KEY TERMS

social insurance	general medical service
social assistance	hospital service
personal service	local health authority service
family allowances	gross national product
panel of patients	

FOR DISCUSSION

1 How are social welfare programs throughout the world classified?
2 Which program is offered by the largest number of countries?
3 Throughout the world, which is more common—social insurance or social assistance?
4 Why is social assistance particularly controversial?
5 What do English, French, and Swedish programs suggest for America?
6 Characterize the major problems in delivery of American health services.
7 Which of the ten principles guiding the British National Health Service would be most controversial here?
8 What will medical services cost for a tourist in Great Britain?
9 How is the National Health Service financed?
10 What benefit is denied to families in France who have only one child?
11 Why is a rent subsidy included in French benefits?
12 In France, with five children the family allowance would provide what proportion of average earnings?
13 Have family allowance programs increased the birth rate?
14 Why is the Gross National Product important to understanding the Swedish welfare system?
15 Compared to other countries, what groups do our welfare programs tend to favor and tend to ignore?
16 What are the strengths of the European Economic Community as an instrumentality for welfare planning and action?
17 What ideas from European welfare programs would be most appropriate for the United States? Why?

PROJECTS

1 Plan and present a debate on this subject: "Resolved, that the United States should adopt the British National Health System."

2   List the services provided to children in France under the system of family allowances. In a parallel column, list the source of each service in the United States. What gaps are revealed?

3   Form two committees—one to summarize social welfare provisions in eastern European countries and the other to consider several developing countries of Africa or Asia. The latest edition of *Social Security Programs Throughout the World* will provide a basic source.

4   Describe in detail the migrant workers' problems in Europe. What are the causes and consequences of mobility?

5   Report on the international social welfare activities of the United Nations. How do their activities compare with those of the European Economic Community?

FOR FURTHER STUDY

Eveline M. Burns, *Children's Allowances and the Economic Welfare of Children*, Citizen's Committee for Children, New York, 1968.

Leif Haanés-Olsen, "Children's Allowances: Their Size and Structure in Five Countries," *Social Security Bulletin*, vol. 35, May 1972, pp. 17–28.

Joel F. Handler, *The Coercive Social Worker*, Academic Press, New York, 1974. A study of English children's services.

Alfred Kadushin, *Child Welfare Services*, Macmillan, New York, 1974, pp. 663–700. One of the few general textbooks with a chapter on services in other countries.

Gaston V. Rimlinger, *Welfare Policy and Industrialization in Europe, America, Russia*, Wiley, New York, 1971.

Social Security Programs Throughout the World, U.S. Government Printing Office. This publication has been reissued every two years and summarizes the program of every country.

Olive Stevenson, *Claimant or Client, a Social Worker's View of the Supplementary Benefits Commission*, Allen & Unwin, London, 1973. Many of the basic issues in social welfare with which we are familiar are considered in terms of the system in England.

Other sources of information include: The British Information Service, 845 Third Avenue, New York, N.Y. 10022; The French Press and Information Service, 972 Fifth Avenue, New York, N.Y. 10021; The German Information Center, 410 Park Avenue, New York, N.Y. 10022; The Swedish Information Service, 825 Third Avenue, New York, N.Y. 10022.

Part Two

Major
Problem Areas

Social workers do not control the means to deal with most large problem areas, but the policies developed by others affect demands for social work services and the objectives of practice. To deal with human needs, large systems employ social workers who collaborate with a variety of people from other fields.

Social policies are developed and promoted by economists, lawyers, and industrialists often with inadequate attention to the consequences for individuals and communities. Such consequences are the concern of the social worker. To demonstrate more political effectiveness, practitioners and social work students need a clear knowledge of the major social problems and the skill to seek effective coalitions with groups that share the same goals. Part Two provides a foundation for that knowledge.

The section includes discussions of two of the top priorities of the social work profession—poverty and racism.

For centuries, we have had widely differing provisions with one set of benefits for people with a history of regular employment and another for those who are economically dependent. Only recently have we had serious proposals to eliminate the resulting inequities.

Racism still persists to create social and economic barriers. We are gradually seeing greater community control of mechanisms for human betterment, but progress is far too slow.

This section will examine:

Work and how employed people obtain security in the face of retirement, work injuries, or unemployment

Approaches to poverty and how well the efforts have succeeded

The critical areas of health, population and family planning, education, and the legal structure

Racism and the responses of its victims

In what areas would you invest your energy?
What approaches to problem solving would you try?

Chapter 5

Economic Security
for the Employed

What economic problems face the employed?
Is social insurance really insurance?
How is economic insecurity reduced?
Can we count on adequate benefits?

The economic well-being of working men and women is an important concern of our society. Social workers are usually not responsible for the direct administration of social insurance programs on behalf of employed people, but they rely heavily on the system as undergirding for other human services.

The alternative to social insurance is economic insecurity, with the hazards of unemployment, work injuries, illness, or dependency after retirement. Economic insecurity is characterized by the threat of a sharp decline in income at the very time when expenses are rising. When a man is injured at work, his wages often stop just as he faces larger medical costs.

Social *insurance* is designed to meet the needs of employed people. Social *assistance* and personal services are utilized to deal with the problem of poverty, the concern of Chapter 6.

Social insurance is provided through the Social Security program, which has grown rapidly in the last forty years. Workers and their employers pay $69 billion a year in payroll taxes for programs for the aged, the disabled, and dependent survivors of workers. More than 30 million beneficiaries in these three groups receive more than $68 billion in cash benefits annually. Unemployment compensation costs an average of $6 billion annually and is paid to about two million, depending on economic conditions.

The principle of social insurance is well accepted. Society agrees that people who are working or who have worked for some years are entitled to assistance with serious life crises. Unemployment benefits are still controversial, because of concern that unemployed workers will not diligently seek work. The beginnings of concern for economic security take us as far back as the Middle Ages.

DEVELOPMENT OF SOCIAL INSURANCE

Employment Security in the Middle Ages

The causes of economic insecurity for the working man have deep roots. Society experimented on a large scale with guaranteeing employment for a lifetime during the Middle Ages in Europe. In the medieval social order every person was dependent on someone else. Nine-tenths of the working population was engaged in agriculture and lived in small self-sufficient villages. No one outside the towns was free to migrate, change jobs, or demand higher wages. The living standards at which people aimed were formed by tradition, not rationality or self-interest. A peasant accepted without question the social convention that he was inherently unequal to his lord and to other social castes. He worked to survive. He had great fear of invention or change and no concept of success or achievement beyond his present place in life. He did not aim to surpass last year's harvest, to occupy a more spacious house, or to send his son to a university. He had succeeded when he had attained a standard of living appropriate to his "station in life."[1]

The peasant in medieval times was not free. He scarcely subsisted from one year to the next. He was not equal to everyone else, but he was at least somewhat secure. Society was close-knit; people were bound by a strong sense of personal obligation to one another. Should a peasant fall seriously ill, grow too old to work, or become badly crippled, he was assured of care from his relatives, the church, or the lord of the manor on which he worked. His possessions were meager and inadequate, but he had access to land which all the village shared in common and to the "wastelands" beyond. His children would have work when they grew up, since they were obliged by tradition to follow in the footsteps of their parents.

The medieval ages offered guaranteed employment under four conditions that individuals would find unpalatable today:

1 Tasks changed very little between generations.

2 Entry into crafts outside agriculture, the supply of products, and market prices were all strictly controlled.

3 Demand for surpluses was confined to a small class of church and secular nobility, because the majority had little purchasing power and villages were locally self-sufficient. Therefore demand rose very slowly, and there was no impetus for high productivity.

4 The population grew little and declined in times of poor harvests and

pestilence. Employment was thus guaranteed by traditional consumption patterns and a system of fixed labor.

The Rise of Capitalism

Between the fourteenth and nineteenth centuries, the manorial economic system gave way gradually to modern capitalism. The main features of a capitalistic economy are respect for private property, pursuit of profit, freedom of individual enterprise, and competition with free prices.[2] Competition and free enterprise can operate effectively only if the labor force is highly mobile; thus men and women have been liberated to seek higher wages and better working conditions. The range of occupational roles is far wider than in the past. However, the old personalized bonds of mutual obligation between employer and employee have been replaced by a highly impersonal organization of labor in factories and large service organizations. People have been freed from the chains of custom but left more insecure and alone in the face of adversity.

Toward an Industrial Society

The Industrial Revolution had its initial impact in this country during the first third of the nineteenth century. Several changes shaped the context in which people work today. Industries became more specialized, producing on a large scale for national rather than local markets. Population began to shift from rural to urban areas. Labor was increasingly engaged in production of manufactured rather than agricultural goods. A proletariat emerged, wholly dependent on wages for subsistence. Science and technology were systematically applied to the production process, so that old ways and old skills were rendered obsolescent. Capital resources were increasingly utilized as the basis for production.[3] Because labor was always scarce relative to capital in this country, wages were higher than in European countries.[4] Finally, the entire social class structure was reshaped. In medieval times class membership was determined by birth and relationship to the land. Class relations were reinforced by traditional loyalties and a set of well-defined services which varied depending on class membership. After the Industrial Revolution, social class membership was determined by a person's ownership or relationship to capital.[5]

An industrialized economy organized along capitalistic principles functioned well to meet the desires of a growing population for a wide variety of goods and services. It often adapted quickly to changes in the preferences of the buying public. The prices of many goods fell over the years, so that most people enjoyed a rising standard of living.

SOCIAL PROVISIONS AND ECONOMICS

The United States as a mature industrial society exhibits two features of crucial importance to social welfare: relatively rapid social change and production of surpluses. Four questions must be answered. (1) How will the surpluses be distributed? (2) What groups will control the apparatus? (3) Will crises and suffering engendered by production of these surpluses be ignored or somehow mitigated by outside intervention? (4) How will future production be determined?

One can let the marketplace decide who gets what and how much is produced. Dollars can be the measure of all value. Individual prosperity hangs or falls on a person's relationship to the productive process. The main indicator of social needs then becomes the price of goods and services. Those who can pay, can get.

The nature of social problems from a market perspective is obvious. Efficiency, mobility, access to capital, knowledge of the market, freedom from economic restraint, and legal protection of property are essential. Social conditions interfering with these objectives can be overcome through inventions to encourage economic movement. The stock market, central banks, investment houses, employment relocation services, the transportation system, and antitrust legislation are all designed to improve the economic system.

Human welfare has been advanced by these inventions. However, our society also holds that individuals have inherent worth beyond their economic roles of laborer or entrepreneur. Because people are valuable in themselves, they have the right to physical comfort, opportunity for self-expression, emotional fulfillment, and equal treatment from powerful institutions.

Value of the Individual   We should not encourage people to be nonproductive or uncreative. Nor should everybody share with perfect equality in the benefits of civilization. What we do say is that all persons are important, and society has an obligation to provide conditions which will enhance their well-being. The level of productivity is not altogether within the individual's control but is inherent in the nature of the industrial way of life. Some persons grow too old to compete; some suffer injury that limits their ability to compete; some are unprepared by their life experiences; and some are prevented from competing by discrimination. Since many problems related to economic insecurity and deprivation are the consequences of industrialization, those affected ought to be compensated by the products of that process. This compensation is provided by social insurance.

SOCIAL INSURANCE IS NOT REALLY INSURANCE

In some ways, social insurance is not really insurance at all. A comparison with private fire or life insurance reveals major differences. Private insurance is designed to cover events that occur independently of each other and that usually do not strike large numbers of people in the same area.[6] Companies reinsure risks with other companies to protect against excessive claims from catastrophes. Earthquake coverage is particularly expensive because of the widespread damage that can occur from a single event.

Social insurance is designed to cover possible widespread unemployment, long-term disability from work-related accidents or injuries, or retirement payments that may extend over many years.

Private insurance is purchased voluntarily, but participation in social insurance is required by law. If claims exceed assets, the private company will eventually go bankrupt. Not so for social insurance. The government may use general tax revenues as well as payroll taxes to pay benefits. Payments can be increased to stimulate the economy or in response to inflation. There is also no responsibility to maintain a reserve large enough to pay all claims.

For these reasons, many argue that social insurance is not *insurance*. It is a tax that provides *transfer payments*, in this instance from people who are working to those who cannot. The only "insurance" is the confidence that funds will be available to pay benefits to present workers who may need them—tomorrow or forty years from now.[7]

THE PROBLEM OF UNEMPLOYMENT

One persistent feature of capitalistic market organization has been unemployment, alternating with overexpansion. The first full business cycle appeared in this country during the 1840s. For the past 130 years, the economy has fluctuated between boom and contraction. Since the Great Depression of the 1930s fluctuations have been less severe. The government has shifted from noninterference in market affairs to a partially managed economy. The Federal Reserve System attempts to control the supply of money and interest rates to promote monetary and price stability. The government through juggling of taxes and expenditures also attempts to stimulate or curb investment and consumer spending. Thus the disruptive effects of the business cycle have noticeably moderated in recent years.

New Workers All the same the threat of unemployment has not disappeared, especially for the 50 percent of the nation's new workers who do not continue their education past high school. They have little prospect of earning high incomes, because they lack the necessary credentials. They cannot make up for lost time by relying on the hope of high salaries in the future. They cannot afford large debts. Most will marry soon after high school graduation. Through no fault of his own a young prospective worker may find himself with all the expenses of a new family and no source of income. Society has implicitly promised that completion of high school means self-sufficiency. When the young person attempts to cash in on this promise, he may find no job available, or only temporary or dead-end employment. Even the well-educated may find themselves unemployed or underemployed.

Pockets of Depression Localized depressions also displace workers. The story of the decline of Appalachia as a coal-mining region is familiar.[8] Less well known are other pockets of depression where one-third of the residents in some counties are welfare recipients, due to disappearance of jobs. It is difficult to hold these workers responsible for their idleness since they are the victims of social change. Social change and the business cycle are unpredictable forces. Even if the worker fulfills his part of the bargain with society by learning a socially useful trade and by actively seeking work, his means of livelihood may be swept away without warning or personal recourse.

Recent Unemployment Trends

The unemployment rate has recently begun to show less response to jumps in national productivity. There has always been a trade-off between inflation and unemployment. When one went up the other went down. However, the United States had a combination of increasing unemployment and rising inflation during the latter part of the 1960s and the early 1970s. While the aim of national economic policy is "full employment," we may have to settle for a permanent unemployment rate between 4.5 and 5 percent. The rate is understated because it does not include those who would prefer to work but have given up seeking employment.

About 75 percent of all unemployed workers at any one time have been out of a job for less than four months.[9] Workers whose job loss is temporary will nevertheless suffer financial injury since they must rely on savings or personal loans if no public support is available. Today people cannot fall back on the family farm or the garden. The industrial worker cannot provide for his basic subsistence unless he has a job. He can no longer pick up "by-work" such as making dolls for wealthy children or whittling cuckoo clocks to support his family. The combination of complete wage dependency and market cantankerousness makes the worker highly vulnerable.

The shift from an agricultural economy to an urban-industrial economy has created other risks to security. In traditional cultures old age brings with it respect and privilege. The aged are honored and often dominate the households of younger children and relatives. Forces in modern society have dramatically altered relationships between the old and the young, often to the detriment of the aged.

THE UNEMPLOYMENT INSURANCE PROGRAM

Unemployment insurance replaces a portion of a worker's income over relatively short periods when he is involuntarily without work. The theory is to give individuals enough money to cover essential living expenses without providing benefits so high that workers lack incentive to return to the labor market.

Financing the System   Under the present unemployment insurance system, all states impose an unemployment insurance tax collected from employers by the federal government and placed in a special trust fund established by the U.S. Treasury. Each state has its own separate account. By law, money from the trust fund must be invested in federal securities, with interest credited to the states' accounts. The federal government pays the costs of administering unemployment insurance programs at the state level. In addition the federal government pays one-half the cost for operation of state unemployment services.[10] This method of financing unemployment insurance has many disadvantages. Unemployment insurance tax rates are more costly for industries with high unemployment histories. Businessmen are therefore strongly motivated to press for inclusion of numerous disqualifying factors in the eligibility criteria of state statutes. Firms also have a powerful incentive to keep benefit levels low and to dispute workers' claims for benefits.[11]

Reforms   What basic reforms are suggested? Program financing must be reviewed and tax rates made more equitable.[12] Duration of benefits should be uniform between states and extended to 30 weeks.[13] Many with high risk of unemployment are currently excluded: domestic workers, farm laborers, workers in agricultural processing plants, self-employed individuals, young people moving into their first jobs, and people who have been out of the labor market for extended periods. Coverage should be universal, with uniform national eligibility rules and liberalized benefit standards.

OLD-AGE AND SURVIVORS' INSURANCE

In the 1880s, about sixty years before Congress approved social insurance for the aged and unemployed in this country, Bismarck's Germany had adopted a system of federally administered old-age pensions. Great Britain, Sweden, Denmark, the U.S.S.R., Belgium, France, and Greece all established pension programs before 1930, though benefit levels and coverage were limited.

Old-Age Insurance in the United States

Here, the Supreme Court remained opposed to old-age insurance. Strongly entrenched individualistic traditions emphasized personal rather than social responsibility for economic well-being. We lacked Germany's paternalistic traditions, although we shared her federalism. Our population was more heterogeneous than that of nations like Sweden, and heterogeneity made agreement on social issues difficult. The land area, size, and dispersion of our population added further obstacles to centralized administration of social programs. The minority group membership of many of our nation's poor contributed to lack of enthusiasm for programs with a strong economic welfare component.[14]

Veterans were the first to receive public pensions. By 1910, forty-two out of the forty-eight states had authorized payments to this group. Eligibility for pensions was contingent on strict residency requirements ranging from fifteen to thirty-five years, depending upon the state. Benefits were minuscule—an average of $14.35 per month in 1934. Industrial pensions were scarcely developed at all. Old people had to fend for themselves, relying as best they could on savings, relatives, and charity.

President Franklin D. Roosevelt in 1933 turned his attention to the task of restoring confidence and economic vigor. There was nothing in his campaign platform about social insurance. These programs were no part of the New Deal package.

By 1934, Roosevelt was distressed to note the widening popularity of two people's movements—the Townsend Movement on the West Coast, with more than a million members, and Huey Long's "Share the Wealth" crusade in the South. Long was possible presidential timber. Townsend, a leader of the aged in California, advocated universal pensions of $200 per month for the elderly with no means test. (If implemented, this plan would have cost one-quarter of the Gross National Product in 1935). The President sensed a direct attack on his administration from these two quarters. Elections were coming up. Furthermore, antidepression policies were not working effectively, and unemployment remained widespread. Old-age insurance might help to rid the labor market of older workers and make more room for younger laborers. Thus social insurance was needed as a counter-offensive for political and economic threats to Roosevelt's policies. The President insisted that leigslation *must* be passed—and it was, in record time. The first Social Security Act of 1935 was so lengthy and complicated that few legislators really knew what they were approving.[15]

Current Provisions   Old Age, Survivors, Disability and Health Insurance (OASDHI) is our major social insurance program. It provides cash benefits to retired workers, dependents of deceased or retired wage earners, permanently and totally disabled workers and their dependents, and medical, hospital, and nursing home payments on behalf of retired workers and their spouses.[16] Benefits are financed by taxes on employees and their employers and on the earnings of self-employed people paid directly to the federal government. The employee's share is withheld from his paycheck. Employers and self-employed persons pay quarterly. Benefits depend upon the earner's income during the productive years, although there are minimum and maximum levels. Because benefits are based on the principle of wage replacement, they are related to the amount earned. More and more occupational groups have been included since the passage of old-age insurance by Congress in 1935, so now only a few occupations are exempt. Migrant laborers and those who never enter the labor market still reach old age without any Social Security benefits under OASDHI.

Costs and Benefits   OASDHI benefits cost $5.5 billion a month for nearly 30 million beneficiaries. The average monthly benefit in mid-1973 to retired workers was $165, and to aged widows and widowers $137.[17] Recent amendments to the Social Security Act have increased benefit levels substantially. This means the tax base has risen too. In 1974, the tax base was $13,200. Automatic increases in the tax base will occur every time benefits are adjusted for inflation. The contribution rate until 1977 will be 5.85 percent of wages from each employee and employer, or a total of $1444 on the maximum income. There is an 8 percent tax rate for the self-employed.[18]

Automatic increases in benefits will occur whenever the inflation rate exceeds 3 percent in any one year. This will be of help to everyone facing higher prices. The first increases from this provision of the 1972 Social Security Amendments came in 1974. Congressional review of benefit levels to keep up with inflation is made unnecessary by this change.

The wages that an older person may earn without affecting full OASDHI benefits were also raised from $140 per month to $175. Above that amount, benefits will be reduced $1 for each $2 earned. In the year a person reaches age 72 and each year beyond, earnings will not reduce benefits at all.

There are some basic similarities between OASDHI and unemployment insurance. In both programs, benefits are related to previous earnings and are paid as a matter of right. Payments are clearly defined in contrast to benefits under public assistance programs. However, OASDHI differs from the unemployment insurance system in several respects:

1   The tax for unemployment insurance is levied solely on employers.
2   OASDHI is wholly federally administered, for unemployment insurance, administration and policy are established at the state level subject to federal requirements.
3   Employers are taxed at a uniform rate in OASDHI, but firms with histories of low unemployment rates are given a tax break on unemployment insurance.
4   The duration of unemployment benefits is limited generally to a maximum of 26 weeks, but OASDHI is provided until death.

5 While private insurance carriers offer policies insuring against old age and sickness, they have refused to underwrite unemployment. The argument is that loss of income due to unemployment is much too unpredictable.

Pay as You Go   OASDHI was originally sold to the American public as an insurance program. Benefits varied with the amount of contributions; the "risk" of old age was spread over a great many people; and a reserve fund was established. However, four years after the Social Security Act was passed, an amendment was introduced to place the whole system on a "pay-as-you-go" basis. The 1972 amendments reaffirm that the trust fund is to be regarded only as a contingency fund. This means that at any one time there is only sufficient money in the reserve fund to pay for one year's claims. The reserve fund has become a bookkeeping fiction. In reality, at retirement no one gets his or her own contributions back, nor are benefits received in proportion to the contribution. Taxes collected from younger workers now on the job go directly to pay for the retirement benefits of those receiving OASDHI. As has been indicated, this is an income transfer. The pretense of a reserve fund may be of little value, especially when such large amounts of federal funds are involved in OASDHI transfers. Social Security might better be financed directly from general revenues.

Use of General Revenue   Financing OASDHI benefits from general revenues would have several advantages. Although employers and employees are taxed at equal rates, many economists feel that the employer tax is shifted to workers either in the form of fewer jobs or reduced wage levels. Payments by workers in conjunction with the personal income tax might be preferable. Social security taxes should also be less regressive. Low-income workers pay proportionately more in taxes than do high-income workers, increasing the economic stresses on the working poor. The issue raises a central conflict: equity versus adequacy. The principle of individual equity, or "equal treatment of equals," is imbedded in the contribution/benefit orientation of OASDHI. Benefits received are proportional to previous earnings. If you earn more, you get more. On the other hand, low wage earners need more of their previous income replaced at retirement to subsist. Consequently they must receive proportionately more in benefits than they have contributed. To the extent that Social Security programs are redistributive and serve to maintain a minimally adequate income floor for retired workers, the equity principle is violated. If general revenues were employed to support OASDHI payments, the program would become more redistributive.[19]

WORKMEN'S COMPENSATION

Workmen's compensation, the most widespread social insurance program among the nations of the world, provides benefits for work-related injuries. Among various social insurance schemes workmen's compensation has been the first to be implemented because:

1 Injuries to workers on the job are clearly related to the work setting, while unemployment and financial problems of old age have more complicated causes. Employers clearly can be held socially resonsible for conditions relating to health and safety under which workers must operate.

2 Since the feudal period, tradition has held that employers have some responsibility for the well-being of employees. This was certainly true in the guilds.

3 The failure of an employer to compensate an employee for an on-the-job injury could result in a costly lawsuit.

American Provisions In the American program, financing comes entirely from the employer. The general rule of thumb is that two-thirds of the income lost due to work-related injury should be replaced by the employer. There are conflicting theories about how to value lost income. Some people argue that psychological anguish should be considered in compensation. For example, the loss of a leg might be more costly to one man than to another. The other view is that psychological factors should be ignored in awarding compensation and only the actual or potential wage loss taken into consideration. The actual amount received by a claimant generally represents a compromise between the two viewpoints.[20]

The workmen's compensation system is the most poorly reported, generally ignored, and inadequate of all the social insurances. There are few federal policy requirements. Each state has its unique act. Casual laborers, agricultural laborers, and domestic workers—about 20 percent of the employed labor force—are usually not covered at all.

Most employers may satisfy the requirements of state law by taking out an insurance policy with a private carrier. Some qualify through "self-insurance," offering proof to the state that they can make payments out of company assets or reserves. One-fifth of the states do not require employers to cover the full cost.

Total disability may be temporary or permanent. In most cases the worker suffers temporary total disability and expects to return to work. Because of waiting periods and other complications, workers generally get only about 50 percent of the average weekly wage. Low-income workers fare somewhat better under this arrangement than do high-income laborers. In thirty-four states workers can receive no more than $55 per week, though the amount varies with number of dependents.

The position of the permanently disabled worker is quite unenviable. In twenty-one states benefits are *not* paid for life but are limited to 330 to 550 weeks, with maximum payments ranging from $10,000 to $30,000.

Laborers can also be compensated for permanent partial injuries, loss of limbs, or more generalized damage to the head or back. The benefits are subject to time limits or state monetary maxima. Death benefits are paid to widows and dependent children. Benefits for widows continue for life (or until remarriage) in only thirteen states.

In recent years employers have begun to extend the scope of coverage to include occupational diseases. However, only thirty-four of the fifty-four jurisdictions now offer this form of protection, and the diseases covered are very limited. There is a special federal program for miners with black lung disease.

Major Shortcomings Serious problems are found in our workmen's compensation programs. State statutory maxima on amounts of benefits allowable have not kept pace with rising wage rates or changes in the standard of living.

Consequently a worker who was permanently disabled between 1927 and 1947 now receives an average benefit of less than $12 per week. The income replacement objective of workmen's compensation is not being achieved. Second, differences between states in scope, coverage, and benefit standards of existing programs raise a serious equity issue. A workman in South Carolina who loses an eye in a steel plant fares much worse than a worker suffering the injury under identical circumstances in Ohio.[21]

Workers not covered, particularly in agricultural labor, suffer disproportionately from severe injuries. Even while recognizing that small employers may find it difficult to offer compensation, some mechanism must be found for providing income security to these groups.

Occupational diseases are too narrowly defined. Workers are under special hardship when they can recover neither medical costs nor lost income due to an uncovered illness. However, the extent of employer liability is often very difficult to identify. Allowances are generally not paid to workers who must undergo rehabilitative training, despite the fact that this training was necessitated by an occupational injury. Total medical costs are often not met due to state statutory limitations. With rapidly escalating costs for medical care, workers are increasingly exposed to financial hardship. Waiting periods before benefits begin may extend several weeks. At the other extreme, workers must often file immediately for compensation before they have any clear understanding of how much their work performance will be affected.

Proposals   The National Commission on Workmen's Compensation made recommendations in 1972 to improve the program. They suggested another commission to conduct further study. Unfortunately the recommended pattern of organization still provides for state-administered programs "enhanced by federal assistance." They also recommended that benefits to widows and other dependent survivors should be reduced by the amount of any payment from OASDHI.

Workmen's compensation then is a skeletal system offering inadequate benefits to a seriously disadvantaged population. On grounds of national efficiency, humanity, and equity, reform should be a compelling issue for social workers.

PRIVATE PLANS FOR EMPLOYMENT SECURITY

Private pension and employee benefit plans have grown concurrently with the Social Security program. These benefits now make up about 25 percent of older people's retirement income. Most plans are designed to supplement, not replace, benefits under OASDHI. For unionized employees, health and welfare benefits are frequently provided under union auspices. Since neither the private firm nor the union has the same stability as the government, a number of special problems developed that led to a new pension act in 1974.

Four questions illustrate the issues:

When Should Vesting Take Effect?   Vesting provides a claim on the employer's contributions to a pension plan. Very few plans give employees that right immediately. Delay in vesting is intended to encourage workers to remain with a firm, and it reduces costs to employers. On the other hand, a short vesting period may be more effective to encourage the security-conscious employee to stay. For short-term employees a brief vesting period results in claims for very small returns that are not worth the effort. Some plans make it impossible for the employee to have a break in service or to leave for any reason without losing benefits. Clearly transfer from one employer to another of pension credits accumulated both from payroll deductions and the employer's contributions is essential.

How Are the Funds Invested?   There are many possible abuses in investment policies. Sometimes the employer's share is simply left in the company, and no earnings are credited. In others, investment of employee contributions outside the company does not lead to adequate return. Plans that are designed to pay a fixed income are of less help when buying power decreases under inflation. Plans that invest assets at least partially in stocks that increase in value with inflation can pay larger benefits if prices go up.

What Happens When a Worker Is Fired or Laid Off?   To gain vesting rights some plans require both continuous service and remaining with the company until retirement. An abuse involves firing or laying off workers who are near retirement to avoid the payment of benefits.

What Happens When a Firm Goes Out of Business?   Failure of a business often involves loss of accumulated benefits from the employer. Unless these contributions are paid in each year to an irrevocable trust, employees are likely to lose. Studebaker was a classic case of a firm with an apparently sound pension plan, but when it went out of business, all accrued benefits were lost.

As a result of abuses and difficulties, we now have greater control of private pension funds. Some proposals suggest replacement by large social security payments. This would provide full transferability.[22] Government insurance of pension programs is now provided for the first time.

Both public and private efforts at employment security will face new problems as the older population increases proportionately and becomes an increasing financial concern. The viability of employment security plans will be more severely tested.

In the next chapter we will consider a minority of Americans but a segment of society that causes much greater concern—those who are too poor to live adequately and the programs that try to provide help for them.

Marilyn Flynn

KEY TERMS

cash transfers	equity versus adequacy
economic insecurity	unemployment insurance
feudalism	workmen's compensation
industrial revolution	disability benefits
business cycle	death benefits
OASDHI	vesting

FOR DISCUSSION

1   What major hazards relate to economic insecurity? Illustrate the statement: "Expenditures often rise at the same time income declines."
2   Which program is least accepted? What are the consequences?
3   What are the values of the marketplace? Which ones does social welfare add?
4   What sources of security did peasants have in the Middle Ages?
5   Is modern capitalism "highly impersonal"? Cite examples in your answer.
6   Why did industrialization result in an increased standard of living?
7   Evaluate the statement: "Unemployment is more often caused by economic factors than by deficiencies of individuals."
8   Do you agree that private health insurance is like social insurance because it deals with large numbers of claimants and may involve long-term problems?
9   What is the most accurate term for "social insurance for the employed"?
10 What is the relationship between the concept of *transfer payments* and the discussion of society's *disposal of surpluses* earlier in the chapter?
11 Should benefits go only to the *involuntarily* unemployed? What groups would this exclude?
12 What is the most controversial reform of unemployment insurance?
13 Why have we been considered backward in insurance provisions for older workers?
14 To which program discussed in the chapter do employees contribute?
15 What would be the effect if OASDHI were financed from general revenue?
16 What is the most serious problem with regard to workmen's compensation? How would you remedy it?
17 What is *vesting* in a private pension plan? Why is it important?

PROJECTS

1   Ask an economist to respond to questions from the class about labor supply and demand, unemployment, or public and private retirement benefits. What new ideas does he introduce, and what values seem of greatest importance?
2   Consult your local Social Security Office, and summarize the current social security benefits for:
    a   A married couple—husband and sole wage earner retiring at 65
    b   A married couple—both wage earners for at least the last ten years, husband retiring at 65 and wife at 62
    c   A wife and two school-age children who survive a husband who had at least ten years of coverage
    d   A wage earner who becomes permanently and totally disabled
3   How will increased cost of living now affect future benefits? Request a statement of your social security credits. Forms are available at your local office. How long does it take to get a response? Compare the information received by each person in the class.
4   Should social insurance benefits of retired workers be reduced if they obtain another full- or part-time job? Discuss the issue, indicating the present regulations as well as the arguments on both sides.
5   You will recall that France has special social security benefits for the family that has a single salary. These payments are much like wages for mothers. What would it cost the government per year for each mother if she received $2 an hour based on a 40-hour week? Should social insurance provide wages to mothers for child rearing in the United States? Set forth the pros and cons.

FOR FURTHER STUDY

Philip Booth, *Social Security in America*, Institute of Labor and Industrial Relations, Ann Arbor, Mich., 1973.

Victor George, *Social Security and Society*, Routledge, Boston, 1973.

Daniel S. Sanders, *The Impact of Reform Movements on Social Policy Change*, Burdick, Fair Lawn, N.J., 1973.

Chapter 6

Poverty
and Income Security

How is poverty measured?
Who are the poor?
Why is public assistance controversial?
Should the poor be put to work?

Poverty as a fact of life in the United States is hard to believe. With few beggars and vagrants on the streets, and with the low-income sectors of the population ghettoized or isolated in rural areas, poverty can be easily overlooked. This country's poor are perhaps the best-dressed in the world. The don't stand out in the city streets or shopping centers. For these reasons, we can say that the poor today are largely "invisible."

For the first time in history, the poor are a minority in American society. Median family income now exceeds $10,000 a year—though in 1933, nearly two-thirds of the nation's families earned $3,000 or less.

In 1962, the President's Council of Economic Advisers estimated that 35 million people—or one-fifth of the nation—were in poverty. Within a decade, the number had declined by 33 percent to 25.5 million, and this trend promises to continue. The "poverty gap," or total amount of money necessary to raise the income of all poor families above the poverty level, is now about $11 billion.[1]

Even though the numbers of people counted as poor have been decreasing, those who remain in poverty today are among the most difficult to assist. Today's poor tend to be the people whom economic progress does not benefit because they lack skills, are subject to discrimination, or suffer from other special liabilities. Furthermore, those who escape from poverty often have incomes hovering only slightly above the poverty line.

CHARACTERISTICS OF THE POOR

The poor are a heterogeneous group of young and old, rural and urban dwellers, white and nonwhite, workers and nonearners.[2] Heterogeneous groups have conflicting interests and are difficult to organize; therefore, antipoverty strategies must reflect a diversity of approaches.

Poverty has a strong statistical association with other social characteristics. The more of these characteristics a person possesses, the more likely he is to be poor. When poverty is so closely correlated with special traits, systematic factors work against certain types of people. Low-income status is not then just a matter of individual laziness, accident, or moral turpitude.

Race About 66 percent are white, but nonwhites are overrepresented in their frequency in the population. Of the 14 million Blacks in America, one in every three is poor. The comparable figure for Whites is one out of ten. Whites have been moving out of poverty at a faster rate than nonwhites.

Sex An adult female is more apt to have financial troubles. Seven out of every ten single poor people are women. Households headed by females are more likely to be poor than male-headed families. The number of female-headed poor families has increased by about 15 percent in the last ten years. Males who are just entering the labor force and older men whose skills have become obsolete are also more likely to be poor.

Age One-fifth of the total poverty population is 65 or over. Although only 10 percent of the population is 65 or older, about 40 percent of them are poor. The rate is higher for single aged people than for aged married couples. The elderly have benefited from recent increases in old-age insurance payments. The number of old people in poverty has declined recently.

Education Sixty-seven percent of the nation's poorest live in families headed by persons who left school before the eighth grade. Another more recent problem is the narrowed average income differential between high school drop-outs and high school graduates. We have commented earlier that society can no longer deliver on its promise that completing high school is a guarantee for work and adequate wages. People on public assistance rolls have more education than they did formerly. About 25 percent of the women receiving Aid to Families with Dependent Children have high school diplomas.[3] The value of a university degree is another matter. Average earnings are substantially greater the higher one goes on the educational ladder, but the number of highly educated people living at poverty level has increased from 2 to 3 percent over the past decade. An eighth-grade education or less is a good predictor for extreme poverty, while secondary education may not free people from membership in the "better-off poor."

Family Size   If you belong to a large family with six or more children under eighteen, you are also more likely to be poor. The more members in a family, the more income needed. Seventy-six percent of all female-headed families with five or more children now live in poverty, as do 20 percent of comparably sized male-headed households. Of the nation's 25 million poor, nearly 10 million are children.

Geography   The majority of poor people now live in the urban areas of the North and West. Of the poor who remain in the South, 64 percent live on farms or in rural areas. Any antipoverty strategy must be aimed both at city ghettos and scattered rural regions. We usually forget the latter and worry over the problems of crowded inner-city neighborhoods.

Employment   What is the relationship between employment and poverty? Logically we could assume that people are poor because they don't work, but among all poor people, 61 percent of the male and 43 percent of the female family heads are employed. Contrary to the general impressions, poor Blacks are more likely to work than poor Whites—77 percent to 59 percent.

It is possible with low-wage employment to work fifty-two weeks a year and still be below the poverty level—a misfortune affecting about a million family heads each year. Other poor people are seasonal, temporary, or casual laborers, who do not have full-time employment. They live on the margin of the economy and are laid off when the value of what they produce is less than the cost of their wage.

Wages account for only about one-half of the total income received by poor people. The remainder is made up almost entirely of benefits from programs like public assistance or social security, with little or no supplementary income from rent, dividends, or interest.

Many poor families and single individuals are altogether without income. Why? About 90 percent of the married men who do not work are ill, disabled, or retired. Nearly three-quarters of the women who are heads of their household and unemployed give family and home responsibilities as their main reason for not seeking jobs. If we are willing to accept the inevitability of sickness, old age, disability, or care of young children, jobs alone cannot be the basis of an antipoverty strategy.

COUNTING THE POOR: A POLICY PROBLEM

How many poor people are there in this country? We have to answer this question before we can design any national attack on the poverty problem. Any time we wish to operate a program to benefit (or exclude) the poor, we must address the issue. Three different approaches have evolved, each with quite different perspectives.

We have seen that poverty may be correlated with nonwhite racial status, limited education, old age, large family size, absence of capital, low-wage occupational status, and being a female head of household. But some of the poor have none of these characteristics.

The poverty line idea uses a minimum budget at which a family can subsist as the cutoff point between poor and nonpoor—e.g., $4,200 for an urban family of four. "Relative" definitions of poverty are based on how income is distributed among all members of society—e.g., the poverty level might be expressed as some percentage of median national income. The social costs of poverty, or "negative externalities" to the rest of society, have sometimes been stressed—e.g., ill health, urban blight, reduced national efficiency, crime, and the costs of public assistance programs.

We have already seen that the number of people living in poverty has declined since 1959. This decline has occurred according to the Social Security Administration, which uses a "poverty line" approach.[4]

However, even though the total number of people in poverty has been decreasing, poor people have not been getting a greater share of total national income. Almost all of the increase in national income since 1947 has gone to workers earning more than $7,000 a year. At present, the lowest 20 percent of income earners receive 5 percent of national income; in 1947 they received 4 percent. Today, the richest 31 percent own 82 percent of all wealth, while the poorest 20 percent hold less than 0.5 percent. To put the problem in even sharper focus, the richest 1 percent own one-third of the nation's total wealth. Almost all the income of poor people comes from wages.[5] We have already recognized that unemployment is therefore devastating.

The "social cost" emphasizes that, altruism aside, almost all members of society should have a vested interest in eliminating poverty.[6] Poverty diminishes the welfare of everyone—admittedly to varying degrees. Programs like Old Age Insurance through Social Security (that directly increase the welfare of taxpayers by relieving them of the necessity for supporting aged parents) should have considerable appeal.

Much of the motivation behind in-kind rather than cash transfer programs for housing, health, nutrition, and education is predicated on the negative externalities concept. If we give cash to the poor, we can't be certain that they will repair their homes, gobble up vitamins to put luster back in their hair, visit a dentist, or buy the Encyclopedia Britannica. They may persist in behavior which has negative consequences for the nonpoor. In-kind transfers are much more cost-effective, in that greater benefits accrue to the nonpoor who pay the necessary taxes. By giving aid-in-kind, actions of poor people can be more effectively controlled to conform to the desires of the giver.

The cost of antipoverty programs, the form benefits will take, and who will be defined as eligible—these problems can be resolved in quite different ways. Society may decide to aid only the poorest-poor, or, at the other extreme, to allocate funds more widely and achieve significant redistributive effects. We may continue with numerous selective, small projects or aim for a program of universal benefits.

EARLY REFORMS TO ASSIST THE POOR

The American response to problems of poverty has been distinctively shaped by English Poor Law precedent, our federated form of government, our economic productivity, and the characteristics of our poverty population. Each of these influences will be examined separately.

English Poor Law Precedent

During the medieval period in Europe, poor relief was a church responsibility. The poor were respected and given alms without question when resources were available. Churches today still care for persons in need, but the main responsibility has shifted to government. This shift began around the mid-fourteenth century. Civil governments made their first significant attempts to legislate on the growing social problems of aid for the destitute, repression of vagrancy, and treatment of the migrant, able-bodied worker. This collection of civil codes has commonly been referred to as the "poor laws."[7]

No European country failed to adopt poor laws of some sort, but the English example is usually selected for special scrutiny. The Elizabethan Poor Law of 1601, the Settlement and Removal Acts beginning in 1662, and the Poor Law of 1834 were particularly important in terms of impact on the United States. These laws were often copied word for word by settlers and later by local governments in this country.

The famous Elizabethan Poor Law of 1601 was really a clarification and remodification of several earlier statutes. Three separate programs were set up for the destitute, depending upon age and ability to work.[8]

"Rogues, vagabonds, or sturdy beggars" (able-bodied vagrants) were to be whipped and imprisoned or sent back to their birthplace upon refusal to work. This penalty applied to any common laborer who would not work "for such reasonable wages . . . as is commonly given in such parts as such persons . . . happen to dwell." Any worker who was unemployed but willing to work could be placed in a workhouse or given raw materials upon which to work at home.

Different provisions were made for the "impotent" poor. These persons were helpless because of severe disability, old age, or blindness. No work could be expected of them. A local magistrate was to decide upon a weekly amount necessary to meet the needs of these dependents and to set a tax rate accordingly, the latter to be levied on citizens of the locality with "visible property." The Overseer of the Poor was made responsible for collecting the "poor's rates," making disbursements, and setting the able-bodied to work. Pauper's children between the ages of five and fourteen for whom the parents could not provide were to be bound out as apprentices.

The Poor Law of 1601 established the principle of categorical relief, by distinguishing between the able-bodied and "impotent" poor. Eligibility was no longer universal. The able-bodied "sturdy beggar" was treated as undeserving and made subject to a work test, while the aged or disabled were viewed as deserving and exempted from work requirements. Financing of public relief was a local responsibility, based on property *taxes*, and administered by a local government appointee. National government took no direct hand in caring for the poor, other than authorizing local governments to do so at their own option. In fact, local communities moved very sluggishly in offering relief out of tax funds. Most governmental units were too small, and the tax base was too fragmented. Benefits were therefore very uneven and often absent altogether. This seems to be an inevitable consequence of local control over income maintenance programs.

Settlement Law   The only other major addition to the 1601 Poor Law was made in 1662, when the first Law of Settlement was passed. Several other pieces of legislation followed on the same subject over the next hundred years, because of the endless litigation which the 1662 statute provoked. This law provided that a destitute person should be given relief only by the community where he was born. (In both England and the United States, any individual automatically has "settlement" by virtue of birth into a community.) Parish officers were allowed to "remove" any poor person who might become dependent on the "poor's rates," sending the luckless pauper back to his birthplace. This measure was conceived of as a way to eliminate vagrants from the parish register, making more funds available for the impotent poor. At the same time, wealthier parishes would be protected from raids on their resources by the paupers from other districts. These depredations in fact never took place, but the fear always existed among local taxpayers that the worst might happen.[9] Wealthier states today have similar fears.

Settlement laws in this country gradually gave way to "residency requirements," which stated that a person was entitled to relief only in the community where he legally had his home. Settlement and residency requirements have never been fully enforced, because people were highly inventive in finding ways around the law. The laws have moreover been very costly, resulting in protracted squabbles between localities and were finally outlawed by the Supreme Court.

The Poor Law of 1834 was enacted as a means of reducing the relief rolls, which grew very rapidly in England with the onset of the Industrial Revolution and the Napoleonic Wars. Use of the workhouse for the able-bodied was required, and the "principle of less eligibility" was formulated. This principle stated that paupers dependent on relief should be supported at a level less than the lowest going wage rate for productive workers. This was an effort to preserve work incentive, and it originally applied only to the able-bodied poor. However, in administrative practice, this principle defined the benefit standard for all recipients. It meant that public relief benefits were pegged at below-subsistence levels. This idea received considerable attention in the United States and was implemented here.[10]

American Concerns about Poverty   After the Poor Law of 1834, a controversy raged in both England and the United States between advocates of the workhouse and supporters of "outdoor relief," or assistance to persons in their own homes. Many Americans feared that politicians were too corrupt to handle public monies for relief purposes. The example of Tammany Hall in New York City was not reassuring. Other people worried about fraud. Early social workers believed that cash handouts might destroy moral fiber. On the other hand, almshouses were generally overcrowded and unsanitary, and contrary to their purpose they offered no activity for the able-bodied. The urban almshouses along the Atlantic seaboard were a major exception; these institutions grew into great teaching hospitals, serving the medically indigent.[11] The issue was finally resolved in America by the Social Security Act of 1935. According to this act, any states wishing to receive matching federal funds for certain categories of public aid were required to give "unrestricted cash grants" to recipients. The era of the workhouse was over.

Our Federated Form of Government

Our nation is a federated republic. This means that the national government shares power, leaving some autonomy in decision making to the states. We do not have a tradition of central control. Provision of welfare benefits is a right expressly given to the states by our Constitution. Therefore, change has always come incrementally in public aid. We have invariably attempted to respect differing values and traditions between localities, rather than make them conform to a single national mold.

One result of state control over public aid programs has been low benefit levels. States must compete with each other for business and high-income residents. If a heavy tax is levied on property in one state for support of public relief, then business and wealthier families may simply migrate elsewhere, leaving poor and dependent families behind. States which have large numbers of poor relative to middle- and upper-income groups must levy higher taxes than states with smaller dependent populations. Either way, state control over fiscal financing for public relief offers few advantages.[12]

The Social Security Act of 1935 required that if states wished to receive matching federal funds for support of public aid programs, assistance programs must be available in all counties within the state under the control of one administrative agency. This provision served to make access to benefits far more uniform across the country. However, no minimum benefit levels were set in this legislation.[13]

Effect of Our Economic Productivity

Historically, increases in national productivity have been associated with successive upward shifts in the general standard of living. Many persons have been lifted from poverty as incomes and the number of jobs increased. The success of our economic system has reinforced the belief that private market solutions would suffice to meet the needs of our poverty population. Public assistance has therefore usually been thought of as a residual program, rather than a basic economic mainstay, for the poor. Until recently, there has been little concerted effort to attract persons of high caliber for work in the agency or to invest resources in improving agency services.

Characteristics of the Poverty Population

After 1900 the majority of poor persons in the East and Midwest were new immigrants from southern and eastern Europe, largely unskilled peasants handicapped by their lack of familiarity with our language. The flow of new immigrants was reduced in 1921 by legislation which set quotas. However, Southern Blacks and Mexican-Americans soon began to move into the cities.[14]

By the late 1940s inflation had contributed to a rise in welfare costs under the new assistance programs established by the Social Security Act. Widows and orphans had shifted in large numbers to coverage under social insurance programs. Liberalization of eligibility criteria for benefits from Aid to Dependent Children and the continuing migration from South to North contributed to a growing proportion of non-Whites and illegitimate chldren receiving assistance.[15] Part of the American reluctance to finance broad programs of social support for the poor has perhaps stemmed from ethnic and racial differences in the composition of the poverty population. Countries with more homogeneous populations, like Sweden and Great Britain, have moved more rapidly and generously in attempting to alleviate their poverty problem.

MODERN PUBLIC ASSISTANCE

The objective of public assistance is primarily to *alleviate poverty*. As is true of the Poor Laws, benefits are provided only to selected groups of the poor. Demonstration of need through a "means test" remains central to the program. The contrast with social insurance programs, where people are assumed to have a right to benefits, is striking.

Deep-rooted cleavages persist in our society over the social purposes of public assistance. Four conflicting program objectives are:

1 Income Maintenance: Guaranteeing adequate standards of living for the poor. This view implies that no family receiving benefits should fall below the poverty line as conventionally defined. In its more liberal interpretation, recipients would be supported above minimum subsistence. Few states now pay benefits that would raise recipient families to the poverty line.

2 Social Stabilization: Reassertion of the traditional role of public relief organizations. Public assistance payments prevent some measure of crime, vagrancy, and other social disorders. Public assistance should operate to give money to the least possible number of recipients. From this view, eligibility criteria would be very strict.

3 Self-realization: Provision of social services, in addition to adequate benefit levels, for recipient families. This objective has never been achieved because social services in public assistance, aside from the investigatory role, have remained undeveloped. Client advocacy, mobilization of individual potential, and multiple supports for family functioning would be emphasized.

4 Labor Supply: A focus on the skills of recipients and the distribution of labor in marginal or seasonal industries. Design of successful work training programs and adjustment of benefit levels to preserve work incentives would be of paramount importance.

The debate about whether public assistance programs are "good" or "bad" cannot be concluded until there is better consensus on which of these objectives society wishes to achieve.

AID TO FAMILIES WITH DEPENDENT CHILDREN

The Social Security Act has established two main programs in public assistance: Supplemental Social Security Income (SSI) to provide benefits to old, disabled, or blind needy adults and Aid to Families with Dependent Child (AFDC) for those who are "deprived of parental support or care by reason of death, physical or mental incapacity of the parent, or continued absence from the home by a parent." The 1962 amendments to the Social Security Act provided for an optional program that was designed to assist married couples who were living together, where the breadwinner was employed no more than 30 hours per week (AFDC-UP). As we have already observed, only twenty-five states have an AFDC-UP program. Definition of "unemployment" can be very narrow. The breadwinner must agree to register with the State Employment Service, seek work actively, and participate in work training programs. AFDC does not afford benefits to all people under 65 who are poor. Healthy single individuals, childless couples, and families with a breadwinner employed full-time (though at low wages) are ineligible.

Federal and State Roles Financing and administration of AFDC programs represent a sharing of federal and state control. The federal government, through the Department of Health, Education and Welfare, writes regulations designed to implement the Social Security laws. States also write their own regulations relating to eligibility criteria, qualifications of public aid staff, benefit standards, and other matters not specifically covered in federal regulations. Program operations are partly financed from Washington, according to a reimbursement formula which favors the poorest states. The states themselves are required by federal law to share in the financing in order to receive federal funds. After accepting money from HEW, the states must follow federal regulations. If a state fails to comply, it may lose federal support.

One example of a federal regulation is the requirement by HEW that all states adopt a simplified method for prompt determination of eligibility. This means that applicants for AFDC must be notified within 30 days whether they will receive benefits.[16] HEW has also required that social services and eligibility determination functions be separated. This means that the person who calculates a family's income requirements will not also be the worker helping with other family needs. Examples of common needs might be day care, transportation, homemaker services. The purpose of this reform was to prevent use of the budgeting process in AFDC for unfair manipulation of family behavior. It was also felt this change would reduce costs, since eligibility determination can be carried out by employees with less training.

About three-fourths of all persons receiving public assistance, or approximately 11 million individuals, are on AFDC rolls.[17] Of this number, less than 1 percent are able-bodied, unemployed men. Approximately half the families on AFDC are white. Among all low-income families headed by women, about six out of ten black families rely on AFDC for support. About 15 percent of the mothers are working, and 8 percent are in work-training programs. Four-fifths say they would gladly find a job if day care, job counseling, and vocational education were available.[18]

The turnover of people of AFDC is substantial. Twenty percent of all cases are closed after four months. Less than 8 percent of AFDC recipients stay on the rolls ten years. The average is about two years.

Over two-thirds of the children in families of AFDC are legitimate. Families get an average of about $40 more per month with the arrival of a baby, not enough to substantiate the charge that it "pays" to have more children if you're living on welfare benefits. Family planning services have not generally been available to the poor, but recipients have demonstrated genuine interest, and there is a reduction in the number of offspring for those who participate in family planning programs. The average AFDC family has three children. The birth rate for welfare families—like that for the general population—is dropping.[19]

Will children born into families on AFDC grow up to be recipients themselves? Are we training whole generations for a life of dependency? The longer a family stays on the rolls, the more social problems children are apt to manifest in their teenage years. Mental illness, delinquency, early marriage, illegitimacy, truancy, and a high drop-out rate all appear in high incidence among children of long-term recipients.[20] Statistics also show that many people on welfare had parents who were also recipients. However, data suggest that most adults on AFDC did not come from families in which welfare assistance was a "way of life." The social problems of children in AFDC families may be attributable not so much to the welfare status of their parents as to noninvestment by society in human capital.

The major difference between AFDC families and poor families that do not make use of public assistance support seems to be in kinship patterns. The nonwelfare poor tend to have much stronger ties with relatives, and all join together in periods of crisis for mutual aid. Fewer assistance recipients have social security coverage than nonassistance families, and more of the nonwelfare poor have union memberships. AFDC recipients tend to have poorer health, less savings, and fewer insurance policies but fewer debts than their counterparts not receiving aid. On the whole similarities outnumber differences for welfare and nonwelfare poor.[21]

The rapid increase in AFDC recipients began about mid-1956. About 8 million people have been added to the rolls since that time. The rate of increase is now leveling off, partly due to pressure on assistance workers to apply eligibility criteria more strictly.

Several explanations have been used to explain the increase—the introduction of AFDC-UP, allowing a new category of the poor to become eligible for benefits; the protracted migration of poor families from the South to the North, where welfare programs are more accessible; inflation and sustained levels of high unemployment; and technological development that invariably creates displacement of unskilled and marginal workers. Other factors may have been community action programs during the 1960s that increased awareness among the poor of public welfare services, stimulating greater demand.[22] Better understanding of the causes of dependency is essential to a more rational framing of public assistance programs. This job remains to be done.

SUPPLEMENTAL SECURITY INCOME

In 1972, Congress created the Supplemental Security Income program to provide public assistance benefits for the needy blind, disabled, and elderly. SSI is federally administered by the Social Security Administration and financed by general revenues at the national level. This program supplants earlier state-administered assistance and sets a national minimum income for the aged, blind, and disabled. Eligibility conditions, which formerly differed widely from state to state, are now more uniform. The purpose of SSI is to assure a minimum income level for people who do not have enough earned income, savings, or benefits from other programs. In computing resources, the value of home or automobile, household goods, personal effects, and life insurance policies under $1,500 do not count. People must be 65 or over or meet the definitions of blindness or disability used under the Disability Insurance program. The definitions are more narrow than eligibility criteria under previous state-administered programs.

When the Social Security Act was passed, Congress assumed that almost all older people would eventually become beneficiaries. However, even though social security benefits have increased by over 50 percent since 1969, about 2 million elderly people still do not have an adequate income by public assistance standards. Today over two-thirds of needy elderly persons get two checks—one for SSI and one for OASDHI. One major impact of SSI has been to increase the overlap between social insurance and public assistance payments.[23]

Implementation of SSI provisions may gradually change the characteristics of the needy elderly, blind, and disabled population served. Until now, the median age of needy elderly public aid recipients has been 77 years. Most were women, most were white, and about 50 percent lived in rural areas. Very few—between 2 to 4 percent—had any earned income. These people were often physically sick, brain-damaged, uneducated, and isolated from sons or daughters. They have needed medical care, a friendly social environment, more adequate income, and protection, but they receive only infrequent attention from public assistance personnel. The states will still have responsibility for social services to SSI recipients.

Needy blind and disabled public aid recipients tend to remain on the rolls indefinitely and have very little potential for work. Most are middle-aged or over, unmarried, and poorly educated. Half of the blind recipients have some chronic physical or mental impairment in addition to blindness. The recipient rates among nonwhite blind persons is almost four times as great as that for Whites. Among disabled recipients, about half are afflicted with chronic diseases associated with the aging process, and another 20 percent are disabled by psychiatric disorders.[24]

GENERAL ASSISTANCE

General assistance is the most anomalous of all the public assistance programs. In a few states, it is still financed and administered largely at the township level. No clearly stated eligibility requirements exist for general assistance—the only program which receives no federal funds. It is supposed to serve those needing temporary rather than long-term financial support. GA is usually funded by property taxes. In large cities like New York and Chicago, the state government contributes heavily toward meeting the costs of GA, but this is unusual. In theory any poor person who cannot meet the eligibility requirements for other federally assisted categorical programs should be able to receive general assistance.

Benefits provided under general assistance are particularly meager, and most of the expenditures are for medical care. A political official may have arbitrary jurisdiction over whether a client gets help. He operates very much like the Elizabethan English overseer of the poor. In rural and moderately sized communities, general assistance is a small program. Benefits are in no sense generous, and in-kind payments predominate. Whenever possible, communities have tried to move applicants from general assistance into federally funded public aid categories, because this reduces local expense.

BASIC AND SPECIAL ALLOWANCES

Let's assume now that a prospective applicant has successfully worked his or her way through the eligibility requirements and has little or no income. The next problem that arises is determining the minimum monthly cash grant to meet subsistence needs. This is called the *basic allowance*. Traditionally it has been composed of two major parts: a *personal allowance* and a *shelter allowance*. The personal allowance is supposed to cover food, clothing, household supplies, and personal essentials for each family member. The size of the cash grant for each of these items has varied, depending on the age of each family member and the total number of persons in the household. Individual allowances are generally reduced as total family size increases.

Shelter allowances have been difficult to establish. State welfare agencies have disagreed as to whether cost should be related to family size, number of rooms in the home, type of facilities provided, or actual rent. Each state has set its own maximum for rent and utilities. The rationale for the maximum is frequently unclear. During the 1960s some argued that public assistance was really subsidizing substandard and slum housing by maintaining low rent maximums. The agency is now empowered in most states to withhold rent checks from landlords if housing is in violation of safety or sanitation regulations.

Once the basic allowance is computed (the sum of all personal allowances for each family member, plus shelter costs), *special allowances* may be added. The family may have occasional needs for expensive purchases, such as school clothing in the fall that cannot be met out of the basic allowance. Or an individual may have unusual disabilities that require services not covered in the basic grant. In these instances the agency will make a special lump-sum grant to supplement the family's regular check. Special allowances may be given on an on-going basis if they are essential to survival or employment. Thus, while the basic allowance may be quite small, recipients can potentially receive important supplementary benefits as needs arise or family circumstances change.

Unfortunately the special allowance program has apparently not been appropriately implemented. In some public assistance offices, "specials" have remained only a paper program. Recipients have never been informed of their eligibility for these additional benefits, and workers have made no offers. Families have then often managed to live—rather miraculously it would seem—on their basic allowance, despite their entitlement to more liberal assistance.[25] Agency practices with respect to special allowances seem to vary widely even within the same state. In one community AFDC mothers may be given special clothing allowances, while in a neighboring community none are given.[26] To eliminate this variance some of the largest states (e.g., California and Illinois) have adopted a policy of "consolidation." Most special allowances have been eliminated. Shelter allowances are averaged and integrated with the personal allowance grant. The advantage is greater uniformity and less likelihood of overpayments or underpayments to recipients. Administrative tasks are simplified. The disadvantage is less program flexibility. A minority of recipients, usually two-person families, receive reduced grants under this policy. Welfare Rights Organizations are therefore opposed. Social workers, too, have been concerned that budgets fail to meet special needs of some poor families. "Consolidation" may be the first step toward a guaranteed minimum income—or so reformers argue. It may also be a convenient means of reducing state expenditures on unpopular programs.

EARNED INCOME

Earned income by recipients in public assistance programs has presented a thorny dilemma. The ideal situation would be for all clients to find a job and get off the rolls. However, incentives must be offered. As the law now stands, female recipients can keep up to $30 a month of any earned income without affecting their allowance from the agency. After the first $30, the grant from public aid is reduced $2 for every $3 of earned income. Mrs. Rooney, who gets $250 a month under AFDC and earns $30 by babysitting, would have total income of $280 per month. As soon as her income from babysitting exceeds $30, her basic allowance will be reduced $2 for every $3 she earns. If she makes $48 on her own, she can keep it, but her public assistance check would then drop to $238. Her total income would be $286. The allowance from public welfare has been reduced by $12 or two-thirds of the amount over $30 which she has earned. Expenses necessary to retain a job, such as transportation, union dues, and social security taxes, are taken into consideration. Reductions are based on net earnings. Most economists agree that this "thirty-and-a-third" rule doesn't offer much work incentive. It's about the same as taxing income at a 66 percent rate.

Many recipients do in fact find work. Thirty-five percent of all cases closed are due to finding employment or achieving increased earnings. However, recipients are not removed from the rolls until their earned income equals the basic allowance after the first $30 plus one-third of the earned income have been "disregarded."

Being on welfare then does not necessarily mean not working. Public assistance may continue to supplement earned income and in fact does so in AFDC for numerous female-headed households. The intermittent use of welfare linked with intermittent employment constitutes a pattern of life for many AFDC mothers.[27] In effect, the government also subsidizes low-wage industries, ensuring that low-skilled labor will be available for seasonal work, part-time employment, and poorly paid jobs in general.[28] Male breadwinners whose families are covered under AFDC-UP are not entitled to any income exemption. Their earned income is deducted at a 100 percent rate.

Congress has been preoccupied with the work and incentive issues, especially since 1965. Apparently there is an unyielding conviction that poor people will give up hard labor for the alternative of a leisurely life at government expense. Certainly states whose benefit standards are below minimum subsistence levels have a better success rate in work-training programs than do other locales.[29] Extreme want is undeniably a strong motive for any recipient who can go to work. Moreover, in cities where there is a large differential between public assistance standards and the lowest going wage, caseloads tend to be smaller. The rolls can be reduced by denying recipients a subsistence allowance or a standard of living equivalent to the lowest-paid production worker.

Low benefits and moving recipients off the rolls rapidly may not be optimum solutions to the welfare problem. Research from the Poverty Institute of the University of Wisconsin reports that recipients who are given a higher allowance with smaller reductions for earned income do not reduce their work effort, although wives in these families are somewhat more likely to remain at home than with a lower assistance payment.[30]

SOCIAL SERVICES IN PUBLIC ASSISTANCE

In 1962, Congress amended the Social Security Act to provide 75 percent matching funds for any state which offered social services as a part of its public assistance program. This amendment was intended "to stimulate and extend services that are designed to help families and individuals use their capacities to attain or maintain self-sufficiency and to function as useful, productive individuals and to lead a more satisfying life." The results of pilot demonstration projects in which social services had been introduced seemed promising. Clients had been moved off the rolls and their life adjustment improved. Congress liked the idea of social services, because rolls might be cut. Social workers were happy because this approach gave new recognition to the profession and advanced the values of client self-realization. State administrators were pleased at the prospect of new federal money. Caseworkers were to be given more latitude in what they might investigate concerning a client, and caseloads were reduced to sixty clients per worker.

"Services" were often interpreted by state administrators simply as an extension of what had gone on before, only now there were federal matching funds. Services might mean general clerical work, quarterly home visits, eligibility determination, some effort to rehabilitate or counsel clients, a change in the credentialing of workers, better administrative management techniques, or in-service training focused on social casework methods. Almost anything a worker did outside of handing over an application form was often called a service.

Stringent questions have been raised regarding the role of social services in public assistance. Poverty lawyers and other social reformers of the 1960s produced an abundant literature that roundly condemned caseworkers.

Is the privacy of clients unduly invaded through the eligibility determination process? Clients feel obliged to answer any question, no matter how personal, because they need money. The application process is demeaning, wtih loss in personal dignity for the individual. Clients may be deterred from seeking assistance because they fear this humiliation. Once on the rolls, clients may be manipulated by their caseworkers and forced to adopt standards of behavior not required by other people. Through imposition of moral codes on recipients, and using the assistance check as a whip, caseworkers can demand thrift, efficiency, temperance, chastity, and hard work. Independence of the individual is curtailed by continual official supervision. Because caseworkers can make decisions on a case-by-case basis, the arbitrary and unfair nature of the public assistance programs is increased. In short, caseworkers have been depicted as vindictive, punitive, interfering, controlling agents in a program that degrades and demoralizes its clients.

Are these charges accurate? Recent studies indicate relatively little intervention by caseworkers in how clients allocate their income.[31] Surprisingly little discussion goes on between workers and recipients about any subject. As a rule the workers tend to avoid sensitive topics like marital relationships or child-rearing practices. Typically, caseworkers initiate contacts with clients at infrequent intervals, and the contacts tend to be short. At intake, discussion is generally confined to financial resources, and the bulk of the time is taken up in calculating individual allowances. Clients do not seem to regard the intake process as coercive, and most recipients have few complaints about their caseworker. Undeniably, some caseworkers have taken an excessive and unwarranted interest in the personal behavior of clients, but this is most characteristic of small, rural communities where relationships are highly personalized. Deviant behavior on the part of clients presents the agency with an acutely difficult public relations problem, since the program is tax-supported. The majority on public assistance may be described as "satisfied clients," principally because welfare benefits provide them with greater economic security.

Judging from research evidence, caseworkers seem to do very little in the way of referral, even when other community resources might help to improve a client's well-being. Workers often fail to inform clients about benefits to which they are entitled within the public assistance program itself. Although there is ample room for tailoring and revising budgets to family need, most recipients operate on allowances that remain fixed. The meaning of "social services" is so watered-down as to be virtually without content.

Initial training for caseworkers is brief, often less than a week. Compare this with the sixteen weeks of training of "field representatives" in the Social Security Administration. Policy manuals are voluminous and in a continuous process of revision—but unindexed. Caseloads may range from 150 to 300 clients. Periodic public crusades against "fraud on the welfare rolls" place workers on the defensive.

When social services are given, do clients get what they want and what they can use? Personal growth, self-realization, insight, and self-mastery—the goals of more sophisticated social services—cannot be established for families operating on a subminimal economic standard under conditions of constant crisis. If "consumer preferences" among recipients were to be used as the measure of what an agency might offer, the first priority among clients is money—with employment as the preferred source of income. Next is medical care. Serious illness is a major problem for the poor and a continual source of stress. Clients would also like housing at rents attainable within their budgets. The rent maximums are never sufficiently high, and clients must divert money from their food or clothing allowances to pay for shelter. Finally, recipients would like more help with concrete everyday environmental problems and emergencies—intervention with creditors, help in finding a lost welfare check, assistance in searching for a runaway child, support in dealing with school authorities or probation officers, or aid in forcing landlords to make necessary repairs to rental property.[32]

These services are far from the rehabilitative and uplifting casework intervention envisioned in the 1962 Social Security Amendments. Studies over the past ten years have shown repeatedly that social casework—even when practiced by skillful caseworkers under relatively favorable conditions of reduced caseloads—

produces negligible behavioral change on the part of recipients. Social functioning of clients shows only marginal improvement when compared with that of
recipient groups receiving little or no service.[33]

Does this mean that casework in public assistance is useless and self-
defeating? No, but some changes are in order. Poor families find environmental
stresses overwhelming. They need support to get sufficiently mobilized just to
make use of already existing programs. In smaller counties with limited
populations, the public assistance office is frequently the only source of public
services. Poor families are also generally ineffective in contending with schools,
business enterprises, and other community institutions. They need an advocate,
someone who can assist them in becoming more socially competent.

The focus of social services in public assistance remains unclear. Amendments to the Social Security Act in 1972 placed a ceiling on the amount of
payments which the federal government will make for services provided by the
states to public assistance recipients. Complete termination of federal support for
social services is possible. Better means of assessing the productivity of service
workers are now being developed. This can help to document more effectively
the need for an expanded social service program in public assistance.

HUNGER IN AMERICA

In the mid-sixties, the nation was shocked to learn that millions of American
children were starving or malnourished. Senator George McGovern initiated
formal congressional hearings on the issue in 1968, collecting volumes of
personal testimony from physicians, poor people, and other witnesses. The
hearings seemed to confirm our worst suspicions. Federal food programs were
strongly recommended by the 1969 White House Conference on Food, Nutrition,
and Health; the 1971 White House Conference on Youth; the 1971 White House
Conference on Aging; and the National Advisory Council on Child Nutrition.

A survey by the U.S. Department of Agriculture on household food consumption patterns revealed a negative correlation between low-income status
and adequacy of diet. Nearly two-thirds of the families with earnings of $10,000 or
more had good diets, while just 37 percent of families earning under $3,000 were
properly nourished, according to the survey. Undernourishment (too few calories) has to be distinguished from malnourishment (not enough of certain food
elements—especially protein). Research also suggests that severe nutritional
deficits in expectant mothers may lead to irreversible brain deficits in the
child—effects traceable to the first trimester of pregnancy. It seemed clear that
the federal government should take a stronger hand in dealing with hunger.

Food distribution programs in the United States are operated in over four out
of five counties under the auspices of the Department of Agriculture. Surplus
commodity programs are no longer important. There are two main programs:
food stamps and school lunches. Expenditures on food stamps rose from $340
million in 1969 to $2.5 billion in 1973. About 13 million individuals participate in
the program. It is not necessary to be a public aid recipient in order to qualify for
food stamps. The school lunch program served 25 million children in 1971 at a
cost of $1 billion. About a third of these youngsters were from poor families.

Food stamps are important because they are available to low-income families who are not assistance recipients. Objections to the food stamp program come from many quarters. Poor people don't like the program because they must "buy" the stamps each month from a fixed percentage of their income. Food stamps act as an income supplement but do not guarantee that the increased purchasing power of recipients will be used to buy more food. Studies indicate that the poor are much more likely to make nonfood purchases. Even if food stamps do increase the *quantity* of food which poor people buy, there is no guarantee that *quality* will improve. Food habits will not be changed by food stamps, nor does the program help to raise the "nutritional literacy" of low-income families. The program does provide a range of choice, however, something the surplus commodity program did not do.

A survey of ten states in 1968–1970 conducted by HEW found virtually no nutritional diseases in any sector of the population—including the poor. Poor people had less iron intake than others, but they consumed more vitamin C. Most dietary deficiencies were associated with family size. Inadequate nutrition was found among teenagers and infants at all income levels.

The basic question is probably buying power, but other approaches can be taken toward remedying deficient diets. Nutrition education can be expanded; new foods can be created; or highly popular nonnutritive foods such as soda pop and potato chips can be fortified. The problem is not just getting food to people, nor is it confined to the poor.

WELFARE AND WORK

We have seen that work requirements have been a part of welfare policy since the first civil codes were passed in the fourteenth century. We have grown more sophisticated in the way we plan and implement work training programs. The last workhouse in this country disappeared by 1920, but the old fear that people want welfare but not work remains.

Aside from historical precedent and innate distrust of the poor, work requirements have been closely associated with provision of public welfare for other reasons. If the number of nonproductive people increases faster than the number of those who are working, the overall economic growth of the country may slow down. Second, to continue their expansion industries must have a mobile labor force. Some jobs are less desirable than others from the worker's point of view. If welfare benefits were high and freely available, workers might stay in one community where they were no longer needed or might avoid taking less desirable jobs.

In 1962, Congress passed the Manpower Development and Training Program (MDT) to help retrain workers with obsolescent skills. When the War on Poverty began two years later, MDT programs were refocused to include the poor—particularly nonwhites with limited educational preparation. Candidates were chosen by state employment offices and then trained either in special centers or on the job, with a subsidy to employers for each MDT candidate they hired.

In general MDT programs have been successful.[34] Program costs, especially for on-the-job training, have been low, and poor people who participated in the program tend to have higher earnings than before. However, the impact on wages and employment of the poor has not been substantial. As with most work training programs, employers tend to take the "cream" among referrals. The hard-core unemployed don't enroll in MDT. Perhaps employers might train most MDT candidates anyway without the government subsidy.

Congress advocated work requirements for public aid recipients since 1962 when the Community Work and Training program was set up. Congress agreed to pay 50 percent of the costs to state welfare departments if they would initiate training programs for recipients. The states weren't very interested, because they could get 75 percent reimbursement for social service programs. In 1964, the Work Experience and Training program was substituted with 100 percent financing from HEW. Every state except Alabama responded under this kind of inducement. Unfortunately little training was provided; jobs involved work relief and not much more.

In 1966, Congress authorized the Department of Labor to create jobs, offer training, and place welfare recipients. The State Employment Services were assigned responsibility for determining employability, training, and finding jobs. State welfare workers were to help when the recipient seemed to be poorly motivated or failed in other ways to participate wholeheartedly in his employment planning.

Congress passed the 1967 amendments to the Social Security Act, creating the Work Incentive Now program (WIN) specifically for welfare recipients. The act requires that every state must refer any employable AFDC recipient to the state employment service. The only exceptions are children under 18 now in school; recipients who are sick, very old, disabled, or residing in remote areas; and recipients who have to stay home in order to take care of an ill or incapacitated family member. The Department of Labor is supposed to set up appropriate training and placement plans for each recipient. The state welfare agencies are responsible for financial aid, health needs, day care arrangements, and other social services. Every family is entitled to keep the first $30 of earnings; after that, the basic allowance is reduced $2 for every $3 the recipient earns. Special grants are made to families participating in WIN projects to cover additional expenses incurred. If an AFDC family refuses to participate in WIN, the welfare department is supposed to reduce the family's welfare check and make all payments directly to merchants in the community. This penalty is generally not enforced, however, because the process is expensive and time-consuming for the agency.

Recent changes in the tax laws give a tax credit to employers for 20 percent of the wages paid to WIN participants, up to a maximum of $25,000 per employer. After that, the tax credit is only 10 percent. Most employers have not responded to this incentive. Many don't even know about the availability of the tax credit.[35]

Compared to the overall size and rate of increase in AFDC recipients, WIN has been a very small program. The first enrollees had a higher educational level than most AFDC recipients; as with MDT, the "hard core" was left behind. Financial incentives do not make completion of training worthwhile. The program has also been very expensive. According to one estimate, it may cost as much as $20,000 to make one successful placement. WIN is also very sensitive to fluctuations in the business cycle. When unemployment is high, WIN participa-

Drawing by Drucker; © 1972 The New Yorker Magazine, Inc.

"There are plenty of jobs around. People just don't want to work."

tion is high. This leads to the conclusion that recipients may substitute WIN for jobs in the private sector.

Women, teenagers, the elderly, those with little previous employment experience, and people with limited education don't do well in manpower training programs. They drop out of training more often. Even if they complete the program, they have trouble finding jobs. Most people on AFDC are not employable, therefore job training will not have much impact on rates of recipiency.

NEW SOLUTIONS TO POVERTY

When Congress was debating passage of the Social Security Act in 1935 the idea of guaranteed minimum income for the poor was considered. This was flatly rejected, mostly due to pressure from Southern congressmen, who saw a minimum income floor as federal interference in what was then termed the "Negro Question." The United Auto Workers succeeded in winning for themselves a guaranteed annual *wage*, but this is quite different from universal provision of transfer income to those with little or no current productivity.

In 1969, President Nixon astounded both Congress and the country with a welfare reform proposal for a guaranteed annual income.[36] He urged passage of a bill which would have paid $1,600 a year to a family of four with no earnings. The size of the guarantee would be increased with family size. Food stamps would be added to the guarantee, bringing total benefits to an urban family of four to $2,200 per year. The guaranteed allowance would be systematically reduced as a family began to earn income. The allowance would drop $1.50 for each $3 of earned income, a 50 percent "tax" rate. Families would have been required to register for work, accept suitable employment when offered, and participate in work training programs.

The furor which followed Nixon's proposal well capsulized current conflicts in our society over the issue of dependency. Liberals attacked the plan because the guarantee was too low. Welfare rights advocates suggested guarantees as high as $6,500 for an urban family of four to provide a "minimum comfort" standard of living to the poor. Food stamps were opposed by liberals, who thought the poor ought to be given full freedom of choice in deciding allocation of income. Finally, an income guarantee of $2,200 without food stamps was proposed, but this satisfied no one.

The President's recommendations were embodied in a bill passed by the House of Representatives. When the legislation reached the Senate Finance Committee, fireworks erupted once more—this time over the issue of work. Led by Senator Russell Long, the committee endorsed a strict compulsory work program for AFDC recipients because the objective of social policy should be an end to "freeloading" and relief for the overburdened taxpayer.

The Senate and the House were unable to resolve their differences in philosophy and approach in joint committee meetings. As a result, no changes were made in the nation's welfare structure. Local experimentation in reform will be sponsored by the federal government over the next four to eight years. Then Congress may reconsider the entire problem.

Between 1968 and 1972, economists, social workers, and other professionals developed welfare reform proposals. Social workers generally favored family allowances; economists favored the "negative income tax." Both strategies would have provided universal coverage to the poor, a guaranteed level of income based only on family size and, in the case of negative income tax, family earnings.

The nation has three choices in policy: We can move to equalize incomes, giving the poor a larger share of the national product. This would mean large-scale income redistribution, probably feasible only through a steep tax surcharge on income above the median level. We could achieve transfers of this magnitude best through the personal income tax system.

A second alternative is to extend coverage under the present categorical system to more of the working poor. Two-thirds of those in poverty do not receive public assistance. Most of them are in the labor market but receive inadequate wages. However, providing benefits to the working poor means that program costs will rise. Even if income supplementation is relatively small, more people than ever would be "on aid."[37] This alternative has been rejected in favor of increasing federal support for human services programs. Education, health, and service programs are receiving six times as much money now as in 1960, comprising 43 percent of all expenditures for the poor. In-kind transfers will probably predominate as our solution to the needs of the working poor.

Finally, our policy could concentrate on reform of public assistance, especially AFDC. Recent steps in that direction have come by separating provision of service from provision of income. Legal Aid Societies have been relentlessly attacking the constitutionality of state welfare laws with a view toward preventing arbitrary and discriminating behavior by program administrators.

What is the immediate outlook? To the Ford administration inflation is the major economic enemy. To cut the federal budget, human services programs are obvious tragets. This policy will create neither more equitable welfare programs nor an ultimate reduction in poverty.

Marilyn Flynn

KEY TERMS

poverty line	general assistance
externalities	assistance standards
English Poor Laws	basic allowance
income maintenance	special allowance
public assistance categories	guaranteed income

FOR DISCUSSION

1 Describe the typical poor person in terms of the social characteristics discussed in the chapter.
2 Respond to the charge: "The poor won't work."
3 What is the difference between absolute and relative measures of poverty?
4 What aspects of poverty impose a cost on others? What is this approach called?
5 Why was it important in England to be able to prove "settlement" after 1601?
6 Which view of public assistance emphasizes the "externalities" approach the most? Why?
7 Why are three programs now less important to local public welfare agencies?
8 What method of payment do federal requirements specify for public assistance?
9 Which states have the highest benefit standards for public assistance?
10 What is the source of money for general assistance? What is the consequence?
11 Why may special allowances in public assistance be considered unfair?

12 What are the most important supplementary benefits provided to recipients?
13 If a family is eligible for $300 a month from AFDC and the mother earns $50 each month, how much total income can be retained?
14 Why are the programs other than AFDC and GA relatively uncontroversial?
15 What is the average stay of families on AFDC rolls?
16 What is the explanation for chronic dependency (children staying on the rolls long enough to become adult recipients themselves)?
17 Other than employment, what is the major difference between the recipient family and the poor nonrecipient family?
18 Explain the failure of the 1962 Social Security amendments that emphasized social services.
19 What two types of nutritional problems does America have?
20 What are major criticisms of the WIN program?
21 Explain a guaranteed annual income.

PROJECTS

1 Use the *Social Security Bulletin* to get the latest data on public assistance costs. Are total expenditures rising or falling? Are per capita payments rising? What is the relative standing of your state on a per capita payment basis? Report to the class on your findings.
2 Now that you are familiar with the general provisions for financial assistance in the United States and some provisions in three countries of Europe (see Chapter 4), indicate the provisions that we should adopt from the European countries, giving your reasons.
3 Present a panel of two or three members of the local welfare rights organization to hear their concerns about public assistance. Include a student as chairman and another as a discussant. Tape the panel as it is being presented to the class.
4 Ask a local public assistance administrator to listen to the tape prepared for No. 3 above, and discuss his reactions with the class.
5 Present this debate: Resolved, that the present system of public assistance should be replaced by a guaranteed annual income.
6 Make a detailed study of the Poor Laws in England. Prepare two or three role-play situations. One example would be bringing a "sturdy beggar" before a local magistrate.
7 Nutritional deficits are most serious for pregnant women. Study the nutritional programs that are available, and indicate the values and shortcomings of each for pregnant teenage girls, considering that the first trimester of pregnancy is most critical in terms of mental development of the child. Distinguish between malnourishment and undernourishment.

FOR FURTHER STUDY

Alan B. Batchelder, *The Economics of Poverty*, Wiley, New York, 1966.
Joint Economic Committee, *Public Welfare Studies Series*, U.S. Government Printing Office, 1972–1974.
Richard L. Morrill and Ernest H. Wohlenberg, *The Geography of Poverty in the United States*, McGraw-Hill, New York, 1971.
Bruno Stein, *On Relief*, Basic Books, New York, 1971.
Clair Wilcox, *Toward Social Welfare*, Irwin, Homewood, Ill., 1969.

Chapter 7

Health

Who needs medical care most?
What has happened to the family doctor?
Have Medicaid and Medicare really helped?
Do we need new legislation?
What is the role of social work in health care?

Income maintenance programs are perceived as the specialty of the social worker. Because public and private social welfare agencies are often managed by social workers and social work is the major activity, they are considered *primary* settings. Hospitals and clinics, agencies dealing with the environment, and the schools are *secondary* settings, but this does not reduce their importance for social workers. These programs spend a substantial proportion of society's resources and have a great impact. Since social workers do not run the programs, status and influence may present problems to them. The contemporary social worker must learn how to work with those in control—the hospital administrator and the physician, the ecologist and the demographer, or the professional educator.

We will begin with *health*. Chapter 8 will consider *ecology* and *population*, and Chapter 9 will discuss *education*.

HEALTH CARE IN THE UNITED STATES

The disappointing record of the United States in maternal and infant mortality has already been highlighted. You have also become familiar with the major provisions of the National Health System in England. Now we will look at our own health provisions and the social worker's role in them. Mental health and rehabilitation will be given more detailed treatment in later chapters.

Factors that influence the delivery of health care in the United States, some of the issues and dilemmas, and the role of social work in health services are the major topics to be discussed.

Heredity and Environment

Health is a product of interaction between a person's genetic characteristics and the environment. Even before birth the environment is extremely important. The mother's diet affects the developing fetus, and maternal malnutrition can cause deficits in intellectual development. Babies can be born addicted to heroin as a consequence of their mother's habit. Food, housing, and sanitation have a major effect on the individual's physical and mental health. Both physical and psychological stress also affect health; thus health and social welfare should be closely allied.

In the United States, the strong emphasis upon treatment of illness coupled with inadequate programs for health maintenance have resulted in *sick care* rather than health care. The system is oriented toward not only sickness but acute rather than chronic illness.

Illness and the Family   Acute illness mobilizes a family so that the patient receives considerable support and special attention. With time the special attention may decrease. If the illness becomes chronic, dependency gradually becomes a major problem and often a major cost. When the doctors "can't do anything more for him," a person is expected to accept their judgment, respond with passive resignation, and be a good patient. The relationship of chronic illness to psychological and social functioning, the major concern of many social workers, is all too obvious. For this reason there is a growing literature on chronic illness and on death and dying.

FACTORS AFFECTING HEALTH

In the last chapter we saw the relationships between poverty and such factors as race, age, and sex. We see similar relationships for health status. The poor get the poorest health services. Since racial minorities tend to be poor, they also get inadequate service. The elderly have special health problems, and because women tend to live longer than men, medical services for the female aged should be emphasized.

Income   Good health and high income are positively related. This is a statement of the obvious, but its obviousness has not led to significant improvements in medical service. Poor people have a higher rate of illness, and medical services are less accessible to them. Impersonal, grudging service also discourages their use of the health services that exist. They are usually denied the opportunity to establish a continuing doctor-patient relationship. Without the financial resources to pay for medical care, they tend to postpone seeing a doctor until their condition is more serious. They are less likely to have insurance, so they enter a hospital at the point of emergency, which results in a longer stay. Low-income families tend to have several hospitalizations per year, suffer from chronic conditions, and have their activities restricted. They lose more days from work because of illness than the rest of the population.[1]

Even though medical resources vary in quality and quantity for the more affluent, the poor suffer acute deficiencies in health care. Poor people are not unconcerned about their health; on the contrary, good health is valued as their first priority.[2]

Understanding of Symptoms   Whether or not a person considers himself ill depends upon his understanding of the cause and course of his symptoms, his expectation of the outcome, and the financial consequences of illness. A college professor or a bookkeeper with a headache may be too ill to work, yet a miner with an advanced case of emphysema or black lung disease still continues on his job. To define himself as ill is to cut off his means of livelihood. Researchers also found that awareness of the symptoms that should be taken seriously varied by social class.[3] Lack of recognition of the importance of major symptoms in lower-class groups may result from inadequate experience with medical services as well as inadequate general knowledge.

Race   Infant mortality is nearly twice as high for non-Whites as for Whites, and life expectancies for both sexes are about seven years shorter for non-Whites—61.3 compared to 68.3 years for white males, and 69.4 to 75.7 for females.[4] The nonwhite poor have a shorter life, greater maternal mortality, and a higher rate of death from tuberculosis, influenza, pneumonia, vascular lesions, and cancer of the cervix.[5]

Age   People over 65 now make up 10 percent of the population, and the percentage is increasing each year. The aged are more likely to be poor and to get sick more often than younger people. They have more serious illnesses, are admitted to the hospital more often, and stay longer. Three times more is spent per capita for health of aged persons than for younger persons, mostly for hospital or nursing home care. Their illnesses are characterized by disability and complexity—arthritis, rheumatism, heart disease and high blood pressure, deficits of hearing, vision, speech, and memory.[6]

COST OF MAJOR COMPONENTS IN HEALTH CARE

Physicians, nurses, technicians, and other medical professional and paramedical personnel; private and public hospitals; convalescent and nursing homes; insurance companies; manufacturers of drugs and technical equipment; and governmental agencies concerned with research and direct and indirect health care for special groups—all are involved in providing health services.

Inflation

The "new national health strategy" in 1971, was no doubt motivated by the striking rise of over 170 percent in medical costs since the beginning of the 1960s and the rise of the federal share from 13 percent to 30 percent. Other criticisms were: variation of care with geography and income, including maldistribution of medical personnel; lack of clarity of responsibility that leads to refusal of care or shunting of people from one facility to another; underdevelopment of preventive services; and uneconomic use of resources, such as overuse of hospital beds.

Seventy-five billion dollars were spent for medical care in 1971, more than half again as much as was spent on education. Hospital care cost twice as much as physician's services. Costs were apportioned as follows:[7]

Type of expense	Percent
Hospital care	39.5
Doctors' services	19.0
Drugs	9.9
Dentists	6.1
Construction	4.7
Nursing homes	4.4
Research	2.7
Public health and others	13.9

HOSPITALS AND NURSING HOMES

The development of medical technology has made the hospital the center of medical care for both in-patient and out-patient services as well as the focus of community health services and planning. Medical schools are combining with community hospitals to take responsibility for teaching, research, and outreach programs. Hospitals are increasingly becoming associated with extended-care facilities where less expensive services can be provided during periods of recuperation and rehabilitation.

Average Cost The cost per patient of hospital service in New York rose from $58 per day in 1965 to $97 per day in 1969. It was $105 in 1973. The employment of more highly skilled personnel, costs of construction, use of sophisticated therapeutic procedures, and the persistence of many inefficient small units have been partially responsible.[8] Third-party financing through private insurance, Medicare, and Medicaid increases costs, since health care vendors know that the money is there, and the demand for services also increases. Temporary price controls stabilized health costs somewhat, but they were removed in 1974.

Until recently hospitals have had little incentive to control costs. Insurance programs cover in-patient rather than out-patient services. This results in serious overuse of hospital services. As nonprofit organizations in a noncompetitive market, the hospitals have expanded, duplicated, and added to the consumer's bill. Hospitals are now being faced with community criticism in connection with consumer demands, high costs, overuse, and tension between physicians and hospital administrators. External controls are increasing.

Nursing Homes

Federal programs for medical care and the increasing number of the aged have focused attention on nursing homes that serve as resources for patients who do not need full hospital services. Unlike hospitals, about nine out of ten nursing homes are established to make a profit.[9] An increasing number are franchised in the same way as restaurants or motels. Many states have investigated complaints of malnutrition, neglect, and physical abuse in nursing homes. Consumer advocate Ralph Nader has provided a dramatic account of nursing home conditions.[10] At the same time, some have superb facilities and excellent services. In view of the variations in quality of care, licensing programs are of particular importance. Few nursing homes have professional social workers on the regular staff, but an increasing number employ them as part-time consultants.

Physicians' Status

Until World War II medical service was dominated by physicians in individual practice. Hospitals assumed a relatively minor role because ill people were generally cared for at home. Then the technology of the past thirty years emphasized the treatment of acute illness, for which hospital facilities are essential. The role of the general practitioner has been devalued. Physicians today are increasingly specialized, and many engage in group practice. The specialized health system has deprived many patients of the personal care they would like. Physicians rarely make house calls, and the emergency room has become the center for crisis care and a variety of out-patient services.

The American doctor is the highest paid professional, earning an average of $42,700 a year.[11] Physicians are concentrated in the high population areas. In 1971, of the 310,845 active physicians in the United States, only 18 percent were in general practice, 72 percent engaged in specialized practice, and 10 percent were involved in nonpatient care such as teaching, research, and administration. The emphasis on specialization in medical education means that doctors are staying in training longer. The large teaching hospitals have attracted the most skilled and ambitious physicians.[12]

ALLIED HEALTH PERSONNEL

Pressures on the health delivery system have brought about changes in the personnel of the health team and its services. Medical technicians trained by the armed forces take further training and serve in hospitals and clinics. New careerists, many of them women and minority group members, have been trained as nurse's aides, social work aides, home health care workers, and community health workers. Indigenous persons have found jobs in neighborhood health centers.

The health team can no longer be limited to the doctor and nurse. Anesthetists, midwives, surgical assistants, pediatric assistants, and various other health workers are important. Teams must be task-oriented and offer services appropriate to the needs of the clients. How social workers participate in these services will be discussed later in this chapter.

The federal government until recently encouraged the expansion of professional schools, training of allied health personnel, preparation of supervisors of subprofessional workers, teachers of allied health professions, and the development of new types of allied health workers through grants and loans. Many federal training programs have been curtailed recently, however.

CONSUMERS

The consumer is a relative newcomer to policy making for health delivery systems. However, with the recognition of the principle of "maximum feasible participation" for affected groups, and the increasing interest of organized community groups in influencing the delivery of services, the health system has been penetrated by consumer interests. Consumer representatives are now included on advisory boards of hospitals, neighborhood health centers, and health planning bodies to enable institutions to understand the dissatisfactions of the public and to enable the consumers to face more realistically the complexity and limitations of the programs. Struggles often develop over the power of such boards and the issue of medical versus nonmedical control.

FINANCING OF HEALTH SERVICES

Private Insurance

Health services are financed by private insurance and by governmental programs. Private health insurance plans take different forms. The major types include Blue Cross and Blue Shield, commercial insurance, and independent nonprofit plans.

Blue Cross and Blue Shield   In 1939 a group of teachers insured themselves against hospital bills through a prepayment plan. Blue Cross has grown into a network of nonprofit organizations. State and local groups belong to the national Blue Cross Association. Blue Cross plans are endorsed by the American Hospital Association.

Blue Shield was established as a separate program to cover doctor's bills. In 1974, 81 million people were covered by Blue Cross and 74 million by Blue Shield. Both are prepayment plans rather than true insurance. A member pays a prorated share of his group's covered medical and hospital charges. About 5 percent of the Blue Cross premiums go for administration. The rest goes for health care.

Other Companies   Commercial companies have entered the health insurance business in large numbers, particularly as a result of organized labor's demands for health benefits. In 1970, commercial companies enrolled 60 percent of those covered, Blue Cross 36 percent, and other nonprofit plans 4 percent. Approximately 80 percent of the population had some private health or hospital insurance during 1970. This left nearly 40 million who had none. For those who had it, private health insurance met 73 percent of hospital care, 48 percent of physicians' services, and 5.5 percent of other health care such as medicine or special glasses.[13]

Problems of private health insurance include:

1 High-risk groups—the poor, aged, and chronically ill—who most need insurance cannot get it economically.

2 Premiums in commercial plans are too high.

3 Coverage is inadequate for preventive or out-patient care, encouraging overuse of hospitals.

4 To prevent small claims, most policies have a deductible provision requiring a cash outlay before benefits are paid.

5 Private insurers exercise little control over rising costs.

6 Programs do not cover the costs of long-term chronic illness.

7 Advertising by commercial companies directly to consumers is often misleading.

GOVERNMENT HEALTH PROGRAMS

Currently the federal government pays 30 percent of the country's health care bill. It participates in the health insurance of federal employees and provides medical programs for families of members of the armed forces and through Veterans Administration hospitals for those who have had military service.

Historical Development

Other countries had begun to develop insured health care in the latter part of the nineteenth century and the early twentieth century. Interest in national health insurance was evident in this country in 1912, when the Progressive Party under Theodore Roosevelt included a national health insurance plan in its platform. Although a national health insurance program was urged in the Social Security Act of 1935, health insurance was finally omitted because it might have endangered the passage of the act.

Legislation for health insurance has been introduced in each session of Congress since 1939. In 1949, President Harry S. Truman urged the enactment of a compulsory system in his State of the Union message. No law resulted. By the 1960s the strategy shifted to securing improved health care for people over 65. The result was the passage of Medicare in 1965 as Title XVIII of the Social Security Act.

Current Programs

Medicare is a dual program. One part is financed by payroll taxes on employers and employees. Coverage includes hospital service, extended-care aid, and some home health care. Initially the patient was required to pay the first $40. He now pays the first $72. The patient must also pay part of his expenses after he has been hospitalized 60 days and part of his extended-care expenses after 20 days.

The other part covering physicians' fees, hospital out-patient services, home health care, physical therapy, and diagnostic X-rays is voluntary. Originally, participants paid $3 a month for this coverage; in July 1972, it cost $6.30 a month. Since 1973 the deductible provision requires the patient to pay the first $60 of his medical expenses. Then the plan will cover 80 percent of the remaining charges. Rates may well rise. The local Social Security Office can provide current rates. Private insurance is available to meet costs not covered by Medicare.

The federal government was careful not to interfere with the existing health delivery system. While the Social Security Administration has overall respon-sibility for the program, intermediaries such as Blue Cross, private insurance companies, and other organizations are chosen by hospitals or physicians to carry out the bookkeeping and payments. This has served to increase the power of the Blue Cross groups, since they make payments to the health providers and set "reasonable" fees.

Advantages of Medicare include participation in coverage of the aged as a right; elimination of negative feelings about health insurance; better benefits than those of private health insurance plans; and improved services to the aged such as home care and extended care.

The problems involve greatly expanded demand for services already in short supply; increased health costs; lack of consumer participation in decision making; overutilization of hospitals; exclusion of drugs and long-term care; and the deductible provisions resulting in the need for additional private insurance.

After years of resistance, health insurance has had increasing acceptance by hospitals, nursing homes, and doctors.

In 1973 through an amendment to the Social Security Act, younger permanently and totally disabled people were also included in the program. However, all the aged and poor persons with long-term disabilities are still not covered.

With the passage of Title XIX of the Social Security Act in 1965, the federal government provided benefits for the medically indigent through Medicaid.

Medicaid differs from Medicare in almost every respect. Medicare is an insurance program based on worker-employment taxes to make it generally self-supporting; Medicaid, like other public assistance programs, is financed by appropriations from general tax revenues. One must pass a means test to qualify. The benefits vary from state to state. Generally they are available to persons on public assistance. The original legislation encouraged states to include coverage of self-supporting persons whose marginal incomes made them unable to pay for medical care. However, this inclusion was not mandatory, and the definition of "medical indigence" was left to the states.

Proposed Reforms

In 1969 Congress placed a ceiling on federal responsibility and created the Task Force on Medicaid and Related Programs, chaired by Walter J. McNerney, President of the Blue Cross Association.[14] The task force report provided a critical analysis. While the stated purpose of Medicaid had been to assure adequate health care to the nation's poor and near-poor, only 13 million of the 26 million people living below the poverty line in 1970 benefited. The report pressed for changes in the purchase of services, management of health services, increased care to prevent illness, consumer participation, and restructuring of long-term care. Further recommendations included:

1 A uniform minimum level of health benefits financed 100 percent by federal funds
2 Inclusion of the working poor as recipients
3 Funds for the development and improvement of health care services and resources
4 Funds for prepaid insurance programs
5 Dental care coverage for children aged five to twelve

PUBLIC HEALTH

Public health services operate at the federal, state, and local levels. They are dependent upon the authority of the state and federal government to intervene in many ways. Nationally, the emphasis has been on research and education, the monitoring of the safety of drugs, and the purity of food. The United States Public Health Service has become involved in more direct services since the creation of the Department of Health, Education and Welfare in 1953.

Functions of Public Health

The first state health department was established in Massachusetts in 1869. On a state and local level, major concerns include water supply, sewage disposal, environmental hazards, control of communicable diseases, and regulation through licensing of health facilities. Public health experts have virtually eliminated a number of communicable diseases such as tuberculosis, polio, and smallpox. Existing clinics generally have been limited to specialized programs such as well-baby care, treatment of venereal disease, and detection of such diseases as tuberculosis, glaucoma, and more recently sickle-cell anemia. A network of community public health clinics staffed by teams of public health nurses, social workers, public health educators, and paramedical personnel could help meet the present crisis in medical care.

Public health education in relation to nutrition, smoking, accidents, suicide, and drug use has been given limited support.

NEW MODELS OF HEALTH DELIVERY

The foregoing discussion suggests that the United States has a multifaceted and fragmented system of health delivery.

Essential Conditions   Somers has identified four conditions essential to a comprehensive system of care[15]—efficient referral, access to health professionals, adequate manpower supply, and peer review, including pricing of services:

1   Every individual must have access to the whole spectrum of health services through referral channels that do not break the primary personal relationship, do not require unnecessary duplication of diagnostic tests or other services, but do provide complete and continuous records of all medical and other health-related information.
2   Every individual must have access to a meaningful personal relationship with at least one health professional, preferably a physician or a specialist who can provide the necessary general coordination and continuity.
3   The supply of doctors, nurses, and other health personnel must be adequate.
4   Health professionals should be subject to an organized system of professional discipline or peer review involving the quality, quantity, and price of services rendered. Every health institution must be subject to some form of price discipline—through market competition, public regulation, or a combination of both.

With these essential conditions in mind, we will consider some models for the delivery of health care.

THREE MODELS OF HEALTH CARE

Private Hospital Initiative

The Montefiore Hospital in New York City began as a home for chronic invalids in 1885. Eventually, services included an extensive program of education and research, primarily for care of the chronically ill. A program of home care was begun for long-term patients after World War II. To ensure proper care, a medical determination and a social evaluation were made. The patient's feelings about his or her illness and the effect of it on relationships with other members of the family were studied. The situation was reviewed to see whether the family had the will and capacity to care for the patient at home.

In 1948, the hospital signed a contract with the Health Insurance Plan of Greater New York (HIP) and formed the Montefiore Medical Group, a prepaid group practice program providing prevention as well as treatment. The newer term is *health maintenance*. The plan meets community medical needs, leading to better control over in-patient care—the source of mounting costs. "Only by providing comprehensive, ambulatory, diagnostic, and treatment services and restricting the use of the hospital for 'hospital sick' patients can we make progress in our attempts to control the total medical care bill of the hospital."[16]

Using the physician–nurse–medical social worker team, the hospital motivated families to seek health services. The hospital determined the kinds of services necessary and compared the differences in the health of those families receiving care from the health team with a control group.

The hospital also developed a community center. Group workers are employed to help bridge the gap between the hospital and the community in connection with psychiatric patients, day care facilities for employees, and special coordinated programs for the aged. The program recognizes community needs and the role of consumer groups.

In association with the Teamsters Union, a major purchaser of health care, and with the Columbia University School of Public Health and Administrative Medicine, the hospital audits the care received, provides specialized services, and carries on research to develop new programs.

Sponsorship by Private Industry

The Kaiser Permanente Health Plan in California was started during the 1930s to provide health services to a group of construction workers. It was greatly expanded during World War II to care for the 90,000 workers in the Kaiser shipyards. When these workers left, the program was opened to the community.

Kaiser Permanente was organized as a nonprofit corporation providing autonomous partnerships of medical groups in each geographical area, group practice, and integration of hospital and clinic facilities with prepayment for services by the members.

No fees are charged at the time of service, and membership is not compulsory. The physicians administer the program. The system encourages doctors to keep patients well and hospital beds empty. Under the fee system patients tend to postpone treatment unless they are very ill. Without fees, the medical system tends to become flooded with a mixture of relatively well people. Garfield, one of the founders of the Kaiser Permanente plan, proposes separating the *well*, the *worried well*, the *early sick*, and the *sick*. He suggests three services: health care, preventive maintenance, and sick care.[17]

The program could be carried out with a well-staffed, well-equipped medical center and a series of outreach neighborhood clinics each providing primary paramedical services.

The preventive maintenance service using paramedical staff under medical supervision provides routine services and supervision for such conditions as obesity, diabetes, hypertension, arthritis, back problems, mental health, aging processes, and rehabilitation. A sick care center similarly staffed includes hospital and clinic facilities, special laboratories, and facilities for both "intensive acute" and extensive care.

The health care service should be staffed primarily with paramedical personnel under medical supervision. Educational and counseling services would be available, as well as nutrition, well-baby, prenatal, adolescent, and family planning services.

Neighborhood Health Centers

In January 1970, fifty-two OEO programs were funded. In addition, thirty-one programs were funded by the Public Health Service under the Comprehensive Health Care or Family Health Care projects.[18] The programs emphasize community involvement and are served by varying combinations of professionals and paraprofessionals. They use paraprofessionals and indigenous workers on teams with physicians, nurses, and social workers.

Community programs have had considerable success in meeting the needs of unserved populations, but their effectiveness with comprehensive health needs is limited unless they operate in cooperation with a hospital. Neighborhood centers should be a part of a national health plan for all citizens. Unfortunately federal funds are no longer available to establish new neighborhood health centers.

PLANNING OF HEALTH CARE

The Hill-Burton Hospital and Construction Act of 1946 was the first national legislation requiring each state to study its hospital facilities, to establish its priority needs, and to plan for expansion. Through this legislation hospitals have been expanded and nursing homes, clinics, and public health and rehabilitation centers built.

Health care planning was greatly stimulated by the 1966 "Partnership for Health" Act:

> The Congress declares that fulfillment of our national purpose depends on promoting and assuring the highest level of health attainable for every person, in an environment which contributes positively to healthful individual and family living; that attainment of this goal depends on an effective partnership, involving close inter-government collaboration, official and

voluntary efforts, and participation of individuals and organizations; that Federal financial assistance must be directed to support the marshaling of all health resources—national, state, and local—to assure comprehensive health services of high quality for every person, but without interfering with existing patterns of private professional practice of medicine, dentistry, and related healing arts.

General Principles   Aid to states in establishing health planning organizations, with advisory councils having a majority of consumer representatives; aid to the development of regional health plans, also requiring consumer representation; and grants for the development of health and mental health programs were included.

This legislation sought to reach every level of government, to relate to both private and public sectors, and to assure the highest level of health for every individual, "without interfering with existing patterns of private practice."

Heart, Cancer, and Stroke   Public Law 89-239 passed in 1965 authorized grants to aid in the planning for regional programs related to heart disease, cancer, and stroke. Included were projects affecting nonprofit universities, medical schools, research institutions, hospitals and health agencies engaged in training and research. Model Cities funds were also provided to assist cities in planning and construction of hospitals and other facilities.

Planning groups will become increasingly important in health programming by government because they represent diverse interests of providers and consumers. So far, however, there has been little change in the delivery system; providers have benefited more than consumers.

Prepaid Health Plans

Congress passed Public Law 93-222 in December 1973 to assist in the development of prepaid health plans known as Health Maintenance Organizations (HMOs). The program is intended to encourage comprehensive health programs for "underserved populations" for a five-year period. The bill provides financial assistance for feasibility surveys, planning, initial developmental costs and research, but not construction costs or subsidies to permit the medically indigent to join HMOs. It removes obstacles of restrictive laws, and mandates employers of over twenty-five people to include in their health benefits plans the option of membership in "qualified health maintenance organizations" where they exist. To qualify, minimum services include physicians, hospitalization, mental health visits, alcoholic and drug abuse treatment and referral, diagnostic laboratory and radiology, home health services, preventive health services, health education, and medical social services—more than any prepaid health plan now provides.

Need for Health Insurance

National health insurance is long overdue in the United States. Even though private insurance coverage is increasing, less than three-fourths of costs of hospital care, half of physicians' services, and only 5.5 percent of other health needs such as medicine and special glasses are covered. The poor, who are most at risk, have no insurance. Even the aged covered by Medicare have no resources for long-term chronic illnesses. In addition, the possibility of serious or extended illness is a critical economic threat to people in the middle-income group.

To begin to meet the present crisis in health care, any national insurance plan must include provisons for regulating and redistributing health care, training health personnel, and emphasizing prevention.

NEW LEGISLATIVE PROPOSALS

The uncontrolled rise in health costs has led to increased support for broad-scale national health insurance programs. Without governmental insurance, many Americans cannot cover the cost of hospitalization in the case of extensive illness. Hospitals cannot survive without assured income. Physicians as well have benefited from insurance. Proposals for national health insurance programs are being made by Republican and Democratic spokesmen, the American Medical Association, representatives of private insurance companies, and organized labor.

Two bills to finance health services introduced in 1974 illustrate different approaches to national health insurance.

The Administration Plan   The Comprehensive Health Insurance Plan (CHIP), introduced to Congress on February 6, 1974, was a three-pronged approach for (a) the employed, (b) the low-income, and (c) those covered by Medicare. It was intended to be administered through private insurance companies. Benefits would begin after the first $150. An individual would pay 25 percent of his expenses until he reached $1500. Low-income people would have a sliding scale of coinsurance and deductibles. Medicare beneficiaries would not have to pay more than $750. Participation in "certified HMOs" was encouraged as an option.

The Kennedy-Mills Plan   Senator Edward Kennedy and Representative Wilbur Mills proposed the National Health Insurance Program (NHIP) on April 2, 1974. Senator Kennedy was identified with the Health Security Act over the past five years. The bill was proposed as a compromise.

It included universal coverage, comprehensive benefits, contributions according to income, cost and quality control, and a Health Resources Development Board to oversee basic reform of the health care system. Contributions would come from employers, employees, and self-employed individuals. There would be deductibles of $150 per person and coinsurance of 25 percent, neither of which were included in Senator Kennedy's original program. For the first time, long-term care would be covered. Under NHIP persons would have to contribute to a maximum of $1,000. Many mechanisms of the Medicare program would be used. Medicaid would be repealed, but the Veterans Administration and the Indian Health Service would contiune.

Approaches   Proposals embody four major approaches. In the mixed *public-private* approach, health insurance would be collected by the federal government and dispersed by private insurance companies that would handle the claims and pay the providers. In the *public* approach, governmental agencies would not only collect funds but also pay the claims. *Tax credits* for the purchase of private health insurance are another possible system. The *catastrophic* approach involves governmental participation only when medical expenses exceed a certain amount.

Several criteria may be applied:

1 Does the proposal improve health delivery to all citizens or only alter financing mechanisms?

2 Will the proposal improve health delivery for those whose needs are not now being met?

3 Will the proposal encourage more comprehensive delivery?

4 Will the proposal maximize utilization of present resources?

ROLES OF THE SOCIAL WORKER IN HEALTH CARE

Dr. Richard C. Cabot introduced social service into the Massachusetts General Hospital in Boston in 1905. Cabot recognized the importance of the environment to the patient's recovery and believed consideration of the patient as an individual would enable him to make better use of the medical care being offered. By 1915, there were social workers in over 100 hospitals. Medical social workers were included in public health programs beginning about 1920 and later in public assistance programs.

Social Work in the Hospital

The main setting for social work practice in the health field is of course the hospital. People come there in times of crisis. Not only do they have worries associated with health problems, they must cope with financial concerns and anxiety about family members. We have already alluded to the special problems of chronic illness.

There are four general areas for the worker—the patient himself and his own resources to meet the crisis, the hospital and its resources, the family, and the community. The preoccupation traditionally has been with the patient and his family, but the hospital and the community in which it is located can be key elements in programs of health maintenance or restoration.

Medical social work, now more often referred to as social work in the health field, has followed the trends of the profession as a whole. It began with a commitment to alter the environment to help in the rehabilitation of the ill client and moved into involvement with psychosomatic medicine and concern about the psychological components of illness. Now there is a broader concept of practice including the internal and external needs of the client and the functioning of the total care system.

Whereas the traditional focus was primarily on direct casework with the individual, medical social workers have also introduced group work and community organization and planning into their practice. Initially they took subservient roles as members of "a guest agency within the host medical agency." However, social workers have become increasingly versatile members of the health team. They provide consultation, training of other professionals, and policy development within various health agencies.

Impetus has been given to the use of social workers in hospitals and extended care facilities by Medicare and Medicaid. The development of community clinics and specialized clinics for family planning, genetics counseling, abortion counseling, and the treatment of alcoholics, drug abusers, mothers and infants, and the elderly has created new opportunities for social workers in the health field.

Patient Care Policies   Social workers have also played major roles in the development of new policies for patient routines. Wider choices of menus, unrestricted visiting hours, and more group activities have been issues on which the social workers' expertise has been useful. Reserved parking spaces for the disabled, more creative use of the funds of local service clubs, and the recruitment and training of volunteers illustrate broader community projects. Social workers are often interested in working in teaching hospitals, where their roles include working with medical students to alert them to social factors that affect the patient's well-being. These hospitals are also more likely to have programs of evaluation and research in which the social worker may participate.

Health Planning

With the new emphasis on health planning, social workers will need to develop increased knowledge in this area. Other skills required include training of indigenous workers and paraprofessionals, particularly in the community clinics, and understanding of effective methods of advocacy. In its policy statement on health care in 1971, the National Association of Social Workers pledged itself to "reorganization of the system and development of resources physical, financial, and human to fulfill the mission of providing quality, dignified health care for all people."

The employment outlook for social work in the health field is good, especially now that a social services department is required by the American Hospital Association as a condition for accreditation. A federal health insurance program will provide additional demands for social workers.

Shirley H. Wattenberg

KEY TERMS

sick care	Medicaid
health maintenance	new careerists
health delivery system	indigenous personnel
allied health workers	Blue Cross–Blue Shield
third-party financing	prepaid group practice
Medicare	neighborhood health centers

FOR DISCUSSION

1   Explain the differences between health care and sick care.
2   Why do social problems such as health vary with income level and race?
3   Why do the aging have special health problems?

4   Why is hospitalization the key to health delivery planning?
5   How does awareness of symptoms relate to social class?
6   "Hospital care costs twice as much as physicians' bills." Do you agree?
7   What are *third-party* payments?
8   Explain the differences between Medicare and Medicaid.
9   What are the major recommendations for changes in Medicare?
10 Smoking, accident prevention, drug use, and nutrition are concerns of what specialty?
11 Summarize the four essential conditions for comprehensive health care.
12 What major barriers impeded consumer participation in planning and control of health services?
13 How is the Montefiore Medical Group financed?
14 What three services are provided in the Kaiser Permanente Plan?
15 What methods are involved in medical social work?

PROJECTS

1   Use the latest *Statistical Abstract of the United States* to give a picture of the costs of health services, the number of health personnel, and other data that you consider important in understanding the health delivery system. Do any of your findings present a different picture from those in the text?
2   Identify the health planning bodies in your community. Make a study of their roles. Attend at least one meeting of each group and report on the discussion. Who was involved? What is your impression of the power structure? Did social workers take any role?
3   Invite one or more directors of social services of local hospitals to talk about the roles of social work and to assess manpower needs. Ask a medical social worker who is not an administrator to make the same assessment. Do their observations differ? If so, how?
4   Interview a representative of Blue Cross–Blue Shield or some other large private health insurance plan. Ask him to explain the benefits available, including their relationship to Medicare. What is his attitude toward comprehensive planning for health services?
5   Ask students in your class who have had extensive medical services to discuss the care given, the costs, and the general outcomes of their experience. What role did medical social workers play? Were the social workers effective? What improvements can be suggested? Was the experience of students who had acute illness different from those who are disabled?

FOR FURTHER STUDY

American Hospital Association, *Essentials of Social Work Programs in Hospitals*, Visual Images, Inc., Arlington Heights, Ill., 1971.
Harriett M. Bartlett, *Social Work Practice in the Health Field*, National Association of Social Workers, New York, 1961.
Eveline M. Burns, *Health Services for Tomorrow; Trends and Issues*, Dunellen, New York, 1973.
Barbara and John Ehrenreich, *The American Health Empire*, Vantage Books, New York, 1971.
E. Matilda Goldberg and June E. Neill, *Social Work in General Practice*, Allen & Unwin, London, 1972.

Emanuel Hallowitz, "Innovations in Hospital Social Work," *Social Work*, July 1972, pp. 89–97.

Sidney Hirsch and Abraham Lurie, "Social Work Dimensions in Shaping Medical Care Philosophy and Practice," *Social Work*, April 1969, pp. 75–79.

Sylvia A. Law, *Blue Cross: What Went Wrong?* Yale University Press, New Haven, 1974.

David Mechanic, *Public Expectations and Health Care*, Wiley, New York, 1972.

Urban Health, the Journal of Health Care in the Cities has been published bimonthly since 1972.

Gary W. Shannon and G. E. Alan Dever, *Health Care Delivery*, McGraw-Hill, New York, 1974.

Milton Wittman, "Social Work Manpower for the Health Services: Problems and Prospects," *American Journal of Public Health*, vol. 64, April 1974, pp. 370–375.

Chapter 8

Population
and Family Planning

What are the worldwide population trends?
What are solutions to the population dilemma?
How can food and water supplies be assured?
Can population be controlled voluntarily?
What roles can social workers play?

Social workers are particularly concerned by overpopulation and shortages of resources. Family size affects family goals. Shortages of food and fuel raise costs for the people social workers serve. Without food surpluses, hunger becomes even more of a problem.

This chapter will begin with the global goals of population control and environmental protection. Then family planning in relation to population control will be examined, along with policy issues that affect the social worker.

The need for family planning specialists provides new career opportunities for social workers. They must respond to controversial issues, including contraception for teenagers, social and legal policy toward abortion, solutions to problems of sterility for those who want children, and possible racist implications in the location and promotion of family planning services. Even if you do not work in an agency that provides family planning, you will probably work with clients who want family planning information.

THE POPULATION PROBLEM

In recent years, the population predicament has received attention as one of mankind's most challenging problems. Along with concern over environmental protection and the energy crisis, public attention has also focused on population. There is agreement that slowing population growth in the developing and the developed areas of the world is desirable for improving the quality of life. The dire consequences of overpopulation have been repeated so often that some people discount them, especially when years pass without any cataclysmic effects from rapid population growth. Still, evidence on the current demographic situation and its impact on the environment and resources warrants continuing concern.

Conflicting Views

Scientists differ in their assessment of the problem, especially in the developed regions of the world. Conflicting policies have been advocated to solve the population dilemma. These range from helping people to act in their own best interests to limit the size of their families to mandatory legal means to regulate childbearing. The Commission on Population Growth and the American Future in 1972 sought a full public discussion of these policies.[1] Unfortunately, the debate centered on the recommendations of open abortion and distribution of contraceptives to minors. Both were rejected by President Nixon.

In January 1973, the Supreme Court in responding to a test of a Texas law found abortion within the first three months of pregnancy to be a matter between a woman and her physician. The impact of this decision may not be clear for years. The reasons for the decision will be discussed in Chapter 10 on Legal Provisions.

Questions of class bias and racism have arisen as to whether or not the poor and the black populations have become the targets of family planning propaganda and services, while the bulk of the middle class, who cause the major population increase, are not included in such campaigns.

POPULATION GROWTH

The population of the world was estimated at 3.86 billion in 1973. With an annual 2 percent growth rate, it will double in 35 years. The increase is 70 to 75 million persons a year.

Historical Perspective   Rapid population growth is a relatively recent phenomenon. During the Stone Age, the world population probably never exceeded 10 million. However, around 8000 B.C., with the onset of the agricultural revolution as man learned how to grow his own food and create settlements, the population grew to about 200 to 300 million. By 1650 it had reached the half-billion mark. This was a population explosion in itself, but in the next three centuries the gain was more spectacular. In the 200 years from 1650 to 1850, the world population reached a billion. By 1930 it doubled to 2 billion, and it reached 4 billion by 1975. By the year 2000 it may rise to 6 or 7 billion without a major reduction in birth rates or increase in death rates.[2]

Reasons for Growth   This rapid growth in population results from several interacting factors. Western civilization was transformed from a rural agrarian to an urban industrial society by an expansion in scientific knowledge and technology, including a revolution in medicine and public health. Mortality in the Western world dropped significantly, leading to dramatic population growth. The developing nations had an even greater drop in mortality, but it was accomplished without an industrial revolution. Unlike the West, where the decline in mortality was accompanied by a drop in fertility, there was no significant reduction in birth rates.

Regional Differences   Birth rates differ by region. The European–North American group has medium to low birth rates, with 16 to 20 per thousand population. The Afro-Asian–Latin American group has high birth rates, wtih 35 to 50 per thousand. Oceania tends to fall in between, with 22 to 26 per thousand. Japan, Argentina, Israel, and Cyprus are exceptions to the general fertility trends prevalent in their region.

The differences between the area of high fertility and low fertility include general economic development, degree of urbanization, dominant occupations, per capita income, communication, and transportation. Population growth is greatest where it can be least afforded, in developing countries that need to concentrate on improving their economic conditions.[3]

Prosperity and Fertility   There is no necessary causal relationship, however, between economic development and decline in fertility. The United States has the highest per capita gross national product, but a birth rate of about 15 per thousand, compared to the 10 to 13 per thousand in many European countries. On the other hand, no nations with a high birth rate have high per capita productivity, although some are more prosperous than others.

Population Growth in the United States

The United States' growth rate, which has steadily declined over the past decade, registered an unexpected decline since 1971.[4] Total births declined 4 percent from 1970, even though potential mothers in the population (15 to 44 years) increased by 2 percent. There were 3.5 million births in 1971. Based on 1970 rates, there would have been over 400,000 more births. The birth rate was 17.3 per thousand, the lowest in U.S. history. Census Bureau analysts placed the total fertility rate at 2.28 children per mother, the lowest since the mid-thirties, when it was 2.24. The rate needed to merely maintain the population is 2.11.

Even though the average completed family is at the replacement level of two children, the Census Bureau estimates that another 50 million Americans will be added to the population in the next twenty-five years.[5] Large numbers of young people born since World War II are still of reproductive age. This group is so numerous that zero population growth would require an average of 1.2 children for about the next twenty years. Such a drastic reduction in fertility is unlikely. The alternative is to bring fertility down to the replacement rate (two children per family) gradually. Zero population growth then will be reached after sixty-five to seventy years.[6]

THE SUPREME COURT DECISION ON ABORTION

A landmark decision by the U.S. Supreme Court overruled state laws that prohibited or restricted a woman's right to obtain an abortion during the first three months of pregnancy. States can impose increasing restrictions beyond that time. The decision came on a 7 to 2 vote of the Court in January 1973.

The national guidelines make possible broadly liberalized abortion procedures. Until the decision, only New York, Alaska, Hawaii, and Washington had made abortion generally legally available in the first months of pregnancy.

The decision for the first three months is now a matter between the woman and her physician. The state's interest in her welfare is not compelling enough to warrant interference. In the last ten weeks of pregnancy when there is likelihood that the fetus is capable of surviving, the state may prohibit abortion if it wishes, except where the life or health of the mother is a concern.

DEMAND FOR NATURAL RESOURCES

What is the capacity of the earth to support people? Any claim that a country's population is too large or too small implies some idea of an optimum size. It implies that growth up to that size is beneficial, and any more growth is harmful. No exact formula can determine the optimum population for a given area at a given time.

Because of the high rate of consumption in industrialized nations, one million additional people in the developed nations is like adding 30 million in the developing nations.[7] The industrialized nations, with their rapidly growing high consumption and high-waste economies, are using up more of the earth's nonrenewable resources and generating greater pollution of water, air, and land than the nonindustrialized nations. As many of the developing countries start to industrialize, the situation will get worse.

Food Supply

The food supply most clearly limits the capacity of the earth to support the increasing population. Harrison Brown estimated twenty years ago that with improved technology the world could eventually support 50 billion persons.[8] Dramatic improvement in the yield of new strains of wheat and rice provides encouraging evidence for this point of view. However, can technology help us with population growth?

The so-called "green revolution" is a mixed blessing at best. High-yield grains require increased use of fertilizers and water. In a country like India both fertilizers and electricity for tube-wells needed to irrigate crops run far short of the demand. Transportation and storage facilities are also inadequate.

More important, though, protein intake rather than total calories remains the most reliable way of measuring the nutritional standard. Widespread protein deficiency is revealed in diseases like marasmus, infantile dystrophy, and kwashiorkor. In 1967 an estimated 20 percent of the people in the developing countries were undernourished (not receiving enough calories per day), and 60 percent were malnourished (seriously lacking in one or more essential nutrients, most commonly protein).[9] Ten million Americans have been estimated to be hungry.

The food supply could possibly be increased by developing new lands, mostly from the tropical rain forests of South America, Africa, and Indonesia. Large amounts of water and sunshine are available in these areas, but they have poor soil and suffer from insect infestation. Twenty-eight billion dollars per year would be required simply to open new lands, not counting the research cost.

Can mankind be saved by harvesting the riches of the sea? The maximum yield from fisheries is 100 to 150 million metric tons.[10] To go over this limit would mean harvesting not only the ordinary fish but plankton. The cost in relation to the yields could be enormous, and more would have to be spent to make the food palatable. Besides, the overexploitation and oceanic pollution would make the venture unprofitable.

Water Supply

Only 3 percent of the world's water is fresh, while 97 percent is salt water. Ninety-eight percent of the fresh water is tied up in ice caps, particularly in Antarctica and Greenland. Some fresh water can be reused, but huge amounts required by living plants cannot be reused immediately.[11]

Water is needed in huge quantities to produce food. A pound of wheat requires about 60 gallons of water, a pound of meat 2,500 to 6,000 gallons. We use an average of 1,500 gallons per person each day in the United States. The supply of ground water reserves will soon be insufficient to meet withdrawal demands. American water requirements in 1980 will be about 700 billion gallons, while only 650 billion will be available.[12] Similar shortages will occur in other areas of the world as more water is needed for agriculture. Also agriculture must compete for water with industry. Fortunately, if pollutants can be removed, much of the water used by industry can be reused.

Desalinization—removing the salt from sea water—is being undertaken, but at such high cost that it is used only for drinking water. Even if the price should drop, the cost of transportation would still make it too expensive to use at any distance from the coast.

Energy Supply

Demand for energy and minerals will be increased both by population growth and by economic development. Whereas it will take thirty-five years for the population to double, the consumption of energy has doubled every twelve years. The United States today is confronted with an energy problem of major proportions. The domestic supply is incapable of meeting our needs, and the nation is forced to turn to foreign sources to an increasing degree. The situation can be partly alleviated by developing the existing potential for producing fuels and energy. The delay in moving in this direction has caused people to suspect that the whole energy crisis is a hoax engineered by the oil companies to squeeze out huge price increases.

The job is further complicated because over nine-tenths of the world's energy consumption is derived from fossil fuel sources (coal, oil, natural gas) and less than ten percent from hydroelectric power, atomic energy, or other sources.[13] New sources of energy that work as well as fossil fuel will have to be found.

Atomic energy is one such source, provided the cost can be brought down and the supply of uranium and thorium holds out. Further development of water power will also help, depending on how many rivers one wants to control with dams. The direct tapping of solar energy in a crowded world presents technological problems. Tidal power has only a fraction of the potential of water power. Many people assume that uranium-based nuclear power will soon replace fossil fuels, but electricity accounts for only 19 percent of the energy consumed in the United States. How soon can pollution-free plants be built and certified? Considerable lead time needs to be allowed. Environmental concerns have slowed nuclear power plant construction.

The consumption of minerals is proceeding so rapidly that both substitutes and mining of low-quality ores will be necessary. With less than 6 percent of the world's population, the United States accounts for over one-third of the world's tin consumption and one-fourth of its steel, phosphate, potash, and nitrogenous fertilizer consumption. When the developing nations industrialize, the demand for these nonrenewable minerals will far exceed the supply.

ENVIRONMENTAL PROTECTION

The increase in numbers of people is not the sole problem. Distribution of population and consumption patterns are related. Heavy demands for extravagances by a large, dense population create more environmental damage than would a small, widely distributed population with a frugal lifestyle.

Direct threats to human health are the most obvious effects of environmental deterioration. The most widely discussed are pollutants that reach us in air, water, and food.

Air Pollution

The United States Public Health Service estimated that our 90 million cars emit 66 million tons of carbon monoxide. The Public Health Service rated as the principal industrial sources of air pollution pulp and paper mills, iron and steel mills, petroleum refineries, smelters, and chemical plants. The fuel for heating houses, apartments, and offices adds its share, as does trash burning. More than 140 million tons of these pollutants are added to the atmosphere—about three-quarters of a ton annually for every person in the United States.[14]

Death rates rise for the very old, the very young, and people with respiratory ailments whenever levels of pollution go up. Pollution contributes to a higher incidence of emphysema, pneumonia, bronchitis, and lung cancer.

Much more can be done to reduce air pollution through enforcement of treatment procedures for pollutants. The reluctance of government to enforce standards and the resistance of industries to comply combine to work against successful pollution control. But even if such control were achieved, population and economic growth would again raise the pollution level.

Water Pollution

In many communities water pollution is a major problem. The U.S. Public Health Service rated the water supply of sixty American cities as "unsatisfactory" or as a "potential health hazard."[15] Reasons included impure sources, tap impurities, infrequent testing for bacteria, and use of nonapproved tests by the water department. Also, sewage treatment facilities were intended to handle a much smaller population. The growth in population generally involves increased industrial growth, resulting in more contaminators in the water (e.g., lead and ammonia). Increased agricultural production can create its own problem of a heavier water-borne load of pesticides, herbicides, and nitrates. The result is pollution of not just the rivers, streams, and lakes, but also of ground water, a more difficult problem.

Solid Wastes

With affluence comes greater accumulation of solid wastes—junked automobiles, cans, bottles, jars, other packaging materials, as well as garbage. Each year this includes 7 million junked cars, 55 billion cans, 26 billion bottles and jars, more than half a billion dollars' worth of other packaging materials, and 150 million tons of trash and garbage.[16] Open dumps and inadequate fills create not only esthetic problems but also public health hazards as breeding grounds for rats and germs. Sanitary landfills can help, but locations are becoming scarce.

Laws to prohibit the manufacture of nonbiodegradable materials and to encourage the manufacture of products that could be recycled are needed. Educational campaigns plus payment of deposits would help in the return of containers. As population grows and land for dumping becomes unavailable, rules will have to be enforced on the grounds of necessity rather than just esthetic considerations.

Chemical Pollution

Lead, mercury, and insecticides such as DDT are considered general pollutants. The symptoms of chronic lead poisoning include loss of appetite, weakness, and apathy—symptoms that are difficult to diagnose. In urban areas, exposure to lead comes from combustion of gasoline. Lead can be obtained from food and water as well as air, but is most hazardous when children eat lead in paint.

DDT has been the most commonly used insecticide since World War II. Studies of laboratory animals have shown that DDT increases the incidence of cancer, affects the sex hormones, and causes changes in brain functioning. Use of DDT has now been prohibited. Efforts are being made to develop a safe substitute that will be just as effective.

FAMILY PLANNING

Family Planning Policies

Governmental population policies are based on what those in authority think people ought to do, but enactment of a law does not assure implementation, especially when financial backing is so meager that the policy cannot be realistically followed. For instance, most of the three-year appropriations for the Family Planning and Population Services Research Act were not released by the administration. Also, policy makers are reluctant to accept the Supreme Court decision on abortion, although nationwide polls suggest public acceptance of liberalized abortion laws.

Since the population of any given area is determined by fertility, mortality, and migration, control of population must involve manipulation of one or all of these factors. Laws on immigration, abortion, and distribution of contraceptives have a direct effect on population; but laws fixing the minimum age of marriage and providing tax exemptions for dependents also have an effect.

Given national goals, the "population problems" of some countries have been a shortage of people. Governments have encouraged reproduction through pronatalist policies that reward large families, as in Russia and France, for example. The programs have been unsuccessful. Australia and Canada increase their population through selective immigration of skilled people.

Family Planning Programs

National family planning programs are governmental efforts to fund and administer birth control information and services *on a voluntary basis* to target populations to lower fertility. By 1970, twenty-five countries—representing over 67 percent of the population of the developing world—had official programs. Fifteen other countries, with 12 percent of the population, provided some governmental support. Other programs were supported through various international agencies.[17]

One Example   India, for example, has a separate department at the national level to deal with health and family planning. Each state also has a department under the directorship of a physician. The program reaches the rural areas through regional family planning centers that run special family planning clinics, temporary camps, mobile units, and already-established maternal health centers and hospitals. An extensive educational campaign accompanies these efforts and is managed by social workers who supervise the basic health workers assigned to the villages.

The most widely used methods in India are vasectomy and the interuterine device (IUD), although female sterilization and other contraceptives are also available. The "pill" has also been introduced on an experimental basis. In 1971, after years of political uproar, the first abortion law was passed. A pregnancy can now be terminated by a physician if it is within the first trimester. The consent of two physicians is required if the pregnancy is between 12 and 20 weeks. Unmarried mothers can have a pregnancy terminated unless they are minors or mentally ill, in which case parental consent is necessary. Despite all these provisions, the government labels the law a social reform and not a family planning measure.

Over one billion births must be averted between 1970 and 2000 to reduce the world's birth rate from 40 per thousand to 20 per thousand.[18] The effect on the birth rate is the ultimate test of the effectiveness of the program. Direct effects of a program are difficult to assess. For example, in India the total population was 546,955,945 million according to the 1971 census—14 million short of the official estimate.[19] Was the drop attributable to family planning programs? Had the death rate declined less than had been predicted? Or was there an undercount of the population? A 1 percent error could account for 5.5 million people!

Evidence shows the effect of family planning. Berelson reported that the family planning programs averted 2.3 million births in 1968, a 3 percent decline in the birth rate.

Public and Private Agencies

None of the developed countries has a significant national family planning policy or program. In the United States the work has been carried on through private agencies such as Planned Parenthood, founded in 1916 when Margaret Sanger opened the first birth control clinic in Brooklyn. Today Planned Parenthood has 190 nationwide affiliates. Family planning information and services are provided by 150 of them at a minimal charge.

Governmental Action

Population has not traditionally been considered a proper concern for government; according to President Eisenhower in 1959, birth control was outside of government policy (a stand he changed a few years later). During President Kennedy's administration, only one staff member was appointed to review world population problems. The first positive statement came when President Lyndon Johnson in his 1965 State of the Union message connected the growth of world population to the growing scarcity of resources. He stated directly that five dollars spent on family planning was worth a hundred dollars invested in some other area of economic development.

The then Secretary of Health, Education and Welfare, John W. Gardner, issued a statement in 1966 defining policy for population dynamics, fertility, sterility, and family planning. For the first time, federal funds could be appropriated to provide family planning services on a voluntary basis to welfare clients. This policy came under attack because of its avowed purpose of reducing the "welfare burden," i.e., by decreasing the transmission of poverty from one generation to another and lowering the illegitimacy rate. The Family Planning Services and Population Research Act of 1970 set up the National Center for Family Planning Services under the Health Services and Mental Health Administration and recognized that family planning was part of the delivery of comprehensive health services for all. In 1971, the Secretary of HEW presented to Congress a five-year plan for a partnership between the federal government and the private sector to achieve research and service goals. Congress made a new attempt to spell out the legislative mandate in 1972 to provide family planning services for all welfare recipients who wanted them. Changes were also made in contraceptive policy lifting restrictions on age and marital status for receiving birth control information and devices. However, a more intensive educational campaign is necessary.

Among Western European countries, England and Sweden provide family planning through the health services. Most Catholic countries have banned birth control, although the pill and condoms are available for "medical purposes" or "disease prevention." Also, late marriages and the use of other methods of contraception such as coitus interruptus and abortion keep the birth rate down. The Soviet Union, other Eastern European countries, and Japan have tried to lower their abortion rate by distribution of contraceptives through government health clinics.

POPULATION CONTROL

Population control is the *deliberate regulation* of population size by *society*. Family planning is the regulation of fertility by individual families. Population control is directed at the rate of growth and takes into account fertility control, the geographical location and movement of population, and problems of economic and social development as they affect fertility, mortality, and total size.

Proposals   Bernard Berelson compiled a list of proposals that go beyond family planning, including use of additives in the water or food supply to temporarily sterilize people, licensing for childbirth, use of time-capsule contraceptives as means of temporary sterilization (with reversibility controlled by the government), and compulsory sterilization of men with three or more living children.[20] Other proposals involve use of incentives—money, goods, or services to couples not bearing children for specific periods. "Negative" incentives include tax and welfare penalties and withdrawal of benefits such as maternity and family allowances after a certain number of children. Social and economic measures could have the effect of lowering fertility, for example, increasing the minimum age of marriage or requiring female participation in the labor force as an alternative or supplement to marriage. Some proposals advocate two types of marriages—one childless and readily dissolved, the other more stable and licensed to have children.

These suggestions may seem "far out" and unacceptable on moral or ethical grounds. However, the research will probably continue, since a compulsory program may become imperative.

CONTRACEPTIVE PRACTICE

Charles Westoff reports a significant increase in the use of more effective contraception from 1965 to 1970.[21] This has been important in the decline in the nation's birth rate. The combined use of the three most effective methods of contraception—sterilization, the pill, and the IUD—has increased from 37.2 percent of contraceptive practice in 1965 to 57.9 percent by 1970. Taking into account also the use of the diaphragm, the condom, and various other methods, the data show that four out of five couples using contraception were protected from unwanted pregnancies. This trend was consistent across varying educational levels and racial groups.

The most popular method of contraception was the pill. Nearly 6 million married women of reproductive age (34.2 percent) were using the pill. The second most popular method was contraceptive sterilization (16 percent). Sterilization was especially popular among older couples (with the wife aged 30 to 44), accounting for one-quarter fo all couples in this age bracket. The use of the IUD has also increased from 1.2 percent to 7.4 percent. The use of older methods declined accordingly—condoms from 21.9 percent to 14.2 percent, the diaphragm from 9.9 to 5.7, rhythm from 10.9 to 6.4, withdrawal from 4.0 to 2.1, and the douche from 5.2 to 3.2 percent. The past few years have also witnessed a growing acceptance and increasing utilization of induced abortion for fertility control.

Socioeconomic Level and Contraception

Westoff estimates that half of the fertility decline in the 1960s might be due to the drop in the number of unwanted births.[22] We do not have wholly adequate data on the differential in unwanted births between different socioeconomic groups. Preliminary investigations into American fertility attitudes and behavior suggest that families in the lowest socioeconomic group express a preference for somewhat smaller families than those in the higher socioeconomic groups, but unplanned births nevertheless occur more frequently. Low-income families depend on less reliable nonmedical methods of family planning, since they cannot afford private medical care. Although the number of people served by family planning programs increased from 400,000 in 1966 to 1.5 million in 1970, only half the counties in the United States had organized family planning programs in 1972.[23]

Despite their higher fertility, births in low-income families account for a much smaller share of the birth rate than births among the nonpoor. During 1960 to 1965, low-income families had 31.8 percent of the children and higher-income families 68.2 percent.

FAMILY PLANNING AND SOCIAL WORK

Schools of Social Work

What efforts are being made to deal with population and family planning in the education of social workers? A questionnaire on the subject sent to the eighty graduate schools of social work by the Council on Social Work Education in 1969 received only thirty replies.[24] Only one school offered a course called family planning. Twelve schools participated in field placements, research projects, or classroom instructional units. Ten schools had integrated family planning into the curriculum, sometimes with only one lecture in an area of concentration. Eight offered no content in this area. More recent data are needed to show how much interest has increased.

Activity is dependent on faculty interest. The schools were not committed to family planning courses. If an interested faculty member left, the program ended. More interest was shown in schools of social work located near schools of public health and centers of population research. However, if social work is to play a significant role in family planning and in social policy related to population problems, the schools of social work have to provide effective educational programs.

Social Agencies

Since social workers function through a variety of agencies, an extensive in-service training effort is necessary before they can effectively provide services in family planning. A welfare department study conducted by graduate social work students at the University of Illinois showed that clients who needed family planning never got to the service.[25] They only received a piece of paper stating that such services were available, distributed with many other forms at the time of the initial interview concerning eligibility. *None* of the social workers saw it as his or her job to provide family planning services. On the other hand, most social workers accept and endorse the need for in-service training, workshops, and simple clarification of agency policy in the area of family planning.

The same results were evident in a survey of two county welfare departments in Michigan and Illinois conducted in 1968. Varela reports that 84.1 percent of the caseworkers felt in-service training sessions would be helpful.[26] Details about birth control methods, counseling techniques dealing with family planning matters, information regarding local family planning services, and clarification regarding agency policy were requested.

Opportunities for Social Workers

Despite current apathy, many roles could best be performed by social workers. There is no more natural setting for discussing family planning than in social work with individuals, families, and social groups. Information-giving on contraception can be organized on a community-wide basis, but the acceptance of service is still an individual or a family decision that often needs support and counsel. Problem clarification and provision of support are also important techniques.

Community organization skills can be used to develop local services and programs and create a climate of opinion to promote the acceptance of family planning counseling as a legitimate service, and will help people feel that such services are not being imposed on them. Communication skills can be used to interpret the needs of people to policy makers so that conflicts and power struggles do not interfere with the effective use of services.

At the policy level social work efforts have been minimal. There has been no discussion in the social work literature of the social implications of adopting a policy of population control. Perhaps with all the emphasis in the profession on individual freedom, social workers have shied away from societal control to solve critical population problems.

Research Needs Topics for social work research should include decision making concerning family size and timing of children, effects of family and peer groups on attitudes toward sex, and analysis of differences in fertility among groups of people of selected demographic factors.

Besides family planning activities in traditional social work agencies, social workers could fill various jobs in specialized agencies that deal with family planning—Planned Parenthood, maternal and child health clinics, public health departments, and obstetrics and gynecology clinics.

Career Opportunities For social workers interested in family planning, opportunities will become more available if the federal government implements population research and family planning services. The plan of the National Center for Family Planning Services seeks to "maximize the delivery of family planning through existing health agencies and channels." It anticipates that voluntary agency coverage will have to double. More social workers will be needed for family planning in social and health-related agencies.[27]

At present, more social workers should be specifically assigned to family planning services and to abortion and postabortion counseling. School social workers have become increasingly involved in family planning activities as part of continued education to sexually active teenagers. Social workers in obstetrics, gynecology, and pediatric departments in hospitals and clinics have organized group discussions and counseling services around the need for family planning. More social workers are being employed by Planned Parenthood to conduct classes in sex education; to provide abortion information and counseling; to establish community contacts for disseminating information on family planning services; and to offer counseling at the Centers. The *Family Planning Digest* indicates some of the job openings.

SERVICE DELIVERY AND SOCIAL POLICY

Social workers need to become familiar with major issues in service delivery in family planning arising out of social policy in population. So far government activity has been largely directed at bringing contraceptive information and services to the poor. Birth control centers have been concentrated in poor communities. Middle-class families get such services from private physicians, but nevertheless it is understandable that members of the black communities have charged that family planning programs are aimed specifically at reducing the black population.

No Antipoverty Measure   Social workers must realize that family planning is not an antipoverty measure. A reduction in poverty can be achieved only by dealing with those probelms in the economy that create imbalances independent of the benefits that limitation of family size may bring. We need to understand the social change occurring in black communities to see why their members would be suspicious of outside efforts to impose any limitation on their numbers. A general fertility increase among all social classes of Blacks has occurred recently because of improved health conditions resulting in decreased death rates. Thus there would be little enthusiasm for limitation of family size, especially when family planning services are not offered as part of a comprehensive approach to health care. The only way such services will succeed is to place them under local community control, which would ease the racial tension and any conspiratorial implications.

Planning of Control   Finally, from a social policy point of view, we must distinguish between a national policy of family planning and one of population control. Family planning depends on individuals making a decision to voluntarily limit the size of their families. It will probably not lead to population control since it does not hold the population growth to a specified number. It only reduces the number of unwanted births. Thus all children might be wanted children, but we might still be faced with a population problem. No country has yet adopted zero population growth as a policy goal. Many scholars believe that family planning is a first step and that we need to develop and disseminate effective family planning services before we think about instituting population control measures. Other scholars disagree and feel that we should have instituted some means of population control long ago. A few years from now we may have to try other measures which now seem unethical or impractical. Utlimately we may have no choice, if the current world growth rate maintains its level. The social worker must be prepared to deal with family planning and population control as both a practitioner and an advocate.

Ketayun H. Gould

KEY TERMS

fertility	sterilization
green revolution	vasectomy
desalinization	condom
family planning	rhythm
population control	withdrawal
zero population growth	douche
diaphragm	"unwanted" births

FOR DISCUSSION

1 How does family size affect family goals?
2 Summarize the Supreme Court decision on abortion.
3 When did the world's population start to grow rapidly?
4 What was the role of medicine and public health in population growth?
5 Why do population trends in some countries run counter to regional trends?
6 Explain the sharp decline in the American birth rate in the 1970s.
7 What are the common population control measures?
8 What is sterilization?
9 Why are condoms recommended for men who have intercourse with several women?
10 Why will we not achieve zero population growth soon?
11 Define *family planning*.
12 What is the major accepted goal in family planning?
13 What social class contributes most to population growth?
14 What social class has the largest total number of unwanted pregnancies?
15 Why are family planning programs charged with class or race bias?
16 Why is a generalist education in social work advantageous for family planning?
17 What is the major problem in developing social work personnel for family planning roles?
18 Why is family planning not an antipoverty measure?

PROJECTS

1 Collect several examples of "optimistic" and "pessimistic" views concerning the future of food and energy supplies in the United States. After a review of the evidence, summarize your own position.
2 Make a study of the organizations interested in conservation, ecology, and public acquisition of open land and parks in your community. Do they cooperate with each other? What are their goals and methods of operation? Evaluate their success.
3 Invite a representative of Planned Parenthood to describe their program and to demonstrate and discuss various contraceptive devices. Does the organization have a program for the treatment of sterility as well as for family planning?
4 Present a discussion or debate on the question: "Resolved, that Blacks should oppose government-sponsored family planning programs."
5 Highway construction and planning are major ecological issues. What agencies are involved? Have citizens' groups organized to oppose any construction plans? What policies will obtain the best system of traffic management and flow and minimize noise, congestion, and pollution?

6 Write a policy statement for NASW on abortion.
7 Present a developmental program for sex education for children. Indicate the goals, methods, auspices, and content for each developmental period. Deal specifically with contraceptive information for adolescents.
8 Collect policy statements and public relations materials on ecology and business from your local Chamber of Commerce. Summarize and evaluate them.
9 Analyze the jobs listed in the *Family Planning Digest*. What skills do they require? Can a social worker fill most of them?

FOR FURTHER STUDY

H. M. Bahr, B. A. Chadwick, and D. L. Thomas, *Population, Resources and the Future: Non-Malthusian Perspectives*, Brigham Young University, Provo, Utah, 1972.

Florence Haselkorn (ed.), *Family Planning: Readings and Case Materials*, Council on Social Work Education, New York, 1971.

John Peel and Malcolm Potts, *Textbook of Contraceptive Practice*, Cambridge Univ. Press, 1970.

Edward Pohlman (ed.), *Population: A Clash of Prophets*, New American Library, New York, 1973.

Chapter 9

Education

Why do public schools vary greatly?
How can they offer greater opportunities?
Is corporal punishment discipline or child abuse?
What is the new model of school social work?

Relatively few of us have had experience with social agencies, but all of us have spent years in school. Our experience as students gives a frame of reference that may be useful in understanding public education as part of the social welfare structure. On the other hand, relying on our own experiences to understand public schools may be limiting, particularly if those schools were inadequate, crowded, regimenting, or nonmotivating.

America has long maintained a belief in the power of the school and a faith in literacy as a means of social problem solving. Since the early part of the nineteenth century, when the states began to pass compulsory attendance laws, the school has been given additional responsibilities in each succeeding generation. Today we have an elaborate system of public education supported by taxation with a continuum of preschool, elementary, and secondary education, continuing education for adults, and institutions of higher learning. Yet at no time in our history has the public school been the object of more dissatisfaction.

This chapter will focus on elementary and secondary public school education. Attention will be given to costs, enrollment rates, and special problems attached to school financing. The often contradictory functions of public school education, current school problems, and the changing role of the school social worker will be considered. We will also amplify the model of school social work introduced in Chapter 1.

SCHOOL FINANCES

A higher percentage of older youth are in school in America than in any other country of the world. About 75 percent of seventeen-year-olds are in school here compared with about 55 percent in Japan and 40 percent in Sweden. Our higher attendance is due to a later legal school leaving age—sixteen in most states—and to emphasis on the importance of a high school diploma.[1]

Developing nations spend on education less than 10 percent of the amount expended by industrialized nations. From 1960 to 1968, expenditures of industrialized nations rose by 145 percent compared to 130 percent for those of developing countries, yet industrialized countries have only about one-third of the world's population. In developing countries, the number of potential school pupils between ages five and nineteen increased by 36 million more than the number of school enrollments. "For hundreds of millions of illiterate people in the world, school can no longer be of help. Moreover, in the developing countries nearly half of the children of primary school age today are condemned, no matter what happens, to grow up without ever having attended a class."[2]

Costs of American Education

Concern has grown about current and projected costs of education in the United States. Total estimated expenditures of public school systems in the 1974–1975 school year are estimated at $60 billion.[3] By 1980 these expenditures will come to $65 billion. If prices continue to rise, costs will be even higher.[4]

In most states, the major costs of elementary and secondary public schools are still paid by local government, mostly from property taxes. Since the establishment of this country, support of schools has been a local responsibility. Income taxes were virtually unknown until this century.

Public educational opportunity available to children and young persons rests upon two key questions: What is the value of the property on the tax rolls, and how many pupils are there in the district? The assessed valuation of real property determines the funds available for educational programs.

Gross disparity in the property values exists due to the movement of population and variations in concentration of industry and natural resources. For example, within Illinois the taxable property per pupil averages about $25,000, but one school board may have sixty times the resources of another board for each pupil it serves.[5] Furthermore, where property values are high, a moderate tax rate will produce sufficient revenues. Where assessed valuations are low, the people have to tax themselves heavily to produce a minimum amount of money per pupil.

Schools in areas with low property values are disadvantaged further in supporting new school construction because statutes stipulate the maximum percentage of assessed valuation for which each district can issue bonds.

Differences also exist among the states in average per pupil expenditures. In 1973–1974, New York spent an average of $1,628 per pupil, and Alabama spent $678.

Following World War II, states passed legislation to attempt to equalize the tax burden between school districts and assure every pupil at least a minimum educational program. State aid was needed to supplement the proceeds of local property taxes so that a "foundation" or minimum financial backing per pupil would be possible in every district. The federal Elementary and Secondary School Act and the Economic Opportunity Act provided additional funds to selected school districts with special problems. Nevertheless, as equalizers these measures have been disappointing.

The power to control public education and its quality for every pupil continues to rest mainly with the states. But even in states that provide the bulk of the money, the local district usually exercises its autonomy, contradicting the traditional belief that power resides with the holder of the purse.[7]

Challenges to the Property Tax

Dissatisfaction of taxpayers with the traditional system of school financing has become widely apparent. A study by the Educational Research Service found that 46.8 percent of the school bond issues were rejected and 47.9 percent of referenda for tax rate increases were voted down because the property tax was rising so fast.[8]

Inequities in educational opportunity as measured by expenditure per pupil led to a strategy for challenging the local property tax as a basis for school financing. The path to social reform of school financing began a decade ago when a group of young lawyers became interested in altering an indefensible and unequal system—spending significantly more on educating a child in one district than in another.[9] Together with a social worker, John Serrano, active in educational affairs in the Mexican-American community of Los Angeles, they filed a class action suit against the state officials who dispensed public education funds. As a result, in 1971 a decision by the California Supreme Court in *Serrano v. Priest* held that the state's reliance on local property taxes for school financing was unconstitutional.[10] It discriminated against the poor by making the quality of a child's education a function of the wealth of his parents and neighbors.

Rodriguez Decision   Another case was decided in 1973 by the United States Supreme Court in *San Antonio Independent School District v. Rodriguez*.[11] Demetrio Rodriguez, who became prominent as a leader in his Mexican-American community, lived in one of the poorest school districts. The state and local property tax allocated for each pupil in his district provided one of the lowest per pupil incomes in the country and less than 5 percent of that allocated in some other Texas communities. In addition the Rodriguez case emphasized racial discrimination.

By a vote of 5 to 4, the United States Supreme Court ruled that the Texas system of financing public school education through primary reliance upon the property tax was not unconstitutional "merely because the burden of benefits falls unevenly. . . . " The equal protection clause of the Constitution, the majority decision said, ". . . does not require absolute equality or precisely equal advantages. . . ." In other words, the Court held that the states could finance their public school systems with property taxes even though this provides more money and better educational facilities for pupils who live in wealthier districts.

The decision criticized the property tax for financing public school education but said that ruling against that system would produce ". . . an unprecedented upheaval in public education. . . ." The Supreme Court in effect gave a breathing spell to the states that had been under pressure to reform their system of school financing.

Forces at work across the country for eliminating or modifying the present financing will persist. The court decision will delay but not turn back reforms. Although reform may be slowed, basic change in school financing seems inevitable in view of the growing awareness that current financing is unjust for children and for taxpayers. Before the Supreme Court decision a variety of alternative methods of school financing were proposed, e.g., a statewide property tax, combining school districts, improving programs for state aid, and a national sales tax.

All of the alternative proposals raise questions about relationships between federal, state, and local units of government for policy making, curriculum planning, and accountability.

FUNCTIONS OF PUBLIC SCHOOL EDUCATION

Public education is closely interwoven with other major social institutions. The cost is very high, and society's commitment is great. The public school has multiple and sometimes contradictory societal functions. Some are explicit and others are not, though they bear directly upon pupils and their parents in adverse ways.

Facilitator of Education   A major manifest function of the school is to facilitate and guide the process of education. We expect the public school to play a major role in directing and helping the child integrate his learning. The school indoctrinates the child in the life of our society and trains him in the use of the implements of civilization. Public education is the medium for a many-sided interchange of attitudes and definitions of situations, techniques, and knowledge about the culture.

Censor and Judge   The school performs a normative function as a censor and a judge of society. It orders its curriculum and procedures in harmony with norms and values. In so doing it passes judgment on the actions of other institutions and seeks to control both the direction and extent of social change. In its discharge of the normative function, what scale of values should the school adopt? It usually conforms to the interests and beliefs of those people who control the school. Individual schools break away to experiment and innovate, but generally the school tends to conserve the existing social order rather than foster change. One can acknowledge the need for these conservative functions of the school and still hold that citizens and school personnel need to shape the school into an effective agency for social progress.

Sorter and Socializer   The school's less explicitly endorsed functions are pervasive and interactive. They remove from the young person a significant amount of self-direction and control of his own fate. The school sorts out individuals for fitness for certain occupations and social positions but does not subject all children to the same kind of sorting. The process is influenced by the child's socioeconomic status, race or ethnic group, initial adjustment to school entrance, behavior in the classroom and on the playground, his parent's relationship to the school, and the reputation he acquires among school personnel and other pupils. By testing procedures, record keeping, reputation diffusion, counseling practices, and disciplinary practices, the school becomes a testing, selecting, and distributing agency—a gatekeeper. Americans have chosen to view the school as an avenue for vertical mobility and as an open environment of fair competition. While it has served this function for some students, for large groups of pupils the school provides limited opportunity and keeps them at the same relative position in society which their parents occupy.

The school socializes children into age, sex, and race roles. Sex and skin color are likely to be the dominant variables in their social relationships. Schools prescribe roles when they use age as a criterion in organizing classes and group activities and in giving various kinds of rewards and recognitions. They withhold opportunity for certain kinds of learning until the pupil reaches a predetermined age. Age in and of itself carries limitations and rewards.

Girls and boys are also taught to see themselves in predetermined sex roles and statuses prescribed by segregated activities, adult expectations of certain behavior, and curriculum materials. Teachers' and counselors' attitudes also are influential, particularly when children violate traditional sex roles.

Pupils' awareness of race and expectations for prescribed race roles are introduced and reinforced by subtle or overt cues from teachers and other pupils, choice of curriculum materials, and participation of selected groups of parents in school policy matters.

Overall, "the favored role model becomes the twenty to twenty-five-year-old, white, university-educated male who has had an outstanding career in athletics. Implicitly and explicitly students are taught that Western culture is a male-oriented, white-based enterprise."[12]

The school may socialize children for failure by using only white middle-class teaching materials, putting troublemaking pupils in low-status schools or curricula, and viewing children as "incompetent" and incapable of helping to direct their own development. Differential counseling in relation to occupations or higher education and disciplinary practices concerning absenteeism also may socialize for failure.

Care Giver   The school performs a child care function for parents both during the school day and in after-school extracurricular activities. Maternal employment would be restricted if the school did not provide care and supervision. Our society has not developed day and after-school care for children on any adequate scale. Thousands of "latch-key" children are left on their own. Furthermore, public education frequently serves as a holding action for young persons whom society is not prepared to absorb into the economy.

These functions reflect or reinforce contradictions between societal values and reality situations:

Value		Reality
Education provides the means for any individual to improve his status.	vs.	Schools educate the child to function in about the same social and economic stratum as his parents.
Public education is a channel for social change.	vs.	The schools preserve and pass on the existing system.
Students have the right to participate in their own education.	vs.	Students are often powerless to share in their own educational planning.
Approval is appropriate to reinforce desired pupil behavior.	vs.	Corporal punishment is a major social control within the school.
Every child has a right to an education to achieve his full potential.	vs.	Too many children are excluded from the school.
An open environment within the school promotes learning.	vs.	The schools are preoccupied with "order and control."

SCHOOL PROBLEMS AND PUPIL CHARACTERISTICS

In the last decade, many articles have questioned the quality of education in the face of our serious social problems. Concern has developed about the ability of the schools to educate the children of the poor or the affluent. This concern has been coupled with a renewed emphasis on the capacity to learn and to provide tools for future education, skills for earning a living, and a mentally healthy adulthood.

Modern theories have brought useful knowledge about how children learn, and this knowledge has focused attention on conditions within school systems that either enable students to grasp opportunity for education or cause them to be pushed aside and to fail. The family and the community also contribute to poor scholastic performance, a factor long recognized in pupil failure. Now increasing evidence suggests that the schools themselves contribute to the educational failure of many children and youth. Because of deficiencies in many school systems, large groups of children are not dealt with effectively, and their life experiences are not utilized in a logical and meaningful way. Harmful school conditions and practices, interacting with pupil characteristics, result in recognizable problem situations.

Attendance Policies

Effective enforcement of attendance statutes has demanded the attention of administrators since compulsory education was first legislated. An early study of nonattendance problems endorsed the need for social workers to serve as school attendance officers. Nonattendance, the investigators said, resulted from the social ills of the community, such as poverty, lack of adequate adult wage levels, illiteracy, and ill health—conditions that existed in many families not known to any social agency.[13] Nonattendance has not been solved. A superintendent or principal in a large inner-city school is still apt to designate absenteeism and truancy as his most difficult problems.

Absenteeism   Sporadic school attendance results when pupils are beset with demands they cannot meet adequately. For example, older children are still kept out of school to supervise young siblings. Children of all ages miss school frequently because preventive health care is not available and they have one illness after another, or because their parents are disorganized and there is no reliable adult support to their school attendance. Secondary school pupils may come to school but roam the building during school hours to evade teachers and classes. These pupils find little satisfaction in school and are alienated from the school environment and isolated from their peers, except perhaps from chronic absentees like themselves.

Truancy   Nonattendance of longer standing is officially identified as truancy. Truants resist the school attendance officer's efforts to return them to school, often leading to a court referral. Difficulties in consistent enforcement of school attendance laws are exacerbated in crowded urban neighborhoods because of insufficient staff, high population mobility, and crime rates that make attendance officers reluctant to make home visits. Persuasion, warning, coercion, and threats have seldom improved attendance very long. Attendance can be expected to improve only with changes in the school-community-pupil relations that produce the problem.

Exclusion   Many children and young persons are absent from school because they have been formally excluded or strongly discouraged from attending. Excluded children may be allowed to leave school or never to enroll because the district has no educational program for them. These children are often from minority groups who do not speak English. Some have physical handicaps or epilepsy and are not allowed to participate in the regular program even though there has been no determination of their abilities. Mentally retarded, emotionally disturbed, and perceptually handicapped children are often excluded, even though no other special education facility exists for them. Any child who is culturally, physically, mentally, or behaviorally different risks arbitrary labeling and exclusion from school in many communities.

Pregnancy   Girls who become pregnant are still systematically excluded from many schools either for the period of the pregnancy or permanently. Some districts have recognized the importance of enabling these girls to continue their education, in the regular classroom, a special classroom, or a program of home-bound instruction. Other districts have given up arbitrary exclusion only after a court has ruled that the policy violates the equal protection clause of the Fourteenth Amendment. Yet despite awareness of the unwed mother's need to complete her education, she is still excluded from many schools.

Behavior Problems   Pupils identified as "troublemakers," particularly at the secondary level, are frequently suspended or expelled. Student unrest and dissent have resulted from political issues, smoking rules, the curriculum, athletics, dress and hair regulations, and racial conflict, for example. Many disruptive incidents have resulted in use of suspension (for a defined and limited period) or expulsion (for the rest of the term or permanently). Sometimes no actual disturbance occurred, but school officials evaluated pupil actions as likely to produce disruption. In other instances disruption ranged from scuffling to serious injuries, from assault to attempted arson. The destruction or theft of school property is another area of concern.

School principals have also used repeated suspension to cope with individual students who distract others in the classroom, come late to class, fail to learn, annoy teachers, provoke peers, or otherwise express their dissatisfaction with school.

Student Rights

Until recently, the right of school boards to suspend or expel pupils was rarely challenged. Courts showed little interest in examining school actions. However, concern with legal rights brought greater attention to such procedures. In general the courts have said that the schools do have the authority to regulate conduct likely to cause disorder and interfere with educational functions, but students must be treated fairly and accorded due process of law under the Fourteenth Amendment.

Freedom of expression has been the subject of court cases. Some were challenges to freedom of verbal expression. One group of students attempted to organize a boycott of the school cafeteria. Some involved freedom of written expression, most often the distribution of underground or unauthorized newspapers or pamphlets. Others concerned symbolic expression. Upon learning that students were planning to wear black armbands to express sympathy for the victims of the Vietnam war, school officials in one city passed a resolution forbidding such symbolic expression on school premises. Five students later wore armbands and were sent home, although no disruption had occurred. Three students and their parents sought court action. The United States Supreme Court finally reversed two lower court actions on the basis that the symbolic wearing of armbands had not been disruptive and had not interfered with discipline nor implied reasonable anticipation of disruption.[14]

In the majority opinion, Justice Abe Fortas said: "First Amendment rights, applied in the light of the special characteristics of the school environment, are available to teachers and students. It can hardly be argued that either students or teachers shed their constitutional rights to freedom of speech or expression at the schoolhouse gate."

Discipline in the Schools

Schools have exercised the right to regulate student conduct under the legal concept of *in loco parentis*—the school stands "in place of the parent." Thus it has almost the same authority over the child at school as the parent has at home.

School personnel may make rules for the educational welfare of the pupils and may inflict punishment for disobedience. Courts have generally held that such actions must be consistent with those of a reasonable and prudent parent.

Physical Force   Corporal punishment at school is permitted by law in most states. This is evidence of the general acceptance of physical force as a legitimate child-rearing practice. For the most part, the only legislative or school policy constraints on the use of corporal punishment define the conditions under which it may take place. A cryptic news item is illustrative: "The school board in Aztec, New Mexico, today banned the use of rubber hoses in public schools for disciplining children. From now on they must use a leather strap."[15]

The history of this country is replete with failures to regard children as individuals with their own rights. School principals and teachers spank, paddle, flog, cane, or beat children with or without parental consent, even though corporal punishment may serve only to teach force and violence as a solution to problems.

Concerned citizens in Dallas formed a National Committee to Abolish Corporal Punishment in Schools and sought unsuccessfully to get the school board to change its policy of paddling. Only the school principal or his deputy could administer corporal punishment without consent from the parent. The school superintendent acknowledged that corporal punishment had increased almost fourfold in 1971–1972 over the previous year as a result of "general unrest resulting from school desegregation." The committee alleged that the incidents involved a disproportionate number of minority pupils and labeled the practice a "tragic admission of racial misunderstanding" that had brought about "increased physical assault on black children."[16]

The courts have been reluctant to become involved in the issue of corporal punishment in schools. The United States Supreme Court turned down without comment an appeal by parents alleging that the schoolteachers in Dallas had deprived students of their fundamental liberties by striking them with paddles and tennis shoes. One student was allegedly knocked unconscious by an assistant principal, who was subsequently suspended. The complaint had been dismissed earlier: ". . . passing judgment on the merits of corporal punishment as an educational tool or a means of discipline is not within this court's function or individual competence."[17]

Other Controls   Attempts to restrict pupil behavior include denial of privileges in extracurricular activities or compulsory counseling interviews. Misbehavior is assumed to result from some problem with the child or from family problems that have affected the child's personality. Such methods tend to ignore conditions in the school or classroom which produce the so-called "emotional problems."

"Dress codes" have prescribed the types of clothing pupils must wear on school premises. If these rules are challenged, they must usually meet the test of reasonableness to be enforced. For example, prescribing certain clothing for physical education classes or "shop" classes may be defended as necessary for the safety of pupils. Forbidding the wearing of metal heel plates is justified on the basis that it damages floors in the school building. Schools pass rules about length of hair or beards and sideburns on the claim that a student's appearance may be distracting and disturbing to others in the classroom. Yet students claim that the right to wear one's hair at any length or in any style is a personal choice. When challenged the school usually has to provide evidence that the noncon-forming appearance has an adverse effect on the educational process.

Many of the criticisms revolve around aspects of the school's climate that fail to promote and enhance self-discipline and self-direction for the student's continued learning. For example, many classroom teachers carefully avoid all but neutral topics; honest expressions of feelings are avoided. Docility and sugges-tibility are prized and curiosity repressed. Many pupils fear failure in a world of confusing demands and irrelevant materials; other pupils are continually bored with an unstimulating, pedantic learning pace.

In such schools conflict among pupils is common. Police are frequent visitors. Pupils tend to move in segregated groups, racially and economically, even though they attend an "integrated" school. The probability of low achieve-ment and failure for large numbers of children and young persons is increased.

Racial and Economic Segregation

Segregation by race or class in the public schools is still widespread and has even increased in central cities of major metropolitan areas. As middle- and upper-income families have moved out of the inner cities, economically segregated groups have remained. The result is that pupils are highly likely to attend schools composed largely of students like themselves, both racially and economically.

The United States Supreme Court in 1954 struck down the doctrine of "separate but equal," holding that racial segregation of schools was inherently unequal.[18] The search for means to integrate the schools was given impetus by findings of the Coleman Report, a national study under the auspices of the Office of Education. Pupil aspirations and achievements are strongly related to the educational backgrounds and performances of other pupils in the same school, this study said. Children attending schools where the level of student achieve-ment is low are more apt to have low achievement than those in schools where overall achievement levels are higher. Nonwhite or low-income pupils (and they are frequently the same) can be expected to attain higher levels of educational performance if they attend schools that are predominantly middle-class or white. Not only does racial and economic balance in schools increase the achievement of minority group children from homes without much educational strength, it does so without reducing the other children's achievement.[19]

Busing

Because prevailing segregated housing patterns do not bring about integration in neighborhood schools, busing of children to other schools out of their neighbor-hoods was introduced to achieve a racially balanced school population. Busing has been a highly controversial and political issue. In some school districts integration of schools through busing has proceeded with minimal difficulty. In others there have been militant protests, parent boycotts of schools, and episodes of disorder.

The issue of busing is affected by a number of factors. Racial integration is no longer a core goal of the black movement. Greater emphasis is given now to such issues as equal opportunity in employment and housing, community control of schools, and recognition of the merits of black identity. White people who supported the movement for civil rights and racial integration in relation to employment, housing, voting privileges, public transportation, and college admissions have been divided on busing of young children away from their neighborhood schools. Leaders in the legislative and executive branches of government are displaying negative attitudes toward busing. Courts are more frequently granting delays in connection with busing plans. Some cities are beginning to cut back busing or to hold off plans to expand it.

Records, "Tracking," and Special Education

Many school systems still have a stereotyped view that most low-income and nonwhite pupils have limited capabilities, that most are "slow learners," and that not much can be done with them. This belief is usually coupled with an expectation that certain school programs and services will be used by certain groups of students. Academic goals are lowered because it is assumed that children are not interested in learning. Children and youth responding to this negative perception on the part of the school staff give the substandard performance that is expected.

Testing   When ability and achievement tests are used as measures of innate potentiality without regard for past learning opportunities and experiences and familiarity with the kind of tasks expected in the tests, they underestimate a particular child's abilities and lower the expectations for his performance.

Grouping   Negative effects of ability grouping or "tracking" are apt to be crucial during the elementary years as the distance between the "slow" and the "fast" learners widens rapidly. In secondary schools students are often grouped in one of several curricular tracks. Criteria for placement include test scores, teacher and counselor judgments, expressed parental preferences, and assessment of student aspirations. Low-income parents frequently do not feel as free to object to the decisions made as do middle-class parents.

Tracking affects the chance to go to college or enter certain occupations. Lower tracks lead to lower status among peers and teachers. Special education rooms for mentally retarded children may fail to achieve the educational purpose for which they were established. Often they become catch-alls for children—frequently minority-group children—with different characteristics and needs who are not retarded but may demonstrate varying manifestations of emotional disturbance.

Parents and some school personnel have begun to raise critical questions about the rights of children as a result of testing and tracking. Evaluation and judgments are often made on unspecified criteria. Without a hearing children are labeled, categorized, and locked into special education tracks which may unfairly limit future opportunities.

With the help of legal services for low-income parents and of civil liberties groups, court cases have focused attention on pupil and parent rights in relation to educational placement. California recently prohibited group IQ tests for children from non-English-speaking countries until they have resided in the United States for two years.

Social Distance between School and Community

Lack of communication between the school and the community and between the school and the home increases the probability of school failure. Schools that serve middle-class families are more apt to be relatively "close" to the community and neighborhoods of their pupils. Middle-class parents are ready to speak for themselves, are generally supportive of education, and often are in reasonably close communication with school personnel. School expectations in relation to parental involvement may be the same for the poor, without recognition that low-income parents see the school as alien, cold, and unwelcoming. Even though studies have shown that these parents place a high value on school achievement for their children, they usually communicate less easily or effectively with teachers, principals, and counselors. When schools make insufficient attempts to understand the surroundings in which their pupils live and the desires of their parents, social distance between home and school is increased.

Parental Participation In some communities, parents have demanded greater participation in the school's decision-making and policy formulation processes. Black ghetto residents of New York City have given leadership in greater community control of schools, and groups of minority parents in other parts of the country have also pressed for a fuller share in planning their children's education.

Even when school-community distance has been lessened through more community control, problems remain. For example, educational issues may be subordinated to political issues and to implicit racial issues. It is also difficult to coordinate the variations in specific educational desires, expectations, and concerns of the subgroups of parents within the community.

SOCIAL WORK IN THE SCHOOLS

School social work is an application of social work principles and methods to the major purpose of the school. Goals center upon helping pupils attain a sense of competence, a readiness for continued learning, and an ability to adapt to change. Increasingly, the focus of school social work is on cognitive areas—learning, thinking, and problem solving—as well as the traditional areas of concern, i.e., relationships, emotions, motivation, and personality.

School social work is related to a particular school system, the outside community, the characteristics of the pupils, and the social conditions they face. Within this framework school social workers endeavor to aid the school to give attention to pupils' individual needs and to offer each pupil opportunity for success and achievement. In addition, school social workers must be concerned with the relationship of the school to other social institutions in the community.

Historical Development

Early Influences School social work began in the early twentieth century. It originated outside the school system. Private agencies and civic organizations supported the work until schools agreed to administer and finance it.

Social work in the schools represented a response to the passage of compulsory school attendance laws, new knowledge about individual differences among children, a realization of the strategic place of school and education in the lives of children, and concern for the relevance of education to the child's life at home and in the community.

Social workers in the settlement houses contributed significantly to the methods of school social work and frequently pointed up the necessity for the school to relate more closely to the lives of its children. For example, from the Henry Street Settlement in New York City came the comments: "Intelligent social workers seize opportunities for observation, and almost unconsciously develop methods to meet needs. They see conditions as they are, and become critical of systems as they act and react upon the child or fail to reach him at all. . . . Where the school fails, it appears to the social workers to do so because it makes education a thing apart—because it separates its work from all that makes up the child's life outside the classroom."[20]

School social work underwent rapid growth in the 1920s following demonstrations in various communities financed by the Commonwealth Fund. The focus was prevention of juvenile delinquency.

Home-school-community liaison continued to be the principal focus of school social work throughout most of the 1920s. Modifications in practice began to emerge in response to the mental hygiene movement: Social workers increased their efforts to develop and define their own method of social casework in the schools, and they began to turn more attention to work with the individual maladjusted child at school.

Developments from 1930 to 1960   A retrenchment in school social work practice came with the depression of the 1930s, but with its end, services were extended rapidly and school social work was accepted as an integral part of pupil services.

During the 1930s truancy and delinquency were given less emphasis. Social workers increased their attention to the individual child in the existing school environment and to the refinement of professional methods and techniques.

By 1940 the transition appeared complete—from the early focus on school and neighborhood conditions and social change to a clinical orientation in relation to individual personality needs. Social casework was the method used, the development of effective relationships the essential technique.

Developments from 1960 to 1970   Beginning in the 1960s, school social work literature began to urge a transition to new goals and methods of work in response to the urgent social problems affecting many school children and youth. A new awareness of the school as a social system was reflected, and the professions of education and social work began to collaborate more effectively on behalf of pupils who were unable to utilize educational opportunities because of social and cultural problems. Group work appeared and was used increasingly by school social workers. Some demonstrations of new approaches to working with the community also resulted. Considerable confusion arose about the roles of the various school pupil specialists that underscored the responsibility of each to clarify his or her function and to measure it against the critical needs of school children.

Organization and Support

School social workers usually are employed by and accountable to local school districts. In the 1960s, state departments of education recommended coordinating and supervising a range of pupil services in the public schools—e.g., guidance, psychology, social work, health, attendance, speech—through "pupil personnel services" or "special services."

By no means do all schools have social workers on their staffs. They are about as numerous as school psychologists or attendance officers. There are far more elementary and secondary school guidance counselors than other "pupil specialists."

Social work is one of the disciplines which may be represented in a state department of public education. When this is so, social workers employed in the public school usually will be required to have a master's degree. In some states, social workers with baccalaureate degrees may be employed. The most desirable staffing pattern involves teams including social workers with different levels of training—master's degrees, baccalaureate degrees, and diplomas from two-year college programs.

Background for Change

School social work has undergone changes in working with pupils, their parents, and school personnel. Early leaders were keenly aware of the strategic place of the school among a community's institutions. They saw the pivotal position for leadership open to school social workers as they were able to move between the institutions of public education and public welfare. They emphasized work in the community and in the neighborhood in an effort to bring school and home closer together.

As casework theory developed and the social work profession became more responsive to the search for psychological causes for their clients' problems, school social workers moved toward a clinical orientation—working with the individual school child in relation to his personal problems. As they did so, they moved away from their focus on school and neighborhood conditions and the need for social change. An analysis of the tasks in school social work produced evidence that professional school social workers primarily favored casework with the individual child in relation to his emotional problems and his personal adjustment.[21] The problems of the child in school were viewed as arising mostly from his personal characteristics or those of his parents. The impact that school policies and community conditions had on pupils was almost unrecognized. School social workers minimized the importance of their responsibilities for leadership in modifying school and community conditions. They also were reluctant to delegate tasks to persons with less than the master's degree in social work. These findings provided impetus to school social workers to reexamine their goals and their staffing patterns.

Present Practice

The traditional clinical model of school social work has been widely criticized as outmoded. Yet it is still the predominant mode of school social work practice in the United States today. School administrators view it as benign intervention and thus acceptable, emphasizing as it does the individual student's need to adapt and adjust to the normative conditions within the school.[22]

In addition, educational systems faced with budget cut-backs view pupil personnel services as more expendable than classroom teachers. Under such circumstances school social workers may be reluctant to undertake a new "change agent" role in the system which employs them.[23] Experienced school social workers who have been trained in casework and have successfully helped individual children may understandably find new models of school social work difficult.

The School as a Social System   One new model being demonstrated is broadly focused on school-community-pupil relations. The school is regarded as a social system, a unity of interacting and interdependent personalities and functions. The social work tasks given greatest priority are to:

1 Facilitate the provision of direct educational and social services and provide direct social casework and group work services to selected pupils.

2 Act as a pupil advocate, focusing upon the urgent needs of selected groups of pupils.

3 Consult with school administrators to jointly identify major problems toward which a planned service approach will be aimed; aid in developing cooperative working relationships with community agencies; and assist in the formulation of school policy that directly affects the welfare of children and young persons.

4 Consult with teachers about techniques for creating a climate in which children are freed and motivated to learn by interpreting social and cultural influences in the lives of pupils, facilitating the use of peers to help a troubled child, or assisting in managing relationships within a classroom.

5 Organize parent and community groups to channel concerns about pupils and school and to improve school and community relations.

6 Develop and maintain liaison between the school and critical fields of social work—child welfare, corrections, mental health, and legal services for the poor. Such liaison facilitates more effective community services for school children and their families, assists with planned change in the community's organizational pattern of social welfare programs and resources, and acts as catalyst to change the pattern of the social structure.

7 Provide leadership in the coordination of interdisciplinary skills among pupil services personnel, e.g., guidance counselors, psychologists, nurses, and attendance officers.

These tasks require adaptations in practice on the part of social workers already in the schools. They must assume greater responsibility for identifying target groups of pupils who present interrelated problems and reactions to strain, failure, or dissatisfaction in the learning situation. They must focus diagnosis and treatment on an understanding of the larger problem complex rather than only on the individual case. School administrators need to establish a contract for service-giving in relation to specified problems. Staff should be assigned for schools where problems are greatest and contracts made with principals regarding the use of staff resources. Service will be most effective if multidisciplinary teams are assigned to particular schools so that the full range of skills among pupil personnel specialists can be brought to bear on major problems.

The pupil welfare team is focused on the public school as a vital and strategic social institution that affects all children during their formative years. This model is geared to the basic purpose of the school, that is, not to serve as a therapeutic center but to provide a life setting where competence can be acquired.

Lela B. Costin

KEY TERMS

assessed property valuation
absenteeism
truancy
suspension
expulsion
in loco parentis
corporal punishment

tracking
community control
school-community-pupil relations
change agent
social system
pupil advocate

FOR DISCUSSION

1 Compare the proportion of youth in school in the United States and in other developed nations.
2 Why have property taxes provided the major means of school financing?
3 Developing countries face what major problem in the growth of education?
4 What is the purpose of state aid to local school districts?
5 Since *San Antonio v. Rodriguez,* will attempts be continued to equalize incomes of schools?
6 What are two major functions of the public school system?
7 Explain how the school also has a sorting function.
8 Evaluate values and realities as set forth in the chapter in relation to your school experiences.
9 Differentiate between absenteeism and truancy.
10 Consider policies and procedures concerning suspension and expulsion. Draft an equitable policy.
11 In view of the power of state government, why do local school districts exercise basic autonomy?
12 What does *in loco parentis* mean in relation to the school's authority?
13 Discuss the use of corporal punishment. Should parental consent be a condition for corporal punishment?
14 What is meant by *tracking*? What are its advantages and difficulties?
15 Contrast the newer model of school social work with the traditional clinical model.

PROJECTS

1 Ask a school administrator to respond to questions on: (1) dress codes; (2) underground newspapers; (3) programs for pregnant girls; (4) explusion and suspension policies in the school. How does he see the issue in *Tinker v. Des Moines Board of Education* concerning the wearing of black armbands?

2　Choose the center city and several differing suburbs. Find out how much money is available to the schools on a per pupil basis from local taxes and from other aid. Do the findings suggest inequities?

3　Invite a school social worker to discuss school rules and policies that need study because they contribute to student problems. Is this change process part of the social worker's role?

4　Discuss or debate: "Resolved, that the age for compulsory school attendance should be lowered."

5　If students in your community are participating in a free school or programs of more "open" education, invite them to describe the programs to your class and to respond to questions.

6　Devise a plan for a day care center for the children of school-age mothers. Consider costs, community acceptance, program, educational goals for the mothers, possible involvement of boyfriends, and location and auspices.

FOR FURTHER STUDY

Lela B. Costin, "A Historical Review of School Social Work," *Social Casework*, vol. 50, October 1969, pp. 439–453.

Mario D. Fantini, *Public School of Choice*, Simon and Schuster, New York, 1974.

Eugene Litwak and Henry J. Meyer, *School, Family, and Neighborhood: The Theory and Practice of School-Community Relationships*, Columbia Univ. Press, New York, 1974.

Rosemary Sarri and Frank F. Maple (eds.), *The School in the Community*, National Association of Social Workers, Washington, D.C., 1972.

Charles E. Silberman, *Crisis in the Classroom: The Remaking of American Education*, Random House, New York, 1970.

Chapter 10

Legal Rights
and Protection

Why does family law differ from state to state?
Why recognize common-law marriage?
What are the special legal problems in adoption?
Why don't child abuse laws punish child abusers?
Can laws help the poor with consumer problems?

Americans are more aware of legal rights today than they were a few years ago. Legal protection is important for buying and selling property, filing tax returns, buying on credit, and resolving family crises. We use legal services so much that prepaid coverage may become common. The poor especially need legal services, but they cannot afford them.

Social Work and Law

Social workers must be familiar with the law in order to serve their clients. Marriage and parenthood; divorce, child custody, and support; child protection; and eligibility for financial assistance all have legal ramifications. Social workers also seek to affect the passage of laws through lobbying with congressmen, state legislators, and local officials.

Several legal concepts have been of particular interest to social workers. Rights of offenders have been recognized in specific requirements for *due process*. Wiretapping and abortion decisions have recognized the right of *privacy*. Groups of people have benefited from suits filed as *class actions*. In divorce, formal grounds with a plaintiff and a defendant are giving way to *no-fault* procedures. Court decisions and legal reforms have resulted in sweeping changes in poverty law, family law, and procedures for criminal justice.

The federal government leaves family law to the states. The result is fifty sets of conflicting laws. Some major issues in family law, important information for the users of social services, and suggestions for legislative social action will be presented in this chapter.

AGE AND THE LAW

Not only does the substance of the law vary from state to state, but standards of legal age also differ. Age provisions are of special interest to college students and other young people who want more legal rights. A major change has been the right to vote at eighteen. As adolescents gain rights, they also tend to take on responsibilities. The eighteen-year-old male who can marry without parental consent has the legal duty to support his wife. Eighteen is gradually replacing twenty-one as the age of majority. This is consistent with physical growth trends, beginning with earlier onset of puberty. On the other hand, adolescents are attaining financial independence at a later age. Women's liberation efforts have been important in eliminating provisions that specify age differences in the law for men and women.

Twenty-one was not selected as the age of majority on a rational basis. One theory suggests that the number seven had religious significance, and three times seven is twenty-one. Until age seven, the child was considered innocent. From seven to fourteen he was growing in responsibility, but innocence predominated; from fourteen to twenty-one responsibility exceeded innocence; at twenty-one the person was fully responsible before the law. Another explanation emphasizes the strength required to manage a complete suit of armor—a task successfully mastered by age twenty-one.

Conflicting Laws Age requirements are confusing at best. Juveniles are considered as adults if they commit game and fishing or traffic offenses punishable by fines. Youth may shop around for legal privileges. They cross state lines to purchase liquor legally and come home to consume it. They may go to another state to get married, but if they do so to evade the laws of their own state, the marriage can be challenged.

Sex Differences The legal age for marriage with parental permission in various states ranges from twelve for females and fourteen for males to eighteen and twenty-one respectively. The most common ages are sixteen and eighteen. Being underage may result in an annulment. Until recently women have been accorded the right to marry without parental permission at an earlier age than men—apparently because they reach puberty earlier and tend to marry older men.

In many states girls have been processed through the juvenile courts, while boys of the same age have been tried in adult courts. In this instance for the girl adult responsibility has been postponed. Apparently girls commit fewer and less serious offenses and are more easily managed in juvenile correctional facilities. Court decisions in several states have found such age differences to be discriminatory.

Support Responsibility   Both the eighteen-year age of majority and the appropriateness of an adolescent's life-style may jeopardize parental support. After majority, apparently parental support is no longer legally required unless the child is crippled or retarded. In one case a father was not required to support his daughter because he disapproved of her life-style.

More Age Differences   Conflicts between state laws and differences in legal age requirements from one activity to another are absurd. The typical eighteen-year-old male can vote and own property, but not make a will. He can be drafted for military service. He may or may not be able to marry without parental permission or to drink beer legally, depending on where he lives. He can sign contracts, but not have to honor most of them. However, educational loan agreements are considered binding obligations. All contracts may become binding for the minor who marries, because he is then considered to be emancipated.

The Illinois Youth Council[1] made up of college and high school students completed a comprehensive study of age requirements. The accompanying table presents their major recommendations and the subsequent changes in laws and regulations.

Differences in legal provisions and age requirements make it easy to see why family law is complex. Different provisions and philosophies among state laws, court procedures, and judges' values affect the major life events—marriage, divorce, the rights of infants and children, adoption, guardianship, child abuse, and handling of juveniles who violate the law—events that social workers find important.

MARRIAGE

Marriage has provided the traditional basis for family formation. With 800,000 marriages ending in divorce each year, laws governing marriage and divorce have special relevance to social workers who engage in marriage counseling or are involved with child custody or support.

Even with technical flaws in the license or in the marriage ceremony, legal policy favors upholding rather than voiding marriages, especially when the parties consider themselves to be married and behave that way. Because states uphold the legality of marriages and divorces that take place in other states people have often sought out those states where marriage or divorce was easier. These options have been available to the well-to-do but not to the poor.

Common-Law Marriage

Some people—especially the poor—live together without first having a marriage ceremony. The laws of the state and the relationship between a man and a woman determine the possible existence of a common-law marriage. Do they "hold

Legal Age Provisions in Illinois

	Legal provisions, 1970	Council recommendations, 1971	Legal provisions, 1973
Citizenship			
Jury service	21	18	18
Parent-Child relationships			
Parental responsibility for one's willful or malicious acts	Over 11—not yet 19	Over 11—not yet 18	No change
Employment			
Entitled to less than adult wages under minimum wage act	Under 19	Under 18	Under 18
Protected under minimum wage standards for women and minors	Males under 21, females under 18	Under 18 for both	Under 18 for both
Driving			
Apply for instruction permit or driver's license	21 or legally emancipated by marriage	18 or legally emancipated	18 or over
Above with parental consent	18; 16 with approved driver's course	Repeal consent provisions	Repealed
Marriage			
With parental consent	Males 18, females 16	16 for both	No change
Without consent	Males 21, females 18	18 for both	No change
Society			
Buy or possess firearms or size to be concealed	18	21	No change
Be tattooed	21	18	No change
Patronize pawnbroker	Males 21, females 18	18	No change
Buy tobacco without consent	18	Repeal	No change
Buy liquor	21	18 for beer, 21 all else	No change
Be executor, administrator of estate	Males 21, females 18	18	18 for both
No longer be tried by juvenile court	Males 17, females 18	18 for both	17 for both

themselves out to the world" to be married? They must publicly and professedly live as husband and wife. Renting an apartment or opening a charge account as a married couple may be evidence enough. There is no uniform time requirement.

Common-law marriage is recognized in the District of Columbia, and in fourteen of the fifty states—Alabama, Colorado, Florida, Georgia, Idaho, Iowa, Kansas, Montana, Ohio, Oklahoma, Pennsylvania, Rhode Island, South Carolina, and Texas.

If a man and woman live together in a state that does not recognize common-law marriage and then move to a state that does, they may acquire such a marriage. If they live in a state that recognizes common-law marriage and then move to a state that would not uphold a common-law marriage originating in its own borders, that state will generally recognize their marriage as valid.

Differing Views   People often live together without a ceremony. Typically they give no thought to common-law provisions. If they are concerned, they can usually get married. The public has disapproved of common-law marriage because it allegedly encourages fraud and vice and debases conventional marriage. These objections have not prevented people from living together. Common-law provisions actually discourage vice because they give living together a legal status. According to one view, "When a woman has performed the obligation of a wife for thirty-five years and then is brutally deprived of all the financial benefits of marriage on the sole ground that the relationship was not signalized by some sort of ceremony, this debases marriage."[2] Common-law marriage reduces injustice and suffering, especially in those social and economic groups that have not accepted middle-class standards—the people most likely to be served by the social worker. It makes the family eligible for benefits under pension and social insurance plans. Recognition of common-law marriage is also desirable for the operation of public welfare programs, because it extends family responsibility. The issue may not become important until financial issues arise from death or separation.

As more middle-class people participate in communes and other "new" family forms typically characterized by living together without a marriage ceremony, they may succeed in removing some of the legal problems, something the poor have not been able to do.

Other Marital Situations

Miscegenation—interracial marriage—was prohibited at some time by as many as thirty states. A Supreme Court decision overthrew such restrictions because they violate the Fourteenth Amendment to the Constitution by denying equal treatment under the law.[3]

Social workers are often asked for advice about marriage for a limited purpose—"to give the child a name"—when the couple do not plan to live together. Such a marriage furnishes only limited protection to the child; he will still be reared by a single parent.

DIVORCE

Divorce refers to the legal termination of a valid marriage. Grounds have been expanded to include such abstractions as incompatibility and mental cruelty. "No-fault" divorce adopted in California and at least thirteen other states[4] recognizes the breakdown of the marriage as the ground without attributing fault to either partner. It is likely to increase in popularity.

Many conflicts in divorce laws are found among the states, but most "divorce mills" requiring very short residency have been eliminated and Mexican "mail-order divorces" invalidated. States accord "full faith and credit" to the divorce laws of other states, i.e., they recognize their validity.

Who gets divorced is subject to misunderstanding. Actually, the working class has higher divorce rates. The poor simply separate. Desertion is known as "poor man's divorce."

The high rates of divorce in the United States have led to proposals for contractual marriage, but contractual marriage may encourage unrealistic expectations and fail to motivate the person to try hard enough to make a marriage succeed. Tensions may develop, particularly at the time a contract is up for renewal. "No-fault" divorce and widely available community legal services may provide most of the advantages of contractual marriage without its liabilities.

Use of counseling in divorce actions, availability of low-cost divorce, and problems of child custody are of special interest for social workers. Laws to require marriage counseling or to impose a cooling-off period to achieve reconciliation have not been successful and have generally been repealed. Counseling is likely to come too late. A compulsory waiting period has not assured serious efforts toward reconciliation. Reconciliation has been the criterion of successful counseling, when in fact there are cases where termination of an unsatisfactory marriage may be preferable.

CHILD SUPPORT AND CUSTODY

Child support involves two major issues. First, support orders are generally issued without relation to fault and are imposed on the father. Legal decisions concerning child custody traditionally tend to favor the mother. Fathers feel they have been "stuck" by the court and may be reluctant to make support payments. As women gain equal rights, support and custody may be decided more rationally and thus earn more compliance. Second, mobility makes it difficult to assure the support of children. A court in Connecticut may order a father to support children, but it cannot enforce that order when the father moves from the jurisdiction of the court without leaving any trace. Reciprocal laws requiring support are unenforceable simply because the legal authorities may not know where to look for the absent parent. Warrants cannot be sent to every county sheriff in the United States on the off chance that a parent resides in that county. Even when the nonpaying parent's address is known, local law enforcement officers may consider serving a subpoena for another county a matter of low priority.

THE RIGHTS OF MOTHERS: FAMILY PLANNING AND ABORTION

The law holds that marriage and the family are needed for control of sexual intercourse and the birth and rearing of children.

Contraception   The last decade has seen many changes in attitudes. In 1942 in a case involving sterilization the Supreme Court held that the right to procreate "was one of the basic civil rights of man."[5] In 1965 another fundamental question was answered in the affirmative: "Do individuals have a right to employ means to prevent conception while they engage in sexual intercourse?"[6] The decision asked, "Would we allow the police to search the sacred precincts of marital bedrooms for tell-tale signs of the use of contraceptives? The very idea is repulsive to the notions of privacy surrounding the marriage relationship."

Abortion   Abortion is defined as "the expulsion of the fetus at a period of uterogestation so early that it has not acquired the power of sustaining independent life." Courts in the nineteenth century had called abortion "a crime against nature which obstructs the fountains of life."[7] Some states had come to allow therapeutic abortions necessary for the mother's well-being. Some also permitted abortions when rape or incest had been involved or to prevent the birth of a potentially defective child. The strictest antiabortion laws still remained in force in thirty-one states. Fifteen have had more liberal statutes that recognized considerations involving the mother's life and health, but only Alaska, Hawaii, New York, and Washington removed practically all restrictions on abortions by 1973. The Supreme Court in *Jane Roe v. Henry Wade* in that year voided state laws that place restrictions on a woman's right to obtain an abortion during her first trimester of pregnancy.[8] For the remainder of the time of pregnancy, the state may regulate abortion procedures for reasons of maternal health and may prohibit abortions in the final ten weeks of pregnancy unless they are necessary to preserve the life and health of the mother.

Like the earlier decision on contraception, the basis was the constitutional right of privacy. During the first three-month period of pregnancy a physician can recommend an abortion "without regulation by the state," and the operations can be conducted "free of interference by the state."

Chapter 9 has already stressed the increasing importance of requests for abortion counseling made to social agencies. The Supreme Court decision has reduced the discomfort of many social workers in providing this service.

THE RIGHTS OF INFANTS: ILLEGITIMACY

The bastard has been of legal concern for centuries. Traditionally, in English law, he had no rights of inheritance from his parents. Upon his death his property went to the Crown. Generally the child has been considered legitimate if the parents married before its birth, resulting in great pressure to marry to "give the child a name." Now in most states he or she may also be legitimized if the father acknowledges paternity and the parents marry after the child is born.

Trends Increases in the rate of illegitimacy have aroused concern. From 1940 to 1968 the percentage of illegitimate births rose from 3.5 to 9.7. The general growth in population was also responsible for a sharp increase in the total number of illegitimate children (from 89,500 in 1940 to 339,200 in 1970).[9] Minority groups receiving public assistance have a high rate of illegitimate births, but, contrary to prevailing opinion, the majority of children born out of wedlock are white.

Annulment and donor insemination also may involve actions at law. In most states the child born after a marriage is annulled is legitimate. When a paternity question is raised in court, however, the child born following donor insemination is considered illegitimate in some states. Legal adoption by the husband may be necessary.

The legal disabilities of the illegitimate child are central concerns. He has no legal claim to inheritance from the father unless paternity is proved. He is also likely to be ineligible for social security and other pension benefits accruing to the father.

Law Reform The conflicts in state laws regarding illegitimacy cannot be solved as long as punishment of the illegitimate child is used to encourage marriage and legitimacy. In an article with the intriguing title, "Bringing the

Bastard into the Great Society," and in a more recent book, Krause has made the strongest appeal for the legal rights of illegitimate children.[10] He presents model legislation based on Norwegian law and a North Dakota statute declaring that all children are the legitimate children of their natural parents. Arizona and Oregon have somewhat similar statutes. The rest of the state laws are more punitive, though some states have proposed to replace the word *illegitimate* by terms like *ante-nuptial*. A model Uniform Parentage Act was proposed in 1973.[11]

Age Differences   The younger mother who wants to rear her child independently has a difficult time in our society—legally, socially, and financially. The minor who is still in school is treated quite differently from the older woman who is self-supporting. The young mother may receive undue pressure to marry and drop out of school or to relinquish the baby. The father may receive an ultimatum to marry her or may be completely rejected because he is a poor source of funds. If he is already married to someone else, he presents a more complex problem. A paternity action against him may obtain few resources for child support and also jeopardize an already established family. If she wishes, the older woman in an urban area may put on a wedding ring, call herself married, keep her baby, and pay for day care, with few questions asked.

Keeping the Baby   White mothers, regardless of their age, generally have tended to give up their children for adoption, while minor black mothers had fewer resources for adoption. As a result, their children were reared as their siblings, or the mother had to drop out of school to care for the child. Now agencies report that mothers of both races have a strong interest in keeping the child as a matter of right. At the same time, their desire is to remain in school. We have already observed that courts are gradually establishing continued education as a right of the mother. Schools and other agencies have begun to provide day care services for children of students. Suits demanding the right to attend school and to make independent decisions about keeping and caring for the baby may still be necessary, however, because of local policies.

With more girls choosing the pill or abortion and more who become pregnant deciding to keep their baby, adoption becomes less important. Paternity, child support, and inheritance rights are the critical issues. Paternity actions have been mainly concerned with money. If paternity is acknowledged, the father and mother may both have legal responsibility for support, but the mother usually lacks financial capability, especially if she is a minor.

Paternity Actions   To determine paternity and to compel support, the mother may make a complaint for the arrest of the alleged father. The state's attorney is often able to convince the father to accept the responsibilities of paternity. If not, a hearing is held to determine whether there is enough evidence for a trial. Blood tests may be used as evidence. If a man is found guilty, a support order is issued by the court. When the order is violated, the man must go to jail or forfeit his bond. Obviously, jailing the father will make financial support impossible, since he will probably lose his job.

Women have been unwilling to press paternity actions. In some cases the mother wants nothing more to do with the father. In others, she hopes for eventual marriage and does not want to involve him in an adversary action.

Sometimes the lack of financial resources of the father may seem to make the procedure pointless. However, when the mother keeps the baby, she should be more interested in the father's financial potential, including social security benefits, than in his present earning power. Establishment of paternity clarifies the child's status equally in relation to both parents.

Support for the illegitimate child has often been regarded as a means to relieve the community of the financial burden rather than to serve the best interest of the child. This philosophy leads to minimal support. Great pressure was placed on AFDC applicants to name the father to obtain support, but these efforts have been declared illegal.

The Father's Rights   Until recently the father had no rights of visitation. Interest in the child is seen as an obstacle to possible adoption. If the child were surrendered, the father's consent was not needed. The Supreme Court in 1973 in *Stanley v. Illinois*[12] accorded parental rights to the father of illegitimate children after the mother died. As a result the father is entitled to a hearing before the child can be offered for adoption. Illegitimate children have also tried to collect damages from their parents for "wrongful birth," but these actions have been unsuccessful.

ADOPTION

Adoption has a special interest beyond the number of children affected because it is seen as an extension of goodwill and altruism toward children. Adoption has been much more important in the United States than in Europe. In Europe each adoption typically required a special bill to be passed. England did not pass a general adoption statute until 1926. The Netherlands passed its law in 1969. Traditionally, property rights related to inheritance are stressed rather than parental nurturance and protection. In America, adoptive parents stress the desire for the child-rearing experience. Nevertheless, divorce or the early death of a parent can often cause serious financial and inheritance problems for the child if the adoption is not legally valid.

Legal Surrender and Parental Rights

In the past twenty years the aim has been to place the child as soon as possible after delivery, preferably directly from the hospital. Recent court actions upholding the right of the natural mother to reclaim the child after placement cast doubt upon one of the major reasons for agency adoption—the assurance of an unconditional surrender and avoidance of contact between the adoptive and the natural parents. New York and other states revised their laws to make surrender final at the time of placement.

In addition to legal provisions for irrevocable surrender before the child is placed, three steps will help to ensure the permanence of the surrender. First, the social agency must avoid duress and pressure to obtain surrender of the child for adoption and should make the mother's legal rights explicit to her. As a result mothers may take a longer time to make up their minds and delay placement. Second, the mother should obtain a lawyer of her own choosing who will set forth her rights, including the implications of a decision to relinquish the child for adoption. Provision must be made to pay the costs of counsel if necessary. Finally, the surrender should be taken in court so the judge can reiterate the mother's legal rights. Following the Stanley decision, the same procedure should be used with the father. These safeguards are likely to reduce the number of children placed, especially in the first few weeks of life.

Children from Married Parents   Traditionally, adoption has been associated with unmarried parenthood, but married parents also relinquish children. They may feel they have too many children already, or they may have a child too early. Sometimes the husband is not the father of the child. Older children are also given adoptive homes when parental rights have been fully terminated for reasons of abandonment, abuse, or neglect.

Adoptions by Relatives   Illness or death of a parent or divorce and remarriage may lead to adoption that usually does not involve a social agency. To the courts, blood ties make detailed investigations unnecessary. Perhaps this provides too little protection for the child adopted by a relative, but in any event social work is unlikely to get a larger role.

Emphasis on the fitness of the adoptive parents has suggested that their place of residence provides the appropriate basis for jurisdiction. Now that surrender has become a legal issue, the importance of obtaining an irrevocable consent may make the place of residence of the natural parents the most logical place for filing for adoption.

Termination of Parental Rights   In adoption, parents acquire a child and the child acquires parents by legal rather than biological means. Since legally a child can have only one set of parents at a time, adoption must involve termination of the rights of the biological parents. If the natural parents live outside the jurisdiction or their whereabouts are unknown, adequate notice must also be given by personal service of papers, registered mail, or publication in the press.

Steps in a Nonrelative Adoption

Four steps are involved in a nonrelative adoption: a petition to the court requesting to adopt the child, an interlocutory (temporary) decree in which the child is placed with the family on a provisional basis, a supervisory process (usually for six months), and the final decree. If parents move from one jurisdiction to another before the adoption is final, supervision must be transferred to another agency. If plans for moving are known, agencies show less interest in making the placement, except in the case of a hard-to-place child.

Petitions to the court should be prepared in a manner that avoids revealing the names of the natural parents to the adopting parents. Also, to avoid making adoptions matters of public knowledge, records of the natural birth and the investigation of the adoptive applicants may be sealed and open to inspection only by court order.

Selecting Adoptive Parents

The steps in investigation of the prospective parents are seldom specified in the law. Agency regulations are dependent to a degree upon factors of supply and demand. Now that we face a scarcity of infants, we may expect regulations to become more strict.

Statutes requiring social work agencies to handle all nonrelative placements have been enacted in several states, including Connecticut, Delaware, Kentucky, New Jersey, and Rhode Island. Concern is expressed about independent placements because of the black market involving the "sale" of children for adoption, disadvantages of direct contact between the natural and adoptive parents, and risks that the child will be unhealthy or the adoptive parents unfit. Rigidity of agency requirements has been one of the detriments to requiring all nonrelative placements to be made by agencies. Also, public agencies may not have the manpower to conduct adequate investigations.

Informal placements are often made by the mother with prospective adoptive parents in advance of application. If the child has lived with the applicants for some months and regards them as his parents, any investigator—social worker, probation officer, clergyman, or private citizen—will be reluctant to remove him from the home except for grave cause.

FROM FOSTER CARE TO ADOPTION

A related issue is the transition from foster care to adoption. Child welfare agencies often held that foster parents could not adopt children under their care when they were freed for adoption. Now, however, many agencies encourage them to do so. Legislation in some states also provides financial subsidies for adoptive parents, mainly for those who take children that are considered hard to place. Subsidies often make it possible for foster parents to adopt the child under their care.

Involuntary Termination

To provide the most stable family life, social workers have an increasing interest in freeing children for adoption through suits to involuntarily terminate parental rights. Parents who cannot possibly rear the child do not want to admit their failure. They always hope for better times. The courts typically support their rights. Legal definitions of abandonment may require proof of a positive intention of the mother to abandon the child. Adequate care for the child by foster parents has also barred a finding of dependency in some courts, even though the natural parents show no interest in the child.

To provide most effective child protection, statutes have to be clarified. Social workers have to be better processors of evidence, and courts have to be more willing to terminate parental rights in the behalf of the child's best interests.

GUARDIANSHIP

Children who are dependent, neglected, delinquent, beyond parental control, or mentally retarded may require a court-appointed guardian of the "person"— someone who is responsible for his direct care. Adults who are mentally retarded, mentally ill, or senile also may be declared wards of the court. If the person has financial resources, such as property or pension benefits, a guardian of the "estate" (or property guardian) is also appointed. State laws define terms in different ways and use varying legal labels. Legal guardianship reduces the parents' tendency to suddenly reclaim the child and also may be required to utilize public funds for the costs of care.

Guardianship Problems

Agencies complain that courts often take the dominant role in diagnosis and planning and consider the agency only as a placement mechanism to carry out unilateral decisions. The agency, on the other hand, may give insufficient attention to the natural family. Temporary guardianship through default too often becomes permanent. Children in stable placements often drift along. On the other hand, if the child goes from placement to placement with unsuccessful outcomes, return to the natural family may come out of desperation rather than out of conviction. The impersonality of guardianship is a problem in large bureaucracies. The head of a child welfare program or his designate may serve as guardian for thousands of children. The major life issues are decided by those who have custody of the child. The guardian should assure that the child is reared affectionately as well as educated and supported.

CHILD ABUSE

Child protection demands legal authority since it requires investigating suspected parental incapacity, neglect, or abuse. Child abuse is considered the most extreme problem requiring protective services. Child abuse laws are intended to give legal immunity from prosecution to persons who report alleged child abuse. Some legal scholars hold that people already have immunity if reports are made in good faith. Other laws establish penalties for abuse, often under the criminal codes. The social worker needs to know the child abuse laws of his own state. He must understand the difficulties of diagnosing abuse, learn the special skills needed to provide services authoritatively, and gain the cooperation of the courts in instances of serious and persistent abuse.

In the only national study of child abuse, 9,563 cases of suspected child abuse were reported in 1967, but only 6,617 cases were confirmed.[13] In the same year 3,000 cases of sexual abuse were estimated in New York City.[14]

Following campaigns by pediatricians, social workers, and citizen groups in the 1960s, every state legislature enacted abuse-reporting laws. Forty-six states require reporting from specified classes of people who may detect alleged abuse. Immunity from prosecution is provided by law to those reporting. While medical personnel are the major potential case finders, varying state laws also specify teachers, nurses, social workers, or Christian Science practitioners. A few states include "all citizens."

Child abuse laws differ widely in the explication of purpose, persons covered, and prescribed investigation procedures. Laws generally cover physical but not emotional abuse. Arizona is the exception:[15]

> Abuse means the infliction of physical or mental injury or the causing of deterioration of a child and shall include failing to maintain reasonable care and treatment or exploiting or overworking a child to such an extent that his health, morals or emotional well-being is endangered.

Some states delegate investigation of reports to the police, some to a social agency, and others to both. The responsibility is accorded to the police in about half the states. In some nineteen states, reports are not required to be directed to a social agency, but these laws are considered inadequate since reporting without the prompt provision of social services seldom results in child protection. On the other hand, if a social worker promises help and then tries to have a child removed, the family may feel betrayed.

Abuse laws do not ordinarily provide the basis for punishing abusers. Criminal laws specify these penalties through such categories as assault. Some of the laws impose penalties upon specified citizens for not reporting. Since child abuse is a matter of judgment, penalties are unenforceable.

Interpreting and verifying evidence are perplexing aspects of child abuse. Bruises and X-rays of healed fractures are major indicators of abuse. Especially with very young children, great skill is required in distinguishing intentional injuries from accidents. In a Pittsburgh study, Elmer reported that many of the cases of alleged abuse reported could not be proved.[16]

A National Center on Child Abuse and Neglect was created by federal legislation in 1974.

Sexual Abuse

Sexual abuse is particularly hard to discover because of family privacy. Studies from protective agencies reveal that sexual abuse usually involves family members or close acquaintances on a recurrent basis—not typically single violent attacks by strangers. Incest is the most common offense. Incidents reported typically involve lower-class families already known to agencies. Sexual abuse also occurs in middle- and upper-class families, but they are better able to maintain privacy. Studies also fail to include instances of sexual activity between siblings and mother-son incest, although both do happen. Sexual abuse is not always simply the victimization of a child. The sexually provocative adolescent may be both aggressor and victim—a familiar story in cases of statutory rape.

Abuse Investigations   Mandatory investigations of child abuse give a social agency defensive and reluctant clients. Delaying abuse investigations may be risky since the children may be injured or killed. Agencies find that investigations and continuing casework may involve different types of manpower. Investigatory police personnel trained in the rules of evidence are useful for gathering facts following receipt of an abuse report. Professional social workers can be used more effectively for continuing services.

Abuse laws should require all complaints to be investigated. When the complainant is unnamed, the agency must take the sole responsibility for legal action. Some agencies, unfortunately, refuse to accept anonymous complaints. This suggests the analogy of the fire department that will not send equipment unless it knows who turned in the alarm.

Abuse reports tend to identify children who have had no regular doctor-patient relationship—children from poor families who are likely to be seen in emergency rooms of public hospitals. Reports from private hospitals and physicians are rare, especially on regular patients. Thus middle-class families are underrepresented in abuse reports.

To be successful, child abuse laws must serve as a case-finding technique.

They require a network of protective services to help families cope with their problems and carry out parental responsibilities more successfully. The primary goal should not be punishment of parents or removal of children from the home, though in some cases one or both actions will be necessary. If the follow-up by the agency is ineffective, doctors, hospitals, teachers, and social workers will neglect to file reports because they will consider them only a ritual.

Child abuse legislation is more complex than it may appear. Legal drafting requires careful definition of terms to cover all those persons most likely to encounter abuse at the outset and to provide the needed supportive services. The laws have worked out better in theory than in practice. In spite of support from the public at large, the laws have not eliminated inadequate reporting or ineffective or delayed investigations.

THE CHILD OFFENDER AND THE JUVENILE COURT

The juvenile court used to be dear to social workers' hearts because it was the one legal mechanism that had been conceived and organized to apply social work principles. The young person in trouble was to receive attention from a "fatherly judge" in an atmosphere that was minimally judicial. Transactions were to be informal, and every effort was to be made to avoid the stigma of delinquency.

The system was not always fair. Punishments were imposed that would not have been tolerated in the adult criminal justice system. Racial and social class bias were likely to result in the informal system.

The Kent[17] and Gault[18] decisions by the Supreme Court ushered in a new era emphasizing due process of law. Kent made it more difficult to process juveniles through the adult courts. In the Gault case, a juvenile was accused of making obscene phone calls, but the charges were rather vague, communication with the family poor, and the time of confinement excessive. As an adult, Gault would have received a maximum sentence of two months. As a juvenile he could have remained in an institution until age twenty-one. The Gault decision specified the explication of legal rights, including formal hearings and representation by counsel.

The current procedure involves provision of counsel to the juvenile and as many as three hearings—for detention, adjudication, and disposition. The *detention* hearing is to determine whether the accused needs to be held for his own protection or that of society or because he may flee. If he is not detained, he is usually sent home to await the next hearings.

In the *adjudication* hearing, the charges are reviewed. Is the child a delinquent, a person in need of supervision, a neglected or dependent child, or none of these? Is he guilty as charged? The adjudication hearing is held as soon as possible if the person has been detained. Otherwise it is usually held within thirty days. The adjudication hearing is guided by rules of evidence prescribed for actions against adults.

The *disposition* hearing is to determine the appropriate action of the adjudication that caused him to remain before the court. In a finding of delinquency, possible dispositions are probation and release to parents, placement in the custody of others (relatives or foster parents), or commitment to a correctional agency.

Since Gault, the more formal procedures have served to satisfy many persons concerned with due process. At the same time, those interested in law and order feel that more informal procedures may not sufficiently impress upon the child the gravity of his action. They have also supported the procedural changes.

For the social worker, the major implication of the emphasis on due process comes in a need for knowledge of the rules of evidence. Unsupported conclusions and clinical "hunches" have no credibility in the present juvenile court system.

COMMUNITY LEGAL SERVICES

Where can the poor get help with their legal problems? Lawyers are expensive, and the poor have been unable to pay for legal counsel. Legal services are guaranteed by the courts by criminal proceedings and in the juvenile court. The federal courts since 1938 have provided an attorney for those who could not afford them. In 1972 the Supreme Court held that the state courts had to provide counsel in all cases involving possible imprisonment.[19] Methods vary from a public defender to casual use of volunteer attorneys without fee to engagement of paid counsel on a case basis. The number of public defenders' offices has tripled over ten years.

Legal aid bureaus were developed first in Chicago and New York and later in about fifty large cities. The bureaus are usually supported by the Bar Association and the United Way. The Legal Service Program of the Office of Economic Opportunity in the 1960s was responsible for the dramatic spread of the community legal services, but we have already discussed the reluctance to provide government support for legal services that take action against government agencies. With the curtailment of the OEO program, legal services have been reduced.

Community legal service is free, and eligibility is based on income. Care is taken to avoid competition with private lawyers. The traditional legal aid bureaus took a very limited range of cases—often excluding divorce. The OEO offices accepted a wider variety—excluding criminal cases, because the courts provided counsel, and personal injury actions that private attorneys would take because of the possible award of damages. Although welfare mothers and other groups have many legal problems, no legal action will solve the problems of income distribution.

Social workers need to know how to obtain legal services for their clients to deal with life crises and with problems of housing and consumer protection. They need to support the network of community legal services, as well as groups interested in legal problems such as the American Civil Liberties Union and the National Association for the Advancement of Colored People. The National Association of Social Workers also has a legal defense fund.

INFLUENCING LEGISLATION

Finally, how can social workers be more effective as lobbyists and advocates? Social workers have not been particularly successful in influencing legislation. Many are employed in governmental agencies and have been subject to the Hatch Act that forbids political activity. They may get more freedom as a result of recent suits contending that the Hatch Act unduly restricts individual freedom. Social work organizations have not had the commitment to lobbying efforts that has characterized such groups as the American Medical Association, nor do they have the resources to carry them on. Social agencies have often worked indirectly through lay board members and other influential citizens.

The Washington staff of the National Association of Social Workers has organized the Educational Legislative Action Network (ELAN) so that interested members can maintain contact with congressmen and be able to act quickly on bills that concern professional social workers. They publish a legislative newsletter called *The Advocate.* Since Watergate, they seem more optimistic about influencing federal human services in spite of Gerald Ford's conservative congressional voting record.

Lobbying is not a dirty word. To react to several thousand bills each session, a legislator needs information from lobbyists who have specialized knowledge. The lobbyist, however, must provide trustworthy information.

Several suggestions are helpful:

1 Know what legislation is being planned. Influencing the drafting of a bill is more effective than responding later.

2 Learn how bills are introduced. The sponsors of the bill and the committee to which it is assigned are the major targets for your views. If you wish to testify, find out when hearings are scheduled and how to prepare a statement. You will not be permitted to testify after the bill has been acted on in committee. Remember testimony will be needed before committees in both houses of the legislature.

3 Personal contacts are generally best. Follow them with a telegram or summary letter to provide a record of your views. Petition or form letters are the least effective. State your own views in your own words. Give reasons.

4 If a bill has a dollar amount attached, it will have to be heard by the Appropriations Committee. This is just as important as a hearing on the substance of the bill. Be prepared to support or refute the financial implications.

5 Get the support of the National Association of Social Workers and other interested organizations.

6 Seek effective coalitions with other groups. Natural alliances on many issues are possible, not only with other professions but with labor unions, the League of Women Voters, Parent-Teacher Associations, Chambers of Commerce, and many others.

Donald Brieland

KEY TERMS

common-law marriage
full faith and credit
no-fault divorce
annulment
illegitimacy
Stanley v. Illinois
interlocutory decree
independent adoption
guardian of the person

child abuse
Kent decision
Gault decision
detention hearing
adjudication hearing
disposition hearing
legal aid bureau
lobbying
ELAN

FOR DISCUSSION

1 Summarize the major issues in age and the law.
2 Identify the age recommendations of the Illinois Youth Council. With which do you agree or disagree, and why?
3 What are advantages and objections to recognizing common-law marriage?
4 What is the criterion for a common-law marriage in a common-law state? Could informal living arrangements of college students be construed as common-law marriage?
5 What are advantages and disadvantages of newer family forms that do not involve marriage?
6 Explain "no-fault" divorce.
7 Why has compulsory counseling been unsuccessful in preventing divorces?
8 Why is child support difficult to collect?
9 What is the major legal right underlying the Supreme Court's decision on abortion? Why would a conservative court make such a decision?
10 Explain how the rate of illegitimacy can go up and yet the number of illegitimate births go down.
11 Describe the present supply and demand situation in adoption.
12 What is the *Stanley v. Illinois* decision, and why is it important?
13 Should married parents be allowed to relinquish their children for adoption? Why?
14 Should all nonrelative adoptions be handled by social agencies? Why?
15 What is meant by guardianship?
16 What is the specific purpose of child abuse laws? Why may these laws discriminate against the poor? Why is emotional abuse rarely covered by the law?
17 What is the difference between the Kent and the Gault decisions?
18 Why do legal services not serve criminal and personal injury cases?
19 What difficulties do social workers have in lobbying?

PROJECTS

1 Poll the class to determine how many members have used the services of a lawyer. What different problems were involved? Did anyone use legal assistance services?
2 Compare the marriage and divorce provisions in two adjoining states. What major differences are found?
3 Study the various legal age requirements in your own state. Which ones have been changed recently?
4 Invite a lawyer to talk to the class about legal aspects of new family forms, including communes and couples living together without marriage. What are the legal problems for them related to the birth and rearing of children?
5 Prepare a discussion on the advantages and disadvantages of recognizing common-law marriages.
6 Select two students with differing views to consider the elimination of the concept of illegitimacy.
7 Invite a social worker who specializes in adoption to present the legal process and the major problems that are involved.
8 Submit questions from the class to a legal aid attorney. Include the types of cases handled and the requirements to be eligible for the service. Ask him to respond to the questions and to discuss the future of legal aid with the class.

FOR FURTHER STUDY

The *Family Law Quarterly* presents articles of special interest to social workers.
The *NASW News* frequently summarizes basic decisions.
The *New York Times* reports Supreme Court decisions in detail.
Leopold Lippman and I. Ignacy Goldberg, *The Right to Education*, Teachers
College Press, New York, 1973.

Chapter 11

Racism

Racism—what is it?
Can we eradicate racism?
Are agencies racist?
How do we get more minority leadership?

Racism is largely unrecognized by the people who practice it, but it is obvious to its victims. Numerically, the victims are predominantly black, but Chicanos and Puerto Ricans have also increasingly publicized the effects of racism. Asian Americans are finally receiving attention. Now we are also becoming more aware of the Native American—the Indian. Because minority group members are likely to be poor, disproportionate numbers of them are known to social agencies.

Defining problems as the responsibility of a minority obscures the central fact that racism is not a problem of Afro-Americans, Chicanos, Puerto Ricans, Asians, and Indians but a characteristic of white people.

ETHNOCENTRISM AND RACISM

Ethnocentrism is based on the superiority of a particular culture; racism results from the belief that skin color and other physical characteristics cause behavioral and cultural differences. Color becomes a more pervasive difference than culture.

For example, the Scots may argue superiority with the Irish, but both have tended to feel that they are superior to any society made up of people of color. In racism, the fact of color becomes the determinant for classifying people as insiders or outsiders.

Racism is usually passive. Most white Americans are not overtly hostile to Indians or Blacks. They did not try to shoot Indians out of the saddle or lynch Blacks, but white American racial values and standards of justice made it possible for Indians to be shot and Blacks to be lynched with little protest and no punishment.

Lack of Knowledge   Many white Americans have never talked to a member of these minorities. Indians are still best known from television movies. Outside of a handful of cities, there are few Chicanos, Puerto Ricans, or Asian Americans. Many communities still have virtually no Blacks.

Emphasis on Hard Work   Most Whites believe that the door of opportunity is open to all and that no barriers exist that cannot be surmounted by ambition and hard work. Racism complicates relationships by introducing inconsistencies. Whites often say that the Blacks or Latinos or Indians could improve their lot

"These social workers think they can blanket us in."

despite their racial characteristics, but Whites also believe these people have limited capabilities. Too few see the contradiction. The way the country runs, members of minority groups find themselves in the role of outsiders as the result of ignorance, indifference, apathy, and unwritten policy.

Stereotypes and Myths

Because color and culture serve as "sorting" mechanisms, unrealistic models are easily built up in the minds of Whites as universal descriptions of members of racial minorities. Unfortunately these stereotypes are taken seriously by Whites and used as the basis for policy. Traditionally, Whites have been taught that Indians cannot use alcohol intelligently. This belief has been translated into laws prohibiting Indians from buying, possessing, and consuming whisky.

Minorities Accept the Stereotypes   Racism is not always obvious. That Blacks have natural rhythm is so ingrained in American culture that many Blacks are firmly convinced of the truth in it. On the surface, it does not sound like a harmful stereotype. After all, music is good and universally appreciated. No laws have been enacted that discriminate against black musicians. The discrimination is subtle. Music is good, but it is essentially play, not work. The belief that Blacks have an aptitude for music may be seen as evidence of their lack of seriousness and productivity. Natural rhythm is then nothing to elicit pride. The belief that Blacks have inborn musical talent no longer sounds harmless but takes on a more significant meaning when infused with racist ideology.

Similar myths and stereotypes, some harmful and some only absurd, persist. They have found their way into common English expressions, such as "lazy as a Mexican" or "colored people's time" (implying lateness). These racist expressions will be used by people who would not use directly insulting terms like "Spic" or "Chink."

Groups Can Gain Acceptance   The consciousness of white Americans about ethnic differences moves in waves. As ethnic groups have become "Americanized," the differences have become obscured and less important, and the ethnic insults lose their sting. Few Americans of Irish descent would become incensed over the expression "give the tablecloth an Irish wash"—to shake it out rather than launder it. The Irish have become more or less integrated into American society. The myths do not dictate public policy, and the ethnic slur falls flat.

If the stereotypical Irishman has physical characteristics that set him apart, they do not have harmful overtones. Dark hair, pale skin, and gray-green eyes coupled with a leprechaun-like body do not threaten white America, and intermarriage poses little threat to racial purity. Clearly the Irish belong to the white race. Even if they are culturally limited, they can be improved! The groups most on the outside have darker skins than most Americans. Skin color has been the barrier to ethnic assimilation in the United States.

Integration and Black Studies   Blacks and their position received dominant notice from white Americans in the 1960s. Ideological and political developments resulted in the civil rights movement. It has been popular even among white

Americans to call for integration of public schools, public facilities, and economic institutions. The demand for recognition of their heritage and culture through new courses and new content in old courses was a major program thrust for groups of minority students. Special study programs were begun at major colleges and universities, and students pressed for a greater role in decisions that affected their special educational desires and needs.

Support of Whites   Preoccupation with the war in Vietnam caused many white students who had formerly been active in the civil rights movement to turn away from the plight of minorities. Antiwar protest reached its extremes in the new radicalism which dissipated into a preoccupation on the part of Whites with their own lives. Minorities learned that they have to press for their own aims by themselves, since Whites and particularly students have not provided continuing support.

This criticism of the white role in the civil rights movement is not intended to deny that Whites made valuable contributions, but Blacks and other minorities realize that they must operate from the base of their own strengths. Whites have to realize that racism is their problem and must work on their own attitudes before they can be of much help to minority groups. In this context, recall the report of the National Advisory Commission on Civil Disorders,[1] and note how few of its recommendations have been taken seriously. Whites do not need to ask what they can do. Read the recommendations of the report and begin there.

AMERICA'S PAST

The United States has always been a racist country. The nation that talked so much about freedom, dignity, and human rights depended heavily in its economic life on slavery. White Americans did not see the contradiction, although there were individual exceptions. Jefferson, although he originally owned slaves, apparently eventually rejected the practice. More frequently the Black was seen as a chattel. The slave was not given the vote and was technically only three-fifths of a man, according to the Constitution.

The Indians were treated as alien to their own lands. When they could be useful, they were courted as allies, but at other times they were only a problem. Westward expansion required their detention at best and their extermination at worst. Today many Indians are wards of the nation and receive less of the benefits of its productivity than any other ethnic group. Had treaties been honored under American law, many would undoubtedly be wealthy.

We will now look more closely at the issues of white racism primarily in terms of Blacks and Asian-Americans. Blacks constitute the largest minority in the United States and have had the most attention from Whites. Asian Americans are included because their situation is dramatically misunderstood. Examples will also be included of the dimensions of the problem for other groups.

Racial Inferiority

Slavery   Many slaves came from cultures that were highly developed, but unfortunately during the colonial period racial and cultural provincialism made people oblivious to values that did not conform to those prevailing in Western

Europe. The African political, artistic, economic, religious, and linguistic experience was not European and therefore of no consequence. Africans were prohibited from practicing and developing their art, their language, their religion, their family life. For want of appreciation and practice, whatever was distinctively African soon died out in America. Although the Black was denied the rights of the white colonialist, the Revolutionary period did produce distinguished Blacks who contributed to America's cultural growth.

Even the great debate over slavery preceding the Civil War took place in the context of white racism. Opposition to the spread of slavery was fed more by the Northern fears of competition from slave labor and the presence of Blacks in the North and West than moral concern for human welfare. Whites who did profess to oppose slavery on moral grounds rarely accepted the principle of racial equality. Abolitionist sentiment reflected paternalistic concern for a "child-like" race as much as indignation over the treatment of fellow men. In a speech in Charleston, Illinois, in 1858, Abraham Lincoln made it clear that opposition to slavery in the federal territories did not mean the acceptance of Blacks as equals:[2]

> I will say, then, that I am not, nor ever have been, in favor of bringing about in any way the social and political equality of the white and black races; that I am not, nor ever have been, in favor of making voters or jurors of Negroes, nor of qualifying them to hold office, nor to inter-marry with White people. . . .
> And inasmuch as they cannot so live, while they do remain together there must be the position of superior and inferior, and I as much as any other man am in favor of having the superior position assigned to the White race.

Jim Crow   Until recently, the relationship of "superior and inferior" described by Lincoln was maintained by two social institutions, slavery and "Jim Crow." Slavery was abolished by the events of the Civil War, but a caste system hardened into a rigid system of oppression known as Jim Crow. The system prescribed how Blacks were supposed to act in the presence of Whites. For example, trains in the South always carried a Jim Crow car where Blacks were supposed to sit. Often this was an old car clearly inferior to the accommodations provided the "white folks."

The Harsh Life of a Slave

Fader in heaven, look upon de poor slave, dat have to work all de day, dat can't have de time to pray only in de night. . . . Fader, when will death come and de poor slave go to heaven?

A slave prayer as recorded by a Northern observer.

From the moment they were captured in Africa through the long, cruel days spent working in the fields, slaves were looked upon not as human beings, but as chattel to be bought and sold. Northerners and Southerners alike saw them in false stereotype as a childish, half-savage people who spoke—or so it seemed to white listeners—in an awkward dialect like the one quoted above.

The violence directed against free Negroes in the North and slaves and free Negroes in the South grew out of a broad popular consensus regarding the nature and character of Negroes and their place in American life—a consensus that was given credence by all kinds of "learned" opinions. Negroes, the scientists said, were weak and imperfectly developed in body and mind. Their color was clear evidence of an elemental inferiority. The blackness, they argued, was caused by the secretion of a greater quantity of carbon, or bilious fluid, and its fixation by uniting with oxygen in the *rete mucosum*, one of the middle layers of the skin. Thus, the membranes, tendons and fluids of Negroes were black, and even their brains and nerves were tinctured with a shade of darkness. Further, the Negro brain was smaller in size and lighter in weight than that of the white man. The distinguished naturalist, Louis Agassiz, declared that the brain of the adult Negro never developed beyond that "observable in the Caucasian in boyhood."

John Hope Franklin, *An Illustrated History of Black Americans.*[3]

Social Control   Slavery and Jim Crow were not merely means by which Blacks were exploited; they were also systems of social control and socialization. During more than three centuries when black labor was ruthlessly exploited, social institutions prevented the outbreak of large-scale black violence and conditioned black people to acquiesce in their own subjugation. The existence of these institutions was inconsistent with the major values in a nation which called itself a democracy.

Insurrections occurred in response to the denial of rights to slaves and the constant policing of their activities. Whippings, mutilations, and hangings were commonly accepted managerial practices. This treatment prevented the development of the slave's individual autonomy and kept him in a state of complete dependence on his master. Maintenance of this dependency required the debasement of the slave.

After the Civil War

Reconstruction   A short-lived and totally inadequate attempt was made by the victorious North to prepare the liberated slaves for first-class citizenship. Although postwar policies protected black voting and civil rights, the federal government failed to launch a comprehensive program of economic and educational aid. Lacking even rudimentary education and having no land, most Blacks soon returned to a state of economic dependence on the same planters who had held them in bondage. Since Northern Whites had never viewed Negroes as their equals, federal protection of black civil rights ended within a dozen years of the North's victory. In 1877 the disputed presidential election of the previous year was resolved by a compromise that ended federal tampering with white Southern "home rule" in return for Southern acceptance of the election of the Republican candidate, Rutherford B. Hayes.

Post-Reconstruction White supremacy was quickly restored. Soon after the reestablishment of home rule, laws were passed requiring racial segregation in schools and public places and prohibiting interracial marriages. This pattern of rigid segregation in the late nineteenth century was designed as much to keep Negroes in their place as to separate the races physically. "Jim Crow" encompassed far more than the social relations between the two races. It also meant the denial of political and legal rights to black people. From 1890 to 1910 Blacks were barred from voting in every Southern state by means of state constitutional amendments. This assertion of white supremacy was not confined to conventional political channels. Blacks who opposed Jim Crow were subject to beatings, burnings, and lynchings. During the transitional period of the 1890s hundreds of Negroes were lynched. Lynchings were public—almost festive—occasions which "taught" black people that challenging white power meant possible death.

Jim Crow required that Blacks be kept submissive and ignorant. Like slavery, Jim Crow socialized black people into accepting their inferior status. Facing constant humiliation and powerlessness, Blacks viewed themselves as inferior to Whites. Thus accommodation was internalized.

World War II and After

On the eve of American entry into World War II black Americans were imprisoned in a rigid caste system. Blacks could migrate north of the Mason-Dixon line, but they could not escape racist stereotypes personified by entertainers like Amos 'n Andy and Stepin Fetchit, nor could their children escape schools that eulogized the achievements of the Whites. Even in the "free" North, Negroes were marked by the effects of a racist culture. Many Blacks internalized white values and covertly regarded themselves as objects of loathing. As two psychiatrists concluded, "Identification with the white oppressor has been the bone of Negro cohesion from the very beginning of slavery, when it took the form of pride in being a house slave, rather than a field slave. This sort of an illusory identification with the master did incalculable harm to Negro cohesion, because it formed one base for class distinction between Negroes."[4] As a result of the Black's identification with the white man, black anger was directed against other Blacks rather than Whites.

Since World War II, black people have generally rejected the role of accommodation and have protested against the inequalities of socioeconomic conditions. In recent years thousands of Blacks have taken part in rebellions against the status quo. An ideology of black revolution has found many adherents in America's urban ghettos.

THE NEW MILITANCY

School Desegregation

As we saw in the chapter on education, a major turning point in the course of black history in the United States was reached when the Supreme Court in *Brown v. Board of Education*[5] ruled that racial segregation in the public schools was unconstitutional. This was a reversal of the *Plessy v. Ferguson* decision of 1896 that "separate but equal" facilities were constitutional.[6] This great legal victory signaled for the Negro an unprecedented opportunity for total integration into the cultural fabric of the United States.

Aggressive Court Actions Since the Supreme Court decision, the Negro himself has added a new dimension to the civil rights picture in the United States—his own preparedness to campaign actively and aggressively for the rights granted him by the courts. This new militancy was at the heart of the civil rights revolution. The 382-day-long Montgomery bus boycott that brought Dr. Martin Luther King to prominence involved effective use of "direct action" for the first time in the South. Its primary objective was to dramatize the effects of racial discrimination on a Negro community.

Confrontation at Tuscaloosa The University of Alabama was the site of the major federal-state clash over school segregation. In February 1956, Miss Auther-ine Lucy, a 26-year-old library science student, was admitted to the university by a federal court order and then barred by university officials. Miss Lucy filed contempt of court proceedings against the school for barring her from the dining halls and dormitories. State authorities eventually prevailed in their decision to expel Miss Lucy, and Alabama remained segregated until 1963.

The Little Rock Crisis In 1957, Governor Orval Faubus summoned National Guardsmen to turn away nine Negro high school pupils, maintaining that they were acting "not as segregationists or integrationists but as soldiers."

At Little Rock, however, a direct challenge was posed to the federal government, which had already approved a desegregation plan submitted by the local school board. When the Negro students were forced to withdraw from the premises of the school, in direct defiance of a federal district court order, President Eisenhower for the first time since Reconstruction sent in federal troops to protect the rights of the beleaguered students. Some 1,000 paratroopers descended on Little Rock and were joined by 10,000 National Guardsmen. The children entered Central High School on the morning of September 25 with an escort of paratroopers. The soldiers remained on call for the entire school year. Little Rock high schools closed for the 1958–1959 school term, but when the school closing laws were declared unconstitutional by the federal court, Central High School was opened to members of all races.

Other Actions The sit-ins of 1960, the freedom rides of 1961, the Albany movement of 1962, the acceptance of James Meredith at the University of Mississippi in 1962, the Birmingham Crisis in 1963, and the Medgar Evers murder of 1963 brought thousands of Whites and Blacks together to protest. To protest, sometimes violently, they joined the Southern Christian Leadership Conference (SCLC), the Students National Coordinating Council (SNCC), the Congress on Racial Equality (CORE), and the National Association for the Advancement of Colored People (NAACP).

The March on Washington The largest protest demonstration in history occurred in August 1963. More than 200,000 Americans of all races, colors, and creeds converged on Washington, D.C., to stage a civil rights protest on the steps of the Lincoln Memorial. The march represented the attempt of Negro leaders to dramatize to the nation the scope of discontent and the enormous appeal of the idea of an open, desegregated society for millions of Americans. Moreover, effectiveness of nonviolence on a large scale had to be tested.

NEW LEGISLATION AND NEW PROTESTS

When the most comprehensive civil rights legislation passed in this century was signed into law by President Lyndon Johnson in 1964, it seemed that the nation had finally entered a more just and serene era of race relations. Although riots broke out in Harlem two weeks later, the belief persisted that basic problems would be solved. This optimism was dampened by riots in other Northern cities that summer and by the Republican nomination of a candidate for the Presidency who had opposed the civil rights bill.

Johnson's triumphant victory in 1964 seemed to mean that the nation had a President who was prepared to attack the problems facing black Americans. His War on Poverty sought nothing less than the total elimination of American poverty, and his civil rights programs were equally ambitious. When the Voting Rights Act of 1965 was signed into law on August 6, President Johnson stated that the act would "strike away the last major shackle" of the Negro's "ancient bonds." One week later the Watts district of Los Angeles was in flames.

After Watts, the nation witnessed several summers of civil disorder, the development of black power ideologies, the radicalization of many black college students, and the organization of local black revolutionary groups. Arguments that Blacks have been reacting to intolerable economic conditions and constant humiliation have not led to massive public and private programs to remedy these ills. Instead, in growing numbers, white Americans have demanded "law and order." In the elections of 1968 and 1972 they gave strong support to candidates who pledged that they would greet civil turmoil with firmness.

Black Gains as a Threat In recent years more and more Whites have become convinced that black gains have led to rising expectations, which have in turn created insatiable demands for power. With some reluctance, these people decided that firmness is necessary to preserve civil order and that Afro-Americans must learn that progress in America is incremental and can only occur through conventional political channels. A majority of Whites believed that massive public expenditures on antipoverty programs would only reward black militancy and encourage Blacks to riot and make unreasonable demands.

The hostility to contemporary black protest stems in part from white ignorance of the realities of black history and the nature of black advances in recent years. Current black radicalism becomes more understandable in light of two central facts of Afro-American history. First, black unrest is not new; during most of our nation's past, black violence was contained only through ruthless repression. Second, current black protest is not the result of black gains but an expression of anger. Despite a generation of advances, insufficient progress has been made toward the elimination of black poverty or powerlessness.

"If we are to end racism in this organization, we've got to roll up our sleeves, get in there and work like niggers."

THE CURRENT SITUATION

Blacks are on the move, physically, economically, and socially. In the 1960s and early 1970s Blacks migrated from the rural South into the cities of the nation's North and West. There, with greater choices, many have been progressing from unskilled low-paid jobs into white-collar and skilled occupations. In search of better housing and better jobs, many have been moving from the city to the surrounding suburbs. A migrant population has been giving way to settled, urban dwellers as increasing numbers are moving economically and socially from extreme poverty into middle-class status.

Many Blacks, however, are left behind both in the rural backwaters of the South and in urban ghettos. In many instances white progress has been so much greater that it overshadows black gains. The Nixon administration was less responsive to racial issues than its immediate predecessors. Social work as an institution has responded to the needs of Blacks in a middle-class way. Social work and social workers have not been responsive to the deep frustrations of the black masses who are still huddled in the nation's ghettos.

The story of the Blacks has its counterpart for the Chicanos. They, too, have moved toward separatism. Their plight is complicated by the large number of them that still serve as migrant farm workers. Mobility makes the development of a strong claim on the benefits of American society more difficult.

RACISM AND ASIAN AMERICANS

Asian Americans are United States residents who have either Mongoloid or Malayan characteristics and whose ancestors resided in East Asia.

Americans believed in white supremacy from the beginning of the nation.

While economic development of the new nation necessitated importation of cheap labor from African and Asian continents, the "colored" people were never meant to be absorbed into the American mainstream. Other Europeans were eligible for full citizenship and privileges if they renounced their continental cultures in favor of at least outward conformity to the American Wasp. "Colored" people, on the other hand, would be excluded from full citizenship rights, but not expelled from the American domain. The "two categories" have been maintained by prejudice, discrimination, isolation, exclusion, and genocide on the part of the white majority.

Early Discrimination

When the first group of Asians appeared on the American frontier in 1850, slavery for Blacks and reservations for American Indians were well established. Unlike them, the first Asian immigrants were neither enslaved nor corralled. America needed a mobile and docile labor force to work uncomplainingly in railroad construction, mines, and new urban factories—jobs which neither Whites nor plantation-oriented Blacks could fill. Lyman[7] proposes that hostile public opinion and violence against the Chinese grew in part out of ignorance, fear, and the threat to jobs, but the overriding factor was clearly white supremacy. Federal and state legislation and judicial decisions handed down since 1854 concerning Chinese, Japanese, and Filipinos provide ample evidence of this attitude.

Racism against Asians can be found in the 1854 decision of the California Supreme Court in *People v. Hall*.[8] The appellant, a white Anglo-American, was convicted of murder upon the testimony of Chinese witnesses. Was such evidence admissible? The judge ruled that Asians should be ineligible to testify for or against a white man, as were Blacks, mulattoes, and Indians.

This ruling opened the floodgate for anti-Chinese abuse, violence, and exploitation. Group murders, lynching, property damage, and robbery of the Chinese were reported up and down the West Coast. Because of the harsh treatment of the Chinese, any luckless person was described as not having a "Chinaman's chance."

Chinese Exclusion Act   Restriction and exclusionary measures against Chinese in employment and property ownership became national in scope in 1883, when Congress passed the Chinese Exclusion Act prohibiting immigration. This act limited the birth rate of Chinese and the development of family life because wives who were still in China could not join their husbands here. The act also excluded Chinese immigrants from naturalization and introduced the category of "Alien Ineligible for Citizenship" used to raise further barriers to other civil rights and privileges. Japanese, Filipinos, and other Asians were later added to the excluded category.

Japanese Immigration   The first group of Japanese immigrants arriving in 1885, a few years after the Chinese Exclusion Act, became the ready target of the anti-Chinese elements on the West Coast. McKee wrote that "the forces that had accomplished the exclusion of the Chinese had developed legend, techniques, and arguments which with little editing could be turned against the Japanese. . . . Politicians and pressure groups had served their apprenticeship in the anti-Chinese crusade. By the turn of the century these veterans were ready to launch a new offensive."[9] To make the situation worse, tension developed between Japan and the United States shortly after the arrival of Japanese immigrants. From 1900 to 1941, Japanese immigrants in California were hostages or pawns in competition for dominance of the Pacific.

An executive order of 1907 prohibited further Japanese immigration from Mexico, Canada, and Hawaii. In the following year, a gentlemen's agreement was signed between the Japanese and the U.S. governments to voluntarily prohibit immigration of Japanese nationals. Excluded from this agreement were the wives of Japanese men residing in the United States. This contributed to a different community organization and development of the Japanese compared to the Chinese.

Imposition of Quotas   "Yellow Peril" agitators, particularly labor leaders and politicians, saw their victory in the enactment of the Immigration Act of 1924. The National Origins Quota System effectively excluded Asian immigration. Thus America made a sharp break with its tradition of free immigration and formalized two policies: the "open door" policy for desirable white northern Europeans and the "closed door" for "colored" Asians.

The Filipino Experience   On the heels of the gentlemen's agreement of 1908 and the Immigration Act of 1924, the Filipinos were lured into the American scene by unscrupulous labor contractors from Hawaii. By virtue of the U.S. trustee-ship of the Philippines, the Filipinos were not considered aliens but nationals of the United States, although rights of citizenship were never granted. The Filipino experiences have been rather similar to those of the Chinese and Japanese.

New Immigration Policies

In 1943, the category of "Alien Ineligible for Citizenship" was eliminated, and naturalization was finally granted to Asians. This amendment also permitted immigration of close relatives of Asian Americans who were already U.S. citizens. Finally, in 1965, immigration laws were enacted that abolished the restrictive national origins quota.

Internment in World War II

The internment of Japanese Americans on the West Coast in "relocation camps" after Pearl Harbor is no surprise viewed against the history and background of persistent and violent anti-Asian agitations. In 1942, some 110,000 persons of Japanese descent were placed in "protective custody." Two-thirds were American citizens by birth, and the other third were aliens forbidden by law to be citizens. No charges had been filed against them, nor had any hearing been held.

This infamous and tragic action apparently resulted from opportunists wanting to eliminate economic competition of Japanese Americans and take over their property, efforts of politicians to exploit public fear, and the influence of the mass media that delighted in inflammatory racist rhetoric.

Several motives were advanced for the internment—dangers of sabotage and espionage, and the need to protect Japanese Americans from mob actions. These appear to be flimsy excuses, particularly when one considers that no similar measures were taken against German and Italian Americans.

The mass internment placed all Japanese Americans under a cloud of suspicion. The internment itself was held as a proof of their disloyalty.

Japanese Americans responded to the internment by requesting to be accepted in the American Armed Forces. Their request was granted. President Roosevelt said in 1943 that ". . . Americanism is a matter of the mind and heart; Americanism is not, never has been, a matter of race or ancestry." The bravery of the 442nd Regimental Combat Team in the European theatre and of other members of the Japanese American military is now well known.

ASIAN AMERICAN COMMUNITIES IN THE UNITED STATES

The predominant Asians and Asian Americans in the United States are the Chinese, Japanese, Filipinos, and Koreans. Burmese, Indonesians, Guamanians, Samoans, South Vietnamese, and Thais are also becoming more numerous. The listing suggests the heterogeneity of history, religion, language, and culture of Asian American communities. Superimposed upon diversity is the differential immigration pattern and accommodation for each group. For these reasons, each Asian community in the United States must be understood and dealt with as a unique entity, but the present perception is to view all Asian communities as homogeneous. This can be likened to viewing all Europeans as a single entity. This does not deny the common basis of Asian experiences in the United States involving fairly uniform and systematic discriminatory practices against them.

Various Asian American communities differ in terms of the numbers, group cohesion, stability, levels of education, and the professional, political, and economic achievements of their members. Asians and Asian Americans tend to cluster around certain locations. Eighty percent live in Hawaii or on the West Coast. The presence of Chinatown, Little Tokyo, and Little Manila in metropolitan areas appears to be a self-protective response of the oppressed. At best, each Asian community can be characterized as a cultural and social community with its unique sets of values, norms, organizations, and accommodation patterns in relation to the host community. As with Blacks, dispersion of second- and third-generation Asian Americans to suburbia from the ethnic enclaves is resulting from the relaxation of discriminatory housing ordinances and from improved socioeconomic conditions.

Wives and Children

Since World War II, between 1945 and 1970, 140,827 Asian women entered as wives of U.S. citizens.[10] Another group of Asians who have entered the United States on a nonquota basis are the 40,000 orphaned or racially mixed children from Hong Kong, Korea, Japan, Taiwan, and South Viet Nam who have been adopted by U.S. citizens.

A study of Korean households in Chicago conducted by a group of Korean social workers in 1972 revealed that 76 percent of the heads of households were under 40 years of age; 85 percent had been in the United States less than four years; 49 percent of the heads of households held professional jobs; and 11 percent held managerial jobs. The average number of children was two, most of whom were of preschool age. Surprisingly, 98 percent of married women worked, 75 percent of them in professional capacities. This raises many questions and speculations about the marital relationships, parental responsibilities, and child care provisions. A third of the college-educated men were engaged in menial jobs due to language difficulties, citizenship requirements, ignorance of community resources, and problems in transferability of skills.[11]

Issues in Asian American Communities

Like other disenfranchised groups, Asian Americans share the disadvantages associated with minority status. Income maintenance, housing, education, health care, unemployment and underemployment, vocational training and retraining are immediate problems. Because of language and cultural barriers and un-familiarity with the institutional arrangement of a community, many needy Asians (particularly aged and new immigrants) do not seek out services to which they are entitled. Equally serious barriers to service delivery are the insensitivity, igno-rance, and inadequacy of community agencies which prefer to maintain the myth that "Asians are successful and they take care of themselves." Serious conflicts are experienced by Asian Americans who are caught between the value systems of their parents and of America. The frustration and anger at the society which has systematically excluded them from the major decision-making institutions must be accepted and dealt with by both the Asian communities and the larger society.

The discussion of the needs and problems of Asians and Asian Americans can be related to three groups: first, the older immigrants who immigrated prior to the Asian Exclusion Act of 1924; second, the immigrants who entered after, World War II—nonquota "war brides," adopted children of U.S. citizens, and quota immigrants, including skilled and unskilled; and third, American-born Asian Americans.

These groups are sufficiently unique to warrant different considerations and approaches by social work and other human service disciplines. Unemployment for the first group is more likely to be related to poor health and marginal job skills. In the second group, it is more closely related to lack of language proficiency in expressing and demonstrating training or to restrictive union or licensing practices, or both. For the third group, alienation or poor educational preparation may be most important.

Responses of Asian Communities

In response to social problems in large metropolitan areas, many self-help "grass roots" organizations have emerged. In Los Angeles alone, more than a dozen agencies provide services to delinquent youth, new immigrants, and senior citizens. The Asian American Social Workers group in Los Angeles was successful in forcing the California State Department of Public Assistance to add bilingual and bicultural Asian social workers to serve the Los Angeles area. More than a dozen projects and programs are proposed along the East and West coasts for provision of services uniquely suited to each ethnic Asian community. A demon-stration and research project to determine and set priorities of the needs and problems of the Asian communities along the West Coast was funded through the Department of Health, Education and Welfare. The Mental Health Training Center for Asian Social Workers trains and develops social work practice models suited for Asian American communities. In New York, the Chinese Planning Council combines direct services with planning and coordinating functions for Chinatown, providing vital linkages between the New York City social welfare community and Chinatown and the Chinese organizations within it.

National Efforts Are Needed

An Asian American Task Force was established within the Minority Commission of the Council of Social Work Education in 1971. This group, consisting of Asian American social workers, students, and faculty, has tried to increase Asian student enrollments and faculty. Since the gaps between needs and service delivery in most of the Asian American communities will be likely to continue, greater involvement of the social work profession in direct service, training, and research is warranted. Collaborative partnerships between Asian communities and schools of social work, social agencies, and national associations will be prerequisites for effective and responsible problem solving in social welfare and race relations.

OTHER MAJOR MINORITY GROUPS

Social agencies and schools of social work have also been targets of criticism from American Indians, Chicanos, and Puerto Ricans. The latter two are sometimes grouped together as Latinos. The groups have both similarities and differences. The various Indian tribes and other subgroups prize their differences from each other.

Rural Background   Like the Blacks, the other minorities trace their heritage to rural antecedents. The Indian has remained the most rural, although there has been extensive movement from the reservations to find work. Chicanos have usually become part of the urban *barrios* or served as agricultural workers. Traditionally they migrated with the crops, but now they are becoming permanent settlers. The Puerto Ricans are the most urbanized in America, but many of them have come from remote rural areas in San Juan to transcend two hundred years of "progress" in the three-hour jet flight to New York.

Language Barriers   All three of these minorities have greater language barriers than the Blacks. Indian children learn English routinely, but often speak it only at school. Limited education is a greater problem for the Spanish-speaking groups. Lighter-skinned adults acquire English more rapidly, probably because they get jobs and are accepted more easily by Whites.

Varied Roles   Different minorities have played different roles. Deloria concludes that our racism led Negroes to be considered draft animals, Indians wild animals, Orientals domestic animals, and Mexicans humorous lazy animals.[12]
Efforts to alienate Indians from Blacks is another interesting theme. In colonial times Blacks often tried to escape to the Indian wilderness and Indians were used to hunt runaway slaves.[13]

All the minorities have shared in poverty. They have all lacked both adequate education and health care. Their work opportunities have conveyed low pay and low status.

A brief sketch of each of the three minorities suggests some of their unique problems.

American Indians

"Native American" emphasizes the Indians' heritage and their claim to America. Their centuries of war with the white man intensified prejudice against them as savages. Earlier in this century they were ignored because of their isolation on remote reservations.

Blacks and Indians   Deloria develops the differential approach to Blacks and Indians. The white man specifically excluded Blacks from all programs, but had to deal with Indians in treaties and agreements. Laws had one goal—"Anglo-Saxonization" of the Indian. "The antelope had to become a white man. Between these two basic attitudes, the apelike draft animal and the wildfree-running antelope, the white man was impaled on the horns of a dilemma he had created with himself."[14]

Indians have received the most paternalistic treatment of all minorities through the Bureau of Indian Affairs. The BIA has become the symbol of Indian frustration and despair.

Privacy of Inner Thoughts   Jimm Good Tracks illustrates some of the problems the outsider will face in working with Indians:[15]

From an Indian's viewpoint, the worker is expected to perform only the superficial and routine administrative functions of his office. . . . The Indian client does not allow nor desire the worker to have any insight into his inner thoughts. . . . The worker's professional function is generally performed within the Indian culture and no foreign interference is desired or contemplated.

The native system provides the Indian people an established, functional, and culturally acceptable remedy in every case.

Economic Development   Generally in this century Indians have been passive, at least until Alcatraz and Wounded Knee. The educational system has prevented the development of strong indigenous leadership, and the reservation life has encouraged passivity. Conditions may improve on the reservations. Economic development projects have had success that will lead to their extension. Tribes have had the advantage of being legal entities that could receive federal grants. Also Indians have obtained highly qualified lawyers to press their historic land claims. Meanwhile the urban Indian is still largely ignored.

Interracial Adoptions   In the social service area, Indians are most concerned about the way interracial adoptions have been used to remove children from their families. Some have even been kidnapped. The Association on American Indian

Affairs has developed a Bill of Rights for Indian Children and publishes an Indian Family Defense Newsletter.

Charles Farris, a Cherokee Indian social worker, recently proposed a White House Conference to call attention to Indian needs. He includes a detailed series of recommendations.[16]

The Chicano

The Chicano is "not Mexican, not Spanish, but a product of a Spanish-Mexican-Indian heritage and an Anglo-Saxon influence."[17] The Chicano resents the stereotypes that demean his people—especially the image of laziness when they perform some of the hardest physical labor in our society.

The movement for Chicano solidarity places strong emphasis on institutional change and the substitution of brotherhood for professionalism.

> Now one must be the advocate of the client. Rather than "keeping the natives down" we must organize clients to have a meaningful influence on our agencies. . . . Individualization—yes—but the individual is a person interacting and transacting with brother, sister, friends—with a community that spells brotherhood, a brotherhood that spells, means power.[18]

Of the three minorities considered here, Chicanos have presented the strongest case for changes in social work that will benefit them. They now have a Chicano-oriented school in San Jose, California. Leaders place great emphasis on the creation of jobs for their people in social agencies. Until more Chicano graduates are produced, those hired will be mainly paraprofessionals. Like the Blacks, they prefer services for Chicanos to be planned by and controlled by Chicanos. So far programs have concentrated on the settled group rather than on migrant workers.

Puerto Ricans

For the Puerto Rican, the Spanish culture has been dominant, but Taino Indian, African, American, and European are also involved. With the pattern of extensive intermarriage great conflict is created for Puerto Ricans who come to a country that defines as black anyone "with a drop of black blood."

Skin Color   In Puerto Rico, identity is based on culture or class, not primarily skin color. Here skin color gets new emphasis. According to Longres[19], four groups are distinguished: the *moreno,* the *trigueno,* the *grifo,* and the *indio.* The first three describe the range from dark to light and the last refers to Indian characteristics. Upon arrival in the United States, Puerto Ricans may find that as a racially mixed group they are generally labeled black. Because of intermarriage, this has ramifications for lighter as well as darker Puerto Ricans. Longres concludes that mental health should be defined within a Puerto Rican cultural context. "Puerto Ricans should emphasize pride in their culture, pride in the racial mixture of Puerto Ricans, and indifference to racial ancestry."[20] That is hard to do if the emphasis of white Americans is not congruent.

Rivera characterizes as unique factors Puerto Rico's status as a United States Commonwealth and its proximity to New York.[21] He also describes the average migrant:

As United States citizens, Puerto Ricans can move freely between the island and the continent. The migration tends to follow economic trends in both the United States and Puerto Rico. The heaviest migrant waves from Puerto Rico came in the early 1950s, encouraged by faster and cheaper air transportation as well as by the demand for semiskilled and unskilled labor.

The average Puerto Rican migrant is young, has little formal education, and comes from the rural areas, in some cases via an urban slum. His move to the United States is not seen as permanent; he intends to go back to the island after making some money. Consequently, he does not see the need to become assimilated and grow roots in this land, nor to give up his language and his culture. In many cases, this fact constitutes a problem in his adjustment to this society, particularly in the establishment of community and political organizations. Some Puerto Ricans are able to save some money and fulfill their dream of returning to Puerto Rico to start a small business or buy a house and retire. Many others return, poor and frustrated, only to find that there is no place for them in Puerto Rico either. Some families are caught in a pattern of traveling between the United States and Puerto Rico without making a satisfactory adjustment in either place. Ironically, many never make it back to the island and their children prefer to stay here.

New York with over a million Puerto Ricans provides the clearest evidence of their problems. They have the lowest salaries, the lowest level of education, and the highest percentage of unemployment and public assistance recipiency.[22]

SUGGESTIONS FOR SOCIAL WORK

Several recommendations appear consistently in the literature of each minority group:

1 Clients are entitled to a general understanding of their culture so they are not served inappropriately out of ignorance.
2 All clients should be served without discrimination or prejudice.
3 Minority clients should have a voice in planning and managing services provided for them.
4 Minority staff members are generally best qualified to serve members of their own group and should be hired to do so.
5 Opportunities for promotion and advancement should be available to minority employees on an equitable basis.
6 Minorities should be accorded special opportunities for professional training. This may mean modifications in educational programs.
7 Minority faculty members are essential. Credentials of experience and skill are more important than academic degrees.

INSTITUTIONAL RACISM

Definition

Racism comes from a recognition of differences, the placing of a negative value on the differences leading to inferiority/superiority, and the generalization of the negative characteristics to all people in the group. Skin color has already been identified as the most evident basis for racism.

Institutional racism results when a society or its organizations use racist values as the basis for laws or formal policies that affect actions. Racist employees can mark an organization as racist through their transactions with the public and with their colleagues, since personal behaviors of staff members get attributed to the organization.

With the federal civil rights acts, executive orders by the governors of most states, and fair housing and fair employment laws, very few social agencies officially and directly deny access to minorities, but this still happens as a secondary effect. Housing patterns have been determined on a racist basis. This affects the educational opportunity for minority students in neighborhood schools, unless busing is used as a remedial measure. Some church-sponsored agencies make it clear that they are designed to serve their own members. If minorities have no opportunity to belong to such churches, they are denied church-sponsored social services.

Three Examples   Informal policies reflect racism:

Quality of service: In an agency with several branch offices, the less skilled staff members may be assigned to the office serving minority people. The explanation may be that other staff "won't go to that neighborhood."

Administrative policies: Rules and procedures may be based on racism. An office in one neighborhood may schedule all intake interviews at 9 A.M., resulting in long waits for some people. If a person is late, he has to come back the next day. Other offices may not have such a rule. The racist explanation is that Blacks are often late for appointments, and it is necessary to be strict.

Services given: Blacks, Asians, or Indians may be told what services they need. When a black family needs help to bring a relative into the home because of a crisis, a request for a bus ticket may be denied, but homemaker service may be offered. Yet the presence of a key member may mean more than anything else to the family, and he or she may actually provide more care than a homemaker. Also, minorities may be referred automatically to public services but Whites to private agencies first.

Personal behavior of staff members is especially hard to control. It may affect:

Hiring and advancement of staff: In spite of civil rights laws, many subtle values operate in staff selection. Reasons may be found not to hire minority members who are well qualified. One is that they may be too militant. On the other hand, recent emphasis on providing opportunities for minorities can lead to charges of reverse racism against hiring Whites. This is sometimes justified as "making up for past wrongs."

Assignment of duties and work loads: Minority staff members may get the undesirable assignments. Minority workers may also be given caseloads made up entirely of minority clients. This is considered racist. We will return to this issue in Chapter 24 on the minority practitioner.

Treatment of persons served: Minority clients complain of curt and rude treatment or condescension from agency staff members. That may or may not be racism. What may be seen as racism can be prejudice against all clients—white and nonwhite—because they are poor, trying to get something for nothing, or too "stupid" to understand the agency forms. Then the attitude of the staff member is hostile but not racist.

In nutritional counseling, staff members often suggest foods that the mother does not want to use or cannot possibly afford. The advice may be based on ignorance or insensitivity, but it is interpreted by the client as racism.

The charge used to be made that minority staff members who were upwardly mobile were frequently punitive to clients from their own ethnic or racial group. As a result, requests were made for white workers. White workers were also preferred because they had more power in the bureaucracy or could be more easily intimidated, or both. With the development of pride and growing recognition of minority identities and group cohesiveness, the frequency of these requests has apparently decreased. One hopes that this is because the behavior of minority staff members has improved, not just because the minority client is now unwilling to challenge a minority staff member whom he wants to consider his brother or sister.

Charles H. Henderson
Bok-Lim Kim

KEY TERMS

racism	*People v. Hall*
Native Americans	Chinese Exclusion Act
Jim Crow	closed-door policy
reconstruction	relocation camps
Plessy v. Ferguson	Asian heterogeneity
Civil Rights Act of 1964	nonquota war brides
"model" minority	institutional racism

FOR DISCUSSION

1 Define racism. How does it differ from ethnocentrism?
2 Why have attempts been made to restrict the sale of alcohol to Indians?
3 How can you reconcile Lincoln's speech at Charleston with the Emancipation Proclamation?
4 Explain the Jim Crow concept.
5 Choose one era of history; identify and summarize the contributions of members of one minority group.
6 How do occupational roles of Chicanos affect their attainment of equity in social services and human rights?
7 Compare the Supreme Court decisions in *Plessy v. Ferguson* and *Brown v. Board of Education*.
8 Why do groups now tend to emphasize separatism?
9 What characteristics advance the stereotype of Asians as the model minority?
10 What was the main implication in *People v. Hall*?
11 Summarize our immigration policy toward Asian Americans.
12 What are special problems of Asian war brides in America?
13 To what extent are Asians alike?
14 Present examples of institutional racism from your own experience.

PROJECTS

1 What organizations in your community are concerned with minority rights or welfare? (Examples might be the Urban League, the National Association for

the Advancement of Colored People, and La Raza.) Invite representatives to discuss their programs and to assess the present status of the particular minority.

2 List five or more terms like "a Chinaman's chance." How do you think each one got started? How common are they now? Are any of the examples favorable?

3 Read the following article: Samuel M. Hersh, "My Lai 4: A Report on the Massacre and Its Aftermath," *Harper's Magazine*, vol. 240, May 1970, pp. 53–84. Discuss it from the viewpoint of racism.

4 Research the confrontation between American Indians and the federal government at Wounded Knee, South Dakota, in the summer of 1973. What were the major issues? How were they resolved?

5 Analyze the admissions and eligibility policies of the social agencies in your community. Is there evidence of discrimination? Interview minority group staff members. What are their reports about the same agencies? How can a fee policy be discriminatory?

6 Prepare and present a discussion on the accomplishments of Cesar Chavez and the United Farm Workers. Analyze the technique of boycotts to gain human rights.

FOR FURTHER STUDY

Ngor-Pei Chen, "The Chinese Community in Los Angeles," *Social Casework,* vol. 7, 1970, pp. 591–598.

Roger Daniles and Harry H. L. Kitano, *American Racism: Exploration of the Nature of Prejudice,* Prentice-Hall, Englewood Cliffs, N. J., 1970.

Vine Deloria, *We Talk, You Listen*, Macmillan, New York, 1969.

Harry H. L. Kitano, *Race Relations,* Prentice-Hall, Englewood Cliffs, N. J., 1974.

Ford Kuramoto, "What Do Asians Want? An Examination of Issues in Social Work Education," *Journal of Education for Social Work,* vol. 7, 1971, pp. 7–17.

Harold M. Rose, *The Black Ghetto,* McGraw-Hill, New York, 1971.

Stan Steiner, *La Raza,* Colophon Books, New York, 1970.

Peter Watson, *Psychology and Race,* Aldine, Chicago, 1973.

Part Three

Social Work Methods

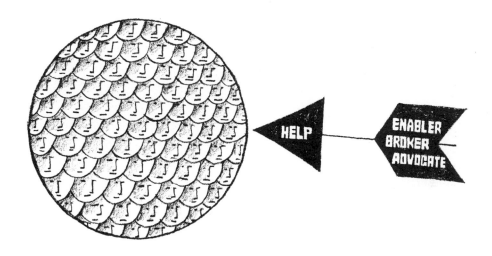

Social work literature has emphasized casework, group work, and community work. Social work theories derived from many fields lead to different views of what is appropriate and effective.

Casework enjoys a preeminent position because it has the longest history of the social work methods and is the technique used by the majority of personnel.

The demand for group work has increased both within and outside of social agencies. New types of groups have created new opportunities and, some feel, new hazards to be explored.

Community work has helped to give neighborhoods more control over their own services and has attracted social workers who are especially interested in advocacy and activism.

Along with these methods come other innovations that create additional options for the student interested in a social work career.

This section will summarize:

Different views of the individual and philosophies and means of helping him
How group activities are effective in the helping process
Efforts to assist communities in social action
Generalist approaches to prepare a social worker effective in all methods

What social work methods appeal to you?
What do you need to know about them?

Chapter 12

Services to Individuals

What is unique about casework?
Why is individualization a key idea?
What knowledge and skills are needed?
Which values are most important?
What are the major casework approaches?

We all face personal problems that we cannot resolve by ourselves. Sometimes other family members, friends, or acquaintances can help, but frequently we need more skilled help to obtain goods and services, to deal with feelings about ourselves, and to cope with marriage or family relationships, problems at school or at work, or sudden catastrophes that change our status or roles. Furnishing personal help is what social work is all about. The majority of social workers spend their time working with individuals in public or private agencies, in schools and hospitals, or in private practice.

Social casework—the focus on the individual and the process of individualization—developed early in the history of social welfare. Older theories of casework are now being questioned. Changes stem from new knowledge about the forces that affect human functioning, new social problems, and new values and goals of society. Social casework continues to focus on (1) understanding the individual and his predicament; (2) changing his attitudes, motivation, and behavior; and (3) making resources available to him. Another element often included is determination of eligibility for the service, a process that social workers would like to deemphasize, especially when eligibility is determined by a financial means test.

TYPICAL CASEWORK ACTIVITIES

The diversity of activities in helping individuals defines the dimensions of casework. Caseworkers talk directly with people who have problems. They are involved with other family members to get information and to enlist their support. They seek services from other agencies in the community and respond to their requests. They relate to hospitals, nursing homes, day care centers, schools, and other helping institutions, as well as to banks, loan companies, and businesses. They deal with the court system and appear in court most often in matters of probation or guardianship. They interpret their services through speeches to community groups, articles, reports, and interviews to the press. A worker who keeps a diary for a few days will be surprised at the variety of his efforts.

A Caseworker's Day Spent Serving the Aged[1]

7:30 A.M.: Telephone call at home from sister of Mrs. A. Mrs. A. has a homemaker who is worried because Mrs. A. had not slept well and still is not feeling well. The doctor will make a home visit. The sister is concerned that hospitalization will be necessary. Will I drop in to see Mrs. A.? We discussed hospital policies, admission, and costs.

8:00 A.M.: Stopped to see Mrs. A. She was dressed and was angry with me. "Why did you come? Who called you? You're no doctor! I'm sick. You can't help me." We talked. She was worried about getting the yard cut, the back porch cleaned, and her recently deceased brother's clothes taken away. She was angry because the house was left to her brothers and sisters. "They're just waiting for me to die." I promised to see about hired help for the yard and porch and suggested giving her brother's things to a clothing center so someone could use them. I reminded her that her brother had left the house to her *first,* giving her life estate, so he thought first of her. If the other brothers and sisters live longer than she, they'll each get a piece of it. She wasn't thinking of it that way.

Mrs. A. was in a better mood by 8:30. She expected the doctor, but her symptoms seemed vague at this point. She said her relatives made her sick last night when they discussed her situation.

8:45 A.M.: Called Mrs. A.'s sister from the office. Told her that the main problems are worry, anxiousness, and anger. She promised to have the lawn mowed and the back porch cleaned this afternoon.

9:00 A.M.: A social worker from another agency came in. We had coffee and discussed developing a joint library for staff use.

9:15 A.M.: Visited the welfare department. Discussed Mrs. B., an eighty-three-year-old client we have in common. She mislays mail, doesn't pay bills, says she has no money, and won't buy food even when someone offers to shop for her. Formerly she did these things herself. Now she has deteriorated. She refused to even consider a nursing home. We talked to the county attorney about guardianship papers but agreed that they should not be served by a uniformed officer. With a guardian perhaps she can continue to live at home as she wants to.

9:40 A.M.: A Salvation Army worker called inquiring about a homemaker. A fifty-seven-year-old man needs someone to look after his wife, who recently came home from the hospital after suffering a stroke. He would like to continue his job, but needs home care for his wife. The man seems frightened. We have no one available, but will look for a homemaker.

9:50 A.M.: Mrs. C. called. She has a heart condition and her husband is recuperating from a broken hip. Their part-time homemaker did not show up this morning. Could we give her the homemaker's telephone number? We asked her to call back if she could not reach the homemaker.

9:55 A.M.: A homemaker who works for Mrs. E., an eighty-two-year-old client, called to report her hours. I'll visit Mrs. E. later and help her make out the check for the homemaker. She will grin when she endorses the check because until a year ago she'd never had a checking account, nor did she "take care of business and all that."

10:15 A.M.: Returned a telephone call to a church group to accept a speaking engagement on "The Later Years." Talks like this are requested every two or three weeks.

10:25 A.M.: Held a conference with our secretary, Mrs. Gray. She had been telephoning members of the men's group to remind them of Stag Day—pool, shuffleboard, and cards—held at City Recreation. Transportation is the major problem here. Also asked Mrs. Gray to invite a seventy-five-year-old client to lunch at a retirement home. She is head housekeeper at a local hotel, but arthritis and reduced stamina are overtaking her. She is interested in group living and will have an opportunity to inspect the home and talk to the manager.

10:50 A.M.: Called Mrs. G., who has been talking about moving away from her son and his wife. She asked that I call again tomorrow. She feels abused and neglected and constantly talks of the wrongs done to her. Her moods are highly variable, and do not seem related to external events. Perhaps psychiatry would be helpful.

11:20 A.M.: Miss H. called. She broke her glasses and can't see a thing. Can we help her? She's on Old Age Assistance and can get new glasses free, but has no one to take her. I offered to get the glasses repaired this afternoon.

Lunch: Attended subcommittee of welfare council on health care. Discussed overuse of hospital emergency room by local citizens for colds and other routine illnesses. Considered ways to get doctors to accept Public Assistance patients.

A FRAMEWORK FOR HELPING INDIVIDUALS

The goal of social casework is *individualization*. This concept characterizes social work practice with individuals. The person to be helped is the unit of attention and the focus for the social workers' activities and agencies' services. Carol Meyer has suggested individualization as both the goal and the process for social work practice.[2]

Individualization means understanding the person as he appears for help—his attitudes about asking for help and the problems as he perceives them. The initial boundaries of individualization are imposed by the dimensions of the problems presented, the help that can be offered, and the kind and amount the client can use.

Taking Help

Most people who are in trouble both want help and are terrified of it. Indeed in most cases the fear of any kind of help that would really induce change or movement is greater at first than the desire for it.

We can understand this fear better, perhaps, if we consider what asking for help demands. The person who asks for the kind of help that will really make a difference to him must, in fact, do four things. He must recognize that something is wrong with him or lacking in his situation which he can do nothing about by himself. He must be willing to tell someone else about his problem. He must accord to this other person at least a limited right to tell him what to do or to do things for him. And finally he must be willing to change in some way himself. This means giving up whatever adjustments he has been able to make to the present situation—adjustments that may have and probably have cost him a great deal to make and have become part of himself and wholly necessary to him—in favor of a new kind of life, which he may have some reason to believe will be more satisfactory but which, at the same time, is an unknown quantity, full of possible dangers.

But the difficulty is greatly increased if up to the time of asking for help a person's experience of permitting another to take some control of his affairs has been that he is taken advantage of; if telling another has meant that his confidence is abused; if his attempts to live a supposedly more productive life have always resulted in defeat. And these have been the experiences of all too many of those who are in need of help.

Yet for the most part this tremendous demand made on the person to be helped has gone unrecognized. People who refuse help are still thought of as ungrateful when all they really are is afraid. Others are thought to be insensitive, not to know there is something wrong, or to lack simple common sense, when in fact they are acutely aware of the wrongness but even more afraid of what it would cost them to put it right. Many are stigmatized as content with unsatisfactory or degrading conditions when all that they are is scared to act on their discontent. . . .

Alan Keith-Lucas, *Giving and Taking Help.*[3]

The Process of Individualization   Problems and needs are explored and clarified by the social worker and client. At the same time the resources of the agency and of the community, the client, and the skills of the social worker are assessed. Out of this comes a mutual definition of the problem. The tasks needed to deal with the problem are agreed upon. Usually a time limit is set.[4] Various problems, needs, and tasks involve different patterns of relationships with clients and different methods of helping. A client may need only information—where to find day care for a child, a homemaker for an older parent, housing, or legal advice. He may need assistance in searching out a resource or in using it effectively. Both emotional support and information may be critical in dealing with an unexpected pregnancy, rearing a defective child, responding to the loss of a spouse, or accepting retirement. A client may require guidance in examining his feelings and actions in marital or parent-child relationships as well as assistance in modifying persistent problem behaviors. A client who is being treated unfairly by a school, hospital, or some other institution will need help to change the system. No arbitrary limits govern the social worker's activity in helping a client.

Termination Ending the casework relationship is important, but unfortunately it does not receive much attention either from social work practitioners or in the literature. Two elements need to be considered: the relationship between client and worker and accountability of the worker. As termination approaches, a client who has met with friendly, warm, concerned, empathetic understanding by the social worker may be loath to give up this relationship because of feelings of loss or desertion. The social worker who experiences the satisfaction of being important in the life of another person also may be reluctant to end the relationship.

Accountability The other element, accountability to the client, is demonstrated through problem and task definition and problem resolution. Since most social workers are employed by agencies to accomplish socially desirable purposes, accountability to the agency and to society is also necessary. It requires systematic information about the nature of the problems and needs, the nature and amount of service received, the use of resources in meeting the need, and final evaluation of the outcome.

THE FAMILY AS THE UNIT FOR HELP

The social worker relates to the communications and transactions of the family as a group. Social workers discovered early that family interactions were instrumental in the development of problems of individual members as well as problems of the family as a whole. Attempts to change were often sabotaged by others in the family.

Since the 1950s the family unit has become an increasingly important focus of attention. The family is seen as a regularly interacting interdependent system. Change in one member affects others. Their reactions in turn affect the whole system. Each family system is influenced by unique patterns of behavior and communication, of role definitions and performances. Family rules that regulate interactions and transactions are frequently not consciously recognized. Each family also has the same developmental tasks that the individual must master— self-control and self-responsibility, intimacy and distance, separateness and dependence, individualization and interdependence.[5]

Short-Term Family Therapy[6]

The R's, a black, middle-class family—father, mother, and three boys—eight, three, and two years old—live in a predominantly white community. The school was concerned about the oldest boy's behavior problems—disruption in the classroom, fighting, and stealing. Two other children had died recently in a trailer fire and the two-year-old had swallowed lye, necessitating extensive surgery.

Since the family had not sought help and both therapists were white, a treatment relationship was the immediate goal. Interpersonal factors and race were discussed frankly during the first home visit. Relationships were established first with the children. The therapists then moved to broaden their perspective to include the whole family unit.

As the sessions developed, the parents talked about the deaths of the other children and about the baby's surgery. With the help of an understanding surgeon, they were able to handle the emotional and financial aspects of that crisis.

The therapists made observations in the school and interviewed school and community personnel. They concluded that a good part of the son's antisocial behavior had been precipitated by subtle racism in the school and the community.

The parents had divergent views on how their son should behave in a white community. The father encouraged passive adaptation, but the mother supported standing up for one's rights. They recognized that they had placed their son in an emotional and behavioral bind.

In a give-and-take discussion the father modified his views. He agreed that their son join a black Boys' Club in another part of town to help strengthen his identity and the ability to assert himself with children of his own age. With the parents' agreement, the therapists shared their impressions with school officials. They recommended changes in the school aimed at removing social pressures. The therapists recommended transfer to a black worker who would continue to see the boy.

Focus of Family Interviews   Individualization consists of family interviews to consider the problems that brought the need for help. The worker and the family unit together become aware of how the family interacts and the dysfunctional elements in the interaction. Transactions reveal role expectations and performance of members; collusions and reciprocal relationships—use of others for one's own ends; expression of feelings; use of defenses; coping mechanisms in response to conflict.

Scapegoating a family member reflects the need for family balance or equilibrium. Communication difficulties result from opposing messages. The mother says something is permissible, and the father says it is not. The double message is another problem. A mother tells her daughter to be "a little lady," but the first gift she sends her at a detention home is a set of seven sexy bras.[7]

Choice of Problem   The social worker and family select the problem to be worked on. If a family's major dysfunctional theme is the expression of aggressive and negative feelings that threaten to annihilate the family, obtaining more cautious expression may be the worker's task. If communication difficulties are the target problem, the worker deals with messages intended, messages received, and the responses given by the family. Some social workers focus almost entirely on communication because when it is adequate other problems tend to be resolved.[8]

SKILLS IN THE HELPING PROCESS

Sensitivity

Skills in interpersonal relationships influence whether or not a person receives help. The first skill is the social worker's sensitivity to the client's feelings and his capacity to communicate his understanding of them to the client. This means sensitivity to the client's fears, anxieties, guilt, and anger as well as to hope and aspirations, communicated openly or covertly. This capacity on the part of the worker is called *accurate empathy.*[8] Second, the social worker must have the capacity to respect and care for the client as a separate person who is allowed to have his own feelings and experiences. This is called *nonpossessive warmth* or *unconditional positive regard.* Third, the social worker has to be *genuine.* The worker is not defensive or phony, but open, real, and honest. The absence of these qualities impedes helping and may make the predicament worse. Also, the skill of the caseworker in conveying realistic confidence and hope for resolution of the problem is an ingredient in successful helping.

Some problems come from outside the individual or family. Then the social worker locates appropriate community resources and helps use them. The worker may need to serve as the advocate to help obtain the rights of clients in the community. Representing the client requires skill in using facts to persuade; influence to achieve goals; mediation to reconcile conflicting stories of clients, professional colleagues, and other agencies or institutions; and pressure without alienating others and jeopardizing the client's cause. We have seen, then, that helping individuals requires concern, warmth, sensitivity, honesty, and self-awareness on the part of the social worker.

Interviewing

A worker also needs expert knowledge about how to conduct an interview. According to Kadushin, this means understanding the process of communication: how to help a client tell his story; how to encourage him; how to interpret the words, the pauses, the physical manifestations; and what words and activities of the worker will convey the desired meaning. He has to know methods of coping and defenses, what sustains a client's problem behaviors, and the importance of social class, cultural, religious, and ethnic influences on the client's perception of his problem.[9]

> A thorough knowledge of the subject matter of the interview is a mark of the competent interviewer. The medical social work interviewer must have at her command a detailed, specialized knowledge of the social antecedents, concommitants, and consequences of physical illness; the psychiatric social worker, of mental and emotional illness; the gerontological social worker, of old age.

Unless the worker has detailed knowledge of the social problem area for which she is offering service, she will not know what questions to raise, what information is most significant, what items need to be pursued in more detail. She needs to know the generalizations which the social and behavioral sciences have made regarding, for instance, delinquency, child placement, or school phobia so that she has some concepts available to make sense out of what the interviewee is telling her. She needs to have sufficient grasp of the relevant generalizations regarding the particular social problem so that she can translate these into appropriate questions, comments, and probes during the interview. . . .

Some statements by the interviewee which have no meaning for an interviewer with scant knowledge will suggest a series of fruitful questions to the interviewer who knows what the remark implies.

Assessment interviews require a knowledge of normative expectations. If the child is toilet trained at 20 months, is it late or early? If he first started talking at 15 months, is this indicative of developmental lag or normal development? What parental behavior suggests "overprotection" and what kinds of separation behavior are normal for a hospitalized school-age child? To know what is unusual, unexpected, or atypical, one needs to know the usual and the typical.

Rights of the Client

The social worker has to know both the rights and entitlements of the individual to the services of the agency.[10]

> The interviewer whose purpose is advocacy, and whose interview orientation is to persuade and convince, needs to have considerable knowledge about the rights and entitlements of his client; he needs to have a good command of the regulations and procedure of the agency. Without such knowledge he cannot challenge, with assurance, any decision denying aid or service. He must understand the agency's structure so that he can appeal, or threaten to appeal, an adverse decision made at a lower level in the agency's administrative structure to somebody farther up the line.

The caseworker needs detailed knowledge of the community resources and the way to obtain them for the client. Finally he has to be able to determine the most effective helping procedures for a particular client and his problems.

SOCIAL WORK AND HUMAN VALUES

Basic to all social work is the belief in human dignity and in the maximum realization of each individual's potential throughout his life.[11] Casework involves a relationship characterized by expressed interest, empathy that is conveyed to clients, integrity on the part of the caseworker, and activity that maximizes the client's participation and safeguards his personal integrity and privacy. This includes a cluster of humanistic values which developed out of both a Judaeo-Christian view of the nature of man and the democratic ideology of this country.

Relationship The importance of the relationship between the worker and client has been emphasized by writers on casework regardless of their theoretical persuasion. Biestek identifies seven needs or rights of clients and enumerates the

related principle for each which guides the worker's activities in the relationship.[12]

Client's needs and rights	Principles for the worker
1 To be treated as an individual	Individualization
2 To express feelings	Purposeful expression of feelings
3 To get sympathetic response to problems	Controlled emotional involvement
4 To be recognized as a person	Acceptance
5 Not to be judged	Nonjudgmental attitude
6 To make his own choices and decisions	Client self-determination
7 To keep secrets about himself	Confidentiality

Correlates of Success Studies indicate that the qualities already identified—accurate empathy perceived by the client, genuineness, and unconditional
positive regard—are the characteristics of helping persons associated with
positive outcomes in counseling and psychotherapy.[13] Mayer and Timms, in their
report of working-class clients' perception of casework, conclude that ". . . only
workers who are perceived as caring, as being concerned, are in a position to
make their supportive efforts felt."[14]

Existentialism Social workers have been increasingly influenced by existential philosophy and values in helping individuals.[15] An existential approach
assumes certain common elements in the lives of all people that make possible
generalizations about man. Man is both free and responsible. The purpose and
meaning of life rests on what he does with his freedom—his commitment and
ability to act upon himself, others, and society. Of equal importance is what man
does with his limitations, his inability to figure out life's absurdities and accidents.
Within both of these spheres man is able to make decisions. Men are capable of
choosing their response to life and to its final limitation, death. Problems arise
when man tries to escape his freedom and responsibility. Freedom, then, means
freedom to choose. Responsibility means facing situations and making choices.
Neuroses, psychoses, being engulfed in a mass identity, and other devices to
avoid facing life are seen as escaping reality, leading an inauthentic existence—
copping out.
   The crucial element is helping individuals to face up to and make choices
about reality. Some people may not know what choices may be open to them.
Others may be so caught up in anxiety that they cannot choose, or are severely
constricted about their apparent choices. Others may be so guilt-ridden that only
self-defeating choices are perceived. The external environment of some is so
limited and impoverished that few choices are available. The self-concept of some
people may be so low that they are unable to perceive themselves as possessing
the right, much less the potential capacity, for choosing. Existentialists see the
helping relationship—the encounter—as being other-centered, the opening of
one's self to the unique importance of the other person.[16]
   Existential values champion the individual, his uniqueness, rights, freedom,
and responsibilities, and offer a basis for helping in situations which hold no

objective or utilitarian happy endings, including chronic illness, old age, and death.

DEVELOPMENT OF SOCIAL CASEWORK

An account of helping individuals comes from France in 1833 when a group of students led by Frederick Ozanam joined together in the service of God to help the poor.[17]

> The poor were to be visited at their own dwellings, in hospitals and prisons, and to be assisted by every means within their power.
> A portion of the very greatest misery of the poor often proceeds from their not knowing how to help themselves out of a difficulty once they have gotten into it; they fall into distress through accidental circumstances, arising from their own fault or other people's and they are too ignorant to see their way out of it. The law frequently has a remedy ready for them, but they don't know this, and there is no one to tell them. Their one idea when they fall into distress is to hold out their hand for an alm, a system which generally proves as ineffectual as it is demoralizing.

Ozanam's young friends responded to the suggestion that

> they should try to remedy this lamentable state of things by placing their education, their intelligence, their special knowledge of law or science, and their general knowledge of life, at the disposal of the poor; that instead of only taking them some little material relief, they should strive to win their confidence, learn all about their affairs, and then see how they could best help them to help themselves.

Charity Organization Societies

Most writers identify the beginning of social casework with the friendly visitors of the Charity Organization Societies during the last half of the nineteenth century, whose job was to control and to alleviate the effects of poverty. We will see that group work and community work also trace their origins to the COS.

The Societies worked personally with individuals caught in poverty. These early caseworkers stressed moral reform of the individual. The poor were divided into two groups—the worthy poor, those who were capable of moral reform; and the unworthy poor, who were not. The former were provided with food, clothing, and further service. The latter were considered ineligible. Investigations were made for "furnishing guidance and knowledge for a long course of 'treatment' by which weak wills might be strengthened, bad habits cured, and independence developed."[18]

Octavia Hill, one of the founders of the Charity Organization Society, commented:[19]

> By knowledge of character more is meant than whether a man is a drunkard or a woman is dishonest; it means knowledge of the passions, hopes, and history of people; where the temptation will touch them, what is the little scheme they have made of their lives, or would make, if they had encouragement; what training long past phases of their lives may have afforded; how to

move, touch, teach them. Our memories and our hopes are more truly factors of our lives than we often remember.

In the next phase social caseworkers amassed long and detailed social histories from which diagnoses could be inferred and treatment plans developed. Histories contained facts to objectify inferences and decisions that previously would have been based on moral judgments. The histories increasingly included material related to the economic, moral, social, and hereditary causes of poverty. Even more important, the histories indicated the personal and social resources needed to serve the client.[20]

APPROACHES TO CASEWORK

Influence of Freud

In the 1920s and 1930s the impact of individual psychology affected the direction and emphasis of social casework. Freud was the dominant influence. Others developed and refined his formulations. Sexual and agressive drives (the id)—the instinctual drives seen as the primary forces underlying the behavior of man— constituted the initial emphasis. Attention then shifted to the defense mechanisms, the devices employed by man to control and channel the basic drives. Repression was seen as the chief mechanism of control to keep basic sexual and aggressive impulses from conscious awareness. A person's early childhood relationships, especially with his mother, determined how drives were controlled or channeled and how well adjusted he would be as an adult. Relationships and deprivations in early childhood were associated with later emotional and mental illnesses and personality characteristics. Clinical evidence was developed to support these associations.

The Freudian formulation of personality development changed the direction of social casework. It included two assumptions that became basic principles of social casework: human behavior is *purposeful* and *determined,* and some of the determinants of behavior are *unconscious.* Social casework was no longer a method to be used only for the poor. These new psychiatric insights applied to all people. Early childhood experiences and memories, rather than external social forces and events between the recipient of service and the caseworker, became the material for social histories and diagnosis.

A close and accepting relationship was necessary to talk about intimate and personal events and to recall early childhood memories that had been repressed. Conscious recollection of events and how one felt about them aided in the solution of problems. The relationship with the caseworker was used to resolve conflicts. Interviews were held one or two hours a week for a year or longer. The need to safeguard the confidentiality of the content of the client's communication was recognized and incorporated into casework practice.

Psychosocial Treatment

As the concept of the ego and ego psychology gradually developed, the focus of social casework moved more toward the social functioning of the individual. Psychosocial treatment became the dominant school of thought within social casework.

Casework has always been a psychosocial treatment method. It recognizes the interplay of both internal psychological and external social causes of dysfunctioning and endeavors to enable the individual to meet his needs more fully and to function more adequately in his social relationships.[21]

Clients come for casework treatment because there has been a breakdown in their social adjustment. This breakdown has three possible interacting sources: (1) infantile needs and drives left over from childhood that cause an individual to make inappropriate demands upon his adult world; (2) a current situation that exerts excessive pressure upon him; and (3) faulty ego and super ego functioning. The degree to which each of these is present varies with different people. Sometimes all three are contributing to the client's dilemma.[22]

Ego psychology is concerned with the adaptive capacities of the individual. How is the individual coping? Are his coping mechanisms appropriate to his situation? Are they effective? How realistic are the person's perceptions of himself and of his outside world? How valid are his judgments based on these perceptions? What is his capacity for control and direction of internal drives and feelings concerning specific elements in his external environment? Further questions also confront the caseworker. What is the nature and extent of the internal stress? What constitutes effective and ineffective coping? How does the person seek and use help?

Increasingly, coping activities have been linked with specific problems or outside pressures. For example, the sudden loss of a spouse or loved one predictably diminishes coping ability. Usually a numbing sense of loss, removal of self from ties with others, physical symptoms, and blaming others or oneself for the loss culminates in reintegration and reinvestment with others. Coping activities also have been linked with the more predictable changes and risks an individual faces. The developmental scheme of Erik Erikson covering birth to old age has affected the practice of many caseworkers, particularly in its stress on basic trust for the infant and identity for the adolescent.

Psychosocial treatment, the most popular conceptual framework, has sharpened the process of individualization and helped to develop insights into human behavior and the helping relationship.

Psychosocial treatment is deterministic. Individuals are governed by their basic drives and by their early life experiences. Psychosocial treatment lends itself best to persons who are intelligent and sophisticated, articulate, and capable of introspection. The focus is on the individual and his adaptive capacity. The pressures of environmental change receive less attention. Psychosocial treatment has not lent itself very well to evaluation, that is, to the development of either an empirical base for practice or effective criteria for judging the outcome.

The Functional Approach

Although ego psychology within the framework of psychosocial treatment has been dominant, the *functional* approach to casework, based partially on the system of psychology of Otto Rank, has also had a continuing influence. The drive to life, health, and fulfillment is seen as basic to man. Man struggles to grow. The process of growth is the central core of activity in working with individual clients.

Man uses human relationships, including the relationship with the social worker, to find and to strengthen his own purpose and to move to its realization. Casework is "a method of administering some specific social service with such psychological understanding of and skill in the helping process that the agency service has the best chance of being used for individual and social welfare."[23]

Emphasis is placed on giving and receiving help. The offer of service unites the person with the skill of the caseworker and the function and services of the agency. This process includes a definition of the service being offered and whether the client can use it. Time limits are set for the help. Empathy with the client in using the help as well as honesty and openness of worker communication are especially important.[24]

The functional approach has emphasized the individual's use of choices in working on his problem. Agency function as well as worker skill are positive elements in helping individuals.

Social Casework as Problem Solving

The problem-solving approach to social casework emerged in the 1950s from the work of Helen Harris Perlman at the University of Chicago.[25] Problem solving involved a branching out from the psychosocial treatment and functional approaches. It also takes into account the individual, the problem, and the agency or institution from which services are received.[26]

> A *person* beset by a *problem* seeks help with that problem from a *place* (either a social agency or some other social institution) and is offered such help by a professional social worker who uses a *process* which simultaneously engages and enhances the person's own problem-solving functions, and supplements the person's problem-solving resources.

Perlman summarizes problem solving as follows:

> On the basis of the assumption of a deficit in problem-solving means—motivation, capacity, and/or opportunity—the problem-solving process consists of actions on the helper's part:
>
> **1** To release, energize, and give direction to the client's *motivation,* that is, to minimize disabling anxiety and fears and provide the support and safety that encourage a lowering of disabling ego defenses, a heightening of reward expectations, and a freeing of ego energies in the task at hand.
>
> **2** To release and then repeatedly exercise the client's mental, emotional and action *capacities* for coping with his problem and/or himself in connection with it; thus to release and then exercise the ego functions of perception, feeling, cognition, comprehension, selection, judgment, choice, and action as they are required by the problem.
>
> **3** To find and make accessible to the client the *opportunities* and resources necessary to the solution or mitigation of the problem; thus to aim to make accessible those opportunities in his environment that are essential conditions and instruments for satisfactory role performance.

The problem-solving approach has received wide acceptance because Perlman clearly specified the guidelines for helping.

Crisis-oriented Short-Term Casework

During the past decade, increasing attention has been given to the vulnerability of individuals in coping with personal crises as well as their capability for using help.

Crisis-oriented short-term casework combines observations about what happens to people in times of personal crisis with the increasing evidence that many people can be helped in relatively brief periods of time. Lydia Rapaport identified the antecedents of a state of crisis:[27]

> Three interrelated factors produce a state of crisis: (1) one or a series of hazardous events which pose some threat; (2) a threat to current or past instinctual needs which are symbolically linked to earlier threats that result in vulnerability or conflict; and (3) an inability to respond with adequate coping mechanisms.

In crisis the individual experiences a high degree of personal upset and helplessness resulting in anxiety, shame, guilt, hostility, and a lessening of ability to think. A person's capacity for confidence about resolutions of his predicament is diminished.

Favorable results in helping can accrue in a rather brief period of time without going into treatment in depth. Helping is characterized by:[28]

> 1 Rapid access to and activity with the person needing help.
> 2 Immediate and direct dealing with the feelings of the individual—a sort of skilled emotional first aid—and at the same time a clarification of the problem and its dimensions.
> 3 Rationally directed and purposefully focused activity on the part of the worker. The worker takes an active role in doing what is necessary in helping to resolve the crisis.
> 4 Worker activity which is geared to enlarging the client's sense of autonomy and mastery of his situation as soon as possible.

The primary values of this approach are immediacy in entering into the helping situation and dealing with emotional upset, brevity of the service, and evidence of effectiveness.

Task-centered Casework

Task-centered casework has been developed by Reid and Epstein.[29] This model incorporates some elements of crisis intervention and the problem-solving and functional approaches. It is based in part on studies by Reid and Shyne[30] of short-term casework.

The problems perceived by the client are considered in the initial interview or two. The target problem is agreed upon by client and worker. A task related to the resolution of the target problem is specified, and the activities of both client and worker in accomplishing the task are delineated. The task represents both an immediate goal for the client and a means of achieving a larger goal. The worker and client decide on the time necessary to achieve the task—usually not more than eight to twelve interviews, say, two to four months. More than one task may be worked on simultaneously, although diffusion of efforts on multiple tasks is not seen as desirable. A succession of target problems or tasks can be worked on through repeating the process.[31] This model provides a basis for evaluation of the service given by both client and worker. The use of defined time limits may well enhance productive activity in problem solving by both worker and client.

Behavior Modification

During the past few years learning theory also has been increasingly applied to helping individuals. All behavior, including social behavior, is considered to be learned. Problematic behavior follows the same laws of learning as nonproblem behavior and is amenable to the careful application of knowledge about learning and modification.[32]

The focus of the helping person is on observable behavior.[33]

> The working behavior therapist is likely to ask three questions: (a) what behavior is maladaptive; that is, what subject behaviors should be increased or decreased; (b) what environmental contingencies *currently* support the subject's behavior (either to maintain his undesirable behavior or to reduce the likelihood of his performing a more adaptive response); and (c) what environmental changes, usually reinforcing stimuli, may be manipulated to alter the subject's behavior?

Behavior generally can be categorized into two classes, operant and respondent behavior.

Operant behavior generally is voluntary. A person emits a response to a situation, and something happens that is contingent upon the response. The modifying techniques used with operant behavior are: positive reinforcement, negative reinforcement, extinction, differential reinforcement, response shaping, and averse stimuli (punishment).[34]

Respondent behavior is not voluntary but is preceded by a stimulus which elicits the response. The techniques used for respondent behavior are systematic desensitization, operant desensitization, and covert desensitization. Generalized techniques used for both operant and respondent behavior include exchange systems, verbal instructions, behavioral reversal (role playing), rule making, model presentation, and positive structuring.

Behavior modification has been criticized as an instrument to control the individual and deal with symptoms rather than causes of problems. Neither of these criticisms is well founded. The cooperation of the client is important in helping in the behavioral approach. Conversely, being free from problematic behaviors and learning new adaptive behaviors can give a client more control over his own destiny. The potential for control, either open or subtle, exists in any system of helping. Behaviorists would answer the second criticism by pointing out that any given symptom implies an underlying causal factor or illness, and that such causes have not been very adequately demonstrated in human behavior.

The behavioral approach directs its focus on behavior as consisting of describable, definable entities. It directs attention to outcome, making evaluation an integral part of helping. It has produced favorable outcomes with a range of problematic behaviors after other approaches have had limited effect.

Behavior Modification: Steps and Objectives

Step 1 - *Inventory of Problem Areas:* To obtain the spectrum of presenting problems as seen by the client and the worker.

Step 2 - *Selection and Contract:* To reach a verbal or written agreement with the client concerning which one of the problem areas needs the most immediate attention.

Step 3 - *Commitment to Cooperate:* To obtain the client's agreement to cooperate fully in the activities associated with assessment and modification.

Step 4 - *Problem Specification:* To denote those specific behaviors of the client and relevant others associated with him that constitute the essential elements of the problem area.

Step 5 - *Baseline of Problem Behavior:* To obtain a preintervention estimate of the frequency, magnitude, or duration of specific problem behaviors. This should be quantitatively expressed and carefully measured for a suitable period prior to intervention.

Step 6 - *Identification of Probable Controlling Conditions:* To isolate the stimuli that precede and follow the problem behavior and serve to control its occurrence.

Step 7 - *Assessment of Environmental Resources:* To determine what environmental resources may be used in the modification of behavior.

Step 8 - *Specification of Behavioral Objectives:* To specify the behavioral objectives of the modification plan.

Step 9 - *Formulation of a Modification Plan:* To select an appropriate behavioral modification role for the worker and the modification techniques to use in achieving the behavioral objective.

Step 10 - *Intervention:* To modify or maintain behavior with respect to the modification objectives and the contract made with the client.

Step 11 - *Monitoring Outcomes:* To obtain information concerning the effectiveness of intervention.

Step 12 - *Maintenance of Change:* To achieve the maintenance and stabilization of the desired terminal behaviors for which intervention was undertaken.

Edwin J. Thomas, "Social Casework and Social Group Work: The Behavioral Approach."[35]

REVIEW AND CRITICISMS OF CASEWORK

Early helping endeavors could be called *moral reform* or *social treatment.* The notion of helping as *treatment* continued in the psychosocial approach. In the functional approach helping was seen as intimate involvement in the *growth* of the individual. Perlman conceived of helping as the social worker and client engaging in a *problem-solving process.* Crisis intervention and task-centered casework use components of earlier approaches. All the approaches have many elements in common. Rivalry has existed between supporters of these approaches as to the best way to help individuals.

Workers Combine Several Approaches

The majority of social caseworkers have been educated in the psychosocial tradition. Some social agencies and caseworkers use one model or approach exclusively. Some agencies and workers use a variety of approaches, depending upon the orientation of the worker or the type of client or problem. The approach of some workers is individualistic—elements of several approaches are fashioned into a single practice modality. Many workers operate pragmatically, untouched consciously by any theory, conceptualization, or the assumptions underlying their activities. The longer the experience of the worker, the less his practice can be linked with his theoretical anchorage, or, for that matter, with the practice of members of other professions serving individuals. Nevertheless, some theory, model, or framework is necessary to learn to work with individuals, to develop confidence and skill in helping them, and to serve as a guide to continued practice.

Effectiveness of Casework

Casework has excluded many of the persons most in need of attention from the caseworker, most frequently the poor.[36] Also excluded are the seriously disadvantaged—the aged and the alienated. Casework has allegedly not been effective in bringing about demonstrable changes.[37] Effectiveness of casework has only recently been given widespread attention. The results of scattered studies are negative or inconclusive.

Casework has also been criticized because workers seem committed to a method or theory rather than to human needs;[38] conceptualizations of ways of helping have stemmed from practitioner views rather than from clients' perceptions.[39] Lastly, caseworkers are criticized because they do not value knowledge based on research and do not use such knowledge.[40]

Generally the criticisms have been directed at "talk therapy" wherein a single individual focused on unraveling the genesis and effects of the person's emotions, an approach which too frequently has been applied to all people requiring individualized services. If clients apparently will not respond to such treatment, they tend to be denied service by agencies.[41] Clients who do not perceive their problems in these terms may not seek service or frequently are dissatisfied if they do. Many people seeking help do not see themselves needing treatment. They need information and advice. They need insight into how bureaucracies function, guidance in getting what they need, and help in being understood and having their rights honored and respected. They may need some social or political muscle to get something done. Finally, diagnostic casework or psychosocial treatment does not lend itself easily to definitions of the process of treatment or to formulating reliable and valid outcome criteria. For those parts of the process, casework practitioners have had to look to their own clinical experience or to the experience of others as their source of knowledge.

Bureaucracy and Accountability

Casework practice in bureaucratic structures and organizations has also been attacked. Caseworkers may become more concerned with maintaining organizational comfort in the bureaucracy than with solving client problems and meeting client needs.[42] Clients may have to accept intensive personal service as a condition to receiving other things they need, such as public assistance, medical care, or admission to an institution.[43] And finally, social caseworkers too often object to being held accountable for the results of their activities.[44]

INDIVIDUALIZATION AS A UNIFYING CONCEPT

Individualization is not hampered by the limitations imposed by a single method of helping. A client does not have to accept being sick or any other label to receive help. The client's perceptions of what is or is not helpful are available to the worker throughout the process. Individualization as the goal for services should have a continuing effect on organizational priorities and behavior. Accountability to both organization and client should be enhanced, since the model has built-in evaluation of task accomplishment and task relevance by both the worker and client. Individualization should produce knowledge about helping clients, since it can be formulated in researchable terms with outcome criteria defined in terms of task accomplishment and problem or need resolution.

The need for individualized services in our increasingly impersonal and mechanistic society is great. To address the problems of children, families, the handicapped, the emotionally disordered, the aged, and offenders, a wider range of individualized services and the personnel to provide them will be needed.

Frank Itzin

KEY TERMS

individualization
empathy
unconditional postive regard
genuineness
Frederick Ozanam
Charity Organization Societies
Freud

psychosocial treatment
functional approach
problem solving
crisis-oriented casework
task-centered casework
behavior modification
moral reform

FOR DISCUSSION

1 Are the majority of caseworkers employed to serve individuals, groups, or communities? Explain private practice of social work.
2 Do you agree that social work began with the poor, came to ignore the poor, and now has rediscovered them?
3 Does our society tend to classify the poor as worthy or unworthy? What are some examples?
4 Explain the influence of Freud and his followers in changing social work.
5 Explain the importance of *coping* to ego psychology.

6 What conceptual framework is most typical for social work? What are its shortcomings?
7 What casework approach particularly emphasizes the agency?
8 Person, problem, and process are basic terms in what approach?
9 What individual is most closely associated with functionalism? Problem solving? Psychosocial treatment?
10 What do you consider the main advantage of the crisis-oriented approach?
11 Explain task-centered casework.
12 Why might behavior modification be particularly successful with a fifth grader of above-average intelligence who has reading problems?
13 What is the major concern of existential casework?
14 What is the evidence for the effectiveness of the existential approach?
15 What are the difficulties of casework as "talk therapy"?
16 Define individualization.

PROJECTS

1 Study one approach to casework discussed in the chapter, and develop a role play to illustrate its characterstics.
2 Ask a member of a local welfare rights organization to discuss the services the welfare workers provide and the additional service needed.
3 Arrange with an agency to sit in on one or more casework interviews. What agency attitudes are revealed by the response to your request? If the agency is reluctant, are the reasons well taken? If you are granted permission, report to the class on the elements of the process without revealing the identity of the client.
4 Analyze the major elements in individual casework and those that family treatment would add. Why do you think family therapy is often more successful than individual counseling?
5 One agency has devised the concept of the child welfare agency acting as parent, which is similar to the functional approach. Read Edith Zober and Merlin Taber, "The Child Welfare Agency as Parent," *Child Welfare,* vol. 44, 1965, pp. 387–392, and report on the position, indicating its strengths and weaknesses.
6 Interview two social workers and find out what approaches they find most helpful. Collect several examples from them that can be reported to the class.
7 Write a short paper on the confusion between public assistance and other activities of professional social workers. Indicate why public assistance is often seen as the prototype of social work activity.

FOR FURTHER STUDY

Howard Goldstein, *Social Work Practice: A Unitary Approach,* Univ. of South Carolina Press, Columbia, 1973.
Allen Pincus and Anne Minahan, *Social Work Practice: Model and Method,* Peacock Publishers, Itasca, Ill., 1973.
Francis J. Turner (ed.), *Social Work Treatment,* Free Press, New York, 1974.
James K. Whittaker, *Social Treatment,* Aldine, Chicago, 1974.

Chapter 13

Services to Groups

Where is group work carried on?
Who provides group leadership?
What are the new group approaches?
Are jobs available in group work?

Group work serves many kinds of people in many different places. It involves school children, youth, offenders, the physically and educationally handicapped, the mentally ill, lonely residents of slum hotels, and the aged.

Social work with groups is practiced in homes for the aged, programs for unmarried mothers, prisons, courts, mental hospitals, physical rehabilitation hospitals, general and children's hospitals, psychiatric halfway houses, public schools, and housing projects. Group workers are utilized in street gang work, residential and day camping, and residential treatment centers, as well as in more traditional settlement houses and community centers.

Helen H. Perlman has described the recent changes in group work:[1]

Social group work is in rapid movement, undergoing almost revolutionary changes. It has burst the too narrow seams of its basketball uniforms and arts-and-crafts smocks; increasingly it appears in the contrasting symbolic garments that bespeak the poles of its present scope—the authority-cool

white coats of hospitals and clinical personnel and the play-it-cool wind-
breaker of the street corner gang–worker.

Its domain has widened . . . to include those agencies and places that
are set up to rehabilitate or restore or reform such social functioning as is
held to be problematic, impaired, deficient . . . the actual treatment of the
individual group member for his particular problems and the relation of such
treatment of personal problems to group membership and process—these
are in the center of group work concerns today.

SOCIAL GROUP WORK—A DEFINITION

Social group work seeks favorable change in clients' communications, awareness,
understanding, feelings, thinking, and behavior. The worker uses program
activities to help group members relate themselves to others and experience
growth in accordance with their needs and capacities. The group becomes a
primary means for personality growth, change, and development. Group work
includes simultaneous concern for the enhancement of social functioning of
individual members, the development of better-functioning peer groups, and the
social contribution of groups in the community.

Goals of Work with Groups

Practice with groups is based on the conviction that people are helped by group
experiences directed toward mutually defined goals, satisfying interpersonal
relationships, and shared decision making. Individual members are helped in
their growth and development by stimulation from the group. Through shared
discussion and activity, expressed and unexpressed needs, problems, and tasks
become more visible. The worker assists the group and its members to achieve
socially desirable but highly individualistic growth. Guided group processes
promote both interpersonal relations and group cohesion.

Social group work as one of the primary social work methods is predicated
upon the belief that people should be helped to acquire skills for membership
and leadership in neighborhood, labor, professional, business, or civic organizations.

The social worker serving friendship clubs or treatment-oriented groups in
clinical settings encourages constructive participation to aid members in achieving an optimum level of functioning. The social worker and members together
plan program activities that will enable members to acquire social, creative, and
practical skills. Along with discussion, the social group worker may employ sports
and games, arts and crafts, dramatics, singing, camping and trips, or parties to
increase member-to-member interaction and group identity.

The worker considers the members' interests, developmental needs, and
physical and psychological functioning as he suggests program activities.

As a unique social work method, group work often is less clearly identifiable
than social casework because there are so many types of groups under such a
wide variety of leaders. Social group work involves professional program planning and direction, although actual leadership may be carried on by nonprofessionals. Many groups have the same objectives as those under professional
leadership but use lay members or volunteers as leaders. In the mental health

area, "professional leadership" may refer to a number of professional specialties in addition to social workers, including psychiatrists, psychologists, and nurses.

Type of Groups

The range of group services may be illustrated through a hierarchy based upon increasingly difficult goals and the need for increasingly skilled leaders. The model is not ideal, however, because a group may choose several goals, and various members may use a group for quite different purposes.

Recreation groups intended to provide activities purely for enjoyment may be practically leaderless. The group service agency may offer little more than physical space and the use of some equipment. If such a group is sponsored by a settlement house or community center, the professional staff may seek a resource person to aid the members engaged in the program. The main responsibility of staff is scheduling a wide variety of such activities to appeal to a broad range of interests. An open game room, informal athletics, and spontaneous playground activities are examples.

Recreation-skill groups provide a task orientation and aim at improving skills as well as having fun. A coach, instructor, or adviser may be assigned activities such as swimming, basketball, leathercraft, or French cooking. Competitive team sports and leagues may evolve, often supervised by professionals trained in recreational leadership rather than social work. Agency administrative personnel must take into account the wide range of members' interests and skills in structuring activities.

Educational groups are devoted to learning more complex skills, often in a more didactic manner. These groups may resemble a class, except that more interaction and group planning is encouraged. Topics may include repair of the home, landscaping, or child-rearing practices, for example. Groups are also used to accomplish purposes other than gaining information. Making new friends is a common goal. Leadership requirements are specialized knowledge, the ability to communicate, and success in involving the group. If human relations topics are chosen for discussion, a social worker may make an excellent leader.

Self-help groups, as we saw in an earlier chapter, should have a special relevance to social work, but they are often antagonistic to any professional leadership, since they stress personal involvement in a problem. Drakeford identified five criteria stressed by self-help groups—responsibility, standards, confession, lay leadership, and action programs.[2] Typical examples are Alcoholics Anonymous, Weight Watchers, Recovery, Inc. (for former mental patients), and parent groups for the mentally retarded. Both Alcoholics Anonymous and Weight Watchers stress confession and testimony. The several hundred Recovery chapters include lessons from the textbook of its founder, Dr. Abraham Low, in each meeting. Some self-help groups operate community programs and spend much time in fund raising. Parents of the mentally retarded often operate schools or workshops that must be funded.

Obviously, many people use self-help groups in the same way that others use social agencies, but their emphasis on lay leadership makes it unusual for social work to play a significant role.

Socialization groups are considered by many as the primary focus of social group work, since their goal is often behavior change and increased social skills of members. Activities are used to facilitate increase in self-confidence and motivation. In a predischarge group in a mental hospital the social group worker strives to help the members to participate in planning for life after they return to community roles. Such groups offer a balance of planned content by the worker and self-determined activity by the members, with the goal of "making it" on the outside. Leadership requires considerable knowledge of how to use the group effort to foster individual growth and change.

Socialization groups also have many goals more limited than re-entry into society. Youth groups are organized for recreation, increase in social skill, reduction of isolation and conflict, and enhancement of cooperation. Leadership may come from a social worker with a master's degree, but typically it is provided by a worker with a bachelor's degree who consults with agency administrative personnel.

The record of the fourth session of a group of adolescent girls shows how behavior and attitudes of group members present problems and illustrates the leader's use of facilitation and control in the group process.[3]

Session 4   *January 11*

PRESENT: BARBARA, BETH, EVELYN, JANE, LAURIE, MARIE, MARSHA

ABSENT: DINA

Dina had called me before the group session to say that she had an assignment in school and that she wasn't able to come to the session. When I questioned her, she became quite angry and said that the teacher had asked her to stay to do something for the photography club and she couldn't tell him no. I said I felt that she couldn't tell him no because she didn't want to and that she did not want to come to the group today. She angrily hung up, after telling me I could think whatever I wanted to think. I told her I would expect her the following week.

When the group began all members were present except Marie, who came about ten minutes late. There was a very long pause with everybody sitting around and looking at one another with an air of discomfort and anxiety. After about four or five minutes I finally broke the silence and wondered what was going on. Evelyn came in to say she guessed that they just didn't have anything to talk about today. I wondered if this were really so and was again met with a long silence. I said that I knew something had happened for all of us at the end of our last session and felt that we were all reacting to this. This statement broke the discomfort and at this point the discussion began.

I wondered what it was that had happened, and Barbara said that she was really scared. When the third session had ended and they were leaving the building, Dina had invited her to go down to the cellar to have a drag with her. Barbara refused, and then Dina asked Barbara to walk her to the subway station since they both went in the same direction. Barbara found an excuse not to go with Dina. She said she didn't want to associate with her and if her mother ever found out about this, she would yank her out of the group. The other group members agreed that they would be yanked out, too. I wondered what they had felt about what had happened. They felt that Dina had no right to challenge me in this way and this was particularly Evelyn's expression. I wondered what she meant by "right." Evelyn very strongly said that smoking pot wasn't right—and certainly not here in the group—and that I couldn't permit it because, if their mothers found out, I would get it. I said I couldn't permit it because I didn't think it was good for Dina or for the other group members and this is where my major concern was. Laurie wondered if I was going to let Dina stay in the group. She felt that Dina might be a bad influence on them. I wondered if Laurie were asking if I would be able to control Dina. Laurie said she didn't think anybody was going to be able to control Dina and felt we should get rid of her. She hadn't liked Dina from the minute she walked in, Dina thought she was a know-it-all and tried to take over. I wondered if Laurie felt that somehow Dina was drawing attention to herself and thus was giving Laurie a little less time to talk about herself. Laurie said yah, that was so, but that wasn't really as important as the fact that Dina might be a bad influence. I felt that Dina was trying to find her way into the group as each of them was. Perhaps it was a shock for all of us to see her taking out the marijuana, but I thought that it was really too early to decide whether we would keep Dina or not. Furthermore, I felt that this was something we would need to talk about when Dina was here and not behind her back. Laurie came in again with her complaints about Dina and how much she disliked her because she thought Dina would be a troublemaker. Evelyn agreed with Laurie. I asked them if they could hold what they were saying until Dina came the next week. I knew that they were concerned and frightened by Dina's behavior but that it would not be helpful either for them or for Dina to talk about it while she wasn't here. We could talk at this time about what they felt about my taking a position in this instance. Barbara said she guessed I told Dina no because I had to. Marsha came in to say that she was very upset by the way Dina spoke to me. She doesn't like it when there are arguments in her home and it upsets her very much when her father yells or her brother yells, and when Dina carried on here it reminded her of home and she didn't like that at all. I wondered if the group felt that I couldn't take it from Dina. Beth said she did know Dina looked like a pretty powerful character. In fact, she couldn't really visualize Dina smoking pot since Dina didn't look the beatnik kind. She looked too sweet. The people she knew who smoked pot had long hair and wore dirty clothes, and this isn't the image that Dina presented. I said perhaps she was talking about me, too, that I didn't for her present the image of being somebody who could really control Dina as Dina did seem so big and powerful. There was a long silence. I told them I didn't really think that Dina wanted to be controlled but that Dina was trying to find a place. Yes, I did need to take a stand and would have to make decisions from time to time as to what was best for the group and certainly Dina's smoking pot here was not in their best interest or her own. I became aware that I was defending myself almost too much in this session, both out of a need to let the girls know that I could protect them from Dina and in response to some of my own disturbed reactions toward Dina. I felt threatened by her taking out this marijuana and did have some question about my own ability to stop her smoking it in the room. I knew that the easiest way at the moment would have been to tell her to leave but I also recognized that this was not what she was asking for, instead she was testing me out. I shared most of this feeling with the group, expressing my own conflict and my own reaction to Dina. I pointed out how easy it was to get scared by her and added that perhaps this was her way of protecting herself. If we needed to protect ourselves by pulling back from her, we would be drifting further away from one another rather than getting closer. Evelyn said that I really could find a reason for everything and that everything they did in this group would be analyzed. Marsha didn't see how this could be helpful in terms of what happened to them at home. I said that this was a difficult idea for her to encompass now but if she could see that Dina or any of the group members could talk to me loudly and angrily and that things could get better instead of worse, this would be good for her since she was so fearful of any loud interchange. Marsha said yes, she was particularly concerned about Laurie and wondered why she had to yell so. Laurie said she didn't know any other way to speak. Evelyn said that Laurie did. She was beginning to learn now that on their trips home Laurie could be quieter. Laurie blushed and hid behind her hood, and I said it was difficult for her to hear something nice. She said yah, nobody ever told her anything good. Jane said it was a shame that Laurie had such a low opinion of herself. Laurie told Jane that she would, too, if all she ever heard was hollering and everything was blamed on her.

Marie had been sitting almost silent throughout this session. As it was drawing to a close, I turned to Marie and the other group members and wondered about her being so silent and our letting her remain so. I wondered where Marie had been and why I had not gotten any response to my letters. Marie said she wasn't able to come, she had been kept after school the first week and the second week her mother didn't let her come as a punishment. She backed off from my question about why she didn't call to let me know, and recognizing Marie's reticence and strong rebelliousness, I didn't go further into this but did let her know that I was glad she was here. She said the reason she didn't say anything during the session was that she didn't see why everybody was getting so upset about Dina's smoking pot. She knew a lot of kids who did it, and if this is what Dina wanted, it was none of our business. I said what happened to each of us was our business here, and what happened in this group was really my business.

Therapeutic groups typically require greater skill in leadership. They are usually composed of people whose behavior is considered maladaptive or destructive. Group participation is often part of a treatment plan following diagnosis by a mental health team. In therapeutic groups, the leader generally plays a more active role in defining basic purposes and procedures. In hospital settings, groups may be created to develop group living and group governance. They also give patients the opportunity to work together with staff and other patients to remove obstacles and increase the institution's therapeutic potential. Healthy social interaction through problem-solving groups is considered an important part of treatment.

Behavioral therapy is an increasingly popular technique in socialization and therapeutic groups. Sheldon Rose[4] provides the following illustration:

Walter: I guess I'm awfully nervous. Dad says I cry too much.

Larry: I get in lots of fights, so they kicked me out of school.

Greg: Just cause I won't do no chores, my ma always yells at me.

Bruce: I don't like rough kids, I don't like to get dirty or get picked on.

Alan: I don't like nothing at all, not you guys, not baseball, not anything.

Martin: No matter what they do, they can't make me go to school. Everybody makes fun of me.

These boys are receiving group treatment. If one watches through a one-way mirror, he observes the therapist responding to desirable behavior (such as one child's offering another a toy) by issuing poker chips or tokens to the giver (reinforcement). The therapist tends to ignore undesirable behaviors (extinction) such as whining or pushing which do not disrupt the group. Should a child get completely out of control, the therapist separates him from the others until he has calmed down (time out from reinforcement), then asks him to return to the group and continue as before. There are many group tasks of short duration during the ninety minute meeting. Some are school simulated activities, others are physical games, and still others are arts and crafts projects. During most of these activities tokens are awarded for specific achievements. At the end of the meeting, each child takes the tokens he has earned and cashes them in for food, small toys, pencils, books, and other items in a "store" in the corner of the room.

Toward the end of the meeting the boys are observed sitting in a circle and discussing what each will work on during the week. One child says he will do at least one chore every day. He signs an agreement (contract) to that effect. Another agrees that he will increase his homework time to thirty minutes a day; another writes in his contract that he will play with his schoolmates a game he learned in the group meeting. A fourth boy is being helped by the others to determine what he could do to make more friends. Each boy eventually receives a behavioral assignment which can be performed before the next meeting and which can be observed by a parent, teacher, or other person involved in his daily activities.

Newer Types of Groups

Many social workers use concepts and techniques developed in encounter groups, sensitivity groups, transactional analysis sessions, and other newer activities. Such groups provide the setting and opportunity for persons to better understand the style and impact of their relationships with others. Immediate here-and-now interaction in the group is established with the aid of the facilitator and is used to further openness, authenticity in relationships, reduced defensiveness, and skill in giving and receiving feedback in the presence of others. As the social climate of the group provides greater safety and as members develop mutual trust, they take greater responsibility for their own interpersonal learning. Perceptions and reactions to behavior of members provide the data for individual and group learning. The intended outcomes are increased self-esteem, successful self-examination with others, and the reward of aiding in the growth of one's peers. These gains from the group experience should carry over to other life settings.

Groups as a Response to Modern Life   Many persons appear attracted to the potential intimacy of groups as a retreat from the monotony, complexity, and stress of life in a modern technological society. According to John W. Bennett, the central problems of modern society are the disintegration of old ties and loyalties and the corresponding loss of personal identity.[5] "The large organization and its fabricated impersonal milieu provides little of value for most people, and by the thousands people move into groups, seeking ties in common interests and

rupturing the old class lines and social categories as they do." Psychologist
O. Hobart Mowrer believes that the great masses of people no longer find in their
everyday lives a sense of personal identity, emotional intimacy, and cosmic
meaning. "The small-group movement represents an attempt to create not just a
kind of 'therapy' but actually a new primary social group or institution which will
compensate for these basic human losses."[6]

The objectives of current self-help, encounter, sensitivity, and marathon
groups parallel those specified for many years in social group work—cooperative
relations, sharing, trusting, responsibility for others, and mutual love and respect.
Practitioners are committing themselves more fully to the need and potential of
specially created groups. The combined experience and knowledge generated by
practitioners and social scientists have enabled us to understand dynamics and
processes as well as to create techniques and tools to enable groups to function
more creatively and responsibly.

Despite the wide attention from the media and the literature of the helping
professions, encounter and sensitivity groups remain controversial. Some self-
proclaimed leaders have been poorly qualified, members for groups often have
been sought through direct and sometimes sensational advertising, physical
intimacy is sometimes used as a come-on, members may be inappropriately
selected, and the short term of some groups may serve to intensify personal
problems rather than resolve them. Most leaders in the new group movement
disclaim the use of encounter and marathon groups as a form of psychotherapy,
but many persons seek out such groups to deal with emotional problems.
Lieberman, Yalom, and Miles conclude from research on the impact of encounter
groups:[7]

> Encounter groups present a clear and evident danger if they are used for
> radical surgery to produce a new man. The danger is even greater when the
> leader and the participants share this misconception. If we no longer expect
> groups to produce magical, lasting change and if we stop seeing them as
> panaceas, we can regard them as useful, socially sanctioned opportunities for
> human beings to explore and to express themselves. Then we can begin to
> work on ways to improve them so that they may make a meaningful
> contribution toward solving human problems.

TWO ISSUES IN GROUP WORK

Autonomy versus Dependence

A basic issue in group work concerns the relative emphasis on peer group
autonomy or dependence on the leader.

Emanuel Tropp discussed the polarization in social group work:[8]

> Robert Vinter . . . sees the group as the means by which the worker can meet
> individual treatment goals—carefully studied, diagnosed, and prescribed for
> each individual in the group—by unashamedly manipulating the group and
> its members to achieve these highly particularistic and differentiated goals.
> . . . At the other pole is William Schwartz, who has developed the

concept of the group as a system of mutual aid and who sees the group and its living experiences as the crucial focus for the worker. He sees the worker and the members as engaged in a common enterprise, that of carrying out the group's purpose. . . . To him the group is an organic whole that develops a life of its own and an integrity of its own, which the worker had better respect if he is to be useful.

Short statements from Vinter and Schwartz point up the differences in their viewpoints more sharply.

Two Views of the Group Work Clientele

Group work as social treatment focuses on its utility in ameliorating the adverse conditions of individuals whose behavior is disapproved, or who have been disadvantaged by the workings of an imperfect society. It emphasizes manifest personal and social problems and the rehabilitative potentials of guided group processes in altering these problems. Persons most appropriate as clientele for such service include the physically or mentally handicapped, legal offenders, emotionally disturbed, isolated, or alienated persons, those lacking effective socialization and the like.

Robert Vinter.[9]

In considering the motive of the client group, what we have before us is a collection of people who need each other in order to work on certain common tasks, in an agency that is hospitable to these tasks. This simple definition combines within it all of the necessary ingredients for a strategy of practice.

William Schwartz.[10]

Leader Direction versus Group Interaction

Group methods permit the social worker to treat more than one person at a time, involving economy in the use of professional manpower, but do not use the dynamics of the group to facilitate behavior change. Group members not involved in an interaction with the leader at a given moment serve as an audience rather than an interacting system. Psychodrama, gestalt therapy, behavior therapy, group psychoanalysis, and transactional analysis all involve more direction from the leader, whereas T-groups, integrity groups, and encounter groups involve more reliance on group interaction. Fullmer and Whittaker provide a more detailed summary of the goals and processes in the various types of group counseling.[11]

HISTORICAL DEVELOPMENT OF GROUP WORK

Social group work's ideological roots were in the self-help and informal recreational organizations—the YMCA and YWCA, settlements, Scouting, Jewish Centers—and in progressive education. Group-serving agencies emphasized programs for the normal rather than for the maladjusted. People came for recreation, informal education, and friendships provided in organized interest groups. Individuals learned to cooperate and get along with others socially; they enriched themselves through new knowledge, skills, and interests, and the overall state of society was bettered through responsible involvement in community problems.[12]

George Williams founded the Young Men's Christian Association in London in 1844 for the purpose of converting young men to Christian ideals. In 1851, YMCAs were founded in Boston and Baltimore. In 1866, the Young Women's Christian Association began in Boston. Other religious and private organizations promoted vacation schools, summer camps, and other youth activities.

The Settlement House Movement

Social work practice in groups developed out of the settlement house movement that began with England's Toynbee Hall in 1884. In the same decade New York City's Neighborhood Guild and Hull House in Chicago became the symbols of the settlement house movement. The movement retains the earlier emphasis upon self-help, community resource development, democratic citizenship, social reform, and social action. Cultural, educational, and recreational programs have continued as basic components in a broader network of community services.

Service to Immigrants   The settlement house and community center movement was related to the flood of immigration to the United States around 1900 as well as to the later migration of rural and farm populations to the larger cities. The idea of "self-help" so dominant in the American social system took form in settlement houses and community centers. People from foreign nations seeking a new prosperity and political freedom often joined with rural Americans moving to urban centers for economic and social betterment to seek solutions to the problems of their densely populated neighborhoods, to retain and advance older cultural ties and customs, and to consider social reform. They aroused politicians and civic leaders to provide health and sanitation services, housing needs, welfare programs, and recreational resources for children and adults. Settlement houses became forums for social planning and reform and educational and recreational programming in response to neighborhood needs.

Social group work has reflected the general purposes of the social work profession. Social group workers, like caseworkers, have sought to enable people to assume greater responsibility in seeking solutions to personal problems and social conditions. Like social casework, social group work aims to assist persons during periods of crisis to reduce environmental pressures and to provide more tangible opportunities to experience satisfaction.

The Settlement—A Solution to Social Problems

The Settlement then, is an experimental effort to aid in the solution of the social and industrial problems which are engendered by the modern conditions of life in a great city. It insists that these problems are not

confined to any one portion of a city. It is an attempt to relieve, at the same
time, the overaccumulation at one end of society and the destitution at the
other. . . . The one thing to be dreaded in the Settlement is that it lose its
flexibility, its power of quick adaptation, its readiness to change its methods
as its environment may demand. It must be open to conviction and must
have a deep and abiding sense of tolerance. It must be hospitable and ready
for experiment. It should demand from its residents a scientific patience in
the accumulation of facts and the steady holding of their sympathies as one
of the best instruments for that accumulation. It must be grounded in a
philosophy whose foundation is on the solidarity of the human race, a
philosophy which will not waver when the race happens to be represented
by a drunken woman or an idiot boy. Its residents must be emptied of all
conceit of opinion and all self-assertion, and ready to arouse and interpret
the public opinion of their neighborhood.

Jane Addams, *Twenty Years at Hull House.*[13]

Social Work with Youth Groups

Paralleling the thrust of social workers and other professionals toward work with
community groups around neighborhood concerns has been the nationwide
movement to create and strengthen leisure-time services for children and youth.
With delinquency and crime in the streets, we hear a renewed plea to "get the
kids off the streets and keep them busy." The development of public playgrounds
started in 1889 in New York City marked a significant beginning of public concern
for the needs of youth for activity programs. Almost all towns and cities have
developed after-school special interest groups, competitive athletic leagues, and
day and resident camping programs.

Boys' and Girls' Clubs, Scouts, 4-H Clubs, Young Judea, B'nai B'rith Youth,
and other organizations supported by private contributions and fees have
flourished. We have already learned that many persons believe middle-class
parents should pay the full cost of community activities for their children, clearing
the way for use of United Way funds for children from low-income families. But as
agencies have reached out, children of all economic backgrounds have become
involved in group programs and many cannot pay their own way.

Youth-serving agencies stress several objectives:

1 Recreational and community service activities and informal education
designed to encourage the development of spiritual and ethical values; love of
home, family, and friends; concern for community and country; and the practice
of responsible citizenship in a democracy.

2 Meaningful interpersonal relationships through participation in friendship clubs, special interest groups, out-of-doors living experiences, and competitive team sports.

3 Service to youth with special problems, such as learning difficulties in
school, conflicts with police, and social isolation, to aid the child in his
adjustment to the family, his peers, and the larger community.

4 The development of indigenous leadership through special training
programs and representative councils.

Group services for the physically and mentally handicapped are still insufficient. For the past two decades innovative youth-serving agencies have begun to identify the needs of these children and either design special programs or integrate them into groups with nonhandicapped children. Much remains to be done to stimulate both agencies and professionals to work with these sepcial populations.

Toward Group Treatment

Following World War II, creative practice of social group work in institutional and clinical settings became a reality. Group workers, as caseworkers had done years before, went into collaborative settings with psychologists, psychiatrists, nurses, and occupational therapists. Social group workers defined a new area of practice in treatment and rehabilitation of the mentally ill.

The innovative work of Fritz Redl with emotionally disturbed children,[14] Maxwell Jones with therapeutic communities in mental hospitals,[15] and Gisela Konopka with group work in institutions[16] paved the way for social group workers to modify social structures considered antitherapeutic, oppressive, and dehumanizing. Social group workers became agents to initiate and maintain diagnostic and therapeutic groups and to help create a social climate in institutions that maximized the therapeutic impact of peer group living on residents.

Federal Support for Group Work Programs

Group work programs received federal support through grants for special projects from the Office of Economic Opportunity, the Older Americans Act, and other federal agencies, leading to numerous preschool and day care programs for children, work training programs for youth, and activities for retired and handicapped adults. Minority group personnel were employed to ensure greater participation by neighborhood residents in the services. Settlement houses and community centers that formerly had received support from the United Way could also compete for federal funds by demonstrating an ability to put innovative and constructive programs into operation to aid neighborhood development. Recently, however, OEO funds have been curtailed, and continued federal funding is doubtful.

Patient Governance Groups

The groups which have been formed in our hospital are parallel to many found in the outside community. Such groups are essential in a psychiatric hospital, I believe, since one of the manifestations of the patient's illness is associated with a breakdown in capacity to cope with problems of community life. These groups offer voluntary opportunities for the patient which will strengthen his capacities to work, live and play with others in a socially acceptable manner.

In our hospital, the governmental group is called the Patient Council. Members are patients nominated and voted on by patients with whom they live. Their function is to assume responsibility for representing them in the council, which has as its assigned task that of calling to staff's attention matters of mutual interest and concern about daily problems of living. The relationship between staff and council is a reciprocal one. Being elected to represent one's fellow patients gives status to the patient member within his particular living unit and tends to strengthen his feelings of self-esteem. In the council, the patient's feelings toward authority are high-lighted around discussion of policy which affects their daily living. This occurs during each meeting as the patient seeks to establish a working relationship with the other members of the council. In the council, patient identification with the administration of the hospital begins to emerge, yet at the unit meetings this same patient may often be fearful of the angry feelings his group may express if he has not been able to accomplish his assigned task. The group worker's participation at unit meetings helps the patient to express the more positive side of his group's ambivalence and to appeal to the strength of his constituents in the unit meetings. In summary, the council provides the patient member three particular areas of relationship experience: (1) his relationship to the group in the council; (2) his relationship to the hospital staff; and (3) his relationship to those whom he represents.

The social worker's role in the council is to affect the total process so that it enhances both the individual patient's treatment and the treatment of the patient group as a whole. This group affords an opportunity for the staff to recognize and deal with the negative influences stemming from the natural associations of patients because many themes of their discussions become a part of the council meeting and thus provide a vehicle for working openly with them.

Minnie M. Harlow, "Group Work in a Psychiatric Hospital; Today a Patient, Tomorrow—?"[17]

BASIC ASSUMPTIONS AND VALUES

The social work profession, according to Werner Boehm, has three major functions:[18] (1) restoration of impaired social functioning, (2) provision and development of social resources, and (3) prevention of social dysfunctioning. Social functioning designates those activities considered essential for performance of roles in the family, church, school, and the work setting. Such role performance requires social interaction between individual and individual, individual and group, and individual and community.

Group experiences were considered by Grace Coyle to be valuable in five ways:[19]

1 *The maturing process.* Just as the family group has remained vital in man's growth and development by providing the opportunity for closeness in human relationships, small face-to-face groups have become essential in man's maturational process. Children increasingly are provided opportunities for nursery school, preschool education, friendship clubs, team sports, dancing instruction, and other interactional activities. Most children choose involvement with acceptable neighborhood peer groups, but others are thrust into neighborhood gangs.

Parents value educational groups, creative workshops, competitive sports, and other group situations where children can gain social competencies, broadened horizons, and skills necessary for living fuller and happier lives.

After children have learned to use loosely organized and more structured play groups, adolescent cliques become important in continuing the development of independence from the parental family, the identification of sex role in company with others of the same sex, the attainment of social skills and attitudes acceptable to one's peers, and exploration and incorporation of the changing values needed as the individual grows from child to adult. As children and adolescents are able to gain acceptance and achievement with their peers in groups and to achieve satisfying relationships, they are better prepared to assume appropriate roles in social groups and to take on adult tasks and responsibilities. Traditional group-serving agencies stress mainly prevention of social dysfunctioning rather than restoration of impaired functioning.

In recent years increased attention has been given by social agencies to group experiences for older adults, to further growth and development and to enrich their lives. Group experiences tend to expand their sense of usefulness and their connection to useful life roles. Old age is seen as an opportunity for the development of interests and skills rather than as a time of retirement and rest.

2 *A supplement to other relationships.* When children and youth are denied the intimate and satisfying relationships of family life or of neighborhood and other peer groups, small-group experiences in agency programs are beneficial. Adults also require stimulation and experience beyond family and home to expand their outlook on life. Older adults need social group experiences and relationships when spouses and friends die and when children move away from home.

3 *Preparation for active citizenship.* Participation prepares members to exercise their rights and obligations as responsible citizens in a democracy. Groups have the potential for educating members about local, state, and national issues and involving them in social action. Members learn how to define common goals and engage in group deliberation and decision making. The concept of "self-government" becomes more visible. Through social action efforts groups become "other-directed" rather than overly concerned with personal needs.

4 *A corrective for social disorganization.* Group experience for dealing with predelinquent and delinquent gangs in large urban areas has received wide attention. Social workers detached from social agencies have established relationship and maintained contact with gangs in their neighborhoods and hangouts. Through the years many group workers have attempted to penetrate the peer gang culture in order to influence antisocial norms of these groups as well as to provide socially constructive outlets for member interests.

Where differing racial, ethnic, or religious groups live in close proximity, group experiences and discussion may lessen tensions. Group work can be an effective instrument for the development of common interests where social differences and misunderstandings have disrupted normal community life.

5 *Treatment of intrapsychic maladjustment.* Specially formed treatment groups may provide restorative, remedial, or cathartic experiences in response to personal crisis or breakdown. Through the mutuality of the group, individuals provide and receive constructive attitudes and advice for dealing with stressful situations. Groups may deter destructive behavior and yet allow persons to examine and test reality in a warm and receptive social climate. The member is aided by the group cohesiveness, realization that life's problems are universal, identification with others, and the hope generated within the group process.

Practice Principles of Social Group Work

The major principles that guide group work practice include the following:

Social group work supports the worth, dignity, and uniqueness of all people and their right to participate in making decisions about matters that directly influence their lives. The social worker enables members to assume increasing responsibility for contributing to the group's efforts and encourages the group as a whole to become more self-directing. Intended outcomes are an improved self-image, acceptance of social responsibility, and increased independence in social functioning. Members are helped to develop trust in their ability to make decisions and to act upon them.

The group's purpose for coming together and the worker's commitment to the group must be clearly articulated and shared. A working agreement negotiated early in the group's existence serves to define respective roles and expectations of individual members and of the social worker. While the definition of purpose and contract may shift as the group gains experience together, such an agreement lends direction and facilitates movement toward change. The contract serves to strengthen the commitment and motivation of the group members and the social worker to work together. The negotiation gives members the opportunity to express feelings and attitudes in contributing to the common purposes of the group. The norms of giving and receiving ideas, opinions, and feedback are established by encouraging members to participate from the outset in group tasks. Unity and cooperation are thereby facilitated.

Particular attention is given to the group's beginning concerns and resistance. New experiences in human relationships tend to evoke conflicting feelings of hope and uncertainty, or excitement and fear of the unknown. Members may unrealistically expect total change through the group, or conversely deny any possibility of meeting that goal.

Problems and special needs of individual members become targets for the social worker's intervention. Often group members require special support, counseling, confrontation, or other types of intervention to enhance their potential contribution to the group. The social worker may meet individually with certain members. Much of the worker's effort is directed toward facilitating appropriate behavior of the individual member in relation to his own goals and to the group's tasks.

Just as the members are individualized in groups, so must groups be individualized. The social worker values the unique character and needs of each group and observes and evaluates the quality of relationships, problem solving, and the group's impact upon individuals. The worker may interpret, question, or limit behavior to facilitate the group's movement toward its declared aims. He may intervene to offer his personal hopes and aspirations for the group as a means of motivating the members toward more responsible and acceptable behavior. He ensures a serious purpose for the group coming together and encourages cooperative relationships to carry out that purpose. With the members, he evaluates the group's progress.

In social group work, as in other human relationships, communication of feelings enriches the group process. The worker values and uses the feelings of group members—excitement, spontaneity, loneliness, uselessness, anger, fear—to further connections between the members and between himself and members. According to Phillips,[20] "The worker's focus as he expresses feeling . . . cannot be his own need to be spontaneous, but must be centered on the group members' need to know and experience the reality of genuine emotion from another, if they, with the worker, are to create something valid for themselves through their group participation." One criterion of development is the movement of members toward regard for others.

Program experiences for the group should be emphasized. Program activities are basic in order to mobilize constructive social interaction, develop diagnostic insights, enable members to learn and practice useful social roles, and ultimately to advance the group's purpose. Selection of program activities by the members and the leader should provide continuity of social experiences, progressive opportunities for skill mastery, achievement, and increased group responsibility. Group activities should further social, recreational, educational, creative, or work values.

Preparing the group for ending their experience together involves evaluating progress toward original objectives. Careful attention must be given to enable groups and members to conclude the program year or to permanently terminate their activities.

EDUCATION AND JOB OPPORTUNITIES IN GROUP WORK

While group work was first taught in a school of social work at Western Reserve University in 1923, not until the 1940s and 1950s did all schools offer such courses. Many larger schools, particularly in metropolitan areas, developed majors in social group work.

Bachelor's Degree Holders Needed For many years group workers with bachelor's degrees have been a vital force in the programming and services of settlement houses, community centers, youth clubs, Y's, residential and day camps, senior centers, and, more recently, community mental health agencies. Euster reported the successful training and deployment of college graduates as mental health workers to perform group work services in Pennsylvania state mental hospitals.[21] Many states have created new and exciting career opportunities for college graduates in human service programs. In-service training programs are widely available for bachelor's-level graduates who wish to enter social work.

A recent survey of the job market for undergraduate social work majors indicated numerous opportunities in group work in medical and psychiatric institutions at the state level.[22] Jobs continue to be available for graduates interested in youth services, Scouting, and community center and settlement house work. Opportunities exist for qualifed persons at both program development and supervisory levels. Correctional, public welfare, and child welfare agencies also have openings for college graduates.

Aging, Mental Retardation, Corrections Just as there was broadened commitment by federal and state government to expand programs focused on poverty and mental health in the last decade, so the next decade may bring expanded emphasis on group work in aging, mental retardation, and corrections. The potential of persons trained in group work to contribute to these areas is unlimited. In large degree, federal policies toward support of social services rather than the need for such services will determine the growth potential of group work.

While social group workers do not have a corner on the group work market, they tend to play important roles in the management of a variety of group service programs and agencies. The further development of bachelor's degree social work programs means more opportunity for direct service to groups. This will create more administrative and management positions at the master's level.

Gerald L. Euster

KEY TERMS

settlement houses
community center
social reform
informal education
indigenous leadership
group treatment
recreation groups
recreation-skill groups

educational groups
self-help groups
socialization groups
therapeutic groups
encounter groups
T-groups
sensitivity training

FOR DISCUSSION

1 What are the recent changes in group work?
2 What activities are important to group work?
3 Explain the hierachy of types of groups.
4 Explain the statement that "groups involve learning both to give and to receive help."
5 On what type group does work primarily focus?
6 Study the specimen group record, and analyze the performance of the leader.
7 How do the views of group work by Vinter and Schwartz differ?
8 How has the clientele of settlements changed since the 1900s?
9 What was Jane Addams's expressed concern about settlements?
10 Discuss advantages and disadvantages of a group that serves both handicapped and nonhandicapped.
11 How can groups serve as a corrective for social disorganization?
12 What is the purpose of a contract in group work?
13 What are the prospects for employment in group work?

PROJECTS

1 Develop a role play of the next session of the girls' group illustrated in the chapter. Set goals for the session in advance, and see whether the class can correctly identify the goals from the role play.
2 Arrange with a local agency to record a group session. Analyze the goals of the group, as in No. 1.
3 Invite a leader of a marathon group to talk about the techniques involved, including advantages and disadvantages of groups operating intensely over a brief period.
4 Make a special study of therapeutic groups, and conduct a brief case

conference about a hypothetical patient to illustrate the group activities involved in his or her treatment. If possible, use an experienced group worker as a consultant.

5 Organize a group to conduct a limited community project (such as repairing toys or rehabilitating a play area). Report on the process of organization and the outcome of the effort.

6 Organize a self-development group from your class that agrees to meet for four sessions. Determine goals and activities. Report on progress periodically to the class.

FOR FURTHER STUDY

Paul Glasser, Rosemary Sarri, and Robert Vinter, *Individual Change through Small Groups,* Free Press, New York, 1974.

Margaret E. Hartford, *Groups in Social Work,* Columbia Univ. Press, New York, 1972.

Carl R. Rogers, *On Encounter Groups,* Harper & Row, New York, 1970.

Harleigh B. Trecker, *Social Group Work: Practice and Principles,* Association Press, New York, 1972.

Emanuel Tropp, *A Humanistic Foundation for Group Work Practice,* Selected Academic Readings, New York, 1972.

Gertrude Wilson and Gladys Ryland, *Social Group Work Practice,* Riverside Press, Cambridge, Mass., 1949.

Chapter 14

Community
Organization

Can a community worker be more than a broker?
Who coordinates the coordinators?
Is activism a new dimension in social work?
What knowledge is needed in community work?

Community organization activities are very different from social casework but more like those of group work. They range from grass-roots neighborhood organizations to local planning bodies to federal and international bureaucracies. Community work has dramatic appeal to some young people because of its emphasis on challenging existing systems in order to reduce inequality in civil rights or social justice. It also provides an opportunity to study and perfect social service delivery mechanisms and makes possible a marriage between interests in research and social action.

WHAT IS COMMUNITY ORGANIZATION PRACTICE?

The objectives of community organization practice in social work generally include coordination of existing services, planning for future services, action to expand and modify services, and the creation and organization of new services. The development of new services in response to citizen demand has led to major recent growth of community work.

A community social worker may specify the nature of the problem; formulate effective, realizable goals; chart logical steps and program strategies, develop models of service delivery systems; identify financial resources; and mount direct action campaigns to secure the service. Community organizers become involved in many social issues, including education, housing, health, leisure-time services, alienation of youth, economic and social control, labor relations, minority-group employment, and child care.

Social issues develop through processes of citizen interest and concern about the imbalance between the needs of people and provisions to meet social ills. Often communications media create, promote, define, and clarify these issues. From issues, action develops among citizens who become caught in the necessity or even the morality of the cause. From issues, slogans develop to promote a familiarity with the problem and its solutions. From issues, social agencies are created and financed after political sanctions define their social value.

PRACTICE SETTINGS IN COMMUNITY WORK

Community councils, health and welfare councils, and the United Way were introduced in Chapter 3. They are major users of the skills of community organizers, but their concern with the existing agency establishment and the resultant conservatism leads some social workers to seek new means to achieve coordination and social change. Others find ways to work within these groups to achieve change.

Neighborhood or Community Councils

The neighborhood council is developed in a small geographical area of a town or city to address area problems. Its concerns may be recreational needs of adolescents, health care, housing problems, or the educational needs of the particular neighborhood. Its name may reflect that of the area: West End Community Council, Over-the-Rhine Council, Avondale Community Council, the Fair Oaks Council, or the Two Bridges Council.

Councils coordinate services and plan new programs for the neighborhood. They are formed by area residents, with representatives from church groups, social agencies, service clubs, study groups, labor unions, and other organizations in the neighborhood. They are staffed by social workers supported by member agencies or assigned from the community health and welfare council. Often, several councils form together citywide or countywide associations that coordinate and plan for a network of service provisions in the given community.

Community Welfare Councils

The community health and welfare council (also called council of social agencies or united planning organization) is composed of a spectrum of public and voluntary agencies to form a centralized planning agency for programming in a community. Usually, such councils are organized into functional divisions including health care, family and child welfare, recreation, youth services, day care, and drug abuse.

The community welfare council also provides services to social agencies in the city, including a social service exchange, volunteer service bureau, case coordinating committee, and community calendar to avoid conflicting scheduling of major events. Six other areas of programming are also provided: (1) program coordination, (2) fact finding, (3) joint action, (4) improving the quality of service, (5) providing common services, and (6) developing public understanding. An organization chart based on a composite of several actual councils is illustrated in Figure 14-1.

The United Way

The United Way, you will recall, is principally concerned with joint financial campaigns. There are over 2,000 such organizations in the United States today. Their main job is to raise funds for community social services under the auspices of voluntary agencies. It has become clear that public monies are needed by volunteer agencies. Urban and rural problems that are national in scope must be attacked from centralized funding sources. When United Funds are faced with large health and welfare needs, they must expand financial resources beyond the voluntary dollar. This need has led to various plans for purchase of services and for obtaining grants.

Figure 14-1   A typical welfare council organization.

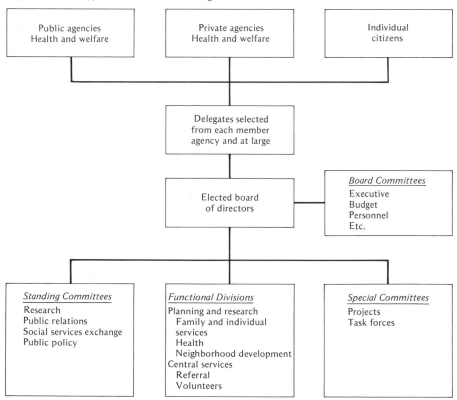

Regional Planning Councils

With increased domestic programming by the federal government, a variety of regional planning agencies have developed with the assistance of federal departments such as the Department of Health, Education and Welfare, the Department of Commerce, and the Department of Housing and Urban Development to assess regional aspects of nationwide problems. Staff members include health professionals, architects, transportation experts, and business and industrial development specialists as well as community social workers.

MAJOR ROLES OF THE COMMUNITY ORGANIZATION PROFESSIONAL

For work in various settings, the community organization professional will use one or more models of operation. Obviously, the model to be applied depends on the job to be accomplished. Since a given situation may involve several roles, the distinctions are not as clear as they may seem. Four major roles will be considered.

The Enabler

The traditional and classic model developed over decades of practice has been the *enabler role*, in which the worker helps people clarify their problems, identify their needs, and develop the capacity to deal with their own problems more effectively. The emphasis is clearly on skill in developing relationships with community residents. The assumption is that self-imposed actions growing out of a community's assessment of its own needs have a value and permanence not found in actions imposed from the outside. The enabler understands individual and group dynamics processes and uses these processes as a central focus in practice. Community self-help is facilitated through the worker's assisting and enabling participation among involved citizens.

The Broker

The broker acts as a guide in the "civilized jungle" of the service network. His function is to put people in touch with community resources that they need but do not know about. For instance, not all people who are eligible for public assistance actually get benefits. They may not know that they are eligible, nor do they know how to apply. Many people may not know how to get food stamps, how to use the child guidance clinic, or how to qualify for public housing. Community organization workers playing the broker role either help people directly to get in touch with these kinds of resources or assist a citizens' group to provide an information and referral center which will do the job. In some large urban areas, the National Welfare Rights Organization has helped to develop storefront information and referral centers as clearing-houses.

The Advocate

Workers in neighborhood community organization programs find that the broker role is frequently insufficiently directive. Therefore, the role of advocate has been borrowed from the field of law. Often the institutions with which local residents must deal are not even neutral, much less positively motivated toward handling the issues brought to them by community groups. They are frequently overtly negative and hostile, sometimes concealing or distorting information about rules, procedures, and office hours. By their own partisanship and practices they create an atmosphere that demands advocacy on behalf of the poor or other clients. If the community worker is to facilitate productive interaction between community citizens and their institutions, it is necessary to provide leadership and resources directed toward eliciting information, arguing the correctness of a position, and challenging the stance of a particular institution. The object is *not* to condemn, censure, or deride the system but to modify or change one or more *particular* institutions.

The worker, both to the community residents and to the institutional representatives with whom he is engaged, is an advocate for the client group's point of view. In employing these techniques, the worker differs from the enabler, broker, expert, consultant, guide, or social therapist. He is a partisan whose expertise is available exclusively to serve client interests. The impartiality of the enabler and the functionalism of the broker are absent here. Other actors in a social conflict may be using their expertise and resources against the client. Thus the community organizer may find himself arguing the appropriateness of issuing a parade permit while the police argue its inappropriateness, or the worker and tenant may take the position that building-code violations warrant the withholding of rent while the landlord denies their existence. There may also be differences among social workers. A community organization worker may claim certain welfare benefits for a group of clients over the opposition of a social investigator, or a community worker and a city housing authority worker may take opposite sides over the criteria for eviction used by the housing authority.

The Activist

Social workers engaged in community organization are going to produce partisan situations. The same logic that legitimizes the roles of broker, advocate, enabler, or social planner leads inevitably to the role of activist.

Morris and Rein establish a framework for the activist role:[1]

> Political knowledge and skill to achieve one's ends have often been considered by social workers to be unprofessional. We have somehow believed that strong advocacy of a particular point of view and the development of techniques to achieve those ends violate our professional commitment to the democratic process. The question for us is whether our commitment to professional neutrality and noninvolvement is to continue to sustain our professional practice.

The traditional neutrality of the social work profession has much to recommend it, but it has been exercised to the detriment of certain client groups. Morris and Rein suggest that if this policy of noninvolvement persists, the function of community organization practice will be limited to coordination. If community organization is to find a role in community development, it cannot be exclusively neutral, hence the role of activist is necessary.

Except for the heroes of the American Revolution, this nation has had a culturally estranged view of political and social activists. Despite their ultimate vindication, abolitionists, suffragists, labor organizers, and pacifists are still viewed as historical mutants by the community at large. Activists are still characterized as "outsiders" and "agitators."

However, the activist role is a legitimate stance for the social worker, especially the community organizer. The passivity and objectivity of the service professions is after all something of a myth. People are urged to action of all sorts—to visit a dentist, sit up straight, curb their dogs, contribute to the Red Cross, and, in some communities, to register to vote or support the PTA. In neighborhood community development, students are urged to stay in school, tenants to keep off project lawns, drop-outs to join the Job Corps, and mothers to use well-baby clinics. Why should not tenants who are without heat also be urged to confront slumlords, parents with grievances to boycott the schools, or citizens without franchise to take to the street in legal public demonstration as a means to redress their grievances?

The section from *Mau-Mauing the Flak Catchers* presents a brief example of activism to get summer jobs for youth in San Francisco. Since it became clear that jobs were being awarded on the basis of organizational power, the delegation had to make a strong impact. Obviously, they succeeded.

Activism Gets Summer Jobs

. . . One morning about eleven o'clock a flamboyant black man in a dashiki turns up at City Hall. And this flamboyant black man, the Dashiki Chieftain, isn't running with any brothers from off the block. He is at the head of an army of about sixty young boys and girls from the ghetto.

. . . He comes marching up the stairs of City Hall and through those golden doors in his Somaliland dashiki, leading the children's army. And these kids are not marching in any kind of formation, either. They are swinging very free, with high spirits and good voices. The Dashiki Chief has distributed among them all the greatest grandest sweetest creamiest runniest and most luscious mess of All-American pop drinks, sweets, and fried food ever brought together in one place. Sixty strong, sixty loud, sixty wild, they come swinging into the great plush gold-and-marble lobby of the San Francisco City Hall with their hot dogs, tacos, Whammies, Frostees, Fudgsicles, french fries, Eskimo Pies, Awful-Awfuls, Sugar-Daddies, Sugar-Mommies, Sugar-Babies, chocolate-covered frozen bananas, malted milks, Yoo-Hoos, berry pies, bubble gums, cotton candy, Space Food sticks, Frescas, Baskin-Robbins boysenberry-cheesecake ice-cream cones, Milky Ways, M&Ms, Tootsie Pops, Slurpees, Drumsticks, jelly doughnuts, taffy apples, buttered Karamel Korn, root-beer floats, Hi-C punches, large Cokes, 7-Ups, Three Musketeer bars, frozen Kool-Aids—with the Dashiki Chief in the vanguard.

. . . The City Hall lifers can envision it already: a liver-red blob of sherbert sailing over the marble expanse of the City Hall lobby on a foaming bile-green sea of Fresca, and the kids who are trying to rip the damned paper off the ice cream in the Drumstick popsicles, which always end up inextricable messes of crabbed paper and molten milk fat, mixing it up with the kids whose frozen Kool-Aids are leaking horrible streaks of fuchsia and tubercular blue into the napkins they have wrapped around them in their palms and mashing it all onto the marble bean of Mayor Angelo Rossi . . . and now Jomo Yarumba and his childstorm are swooping up the great marble stairs of the great central court toward the first gallery and the outer office of the Mayor himself, and the City Hall functionaries are beginning to confer in alarm. By and by a young man from the Mayor's office comes out and explains to Jomo Yaruba that the Mayor regrets he has a very tight schedule today and can't possibly see him.

"We'll wait for the cat to get through," says the Dashiki Chief.

"But he's completely tied up, all day."

"Hell, man, we'll stay here all night. We'll see the cat in the morning."

"All night?"

"That's right. We ain't budging, man. We're here to tend to business."

Tom Wolfe, *Mau-Mauing the Flak Catchers*.[2]

HISTORICAL PERSPECTIVES

Community organization has developed out of a conglomeration of practical programmatic efforts. The term "community organization" was initially introduced considerably after the birth of community social work practice. As we will see later, community social work began in the last decades of the nineteenth century. In the United States, community organization was first introduced by sociologists and adult educators during World War I. As a discipline, it has been taught principally in schools of social work since the 1940s.

Charity Organization Society Movement

Like other social welfare activities, community work had its roots in the Charity Organization Society movement (COS) during the 1800s—the first major attempt in the United States to achieve some degree of rational order out of the chaos of emerging health and welfare services. With an economic depression in 1873, severe changes led to new demands for voluntary assistance. Rapid urbanization had begun to occur as rural people moved to create urban industrial work forces. Industrialization was also accompanied by massive immigration.

Patterned after the London Society for Organizing Charitable Relief and Repressing Mendicity, the society was to provide a solution for the chaos of indiscriminate giving, fraud, duplication, and other evils of benevolent charity.[3] In its early attempts to bring voluntary social agencies together, the COS assumed that financial assistance had to be closely supervised and coordinated. If not, the fear was that the poor would exploit the available resources and further undermine their already questionable moral character. "Pauperism" was more of a concern to communities than was the bitter wretchedness of the poverty being endured. The COS movement caught on, since the philosophy at that time viewed economic deprivation largely as a result of moral failure and depended on moral uplift and proper education for the assimilation of the poor.[4] Obviously, this explanation for poverty is still widely accepted.

The New York COS initiated the *Charities Review,* merged into the *Survey* in 1907. In the same year, the New York COS stimulated the Pittsburgh survey "for the improvement of social and living conditions in the United States" financed by the Russell Sage Foundation. The survey brought together social workers and students of social problems for "the study of wages, hours of work, work accidents, other industrial conditions, family budgets and home conditions, contagious disease and other health and sanitary problems, housing, taxation, the public schools, city planning, hospital and other institutional needs and certain phases of the crime situations." The survey was a forerunner of numerous other studies of welfare needs and methods of care in many other sections of the country. The COS and the settlement movements represent the successful combination of the reforming zeal of the social worker with the philanthropic spirit and civic consciousness of well-to-do individuals.

SOCIAL CONTROL VERSUS SOCIAL JUSTICE

As we have noted in other chapters, social work is not characterized by a monolithic ideology. We see various social, political, and economic philosophical positions. Community organization charts its history out of both social control and social reform. The moralistic and social control aspects have always been most prominent in programs related to economic support for the able-bodied poor. The reformist approach is seen in the history of services for certain categories of people—the aged, handicapped, mentally ill, and dependent and neglected children, for example. This process was characterized by a movement away from institutional placements toward community-based programs providing new opportunities. Boarding homes, halfway houses, and foster care evolved out of social reform philosophies.

Much of contemporary community organization and planning continues along categorical lines. Although greatly expanded services in such fields as mental health, job training, care of the aged, and helping the retarded were developed after World War II, their service structures and systems often go back to the nineteenth century.

The Settlement House Movement

Settlements started in the United States in 1886. Community houses and later social and community centers provided a focus for a variety of health and welfare campaigns. Staff workers in settlements went to live in the neighborhood they were serving. As "settled-in neighbors," they worked with individuals and families in problem solving for improved sanitation, better schools, adequate health facilities, etc. These pioneers were sensitive to the deep human needs growing out of a social environment which was contributing to social problems more rapidly than established programs could either meet or recognize.

Hull House was established by Jane Addams in 1889. This settlement was located on Chicago's near-West side and served as a focal point for immigrant groups arriving from Europe. Students of social problems and leaders in social movements became Hull House residents, making Chicago the laboratory for studies of factory and sweatshop conditions, wages, employment conditions of women and children, industrial diseases and accidents, and the difficulties of the immigrants. These activitists also pressed for court reform and improvements in correctional agencies.

By 1911, the number of settlements in cities across the country made possible the National Federation of Settlements for the sharing of information, joint planning, and lobbying for increased funds. Now renamed the National Federation of Settlements and Neighborhood Centers, the organization provides training, offers publication services, and conducts national conferences and workshops.

The intensified social problems that accompanied industrialization became particularly evident in the twentieth century. For example, in 1900, twenty-four states and the District of Columbia had no minimum age for child labor, and other states had very inadequate provisions. There were few safety standards or sanitation facilities in factories and workshops; the employer was not considered liable for workers injured in industry. There was no legal protection for women in industry; wages and hours were unregulated, and there was little organized interest in the health or housing of the workers. As the widening gap between the rich and the poor attested to the inequalities in wealth and income distribution, a few were attracted by radical schemes for changing the prevailing system of individual business enterprise into state socialism, but for the most part the efforts of organized labor, social reformers, and social workers were focused on ways and means for easing the hardships of the working population rather than on changing the basic economic structure. These objectives were being furthered after 1900 by more liberal and more honest administration in some state and local governments, and by growing competence and understanding on the part of the leaders of social work and social reform. A spirit of optimism that the problems arising from the industrial era could be overcome began to replace the pessimistic belief that poverty was a permanent and insoluble condition.

Supporters of progressive movements became convinced that social progress could be achieved only through legislative reform. These reformers thought that it was possible to legislate out of existence such evils as child labor and that government or industry could provide compensation for accidents and for involuntary unemployment. They also advocated the use of the state's taxing power to provide pensions for the aged and mothers of dependent children. Social workers participated in the formation of the National Child Labor Committee in 1904 and the American Association for Labor Legislation in 1906.

After 1900, social workers constituted a growing politically active element in American society. With the support of philanthropic foundations they made intensive surveys of labor conditions, the causes of poverty, and means of alleviating distress. They envisaged use of state power to accomplish rearrangements of economic relationships. Professional social workers, students of labor problems, and leaders of advanced social opinion sought to affect national priorities on behalf of the powerless.

A Settlement House Staff Loses Its Building

The church group that supports our settlement house notified us that they would continue support of our service, but not of the building. We were free to finance it ourselves or redirect our services. I regarded the letter as a mixed blessing. The settlement house had been operating for forty years. Our traditional programs seemed a far cry from the community's needs. The schools were bad and the whole area was very tense. There had been three police-community confrontations during the month and a bombing of a retail store.

My first response to the letter was, "Hell, they're giving these people the shaft again." When I cooled down, I realized that we had been too tied to the building. We had done too little to move out to handle community problems. I discussed the letter with key board members, especially the chairman of the program committee, and with the full board. The board told me to do three things: determine the problems of the area, the services that were needed and how we could help, and whether we needed the building to offer our services.

We involved all the board members in meetings with community and neighborhood groups. We involved the "respectable" community leaders, the agency people, and some of the political leaders. We also asked to be invited to meetings of other community groups. I told them of our dilemma: what were the real needs and could they be met with the program in our building?

After nine or ten meetings, certain themes emerged that provided the basis for task forces: the community needed recreation and social services, day care and pre-school services, and expert help in running organizations.

The recreation and social services task force visited every local agency. They found that services needed to be pulled together and integrated. After documenting the needs for day care, the second task force began negotiating with an antipoverty program for a demonstration project. The community organization task force had to determine whether we should form a community council ourselves or help other groups get organized.

The board examined the findings of the task forces and voted to accept eviction. We decided to stop being a settlement house and to become an action agency. The reaction of the church was positive but we had some question about the welfare council. They provided us with fifty percent of our budget. The council had been jealous about its planning function. But they can't get down to the neighborhood level and we were right there. I was sure we could convince them that we were on the right track.

Abridged and adapted from Joan L. Ecklein and Armand A. Lauffer, *Community Organizers and Social Planning*[5].

Progress toward enlightened welfare legislation to improve industrial conditions was beset with legal and other obstacles. In 1893, Illinois enacted the first enforceable eight-hour law for women, the result of the labor of Florence Kelley (associated with Hull House), only to have the State Supreme Court nullify the measure two years later. New York succeeded in enacting a similar statute in 1896 limiting women's work to 60 hours a week. In 1898 the U.S. Supreme Court, reflecting the rising liberal trend, affirmed that it was the duty of the state to protect the health and morals of its citizens through its police power, thus making it constitutional to limit the hours of labor in dangerous occupations.

PRACTICE PRINCIPLES FOR COMMUNITY SOCIAL WORKERS

In community social work practice, community organization is often distinguished from community planning. Others prefer to divide community organization into processes of directed social change, management of social conflict, and planning.

Two examples illustrate the extremes and suggest the differences in the needed knowledge base. A local health and welfare council plans for the distribution of funds to various member agencies within a community's voluntary network of services. In the course of activities a community social worker would recommend additional services based on a survey of assessed need. Other tasks could include agency mergers, improving accountability systems, interagency coordination, and grant applications.

Planners and organizers need to understand the social fabric of society, community sociology, social problems, community psychology, social planning, and social policy in relevant areas such as health, housing, child care, mental health, and leisure-time services. Equally important is a knowledge of social welfare organizations, communications theory, fund raising, and public relations technology. Finally, skills in business management, social welfare law, and human behavior are useful tools.

At the other end of the spectrum is the activist employed in agencies, organizations, or governmental units which are in the business of social change. These practitioners should be prepared as social movement organizers. They need to know about community sociology, political organization, labor and industrial relations, group dynamics, political influence, social policy, and community planning. Subjects such as collective behavior, mass movements, history, and social psychology are also of benefit.

Rothman sees community organization in terms of locality development, social planning, and social action.[6] The table on pages 248–249 develops these three approaches for twelve practice variables.

JOBS IN COMMUNITY SOCIAL WORK

Employment opportunities are available on a basis of skill, experience, and educational achievement. While not expanding as rapidly as they were during the later 1960s, jobs are available for practitioners.

The concept of the community outreach worker was expanded during the last decade so that paraprofessional staff with little formal training are employed in their own neighborhoods as advocates, organizers, and referral agents. They might be attached to a neighborhood health center and organize a block health education group or carry on a local campaign to urge residents to seek treatment for a particular contagious disease. They are discussed further in the section in Chapter 22 on the indigenous worker.

Programs organized by the federal volunteer agency, ACTION, such as VISTA, RSVP, and SCORE* employ staff for direct programming among low-income people. State agencies dealing with drug abuse, health, child welfare, and mental health also employ some paraprofessional staff to do community social work in the category of "community outreach" person, "neighborhood worker," or "area liaison" representative. New Careers programs sponsored by the Department of Labor also have training and placement programs for paraprofessionals in the field of community social work.

An innovative form of community social work is the community collective movement. Collectives function as settlements of activists who do community organization in neighborhoods. Often workers live together and share income from employment. Sometimes they provide a specific service such as a drug crisis center or a runaway halfway house, or they do more generalized community work.

Community social workers with a bachelor's degree are doing most of the tasks outlined in this chapter—the creation of new services, the coordination and realignment of programs, and issue-centered grass-roots organizing. Workers trained in a four-year social welfare undergraduate curriculum are prepared for

*Volunteers in Service to America, Retired Senior Volunteer Program, and Senior Corps of Retiree Executives.

Rothman's Three Models of Community Organization Practice According to Selected Practice Variables[6]

	Model A (locality developmental)	Model B (social planning)	Model C (social action)
1. Goal categories of community action	Self-help; community capacity and integration (process goals)	Problem-solving with regard to substantive community problems (task goals)	Shifting of power relationships and resources; basic institutional change (task or process goals)
2. Assumptions concerning community structure and problem conditions	Community eclipsed, anomic; lack of relationships and democratic problem-solving capacities: static traditional community	Substantive social problems: mental and physical health, housing, recreation	Disadvantaged populations, social injustice, deprivation, inequity
3. Basic change strategy	Broad cross section of people involved in determining and solving their own problems	Fact-gathering about problems and decisions on the most rational course of action	Crystallization of issues and organization of people to take action against enemy targets
4. Characteristic change tactics and techniques	Consensus: communication among community groups and interests; group discussion	Consensus or conflict	Conflict or contest: confrontation, direct action, negotiation
5. Salient practitioner roles	Enabler-catalyst, coordinator; teacher of problem-solving skills and ethical values	Fact-gatherer and analyst, program implementer, facilitator	Activist-advocate: agitator, broker, negotiator, partisan

entrance-level positions. Many employment opportunities were developed by the antipoverty program and later have become institutionalized by state and local governments. Crime control and corrections, child welfare, drug abuse programs, and the expanding health services field employ bachelor's-level workers.

Persons with the master's degree become engaged in all types of community work. The M.S.W.s in community organization can manage the community councils, the health and welfare councils, and the United Funds. At the state or federal governmental level, they supervise and manage large programs. They direct settlement houses or neighborhood centers. As community planners,

Rothman's Three Models of Community Organization Practice According to Selected Practice Variables (*Continued*)

	Model A (locality developmental)	Model B (social planning)	Model C (social action)
6. Medium of change	Manipulation of small task-oriented groups	Manipulation of formal organizations and of data	Manipulation of mass organizations and political processes
7. Orientation toward power structure(s)	Members of power structure as collaborators in a common venture	Power structure as employers and sponsors	Power structure as external target of action: oppressors to be coerced or overturned
8. Boundary definition of the community client system or constituency	Total geographic community	Total community or community segment (including "functional" community)	Community segment
9. Assumptions regarding interests of community subparts	Common interests or reconcilable differences	Interests reconcilable or in conflict	Conflicting interests which are not easily reconcilable: scarce resources
10. Conception of the public interest	Rationalist-unitary	Idealist-unitary	Realist-individualist
11. Conception of the client population of constituency	Citizens	Consumers	Victims
12. Conception of client role	Participants in interactional problem-solving process	Consumers or recipients	Employers, constituents, members

M.S.W.s are involved in new program development, employed perhaps by a union, a health planning council, an antidelinquency board, or an area planning office for services for the aged. In this kind of job, a worker may research legislation and program guidelines for new funding and develop proposals for submission to foundations or governmental subdivisions.

New agencies in the fields of women's rights, drug treatment, child welfare, public and mental health, and services for the elderly develop their programs with community social work manpower. The demands for workers vary with the political and financial support for social services.

Much of the work to be done by community social workers is also done by other disciplines. Students gaining master's degrees in community psychology, recreation, urban and regional planning, health planning, or corrections planning and administration are competing with social workers for similar employment opportunities. Opportunities for members of minority groups are available. Increasingly, positions are opening for Spanish-speaking persons and Blacks, but for Whites jobs working with minorities are hard to obtain.

Only one out of every twenty professional social workers is employed in community organization agencies.[7] Job opportunities in the newer types of community work agencies vary. Some of them employ non–social workers as a matter of conviction, but many that prefer social workers have difficulty paying an entry salary of $10,000 to an M.S.W. They may then hire a paraprofessional. Some jobs require special knowledge about mental retardation or drug programs, for example. Some agencies show strong preferences for women, while others feel that neighborhood night meetings are too dangerous for a woman. Such special requirements reflect conservatism, but they do have a bearing on opportunities.

Arnold Panitch

KEY TERMS

coordination	activist
community council	noninvolvement
community welfare council	Charity Organization Society
regional planning council	surveys
enabler	child labor
broker	community planning
advocate	

FOR DISCUSSION

1 What is an example of a grass-roots neighborhood organization?
2 Differentiate between a community council and a community welfare council.
3 Give examples of coordinating, creating, and expanding social services.
4 Is brokerage to help people qualify for public assistance a legitimate use of social work skill?
5 Give an example of conflict between a community worker and another social worker.
6 What are the major differences between advocacy and activism?
7 Explain the difference between the worthy poor and the unworthy poor.
8 What services evolved from social reform?
9 What social issues had major importance for settlement houses?
10 Why is owning their own building a controversial question for community work programs?
11 Why are so few professional social workers employed in community work?

PROJECTS

1 Make a list of the local community work agencies. Telephone the executive of each one and ask how he or she would define *community organization practice.* List the various responses and analyze the differences.
2 Survey the members of the class to determine how many of them have been involved in demonstrations, picketing, or other sorts of activism. How was each activity organized, and what success did it have?
3 Read *Reveille for Radicals* and present a report on the methods of community organization used by Sol Alinsky.
4 Have a small panel discuss the techniques used in *Mau-Mauing the Flak Catchers.* What elements are presented in the full text that are not included in the excerpt? What alternative techniques would you suggest?
5 Discuss the advantages and disadvantages of professional neutrality for social workers. What conflicts arise between their professional roles and their responsibility as citizens?
6 Interview the head of the local welfare council to find out its present role and how it has changed. Ask him or her to respond to the typical criticisms of such organizations. What innovations would he or she propose?

FOR FURTHER STUDY

A. Michael Washbum and Charles Beitz, *Creating the Future,* Bantam Books, New York, 1974.
George Brager and Harry Specht, *Community Organizing,* Columbia Univ. Press, New York, 1973.
Charles Grosser, *New Directions in Community Organization,* Praeger, New York, 1973.

Chapter 15

Newer Approaches
to Methods

What is a generalist?
How do generalist programs differ?
Should a social problem shape the curriculum?
Will management be the new M.S.W. role?
Where does a research major lead?

At one time, if you had a college degree you could become a professional social worker in one additional academic year. The job of schools of social work in the 1920s and 1930s was to turn out specialists. To be a medical social worker, you took one set of courses and received practical experience in a hospital or a clinic. To become a child welfare worker, you took a different set of courses and had different field assignments. Psychiatric social work was a similar specialty.

Dissatisfaction resulted from this approach because a one-year professional program was too short. Also, the specialties had a common knowledge base, and people often moved from one specialty to another. Thus social work took two steps simultaneously—the educational program became generic, and the time for the professional master's degree was lengthened to two academic years. The student was expected to be able to learn the basic principles and techniques of the casework method that would be applicable in work with medical patients, mental patients, children, offenders, the disabled, and the aged, to name but a few types of clients. His special interests were accommodated in field placements, but the courses tended to be broader and more general—applying psychoanalysis and social science knowledge to problems of the human condition. Meanwhile, group work and community work were developing as additional methods requiring a different knowledge base and different skills.

In the last few years, attempts have been made to emphasize the need for an understanding and an application of all three methods, plus other new "tracks" or "majors." This chapter summarizes the newer approaches. One is the generalist—the social worker capable of using all three methods. Others are the social problem approach; social policy analysis and development; management and administration; and research.

THE GENERALIST

The generalist is most clearly conceptualized in programs of social work education, but agencies are also recruiting generalists. Generalists often develop their varied skills on the job, but they have greater confidence if they have had academic preparation to fit their roles. Since the generalist may still identify himself or herself by a primary social work method, the number of generalists in the profession is impossible to determine.

Solving Human Problems   Until social work developed, solutions to human problems were never thought of in terms of casework, group work, or community work. The individual, his family group, other people similar to him, and his community have been there for centuries, and they have always had to be reckoned with. As the efforts of the nonprofessional helpers and the social reformers were described and analyzed and social science knowledge increased, systematic methods for helping individuals resulted. As the discussion in Chapter 12 has suggested, eventually a marriage with psychiatry was consummated, and casework adopted a medical model that emphasized personality change through psychosocial treatment. But many social workers were not influenced much by the medical model. They continued their concerns with helping a person get more marketable skills and a better job, reducing family conflict by talking with other family members, trying to provide child care, and improving housing. These activities, however, were usually considered secondary to treatment which has centered directly on a better self-concept or an increase in ego strength.

Use of Groups   To help people in their personality development groups were used increasingly. Learning to share with others in organized activities provided transferable skills for learning to work with others. Recreational skills enhanced personal satisfaction and group acceptance. Cooperative projects under effective leaders taught skills in personal interaction. People with particular problems or handicaps were able to see that others had the same difficulties and that better means of coping could be learned from each other as well as from a leader. Groups could plan to do things together that they never would have considered doing as individuals. The family was discovered by both caseworkers and group workers as the most significant small group. Goals for the individual were often facilitated or constrained by other family members, so caseworkers began working with total family groups. Agencies with group services also hired caseworkers to supplement group sessions.

Community Work   Meanwhile, the social work community was developing its own organizational structure. Welfare councils did community planning and coordinated agency programs. Neighborhood improvement groups were formed to obtain concessions from the city council, to put pressure on local property owners, to sponsor or oppose political candidates, or to apply for grants. Often the major task was to work not with the whole community but with subgroups. To affect decision making, the community worker also had to single out individuals to try to change their values and to change their minds on issues.

A Combination of Skills   A variety of skills are often needed in the same person. Just as social workers did not want to be limited to one field, they also began to see one method as too limiting. Schools of social work looked for new ways to skin the cat—to somehow combine the skills and experiences required for the three methods in a more adequate package. Sometimes the attempt was complete; in others it was partial.

One approach was to skin the old cat very carefully and to skin another one or two quickly—to concentrate on a major method and supplement it with a survey of the others. Casework students, for instance, were expected to have knowledge of group work or community work for caseworkers, or both. Students often felt they got only a smattering of the "minor" methods unrelated to the primary method.

Another approach was to cross-breed the three cats into two. Casework and group work were put together as "social treatment." Group work and community work were combined into "intervention with groups and communities."

A more exciting way was the generalist model, a different cat. This model involves identifying and analyzing the interventive behaviors appropriate to social work and providing experience with them. The worker must perform a wide range of tasks related to provision and management of direct service, the development of social policy, and the facilitation of social change. As paraprofessionals perform more of the direct service tasks, the professional social worker is encouraged to move into middle-level management of the social services, thus enhancing his role as a generalist.

A specific definition of a social work generalist is difficult. A short definition is about as satisfying as the psychological definition, "Intelligence is what the intelligence test measures": A generalist is as a generalist does.

The Generalist Is Not New

The generalist label is new, but the generalist is not. Especially in rural areas, social workers have been expected to undertake a range of intervention strategies. Their own inventiveness has extended that range. Their roles have included services to individuals and groups. Community planning and advocacy efforts have often been born of necessity more than design. Workers gained versatility and competence through practical experience and an occasional short course or workshop. These generalists have most often been women who changed jobs

"A famous generalist."

infrequently and had deep roots in the community. They knew everyone, and everyone knew them. They were publicly identified with social work practice and had no desire to hide in a bureaucracy. As client advocates, they expected to be equally effective with clients and with the power structure. They did not hesitate to enlist other agencies on behalf of a client and often called staff members of several agencies together to plan jointly on a case. Organizing and leading groups, developing new resources and facilities, promoting better schools and improved housing was their responsibility, too. Hours were spent in meetings outside traditional work time. Roles as agency employees and as concerned citizens were seldom clearly separated. What these social workers did and how they did it were highly individual, and there was little documentation of methods or outcome.

Although the home-grown generalists developed mainly in rural areas, a similar need exists in urban agencies. *Service advocacy* that pushes all relevant community institutions to meet a client's needs is essential. Family treatment typically requires the application of both individual and group principles. Community centers find that individual counseling is needed to supplement work in groups. The leader in many instances may also work best with individuals from the group. In affecting the behavior of an individual or of a group, changes in the environment or the opportunity structure may be required to make individual change possible. The worker serving the client may be best equipped to carry out this role. This suggests the close linkages among individual, group, and community intervention. Living in the community where he works helps, too. Then both his skills and concerns may be much more sharply focused.

To tie one's expertise to one single method may be uneconomical and unpromising. The small voluntary agency finds that it cannot afford a variety of specialists, and the large public agency has learned that to be effective it cannot separate individual and family improvement from societal change. For those who see the world in holistic terms, the generalist has come to represent the most promising solution.

Educational Formats

The Bachelor of Social Work* program is seen by some social workers as the most appropriate point to emphasize generalist preparation. The generalist is capable of making a diagnosis, that is, an accurate evaluation of a given situation, and is competent to deal with the more usual forms of dysfunctioning while able to work with different targets, individuals, groups, organizations, and communities.[1]

The Southern Regional Education Board defines the core of competence of social welfare as "all of that area of human endeavor in which the worker uses himself as an agent to assist individuals, families, and communities to better cope with social crises and stresses, to prevent and alleviate social stresses, and to function effectively in areas of social living." The following areas are included: public welfare, child welfare, mental health, corrections, vocational counseling and rehabilitation, community action, and community development.[2]

Other Variations   The generalist emphasis can provide a foundation for specialization. The generalist B.S.W. may be followed by a specialized M.S.W., or a generalist program for the first year of graduate education may precede a second year that involves specialization. Another format begins with the more tangible specialization and follows it with generalist content and experience.

There are also generalist models for the total M.S.W. The program at the University of Chicago presented this statement of rationale:[3]

> Encouraged by support and clarification of our concerns and intentions and the implied specification of new directions for exploration, we proceeded to define and develop our view of a generalist form of practice. We believed that such a practice must be marked by a solution-seeking emphasis as opposed to the methods orientation of traditional practice or combined methods. A generalist practice could be developed, we concluded, by (1) being responsive to leads from practice; (2) utilizing a problem-solving approach as the major organizing principle; (3) turning to the practice literatures and skills of all three practice methods for intervention, planning, and implementation; and (4) focusing on the relationships between change and stability that are germane to each problem situation.
>
> Our particular approach to generalist practice as it finally evolved was developed in response both to renewed and changing awareness of the dynamic interrelationship of the individual to his total environment and to an increased awareness of the limitations imposed on the worker's role. We contended that a strict adherence to a methods orientation limits the perceptions and activity of social work practitioners. This point of view gave us a new feeling for the long-held social work principle that human

---

*The terms for the degree may differ, but should be considered interchangeable. Bachelor of Arts in Social Work, Bachelor of Science in Social Work, and Bachelor of Social Service are common titles. Bachelor of Social Work is used here for the sake of simplicity.

problems, multi-caused and multifaceted as they are, result in far-reaching cause-effect spirals. We also believed that agency structure, policy, and procedures too often hinder problem-solving activity rather than encourage or support it. The nature of the problem is the crucial determining factor in interventions. It follows that solutions to and prevention of problems frequently require a multiplicity of methods in the interventions; agency flexibility and expanded community effort are essential to support practice that is guided by the nature of the problem.

Our conception of generalist practice requires a worker to assist individuals, families, small groups, and larger social systems to work on change that promotes the best possible relationship between people and their environment. In this process, all social work methods, traditional and innovative, are utilized singly or in combination to meet reality needs and to alleviate stresses in ways that enhance or strengthen the inherent capacities of client systems. Generalist practice is addressed to the solution and/or prevention of problems at all levels of intervention—intrapersonal, familial, interpersonal, organizational, community, institutional, and societal. Commonly, more than one aspect of a given problem may be dealt with simultaneously. There is an effort to establish and review the necessary balance between change and stability in every situation and to identify areas that may require stabilization if the desired change is to take place and to survive.

The generalist social worker is a practitioner who usually is first involved in the problem-solving process with individuals or groups who are having problems in social functioning. Social functioning refers to the life-tasks required of people and their efforts to cope with them.[5] Exploration of these problems focuses on those social, cultural, and institutional antecedents in the larger social system that are adversely influencing the clients' lives and coping efforts. This process of problem identification and definition is the joint endeavor of client and worker. Plans are also formulated collaboratively and interventions leading to solutions are outlined. In these two stages of the problem-solving process (problem identification and problem assessment) the worker has two judgments to make. One is the level or levels at which intervention should take place. The other is the specific plan of action to guide the actual interventive efforts. Systematic assessment guides the first decision in ways that avoid premature closure on the object of change (problem) and the means to be employed. Assessment also assists in the determination of the social problem context in which the problem-solving will be done.

A specific assessment and plan for action may be drawn from any one or any combination of the practice methods. Each practice method is seen as a repertoire of specific approaches. To analyze and address each problem situation, the worker attempts to match specific approaches to the problems. In this way, already established knowledge is eclectically utilized, and additional modes can be developed to meet new challenges to the profession.

How Programs Differ   The key differences among generalist educational programs come in the independence or integration of generalist and specialist training, the extent of versatility expected in role behaviors, and the terminal level of skills considered to constitute successful outcomes of professional education. Many social workers and students believe that the generalist concept represents the essence of social work. They see the worker as an advocate who should make societal systems responsive to the needs of those he serves. He deals with the client's feelings and gives him more confidence. He helps the client define his problems and their priorities. He may need to bring his client together with other similar people for better understanding or for the greater power that comes from group membership. The generalist represents the client in dealings with other agencies or groups—not with vague or routine referrals, but as one who helps him negotiate the system. He looks at the adequacy of existing services and their implied values and operating policies. Often the major goal is to make existing services more accessible or more responsive. When there are significant gaps, he may have to help organize new programs and negotiate their acceptance by power groups and by the public. When there are policies that are unfair, he may be able to break down the barriers. When money is needed, he has to find it. When a program is inefficient, he can make that judgment accurately and determine the reasons why.

Like the early heroes of American social work, the generalist sees that the environment can be the major target for change and that the environmental change often must precede changes in the psyche. As a citizen in his time away from the job, he is active in a range of organizations that can use both his knowledge and his energy. Protest is often useful, but he also appreciates and uses more subtle forms of persuasion. He is critical of his own organization as well as of others. He must also be able to challenge the effectiveness of his own efforts. When there are ethical conflicts, he may have to risk his job for what he believes.

Field Experiences for the Generalist

The development of bachelor's-level programs makes it much easier to provide a generalist foundation, including an appropriate field placement. Students should be able to complete a master's degree in one additional year and have the range of experiences needed to meet the goals of the generalist model.

Types of Placement   For the generalist, a *block* field placement—in which the student is available virtually full time to work intensively with the social services of the community—is generally preferable to a placement operating concurrently with classroom work. Availability of the student to meet crises is especially important. If placements are *concurrent* with classroom work, the student does not have the same opportunity for sustained effort, and there may be tension between field and classroom demands. Most concurrent programs do not succeed in integrating classroom and field experience, although integration is a potential advantage.

A Key Element   Perhaps the greatest test of generalist programs comes in the available field placements. Whereas students may see themselves as potential agents of social change, their practical experience may still be limited to one traditional social work method. Then the experience is inadequate.

The content of field instruction is important. Special faculty skills are needed to provide the necessary variety of experiences often beyond the limits of a single agency. Schools of social work have found that operating their own service units or having direct control over an agency program may make it possible to provide a better generalist learning experience. Schools have also provided student placements in their own service projects operated through grants. Sometimes agencies that employ no other social workers are used effectively if a faculty member is responsible for planning and monitoring the learning experiences of the student.

THE SOCIAL PROBLEM APPROACH

Schools of social work have also been innovative and built their curriculums around the study of intervention in selected social problems. Some of the problems selected are broad, others are more narrow. Examples include (1) poverty and income security, (2) delivery of health services, (3) corrections, and (4) the unmarried mother and her child. The social problem approach may be used either for development of generalists or for students who are interested in the traditional social work methods.

In a fully integrated curriculum, courses in social policy and planning, human behavior and social environment, social work intervention, research, and administration can all concentrate on the same social problem.

An Illustrative Problem

Taking the unmarried mother and her child as the social problem, for example, social policy courses may concentrate on legal rights and constraints and on service issues, with particular emphasis on school attendance policies and provisions of medical care. In connection with human behavior, the differing problems of the fifteen-year-old and the twenty-five-year-old unmarried mother can be compared. Nutrition and prenatal development is a major topic, involving possible mental retardation. Maternal employment and day care are important too, especially when the unmarried mother is likely to want to keep her child. Obviously adoption is another relevant subject for those who surrender a child.

Research   Projects can be developed to study the client group, the provision of service, or public attitudes toward unmarried motherhood. One group of students found that their social action efforts could also be effective; over a two-year span they were able to eliminate a regulation that had barred women with more than one illegitimate child from being accepted for public housing.

Intervention   Extended examples of help required by this group of unmarried mothers can be developed for courses in intervention—work with the pregnant girls individually and in groups, ways to deal with family concerns related to the pregnancy and to possible marriage; goals and techniques for involving the girls and sometimes their boyfriends in groups; access to the medical care system; preparental education; school policies and peer-group reactions to pregnancy; and facilitation of independent study if the girl is to receive home instruction.

Administration   In administration courses, unmarried motherhood can be studied in terms of the major decisions faced by administrators in public assistance, foster care agencies, maternity homes, and group-serving agencies.

Administrative decision making is particularly interesting because maternity homes are slowly disappearing or finding other roles. A community analysis can be made of the barriers to service faced by the girls. The findings can be presented to city officials, school personnel, public health nurses, and other interested groups.

Field Instruction   The social problem approach has special implications for field instruction.[4] Field placements are selected so that the group will gain experience working on aspects of the problem, although they may not (and probably should not) serve unmarried mothers exclusively. The social problem model makes the assumption that students will generalize from this problem to others, since by no means all of them will be employed to serve unmarried mothers. Although poverty and health care are broader topics, a program using these problems relies on the same assumptions concerning generalization of experience.

POLICY ANALYSIS AND DEVELOPMENT

One of the major interests of social workers is changing ineffective social policies and developing new ones. As a result, programs at the master's and doctoral levels now also seek to produce policy specialists.[5] These tracks emphasize the need for increasing knowledge from the social sciences—especially economics and political science. Courses also help students to become familiar with major policy issues and techniques of analysis and evaluation. Block field placements are often available to governmental agencies at the state and federal level concerned with public policy and the development of regulations to implement it. Students may obtain interesting jobs with social agencies and as policy advisers to legislators, or as social welfare reporters for larger newspapers and magazines. Demand is also increasing for policy specialists for the faculty of schools of social work and for public administration.

SUPERVISION, MANAGEMENT, AND ADMINISTRATION

Recently many efforts have been made in the schools of social work to include supervision, management, and administration to accelerate the career line of outstanding students. In the past, leadership positions covering a wide range of autonomy and authority have been filled by promoting people who have provided direct services. Especially with developments in administrative science and management that involve specialized knowledge and skills unavailable to the traditional social worker, the apprenticeship system is inefficient as a means of leadership training. Only recently have students considered work measurement, cost analysis, and planning techniques. Along with efforts to train administrators, emphasis is put on educating students to become supervisors or team leaders—managers of direct service activities.[6]

Management Roles

Anyone who has responsibility for the work of others is exercising a management function. He must constantly evaluate the efforts of his work group in terms of the purposes and goals of the organization. Schools of social work and agencies are increasingly interested in training social workers to be responsible for the direct service efforts of teams of employees involving a variety of skills, educational levels, and job titles. By serving as assistant team leaders and gradually assuming greater responsibility during their field placements, they learn to supervise others. These career objectives are realistic, since most of the M.S.W. graduates are offered opportunities to serve in a supervisory role within two or three years after graduation, if not sooner. The service management curricula include special attention to decision making, the effectiveness and efficiency of work, work measurement, and work satisfaction. Their study of group techniques is focused on both client groups and staff teams.

Training for middle-range management includes the development of staff specialists, program planners, and consultants. Especially in large public agencies, recent graduates are not expected to direct programs for adoption, homemaker services, institutional care for the aged, and many other similar specialties. Special courses and field placements involving work with comparable specialists are included.

Curriculum Content   Schools of social work have long had administration courses, but now students interested in executive management are encouraged to take courses in organizational sciences, the functioning of bureaucracies, and fiscal planning and budgeting. The administrator will require detailed knowledge of many laws, skills in personnel management and negotiations with unions, and use of data processing, as well as general courses in management. Schools of social work are increasingly involved in cooperative arrangements with other professional schools and academic departments to provide an enriched program. In their field placements, students serve as assistants to top-flight administrators in federal, state, or local agencies.

RESEARCH

Some schools of social work offer a research major to provide advanced education in research methods and statistics, with an appropriate specialized field placement. Welfare councils and other planning groups have been the major employers of such social workers. Researchers in individual service agencies have been limited mainly to projects. Research training is of special importance to social work students who expect to go on to the doctorate. The vast majority of dissertations are experimental studies that require skills in problem formulation, data gathering, and analysis. With modern computer technology much of the "busy work" can be eliminated. At the same time, schools of social work are interested in providing an understanding of research for all students so that they can read and understand published studies and participate intelligently as subjects. For both doctoral and master's programs in research the resources of other academic departments are essential.

FOR MORE INFORMATION

Social work is more than casework, group work, and community work. New opportunities are available for those who want more versatility as a generalist or who want to study social problems in considerable depth. There is a need for more "movers and shakers" concerned with social policy and social change. Vast new opportunities present themselves for team leaders, specialists, and administrators. The researcher has challenging problems and much more efficient tools to use in dealing with them.

Except for the generalist, most of these opportunities require a graduate degree. Some of the block placement programs offer paid field experiences as a financial incentive.

New programs are developing rapidly in agencies. Schools of social work have many new approaches—some so new that their catalogs may not list them. If you are interested in any of the approaches discussed here, inquire at the admissions office of several schools to see what they provide.

Donald Brieland

KEY TERMS

generalist model	policy analysis
service advocacy	managment training
block placement	middle management
concurrent placement	research major
social problem approach	computer technology

FOR DISCUSSION

1   What is a generic caseworker?
2   What is the major criticism of courses such as "casework for group workers"?
3   What two methods are combined under social treatment?
4   What are the three task areas of the generalist?
5   Explain how social workers have functioned as generalists even if they did not know the term.
6   What is a client advocate?
7   What are the two major questions that arise in connection with generalist programs?
8   How would you answer the two questions cited in No. 7?
9   Identify the various generalist formats.
10   What are the advantages and disadvantages of a block placement for a generalist?
11   Select a major social problem. Show how it could shape the various aspects of the curriculum.
12   Is there a demand for full-time policy analysts?
13   When does the social worker begin to function as a manager?
14   Why is the team discussed in connection with management training?
15   What are the most important skills for a research major in social work?
16   Why is change in social work education so rapid?

PROJECTS

1   Develop and compare a course of study for a social work generalist at the B.S.W. level. Assume that 30 semester hours of social work courses were

required. What social science courses would you require from other departments?

2   Find out from the local Welfare Council which agencies employ generalists. Interview several of the staff members, preferably from different agencies. Compare their roles. What proportion of their efforts would be classified under each of the three traditional methods?

3   Develop a role play for the meeting of a team in a specific social work agency. Show how the team method leads to different methods of communication. Describe the use of the secretary. (References on teams in the chapter will be helpful.)

4   Organize a panel discussion on how management of nonprofit agencies differs from that of businesses making a profit. Previous chapters in this book will suggest some of the specific issues.

5   Get examples of annual reports of agencies. What kinds of data are reported? Are any of the agencies conducting special research studies? Find out more about them. Are social workers in charge of the studies? If so, what are their qualifications?

6   Poll several agency executives to find out what kinds of research they would like to see carried out. Determine whether the questions proposed are significant and reasonable.

7   Organize a faculty panel to describe and assess new developments in curriculum formats, including those in the chapter. Compare their responses with your own ideas.

FOR FURTHER STUDY

Curriculum Building for the Continuum in Social Welfare Education, State University System of Florida, Tallahassee, 1972.

Carol H. Meyer, *Social Work Practice: A Response to the Urban Crisis,* Free Press, New York, 1970.

Robert J. Teare and Harold L. McPheeters, *Manpower Utilization in Social Welfare,* Southern Regional Education Board, Atlanta, 1970. This publication presents a generalist model for the B.S.W.

Harold H. Weisman (Ed.), *The New Social Work,* Association Press, New York, 1969.

Part Four

Target Groups
for Social Services

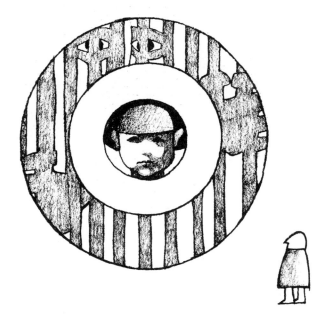

While social workers are involved with a wide variety of people, knowledge of the special problems of several target groups is increasingly needed. Many social workers become specialists with a particular clientele.

This section will consider:

The child and the family, including the child without an adequate family
The person with emotional problems and the complex of mental health services

Handicaps and the means of rehabilitation
The offender and the corrections systems
The aged, who challenge us to "add life to their years"

What target group particularly interests you?
What special skills are required to serve it?

Chapter 16

Children in Need
of Protection

Do children have any rights?
Does child abuse happen by chance?
Day care—for whose children and why do we need it?
Are there any social utilities for children and their families?

Children in need of protection usually become the concern of "child welfare" that attempts to further the well-being of individual children, to strengthen family life, and to advance the welfare of all children and young persons.

CHILD WELFARE—A DEFINITION

A narrow definition of child welfare that persists in many communities is the arrangement of long-term care of children outside their own homes. Children who need this service have lost their homes through parental neglect or abuse or through unfortunate circumstances beyond their parents' control. In this chapter we shall consider children in need of protection from a broad perspective of programs and public policy issues directly related to the fulfillment of the rights of all children and young persons.

Other Disciplines In child welfare, unlike health and corrections, services are under the primary control of the social work profession. Nevertheless, child welfare practice joins with other disciplines and interests in taking responsibility for individual children. Child welfare workers and administrators are called upon to collaborate with police, court staff, public school personnel and early child-hood educators, medical personnel, and psychiatric and psychological staff of clinics and hospitals, as well as a variety of public officials. These persons must cooperate closely if the best interests of children are to be served.

Social agencies giving service to children and their families may offer a variety of programs—counseling of children and their parents, either individually or in groups; day care of children in family homes or centers; advising and planning with an unwed pregnant girl about abortion or completion of the pregnancy and keeping the baby or adoption; helping parents of children who are neglected or abused; placing a homemaker with a family during a period of crisis which prevents the mother from caring for her children; studying child care situations and making decisions about issuing a license; and placing children in foster or adoptive homes. Some agencies specialize in only one or two of the services, typically foster care, adoption, or child protection.

Sponsorship Child welfare service may be under public, voluntary, or proprietary auspices (sometimes referred to as "commercial" to identify its profit-making intent). Social services are also provided for children in the public schools, courts, and hospitals.

Educational Requirements Child welfare agencies employ social workers with different levels of education and training. Most direct service is given by persons with bachelor's degrees. Supervision, consultation, program development, and other service management tasks usually require graduate social work education. Persons who have completed high school or a two-year community college program frequently are employed in a range of child care duties and direct service activities.

WHY DO SOME CHILDREN NEED SOCIAL SERVICES?

Child Population

The 1970 White House Conference on Children reported that children under eighteen years of age—about 71 million of them—make up over one-third of the nation's population. About 94 percent of our population live in family units. Most children, over 85 percent of them, live with two parents. For 10 percent their mother is the single head of the family. (In one-fourth of this 10 percent, the father is dead; in one-half there is divorce, desertion, separation, or illegitimacy; in the remaining fourth the father is in military service, an institution, or working continually away from home.) One percent of children are cared for by relatives or by non-family members.[1]

Most children and young people are city dwellers; two-thirds live in or near a city. The majority of urban nonwhite children live in central cities, while the majority of white children live in suburbs. Yet three times as many white as nonwhite children live in central cities. For an accurate understanding one must distinguish between *numbers* and *proportions*.

The majority of nonwhite children are poor; yet the majority of poor children are white.

Problems of Children and Young Persons

Millions of children grow up under economic, social, or psychological conditions which hinder their optimum development. Conditions within the neighborhood and community are the primary cause of many problems. National issues and influences and the resultant neglect of the family as a unit of attention and concern in public social policy are also important.

Effects of Poverty For many children there is destructive or poorly functioning family life due to poverty. The unfavorable influences of poverty begin early for children, even during the prenatal period, and continue for a long time—too often through all their lives. Poverty and slum conditions deny children adequate nutrition, clothing, medical care, and even sleep and rest. Their housing is usually dilapidated and crowded, and they are likely to have to share it with others in addition to their own parents and brothers and sisters. Their neighborhoods, too, are usually drab and ugly and lack the quality of public services found in higher-income neighborhoods. The street with its hostilities and violence must be their playground, not spacious lawns or parks.

Migrant Labor Despite child labor laws, some children lack sufficient protection from harmful work situations, especially children of migrant agricultural workers, who most often are black, Chicano, or Puerto Rican. An investigation of child labor abuses on farms in the 1970s found widespread unregulated child labor, with children "stooping and crawling" in intense heat for 10 hours a day. Because many such working children never appear on school census reports or employment records, the exact number of child laborers on industrialized farms is unknown. Estimates run as high as 300,000. In the Willamette Valley of Oregon (the area with the largest population of migrant and seasonal farm labor), 75 percent of the seasonal work force harvesting beans and strawberries are children.[2] The result is reminiscent of child labor in tenement sweatshops and factories—children deprived of a normal period of growth and education by too little food and rest and too much work at too early an age.

Impersonal Guardianship Although most children live with their own parents who serve as their legal guardians, many children lack the protection of guardianship. Without an adult protector, guide, or advocate these children are even more vulnerable to a disregard of their individual rights. For thousands of children who must live in institutions or in other forms of substitute care, their court-appointed guardian is an officer of the state or an administrator of a large child care agency. This practice fixes legal responsibility for the child but denies him an ongoing personal relationship with a concerned adult.

Neglect or Abuse Children are frequently brought to the attention of social agencies because of complaints from the community that they are neglected or abused by their parents or other caretakers. A child welfare agency must then investigate the complaint and attempt to help the parents improve conditions and child care methods within their home. Arrangements must be made for many of these children to live full time away from their own parents in foster homes or institutions.

Delinquency Child welfare agencies also attempt to help "incorrigible" children whom the police or juvenile court staff discover to be in trouble in the community because of alleged delinquent acts or because they appear to be beyond the control of their parents. They are then "in need of supervision."

Family Relationships Many families who voluntarily seek help on behalf of their children reflect faulty personality functioning and conflict in the marital or parent-child relationship. Some parents exhibit serious behavior problems that impair a child's chance to develop normally. At all socioeconomic levels a parent may steal or lie, have destructive attitudes that affect success in employment, be addicted to drugs or alcohol, or be sexually exploitive or aggressively hostile.

Running Away The last decade has brought greater attention to the problems of many teenagers. Some are without friends or interest in school. Frequently they do not learn or acquire the basic competence needed in today's world. Some feel alienated from their families, schools, and communities. Considerable numbers run away to another city or to the home of friends whose parents permit them to stay for indefinite periods. Many are trying to escape conflict with family members or with their parents' way of life or are attempting to find individuality or adventure in a new environment. For many of these youth the experience is one of loneliness, untreated health problems, precipitous experimentation with sex, harmful use of drugs, and disillusionment. Social agencies are faced with new problems in helping parents locate their children and reestablish communication with them. New forms of help are urgently needed for these troubled teenagers.

Mental and Physical Problems Mental deficiency or mental or physical illness of parents may sharply limit their capacity to care for children. Others have been poorly prepared for parental responsibilities and show signs of family management problems—inability to handle income efficiently, obtain and keep appropriate housing, organize and execute housekeeping tasks, get children to school regularly and on time, or protect them from health hazards. Parents also frequently use damaging methods of discipline or supervision. Many parents have unwanted children because they lack the help they need to plan the size of their family or to use contraception effectively.

Unwed Parents Some children's problems stem from birth outside of marriage. Their unwed parents are faced with critical problems about whether to keep them or surrender them to the care of others. If they keep their children they will face problems of housing, economic support, and societal roles. When the unwed parent is a teenager, her own problems as well as those of her child are compounded.

One-Parent Families   Families with only one parent are handicapped in providing a suitable child-rearing environment and normal family relationships. The parent may be overwhelmed with the total responsibility for home management and rearing of children. There may be lack of adequate adult models of both sexes, insufficient financial and emotional support, difficulties in visiting arrangements by the absent parent, or trauma if the parent's absence is due to death.

Need for Day Care   Millions of the nation's children from all socioeconomic groups need daytime programs for their care and development. The primary need for day care may be related to different kinds of disadvantages that poor children experience in their restricted environments, to the mother's absence at work, or to parental illness and hospitalization. Mental retardation, emotional disturbance, physical handicaps, or other circumstances of family life make day care necessary for many preschool and school-age children.

All of these problems directly affect the well-being of the nation's children and are appropriate for attention by child welfare agencies.

EFFECTIVE CHILD WELFARE POLICY AND PRACTICE

Children and families with serious problems need social services to support and strengthen their family life, to supplement parental care of children, or to substitute for inadequate or unavailable care by a child's own parents. In addition to these forms of care and social service, child welfare services must be directed toward social conditions that are unfavorable to family life and infringe on the needs and rights of children and youth.

1   *Social services are not a substitute for inadequate income.*

For children and their families, obtaining food and clothing, keeping a place to live, and getting medical service for emergency health problems must receive first attention. When families are continually bound down to meeting these daily demands, it is unrealistic to expect social services to overcome the loss of a reliable income, decent housing, the acquisition of marketable skills, and employment opportunities free of discriminatory practices.

An early child welfare reformer, Julia Lathrop, who gave leadership to the establishment of the Juvenile Court and later became the first chief of the United States Children's Bureau, recognized the importance of adequate income to families if child welfare services were to succeed in their purposes. In an address to the National Conference of Charities and Corrections in 1919 she commented, "Children are not safe and happy if their parents are miserable, and parents must be miserable if they cannot protect a home from poverty. Let us not deceive ourselves. The power to maintain a decent family living standard is the primary essential of child welfare."[3] Yet the effects of poverty on children and their families continue to manifest themselves throughout the child and family welfare service system and prevent the full attainment of social service goals.

2   *Social services for children must be reexamined to identify and remove the influences of long-standing racism.*

From a study of black children and child welfare by Billingsley and Giovannoni, racism manifested itself in three ways: (1) The kinds of services available are not sufficient to the special situation of black children, who should be seen as members of black families and black communities in all their variety and complexity; (2) within the system of services that exists, black children are not treated equitably; and (3) efforts to change the system have been incomplete and abortive.[4]

A historical review of the development of child welfare services brings numerous examples of stereotypes and inequities in designing and extending services. For example, a study of "suitable home" policies applied to the Aid to Families of Dependent Children program documents discriminatory practices in implementing the Mother's Pension statutes enacted in the early part of this century.[5] "Suitable home" eligibility conditions permitted adaptation to local and regional mores by those who made decisions as to which mothers would receive aid. The result was a Mother's Pension clientele—considered to be "worthy" and "fit"—which consisted mostly of white mothers, most of them widowed. These early state programs were the forerunners of AFDC.

Adoption resources for children of unwed mothers provide another example of racial and socioeconomic discrimination. Social workers showed ambivalence when they attempted to come to terms with the racial component of the illegitimacy problem.[6] Ruth Reed found that black families were more likely to keep an illegitimate child and that social workers believed that a black unmarried mother was less likely to wish to surrender the child because of her "natural affection," fewer social pressures, and the presence of relatives who were likely to be willing to help her. At the same time, however, social workers acknowledged that "facilities existing for the care of the dependent Negro child are far less adequate than the same facilities for the dependent white child, and that, even if the Negro unmarried mother should wish to surrender her child, she would have more difficulty in doing so."[7]

For a long time it was assumed that black illegitimate children were accepted in a matter-of-fact way, that they were not faced with social ostracism, and that the black community's readiness to care for illegitimate children should be seen as a positive innate characteristic rather than as a response to a lack of social services. Social workers now question these generalizations and point out that the stereotyped assumption that Blacks accept illegitimacy leads unfairly to the premise that no action needs to be taken on behalf of black children.

3 *Recipients of child welfare services should have a part in the plan for social services.*

The importance of "consumer involvement" has become recognized in delivery of all social services. Social workers adhere to the principle that solutions to problems cannot be enforced upon persons affected by those problems; people must be helped to help themselves. Their individual capacities must be identified and strengthened to cope with their particular personal and social problems. In addition, children and adults can sometimes help each other. Sixth-grade children can successfully tutor lower-grade elementary children who are not achieving well in school; older teenagers can best identify recreational interests and readiness to participate in activities on the part of younger adolescents; parents with common problems in relation to their children can frequently help each other, particularly if skilled professional direction is available.

The last few years brought additional demands for participation on behalf of children. Parents should be given a responsible role in program development and policy making in matters that affect their children. Groups of adoptive applicants and successful adoptive parents came together in Councils for Adoptable Children or Open Door Societies to persuade adoptive agencies to modify their perceptions of the readiness of many couples to care for "hard-to-place" children. Representatives of the black communities organized to lobby in Congress for day care programs with a child development focus that requires attention to neighborhood patterns and life-styles and parental preferences in child care. Foster parents have also come together in organizations that sometimes make demands on sponsoring agencies.

4 *Effective child welfare services should be available to all children and families who need them—universally, not selectively.*

Most social services are geared toward certain groups identified by categories of income or special need. Services continue to be "residual," and they are provided only after the family or the market economy has failed to meet the needs of an individual or group. Services rest on an underlying assumption—often denied or unacknowledged—that adequate and competent families do not need help. As a result, services have been provided only after the family has endured hardship and trouble, and the community has stood by while breakdown or family disintegration goes on. The residual approach to social services, then, focuses on breakdown, economic depression, pathology, inadequacy, and need for treatment.

By contrast, an "institutional" conception of social welfare holds that many normal and adequate families have common human needs and require help at various times. Therefore, services for children and families should primarily be preventive, easily available without stigma, and aimed toward supporting and holding families together and helping parents and their children toward self-fulfillment. This conception of child welfare services necessitates a much fuller development of supplementary services, i.e. social supports or "social utilities" necessary to help families meet the realities of family and community living.[8] Social services should be made generally and easily available to all families at the points of normal stress in the family life cycle rather than only to those who are casualties of modern life and in need of protective or therapeutic services.

Experience shows the wisdom of planning services with the needs of all the population in mind. Services for poor children tend to be poor services. Services designed for the middle and upper classes tend to be services of higher quality.

5 *Social services for children and families should be comprehensive rather than islands of services that result from fragmentation.*

Although child welfare services vary greatly, no community in this country can claim a truly comprehensive child welfare service. Early historical influences prompted private citizens to establish social service agencies to protect special groups of children and special adult interests. For example, numerous sectarian children's agencies emerged from the foster care movement. In addition to the humanitarian motive to provide rescue and care to homeless children, the founders of these early agencies intended to ensure that children needing care outside their own families should be guaranteed their religious faith. Such agencies have provided a volume of service for many children, but, depending upon their religious identification, not all children have been eligible for service, nor has equal service always been available elsewhere in the community.

An example of the social service system's fragmented organization is found in the development of day care. In planning and administering such programs, specialists have sometimes emphasized the child's need for care and protection. In other instances, the focus has been upon his or her need for experiences to further social and intellectual development. The social work profession usually has stressed components of emotional care and protection and has termed its programs "day care service," a form of supplemental family care. The education profession, on the other hand, has given greater consideration to the child's social and intellectual development and has applied such terms as "nursery school" or "compensatory preschool education." Neither profession has fully explored or conceptualized day care as a service for older children outside of school hours. In no community can parents of any socioeconomic group find acceptable day care easily available at a price they can afford.

The insufficiency of day care for children is particularly unfortunate since this type of care can be a means for parents to seek help with a variety of problems. Parents can often be reached through their children's needs. Yet most day care is still custodial, geared for children whose parents are working.

Fragmented child welfare services also exist in the care of emotionally disturbed, physically handicapped, and mentally retarded children sent to live in residential institutions far from their own family and community. Children are often treated successfully in these centers, particularly considering the severity of their disorders. But in many instances they are not prepared to return to their communities and families; nor are parents helped to prepare for their return to the family group. As a result, mentally and physically handicapped children are likely to remain in institutions.

Still another example of the adverse effects of this nation's fragmented approach to the field of child welfare can be found in services to unmarried mothers. Frequently, the only agency help available is medical care, a place to live during pregnancy, and adoptive placement of the baby. Yet the majority of unmarried mothers keep their children rather than surrender them for adoption. Social policy concerning illegitimacy will be most profitably defined in relation to the larger context of the institution of the family and family life problems.

6 *Fully effective social services for children and their families will require a commitment to the rights of the child and the importance of the child's own family and an active role for government in protecting children against the hazards of life.*

For many voters, the extent to which government should intervene in the affairs of children is debatable. In this country not all areas of national life are considered equally suitable for social planning. There is a wide difference of opinion as to the role the government should assume for a comprehensive approach to family policy. In what ways does government have the right and responsibility to exercise authority in behalf of children? For one, it can set up regulations for the protection of children generally. By exercising its regulatory powers, it can compel parents to send their children to school or impose restrictions on employers who hire children to perform certain kinds of work. It may also apply regulations to foster parents and social welfare agencies that give care to children. These regulations consist of prescribed standards of care and treatment to which all foster parents or child care agencies must adhere. The intent in the state's use of its regulatory authority is to represent society's interest in all children by setting standards which apply to all children or to all parents or to other adults acting in relation to children.

The state can also intervene in the relationship of parent and child in the life of a particular family. When parental care falls below a level allowed for by law, or when a child or young person engages in delinquent acts prohibited by law, the state has a responsibility to intervene and to exercise the ancient principle of *parens patriae,* under which the court acting as a protector of the dependent child uses its power to require a better level of care or treatment for a particular child. This can result in removal of the child from his own home to a foster home or institution.

A third power lies in authority to legislate for the development of various child welfare services. For example, the federal government can provide grant-in-aid programs to the states so that they can develop their own plans of social services to children and their families. State governments have the power to adopt statutes which provide for the development and financing of a range of social services on behalf of children. The importance of the state's authority to legislate for the development of social services to children and their families cannot be overemphasized. How successfully children are helped often depends upon the extent to which the statutes of a state reflect modern knowledge about children, respect for their rights, and readiness to tax and appropriate money for professional services and facilities to meet the needs of children.

Providing basic support for children in need of protection is a public responsibility. Furthermore, only government has the resources to make a significant impact on poverty and to extend basic child welfare services to all children who need them.

We will now turn to day care, services to protect children from neglect and abuse, and foster care of children. You may also wish to study other important services for children, including the child and the juvenile court; the nature and use of guardianship for children; the variety of services used on behalf of children in their own homes, such as casework and group work approaches to counseling and therapy and the use of homemakers; the provision of services for unwed parents and their children; adoption services and the regulation of out-of-home care.

DAY CARE

Some children require planned experiences outside their own homes. Many others can benefit from them. Day care encompasses a variety of provisions for children's daytime care and development. The perceived need for day care, terminology, auspices, and parents' reasons for using it differ. Nevertheless, all day care programs should include: programs based on understanding a child's individual needs and stage of growth, consistent nurture, supportive emotional response, attention to health and physical progress, and a stimulating experience to contribute to cognitive and social development. The child is not well cared for and protected if his need and capacity to learn and acquire competence are not given careful attention. His success in learning even in carefully devised educational programs is hampered if there is no appropriate response to his feelings and emotions. Neither his education nor his welfare can be well looked after if he has unmet health needs, handicapping conditions, or insufficient food and rest.

Auspices

A variety of sponsors plan and administer day care programs in family or group settings. Some are under the direction and control of state or local public welfare agencies, using tax funds made available through the Social Security Act. Public funds are also used in the Head Start program. In some localities public health departments or teaching hospitals have developed day care centers for the care of children with special health problems. Many of the experimental group programs of compensatory education are sponsored by colleges or other centers for the study of child development.

Voluntary family and children's agencies may provide group care centers or family day care homes, or both, financed from voluntary contributions, public funds through a purchase of care, and parents' fees. Churches sometimes provide day care. Parents who want additional opportunities outside their homes for their children's development may choose to operate nursery schools cooperatively.

Thousands of children receive day care under commercial auspices—centers operated as a business or day care homes where a woman takes one child or more into her home during the day for pay. Other types of commercial day care have appeared. Some employers operate day care programs to attract women employees and reduce absenteeism. Franchised businesses guided by companies of stockholders have developed day care centers on a regional or national basis, carrying such names as Mary Moppet's Day Care School, or Alphabetical Pre-School Center. Their intent is to plan more extensive operations than the family or individual owner, to develop a clientele among the better paid working women, and to operate on a contract basis with industry, labor, and public welfare. Franchised centers have encountered problems of financing and criticisms about motives and quality of program. As a result, their potential for growth in the future is not clear.

Federal funding sources with different eligibility criteria and program standards have caused confusion. To lessen this effect, more than 150 Community Coordinated Child Care Programs (4 C's), administered by the federal Office of Child Development, have tried to coordinate various day care programs in local communities and make use of funds, staff, and facilities as effectively as possible. Overall, the financing of day care has depended heavily upon parent fees, a practice which has provided an inadequate financial base and retarded growth in quality day care services.

Children of Working Mothers

The most frequent need for day care comes from mother's working. The numbers and proportions of working mothers have increased markedly for a quarter century. Recent increases have come from mothers of young children joining the labor force.

Working mothers are not new in America, however. Even before the Industrial Revolution, mothers worked many hours a day in their homes and on farms to produce goods and services to supplement their husband's income. This essential work often resulted in divided attention to children. Only in this century have large numbers of women been able to choose to be "full-time mothers," having been relieved of much housework, food preparation, sewing, and gardening by labor-saving machines and ready-to-use foods and clothing. Viewed in this way, the high rate of maternal employment today is not a radically new phenomenon, but an old one modified by new occupations, changed work locale, relationships, and rewards.

Mothers work for varying reasons. Most often, a felt pressure to earn is a major factor. Employed mothers are drawn disproportionately from low-income strata. In other families, the mother works to raise the standard of living beyond the attainment of necessities, or to help meet major expenditures such as the cost of college education or a larger house for the family. An inflationary cycle has

"Ask what's-his-name how he likes the day-care center."

caused many mothers to begin work in order to help maintain the family in its accustomed standard of living.

Other factors besides economic reasons are involved. Value attached to achievement and recognition outside the home, a means of self-fullfillment, desire to use special skills—all these induce mothers to work. Some work just because they enjoy the variety it adds to their lives, or they want to be with adults. Nonwhite mothers work in higher proportions than white. The higher the mother's education, the more likely she is to have a high commitment to her work. Marital status is another factor. Mothers who are widowed, separated, divorced, or single are more likely to work. Yet despite the greater likelihood that mothers will work if they are heads of families, in the total distribution of working mothers, 85 percent are married and living with their husbands.[9] This fact warrants attention in developing day care services.

Child Care Arrangements   Day care for the children of working mothers is most often an informal arrangement between private individuals, with no organized community involvement or sanction. The children of three-fourths of the working mothers are cared for in their own homes, most often by their fathers, siblings, grandparents, often themselves, or babysitters. In at least 7 percent of instances, the child is left alone. Outside the home the child may be cared for by relatives, neighbors, or friends in unlicensed family homes, in centers and nursery schools, or on playgrounds or in recreation facilities.[10] A consideration of distribution of children in these arrangements suggests the need for a considerable expansion in licensed, quality-care day time centers or homes.

Policy Issues

Prior to the 1970s there was no public policy to give national direction to the development of day care. The absence of a reliable day care system has become a source of concern. The result is that in the politics of day care a variety of interests seems to be coming together.

The absence of day care has been an obstacle to persons interested in welfare reform as they have tried to get public assistance mothers into the work force. Those newly admitted into the "working poor" are equally frustrated as they find themselves thrown back onto welfare rolls when informal child care arrangements prove unreliable or centers close for lack of funding. To child development experts interested in the social and intellectual potentialities of young children, the failure to achieve an institutionalized approach to day care represents a lost opportunity. The adherents of the women's movement see the lack of day care facilities as a form of sex discrimination. To the extent that these interests are converging politically, legislators and social planners are required to consider a federal policy and a feasible program for child care.

Kahn argues for the provision of day care as a service to which a child has a right by virtue of his status, rather than special problems. According to such a concept of day care, the child would become eligible in ways similar to those in which she gains admission to elementary school—on the basis of age, health, local residence, innoculation, but the family would not have to establish in an intake evaluation that day care is "good" for one or "necessary." Day care in an advanced industrial society, Kahn says, should be a social utility.[11]

In any event several issues must be resolved. What is the real need for new day care facilities? Do projections of need take into account the substantial amount of unlicensed family home care now in use which is not entirely unsatisfactory, or are the projections only in relation to existing licensed facilities? What shall be the sources of funding? At what income level will parents be required to pay part or all of the cost? What governmental or voluntary agencies shall qualify as sponsors for receipt of federal funds? To what extent should day care become an extension of a tax-financed school system, considering the problems with which the public schools are presently faced? How can child care personnel be trained to enhance child care as an occupation to the benefit of children? Considering the variety of forms of day care which parents seek, how can a national day care policy allow for a pluralistic system and a role for parents in planning the day care program? Can day care become an economical way of freeing low income mothers with limited skills and education for work or should it be viewed as a public investment for the development of all the nation's children?

But inevitably public child care programs will increase and some fixed public policy will come, either by rational planning, or by default.

SERVICES TO PROTECT CHILDREN FROM NEGLECT AND ABUSE

Neglect, abuse, or exploitation of a child by parents is by far the most frequent problem to come to the attention of child welfare agencies. Children who are found to be neglected, abused, or at high risk in their family situations require specialized protective services from the community and its social agencies. Even though the intent of protective services is to help parents improve their level of care and keep the family together, neglect and abuse constitute the major reason for placement of children in foster care.

Child protective services are involuntary. The protective agency initiates the service by approaching the parents about a complaint from someone in the community—police, schools, public health nurses, neighbors, relatives, or other persons. Thus, the service is involuntary for the parents. That the agency approaches a family about its problems without a request from the family implies some invasion of privacy, however well motivated the services may be.

Child protective services carry increased social agency responsibility, since they are directed toward families who have children at risk. Children cannot make effective claims by themselves for the enforcement of their rights; if prompt and effective initiation of services does not follow a complaint from the community, a child may experience lasting harm through physical abuse or continued neglect. Moreover, the social agency cannot withdraw from the situation if it finds the parents uncooperative or resistant (as it can when individuals have voluntarily sought help).

Child protective services involve a special mandate to the agency from the community. Statutes or terms of their charters charge particular agencies to receive complaints about alleged neglect and abuse of children, to investigate those complaints, and if necessary to initiate service to the parents. A voluntary agency sometimes has a sanction in its charter to give protective services, but even when voluntary services are offered, the provision of child protective services is a fundamental public agency responsibility, one as essential for children as the provision of education.

Protective services require an effective and just balance in the use of the agency's authority. The social worker who extends child protective services is given authority by law to act to protect children from neglect and abuse. Parents usually feel this to be a threat. An agency representative has come without being asked and has reported a complaint about their child care. When the complaint is well founded, parents must either seek ways to improve the level of child care or face the possibility of the child's removal from their home through a court order.

The social worker has the difficult task of maintaining a fair and constructive balance in the use of the agency's authority in relation to the child at risk whose rights and protection depend upon other persons, to the parents whose right to rear their children without outside intervention is being questioned, and to society that has delegated a responsibility for the protection of children from neglect or abuse.

Causes of Child Neglect and Abuse

Conditions leading to the neglect or abuse of children are multiple and interacting. In some families, there is clearly recognized individual or group psychopathology in the neglectors or abusers and other family members. In other instances neglect and abuse are more directly traceable to the social conditions and environmental stresses that bear harshly upon parents. Usually elements of both psychopathology and of stressful social conditions can be identified.

Parental Experiences   In most cases of abuse and neglect the effects of the parents' own deprived childhood and their lack of relationships to caring, reliable adults can be traced. They may try to cope with these early experiences by withdrawing from parental responsibility or by striking out against their children, who are vulnerable symbols of their own deprivations and failures. Other factors are the added stresses which accompany untreated poor physical health, unwanted pregnancies, or lack of supports which more fortunate parents take for granted—e.g., adequate income or helpful and reliable relatives.

Environmental Conditions   Lack of parental control over some situations also contributes to child neglect and abuse. Negative influences exist within a community's system of social services; for example, there may be a lack of social utilities, so that families and children receive attention long after the onset of trouble or stress, or agencies may fail to follow through on referrals or to establish effective communications when referrals are finally made. Serious social problems in our communities increase the incidence of child neglect and abuse— problems such as large-scale incidence of mental ill health, unequal medical services, poverty in the midst of affluence, lack of jobs for youth and heads of families, deplorable housing for many families, high rates of delinquency, or inadequate or irrelevant education for the nation's youth who become the new young parents.

Symptoms of Child Neglect

The label "neglect" is attached to those symptoms which suggest parents' failure to perform adequate, essential child care tasks. The child may be poorly fed, resulting in lack of proper growth, low energy levels, apathy, restlessness, or susceptibility to chronic infections. He may be shabbily clothed. He is often dirty. Sometimes the neglect involves failure or refusal to obtain essential medical care. Frequent and persistent absence from school may be a symptom of parental failure to get him up on time in the morning, to start him off feeling prepared for the day's demands, or to support him in his school life with interest and approval. Preschool children who belong to multiproblem disorganized families often show distinctive and handicapping deviations in their psychological development. Some infants and young children show a general failure to thrive even when no organic basis can explain their lack of healthy growth and development. Children of all ages may reveal parental neglect through a range of maladjusted behaviors and emotional disorders.

A child's neglect may be directly observable in home conditions that affect him adversely, including dilapidated housing without the essential material equipment for normal family life, overcrowding, and lack of privacy. The child may experience eviction and homelessness. His parents may maintain such low housekeeping standards that the family lives in squalor. He may not have an adequate place to sleep. If he is young, he may be left alone or be poorly attended when his parents are away. The home may contain physical hazards to his safety or unwholesome or demoralizing circumstances—violence, excessive quarreling, parental dishonesty, defiance of authority in society, or lack of love and concern for each other's welfare among family members.

. . . Although child neglect sometimes has striking and bizarre aspects, it most often takes place silently and routinely in the lives of children who are reared by their own mothers in their own homes.

Norman A. Polansky et al., "Child Neglect in a Rural Community."[12]

Symptoms of Child Abuse

With its connotations of violence and injury inflicted upon the child's person, child abuse is a phenomenon of medical, social, and legal significance. Each year in this country large numbers of children are beaten, cut, or burned by their caretakers in circumstances which cannot be explained as accidents. Moreover, their injuries usually result from recurring acts of violence rather than from a single expression of anger or loss of control by the adults who care for them. The severity of such injuries ranges from a mild form of abuse, which may not come to the attention of a doctor or other persons outside the home, to an extreme deviancy in child care which results in extensive physical damage or even death to the child.

How Children Are Abused   Children are severely and repeatedly hit with a hand, hair brush, or fists, or are beaten cruelly with sharp or heavy objects, or straps, electric cords, ropes—sometimes baseball bats. They are cut with knives and broken bottles. They are assaulted by adults who sexually molest them or administer overdoses of drugs or expose them to noxious gases or other toxic substances. Sometimes infants are thrown against a wall or downstairs or are held by their legs and shaken hard. Children of all ages may be viciously yanked or shoved. They are burned by having hot coffee or scalding water thrown at them. Their limbs may be held over open flames or pressed against steaming pipes. Sometimes they may be burned systematically by lighted cigarettes. Sexual abuse of children occurs even more frequently than do other forms of abuse and is ignored for the most part by families and communities.

The Social Worker's Role in Protective Services

Working with the seriously disorganized families referred for protective services places special demands upon social workers. Requirements include understanding the state's legal definition of abuse and neglect as well as the community's own definition reflected in the kinds of situations that result in a "complaint" about child care. It is also important to understand the source and use of the authority implicit in the nature of "protective" services. To give social workers support and to be fair to parents complained about, the agency must establish clear and objective criteria as a basis for intervention into the privacy of family life. The social worker must be prepared to use a broadly based treatment approach with attention to individual, family, and neighborhood dynamics.

Do Protective Services Improve Family Functioning?

Protective services do not achieve their goals very well. Many social workers engaged in work with neglecting and abusing parents believe that they effect improvement with a fair number of these families, and this encourages them to continue. Their cautious optimism is borne out by studies of protective caseloads in some agencies. Whether the gains occur mostly in cases of moderate rather than severe neglect or abuse is not clear. Certainly helping the multiproblem family or the severely abusing family out of its problem-producing cycle is extremely difficult.

Protective intervention through social services comes very late in a family's problems, after heavy stresses have led to neglect or abuse. New ways of "reaching out" are needed to help parents use help voluntarily, requiring auxiliary services adapted to the needs of these deeply troubled families such as birth control, day care, homemaker service, recreation centers, and family life education.

Finally, an agency's protective service must be defined and organized in relation to all of a community's social, medical, and legal services, with attention to coordinating these services effectively for the community's most vulnerable children.

FOSTER CARE

Characteristics of Foster Care

As a child welfare service, foster care is arranged by a public or voluntary social agency (although an unknown number of children are living in foster homes or institutions under arrangements made by their parents independent of a social agency). Responsibility for the child's daily living usually has been transferred from his parents because of some serious situation—a set of conditions or parental characteristics which leaves them unable to continue to care for their child and thus necessitates community assumption of responsibility.

Foster care is full-time care, twenty-four hours a day, outside the child's own home. It may be given within a foster family home, a small group home, or an institution.

In contrast to adoption, foster care implies a temporary arrangement—an expectation that the child may be enabled to return to his parents' home. Using social work methods, the agency intends to play a major role in planning and carrying out the child's care as long as he needs it. To be effective, this broad child-rearing responsibility has to be shared with his parents, the court, and other institutions of the community.

As a consequence of the difficult experiences of children who enter foster care and the unresolved conflicts in relation to their parents, effective foster care is not supplied by a change of setting alone; attention must be given to the child's previous experiences and continuing total development.

Conditions Leading to Foster Care

Parental characteristics and social conditions that precede foster care in most instances are not easily corrected by existing services. Although the child welfare concept of foster care emphasizes its temporary nature—substitute care until the child's own parents can be helped to restore their home—foster care often is long-term. Furthermore, children may experience a series of foster living situations.

Contrary to popular belief, most children in foster care are not orphans; at least they have not lost their parents through death. Their biological parents may or may not visit them or assume any responsibility for them. As a result, children in foster care have been termed "orphans of the living" to emphasize the emotional, social, and legal limbo in which these children frequently live. Too often they are tied to their parents by unmet needs and unresolved conflicts, with a future which promises only a succession of foster homes or institutions.

The Child's Identity

As children move into foster placement, many show an intense need to understand the circumstances of separation from their parents. Their feelings tend to be most accessible early in foster care, offering the social worker an opportunity to help them talk about their experiences so they can begin to understand and accept them. Leaving the child alone with his feelings of confusion and rejection over what has taken place or avoiding his stressful feelings by giving him too ready reassurance about the future will fail to alleviate the child's real hurt. Also the social worker is apt to lose a critical opportunity to forestall the hazards of denial or repression of the true situation or of the child's fantasy about his troubled parents.

The need to help children connect their present life in foster care to their past experiences with their own parents has not always been recognized in social work practice. In earlier years, most agencies sought to break as completely as possible all continuity with his parental home when a child was moved into a foster home, on the assumption that the child would adapt more completely in his new home if he were not remembering and yearning for people and conditions in his former home. But physical separation of a parent and child does not necessarily interrupt the influence of the parent upon the child. Children can modify their relationships to parents more effectively if their parents are not denied to them and if they are not expected to abandon them completely. For the significant persons in the foster care system not to talk to a child about his experiences with his parents increases his confusion about his identity.

Foster Care Facilities

Foster Family Care   Family homes differ from other forms of foster care by the opportunity offered the child for experiences of family living. In the foster home the child has a chance to form emotional relationships with substitute parents and the rest of the family and their friends as well as to learn about modes of behavior and family roles and responsibilities. Mainly for these reasons, the foster home has been regarded as the preferred form of care when children cannot live with their own parents.

Foster parents are selected by means of a social study from persons in the community who apply to give care to children. They usually receive payment for their service, but the payment in most cases is low, especially in view of the service they provide.

Better Homes Needed   A wide gap is evident between the quality of foster homes needed and those that are available. Although children's agencies can all cite gratifying examples of effective, reliable foster parents who give good care to children, the average foster home falls far short of what is needed. Studies have shown that foster parents are recruited generally from lower socioeconomic groups. They are persons with limited education who are older than the foster children's own parents. They often show ambivalent attitudes toward the disturbed children they care for and may be unable to withstand the impact of aggression that is common among foster children. Foster parents do not have a clear understanding of their role because of lack of foster parent training, and they frequently are without constructive techniques to use in child rearing. Amid great obstacles and little reward from the community, foster parents give an essential child care service, but overall they lack the qualifications necessary for an effective foster care program.[13]

Parents Organize   Foster parents are beginning to develop and use their own power. We have already mentioned foster parent organizations. Foster parents are also more likely to use legal means to assert their rights. Suits have been filed to prevent children under their care from being placed with others for adoption without according the foster parents due consideration.

Institutions   Foster care institutions have existed in this country for more than 200 years. Today they are being asked to provide specialized care and treatment for more children and young persons who are handicapped emotionally, socially, or intellectually. The shortage of good foster homes for children has been a factor in the widespread use of institutions.

Because of their characteristics, some children who enter foster care today are able to make better therapeutic use of a group living experience than of the more intimate and autonomous foster home setting. The successful use of different forms of group care for child rearing in other countries has led to interest here in new forms of institutional care. Also, research findings have seriously questioned the traditional view that living in an institution necessarily has devastating effects upon children.

Group Homes   Many children who need foster care have characteristics which make them unsuited for either foster homes or institutions. Serious unresolved conflicts in relation to their parents may make it difficult for them to accept the traditional foster family setting; yet they need opportunities for more informal living and casual community experiences than institutions permit. To meet this need, some agencies have developed small group homes for preadolescents and adolescents.

The group home is usually a house or apartment, owned or rented by an agency, and located in a residential area. From four to twelve children are usually cared for. Child care staff are viewed as counselors rather than as foster parents. Other professional personnel are also involved—social workers, psychiatrists, psychologists, tutors, among others. In view of their potentiality for effective care and treatment, many more group homes are needed.

For older adolescents, independent living arrangements are increasingly common. The young person obtains a room in a private home, at the "Y," or in an apartment with age-mates. A social worker or an older lay advocate provides help and minimal supervision. This plan is superior to a group home for some adolescents who are self-motivated and responsible.

Assessment of Foster Care

A study of foster care practice in nine communities marshaled concern about the plight of children who are in danger of staying in foster care throughout their childhood years.[14] How to decrease the numbers was a challenge recognized throughout child welfare. Yet despite some gains, the central problems are still unsolved: (1) the limited use of evaluation by agencies while children are in care or after they are discharged; (2) the limits on effectiveness because of staff shortages and turnover; (3) maladaptative ways for the court and social agency to meet their mutual responsibilities for children; (4) minimal professional concern about certain groups, including young persons in correctional institutions, children in private boarding schools, and American Indian children who must live away from their parents because of critical social and educational deficits in their own communities; (5) the acute shortage of foster parents who can effectively serve children with emotional, educational, and physical handicaps; and (6) the confused identity characteristic of many foster children.

The problems in foster care are critical. But there is substantial reason to be hopeful in view of the fact that the need for change in the present system of foster care is clearly recognized by those in social work practice.

EMPLOYMENT OPPORTUNITIES

An assessment of child welfare must take serious note of the continued fragmentation of social services for children and their families and the lack of comprehensive social planning in their behalf. While steps have been taken in most states to integrate public child welfare services with social services extended to AFDC families, this has not been fully effective. The United States continues to be the only industrialized nation that has not legislated a program of children's allowances—financial benefits to parents regardless of need—to act as a base of protection for children. Family and child interests are only sporadically represented when public social policy is formulated which explicitly or implicitly affects family life.

Some positive trends brighten the outlook for children and make child welfare an attractive field of practice for new professionals to enter. Child welfare services have always drawn a large proportion of social workers into employment. It is an expanding field of practice, not only in quantity of services but in variety. Persons entering the field can expect to find opportunities to work in newer ways intended to be especially responsive to the needs and interests of minority groups and parents. We all need to work to extend the rights to which children and young persons are entitled.

Lela B. Costin

KEY TERMS

social utility	commercial care
child neglect	child abuse
fragmented services	day care
foster family care	agency group home
parens patriae	regulatory power

FOR DISCUSSION

1 Why are services to children in their own homes important but less well developed than foster care and adoption?
2 What are the political questions in expansion of day care for children?
3 Describe the variety of settings in which day care is offered.
4 Where and by whom are most young children cared for while their mothers work?
5 What are major causes of child abuse? What treatment is appropriate?
6 Discuss symptoms, persistent causes, and treatment of child neglect.
7 What typical conditions make foster care likely?
8 Suggest means to reduce the incidence of foster care.
9 Who are the "orphans of the living"? What characteristics make adoption unlikely?
10 What significant factors adversely affect foster family care?
11 How does foster care differ from adoption?
12 What kinds of children are available for adoption?
13 What innovations in child placement have given homes to children who were formerly seen as unadoptable?
14 Identify major trends and issues in child welfare. How do they compare with those in other fields of practice?

PROJECTS

1 Visit a children's institution. Interview the executive director or the head of social services about the purposes and methods of the program. Interview several of the children served. What is the content of a typical day? Is the program custodial or treatment-oriented? Do the perceptions of the staff and of the children differ?
2 Obtain the latest statistics of child abuse for your state from the local or state child welfare office. Report on trends over a period of time, program changes, and future plans.
3 Describe the possible family structures for a child who is placed in foster care after his parents get a divorce. At a given time, how many "parent figures" maximally is such a child likely to have? (Most students have said seven; why?)
4 Invite a judge to talk about the role of the public child welfare program in his

jurisdiction. Tape the talk, and ask a child welfare supervisor to listen to it and indicate areas of agreement and disagreement.

5 Make a chart listing all the child welfare services mentioned in the chapter. Identify where each one can be found in your community. Indicate the gaps.

6 Prepare a discussion or debate on this topic: "Resolved, that foster parents should be given first consideration when the child they are caring for becomes available for adoption."

7 Obtain and evaluate the annual report of a public child welfare agency. Suggest any changes in program emphasis, and indicate your reasons.

FOR FURTHER STUDY

Andrew Billingsley and Jeanne M. Giovannoni, *Children of the Storm: Black Children and American Child Welfare*, Harcourt Brace Jovanovich, New York, 1972.

Lela B. Costin, *Child Welfare: Policies and Practice*, McGraw-Hill, New York, 1972.

Joseph Goldstein, Anna Freud, and Albert J. Solnit, *Beyond the Best Interests of the Child*, Free Press, New York, 1973.

Phyllis Harrison-Ross and Barbara Wyden, *The Black Child: A Parents' Guide*, Peter H. Wyden, Inc., New York, 1973.

Alfred Kadushin, *Child Welfare Services*, Macmillan, New York, 1974.

———, *Child Welfare Services: A Sourcebook*, Macmillan, New York, 1970.

Alfred J. Kahn, *Planning Community Services for Children in Trouble*, Columbia Univ. Press, New York, 1963.

Chapter 17

Serving the Family

Are crises in family living normal?
How do new family forms affect agencies?
What services do family agencies provide?
Will advocacy succeed?

The family, like the biological organism, goes through progressive changes that may entail crises. As a social unit it usually includes several individuals at varying levels of maturity who must cooperate and interact appropriately to accomplish necessary tasks. Duvall[1] defines family developmental tasks as "growth responsibilities" that result in satisfaction or unhappiness depending on the degree of success in meeting those responsibilities. Marriage is the generally accepted beginning of a family, and death of one partner is the end. The family goes through identifiable stages:

1 Marriage—one or more times
2 Entrance of the first child into the family through birth or adoption
3 Entrance of the first child into the community
4 Entrance of the last child into the community
5 Exit of the first child from the home for marriage or independent living
6 Exit of the last child from the family
7 Retirement of the major wage earner
8 Death of one of the partners, usually the husband

Variations include families without children, children remaining at home longer than usual, and extended family relationships that occur when parents or parents-in-law spend their later years with their children.[2] With multiple marriages, "his," "hers," and "ours" may characterize children in a family.

FAMILY PREHISTORY

The events that precede marriage, including dating, courtship, and engagement, are important because the family "prehistory" reflects the strengths and weaknesses that the partners bring to the newly established family.

Dating, courtship, and engagement represent varying levels of obligation and commitment prior to marriage. Dating represents the least commitment; at this stage there is freedom to relate to many people, one of whom may eventually be selected as a future partner. The old-fashioned term "courtship" is still used to identify the point of serious commitment. Not only do the two individuals involved in the relationship have expectations, but society also has its expectations of them. The two sets of expectations may or may not be congruent. Engagement involves testing a selected marriage partner. Similarities and differences in personality, values, and attitudes, as well as possibilities for patterns of later adjustment, are often discussed and evaluated. This process becomes especially important if marriage is regarded as a lifelong commitment.

New Dating Patterns The idea of dating leading to a lifelong commitment is considered outmoded by some people. There may be very little dating in the sense of pairing off or "going steady." Activities in larger groups may continue. When large-group activities persist into late adolescence, those who want to follow a traditional dating pattern and become more serious may develop concerns about their own adequacy and their own future. Sexual relations, which used to serve as the culmination of a relationship, have now become for some the means of testing a relationship. Sexual relationships may precede knowledge of other interests and values. Sexual intercourse may also imply very different expectancies for one partner than for the other.

When courtship and engagement are replaced by living together, quite a different kind of trial is provided. Living together may be a serious test of the potential for marriage or a more casual day-to-day companionship with little serious regard for the future.

Not only changes in the standards of society but the widely differing goals and commitments of individuals in the various living patterns provide new challenges for the family agency that offers educational and counseling services. Both teenagers and adults have new problems and new ways of coping that make the individual's goals more important and the behavioral norms as defined by society less relevant.

STAGES IN FAMILY DEVELOPMENT

Marriage

Marriage is the public joining together under socially specified regulations of a man and a woman as husband and wife. The question of when to marry or whether to marry at all arises without the solace of "easy" answers. Marriage-like relationships are discussed increasingly, using such terms as "probationary marriage," "renewable contract," and "nonlegal voluntary association." The question of who should marry also becomes an issue. Is it discrimination when two men, two women, or a whole community are denied the right to marry? Attitudes and behavior will be influenced by the values instilled within the family and by the modifications which take place as an individual interacts with the larger society. Legal controls affect the decision to marry and the expectations and responsibilities of the marriage partners. The legal aspects of marriage were considered in Chapter 10.

Marriage involves a set of expectations and affectional patterns for each partner, including financial dependence or autonomy, ethical and moral values, religious beliefs and practices, attitudes toward having children, and many other questions involving varying degrees of unity and autonomy.

Marital Problems   Crises in the early stages of living together with or without marriage may come from failure to recognize and understand the feelings of the other partner, problems occasioned by the close association, affiliation with or alienation from parents and other relatives, power elements in decision making, and achievement motivations related to work roles. For many couples professional help is desirable to resolve marital problems. Marriage counseling is often the major activity of the family agency. Here again, however, the agency cannot merely represent society's traditional strong desire for marital stability. Although it aims at strengthening family bonds and reconciling of alienated persons when possible, the agency's role is to facilitate separation and divorce when problems are insoluble.

The consumer role is a critical aspect of the marital relationship. For many couples, interpersonal stress and management of finances may be closely associated. Innovative programs of financial and debt counseling have been developed by social agencies, often in cooperation with banks and other financial institutions.

Birth of First Child

The entrance of a child into the family may disrupt the previously established routine. Sometimes marriage follows pregnancy, presenting the tasks of child-bearing so early in the relationship that normal stress is exacerbated. Pregnancy for a couple living together may be the event that leads them to marry—because of the emphasis of society on legitimacy, if for no other reason.

New Roles   When the first child is born, the couples must work out the mother/wife and husband/father functions. While tasks are increasingly shared and sex roles more interchangeable, there are many new demands on each person. Decisions may involve whether both parents will still work, what home tasks will be shared, and how privacy will be provided in the expanded family. The mutual social and emotional investment of a husband and wife may be enhanced when shared with a third person, but a child may lead the husband to feel alienated and neglected or the wife to feel overworked and overwhelmed.

Socialization of the child to become a part of the family and of society by learning approved behavior will be a primary task, because the family is the first influence from which the child learns acceptable attitudes and behavior.

Family agencies often provide parent education programs to consider child-rearing techniques and to discuss parental attitudes toward such areas as emotional and social development, discipline, and sibling relations.

Entrance of the First Child into the Larger Community

The child's socialization is expanded as he participates in the larger society with its widened social and emotional relationships. The child enrolled in a preschool program begins to be influenced by the larger community at an early age. Infants in day care are involved even earlier. Friendships with other children and with outside authority figures are important elements of group experience. Learning that has taken place in the family is put to the test through feedback from peers and others. The family must adjust to the increased individuality and in-dependence of the child. The family agency often works in partnership with the schools to carry on educational projects and to provide special counseling to school-age children and their parents.

Entrance of the Last Child into the Community

As the last child enters the larger society and forms other social and emotional relationships, parents have necessarily relinquished many of their controls. At this time mothers often return to the labor market. As the children reach adolescence, they need to be more independent and more responsible for their own decisions. Both parents and adolescents are usually ambivalent toward increasing independence. Family agencies may provide counseling programs especially for teenagers in their transition to adulthood.

Exit of First Child from the Family

A child may leave the family to marry, to go away to school, or to establish other independent living arrangements. This thrusts the family members into different roles. Parents and remaining children have to redefine their relationships. In our culture, moving away may not convey financial independence. Financial help from parents may cause conflict between them and the child, who is now an adult.

Exit of Last Child from the Family

After more than two decades of rearing children, a husband and wife often find that they are alone. No longer does one of the children consider it his responsibility to stay home to care for the parents. Parents must begin to rediscover each other—a real test of the quality of the relationship built over the years. With the cessation of active parenting, many marriages fail. The result is a special demand for marriage counseling in middle age.

Early marriage and early childbirth have produced younger grandparents. The importance and value of grandparenting is demonstrated in the extension of the socialization process with grandchildren.[3]

The possibility that the child models himself after grandparents as well as parents or that at least patterns of behavior are transmitted by a modeling process from parent to child in succeeding generations can lead logically to the possibility of continued modeling and socialization throughout adulthood, particularly if parents survive into old age to serve as models for later stages of adult development.

Retirement

A few industries have sought the help of social agencies to develop preretirement counseling programs involving ways to phase out the work role rather than to terminate it abruptly. For the wife, especially if the marriage has been unhappy, having the husband at home all day can be a major problem. Retirement is creating difficulties for working wives, too, because they no longer have the contacts with the adult world that they have come to value. Retirement counseling often comes too late. Planning for this event should be a part of the entire adult life span, but it rarely is.

Death of One Partner

In the last stage of the family life cycle, the couple must face the aging process and the fact that they will be separated by death. The prospect of nearly a decade of widowhood should be a part of the long-term planning process, so that decisions involving housing and finances need not be made under crisis conditions. Other specific issues will be considered in the chapter on aging.

ORGANIZATION OF FAMILY AGENCIES

How did family agencies arise and what services do they offer?

Family agencies in the United States trace their origins to the Charity Organization Society established in Buffalo, New York, in 1877. The first training course for family service workers was begun in 1898. The Family Service Association of America (FSAA), the national organization of family agencies, was established in 1911 and now includes 340 member agencies. It accredits agencies and also publishes the journal *Social Casework.*

The family agency typifies the voluntary social welfare organization discussed earlier in Chapter 3. Traditionally, the older family agencies provided financial aid to the poor, but with the depression of the 1930s this function was largely taken over by public agencies because of the vast resources required.

Family agencies and those offering child welfare services often have overlapping functions. As a result, there are 120 combined family and children's agencies that are members of the FSAA. Also, the activities of the family agency are often closely related to those offered by the out-patient mental health center. Thus twenty-eight combined family and mental health agencies have resulted from mergers or have been newly established.

Ethnic Agencies   The development of racial and ethnic identity has led to demands for greater attention to making service effective for minority groups. A few new family agencies serve only members of a specific minority group. For family agencies in general, there has been an emphasis on more minority staff and greater participation in agency leadership.

A black caucus serves in an advisory capacity to the Family Service Association of America. Some of the concerns of minority groups have already been presented in earlier chapters. Minority practitioners emphasize the dangers of stereotyping the minority family as matriarchal, unstable, and in a perpetual state of disintegration. They stress family adaptability, the result of strong kinship bonds, achievement and work orientations, and religious affiliations. Only a quarter of black families are now classified as *extended*. About one-tenth have incorporated nonrelatives into the household.

SERVICES OF FAMILY AGENCIES

As voluntary social welfare organizations, family agencies have discretion to offer whatever programs their board considers necessary, resulting in wide variety. Four examples of services will be discussed: counseling, family life education, homemaker service, and services for senior citizens. There is obvious overlap in these four categories. Other types of service will be identified. The range is shown in Figure 17-1, prepared by the FSAA.

Counseling

With the development of casework treatment, counseling became the major function of family agencies. People who had the ability and desire to verbalize their difficulties generally received the most effective help. As a result, family agencies have served a high proportion of middle-class people. Agencies also charge for counseling service based on the ability to pay. More recently, special efforts have been made to serve more low-income families.

Models   Counseling now takes several forms. The one-to-one interview involving a psychosocial approach has been augmented by group treatment, in which couples or other adults with similar problems come together to discuss them with a professional leader. Another major counseling technique has involved seeing the couple or all family members together, with problems in interaction providing the focus for treatment. The discussion of the family life cycle has shown that counseling is often provided for varying age levels—teenagers, persons contemplating marriage, couples with marital problems, adults looking forward to retirement, and senior citizens.

The prevailing model used to be long-term casework service, with one or more weekly sessions sometimes continuing for months or years. As the chapter on services to individuals indicated, new approaches often involve shorter-term treatment focused on specific limited problems—major elements in a crisis rather than more general concerns. The worker and the individual client, couple, or family often agree to work together for six to eight sessions to see what can be accomplished. Whether to continue is a decision made jointly.

Counseling with low-income families has pointed up the special need to effect changes in the environment on their behalf. Obtaining adequate housing, jobs, and needed health services are but a few examples.

Family Service Advocates Action Based on Urgent Needs of Families

Problems of Families and Individuals

A marriage breaking up

Pre-marriage concerns

A youth dropping out of school

An emotionally disturbed person unable to hold a job or continue training

An emergency due to illness or death

An under-achieving child in school

Broken families

Unwed parents

Alcoholism

Drug use

Retirement and growing older

Need for information about resources

Problems related to unemployment, housing or need for health and welfare services

Counseling and Specialized Services

Individual counseling

Family and group counseling

Family life education/plays for living

Research

Homemaker service

Help to neglected children

Training center for the profession

Agency training for social work aides

Consultation to other organizations

Counseling alcoholics and their families

Foster home placement/adoption

Legal aid/aid to travelers

Community Conditions Hurting Families

Inadequate income for basic needs

Unemployment or unsuitable job

Poor job opportunities

Poor or no job training

Discrimination (racial, ethnic, religious)

Housing problems

Poor schools

Unsafe neighborhood

Heavy drug use in area

Poor police protection

No day care for children

No home care services

Poor recreational opportunities

Poor or costly transportation

Poor health resources

Action and Advocacy Programs

High-priority services for minority and poor families

Seeking institutional adaptations to solve new problems

Involving people themselves in problem solving

Intervening with public services to meet needs

Effecting systems change to serve families

Strengthening families through advocacy

Developing social policy to strengthen families

Special projects

Deploying and training staff for family advocacy work

Enlisting volunteers for action programs

Informing community on acute family problems

Closing gaps in services

Figure 17-1   The range of family agency services.[4]

Family Life Education

Family life education may have considerable overlap with counseling but usually implies more emphasis on knowledge and information giving to groups. Lectures and informal methods are used. Sessions may also be organized into courses, with or without academic credit. Sex education, money management, first aid and home health, and drug abuse are popular topics. Family life education programs may also involve the training of laymen who act as leaders of self-help groups. In view of the vast amount of information given out by the media, parents may be better informed than they used to be, but it is still important to consider values and attitudes involved in using information. This process requires greater skill than does information giving. Family life education programs are often cosponsored by day care centers, Parent-Teacher Associations, or parents of handicapped children.

Homemaker Services

Trained homemakers are used by child welfare and health agencies as well as by family agencies. Homemakers generally either provide direct service in case of illness or other family emergencies (i.e. child care, cooking, marketing and general housekeeping), or they serve as teachers for people who lack skills in homemaking. People who need the service are expected to pay the cost to the extent they can, but homemaker service is never self-supporting. With administrative costs and the need to serve low-income families, it cannot possibly be so.

While the service is usually considered temporary, homemakers assisting the aged for a few hours a week can help old people maintain themselves in independent living, often for years.

Services for the Aged

Services for the aged involve a wide variety of group activity programs emphasizing socialization, skills, and public service. Individual services are also increasing. Programs now tend to delegate more authority in decision making to the users of these services. Individual and group counseling may focus particularly on health problems or on relations with other family members. Programs are gaining greater effectiveness in outreach to isolated aged persons through the use of volunteers as well as professional staff. Senior citizens themselves also serve the agencies as volunteers in many different ways. Family agencies are generally committed to the goal of continued participation for the aged rather than to the theory of disengagement.

Other Services

Family service agencies serve other groups—the mentally retarded, discharged mental patients, drug abusers, alcoholics, and travelers who encounter crises. They also act as the sponsor for legal aid services in some cities. Recently in their advocacy programs they have taken a much greater interest in the delivery of social services by other agencies, in civil rights legislation, and in other aspects of social policy.

The FSAA publishes an annual summary of special service projects conducted by member agencies, including the sources of funds for them. These reports reflect the increasing involvement of family agencies with other community institutions.

OUTREACH AND ADVOCACY

Although family agencies have traditionally served individual families, since the latter part of the 1960s the FSAA and its member agencies have been involved in several large efforts directed toward outreach and advocacy. In Project ENABLE, FSAA cooperated with the National Urban League and the Child Study Association of America in an effort to achieve several major objectives—weekly parent group meetings with poverty-level people, using a community action approach to problem solving; employment of indigenous personnel; development of close relationships with the community action program of the OEO; outreach to the poor by the agency; and liaison with other poverty or self-help organizations. Sixty-four family service agencies participated. Funding came from the OEO. The project operated in 1966 and 1967, serving 30,000 parents in 600 separate parent groups, and used 145 specially trained group leaders as well as 200 neighborhood, nonprofessional social work aides.[5]

> Through ENABLE, the poor began to see themselves in the new roles of spokesmen and change agents. They entered into the educational process of community organization. They began to understand the workings of agencies and bureaucracies with which they contended. For them, education and action became inseparable and intertwined.
>
> From mute and unknowing isolation many parents advanced to the idea that participating in decision-making is sharing community. In their neighbors and in themselves, as human mirrors, they found motivation. One person's problem was another's revelation. And since their discussion subjects came out of the group, rather than from some outside professional agenda, the solutions belonged to the poor. By their own education and action the alien poor acquired a stake.
>
> Though created at the national level ENABLE was in practice local and personal. ENABLE opened playgrounds, paved streets, battled tuberculosis, erected traffic signs, sent kids to camp, enforced housing codes, established surplus food distribution centers, got out the vote, and started adult education programs.

Experience with project ENABLE and other OEO programs led the Family Service Association and its member agencies to emphasize advocacy and social action. *Family Advocacy, A Manual for Action*[6] was published in 1973 to define advocacy. Two illustrations are presented here.

> Family advocacy is a professional service designed to improve life conditions for people by harnessing direct and expert knowledge of family needs with the commitment to action and the application of skills to produce the necessary community change. The purpose of family advocacy services is to insure that the systems and institutions with direct bearing on families work for those families, rather than against them.
>
> Family advocacy goals include not only improvement of existing public

and voluntary services and their delivery, but also development of new or changed forms of social services. Any institutionalized service such as housing, employment, welfare, education, health care, recreation, transportation, police and courts, and social agencies including family service agencies may be in need of change to achieve its stated purposes in today's world. Advocacy may also aim a concerted action at the solution of common problems such as drug abuse, alcoholism, mental retardation, and abuse of civil rights, which affect many families in a community.

Family advocacy service is needed by families at all socioeconomic levels, since it is concerned with provision of a humane social environment for all and is related to problems common to all. Priority for advocacy service should go to families, neighborhoods, and communities in the greatest jeopardy, who have suffered most acutely from the impact of racism, dehumanization, poverty, injustice, and inequality of opportunity.

One illustration indicates how a playground was obtained in Baltimore:

When a family service agency foster mother deplored the fact that the street was the only play space in the neighborhood, a family service graduate student worker assured her that the family service board and staff would act as intermediaries with the city officials if the neighborhood citizens developed a self-help project. Available through the owner, who offered to deed it to the neighborhood, was a 110-foot-square lot filled with broken glass and junk. A group of citizens had tried unsuccessfully to raise money to pay taxes and insurance on it and to equip it. The worker then met several times with the group, which incorporated and elected officers. The major project was a rummage and bake sale to secure funds and to arouse the community's interest and support. On the day of the sale there was a large crowd, including the city council president, the executive director of the family service agency, and many of the agency's volunteers. The council lauded the efforts of the citizens toward self-improvement of their neighborhood and pledged $1,000 from the city for equipment. The lot was furnished with swings, a jungle gym, seesaws, and benches by city officials, who were impressed by the efforts of parents who raised money to pay the back taxes.

This project demonstrates how a student in a family service agency stimulated a previously defeated people to organize and improve their own community. The involvement of the agency, the Family and Children's Society of Baltimore, Maryland, also resulted in recruitment of more foster parents.

A more complex issue involving maintaining the trust of adolescents and achieving legal protection was dealt with in Philadelphia and ultimately in the Pennsylvania legislature.

Counseling of minors without the consent of their parents has been for many years a difficult problem that has troubled not only family service agencies, but psychiatric hospitals, child guidance clinics, and mental health clinics, as well as private physicians who have been asked from time to time to provide treatment for their underage patients without the knowledge of their parents.

In 1970, Jewish Family Service began its Project on Troubled Youth in the western suburbs of Philadelphia. In order to reach these adolescents, they were assured that the agency would not get in touch with their parents without their consent. Simultaneously, the agency was engaged in running "rap sessions" in its northwest district office where the same ground rules were used. While it was felt certain that this was the best way to proceed in order to involve the youth on a free-choice basis, the agency was advised by legal counsel that there were a number of risks involved in such practice. The only thing that provided reassurance for the agency was counsel's opinion that, as long as it eventually intended to involve the parents, it did not run a great risk of jeopardy. However, the problem still remained a troubling one because of the legal aspects.

The public issues committee, following study of the issue, recommended to the board of directors that the agency attempt to get immunity legislation passed by the state legislature. By using the resources of Community Services of Pennsylvania, a voluntary, statewide citizens' advisory agency, and the knowledge and interest of several of the board and committee members, the committee canvassed the available legislation, both existing and proposed, to see if there was any way for the agency to have either a bill or an amendment on existing legislation enacted.

The chairman of the advisory committee, a young, politically knowledgeable attorney, provided the political expertise necessary. The consensus of the public issues committee, after a review of existing and proposed legislation, was that it would be more practical to seek an amendment to some proposed legislation than to try to get a bill offered *de novo* in the legislature.

A bill was selected that was being offered in the state senate to provide immunity to physicians treating youths with drug problems. This bill was seen as having the greatest likelihood of success because of the political influence of physicians and the fact that the bill, if enacted, would not cost the taxpayers of Pennsylvania any money. Although the bill had many legislative sponsors, the agency was fortunate that one of them was a state senator from Philadelphia, and this was one of the reasons why the bill was chosen. Contact was made with this senator, through the good offices of one of the members of the JFS board of directors, who was of the same political persuasion as the senator, and who had considerable behind-the-scenes political influence within the city. The senator was invited to a meeting of the public issues committee, at which time the agency's proposed amendment, allowing accredited family service agencies of Pennsylvania to counsel adolescents, was introduced. The senator was agreeable, providing the medical society had no objections to an amendment being tacked on to a bill which was originally offered on their behalf. JFS undertook the responsibility of clearing this with the local medical society, which sent a letter to the chairman of the Committee on Public Health and Welfare indicating their support of the amendment. It was also cleared with the general director of FSAA.

At the same time, the public issues committee involved the twenty-two member agencies of FSAA in the state of Pennsylvania to enlist their support in writing to their state senators and representatives on behalf of State Senate Bill No. 1034 which was being offered in the senate. JFS also provided the senator with copies of the agency's hundred-year history as well as material about FSAA, including its concerns about standards and accreditation. The senator had requested this as background information in order to reassure himself—and legitimately so—that the agency and its accrediting bodies were not "fly-by-night outfits."

When next the agency heard from the senator, State Senate Bill No. 1034 had been incorporated into House Bill No. 850, which was part of the comprehensive drug bill which reevaluated all the state's involvement with drug usage, changing several laws and modifying others. Most important for family service agencies was one section allowing agencies and clinics "to offer counseling to youth who were involved in drugs without the obligation of involving the parents, if this was counter-indicated either by the youth's wishes or because of treatment considerations." The bill was signed into law in May 1972 by Governor Shapp.

. . . This, in effect, represents the summation of over two years' concentrated work in the political arena, to provide immunity legislation for family service agencies.

Advocacy efforts have greatly broadened the scope and increased the impact of family agencies. Like the new model of school social work, the emphasis on systems change has greater impact and a more lasting effect than programs only emphasizing services to an individual or to a family.

FINANCING OF FAMILY AGENCIES

Family agencies are primarily financed by contributions and user fees. Some of the older agencies have substantial endowments. Bequests and foundation grants also are important. Family agencies now also receive substantial income through purchase of service from governmental agencies. They are more likely to be reimbursed for homemaker service than for counseling, which is less tangible. The community-based programs developed under the OEO have led to closer financial relationships with governmental agencies, including school boards as well as welfare organizations.

Two problems are presented by user fees. There may be a tendency to serve middle-class clients in preference to those who cannot pay but who still have a great need for the agency service. United Funds are giving higher priority to those agencies that concentrate on the poor. At the same time, those who can pay the full cost may prefer to see a psychiatrist or a social worker in private practice. They often do not want to be associated with a charitable program.

Advocacy efforts are important to provide community leadership and to encourage social change, but they may also incur more opposition from givers than do the more traditional services.

Member agencies of the FSAA raise over $90 million a year. The major source is the United Way, accounting for 58 percent. About 13 percent comes from governmental sources, and another 10 percent from user fees.[7]

JOB OPPORTUNITIES IN FAMILY AGENCIES

With their emphasis on professional casework services, family agencies have tended to require high educational standards for their social work staff. Many agencies would not hire a person without the M.S.W. degree and a field practicum in a casework agency. Since there were no established homemaker training programs, agencies developed their own recruitment and training programs for these personnel.

While casework service is still the major activity, the agencies increasingly make use of individuals with a greater variety of training and experience. They find that bachelor's-degree personnel can perform many of the tasks needed, though they may insist that a worker obtain the M.S.W. within a specified time. They also employ professional personnel from other fields and use volunteers in many creative ways. They have been impressed with the value of indigenous workers and of family advocates from the recent projects summarized earlier in this chapter.

Family agencies have always had appeal for social work students because they have highly motivated clients, some of whom want long-term service. The agencies pride themselves on providing careful supervision to new workers, and they offer small caseloads compared with public agencies. Their newer services provide greater opportunities for group workers and community workers, especially for the generalist who wants to be involved with all three social work methods.

Ruppert Downing

KEY TERMS

family stages
family prehistory
socialization of the child
Family Service Association of America
individual counseling

family treatment
family life education
homemaker services
Project ENABLE
user fees

FOR DISCUSSION

1   Evaluate the concept that marriage is the beginning of a family.
2   Why are modern birth control methods considered an important influence on family life patterns?
3   Why is "prehistory" important to family development?
4   Should two persons of the same sex be permitted to marry?
5   Why is widowhood as a life crisis particularly important?
6   What problems are occasioned by premarital pregnancy?
7   How are family agency programs combined with other services?
8   How are some minority groups seeking to obtain family services?
9   What service receives the greatest attention from family agencies?
10   How does homemaker service broaden staff composition of a family agency?
11   What kinds of advocacy should a family agency provide?

PROJECTS

1   Assign several students to interview one of their grandparents and make brief talks on the family life cycle as the grandparent views it and as the students view it. Use the basic stages provided as a uniform outline.
2   Show a film on marriage counseling and analyze the process. Your audiovisual department can suggest new releases on this topic.
3   Look at a recent issue of *Social Casework* and classify the articles. How much

attention is given to community work and group work? Is advocacy considered?

4 Develop a role play involving a short interview with a family. Choose and develop a typical family problem. Have one of the students serve as the social worker. Repeat the role play with the instructor in the social worker's role.

5 Present for debate: "Resolved, that marriage is obsolete" or "Resolved, that childless marriages are preferable in American society."

6 Ask the administrator of a local family agency to discuss the current program and the funding of the agency. What changes have taken place recently? What directions would he like to see followed? Use the discussion in the text as the basis for questions from the class.

7 Prepare a description of a low-income family, indicating its size and financial resources. Independently, prepare a budget for the family. Compare the budgets of the various members of the class.

FOR FURTHER STUDY

Bernard Farber, *Family and Kinship in Modern Society*, Scott, Foresman, Glenview, Ill., 1973.

Robert B. Hill, *The Strengths of Black Families*, Emerson Hall, New York, 1972.

William G. Hill and Stanley C. Sibler, "Reciprocal Aspects of Mental Health and Family Service," *Social Casework*, vol. 53, December 1972, pp. 623–630.

Gordon Manser, "Implications of Purchase of Services for Voluntary Agencies," *Social Casework*, vol. 53, June 1972, pp. 335–340.

Richard G. Niemi, *How Family Members Perceive Each Other*, Yale Univ. Press, New Haven, 1974.

Ivan F. Nye and Felix M. Berardo, *Emerging Conceptual Framework in Family Analysis*, Macmillan, New York, 1966.

Atlee L. Stroup, *Marriage and Family, A Developmental Approach*, Appleton-Century-Crofts, New York, 1966.

Chapter 18

People with
Emotional Problems

Who provides mental health services?
What will be the next "psychiatric revolution"?
Why is the medical model controversial?
New knowledge—new hope?

All of us encounter problems in living that affect our thoughts and emotions as well as our physical and social functioning. Ordinarily we learn to deal with these problems in our own way. However, people who are seriously troubled need professional assistance. Social work has traditionally attempted to help troubled people learn to cope with the social and emotional factors in their lives. This psychosocial orientation to the person in his situation has been accompanied by a special commitment to the poor, the handicapped, and the disadvantaged. Social work has also emphasized the importance of helping people within the context of their family and community.

EMOTIONAL PROBLEMS IN PERSPECTIVE

Emotional problems vary in degree and kind and are manifested in different ways and in different places. For example, some people are caught up in interpersonal difficulties or cannot cope with the effects of environmental stress. Still others suffer from serious distortions in their relationship to reality.

Public and Private Resources Emotional problems that seriously interfere with the adult's or child's functioning or orientation to reality are dealt with in mental health clinics or psychiatric hospitals through individual or group psychotherapy and psychotropic medication. Less serious emotional problems, such as reactions to interpersonal and environmental stress, are helped by individual counseling and family therapy in family service agencies. However, this division of responsibility does not always apply. A study by the Illinois Department of Mental Health and the Family Service Association of America demonstrated overlap in the kinds of problems treated and the services provided by mental health clinics and family service agencies.[1]

Many social agencies and institutions, including schools, courts, public welfare agencies, hospitals and clinics, and the military, have also established sections or departments to deal with social-emotional stress related to the primary mission of the agency. Social workers are employed in these agencies because of their ability to deal with both the social and psychological dimensions of people's lives.

Other Mental Health Resources Psychiatrists and psychologists in private practice, particularly in urban areas, furnish individual and group psychotherapy for a variety of emotional problems. Also a small group of well-trained and experienced social workers in full- or part-time private practice provide clinically oriented services to individuals, families, and groups similar to those furnished by psychologists and psychiatrists. Since these private practitioners charge relatively high fees, they do not treat many poor people.

Other persons in the community also provide an opportunity for troubled people to engage in "talk therapy." These include friends, neighbors, clergymen, and even bartenders. Their willingness to listen and to offer emotional support and counsel sometimes enables people to obtain a new perspective.

State Mental Hospitals The chronically mentally ill, the aged, and the poor who are unable to afford other resources use these hospitals as a last resort. Unfortunately, the "treatment" in many state hospitals is inadequate due to overcrowding and understaffing. Some people have gone to state hospitals to avoid problems in community living, only to develop more severe problems there as a reaction to what Irving Goffman calls "total institutions."[2]

Views of Mental Illness

The more serious emotional problems have been viewed as manifestations of mental illness stemming from brain damage or conflicts over the inner life of instincts and inherited drives. This assumption of underlying internal causes for serious emotional disorders has been extended to less serious emotional problems in living, resulting in a medical model to conceptualize the causes and treatment for all emotional problems. The medical specialty of psychiatry has assumed primary responsibility for designing and delivering mental health services.

In the past ten years we have seen a shift in emphasis from mental illness to community mental health and the behavioral consequences of social problems and maladaptive learning. Some authorities question the existence of mental illness.[3] They suggest that medical concepts be reserved for behavior disorders that demonstrate direct pathology of the brain. This view of emotional problems brings them closer to the psychosocial orientation of social work. Indeed, the developing subspecialties of community psychiatry and psychology increasingly emphasize social work's traditional concern with the mental health aspects of social and environmental problems, the importance of the family and community, and the delivery of services to minorities and disadvantaged members of society.

Paradoxically, the nonmedical approach to mental health has accompanied new discoveries about the genetic and biological bases of selected behavior disorders. Since current literature and practice still make use of them, the terms mental *illness* and mental *patient* will be retained here, except where other terminology would better describe the ideas being discussed. Nonetheless, the orientation in this chapter is psychosocial rather than medical.

MENTAL ILLNESS AND MENTAL HEALTH

One cannot consider mental *illness* without a simultaneous look at mental *health*. This latter term is poorly defined, despite efforts directed toward its promotion. Freud's dictum that the mentally healthy person is one who is capable of working and loving is well known. Not everyone would consider these characteristics sufficient indicators of sound mental health. Moreover, anthropologists have documented the wide variety of behaviors considered normal or abnormal among different societies of the world. The recent cultural revolution in the United States has produced increasing recognition of how subcultures and diverse life-styles affect fundamental aspects of behavior and standards of normality—a marked contrast to an earlier period in American history when acceptance of cultural and behavioral diversity was limited by a commitment to a "melting pot" ideology and the American dream. Today we accept the reality of a pluralistic society, but we disagree on standards of behavior considered normal or abnormal and on the elements of mental health and mental illness.

Social and Interpersonal Dimensions of Human Behavior   From this perspective the mentally healthy person demonstrates personal and social effectiveness within the context of his particular society. Effectiveness is revealed by a person's level of functioning in carrying out his significant life roles in the family, school, employment, and the community. Thus, the problems of mental illness are manifested in varying degrees of personal and social ineffectiveness in role performance.

Need for Treatment   We read that one person out of ten is in need of some type of help for emotional problems, but this statement is deceptive and subject to misinterpretation. Epidemiological methods have not been sufficiently standardized to accurately measure the impact of culture-bound aspects of normal and abnormal functioning. The National Center for Health Statistics and other public health agencies are working toward more satisfactory approaches for defining and assessing the incidence and prevalence of behavior disorders.

Measurement and classification of mental illness are equally problematic. Widespread use of psychological projective tests, social histories, and clinical assessments have established low levels of agreement on all but the grossest deviant behavior. Attempts to reliably classify the various types of mental disorder also pose difficulties, despite continuing efforts to refine diagnostic schemes.

A Dramatic Experiment   Psychologist David Rosenhan discovered that the professional staff in psychiatric hospitals could not distinguish sane people from insane patients.[4] Rosenhan and seven "normal" associates walked into twelve psychiatric hospitals in five different states on the East and West coast. All eight were admitted to the hospital by feigning the same symptoms of hearing voices. After admission, the pseudopatients reverted to their normal behavior. They remained hospitalized for periods ranging from 7 to 52 days, with an average of 19 days. The psychiatric staff was unable to distinguish the pseudopatient's sane behavior from that of the "insane" patients. All of the pseudopatients were discharged with a diagnosis of "schizophrenia in remission." Since some of the hospitals in the study were quite new and research-oriented, the findings of the experiment are particularly depressing. The study points up the questionable validity of current diagnostic and classification procedures and raises serious concern about people whose lives have been shaped by the misapplication and consequences of psychiatric labeling and hospitalization.

THREE REVOLUTIONS IN PSYCHIATRY

The First Revolution

Three revolutions in psychiatry involve different views of the mentally ill and their treatment. The first revolution was typified by the "striking off of the chains" of the patients at the Bicêtre Hospital for the Insane in Paris in 1793 by its director Philippe Pinel, signifying the end of a period going back to primitive times when individuals with behavior disorders were considered to be possessed by the devil. The accepted treatment in many parts of the world was to isolate and punish those who were "possessed."

From Moral Treatment to State Hospitals   The humanist concerns of Pinel and others led to the era of "moral treatment" and the substitution of an accepting human relationship for punishment in treating behavior disorders. Institutions for the mentally ill practiced moral treatment in Europe and the United States for fifty years, until about 1855. The major characteristic of moral treatment was the creation of a total therapeutic environment where staff and patients were expected to treat each other with acceptance, respect, and good example. This emphasis was the forerunner of the modern-day "therapeutic community." The staff viewed patients as having problems in living for which they needed hope, guidance, and support. Improved social functioning was expected and reinforced. Chronic patients were rare. Most institutions were relatively small, and the staff came to know the patients and their families quite well. Moral treatment flourished in the United States prior to the time of large migrations of immigrants from central and southern Europe. The staff and patients shared a common culture and language that enhanced their communication and interpersonal relationships, leading to a relatively high "cure" rate.[5]

Not all of the mentally ill received the benefits of moral treatment. The thousands of emotionally disturbed people who were kept in jails and almshouses under deplorable conditions became the object of reform for the crusader Dorothea Dix.[6] She was remarkably successful in convincing state legislatures to expand existing hospitals and to build new ones. She visited the hospitals on inspection tours and was influential in selecting their directors. By the 1880s almost all emotionally disturbed people had been transferred from jails and almshouses to the new hospitals. Unfortunately, the combination of large hospitals, an influx of many chronically ill patients, and immigrants who were unable to speak English diminished the effectiveness of treatment. The atmosphere changed from hope and enthusiasm to concern about management and routine. Along with the change came a new emphasis on medical diagnosis and treatment. As recovery rates decreased, mental illness was seen as an organic disease of unknown origin and poor prognosis. Since that time, state hospitals have generally served a custodial rather than a treatment function.

The Second Revolution

Contributions of Freud   Sigmund Freud in 1893 evolved the technique of free association to enable people to speak freely about their troubled feelings. He brilliantly analyzed the verbalizations of his patients and constructed a theory of psychoanalysis and a method of treatment. His experiences with patients led him to hypothesize the existence of psychic energy and tensions related to inborn biological drives. Freud proposed a psychosexual view of human development emphasizing oral, anal, phallic, latency, and genital stages. He viewed neurosis as the symptoms of a struggle between the instinctual demands of the *id* and the prohibitions of the conscience or *superego*. In this struggle the mediator of the mind, called *ego*, employs a variety of energy-depleting defenses. These defenses consist of exaggerated forms of behavior which appear as the symptoms of neurosis. Phobias, for example, are displaced fears which result in unrealistic efforts to avoid the feared object. Freud concluded that much of our behavior is due to the workings of the unconscious. He devised a systematic method for analyzing unconscious mental conflicts. Freud employed this method to help patients achieve insight or emotional awareness of how early life experiences determined their current behavior.[7] Despite their dynamic aspects, these theories were rooted in the medical tradition and emphasized treating underlying pathological causes of behavior.

Although Freud died in 1939, his concepts still enjoy wide but diminishing acceptance. Moreover, they have been embellished and modified over the years by his followers. Perhaps the most important addition to Freud's individually oriented psychology came from the psychiatrist Harry Stack Sullivan, who introduced the importance of interpersonal relationships into the stream of psychoanalytic thought.[8] Even though Freud's contributions about the mind and its workings have been widely disseminated, the psychoanalytically oriented treatment of the mentally ill has generally been limited to the educated, verbal, middle- and upper-class segments of society.

The Third Revolution

Community Mental Health   The third psychiatric revolution is still in process. During and after World War II a shortage of professional mental health workers necessitated the use of group therapy and the therapeutic use of environmental manipulation. Psychiatric practice and research in England and the United States began to demonstrate how group and social processes could involve hospital patients and staff in a new kind of therapeutic community that went beyond the contributions of moral treatment. The evolution of "social psychiatry" into "community mental health" was precipitated in this country by research on the sociology of mental illness and a series of legislative and policy changes stemming from congressional and presidential concern over mental health.

COMMUNITY MENTAL HEALTH LEGISLATION

The report of the Joint Commission on Mental Illness and Health to Congress in 1961 recommended a series of progressive reforms emphasizing a stronger role for the federal government. The personal concern of President John F. Kennedy resulted in the Community Mental Health Centers Act of 1963.[9] The act provided for transferring the care and treatment of the majority of mentally ill persons from state hospitals to their home communities. The emphasis was to be on local involvement, with provision of comprehensive services to underprivileged areas and people. Continuity of care would be provided through early diagnosis, treatment, and return to the community. The five basic components of comprehensive service are: (1) in-patient care; (2) out-patient care; (3) partial hospitalization (i.e., night-day hospitals); (4) emergency care; and (5) consultation/education. Comprehensive mental health centers offer diagnosis, rehabilitation, training, precare and aftercare, research, and evaluation. These services are expected to relate to a wide range of problem areas and population groups, such as the retarded, the aged, and minorities.

The process of financing, administering, and delivering services in such an ambitious program is compounded by the complex relationships and structures in our political system. The federal government established standards and guidelines for the fifty states to be eligible for federal funding of local community mental health centers. The states in turn drew up rules and standards for local units of government interested in establishing community-based centers.

Problems of Definitions   A primary difficulty lies in the use of the ill-defined term "community mental health center." Does this mean a more elaborate type of traditional psychiatric hospital, or an entirely new concept in the design and delivery of mental health services? In some instances, organized psychiatry has defined the term to substantiate the need for high-quality traditional services in bigger and better hospitals available only to a limited number of people. On the other hand, some militant groups have viewed community mental health as an opportunity to attack psychiatry and to confirm their belief that mental illness can be eradicated solely through social and political action.

Federal regulations required that mental health centers be located "near and accessible to" the populations they serve and that centers be established on the basis of "catchment areas" containing between 75,000 and 200,000 people. This imposition of a federally designed community often runs counter to the reality of logical local community boundaries.

Social and Political Forces   Despite such differences, the shift to a community mental health focus has resulted in clear recognition of the effects of the political and social environment on behavior. It has also allowed other disciplines and nonprofessionals to contribute to the provision of mental health services. Community mental health programs have helped to emphasize the damaging effects of discrimination, poor housing, and urban dislocation. Mental health center personnel have experimented with social action techniques to eliminate or mitigate the emotional impact of negative social forces. The mental health team has been modified in some centers to include lawyers, paraprofessionals, and indigenous community workers. Citizen participation in the design and delivery of mental health services has been achieved, resulting in closer and more positive relationships between center staff members and the people they serve. As community-based programs increase, the cost of maintaining large state hospitals has become prohibitive. Thus, many of them are being closed.[10]

Evaluation   These positive contributions are difficult to evaluate on a nationwide basis since few systematic studies have been done on the impact of community mental health centers. The National Institute of Mental Health has acknowledged this shortcoming, and program evaluation is now being built in. In the meantime, available research indicates that some community mental health services are inadequate and ineffective. The National Institute of Mental Health's Center for the Study of Schizophrenia has discovered that people with this most prevalent mental illness still have high readmission rates and very inadequate levels of adjustment to the community.[11] A report by Ralph Nader's Center for Study of Responsive Law documents the inability of community mental health centers to deal with the personal and societal problems of significant numbers of poor people.[12] The study also shows that the transfer of patients from state hospitals to foster home care in the community often results in worsening of a patient's situation. In many instances, so-called comprehensive community mental health centers provide little more than traditional medical out-patient and in-patient treatment for middle-class patients. Consultation and prevention services have often been neglected. The inadequacies of the community mental health model have also been criticized by client groups and by an organization of "radical therapists" who propose social action to bring about necessary changes.[13]

While the third psychiatric revolution continues, evidence thus far indicates that the promising theory of community mental health needs better implementation if it is to live up to its designation as a bold new approach.

CONCEPTUAL VIEWS OF BEHAVIOR DISORDERS

What are the major approaches employed in current practice? The medical specialty of psychiatry continues to dominate the established programs for treating the mentally ill. The psychologist O. H. Mowrer has called the *diathesis-stress hypothesis* the most widely espoused position in psychiatry. This hypothesis holds that mental illness is most likely caused by the interaction of genetically determined predispositions and environmental or experiential factors. Because of its inclusion of nonmedical components, the diathesis-stress hypothesis has been instrumental in promoting interdisciplinary cooperation and the team approach in treating the mentally ill. Mowrer has conceptualized the diathesis-stress hypothesis into a fourfold approach to mental illness based on (1) genetics, (2) biochemistry, (3) social processes, and (4) reeducation.[14]

Heredity

Some people reject the idea that mental illness may be at least partly determined by one's genetic inheritance. They prefer to view behavior problems as a reaction to one's life circumstances. After all, circumstances can be changed, and democracies have proved particularly adept at providing the opportunity for their people to do so. Nonetheless, evidence indicates the importance of heredity. Research has repeatedly shown higher percentages of schizophrenia and depression for monozygotic (identical) twins than for dizygotic (fraternal) twins. Carefully designed studies in Europe and the United States over the past twenty years have led to the conclusion that complex genetic factors are instrumental in transmitting the potential for both of these disorders.[15]

Research since 1961 has reported that inmates of penal and mental institutions have a higher prevalence of an extra Y or male-determining chromosome than persons in the general population.[16] These findings have resulted in both interest and controversy, but research thus far does not substantiate that particular behavior patterns are preordained and unremedial. However, research continues. The next decade should provide additional data to clarify chromosomal abnormality and its possible effects on deviant behavior.

Biochemistry

Since early times we have known that drugs can influence behavior. Researchers have often attempted to associate biochemical processes with normal and abnormal functioning of the mind. However, interest in the use of medication to treat behavior problems was dramatically reawakened in 1954 with the introduction of the tranquilizers chlorpromazine and reserpine. These drugs helped to initiate a new era of drug therapy based on their dramatic ability to ameliorate excited behavior without marked impairment of motor function or consciousness. The increasing use of tranquilizers and other drugs has made it possible to calm large numbers of disturbed patients so they may function more adequately in the hospital or return to their home community. The marked decrease in the number of resident patients in state hospitals from a peak figure of 555,033 in 1955 to 275,995 in 1972 is largely due to the employment of psychotropic drugs.[17] Antipsychotic drugs are especially successful in treating schizophrenia. The antidepressant drugs have been less impressive, but they continue to be important in restoring the functioning of a large number of people. Antianxiety drugs have been used to modify crippling tension and as an adjunct to other forms of treatment. In addition to their therapeutic function, the ability of certain drugs to bring about altered states of consciousness opens up new possibilities for creative endeavors.

While the effects of the various drugs are often clearly demonstrated, many of their specific actions are still poorly understood. In addition, the widespread use of psychotropic drugs has had some negative consequences. Complications and side effects involving the central and autonomic nervous systems, as well as allergic and toxic reactions or metabolic and endocrine problems, can usually be prevented by careful medical management. Less easy to manage is unsupervised use of drugs to alter one's perception of life experiences. The growing problems of drug abuse through use of hallucinogens, barbiturates, amphetamines, sedatives, and opiates are perhaps an unavoidable consequence of the biochemical advances of the past few years.

Social Processes

Social and environmental factors in the cause and treatment of mental illness have received increasing recognition during the past twenty-five years. The cultural and civil rights revolutions in American society also fostered the development of the community mental health movement. Accumulating evidence and concern about the damaging emotional effects of racial and sexual discrimination, urban blight, and advancing technology shifted the emphasis from intrapsychic to psychosocial causes of stress. One approach has been the investigation of poor communication patterns in the families of schizophrenic patients.[18] This investigation was stimulated in 1956 by the "double bind" hypothesis of Gregory Bateson and his associates, namely, that in some cases the developing infant is repeatedly exposed to contradictory messages about love and acceptance, usually from a rejecting mother.[19] As a result, the infant has difficulty in accurately discriminating the messages it receives. Perceptions and concepts of self and the world become distorted, thus forming the potential nucleus for eventual schizophrenia. This hypothesis has also influenced family therapy. However, evidence to support the hypothesis is still inadequate, and better controlled studies of family communication are needed.

The 1960s saw a new line of investigation that highlighted the antitherapeutic aspects of the hospital environment. Irving Goffman,[20] Thomas Scheff,[21] and other sociologists made use of symbolic interaction theory and the concept of deviancy to analyze the initiation and maintenance of the mental patient's career.

The symbolic interactionists have shown that the perception of one's self is influenced by the definitions of others. They have described how the imprecise concepts of mental health and illness result in a subjective labeling of certain less common behaviors as deviant. Once a person demonstrates these behaviors, he is labeled mentally ill. A series of consequences places him in the status of mental patient. His actions then confirm the negative expectations others have of him. People respond to him accordingly and reinforce his deviant behavior.

Apparently the general public is becoming more accepting of people who have encountered emotional difficulties in their lives. However, there are prejudices and negative consequences associated with the experience of having been a mental patient. This fact was demonstrated in the forced resignation of Thomas Eagleton as vice-presidential nominee in the 1972 elections because of a history of depression and treatment with electroshock. While some people were willing to accept the nominee's current adequate functioning as the test of his qualifications, others were unable to forget that he was once labeled mentally ill.

The concepts of family and social interaction, deviancy, and labeling have made a significant contribution to our understanding of mental illness. However, they do not sufficiently account for the fact that the mental patient also helps to determine the way others treat him and how they define his behavior.

Reeducation

Reeducation involves psychological methods and techniques to bring about more effective and satisfying behavior. People function and interact with one another on the basis of thinking, feeling, and acting, but many psychological approaches to human functioning and behavior disorders typically emphasize one of these components rather than their integration.

The two best known approaches are derived from psychoanalytic theory and learning theory. Psychoanalytic theory and its variations provided the major orientation to the understanding and treatment of mental illness during the first half of the century. The discoveries of Freud mentioned previously were elaborated and extended from neuroses to other major emotional disturbances such as psychoses and character disorders. They were also applied to a wide variety of individual, family, and group problems. The early learning theory approaches of the Russian Ivan Pavlov and American psychologists like E. L. Thorndike and John B. Watson were not initially seen as having broad human applications. However, recent applications of learning theory have provided a major alternative to psychoanalytically derived methods.

During the 1960s the "human potential movement" came into prominence and focused attention on the feeling aspects of behavior. The widespread popularity of encounter-sensitivity training groups and gestalt therapy was seen by some people as a reaction to the thinking and mechanistic approaches to human behavior. While the human potential movement is concerned primarily with "normal" people, its techniques for intensifying the awareness and expression of feeling have been increasingly incorporated into work with severely troubled individuals, families, and groups.

THINKING AND INSIGHT— THE PSYCHOANALYTIC APPROACH

Freud was trained in medicine. From his experience with a limited number of patients he formulated his theory of behavior around the medical model of diagnosis and treatment of underlying causes. Nevertheless, Freud believed that psychoanalysis should not be restricted to the profession of medicine. As a result, many of Freud's European followers were nonmedical analysts. In the United States, the nonmedical professions of psychology and social work embraced many of Freud's ideas and integrated them into their practice beginning in the 1930s. Today some people consider that this was a mistake, because social workers concentrated on their clients' intrapsychic conflicts rather than on the need for social and institutional change. However, since social work must deal with both personal and public concerns, it is not surprising that the profession was influenced by the psychoanalytic theory of human functioning and treatment, which went far beyond the previous limited state of knowledge.[22]

Psychoanalytically oriented approaches assume that the behavioral symptoms of mental illness can best be treated by determining and dealing with their causes—causes presumed to be rooted in past unresolved experiences of which the patient is often unaware. A major goal of diagnosis is to identify and understand the meaning of the patient's conflicts and ego defenses. Treatment is aimed at increasing insight into these conflicts and defenses. Insight presumably leads to modification of attitude, which is seen as a necessary condition for behavior change. Problematic behavior is thus thought to be a symptom of underlying emotional difficulties. Therefore, changing behavior without dealing with its causes will produce a new set of symptoms.

Freud's original model of behavior and his system of treatment have been modified in recent years to emphasize the positive, adaptive functions of the ego and ways of building "ego strength." Thus, the modified approaches are described as "ego psychology" rather than psychoanalytic theory. Despite the departures from Freud's individually directed theory, his ideas continue to be apparent in new and popular systems for the interpersonal understanding and treatment of behavior. For example, in transactional analysis, concepts like superego, ego, and id are replaced by counterparts with simpler terminology, i.e. parent, adult, and child. The goal of treatment is not to develop ego strength, but to accelerate the appropriate operation of the adult in transactions with others.[23]

ACTION AND BEHAVIOR—BEHAVIOR MODIFICATION

In contrast to Freud's medical model, learning theory is a composite of broad generalizations, specific laws, and deductive theories from the experimental laboratory. The two major figures are Pavlov and B. F. Skinner. Together, their basic ideas about learning provide a major alternative to Freud's views on behavior and its modification.

Learning theorists emphasize the connection between an environmental stimulus and a behavioral response. In many respects, this orientation is more congruent with the psychosocial commitment of social work than is psycho-analytic theory, with its emphasis on underlying causes of behavior. From a learning standpoint, there is no qualitative difference between normal and abnormal behavior, since all behavior is learned.

Learning can take place in two ways: (1) According to Pavlovian, classical, respondent conditioning, a stimulus precedes and elicits a response. A classic example of this kind of learning was described by Watson and Rayner in 1920.[24] They determined that an eleven-month-old child named Albert was not afraid of a white rat. They knew that children his age were frightened by loud noises. The white rat (a neutral stimulus) was given to Albert, followed immediately by a loud noise (unconditioned stimulus). After repeating this sequence several times, the rat without the noise became a conditioned stimulus and elicited a fear response from Albert. This type of learning occurs in many common experiences. For example, an accident may elicit fear of riding in automobiles.

(2) In Skinnerian, instrumental, or operant conditioning, the situation is reversed. Here a person first responds to a situation, then an environmental event happens which is contingent upon the behavior. This takes place when a child has a temper tantrum and his or her mother gives the child attention. The child then engages in frequent tantrums. If an event following some emitted behavior increases the rate at which the behavior is emitted, it is called a reinforcer. Thus, the mother reinforces tantrum behaviors by her attention. Behaviors that are reinforced are likely to increase in frequency.

From such concepts, a series of techniques has evolved for increasing desired behavior or decreasing unwanted behavior. For more than a decade, behavior modification has been used to help people with a variety of problems. These range from socializing an autistic child to quieting a classroom of unruly adolescents. "Token economies" have been established in institutions for the mentally ill and retarded where prosocial behaviors are rewarded with tokens which can be exchanged for material rewards. These primary reinforcers are gradually phased out, and patients are taught to modify their behavior in response to verbal praise and attention.

B. F. Skinner has proposed that society be redesigned to take advantage of the fact that behavior can be determined by its consequences.[25] He advocates that societal control be placed in the hands of the behavioral scientists. However, considerable resistance is expressed to exchanging freedom for scientific control of society. Nonbehaviorists are concerned about the amount of control the behavior modifier may exert over the people he works with. Nonetheless, research indicates that more traditionally oriented therapists also shape the verbalizations and behavior of their patients. Thus, the issue becomes one of recognizing overt versus covert control of deciding who will determine the nature of the behavior that is reinforced. Despite the continued debate, learning theory is increasingly being employed with individuals, families, and groups in the home, community, and institutions. Social workers apply behavioral techniques in many practice settings.

"HERE AND NOW" ENCOUNTER GROUPS

Concern with the feeling aspect of behavior is not new. Psychoanalytically oriented therapists and behavior modifiers certainly take feelings into account. However, a popular interest has developed aimed at fostering human awareness and interpersonal encounter as a response to the alienation experienced by large numbers of Americans. Alienation is presumed to be associated with the significant changes that have occurred in the previously stable institutions of the family, the church, the school, and the neighborhood. A means to communicate on an authentic feeling level is viewed as essential to help people achieve self-actualization and a renewed sense of community. The theoretical methods and techniques for accomplishing this goal are varied. They range from the gestalt therapy of the late Fritz Perls[26] to the encounter groups of Carl Rogers[27] and the varied programs of the Esalen Institute.[28] They all share the goal of plumbing the senses and emotions. These approaches were introduced in Chapter 13 on services to groups.

Increasing human awareness and interpersonal communication is achieved through group interaction. A leader or facilitator teaches group members how to modify their behavior by experimenting with a variety of sensory experiences. Unrestrained dialogue, games, touching, and weekend marathons are used to achieve a new depth of self-understanding and intimate communication with others.

Training—Not Treatment Encounter-sensitivity training groups are for ostensibly "normal" people who wish to develop their human potential. The emphasis is on training rather than treatment. However, people with emotional problems find their way into such groups—occasionally at some peril to themselves. While most groups are led by professionals such as psychiatrists, psychologists, and social workers, untrained leaders have also operated groups. The American Psychiatric and Psychological Associations are concerned about the absence of standards for leaders or facilitators.

A recent detailed study of encounter groups shows that people can learn how to experience many deep feelings and relationships in these groups. However, evidence indicates that such experiences may not necessarily produce lasting changes.[29] Despite these findings, various groups in the human potential movement have contributed much to our understanding of the importance of feelings and emotions. Many of the techniques from this movement have been incorporated in the treatment approaches to people with serious emotional problems. As further research becomes available, we should learn more about the interrelationship of thinking, feeling, and behavior.

SOCIAL WORK CONTRIBUTIONS TO MENTAL HEALTH

Social workers began obtaining social histories from relatives of patients newly admitted to Manhattan State Hospital in 1906. Since then many social workers have been associated with the field of psychiatry in providing a variety of diagnostic and treatment services. For example, social workers were instrumental in originating foster home care for discharged mental hospital patients, and they continue to furnish the major supervision in these programs. In the 1920s social workers first became an integral part of the mental health team with psychiatrists and psychologists. This began in the child guidance clinics established by the Commonwealth Fund. The psychiatrist coordinated the services and treated emotionally disturbed children. The psychologist provided projective and intelligence tests. The social worker interviewed the child's mother to obtain a social history. He or she also dealt with the family's social situation and helped the mother modify her behavior in relation to the child.

Interchangeable Roles   Over the years the emphasis has moved from the child to the total family as a unit. Psychiatrists, psychologists, and social workers now function interchangeably as individual, family, and group therapists. The resulting role diffusion in the psychiatric team has been accentuated in recent years with the addition of nurses and other professionals as well as nonprofessionals. While social workers have blended their skills with those of the other team members, their training and experience equip them with particular knowledge about family relationships and community resources. Thus social workers continue to provide specific services related to these dimensions of the mental patient's life.

Social work methods have been expanded over the years to keep pace with changing client needs and new developments in helping methodology. While social workers continue to treat individuals within the context of ego psychology, they also work with groups and families and employ alternative approaches such as behavior modification.

Self-Help Groups   Clients who do not depend on professional leadership also deal with a variety of behavior problems such as alcoholism, drug addiction, mental illness, obesity, and alienation through self-help groups. The clients employ small-group techniques such as self-disclosure, confrontation, and support—all aimed at behavioral change. Social workers refer clients to these groups and maintain liaison with them. They also provide direct help to some groups. To do so they must shorten the social distance between themselves and the clients by also engaging in self-disclosure, confrontation, and support. Social workers also perform special functions by initiating and facilitating group interaction, doing research on the group's helping procedures, and providing ideas for further development of the self-help group.[30]

THE VARIETY AND SCOPE OF BEHAVIOR DISORDERS

Despite the difficulties encountered in attempting to define and classify mental illness, medical and legal considerations support the continued practice of classification. The *Diagnostic and Statistical Manual of the American Psychiatric Association* presents the most widely used system.[31] The second edition (DSM-II) was published in 1968 and reflects international collaboration through the World Health Organization. The major disorders include:

1   Organic brain syndromes
2   Schizophrenia (psychotic and not psychotic)
3   Affective disorders (depressions and manic states)
4   Neuroses
5   Personality disorders (including alcoholism and drug addiction)
6   Psychophysiologic disorders
7   Transient situational disturbances
8   Behavior disorders of childhood and adolescence
9   Social maladjustments without psychiatric disorder (including marital and occupational maladjustment)
10   Mental retardation

People are classified as neurotic if their emotional difficulties produce subjective distress and loss of effectiveness without manifesting gross distortion or misinterpretation of reality and personality disorganization. The psychotic category is reserved for people whose mental functioning is impaired to the extent of distorting their ability to recognize reality. The "personality disorders" category is used for people with lifelong patterns of maladaptive behavior which differ in quality from those of the neurotic or psychotic.

Patient, Family, and Community   Many emotional problems are unrelated to organic dysfunction. Help for people with any of these disorders is oriented to both the patient and his family and is coordinated with the medical treatment provided. The social worker's efforts are directed toward mobilizing the motivation and capacity of the patient and his family and the resources in the community. A systematic assessment of the patient and his situation is followed by the skillful employment of a variety of intervention techniques; these range from reinforcement of self-help activities by the patient to serving as his advocate with community agencies and society at large. The severity of the patient's illness will determine the extent of his effectiveness in relation to his family, his employment, and society. The overall social work goal is to enable the patient to achieve and maintain the highest level of psychosocial functioning possible within his family and the community.

With or without the label of mental disorder, marital, social, and occupational problems have been the major concern of social workers. Marital and family problems are probably treated more often by social workers than by any other professional group. Job finding, job adjustment, and financial provision for the unemployed are also major social work concerns. While DSM-II's first category, organic brain syndrome, is obviously a mental disorder calling for the services of a medical specialist, the category of social maladjustments raises serious questions about applying the ubiquitous labels of mental health and illness to everyday problems of living.

MENTAL RETARDATION

Mental retardation is considered apart from the emotional disorders because of the biological and cultural conditions instrumental in its development. Of course, mental retardation may also occur in individuals with emotional problems such as neurosis or in those who have organic brain damage.

Retardation is evident in the slowed maturation of the young child, the school-age child's learning disability, and the social inadequacy of the adolescent and adult. While approximately 6 million Americans are affected with varying degrees of mental retardation, a large number are capable of supporting themselves and making an adequate social adjustment.

For the 25 percent whose functioning is most severely impaired, the causes of mental retardation are primarily medical, including genetic chromosomal defects, birth injuries, disturbances of metabolism, and infections during the mother's pregnancy. Most retardation occurs as the result of a complex interaction of genetic factors and psychosocial experiences within the family and society.

New Hope   For years the retarded were considered beyond hope by professionals and the general public. The personal concern and imagination of President Kennedy in 1963 laid the groundwork for a broad program of prevention, care and treatment, research, and community planning. The maternal and child health and mental retardation amendments to the Social Security Act brought a new emphasis on prevention through provisions for improving service. Support for research and training encouraged the development of new facilities and techniques for helping the retarded and their families.

Approaches to Retardation

A reawakened interest in poverty and civil rights has highlighted the disproportionate amount of cultural-familial retardation in disadvantaged people in both urban and rural areas. Renewed controversies over nature-nurture contributions to retardation have pointed up the difficulty of trying to separate the effect of the two on intelligence and social behavior.

Widespread use of behavior modification techniques with the retarded in institutions, the home, and the school attempts to reinforce self-care and to improve social and intellectual functioning. These techniques have given new hope by demonstrating that the retarded child can be toilet-trained and taught self-care activities even in the home. Social workers and other professionals now have more than emotional support and custodial care to offer the retarded and their families. Many social workers are engaged in helping parents and teachers learn behavioral techniques to shape and enhance the physical, social, emotional, and intellectual functioning of the retarded.

Groups of parents of the retarded have organized to promote legislation and social policy on behalf of their children. However, much remains to be done in the four important areas of prevention, care and treatment, research, and community planning.

LEGAL CONSIDERATIONS AND CIVIL RIGHTS

Despite the progress made in understanding and treating the mentally ill, our laws still permit the curtailment of a patient's liberty against his will. Infringement of civil rights for the mental patient usually occurs in relation to enforced hospitalization. While state laws differ, in many jurisdictions a person may be hospitalized for many years without due process of law. A person may be sent to a mental hospital for "treatment" on the statement of a physician. However, he often receives no adequate treatment even after several years of confinement. The sad truth is that most large state hospitals are too understaffed to provide anything but custodial care.

American Patients but Foreign-trained Doctors   A particular irony is seen in the staff and patient populations in today's state hospitals. One of the reasons for the decline of moral treatment was the breakdown in communication between American psychiatrists and an increasing population of immigrants with a different culture and language. Today, most of the patients in state hospitals are American-born. However, in many instances, their "psychiatrist" may be a foreign-trained physician who is a recent immigrant to this country.

Abuses of Civil Rights

Treatments such as electroconvulsive therapy pose a real dilemma for the seriously disturbed who are often unable to make rational choices for their own welfare. In such instances, the permission of relatives is obtained. Nonetheless, this still denies the patient his fundamental rights.

Enforced hospitalization and treatment are often imposed on elderly people who might be more appropriately cared for outside of state hospitals. Some states have enacted progressive mental health legislation to safeguard the rights of those who are labeled mentally ill. The psychiatrist Thomas Szasz and other civil libertarians continue to focus our attention on the need for due process for all of our citizens, irrespective of their behavior.[32]

AVAILABILITY AND QUALITY OF SERVICES

Good mental health service is expensive, and availability varies with location and economic circumstances. Mental health professionals and facilities are concentrated in large urban centers, with very few resources in smaller cities and rural areas.

The research of Leo Srole and his colleagues in Manhattan showed higher percentages of mental health impairment among people in the lower social class.[33] Hollingshead and Redlich discovered that in the New Haven, Connecticut, area a larger number of people from the lowest social class were receiving psychiatric care than one would expect by chance.[34] The lower class received custodial or physical care, while people in the upper social classes received psychotherapy. Other research also confirms that poor people often need mental health services that are unavailable to them.

Comprehensive services are becoming available to a larger segment of the population from (1) the establishment of community mental health centers described earlier in this chapter; (2) the decentralization of mental health resources and the availability of psychiatric care in local community medical hospitals; (3) payment for psychiatric care under the provisions of new welfare legislation; (4) a movement of professionals from urban centers to outlying areas; (5) self-help groups to deal with problems previously treated by professionals; and (6) involvement of client groups in the design and delivery of mental health services as agency board members and indigenous workers.

EMPLOYMENT OPPORTUNITIES

Until a few years ago, social work in the mental health field was practiced in relation to psychiatry, but since the problems of mental health are problems in living, they transcend the boundaries of traditional psychiatry. The social worker interested in this field now has a broader opportunity for service.

Hospitals and Clinics Numerous employment possibilities are found in hospital and clinic settings, particularly in large urban areas. Outside of state hospitals, this type of practice is usually centered in an office or ward working with verbal, upper- and middle-class children and adults. The psychiatric team typically consists of psychiatrist, psychologist, social worker, and nurse. The social worker will usually be able to provide individual, group, and family therapy. Treatment approaches differ among agencies. Most employ methods based on ego psychology or behavior modification or a combination of the two.

Community Programs The new programs under the ill-defined mantle of comprehensive community mental health services are often more challenging. The emphasis is on providing services to a more heterogeneous population, including the underprivileged, the retarded, the chronically mentally ill, and the aged. Clients are sometimes worked with in the office, but more likely in the home and community. The commitment to continuity of care enables the social worker to experience in-patient and out-patient services, partial hospitalization, emergency care, consultation and education, prevention, and after-care services. The mental health team in these settings is made up of many different professionals and nonprofessionals. Treatment methods are more varied and eclectic than in traditional settings, with less emphasis on psychodynamic concerns and greater concern with the social antecedents and consequences of observable behavior.

The social worker in the mental health field today is operating from the standpoint of both yesterday and tomorrow. The concepts and terminology of yesterday's medical model are being transformed by new discoveries about learning, small groups, and psychosocial forces that will emphasize education and prevention. Everyone needs to learn more about the mental health consequences of their life circumstances and behavior and the way in which legislation and social policy affect emotional well-being. Social workers have an important role to play in helping us cope with the emotional problems of living.

Anthony J. Vattano

KEY TERMS

mental health
mental illness
psychoanalytic theory
learning theory
social processes
symbolic interaction
diathesis-stress hypothesis

double bind
community mental health center
self-help groups
DSM-II
neuroses
psychoses
personality disorders

FOR DISCUSSION

1 Why do mental health centers and family agencies see similar clients?
2 Why has mental health treatment been a medical specialty?
3 Contrast the "melting pot" and pluralistic ideologies.
4 Criticize: "One out of every ten people needs mental health treatment."
5 What are the implications of Rosenhan's findings about the difficulty in identifying psychiatric patients?
6 Why was moral treatment successful?
7 What were the three revolutions in mental health?
8 Identify the five components of comprehensive mental health.
9 Explain the dramatic decrease in the number of mental hospital patients.
10 What are the shortcomings of the Freudian emphasis in social work?
11 How is conditioning used to alter behavior?
12 What knowledge and skills do social workers bring to the mental health field?
13 Distinguish between neurotic and psychotic.
14 How are the mentally ill denied due process of law?
15 What are the employment opportunities for social workers in mental health?

PROJECTS

1 Compare the services of mental health and family agencies in your community. How are they alike and how do they differ?
2 Prepare a report on hospitalization for mental patients in your state since 1950. What trends are shown in admission rates, length of stay, and cost of care?
3 A Long Island community recently passed an ordinance to try to prevent mental patients from living there. What would lead a community to take that action? If you were a mental health professional, how would you respond?
4 Invite representatives from Recovery (or a similar program for former mental patients) to discuss programs for self-help. How are social workers involved, if at all?

5 Reserve two class sessions. Ask a social worker from a mental hospital to describe the hospital program in the first meeting, and a worker from a community mental health center to make a similar presentation on the center at the second meeting. Be sure they discuss their professional activities. How do the two programs differ?

6 Debate this topic: "Resolved, that serious emotional problems are best described and treated from a medical viewpoint."

7 Interview the local representative of the State Mental Health Association. How is it funded? How do its activities relate to mental health programs in the community?

FOR FURTHER STUDY

Lawrence C. Kolb, *Modern Clinical Psychiatry*, 8th ed., W. B. Saunders, Philadelphia, 1973.

Theodore Millon, *Theories of Psychopathology and Personality*, 2d ed., W. B. Saunders, Philadelphia, 1973.

Stephan P. Spitzer and Norman K. Denzin, *The Mental Patient: Studies in the Sociology of Deviance*, McGraw-Hill, New York, 1968.

Chapter 19

The Handicapped

Who needs rehabilitation?
How does the social worker help?
How does disability spread?
Must the handicapped be employable?

The physically disabled have been identified throughout history as a group to be set apart from the rest of the population. The Bible lists twelve physical blemishes as sufficient to disqualify a priest from officiating. These include "a blind man, or a lame, or he that hath a flat nose, or anything superfluous, or a man that is brokenfooted or brokenhanded, or crookbact, or a dwarf, or that hath a blemish in his eye or be scurvy or scabbed or hath his bones broked. . . ." Later Talmudists extended this list until it included 142 bodily imperfections. Even to this day a candidate for the priesthood must be free of physical infirmities.[1]

CHARACTERISTICS OF THE HANDICAPPED

More than 22 million persons, or 11.5 percent of the civilian, noninstitutionalized population of the United States, are limited in their activities due to chronic health conditions.[2] Heart conditions, arthritis, and rheumatism afflict approximately 50 percent of all disabled. Other major disabling conditions include impairments of the back or spine, lower extremities, and hips; mental and nervous conditions; visual impairments; and hypertension.

Disabling conditions vary with age. Among persons under seventeen, asthma and hay fever are leading disabling conditions. Among those seventeen to forty-four years of age, the major disabler is impairment of the back or spine, and among persons forty-four years and over it is heart disease. Although people at all ages are vulnerable to disability, the aged are most affected. With age the rate of acute and chronic disabling conditions increases dramatically. Between the ages of seventeen and forty-four, 7 percent of the population have some chronic illness or disability. Between forty-five and sixty-five the rate increases to about 19 percent, and in persons sixty-five years of age and over to 46 percent.

The incidence of chronic disability also varies with race. The proportion of severe disability is more than twice as large in the nonwhite as in the white population.[3]

Finally, chronic disability varies sharply with family income. Chronic limitation of activity is most prevalent among low-income families. Approximately 26 percent of persons in families with incomes of less than $3,000 per year have some degree of chronic limitation of activity. This proportion decreases steadily to only 7 percent in families with incomes of $15,000 or more.

The relationship between disability and poverty tends to be cyclical. The poor get sick more frequently, seek and receive less medical treatment, take longer to recover, and suffer more from disabling conditions than those with higher incomes.[4] In addition, the poor who become disabled are usually hindered in finding work not only by physical disability but also by poor education and lack of skills.

REHABILITATION OF THE DISABLED: A DEFINITION

The National Council on Rehabilitation has presented the following definition: "restoration of the handicapped to the fullest physical, mental, social, vocational, and economic usefulness of which he is capable."[5] Rehabilitation involves a combination of disciplines, techniques, and specialized facilities to provide physical restoration, psychological adjustment, vocational counseling, training, and placement. The general philosophy of rehabilitation was well summarized in principles from the proceedings of a conference of psychologists in the field.[6]

1 Every human being has an inalienable value and is worthy of respect for his own sake.

2 Every person has membership in society and rehabilitation should cultivate his full acceptance.

3 The assets of the person should be emphasized, supported, and developed.

4 Reality factors should be stressed in helping the person to cope with his environment.

5 Comprehensive treatment involves the "whole person" because life-areas are interdependent.

6 Treatment should vary and be flexible to deal with the special characteristics of each person.

7   Each person should assume as much initiative and participation as possible in the rehabilitation plan and its execution.

8   Society should be responsible through all possible public and private agencies for the providing of services and opportunities to the disabled.

9   Rehabilitation programs must be conducted with interdisciplinary and interagency integration.

10   Rehabilitation is a continuous process that applies as long as help is needed.

11   Psychological and personal reactions of the individual are ever-present and often crucial.

12   The rehabilitation process is complex and must be subject to constant reexamination—for each individual and for the program as a whole.

ROLE OF THE SOCIAL WORKER IN REHABILITATION

Rehabilitation services are provided in many facilities, including hospitals, rehabilitation institutes or centers, sheltered workshops, vocational training schools, and special institutions or schools for particular disabilities. Professionals in rehabilitation services include physicians, nurses, physical therapists, occupational therapists, corrective therapists, speech and hearing therapists, manual or industrial arts teachers, special education teachers, prosthetists, directors and administrators, social workers, clinical psychologists, counseling psychologists, and guidance counselors. In most rehabilitation settings, professionals from various disciplines work together as a team. The team is primarily medical, with the physician at the head. Emphasis is on the physical functioning of the person. The social worker, however, is primarily concerned with the patient's social functioning. The roles performed by the social worker in hospitals and rehabilitation centers usually include:

1   *Obtaining information about the client's family background and present status through a social history.* The social worker is expected to provide the rest of the rehabilitation team with information about the patient's life outside the hospital, both as it was before he entered the hospital and as it potentially might be upon discharge. What are the relevant family relationships? Will the patient be able to return to the home environment? What kinds of supports are offered? What problems exist? This information is gathered through contacts with the patient and his family at the center, in visits to the patient's home, and from case records of previous contacts with social and medical agencies.

2   *Communicating with the patient about the treatment facility and his treatment program.* The impersonal atmosphere of hospitals and rehabilitation centers is aversive to most patients. Unfamiliarity, strangeness, and uncertainty about the environment and the procedures to be employed add to the patient's negative feelings. Routine hospital procedures often make the patient anxious because he does not understand why they are being done and may misinterpret their purpose. To help overcome these feelings, the job of the social worker includes ensuring that the patient has a good orientation to the institution, the equipment to be used, and the procedures to be performed.

3   *Communicating with the patient and his family about the patient's physical condition.* The doctor explains the particular medical condition to the

patient. The social worker explores with the patient and his family the practical implications of his medical condition. What will his medical outlook mean in terms of his ability to function in his home and in his vocational and social life? For the social worker, this requires a basic knowledge of various medical conditions and terminology.

4 *Acting as liaison between the patient's family and the rehabilitation staff.* The social worker may arrange meetings between the physician and other staff and family members or pass on information from the physician to the family or from the family to the physician.

5 *Helping the patient and his family make use of community resources.* Familiarity with the procedures and programs of agencies such as the welfare department and vocational rehabilitation department is essential to educate the physician, the patient, and his family about appropriate use of these resources. The social worker may also carry out the arrangements for prosthetic devices, wheelchairs, assistive appliances, financial assistance, or special job training. The worker may process forms and try to prevent delays in agency procedures.

6 *Making arrangements and recommendations for discharge.* The information necessary for discharge planning comes from the social worker's knowledge of the patient and his family and their preferences. If the patient cannot return home, the social worker needs to provide information about other available facilities, including the services they offer and their cost. The worker may arrange for care and for financial aid.

7 *Counseling the patient and his family.* Counseling involves helping the patient adjust to the rehabilitation program and helping him and his family accept his disability and the changes that it may involve in his functioning. Dealing with problems created by new role relationships is essential. Counseling requires specialized knowledge of the psychosocial, familial, maturational, interactional, and employment aspects of disability.

PSYCHOSOCIAL ASPECTS OF REHABILITATION

Initial Reactions to Disability

Work with a disabled person will be influenced by the patient's own response to his disability. Reactions differ. Some people first feel shock comparable to that at the death of a loved one. During this period, the individual compares the past with the present. He focuses on the things he will now be unable to do and what his loss means in terms of personal and social satisfaction denied him. These feelings are well expressed by Harold Russell when he became aware that he no longer had hands. In his book, *Victory in My Hands*, he recounts how he depended on his hands, how efficient they were, how valuable, and how perfect.[7] During this period, the individual is often seriously depressed and preoccupied with the question, "Why me?"

Daily Demands   Several processes may move the person from his preoccupation with loss. The sheer necessities of living may help the person deal more with the present and less with the past. The blind individual becomes concerned with learning to eat and learning to move around. Learning to master activities of daily living focuses attention on the present. In an effort to help the patient focus on the present and recognize his abilities to cope with it, the rehabilitation team may introduce instruction in daily living skills quite early.

Social Relations   Association with other individuals who are also disabled may provide some measure of objectivity. For example, the blind individual begins to realize that he is able to walk, use his arms, and hear things being said—abilities that other patients may lack. Through this type of comparison, he becomes aware of his own assets and that he is not so "badly off" after all.

Time Restores Confidence   Finally, a single emotional state is time-limited; the person tends to become satiated with the emotion and then is ready to move away from his preoccupation with loss. A woman discussing her own reaction to becoming blind noted: "At first, I said, 'I cannot believe it,' and then I said, 'I will not believe it,' but finally, fatigued beyond measure, I said, 'I suppose I must believe it.'"[8]

The Congenitally Disabled

These stages apply mainly to individuals disabled in late childhood or older. A different process of adjustment is involved for the congenitally disabled or those disabled in early childhood. The very young child is unlikely to be aware of his disability. However, the passage of time and interaction with others bring growing awareness. The child learns that he is different and that a negative value is placed on this difference. In his autobiography, Christy Brown, who was born with cerebral palsy, describes the process. While growing up, Christy was taken everywhere in a wagon by his sisters and brothers. One day the wagon broke, and he couldn't go out with them.[9]

> I was now just ten, a boy who couldn't walk, speak, feed or dress himself. I was helpless, but only now did I begin to realize how helpless I really was. I still didn't know anything about myself: I knew nothing beyond the fact that I was different from others. I didn't understand what made me different or why it should be I. . . .
> I couldn't reason this out. I couldn't even think clearly about it. I could only feel it, feel it deep down in the very core of me, like a thin sharp needle. . . .
> Up to then I had never thought about myself. True, there had come sometimes a vague feeling that I wasn't like the others, an uneasy sort of stirring in my mind that came and went. But it was just one dark spot in the brightness of things; and I used soon to forget it. . . .
> Now it was different. Now I saw everything, not through the eyes of a little boy eager for fun and brimming with curiosity, but through those of a cripple, a cripple who had only just discovered his own affliction.
> I looked at Peter's hands. They were brown, steady hands with strong, square fingers, hands that could clasp a hurley firmly or swing a chestnut high into the air. Then I looked down at my own. They were queer, twisted hands with bent, crooked fingers, hands that were never still, but twitched and shook continually so that they looked more like two wriggling snakes than a pair of human hands.
>
> I began to hate the sight of those hands, the sight of my wobbly head and lopsided mouth. . . .

Christy's awareness involved several steps: (1) avoidance of thoughts of himself; (2) a vague but hurting feeling that he was not like others; and (3) a focus on the different and negative meaning of it. A critical incident, not being able to go out, led Christy to focus attention on his individual characteristics. For many children the critical event occurs when they first attend school and are ridiculed by others.

Parental Attitudes   An additional determinant of the child's adjustment to his disability is his parents' reaction. Many parents blame themselves for their child's handicap and experience feelings of shame and guilt. A study of thirty sets of twins in which one twin of each set had cerebral palsy suggests that handicapped children are often treated by their parents as though they are "sick," with all the social role connotations commonly associated with sickness. The child is offered less responsibility. Fewer limits are placed on his behavior, there is increased tolerance of his deviant behavior, and his personal whims are indulged more often than those of other siblings. Whatever the reaction, parental behavior strongly influences the child's attitudes and behavior.[10]

Cult of the Body Beautiful

Handicapped persons must deal with specific societal attitudes and expectations, as well as with their own internalizations of these beliefs. Our culture places a heavy emphasis on the value of a perfectly formed physique. From childhood the importance of physical perfection is stressed. This focus is present in teaching through books, movies, and television. Even early fairy tales embody the value of physical perfection. The beautiful Snow White was good, the ugly witch evil. In the story of Peter Pan, Captain Hook can be recognized on first sight as "bad" by his short fat body and the hook that replaces his missing hand. Beauty is identified with goodness and physical ugliness with evil. Physical attractiveness, children are taught, leads to the "good life." By contrast they learn that the person who is physically imperfect is considered inferior. Evidence suggests that all children, disabled as well as able-bodied, incorporate these values into their thinking. One study found that ten- and eleven-year-old able-bodied and disabled children of various races and different social and cultural backgrounds consistently rank-ordered pictures of children with and without physical disabilities in the same manner. In all cases the picture of a child with no disability was most preferred. Apparently, the disabled individual, having been brought up to value physical perfection, regards himself and is regarded by others as less desirable.[11]

Societal Values   The cultural values that emphasize perfect physique, physical power, and strength are learned as a part of socialization. They can be unlearned. Other values may contribute even more to a person's worth. Kindness, helpfulness, and maturity are all values of importance. The society needs to revise its values, and the social worker can help the handicapped person alter his own values.

In the process of reevaluation the handicapped person is faced with contrasting personal and societal attitudes as he tries to build an image of himself. Katherine Butler Hathaway, a dwarf, describes an anguishing process:[12]

One day I took a hand glass and went to a long mirror to look at myself. . . . I didn't scream with rage when I saw myself. I just felt numb. That person in the mirror couldn't be me. I felt inside like a healthy, ordinary, lucky person—oh, not like the one in the mirror! Yet when I turned my face to the mirror there were my own eyes looking back, hot with shame. . . . When I did not cry or make any sound, it became impossible that I should speak of it to anyone, and the confusion and panic of my discovery were locked inside me. . . .

Over and over I forgot what I had seen in the mirror. It could not penetrate into the interior of my mind and become an integral part of me. I felt as if it had nothing to do with me; it was only a disguise. . . .

I looked in the mirror (again) and was horror-struck because I did not recognize myself. In the place where I was standing, with that persistent romantic elation in me, as if I were a favored fortunate person to whom everything was possible, I saw a stranger, a little, pitiable, hideous figure, and a face that became, as I stared at it, painful and blushing with shame. . . .

Every one of those encounters was like a blow on the head. They left me dazed and dumb and senseless every time, until slowly and stubbornly my robust persistent illusion of well-being and of personal beauty spread all through me again, and I forgot the irrelevant reality and was all unprepared and vulnerable again.

The Spread of Disability

In addition to being seen as inferior physically, the disabled person may be perceived as less capable in other respects. His physical aspects may tend to dominate the entire perception of him as a person, so that his handicap appears to spread to other areas. We tend to talk more loudly in the presence of a person who is blind; if a person cannot see, an assumption is made that he also has trouble hearing. Another example involves treating a physically disabled person as if he were socially and mentally retarded. Larry B., a twenty-year-old college student, gave the following account:

I'm in church with my father and my father is standing beside me and I'm in a wheelchair. I'm relatively intelligent, but I'm disabled. I'm sitting there like anyone else. And somebody comes up to my father and they're about as far away from me as from him and they say to my father, "How's he doing?" "Well, he's looking pretty good." And I just want to kick him in the stomach.

Generalization of disability can also influence the behavior of the person with a handicap. Recognizing his disability in one area, he may begin to believe that he is less able mentally and socially. Unfortunately, the behavior of others reinforces the disabled person's beliefs. A social worker may help the person with a disability to see that there is no inevitable connection between his physical disability and other traits. He can be helped to recognize his potential as an intelligent, warm, good, socially able individual.

Other Causes than Disability   The social worker must also be careful not to overgeneralize the effects of disability. Problems with a spouse or children or a job can be caused by many other factors. Although the individual with a physical handicap may have to cope with many social and psychological problems, he usually meets them about as well or as poorly as the able-bodied individual. In studies of the adjustment of the disabled, 35 to 45 percent of the subjects were reported to be at least as well adjusted as the average able-bodied individual. The maladaptive behaviors shown by the handicapped were similar to those shown by the nondisabled, and there was no relationship between the type of physical disability and type of adjustive behavior.[13]

Requirement of Mourning

Another of society's attitudes affecting personal adjustment is that the disabled person "ought" to feel inferior—"the requirement of mourning."[14] People have a need to safeguard their values; they need to see a person who is unable to attain their values as suffering and inferior. An able-bodied individual who is valued for his physical attractiveness needs the disabled person to suffer as a sign that the values of "body beautiful" are worthy and important. Consider attitudes toward the mentally retarded. Society tends to believe that intelligence is of prime importance, and that individuals who do not have at least normal intelligence are unfortunate. If they do not suffer, the tendency is to infer that they are "too stupid to know better."

Out of this attitude come conceptions of the disabled person as someone to be pitied. He is less fortunate and should be helped. Oversolicitude and patronizing attitudes are the result. The social worker must develop self-awareness so he can view the client as a peer, not to be protected from the world but to be helped to become part of it.

IMPORTANCE OF THE FAMILY

The effectiveness of a rehabilitation program depends upon support from the family. If it fails to provide an atmosphere of warmth and encouragement or is unwilling to accept the person's performance, the aims of a therapeutic program may be seriously hampered.[15]

Family solidarity and encouragement are important factors in rehabilitation. The disruption of family roles and strained interpersonal relations that occur when a member becomes ill or disabled must be recognized. Whenever a family member becomes disabled, new expectations result that influence the roles of family members. Conflict and stress among family members are likely to occur. Numerous adjustments must be made. The social worker must explore how the disability affects all family members. A mother's inability to cook and clean may mean that these tasks fall to the oldest daughter. The daughter, feeling cheated of time to do other things, may resent her mother, or the mother may resent the new dependence upon the daughter.

INDIVIDUAL MOTIVATION

Influence of Other Patients

Effective rehabilitation will also depend on the motivation of the individual to further his treatment plan. A source of support for the patient may come from other patients, as well as from the family. To utilize this resource the social worker may organize a group of patients to enable them to receive assurance and support from each other. Peer-group members are usually anxious to share their experiences and are in a good position to offer realistic advice and support. The group may encourage one another to carry out prescribed therapeutic planning and be critical of those who deviate. Members may also use each other as a comparative reference group. Members who are further along in the rehabilitative process may serve as role models for others, their level of progress becoming a goal. For example, one member may hear that another member with a similar injury is able to dress himself completely; this may then encourage the other patient to work until he also is able to do so.

Dependency in the Hospital In rehabilitation centers people live very dependent and sheltered existences for long periods of time. Each day their needs for food, shelter, and activity are taken care of within the confines of the center. Sympathetic physical therapists, occupational therapists, nurses, nurse's aides, and social workers meet their needs. The individual adjusts to the center, even though it may often be boring and routine. It is a place where the individual feels comfortable.

In contrast, the outside world often seems scary and uncomfortable. It is easier to get around in the rehabilitation hospital than in the outside world. People in the hospital are friendly and interested; people outside are usually either hostile or patronizing. Ex-patients may voluntarily return to the rehabilitation center because they like it there.

To counteract the lack of motivation to return to the outside world, more halfway houses should be set up. After completing a rehabilitation program, patients can live in the halfway house while they begin adjusting to the world again. Gradually they take on all the responsibilities of daily living.

INTERACTION WITH THE NONHANDICAPPED

People tend to end interactions sooner with a handicapped person than with a nonhandicapped person.[16] In social situations with handicapped persons, appropriate behaviors are not clearly known, making interactions uncomfortable. For example, if the nonhandicapped person makes a direct remark about the disabling condition, he feels he may be too outspoken. Yet if he tries to completely forget the disability he may make impossible demands on the handicapped person or unthinkingly slight him. There may be guarded references; common everyday words suddenly are avoided; and there may be a fixed stare away from the person, an artificial seriousness, or compulsive talking on the part of the nonhandicapped person.

The handicapped person in turn is usually sensitive to these interactional strains:[17]

I get suspicious when somebody says, "Let's go for a uh, ah [imitates confused and halting speech] push with me down the hall," or something like that. This to me is suspicious because it means that they're aware, really aware, that there's a wheelchair here, and that this is probably uppermost with them. . . . A lot of people in trying to show you that they don't care that you're in a chair will do crazy things. Oh, there's one person I know who constantly kicks my chair, as if to say "I don't care that you're in a wheelchair.

I don't even know that it's there." But that is just an indication that he really knows it's there.

The handicapped person is aware that his preferred definition of himself as someone who is merely physically different but not socially deviant is being denied.

Social Workers May Be Uneasy   Establishing an honest comfortable relationship with the person who has a physical or mental disability may be difficult for many social workers. Their ability to overcome this feeling of uneasiness is essential to a relationship with handicapped clients. Attitudes of the social worker toward physical disability will influence his ability to help the disabled client, who may quickly detect covert feelings of pity, horror, or aversion. The social worker must consider disability not as a disaster but as a deviation to which one can adjust. The successful social worker reacts to the client as a person, and not to the physical disability.

EMPLOYMENT

Productive employment is the goal of most rehabilitation programs. The individual may be well qualified yet unable to get a job because of the employer's attitude toward the disabled. Employers generally hire the able-bodied rather than the disabled. The social worker can often help by showing the employer that the disabled client is right for his job because he is the best-qualified applicant. It means demonstrating that although he is limited by his disability, he can perform effectively in other areas of functioning.

Architectural Barriers

After successfully completing a rehabilitation program the handicapped individual may not be able to accept a position because the place of business is inaccessible. To the individual in a wheelchair, a flight of steps that can't be ramped or bathrooms that are too small mean no job. In 1967 the National Commission on Architectural Barriers to Rehabilitation of the Handicapped found that the biggest obstacles to employment were the physical features of the buildings. More than 20 million physically disabled were excluded from normal living by steps and curbs, steep and narrow corridors, narrow or revolving doors, inaccessible toilet facilities, unreachable light and alarm switches, and a lack of Braille lettering for the blind on doors and elevators.[18]

Federal legislation was passed in 1968 to alter this situation. Public Law 90-48 requires all buildings that are designed, built, or altered using federal funds to be accessible to the physically handicapped. Similar legislation needs to be enacted by each state to cover all public buildings, and the laws should be enforced.

REHABILITATION PROGRAMS

Thus far we have been discussing the social worker's role in dealing with the disabled client and assuming that he will be involved in a rehabilitation program. What are these rehabilitation programs? Who is eligible to use them? How are they paid for?

History of Programs for the Disabled

Rehabilitation programs reflect a history of changing attitudes and customs, beginning with unorganized alms-giving to help the disabled. Begging was the main occupation of the disabled in Europe, and those in the American colonies followed suit. Towns and counties were usually willing to maintain their own beggars, but strict laws prevented residents of other villages from begging in their town. Disability was viewed primarily from a moral perspective. An association was made between physical malformation and evil. Disability represented a punishment for sinful behavior and sometimes as evidence of witchcraft.[19]

Toward a Medical Emphasis   Slowly, with the development of hospitals during the early 1800s, emphasis shifted to treating the sick and disabled. Great advances were made in orthopedic surgery for restoring the bodies of persons crippled by disease or injury. Special facilities for the disabled were established. The Hospital for the Ruptured and Crippled and the New York Orthopedic Hospital and Dispensary were both opened in the 1860s; the first educational institutions for the disabled were also established about the same time.

Industrial Accidents   Parallel to these developments was the growth of the Industrial Revolution. Workers in factories labored long hours at fatiguing, often dangerous tasks. Injuries and illness resulting from these conditions were common. The employer and larger society took no responsibility for compensating the worker. However, some segments of society began to feel that help should be given to persons disabled in industrial accidents and to those disabled by other external forces. Charitable organizations began to offer help to those whose problems were not of their own making through work, and training for work.

Legislation

Through organizations set up to help the disabled, influential citizens became personally involved with the problems of disability. They also became aware of the limited impact of private or voluntary efforts and began to educate fellow citizens to the need for the assumption of public responsibility. In 1918 Massachusetts passed the first state law that set up public provisions to help the disabled. In this same year the federal government passed legislation to help rehabilitate handicapped veterans of World War I.

Several factors now combined to provide a basis for support of national legislation for civilian rehabilitation: success of the veteran's rehabilitation bill; increased awareness of the needs of the disabled, especially those injured in industrial accidents; and an awareness that our growing economy was dependent on an ever-increasing supply of able-bodied manpower. In 1920, the Smith Fess Act—The Civilian Vocational Rehabilitation Act—was passed to encourage states to undertake rehabilitation services for disabled civilians. This was the first legislation to provide federal "grants in aid" for support of social services on a 50-50 matching basis providing vocational guidance, vocational training, prosthetics, and job placement services.

Economic and Humanitarian Goals Legislation relied on two kinds of justification, an assumption of social responsibility to help the disabled and an awareness that our economy needed this rehabilitated manpower. From 1920 to 1970 the expansion of federal-state programs of vocational rehabilitation led to increasing tension between the economic and humanitarian justifications of the rehabilitation program.

By the 1960s humanitarian considerations were stressed in the extension of rehabilitation. Emphasis was on helping every individual develop his full potential apart from his contribution to the economic system. Accordingly, services were provided to a wider range of individuals. Clients who had been considered too physically or mentally handicapped were now eligible to be served. Vocational objectives were no longer defined only in terms of competitive employment. Sheltered workshop employment and the development of skills for personal living were considered to be acceptable goals.[20] However, this growing humanitarian concern did not eliminate economic concerns. While attempting to give service to all who needed it, the program was still justified to Congress on economic grounds. Data were used to show the economic values of rehabilitation to society:[21]

> The average cost of rehabilitation is returned fivefold in income taxes paid by the employed handicapped worker; the average rate of income after rehabilitation is seven to ten times greater for the average person than before rehabilitation; and vocational rehabilitation of a handicapped person on public assistance can be effected at a one-time cost comparable to the cost of supporting him on welfare during a one-year period.

The economic appeal of such statistics tended to make Congress very supportive of the program.

The Rehabilitation Act of 1973 continues the dualistic purposes. It furthers humanitarian objectives by providing services to severely handicapped individuals. On the economic side:

> This bill keeps the Federal vocational rehabilitation program focused on its original and proper purpose, that of preparing people for meaningful jobs, rather than burdening that program with broad new medical or welfare functions better performed elsewhere.[22]

HOW THE VOCATIONAL REHABILITATION PROGRAM WORKS NOW

An individual is eligible for service if he has a physical or mental disability that substantially interferes with his ability to obtain employment, and if there is a reasonable expectation that service will enable him to obtain gainful employment or be more productive.

An individual contacts the state rehabilitation agency and explains his situation to a counselor. A medical examination is given free of charge to determine the extent of the applicant's disability, the general state of his overall health, and the presence of any other handicapping conditions.

On the basis of medical findings and recommendations of the rehabilitation counselor, the agency determines whether the applicant is eligible. The program of appropriate services may include:

1 Individual counseling and guidance
2 Medical, surgical, hospital, or other services that will lessen the individual's disability or correct any other handicapping conditions that may be found through medical examination
3 Special equipment such as prosthetics, hearing aids, canes, guide dogs, or wheelchairs
4 Special training in areas such as reading, sign language, or social adjustment; training at a rehabilitation facility, a public or private college, or on the job
5 Money for living expenses and transportation during the training period
6 Help in attaining a suitable job and necessary tools, equipment, licenses, or stock for a small business
7 Follow-up to see if the client and employer are satisfied

The services provided depend both on the individual needs of the client and the current financial resources of the state rehabilitation agency. An individual may be eligible, but for financial reasons the state agency may be unable to provide service.

If a State is unable to serve all eligible persons who apply for service the state agency establishes a system of priorities for determining the order in which individuals are accepted for service.[23]

Thus it can decide, for example, that priority is to be given to the individual who needs vocational training over the one who requires medical restoration. Each state also determines whether an economic means test is to be used to determine the applicant's entitlement for certain services.

ASSESSMENT OF SERVICES

Studies by the President's Task Force on the physically handicapped showed that only one-third of the people in need of the services were receiving them. Several problems were identified in the current system of services: (1) Policies and procedures of agencies tended to be too complex and confusing to be understood easily by those who needed service. (2) Varying eligibility requirements had little relationship to the actual service needs of the individual. (3) Coordination between government programs, and between government programs and private or voluntary programs, was very poor. (4) The geographical distribution of resources for the handicapped was uneven, resulting in overutilization of some programs and facilities and underutilization of others. (5) There was a lack of consumer representation or advocacy in the planning and evaluation of services. (6) There were serious gaps in services for children.[24]

NEEDED: PUBLIC UNDERSTANDING

A beginning has been made in meeting the physical needs of disabled persons, but there is still a significant lack of public understanding and social acceptance of the disabled. Often the largest disability for the physically handicapped is not the physical defect itself, nor the unavailability of needed services, but the ignorance and oversolicitude of others concerning handicapped persons. The prevailing attitude seems to be that such "blighted creatures" must be protected from the world, instead of helped to become part of it.

Ideally, the disabled individual's behavior should be limited only by the physical restrictions imposed by his impairment. The psychological and socioeconomic handicap of the disabled person frequently far outweighs his actual physical limitations. Until the handicapped person can be given an opportunity to obtain an existence as close to normal as possible, social services will be only partially effective.

Nancy Weinberg Asher

KEY TERMS

rehabilitation
handicap
requirement of mourning
disability spread

"body beautiful" cult
National Commission on Architectural
Barriers

FOR DISCUSSION

1 Identify possible reasons for not accepting people with serious physical disabilities in professions.
2 Why are disabilities related to age?
3 Explain the relationship between disability and poverty.
4 Define the goal of rehabilitation.
5 Of the twelve principles of rehabilitation, which two or three do you consider most important? Why?
6 Why is the social worker in the rehabilitation hospital sometimes identified as the "family helper"?
7 How do reactions to congenital handicaps differ from those to handicaps acquired later?
8 Cite examples from literature other than the text that show the association of disability with evil.
9 What is meant by the spread of disability?
10 How much does a handicapping condition change personality?
11 Why are self-help groups often important in rehabilitation programs?
12 Explain why social workers may be uncomfortable with handicapped people.
13 What has been the major clientele of public rehabilitation counseling programs? What other groups are being added?
14 Why do some agencies show especially outstanding records of job placements?
15 Why should rehabilitation programs provide more services for children?

PROJECTS

1 Ask two or three handicapped students to visit the class to discuss rehabilitation services that they have received, problems occasioned by self and others, and use of self-help groups.

2 Analyze various areas of the community in terms of architectural barriers for the handicapped. Also consider construction of sidewalks and parking accommodations. What means could be used to improve the situation?
3 Read a biography of a handicapped person and discuss means of coping. Your choices might include Clara Barton, Ludwig von Beethoven, Demosthenes, Thomas Edison, Helen Keller, John Milton, and Franklin D. Roosevelt.
4 Invite a staff member from the public rehabilitation agency to discuss programs for the disabled and for other groups such as former mental patients, alcoholics, and the poor.
5 Make a study of the development of the wheelchair. What improvements are still needed? What are the advantages of manual and battery-powered types?
6 Visit a rehabilitation hospital or clinic. Find out all you can about the roles of the social worker. What other staff members are involved?

FOR FURTHER STUDY

Israel Goldiamond, "A Diary of Self-Modification," *Psychology Today*, November 1973.
Elizabeth E. May, *Independent Living for the Handicapped and the Elderly*, Macmillan, New York, 1974.
James McDaniel, *Physical Disability and Human Behavior*, Pergamon Press, New York, 1969.
Harold Moses and C. Patterson (eds.), *Research Readings in Rehabilitation Counseling*, Stipes Publishing Co., Champaign, Ill., 1973.
Julian Myers, *An Orientation to Chronic Disease and Disability*, Macmillan, London, 1965.
Isabel P. Robinault, *Functional Aids for the Multiply Handicapped*, Harper & Row, Hagerstown, Md., 1973.
Constantina Safilios-Rothschild, *TheSociology and Social Psychology of Disability and Rehabilitation*, Random House, New York, 1970.
Melvin E. Schoonover, *Letters to Polly . . . On the Gift of Affliction*, Eerdmans, Grand Rapids, Mich., 1971.
SCI Source Book, Veterans Administration, 1973, Government Printing Office, No. 5100–00063.

Chapter 20

The Offender

Who are the offenders?
Do most offenders go to prison?
What does social work accomplish in corrections?
How do probation and parole differ?

"Criminal offender" and "corrections" suggest sensational events and exposés. The Attica prison uprising, resulting in the killing of ten guards and twenty-nine inmates, has been called by the New York Special Investigative Commission the "bloodiest one-day encounter between Americans since the Civil War."

Periodically, the news media remind us of the continued use of armed "trusties" in a number of correctional facilities—a select group of inmates trusted by the administration who are given authority to direct work crews and to guard and discipline their fellow prisoners. These examples demonstrate that the correctional system suffers from a variety of problems that hinder its avowed goal of rehabilitation.

Social workers and others concerned about the problems of the offender must be prepared for a lengthy struggle to eradicate those elements of the system that tend to dehumanize its clients and to foster elements that contribute to their rehabilitation. Working with offenders is an increasingly important career in social work today. Current correctional policy and procedures now require more social workers. A brief look at the criminal justice system will clarify their roles in different settings within the system and suggest various roles for the future.

SOCIAL WORKERS IN CORRECTIONS

Although social workers have been working with criminal offenders for a long time, mainly as probation or parole workers, they have generally preferred to work in other settings and with other clients—the "deserving poor" or those who get into trouble through no fault of their own. Offenders, by contrast, get into trouble from their own acts, not as a result of a misfortune over which they have had no control.

Preference for Voluntary Clients Social workers have preferred voluntary clients who come because they want help and believe that social workers can provide it. Presumably the client and worker will then perceive the problem in about the same way and can work out a mutually acceptable solution.

The offender has probably been ordered to see the social worker, and he may not think that he needs help—at least not the type the social worker is prepared to offer. An offender who was "busted" on a drug charge may describe his problem: "The fuzz are picking on me. There are lots of guys on the street doing worse. Why don't you get the cops off my back?"

The social worker, on the other hand, may define the problem in terms of the offender's drug use. He may want the client to talk about why he is using drugs and how he could break the habit. Such a disparity in the definition of the problem can prevent a productive helping relationship.

Use of Authority In a correctional setting the use of authority for many social workers is an additional complication. In a private child guidance or a mental health clinic, a client seemingly comes for help because he wants to. If he doesn't like what the social worker has to offer, he is free to quit coming, and many do so. In corrections the client is forced to report at stated intervals and is punished if he does not, sometimes by being sent to prison. Many offenders regard their social workers more as agents of social control than as sources of help. But is the mentally ill patient who may have been committed to a mental hospital against his will really a voluntary client? When a public assistance worker denies a client further assistance because he does not conform to stated rules, is he not acting authoritatively? Recognizing the coercive element inherent in much social work practice is a first step for the social worker who must learn to use authority constructively.

Value Conflicts Social workers are sometimes reluctant to work in correctional settings because many of their co-workers may not share some of the basic values of the social work profession. For instance, a probation or parole officer often has to work cooperatively with the police. Correct police procedure can look like harassment to the offender or to the social worker, who is more concerned with the welfare of his client than with the protection of the general public.

For instance, Joe, who has been convicted of burglary and armed robbery, is out on parole and has just found a job with the help of his parole officer. A week after he begins work, an armed robbery is reported in the vicinity. The police ferret Joe out, because he has a history of similar crimes, and bring him to the station house to question him. He misses a day of work, and his employer, who was reluctant to hire a man with a known record, fires him. The parole officer is furious. He knows how hard it is for an "ex-con" to find work and thinks that the police should have given him a break instead of bringing him in on the slightest suspicion. The police, on the other hand, followed the procedure most likely to solve the crime. From their point of view, any person with Joe's history is a prime suspect. They would have been derelict in their duty if they had not checked him out.

Income and Status   In the past, social workers were reluctant to accept employment in correctional settings because they did not enjoy pay and prestige equivalent to that of other social workers. These disparities are gradually decreasing, partly because the correctional system is relying more heavily on social work, with its greater emphasis on rehabilitation than on custody. Cost analysis shows that even relatively well-paid social workers are less expensive than custody in prisons or jails. Accordingly, the proportion of convicted offenders put on probation in the community rather than being put in prison has increased steadily. In 1965 about 53 percent of the convicted offenders were put on probation. In some localities, over 80 percent are on probation.[1]

The need for additional social work staff, especially as probation and parole officers, is overwhelming. The President's Task Force estimated that in order to handle the juvenile offender population alone 23,000 staff are needed, three times the number available in 1965. For adult offenders three times the number of probation and parole officers are needed just for major adult offenders (felons).[2]

A PROFILE OF OFFENDERS

None of the statistics on the offender population gives a true indication of the extent of crime or of the number of offenders. The statistics reflect only those who come to the official attention of the police, courts, and correctional agencies. Less than 20 percent of all situations that warrant an arrest actually lead to one.

Social workers in corrections deal more with criminal offenders than with those involved in such civil offenses as breach of contract. They are rarely asked to treat extortioners or operators of confidence games. Those who participate in organized crime are also unlikely to seek or receive social work services.

Criminal offenders are generally young people, although the typical age varies with the type of offense. Auto theft (usually joy-riding), burglary, and larceny (including shoplifting) are primarily committed by fifteen- to seventeen-year-olds, whereas embezzlement and gambling are usually committed by persons over twenty-four years of age.[3] Some of the most common crimes, such as running away from home, truancy, or curfew violations, can be committed only by minors because these acts are not considered crimes when committed by adults. Accordingly, you may expect an increase in crime over the next few years because children born during the baby boom of the second half of the 1950s are now teenagers and young adults.

Offenders are predominantly male and white. Blacks have a higher crime rate than Whites but constitute a smaller number of offenders. In recent years the rate of increase in crimes among females has been much greater than among males, but still almost five times as many males as females were arrested in 1970.[4]

There are relatively few murders (homicides), but many auto thefts. Misdemeanors (petty offenses) are far more common than felonies (serious offenses), and crimes against property, e.g. theft or vandalism, are much more common than crimes against the person, e.g. aggravated assault or manslaughter. About one-third of all arrests are for drunkenness.[5]

Plea Bargaining   Don't conclude, however, that there is no real crime problem. The offense for which a person is convicted is frequently much less serious than the one of which he was originally accused. As a result of plea bargaining, many charges of assault are reduced to disorderly conduct or drunkenness. In charges of drunkenness, very few of those arrested were only intoxicated. Many were involved in fights or constituted a nuisance to others. Others are arrested because they were discovered in a public place unconscious from intoxication. The police may have charged them and taken them to the local lockup to "dry out" or to "sleep it off" to protect them from exposure and other dangers. Recorded offenses are a poor reflection of actual law-violating behavior, but they are the best indicators we have.

Estimates of selected offender characteristics are shown in Figure 20-1. The total offender population has increased by about 40 percent. The distribution of

Figure 20-1   Average daily population in corrections.[6]

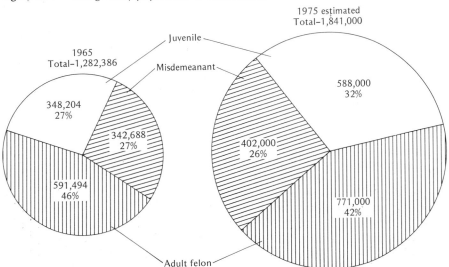

offenders among the three categories has not changed radically. The greatest increase comes in the juvenile offender category. Adult felons constitute a smaller proportion of the total offender population. However, changes in labels may affect crime rates. If victimless crimes, such as private use of drugs, prostitution, and intoxication, are removed from the criminal code, we may see a marked drop in the number of offenders. If juvenile codes eliminate running away and curfew violations from the list of offenses, delinquency rates will go down. There is strong support for limiting juvenile delinquency to those offenses against persons and property that would be crimes if they were committed by adults.

Similarities to Other Clients   Criminal offenders share many of the characteristics of other types of clients. They tend to be poor, to live in slums, to have a low level of education and a spotty employment record, and to show a history of failure at home, at school, and at work. Many suffer from mental or physical disease, and a large fraction are known to other social agencies. The offender population is not radically different from social work clients in other settings, and the techniques of intervention are essentially the same: casework, group work, community organization, and client advocacy. The intervention chosen depends upon one's theories concerning the cause of crime.

CAUSES OF CRIME

One of the nagging questions is why people commit crimes. The following theories have been put forth to answer this question.

The Offender Is "Sick"   Many theories imply some version of a medical model. Something is wrong inside the offender which causes him to act as he does. The cause can be genetic. An individual with an extra chromosome may be more prone to commit violent crimes; the cause can be physical (such as hyperactivity) or psychological (such as neurosis, immaturity, or the inability to control impulses). Psychologically oriented casework treatment is compatible with the medical model.

The Company Is "Bad"   Another theory suggests that since most crime is committed by several persons acting together, the primary cause of crime lies in the offender's associates. The offender is led astray by bad companions, resulting in an emphasis on changing the peer group, primarily through group work. The aim is to alter the orientation of the peer group from pro- to antidelinquency. The strategy is to forbid an offender to associate with anyone who has a criminal record—a common condition of probation or parole.[7]

Society Is Unjust   The main cause of crime may lie in the lack of legitimate opportunities for employment and recreation available in the inner cities. Offenders commit crimes not because they choose to but because their legitimate goals can be fulfilled only by illegitimate means. Programs built on this theory attempt to create a variety of legitimate channels for work and play as a way to combat crime. Society at large or specific institutions are at fault, rather than a given individual or group of individuals. Social workers involved tend to rely heavily on community organization programs that place greater emphasis on preventing crime than on treating criminals, a perspective that is gaining increasing public support.

Definitions Are to Blame   Finally, "labeling" theory suggests that there is no such phenomenon as a delinquent or criminal per se. Delinquency is what the judges or society or the police say it is. Criminal acts are acts that are defined as criminal. Definitions can and do change and depend on who is in a position to do the defining.[8] Consider drug offenses; the use of drugs was widespread in the 1920s and early 1930s, but possession did not become a serious federal crime until after the Marijuana Tax Act was passed in 1937 as a result of the legislative efforts of the Federal Bureau of Narcotics. Today we are moving toward decriminalization of minor narcotic offenses partly because these behaviors have become so widespread that enforcement is virtually impossible. Obviously, one method of coping with the "crime wave" is to promote decriminalization, especially for crimes without victims, and to limit the types of persons who can be considered offenders, excluding children under fifteen or alcoholics, for instance.

TREATMENT APPROACHES

The table that follows shows the relationship between theories of crime causation, methods of dealing with offenders, and the characteristic setting in which tasks are carried out.

	Theory of crime causation	Method of intervention	Type of setting
1	Medical model—the problem lies within the offender	Counseling or casework service to change the individual offender	Probation
2	Influence of crime-prone associates—the offender is led astray and/or is part of a delinquent sub-culture	Group work to change peer group orientation from pro- to anti-law-violating behavior	Correctional institution
3	Lack of legitimate opportunities to fulfill social-ly acceptable goals	Community organization to change social institutions and to establish legitimate channels for work and play	Parole and programs for crime prevention
4	Labeling theory—crime is whatever the person in a position to do the judging decides that it is	Decriminalization of acts currently labeled as criminal	General political arena

The relationship between the theories of crime causation and method of intervention is less ambiguous than the relationship of either of these two factors to type of setting. Many parole officers give as much casework service as probation officers. Group work is possible whenever a group of clients can be collected in one place at one time.

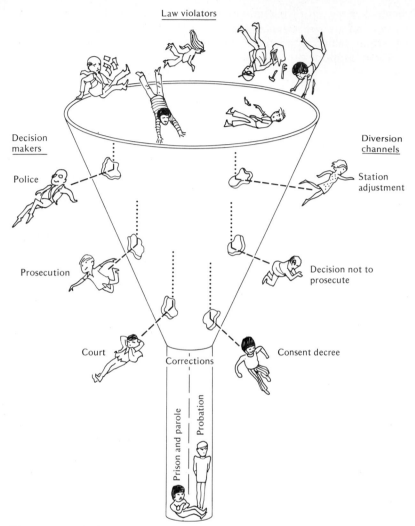

Figure 20-2   The leaky criminal justice funnel.

WHAT HAPPENS TO THE OFFENDERS?

To understand social work with offenders, knowledge of the various institutions
that process the offenders is important: the police, prosecution, the courts, and
the correctional system. Primary emphasis will be put on the correctional system
itself where social workers play a prominent role.

Diversion from the System

The criminal justice system can be thought of as a leaky funnel (see Figure 20-2). It
continues to function only by means of perforations along the sides through
which it can "leak out" (i.e., divert) perhaps 50 percent of the cases, thus relieving

the pressure. Each of the major decision makers listed on the left of the illustration can use various mechanisms for diverting offenders, such as those listed on the right. When an offender has been diverted, he has been removed from the criminal justice system—at least for the present. Diversion is much more frequently used with juveniles than with adult offenders, but many adults are diverted, too. The number of offenders who reach every later decision point is smaller than the number at an earlier level. Despite the frequency of diversion, many persons charged with a serious crime may have to wait six months to a year before trial.

The Police

The police are often called the gatekeepers of the criminal justice system. Anyone who wants to function effectively within the criminal justice system must understand their problems and perspective and find a basis to work cooperatively with them.

Not all of those who appear to have committed chargeable offenses will be subject to official action; it is the police who decide. This suggests the significant role police play in regulating human conduct and the need to develop objective criteria against which to test individual judgments. Prosecutors, juries, and correctional officials make decisions concerning only the 20 percent who have been arrested.

Police are referred to as "5 P.M. to 8 A.M. social workers" because only about half their time is taken up with crime-related problems. Much of the rest is spent in social work activities such as helping to settle family disputes and procuring treatment for the physically and mentally ill. Contrary to popular belief, the police attempt to divert people from the criminal justice system.

Station Adjustment   A juvenile is brought into the police station, but instead of being referred to court for formal processing, he is given informal supervision by the police. This service gives the juvenile another chance to "go straight" and avoid the more serious court procedure. In some communities formal referral channels between police and social agencies have been established so that the police can bring drug users or alcoholics to treatment centers instead of to jails. Sometimes the police become hosts to social agencies who share their offices. Social workers in such settings may provide diagnostic and treatment services to vagrants, homeless children, or other persons who might otherwise be placed in jail, not because they constitute a danger to society but because no other alternatives are readily available.

As a result of recent demonstration projects, many police agencies have incorporated social work techniques in staff development programs and worked cooperatively with social work practitioners.[9] Many police training programs teach fundamental principles of psychology and sociology and related techniques.

Noncriminal Problems   Law enforcement staff tend to feel frustrated when dealing with chronic runaways, drunks, and drug users because the usual techniques of charging, booking, and detaining do not deter the offender. For this type of offender the police station and the jail have a revolving door. Almost as soon as the offender is released, he is brought in again for a similar offense. For treatment to be effective, the underlying problem that brought the offender to the attention of the police must be dealt with.

Social workers in police settings are helpful both as consultants to the police and as sources for referral. Often when the police are called upon to deal with someone who behaves in a bizarre fashion, they turn to a social worker to determine whether to ignore the behavior, bring the offender to a mental hospital in hope of getting him admitted, or charge the offender with an offense, possibly curfew violation, disorderly conduct, or vagrancy.

Relations between police and social workers have been strained as a result of mutually unflattering stereotypes based on ignorance. Police tended to regard social workers as soft-headed do-gooders. Social workers regard police as hard-boiled and punitive, if not brutal. Recent efforts at cooperation have served to dispel or at least soften these negative images. However, friction is to be expected because of differences in occupational goals and loyalties. The primary function of the police is to protect society, with the needs of individuals coming second; for the social worker the priorities are reversed. However, these

"If you'll plead guilty, I think I can get your bigamy charge reduced to proceeding too fast for conditions!"

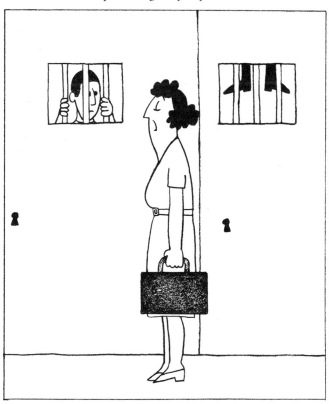

differences may not be as unreconcilable as they seem. Helping individuals may in some cases constitute the best possible long-range protection for society. The police function of social control is also helpful for some social work clients.

Prosecuting Attorney

The prosecuting attorney, often known as the District Attorney, represents the state in criminal matters and decides which of the cases brought in by the police warrant prosecution. Many cases are dismissed at this juncture because of insufficient evidence. Even in cases that get to court the prosecution and the defense lawyer frequently engage in some form of plea bargaining, whereby a criminal charge and/or a sentence are reduced in return for a plea of guilty by the defendant.

Plea bargaining speeds action of the judicial process and often makes the accused feel that he is getting a good deal. If every case were handled in the formal fashion prescribed by theory, the traffic jam in the flow of court cases would be disastrous to the cause of justice. Even now for many cases months elapse before a trial takes place. Meanwhile, the offender may sit in jail. He will have lost his job, with untold suffering to himself and his family. In addition, as a result of pretrial detention he may also jeopardize his chances to prepare an effective defense to reduce the possibility of conviction and imprisonment. Plea bargaining, however, is not officially recognized by the courts nor surrounded by enough procedural safeguards. No one knows how many innocent defendants have pleaded guilty under threat of more serious punishment if found guilty as a result of formal processing. Plea bargaining sometimes results in gross injustice, but without it the criminal justice system might be so slowed as to produce injustice by failing to provide the defendant a speedy trial in keeping with his constitutional rights.

The Courts

Of the small proportion of all offenders who reach the courts, many are handled informally, especially juveniles. Social workers often play a crucial role. Commonly a decision may be made to give the juvenile another chance. A "consent decree" may be drawn up that formalizes the terms of an agreement between the intake officer of the court (who may be a social worker), the offender, and his parents. The agreement will specify the conditions that the juvenile agrees to fulfill (e.g., regular school attendance, periodic reports to the courts, and compliance with curfew regulations). If the judge approves the agreement and the offender abides by it, no formal petition need be filed, and the juvenile may escape having an official record. If the juvenile violates the terms of the agreement, he becomes subject to official processing for the original offense. The desirability of not acquiring an official court record for an alleged offense is obvious, but consent decrees or "unofficial probation" may violate the juvenile's constitutional rights, since without a formal hearing he may not have adequate legal protection.

Pretrial Detention   Many procedures are currently employed to permit a maximum number of nondangerous offenders to remain free while awaiting trial.

The use of *summons* (ordering a suspected offender to appear at a subsequent court hearing without arrest and booking) and *release on recognizance* (release after arrest and booking without financial security such as bail or cash bond) permit an offender to remain in the community on the basis of his promise to appear when necessary. Other programs allow juveniles who normally would await trial in a detention home to remain in their own homes or under close supervision until their court hearing. Any program that reduces pretrial detention constitutes a temporary diversion from the criminal justice system and can result in significant savings in dollars and in psychological and social costs.

In general, the social worker does not enter any legal case until after the offender has pleaded guilty or been convicted. As a result, the social worker has no opportunity to modify stressful experiences that the offender may undergo at earlier stages, particularly in attempting to raise bail or in pretrial detention. The main rationale for minimizing social work intervention until after conviction is to ensure that the determination of guilt or innocence is based exclusively on legal facts and is not influenced by the type of psychological and social information that the social worker collects to aid in posttrial disposition.

The Presentence Report   After the adjudication proceedings, if the offender has been found guilty, the social worker plays an important role, especially for juvenile offenders and for adult felons who are legally eligible for probation. The social worker may be asked to draw up a presentence report to give as full a picture as possible of the offender as a human being and of his social situation. This report becomes the major source of information on which the judge decides among sentencing alternatives—a fine, suspended sentence, probation, incarceration. The social worker, here usually called a probation officer, can exert a decisive influence on the offender's disposition. An offender's sentence is determined not only by legal criteria but also by the question: "Which disposition will most help to rehabilitate a given offender?" This approach shows the changing philosophy of corrections.

The Correctional System

The fortress-like maximum-security prison is regarded today as an obsolete monstrosity. It was built when offenders were required to "do time" as punishment until they became penitent (therefore the term "penitentiaries") or reformed (therefore *reformatories*). Many modern social reformers regard prisons as medieval, but historians have shown that the concept of imprisonment as punishment is a relatively modern phenomenon. It wasn't just the Queen in *Alice in Wonderland* who said, "Off with his head." Execution used to be a common form of punishment for crimes as minor as begging and vagrancy. The biblical law of retribution (*lex talionis*), "An eye for an eye . . ." can be traced to Hammurabi's Code in about 2000 B.C. Until the nineteenth century, prisons—if they existed at all—were generally way stations where offenders were held until they could receive punishment. Imprisonment was not considered a form of punishment in itself.

Prisons Handicap Rehabilitation   Although we have largely abandoned such harsh forms of physical punishment as mutilation and execution, even milder forms of punishment such as imprisonment can constitute a serious handicap to a rehabilitation program. Prisons are normally located in rural settings, whereas most offenders come from urban areas. This creates difficulties for maintaining family contacts and for working out family problems that may have contributed to an offender's propensity to commit criminal acts. The regimentation of prison life and lack of opportunities for work and training make it difficult for an offender to learn vocational, academic and social skills to help him to "go straight" after discharge. Too often prisons inadvertently become schools for crime.

Parole Reports   Social workers (often called counselors) employed in many prisons constitute a small fraction of the staff and spend most of their time preparing reports for parole boards. These reports, like the presentence investigations prepared for the judge, serve as the basis for decision making. They include a summary of the offender's activities while incarcerated, his performance of assigned duties, his willingness to involve himself in voluntary educational, cultural, religious, and psychological therapy programs as well as his general behavior and attitude or record of rule infractions. Depending on the board's assessment, an offender can be discharged when a fraction of his minimum sentence has been served or kept in confinement until his maximum sentence has expired. Few social workers in these settings have much opportunity to offer treatment to offenders.

Treatment in Corrections   Obviously, many of the newer types of correctional institutions and programs offer greater scope for social work treatment. They tend to be smaller, more flexible, more therapeutically oriented, and considerably less expensive than the traditional prison. Halfway houses, for instance, offer discharged prisoners a temporary transitional setting until they feel prepared to live independently in the community. Some also serve as "half-way-back" houses for short periods of reconfinement of offenders who have demonstrated that they were not ready to "make it" on the outside. Work release programs are implemented to permit an offender to carry a job while he is "doing time" in a correctional institution. The offender returns to the institution after work and on weekends. With work release the taxpayer saves, because the offender pays for his own upkeep and for the support of his family out of his earnings. The program also facilitates the offender's reintegration into the community. One of the main tasks of the parole officer who supervises the offender after discharge from the prison is to help him find and hold a job, a task that is considerably easier when the offender has learned work skills and has a record of steady employment.

Probation and Parole

Probation and parole are forms of community treatment roughly equivalent to out-patient care of the mentally ill. Although probation and parole are alike in that they both involve supervision of offenders in the community, probation is generally used in lieu of incarceration, whereas parole is used along with incarceration. A judge places an offender on probation directly after conviction. A parole board places an offender on parole during his prison term.

Conditions of Probation and Parole   In some jurisdictions probation and parole are part of the same agency, as in the federal system. Generally, however, the probation service is under the jurisdiction of the court, and the parole service is part of the state correctional apparatus that also runs the prison system. In both probation and parole the client does not enjoy all the rights and privileges of a free man, but he has more freedom than if he were in an institution. Generally he is required to sign a contract setting out the conditions of probation or parole—prohibitions against use of alcohol and against associating with known offenders, the requirement that he report to his officer at stated intervals and that he secure his permission to leave the state, get married, or make a change in occupation. Probation/parole is subject to revocation, and the offender may be returned to court or to prison for having violated the probation/parole conditions even though he may not have committed a new crime. Since the probation/parole officer can recommend revocation, he has considerable authority over the offender. Both he and the client must recognize this power if the use of probation/parole is to be productive.

Major Differences   Although supervision in probation and parole are similar in many respects, some of the tasks are different. The probation officer may need to persuade a client to break off his relationship with a group of friends who may be getting him into trouble with the law. He may have to teach his client to change his characteristic attitudes and patterns of behavior without giving him a chance to "make a clean break" in a new environment.

The parole officer has to help his client adjust to a new environment by acquiring the skills needed to function in the free community. These may be very different from skills needed in the prison setting. For instance, an offender may have developed unquestioning obedience while in prison, whereas outside the institution he will be expected to show initiative and to accept responsibility. In contrast to the probationer, the parolee will need help to establish new associations more than to weaken old ones.

Comparative Cost   Probation and parole as forms of treatment are becoming increasingly popular because they are much less expensive and probably at least as effective as incarceration for many types of offenders.

A Comparison of Institutions and Community Treatment[10]

Category	Offenders	Operating costs	Employees
Institutions			
Juvenile	4.9%	22.5%	26.2%
Adult felon	17.3	43.3	42.8
Misdemeanant	11.0	14.7	15.8
Subtotal	(33.2)	(80.5)	(84.8)
Community treatment			
Juvenile	22.2	9.3	8.0
Adult felon	28.9	7.3	5.2
Misdemeanant	15.7	2.9	2.0
Subtotal	(66.8)	(19.5)	(15.2)

The bulk of the offender population is located in community-based treatment, primarily probation and parole, whereas most of the cost of maintaining the correctional system and most of the personnel who run it are working in institutions, as the table given here illustrates. It costs approximately ten times as much to keep an offender in an institution as under supervision in the community. Today caseloads are large, two-thirds of adult felons being carried in caseloads of over one hundred, whereas loads of thirty-five are recommended.[11] We can afford to spend considerably more on community supervision and still save money if we are willing to reduce the number of offenders who are imprisoned, reduce the length of time that they spend in prison, or shift our incarcerated population from maximum- and medium-security prisons to minimum-security institutions and halfway houses.

Priorities for Reform

The first order of business should be to remove from prison and/or jail any inmate who is kept in prison or jail because alternative programs are not available. Children are still locked up in jails because they are dependent and neglected and no other facilities are available. Mentally ill and mentally defective offenders who belong in treatment hospitals or in benign custodial facilities are found in maximum-security correctional institutions. Their maintenance in these settings is extremely costly, and they fail to receive the type of treatment that might result in their eventual rehabilitation. Offenders are still sent to prison because judges are dissatisfied with the services offered by probation departments. They sometimes remain in prison after they are eligible for discharge because parole officers have not been able to locate jobs or satisfactory living arrangements as a condition for discharge.

SOCIAL WORK INTERVENTION

Only a small fraction of the social workers who work with offenders have a professional degree. A few agencies, like the Federal Probation and Parole Service, require a master's degree. Usually staff with master's degrees are primarily involved in supervision, administration, and staff development. Most of the direct treatment of offenders is carried out by persons holding bachelor's degrees or less. The more highly qualified staff often supervise the treatment process and prepare the official reports, presentence investigations for the court, and reports for parole boards.

Need for a Variety of Personnel Staff with a variety of interests, backgrounds, and levels of training are needed for working with offenders. Volunteers can be extremely effective both as extensions of and substitutes for the professional staff. Because volunteers are usually not invested with the same degree of authority as a probation or parole officer, a client may feel freer to confide in them and seek help without fearing that such information may be used against him later. Volunteers usually carry a very small caseload and are available when the offender needs a steady friend or parent substitute to help him over the rough spots.

Ex-offenders as Staff Members One of the recent developments is use of ex-offenders as treatment staff. They can make a special contribution. Their background and the environment in which they live are usually similar to the offender's, which helps them to understand his situation and facilitates communication. Because they have themselves been through the correctional process, they can sometimes understand and empathize with the offenders more effectively than many middle-class professionals. Because they are ex-offenders, they become an important role model to the client. Their presence says, "It can be done. You too can learn to go straight." At the same time the process of helping the offender on probation or parole can help the ex-offender to stay out of trouble. Self-help groups such as Synanon and Alcoholics Anonymous have demonstrated that the "ex" is very effective in treating the current addict or alcoholic and that the treatment process has positive effects for the treater as well.

ORGANIZATION OF SERVICES

Local Control

From the chapter on public agencies, you will recall that correctional services are provided within the public sector. Since by definition, the state is generally the aggrieved party in a criminal proceeding (in the sense that the offender has violated a law), the state in the guise of the police officer catches the offender. It brings him to trial in the courts. If he is found guilty, the state punishes and hopefully rehabilitates him. In general, law enforcement, jails, the courts, and probation services are locally controlled. Correctional institutions such as prisons and training schools as well as parole services are state-controlled. The federal government has its own system of law enforcement, the Federal Bureau of Investigation, its own system of federal courts, a network of prisons organized and administered by the Federal Bureau of Prisons, and combined probation and parole services for those who violate federal law. However, federal offenders constitute a small fraction of the total offender population.

In terms of cost, by far the most expensive branch of the criminal justice system is the police, with corrections in second place and the courts third.

More Federal Involvement

The organizational pattern is changing. Today more federal money is being used to finance state, local, and privately organized and administered correctional programs. The federal Law Enforcement Assistance Administration, through its state branches, finances a number of innovative correctional programs, such as Youth Service Bureaus and halfway houses, which may eventually point the way to more productive approaches in corrections. The National Council of Crime and Delinquency is a private national organization that sponsors research and provides technical assistance and educational services in the field of corrections. Such funding sources help to keep correctional services from hardening into a single mold and provide needed encouragement for continuing experimentation and change.

EVALUATIONS OF CORRECTIONS

The field of corrections, like other fields of social service, suffers from unreasonable expectations. The public faults corrections for the continuing existence of a "crime problem" and especially for recidivism. It demands that the number of crimes decrease and that offenders not reappear—especially not for offenses similar to those for which they have been "corrected." It is unwilling to accept the unpalatable reality that there will always be a crime problem so long as we have (1) laws that prohibit behaviors practiced by some citizens and (2) machinery to label and process persons who are guilty by the standards we have established. We need to understand and to educate others to accept the fact that there will probably never be an equivalent of the Salk vaccine to protect us against crime.

Criteria for Evaluation Once we learn to accept this reality, instead of proclaiming every seemingly promising innovation a panacea for all our problems and then being disappointed with the results, we may learn to analyze innovations rationally. For how many and what types of offenders will the new method work? What are all the effects (both intended and unintended) of this particular method? Why does it produce the observed results? How much does it cost in dollars and cents and in long-range psychological and social effects? How do these costs compare with costs of alternative approaches? How do programs that are equivalent in effectiveness compare in terms of cost, and, conversely, how do programs that cost about the same compare in effectiveness?

There has been a tendency to regard such questions as peripheral to the important issues or to assign them to a researcher who has played the role of rejected stepchild in the field of corrections. The doer has generally been given precedence over the thinker, even though the field could benefit considerably from a judicious and systematic evaluation of new techniques.

Success in Returning to Society Evaluation becomes even more important today as we recognize that virtually all offenders return to society sooner or later. We must ensure that they will return with skills and motivation to "make it" in legitimate activities instead of the skills for crime and the motivation to "get back" at society for unjust and capricious punishment. To accomplish this, a way must be found to change our correctional programs from schools for crime to schools for life. As the philosophy for dealing with offenders has moved from an emphasis on secure custody to one of rehabilitation, the spotlight has shifted from the prison guard and security technology to treatment, individualization of programs, and training technologies—teaching machines instead of locking devices. Perhaps we are learning to set more realistic standards and to place greater emphasis on the offender's needs rather than on his crime. As a professional social worker, a volunteer in a social agency, or an interested citizen, you can do a great deal to meet his needs.

Ellen Handler

KEY TERMS

labeling theory	decriminalization	consent decree
probation	recidivism	bail
parole	incarceration	presentence investigation
diversion	pretrial detention	halfway house
plea bargaining	posttrial disposition	work release

FOR DISCUSSION

1 Why have social workers had little to do with corrections?
2 How is police–social work collaboration hindered?
3 What types of offenders are most likely to be served by a social worker? Least likely?
4 Identify major police functions in addition to law enforcement.
5 How are offenders diverted from the criminal justice system?
6 What is the purpose of a presentence report?
7 In what ways do institutions hinder rather than help offenders?
8 How can work release programs be justified?
9 Identify the advantages of community-based programs over institutions.
10 Differentiate between probation and parole.
11 Why may volunteers be more successful than regular probation officers?
12 Why are "ex-cons" often effective as probation or parole officers?
13 Should prostitution, personal use of drugs, and other "victimless crimes" be removed from the criminal code? Why or why not?
14 What are some of the philosophical differences in running programs for juvenile offenders and for adults?

PROJECTS

1 Select subjects whom you do not know personally. Interview five adults each on two questions: How should you deal with a juvenile who is found guilty of stealing a car—a first offense? How would you proceed if it were his third offense? Code, tabulate, and analyze the results. Write a brief summary report.
2 Write an account of the Attica prison riots, indicating the main issues and their resolution.
3 Choose several of the behaviors listed below and indicate whether they should be considered legal offenses for juveniles. What means would you follow to deal with them? Truancy, curfew violations, running away, persistently disobeying parents, drinking liquor or driving under the legal age, using marijuana occasionally.
4 Examine the argument in the chapter that the corrections field is not unique because in many other situations clients also do not choose social services voluntarily. Why are young social workers being attracted to the corrections field?
5 Determine how social workers are being used in probation and parole services and in penal institutions in your area. What are the job opportunities at various educational levels?
6 Determine whether there is a program available in your area to help former prisoners. Invite its director to talk to the class or with a student committee. Is there a role for social workers in the program?
7 Choose one of the following positions to defend in class discussion. Crime is caused mainly by (a) emotional disturbances, (b) influence of undesirable companions, (c) injustices in society.

FOR FURTHER STUDY

D. R. Cressey and R. A. McDermott, *Diversion from the Juvenile Justice System*, National Assessment of Juvenile Corrections Project, University of Michigan, Ann Arbor, 1973.

Vernon Fox, *Introduction to Corrections*, Prentice-Hall, Englewood Cliffs, N.J., 1972.

David Glaser, *Adult Crime and Social Policy*, Prentice-Hall, Englewood Cliffs, N.J., 1972.

Keith D. Harries, *The Geography of Crime and Justice*, McGraw-Hill, New York, 1974.

Norval Morris and G. Hawkins, *The Honest Politician's Guide to Crime Control*, University of Chicago Press, Chicago, 1970.

Lloyd E. Ohlin (ed.), *Prisoners in America*, Prentice-Hall, Englewood Cliffs, N.J., 1973.

Chapter 21

The Aged

Are the aged mainly a social problem?
What are storage? Accommodation? Participation?
Home-based services—a major gap?
Can we add life to the years?

Old age is often portrayed as the drab and dismal terminal period of human existence. Social workers especially may see it that way, because the old people who come to social agencies generally have problems in coping with life's demands. Society's attitude is also a problem, because the aged have not been accorded the status they deserve. We should remember two characteristics of human development in assessing aging. First, the aged person will be more or less the same as he was when a younger adult—personality usually does not change drastically. Thus, adjustment to old age can usually be predicted from previous functioning. Second, certain conditions promote successful aging— especially physical health and an income adequate to maintain a way of life resembling that of the earlier adult years. Other important factors are a range of skills and interests so that life is considered rewarding, an intact and generally happy marriage, and satisfying ties to children and other relatives. Many older people can fulfill these conditions. As a result they can add life to the years and find aging a time of great satisfaction.

Two very different problems are seen: first, how to provide adequate societal provisions for the minority, especially the very old, who don't have health, money, or family; second, how to change societal institutions and facilities—from retirement rules to public parks—enough to permit the capable majority of older people to live fully and contribute to society from their experience.

THE AGED AS A SOCIAL PROBLEM

What has social work to offer the aged? Social workers have always worked with older people through family welfare services, old-age assistance programs, mental hospitals, and nursing homes, yet the field of social work has not taken a significant leadership role in special programs for the aged.

The aged, the middle-aged, and youth have different views of the aged as a group. Old people resent being labeled as a social problem. People in middle age who have responsibility for one or both of their parents know that old age is a social problem. Adolescents are likely to see people over thirty as an undifferentiated power structure. Unless they have a grandparent in the home, they may not see old age as a special problem.

Why are old people more of a social problem here than in South America or Asia? Why are the aged a special subject of public debate now? Are old people different now? What will be the effects of changes in population, changes in society, and changes in our standards and expectations?

Jessie Bernard points out that a "social problem" poses three kinds of difficulties: pain or anxiety imposed on individuals, a "social cost" to society in general, and a threat to the functioning or solidarity of the social system.[1] Does growing old involve pain or anxiety for the aged? How do old people become a cost and a threat to society?

AGING: SOCIETAL IMPLICATIONS

The aged are a problem because there are over five times as many old people now as at the turn of the century. As the accompanying table shows, there are *proportionately* over twice as many.

U.S. Population Age 65 and Older[2]

	Year			
	1900	**1950**	**1970**	**2000**
Number of older persons in millions	3	12	20	28
Percent of total population	4	8	9.5	10

Demographers give two reasons for the phenomenal growth of the older population. First, people now survive the diseases of infancy and childhood that used to be fatal to one or two in every large family. We also survive the infectious and epidemic diseases of middle age, thanks to new drugs and better sanitation. Now a person is likely to survive into his sixties.

The second reason for the increasing proportion of old people is that we are having fewer babies. If the one-child family and the no-child family are here to stay, the proportion of old people by the year 2000 will be substantially higher than the estimate shown in the table.

Aging of the Older Population

Old people are a problem because *old people are older*.[3] Over a million people in the United States are eighty-five or older. The median age of people over sixty-five is now age seventy-three—a substantial increase in the last generation. The numbers of "old old"—those over eighty—will almost *double* in the current generation. They have the lowest incomes, and they require the most medical services and the most care.

Earlier Retirement and Its Social Cost

Old people are retiring earlier with higher income. The working population must pay the cost of ten, twenty, or even thirty years of retirement for millions of fellow Americans.

One might think that old people would work longer today; they are healthier on the average, and our occupational structure includes more service jobs and fewer physically demanding jobs. But older people are increasingly forced to retire younger, or enticed to retire younger, by public and private policy. Being still vigorous in most cases, they are apt to seek a job to supplement retirement income. The result is a high social cost for retirement.

Public Policy and Early Retirement   In a recent national study, over half the companies reported that retirement prior to age sixty-five increased in the past ten years. Only 2 percent reported a decrease. More companies had policies to encourage early retirement, and many of the retired proceeded to find another job so they could earn as well as draw retirement benefits.[4] Our public policy, as exhibited by the massive social security program paying benefits to nine-tenths of all older Americans, supports early retirement and second jobs. Retirement under social security can come as early as age sixty-two. Pension plans of some craft unions and companies make it attractive to retire as early as fifty-five. Armed forces retirement on full benefits at age thirty-eight after twenty years' service is the extreme case. Most public and private plans permit additional income while receiving full benefits.

For many workers, early retirement with good income supplemented by another job is becoming easier. That fact is reassuring for the half of the labor force in favorable situations, but it is alarming for society since the total bill for such retirement is already huge and still growing. It would be far better if workers who are still productive could stay on their original job longer on a part- or full-time basis, rather than taking other jobs that are often of lower status.

Health Problems and Cost of Care

Older people go to the hospital twice as often and on the average stay twice as long for each confinement. Medical costs are especially high. Of the $65 billion annual personal health care expenditures, 27 percent was spent by or on behalf of the aged, who make up only 10 percent of the total population. Almost 7 percent of our national income goes for personal health care, but over a quarter is spent for the one-tenth of our population who are old. The societal impact is even greater. Through health insurance, Medicare, and Medicaid, we have socialized more of the cost of health care for the aged than for other groups. Public funds paid two-thirds of the aged's 10-billion-dollar health care bill, but only one-fourth of the 47-billion cost of health care to persons under sixty-five. A major problem is organizing and paying for the care to chronically ill older people—a rapidly increasing group. Over three-quarters of the aged have one chronic condition, and almost half have two or more.[5] Our hospitals and clinics are organized for quick and intensive care, not for care of the chronically ill.

Social Roles and Status

In both a physical and social sense we have no place for large numbers of older people. Community facilities—subways, parks, libraries—are oriented to children and young people. A suburban ranch home for parents and children is the typical housing model. We literally have no physical space for the growing numbers of the old. Society also has little place for the old people in social space and *little use for them*. Our social structure—the vertical space between high and low status and the horizontal space between different communities, associative groups, and races—is based on the occupational system. When a person is not in an occupation, his status and his power and his self-esteem may be lost.

Rural and Urban Differences   Where most workers are employed in agriculture and live on farms and in small towns, there is a place for old people. Older men can retire gradually; and since families are larger, the advice and housekeeping skills of older women are needed. When a person's property is in land rather than a job, he can retain his importance and esteem to an advanced age. But today almost three-quarters of our population is urban. Few workers are self-employed, and more and more jobs involve specialized and changing technical skills. In an advanced industrial economy with high-density urban living, there is little place for the aged.

Magazine Fiction   An illustration of the "role-lessness" of older people was found in a content analysis of popular magazine fiction. A "census" was conducted among leading characters in a large sample of stories in popular magazines for 1900 and 1950. In 1900 there was a goodly number of old people, about as many as their proportion in the population at that time. Many played leading parts in the stories. The occupation of these old people was not clear, but in 1900 the occupation of most characters was not emphasized. Rather, people were identified by their home town and family. Among all the 1950 stories in three popular magazines, the only person who appeared to be over thirty was a man "in his fifties" who was as active as a young man and sailed his own boat! Thus a census in the world of popular fiction led to the same conclusion as more scholarly social analysis—our society has no place for old people unless they act like young people.[6]

From the economist's viewpoint, the problem posed by old people might be characterized more succinctly—no production, but high consumption. Now that medical science has extended the typical active life after child-rearing from age

Drawing by O'Brian; © 1971 The New Yorker Magazine, Inc.

"Believe me, Mrs. Parkson, you have our deepest sympathy. But retirement at sixty-five is mandatory. The fact that he will be under your feet all day is, unfortunately, something we are powerless to do anything about."

fifty to seventy, so that more and more people can retire and have the potential to enjoy life, we are puzzled about what to do with them.

Sources of Help   Where do older people turn for visiting, friendship, and help? A study by Rosow indicates that the active aged, especially working-class people, found their friends among neighbors who were also older. Contacts with family were important. For two-thirds or more of the aged who had family nearby, their families cared for them when they were ill.[7] Studies suggest two possible answers to the question of what to do with old people. One, they should live among other older people, and two, they should be cared for and attended to by their children. But as a general solution neither of these answers seems satisfactory. Mutual aid and family help are important for many older people but are not available to all; and the chronically ill need more care than family and friends can provide.

Sexuality in Old Age

Older people have not been expected to be interested in sex. The "dirty old man" is a common stereotype. With the increasing sexual freedom and greater willingness to discuss sexual practices, however, many older people indicate strong interest and a satisfying sex life. The attitudes of others create problems. While married couples have more freedom to behave as they choose, the widow or widower faces strong pressures from other family members against remarrying in old age. Old people are given the feeling that they should not be interested in members of the opposite sex and certainly not in establishing new sexual relationships.

Negative attitudes are often strongest when an older person shows an interest in someone younger who will become the heir if the old person dies. Another deterrent to remarriage is the loss of pensions. If a widow remarries, she generally loses survivors' benefits from her husband's entitlement.

Living Together without Marriage   With the changing attitudes of younger people to alternatives to the traditional family, some older people are finding informal arrangements for living together attractive. The couple who do not have a marriage ceremony can share all the companionship and sexual satisfactions without upsetting inheritance rights and retirement benefits. When they become aware of it, their children may accept such a pattern because they find it preferable to remarriage. We have no idea of the numbers that are involved, but the old as well as the young have new options as societal norms change. The popularity of living together without marriage will probably increase.

Political Potential

Old people are also a problem for society because they vote. Currently, persons over sixty make up less than 15 percent of the population but constitute between one-fourth and one-third of the voters in each election. The biennial increases in social security benefits just before every election have become a familiar and dependable ritual. Older people do not vote in a bloc, but political parties tend to woo them with irresponsible promises.

Why is it a problem that older people vote? In our system we expect everyone to vote their interests. The political power of older people becomes a problem only when opportunistic politicians seek to exploit that vote. In some local communities where many homes are owned by older people, the aged are accused of always voting down bonds for schools and parks because of property tax increases. This is more likely to be the result when the aged have low incomes.

The discerning reader will have already noted some peculiar discrepancies in our society's handling of the aged. We are alarmed at the cost of retirement and puzzled at how to keep older people active in society, but at the same time we continually reduce the retirement age. Both the political power of older people in national elections and the need for jobs for younger people apparently explain the discrepancy.

AGING: A PROBLEM FOR OLDER PEOPLE

We asked earlier how the aged trouble society. One can turn the question around and ask, "How do society and its organizations make life difficult for the older person?" This is the other part of the definition of a social problem. What pain and anxiety is involved in being old? What is the typical process of aging in the United States? What does it mean to be old?

The process of growing old should be divided into at least two stages, from sixty to seventy-five and from seventy-five on. Typical experiences and problems change a great deal between ages sixty and ninety. The establishment of sixty-five as the onset of old age was a historical accident. Most observers argue that the awareness of old age begins at about age sixty.

Retirement and Slowing Down, Age Sixty to Seventy-five

By age sixty workers are planning how to deal with retirement. For manual laborers, marginal workers, and women with low education, employment problems caused by aging may well start in their forties. There is a steep decline after sixty in participation in the labor force; by age sixty-five only half of all men are participating and by age seventy only one-third. At age seventy-five one man in five is participating, usually only part-time. Female participation in the labor force drops between ages sixty and seventy, from one-third to about one-eighth.[8]

Income Trends   In our materialistic society, life satisfaction is constrained mainly by income. Income is determined mainly by work. What happens to the income of our typical sixty-year-old? Surveys, census data, and social security reports indicate that older people have less than half the income of younger adults and that average income declines with age.[9] The big drop in income, like the big drop in working, is from age sixty to seventy. Since consumption patterns, leisure activities, travel, and need for food do not drop suddenly at age sixty, a considerable adjustment is involved.

Two out of three typical Americans aged sixty to seventy-five are living with a spouse in their own home. Median income for married couples age sixty-five to sixty-nine in 1966 was about $4,200, or just above the moderate standard as defined by the Bureau of Labor Statistics. Median income for the nonmarried was under the poverty line of $1,600 defined by the Social Security Administration at that time. Only two-fifths of the nonmarried had their own homes.[10]

Social Adjustment   Interviews with people in their sixties show that men share more of the household duties and that in general couples seem to draw closer. There is more interest in grandchildren. Most older people would like more contact with their families than they have. Relations of the aged with their children are marked by visiting, emotional support, and solicitude. There are few well-developed programs of community activity, civic service, recreation, or adult education to use the energies of older people. The contrast between "haves" and "have-nots" is sharpened with old age. The "haves"—those who have strong family ties, health, and property—can find a satisfying life as long as they keep in good health. Those who have no such resources, especially the ill, are denied whatever social satisfactions they received earlier from work and recreation.[11]

Physical Trends   The average older American declines between ages sixty and seventy—but no more, apparently, than between forty and fifty or fifty and sixty. A wide range of indices for physical functioning—lung capacity, sexual activity, return of heart to normal after exercise—shows steady and regular decline after age thirty, with no special changes at age sixty.[12]

For physical impairments, chronic diseases, and resulting limitations on activity, the picture is different. Only one in five reported any impairment from age forty-five to sixty-four. But almost two in five at age sixty-five to seventy-four had some impairment. After age seventy-five the proportion was three in five. Chronic diseases, like impairments, increase rapidly in the last third of the life span. Over a quarter of older people report that they suffer from arthritis or rheumatism and 15 percent from heart disease. The proportion of aged with limiting health problems rises rapidly after age sixty and becomes very high after age eighty.[13]

Health problems also have an economic aspect. The cost of medical treatment and hospital care has risen more rapidly than the cost of living, and home help is unavailable. Health problems combine with the suddenly diminished income of the aged to present major problems in finances and independent living.

Mr. and Mrs. Typical American in their sixties, in summary, do not look very different from the way they did in their fifties. They still own their own home. They have greater interaction with each other, but society has decreed that they leave the labor market. This means suddenly lowered income and the loss of the prime status, the occupational role. Reduction in social activity, problems over purchase of health service, and increased worry about the future follow naturally from these fundamental changes.

Older Old Age—Seventy-five and Over

During the decade of their seventies, Mr. and Mrs. A. truly join the ranks of the aged. Some old people are sick and lonely in their sixties while others work and enjoy an active life into their eighties—but they are exceptions.

The pattern of associations, activities, and living arrangements changes greatly for Mr. and Mrs. A. during their seventies. In their late sixties people living as married couples outnumber nonmarried people, two to one. During the next decade of life the proportions are reversed. One of the partners dies during this decade, usually the husband. The difference in life expectancy in favor of women begins to have a dramatic effect. At age fifty-five to fifty-nine in 1970, there were 109 women for every 100 men. But at age seventy-nine there were 155 women for every 100 men. In the intervening years about half of the group has died—more men than women, obviously.[14]

By age seventy-nine the typical older American is single. Two-thirds are living in households with others, one-third with their spouse; another one-tenth are family heads, and over one-fifth live with relatives. Most of the remaining one-third are living alone, and most are women. Only 7 percent are in group living arrangements such as nursing homes or mental hospitals.[15]

Income is lower for people in their seventies than in their sixties. The median income of the nonmarried in their seventies is below the Social Security Administration poverty line, which is only half what the Bureau of Labor Standards calls a "moderate" income. Couples over seventy are below the poverty line in about one-third of the cases.

The typical American aged seventy to seventy-nine, then, experiences further loss in income, in close family members and friends, and in functional capacities. New living arrangements are necessary, and he or she is truly "aged." For the tpyical American as he passes age eighty, life experiences can be inferred from the trends already mentioned. There are 184 women for every 100 men. Almost one-half of the women live in poverty. Over one-half have two or more chronic conditions, and a majority suffer some impairment. This group averages three to four weeks of bed-disability per year. One-tenth or more are living in institutions. In 1970, there were almost 4 million persons age eighty and over. This is the most rapidly growing segment of our population.

SOCIETY AS A PROBLEM FOR THE OLD

How is society a problem for older people? The answer is obvious. Society is organized for the young. The labor market forces retirement and requires full-time participation, with frequent shifts in jobs and skills. Health facilities are centralized and provide quick expensive treatment with no follow-up. Transportation has been built around the automobile. Most housing is designed and priced for the young couple with one or two children and an annual income of at least $10,000. Private and public recreational facilities are geared to the activities of the young.

What should society do about the aged? Aging is an urgent concern for welfare planning because our artificial retirement age of sixty-five has created a growing dependent population who still have the capacity to work or contribute to society in other ways. From age sixty-five to seventy-five, most people retain their ability and desire to continue as producers, as consumers, and as participants in all aspects of society. However, this choice is not permitted by society for most people over sixty-five.

The needs of the most disadvantaged old people make aging a concern. Among the 8 million Americans over seventy-five are concentrated the multiple handicaps of living alone and being a woman, poor, and ill. What should our government do? Now we will consider the present pattern and future possibilities for provision of income, care, and services to the aged.

AGING: A PROBLEM FOR
HUMAN SERVICE PROFESSIONS

Like other service professions, social work has not done well by the aged. In reviewing social programs we see how little the aged figure in community service caseloads.

Our development and personality theories are oriented to infancy and childhood. Only recently have students of human development begun to study the adult development problems of adjusting to children or to having the children grown; of widowhood; of mid-life loss of drive.

Future Orientation   Professionals, like our society in general, are future-oriented. The ancient Catholic rule that the child shall be saved rather than the mother finds its counterpart in remarks by doctors, social workers, and psychologists that treatment of the child is especially important "because he has his whole life ahead of him."

Reluctance and Passivity   Also, older people are often hesitant to seek service. Most professionals who have worked with old people have observed a lack of aggressive self-confidence. "Why bother with me?" is the keynote. Professionals, like all other humans, are prone to respond to the most urgent plea. Many older people seem to have incorporated society's judgment that they are only waiting to die and do not have a strong claim on society's energies.

A Successful Project   Physical limitations combine with low self-esteem to make older people poor consumers of social, educational, and health services. One project provides a striking example. A "Golden Age Stag Club" was started. Almost no one came. When old men who had expressed interest were interviewed, they reported that bus service was irregular and took too long. A panel truck was found, turned into a bus, and a seventy-four-year-old volunteer driver recruited. Even then the driver often had to help the old men dress themselves and jolly them out of their blues to get them into the bus. The old men enjoyed their stag evenings immensely when they finally got there and talked about each meeting for days afterwards.

Typical Barriers   The mental health clinic in a shopping center with no bus service, the adult education class with a $15 fee, the visiting nurse service requiring referral from a family physician—in each case unintended barriers are erected against the aged. Since the aged have not been organized and vocal in pressing for their rights, their needs have a low priority.

Nursing Homes as a Special Problem

The docility of the aged and the apathy of professionals and the public come together most poignantly in our nursing homes. Created as an alternative to expensive hospital care, and primarily supported by over $2 billion of public funds through Medicare and Medicaid, nursing homes and other extended-care facilities are now under attack. The Nader report collected instances of brutalized patients tranquilized and kept alive in a stuporous but manageable state, kickbacks to home administrators from druggists, use of patients as guinea pigs in drug experiments, and abysmal neglect and dehumanization.[16] Well over half a million older people live in extended-care facilities. The existence of many poor facilities is an indictment not only of opportunistic nursing home operators but also of community professionals who ignore the homes and their patients.

NATIONAL POLICY FOR THE AGED

We do not have a policy for the aged, but only a wide variety of federal and state laws and programs. The social security program pays billions of dollars every year to 18 million retired people and their families. Medicaid was passed to help states pay doctors and hospitals for health care of the aged poor. Special bus rates are offered to old people in many cities. Property tax relief is available to the aged in many states, and we have a special federal income tax deduction for people over 65. Special housing projects for old people are built by local sponsors with the help of the Department of Housing and Urban Development. In public housing projects spaces are set aside for activity centers for older people from both inside and outside the project. We have federal grants for training and research in geriatrics and in social gerontology. A new federal program has been started to develop congregate feeding for older people to improve their nutrition. We have

---

Aging—A Double Standard

. . . Growing older is mainly an ordeal of the imagination—a moral disease, a social pathology—intrinsic to which is the fact that it afflicts women much more than men. It is particularly women who experience growing older (everything that comes *before* one is actually old) with such distaste and even shame.

. . . The double standard about aging shows up most brutally in the conventions of sexual feeling, which presuppose a disparity between men and women that operates permanently to women's disadvantage. In the accepted course of events a woman anywhere from her late teens through her middle twenties can expect to attract a man more or less her own age. (Ideally, he should be at least slightly older.) They marry and raise a family. But if her husband starts an affair after some years of marriage, he customarily does so with a woman much younger than his wife. Suppose, when both husband and wife are already in their late forties or early fifties, they divorce. The husband has an excellent chance of getting married again, probably to a younger woman. His ex-wife finds it difficult to remarry. Attracting a second husband younger than herself is improbable; even to find someone her own age she has to be lucky, and she will probably have to settle for a man considerably older than herself, in his sixties or seventies. Women become sexually ineligible much earlier than men do. A man, even an ugly man, can remain eligible well into old age. He is an acceptable mate for a young, attractive woman. Women, even good-looking women, become ineligible (except as partners of very old men) at a much younger age.

. . . Most women share the contempt for women expressed in the double standard about aging—to such a degree that they take their lack of self-respect for granted. Women have been accustomed so long to the protection of their masks, their smiles, their endearing lies. Without this protection, they know, they would be more vulnerable. But in protecting themselves as women, they betray themselves as adults. The model corruption in a woman's life is denying her age. She symbolically accedes to all those myths that furnish women with their imprisoning securities and privileges, that create their genuine oppression, that inspire their real discontent. Each time a woman lies about her age she becomes an accomplice in her own underdevelopment as a human being.

Susan Sontag, *The Double Standard of Aging.*[17]

an Administration on Aging within the Department of HEW, and every state has designated some office or bureau to plan for the aged. Most of these programs have grown up in the past few years as we have discovered the size of our older population and have begun to respond to their problems. We can ask about their intent and the overall impact. How do these many separate actions add up as a national policy for the aged? Later, as a way of understanding the impact of these programs, we will review what older people actually get.

Three policies can be defined: storage, accommodation, and participation.

A Policy of Storage:
Warehouses for the Aged

The Nader report on nursing homes claims our policy is to store old people away. The report quotes a witness at a Senate hearing on nursing home care: "The Eskimos used to freeze their old people to death, we bury ours alive." In a section titled "A Modest Proposal" it is noted that when we have a beloved pet who becomes aged and sick, we put him away. Nader continues in a bitterly facetious vein: "To treat the aged similarly would be inhumane, but there is another scheme that should work just as well. In fact, the government has actually been perpetuating the idea for some time. The government's unquestioning support of the nursing home industry has helped keep the aged away from society."[18] While the cost of nursing home care is high, it ought to be considered cheap when the benefits are taken into account. Few survive for long in a nursing home. The more bedridden patients the better, because government payments become higher. Patients may be tied down and bedsores encouraged. Sedatives can be used freely and call buttons put out of reach. Food may be unattractive and inadequate. Disturbed patients from a state hospital can be moved in. Patients can be burned to death by allowing them to smoke in bed, or frozen to death in cold weather. "The advantages are clear . . . fewer mouths to feed . . . more money for education and schools, and on the whole, a younger, more attractive population. The beauty of the plan is that it may be executed out of sight of the public. It may even be worth considering a compulsory age for entering a nursing home, shall we say seventy?"

Nader is actually describing a policy of storage with extinction, but we could also follow a policy of benign storage with two elements: separation of old people from the rest of society, and minimum attention congruent with humane standards for decency. The Rosow study showed that older people formed their associations among their own age group. From a practical viewpoint there would surely be an economy in providing social and health services—such as the congregate meals program or a geriatric clinic—on a large scale for concentrated groups of older people. The "disengagement theory" put forward a few years ago would be used to support such a policy. Cumming and Henry presented a theory of aging and society that has been a focus of controversy in social gerontology.[19] The central hypothesis was well stated by Rose in a critique of the theory: "The society and individual prepare *in advance* for the ultimate 'disengagement' of incurable, incapacitating disease and death by an *inevitable, gradual, and mutually satisfying process of disengagement*."[20] The withdrawal of the older person from society is seen as natural and universal among societies. Disengagement minimizes disruption of society and is good for the individual as preparation for death.

Rose, in opposition, argued that disengagement of the elderly was a *fact* that could be explained by social values, structure, and process, but not a *necessity* for social solidarity.

Rejecting the Disengagement Theory   Rose observed that in many societies, including our own, there is the development of new roles and the possibility of reengagement for older people. Further, on the grounds of social welfare, segregation with minimal maintenance of any group—mentally ill, prisoners—has always led to neglect, exploitation, and a loss of human potential. At the turn of the century many older people ended up in county poor homes. During the 1920s fraternal groups such as the Moose established homes for their older members and exposed the condition of public poor homes as a scandal. In the 1940s and 1950s, several hundred thousand old people were also stored in mental hospitals. Care was minimal, and neglect was general. The community mental health movement capitalized on the success of drugs for management of chronic patients and the Medicaid funds of the late 1960s to effect wholesale transfer of older state hospital patients to "the community." Community care turned out to mean nursing home care. Only a few years later we have had the Nader indictment of conditions in nursing homes. Neither the welfare of older people nor the sensibilities of the public will permit a policy of storage.

A Policy of Accommodation:
Make Room for Old People

A second possibility for a national policy would be accommodation. To effect an accommodation policy we obviously need to encourage independent living and self-care by older people, with maximum opportunity to use community services and interact with others. Older people are not defined as objects to be stored. Most policy debates for the aged focus on the "old old" with disabilities and ignore over 10 million citizens past the age of sixty-five who are capable in most respects—occupationally, socially, politically, and sexually—but who are denied full social participation by society. Under an accommodation policy, the aged are not viewed as potential full participants. The policy views older people neither as objects to be shelved nor, at the other extreme, as fellow citizens.

Recently the federal administration's policy has been one of accommodation:

1   Protecting the income position of the elderly
2   Upgrading the quality of nursing home care
3   Helping older persons live dignified, independent lives in their own homes
4   Expanding opportunities for the involvement of older persons in community life
5   Organizing the government to meet their changing needs

A 5 percent increase in income from social security was proposed, with a similar increase in public aid for the neediest aged, the property tax relief through revenue sharing. Regarding nursing homes, it was noted that progress had already been made in better inspection and more training for personnel. For "independent living," $200 million was asked for supporting programs "to enhance and maintain the independence of older citizens." These programs include information and referral services, nutrition programs, public transportation, and subsidy of about 80,000 units of housing for the elderly. On "opportunities for involvement," three programs were designated, costing about $65 million; $25 million to pay 11,500 "foster grandparents," $15 million to pay up to 75,000 Retired Senior Volunteer Program workers; and $26 million to pay up to 10,000 workers in such projects as Green Thumb and Senior Aides. As the names suggest, these programs pay old people to engage in needed public service work. Strengthening the Advisory Committee on Older Americans in various ways was also suggested.[21]

The administration program was changed greatly before passage; we need not follow that story, however. Our concern is with the nature of public policy, not the political process. The administration program of 1972 consisted of (1) just enough of an increase in social insurance and assistance to keep up with the cost of living, (2) small amounts for public works projects, (3) encouragement of industry and local government to do more for the aged, and (4) resistance against new federal bureaucracy. In short, an "accommodation" policy. The 1972 administration program would not use government powers to replace lost income at higher levels or to open new opportunities. Rather the emphasis is on a variety of small actions to prod society into giving older people a somewhat larger place in the scheme of things.

A Policy of Participation:
Both Expectations and Rewards

Storage and accommodation can be depicted clearly, since these two themes have characterized national policy. A policy of participation is harder to define but would provide expectations and rewards for optimum role performance of older people. It would systematically identify barriers to participation and remove them. Such action would involve a higher income guarantee, comprehensive planning for health and home help services, and changes in private employment practices. Public employment might be required. It would try to maximize use of skills emphasized at the outset of this chapter.

The cost of a participation policy would be acceptable perhaps only if there were clearly visible contributions from older people to offset part of it. The 1971 White House Conference on Aging produced many recommendations on government action for older people, such as more income and more medical service. Full participation and particularly the key question of reciprocal obligations was not addressed by the conference. Most recommendations called for more benefits; a $4,500 income floor and higher unemployment insurance are just two examples. The recommendations on roles for aging and young are particularly disappointing. Young people were to be educated about the old, and voluntary programs established to inform older people about services, to give them direct service, and to be their advocates. There was no coming to grips with the problem of participation—older people were seen in terms of their needs but not their capabilities.[22]

SOCIAL PROVISIONS:
WHAT SOCIETY DELIVERS TO THE AGED

Examination of policy pronouncements and program proposals, or even a careful analysis of federal and state law, does not give a coherent picture of social provisions for older people. It is instructive to examine the "delivery" element of our national welfare service delivery system. Does a study of services actually delivered reflect the current emphasis on accommodation and independence?

The New Concept

Here, then, lies the challenge of aging, both individually and socially. There are organic and mental changes characteristic of aging. They are gradual, however, and need constitute little or no serious impairment until much later than has been commonly supposed. There are situational changes to which adjustment can be made and some of which offer new opportunities.

Attainment of middle age may be viewed as bringing us to the threshold of a new phase of life—a phase that can represent a new stage of development, growth, maturity, and social contribution. Freed to an increasing extent from the responsibilities of early adulthood, we find ourselves ready to make further and broader contributions to the social welfare, effective because they grow out of half a century of experience gained through living. And this, we submit, is the role older people would choose for themselves. . . . Older people want activity, friendships, emotional security, a sense of usefulness. Socially our aging people constitute a huge natural resource eager to be exploited.

Clark Tibbitts and Harry D. Sheldon, "Introduction: A Philosophy of Aging."[23]

In one of the few studies of community services for older people, social provisions were defined as all income, services, or institutional care subsidized by taxes or voluntary contributions and available on an ongoing basis to community residents. During 1969 data were collected from fifty to eighty agencies and organizations in three Illinois counties.[24] The survey included recreation, adult education, public health, mental health, employment, churches and fraternal groups, income maintenance groups, and social welfare services.

This survey showed that society provides something for most older people. In each county 75 to 80 percent of older people received something from a social provisions network, usually in the form of money payments through social security or public assistance. Socially provided income accounted for 30 to 40 percent of total personal income for persons age sixty or over in the three counties.

The government overshadows voluntary health and welfare organizations as a provider of care and services as well as income. Local services under the United Fund, churches, or other charitable auspices that occupy so much newspaper space and so much of the energies of middle-class citizens on their boards and advisory committees seem to have little actual impact on the elderly. Of some 55,000 persons age sixty and over, about 35,000 received some socially provided income but only 3,700 received any services. Only 450 received them under voluntary auspices.

Government is the only provider of income programs, and two-thirds of all patients in nursing homes, local hospitals, and state mental hospitals were supported by public tax funds.

COMMUNITY SERVICES: THE MISSING LINK

The most significant question has to do with the distribution of effort among the provision of income, the provision of care, and the provision of a variety of local services. Community services to sustain independent living and encourage participation were trivial. The table shown here permits a comparison between provision of income, services, and care. Home-delivered services have been separated out because of their importance for the policy questions of accommodation and participation.

Type of Social Provision to Population Age Sixty and Over by Number Receiving and by Estimated Cost, in Three Illinois Counties[25]

Type of provision	Numbers served	Estimated cost
Total	43,600	$5,468,000
Income	35,500	3,900,000
Care (general hospital, nursing home, etc.)	4,400	1,500,000
Services: not home-delivered	3,100	60,000
home-delivered	600	8,000

Income provision totaled 71 percent of the cost of all social provision. Income provisions consisted primarily of social security payments but also included veterans pensions, public assistance, and township relief.

"Care" involved only 10 percent of the older people but accounted for over one-fourth of the total cost.

Social workers are particularly interested in the category of service. In this study, service included all direct person-to-person contacts with the elderly by helping welfare organizations or voluntary groups, including counseling and psychotherapy; information and referral; friendly visiting; organized recreation; out-patient medical attention and home-help visitation; and personal services, such as transportation, errand-running, or other special accommodations made for the comfort of elderly individuals.

The number receiving service was even fewer than the number receiving care, even though the care group is presumably an especially problem-ridden minority. Service accounted for 9 percent of the number served, with 1 percent of the total cost. The 3,700 people needing some service had to search out services among several dozen community agencies.

Lack of Home-based Services

What is the significance of this study for the future of social services for old people? As a society we do not "put our money where our mouth is." We talk about independent living and social integration of older people, but we provide a stipend insufficient to avert poverty and expensive residential care—nothing in between.

Is this study typical for the United States? The data came from three communities with above average personal income, and with well-developed social service networks. The methods were sufficiently thorough that underreporting was not a problem. The data reported do not understate society's provision of services in between completely independent living and residential care. Support also comes from the earlier review of national programs. Policy has been oriented to providing several billion dollars for income and health payments but not much federal money for the other "in between" services. In *Old People in Three Industrial Societies*, Shanas reports on the situation of old people in three countries in Northern Europe. Even in the highest age group, age eighty-five and over, less than a quarter of the old people were receiving any personal welfare service. The same conclusion is reached—society calls for participation by older people but provides a set of services which offer almost nothing between complete self-maintenance and complete institutionalization.[26]

"In-between" services

What services might be useful for old people? One study included 300 people age seventy and over in a South London borough referred to the welfare department for services.[27] In England the "welfare" department does not administer income programs, nor does it operate institutions. The welfare department is responsible for a wide variety of personal social services, especially home-delivered services.

England has a higher proportion of older people than the United States (12 percent age sixty-five and over), less fear of government provision, and a wider variety of in-between services.

Seventy-two percent of 300 aged referred to welfare were already receiving at least one home service. Many persons received more than one service. Practical help with housework and household maintenance, preparation of meals, and attention to health or social needs in the older person's own home were common.

Service	Percent
Home help (housework and chores)	55
Meals on wheels (home-delivered meals)	31
Chiropody—welfare or private	27
Voluntary visitors (church, volunteer corps)	23
District nurse (visiting nurse)	11
Regular welfare visits (social or health workers)	2

The London study also listed "additional needs" of the 300 older people.

Living arrangements and material aid were needs for a surprisingly small proportion. The four main types of problems were health attention, home help, recreation, and social work visiting.

These data are not presented as a scientific sample of typical needs of all older people. The list of services and needs for independent living, however, does give a realistic picture of the kinds of services that have to be considered if we seriously pursue a policy of accommodation or of integration. Of people over sixty, only 700 out of 55,000 in three different counties were receiving *any* home services.

In the next section we consider possible lines of development for national policy and for welfare services to older people, and we ask what role social work will play in these developments.

SERVICES FOR OLDER PEOPLE IN THE NEXT GENERATION

Society wants something done about the aged. Older people are a threat to society—their growing numbers, many needs, and their power are worrisome. Aging is unpleasant for older people themselves, beyond the inevitable restrictions of physiological aging. Older people are excluded from employment; social facilities are not convenient for them; they cannot find useful roles. National policy is not well developed. We are moving from storage to accommodation but without effective programs. Health and welfare services for older people are not satisfactory to anyone. Society provides several billions of dollars for income and health care at inadequate levels but virtually none of the local services that would support satisfactory community living. Clearly, in the next twenty-five years social work will recognize the greater importance of services to the aging.

Policy Trends

Four lines of development may define new policy directions. First, community health and welfare agencies will become more responsive to the aged and serve them better. All human service professionals tend to ignore the aged. A 1960 survey showed over 5,000 social workers in children's institutions and a like number in general hospitals and mental hospitals, but only about 800 in institutions for the aged.[28] Family service agencies, mental health clinics, and other settings preferred for employment by social workers have shown low proportions of aged in their caseloads and smaller amounts of attention to those served than to younger people.

New Interest in the Aged Faculty in many schools of social work have observed that students only recently have expressed interest in working with the aged. With some prodding from federal specialists in aging, social work agencies and schools are establishing special programs for the aged. Normal social agency practices must also be adjusted to accommodate older people. Interviews move at a slower pace, field visits are more feasible than agency visits, and workers must have knowledge of personality changes in old age just as child care workers need to know child development.

A second trend will be the development and administration of a variety of personal social services for older people: service centers, visiting nursing services, information and referral, foster homes, and help with transportation. These services do not employ the traditional social work methods of casework and group work. They must be organized, tailored, and delivered for individual older people; they cannot be set up on a mass basis. Current federal planning emphasizes nutrition and feeding programs, transportation, and information and referral services to put the aged in touch with community resources.

Social work's role may be the design and organization of local, practical programs to support independent living. The programming of new services requires skills different from those used to provide direct service. To take on this role effectively social workers will have to develop more skill in agency budgeting, estimating costs, surveying needs, preparing job descriptions, and training people to fill the jobs. If professional schools can teach these programming skills along with social work's traditional techniques for individualization and interpersonal helping the next generation of graduates can lead the way in creating the needed services.

Policy and Advocacy Planning   A third role for social work is policy planning and advocacy planning. The policy planning task can best be seen in the state offices for the aging, in the regional planning organizations created with the help of federal money, and in federal departments where aging specialists are becoming more common. The state offices have the tasks of helping communities apply for federal funds; of reporting to governors and legislatures on the needs of older people; of consulting with organizations which are starting new programs for older people; and of coordinating the efforts of state departments of mental health, public aid, and health in serving the aged. Regional planning requires some study of census and other data to describe the older population in the area, identify existing services, and form recommendations for new programs.

Advocacy planning is different from official planning because it operates outside the system and challenges the system. The Nader report on nursing homes as an example of advocacy seeks the deliberate organization of older people for protest and political pressure. Such organization violates the stereotype of older people passively withdrawing from social engagement and having lower levels of desire and aspiration than younger people. Since older people clearly do have strong desires and interests, self-help organizations concerned with aging will increase. The Townsend movement in the 1930s was a key factor in passing the Social Security Act, and the McLain movement in California was also organized for higher income provisions. At present a number of retired persons' organizations are active in lobbying at the national level. The 1971 White House Conference on Aging faced a near-rebellion of delegates when it became clear that the administration was not interested in large new spending programs.

SOCIAL INTEGRATION OF THE AGED

A fourth role for social work is in developing new policy directions to achieve full participation rather than storage or accommodation. How can older people be integrated? From an economic viewpoint, we can hardly continue the present

A Nutrition Activity Program in Salt Lake City[29]

The project provides a nutritious lunch, nutrition and and consumer education, enrichment and recreational activities. For participants who have serious personal problems, the project has been a major factor in assisting them to lead more nearly normal lives.

An outreach worker visited Mr. and Mrs. Jon Dekker at the time the nutrition program was started at Lincoln Junior High School. Mr. Dekker had suffered a stroke and spent most of his time in a wheelchair. Usually, the only time the couple left the house together was to go to the doctor's office. Both were in their mid-60's, and had one son who lived out of the state. Mrs. Dekker said that many of their friends were sympathetic when Mr. Dekker first suffered his stroke, but now they were left alone and ignored much of the time.

Soon the Dekkers were among the regular participants, two days a week. They enjoyed the meals, the fellowship, and the activities. Mr. Dekker liked working with his hands and usually would take part in the crafts class. His speech improved as he talked with others. His walking also improved.

One year later, Mrs. Dekker became bedridden with cancer. She insisted that Mr. Dekker continue to participate in the nutrition program, even though she had to remain at home. One woman participant visited the home almost daily and assisted with the cooking. The project staff instructed Mr. Dekker about frozen and convenience foods—anticipating the day when he would be on his own.

Since Mrs. Dekker's death, Mr. Dekker has continued to live in his home and to participate in the nutrition program.

policy of pushing people out of the labor market at an earlier age. The cost of retirement pay plus the cost of health care for the growing number over the age of eighty will be prohibitive. Friedman has put the problem well: "The magnitude and suddenness of the explosion of our aged population have created a surplus of aged for the proportion of roles which have previously been allotted to them."[30] He suggests that integration of the aged will depend on opportunities afforded them for participation, not on society's ability to maintain them. Part of the answer is the continuation of old roles, and part is the development of new roles.

Programs to pay older people to be foster grandparents, or to maintain public rights-of-ways, or to give the telephone and visiting services to other people are attempts to define new social roles as well as to provide some income to the aged. Cottrell suggested that the degree of adjustment to roles in a society varies with the clarity with which such roles are defined, with the degree of importance attached to them, and with the definiteness of the transitional procedures used by the society in designating the change in roles.[31] Sussman commented, "Not only does the older person need a definite role, but he also needs individuals who will become responsible socializing agents."[32]

New roles need to be clearly defined and recognized by others. Reciprocal obligations, the key to role definition, must be spelled out. Further, there must be a system of preparation and training for assumption of the roles.

Social workers are in a good position to lead the innovation of new roles. They have a view of the impact of social institutions on older people, and they administer programs of human service that are chronically short of manpower to meet obvious needs. Yet social agencies have not taken advantage of opportunities to obtain government money to employ old people in service jobs. Where the aged are concerned, social workers may need to see themselves more as organizers of service rather than the persons who perform the service.

Merlin Taber

KEY TERMS

early retirement	disengagement
chronic illness	accommodation
rolelessness	home-delivered services

FOR DISCUSSION

1　Explain the increased proportion of aged in the population.
2　Why are the aged considered a problem group?
3　Explain the increased cost to society. How is the cost to society of retirement from the labor force increasing?
4　How are age and average income related after age sixty?
5　What health facilities and services are most important for older people?
6　Identify difficulties in gaining access to community health and welfare services.
7　What major provisions does our society make for the aged?
8　Contrast the policies of accommodation and of storage.
9　What are the difficulties in integrating old people into society?
10　Summarize income, service, and care provisions as indicated in the Illinois study.
11　What are the obstacles to advocacy planning for the aged?

PROJECTS

1　Research and debate the question that retirement ages should be increased rather than decreased.
2　Visit a home for the aged and interview several residents on a social issue of your own choosing. An example is: "People would be better off if both prices and wages were lower." Tape-record the answers and compare them.
3　Invite two people of about the same age—a housewife and a man who has retired from his job several years ago—to come to a class session and discuss their present activities and interests with a small student panel. What similarities and differences are revealed?
4　Consider old age for your own parents. To what extent will they depend on you financially? Psychologically? What provisions have they made to maintain their own independence? Do you expect that one or both may live with you at some time?
5　Analyze the problem of inflation as it affects the aged who live independently and those that must have special care.

6 Organize the class into a survey team to determine what programs the local churches have for the aged. What methods of outreach are used, and what is the response?
7 Discuss the differences between disengagement, accommodation, and participation as basic philosophies of planning for the aged. What are some of the barriers to full participation?

FOR FURTHER STUDY

Robert C. Atchley, *The Social Forces in Later Life: An Introduction to Social Gerontology*, Wadsworth, Belmont, Calif., 1972.

Zena Smith Blau, *Old Age in a Changing Society*, F. Watts, New York, 1973.

Ewald W. Busse and Eric Pfeiffer (eds.), *Mental Illness in Later Life*, American Psychiatric Association, Washington, D.C., 1973.

Mary Adelaide Mendelson, *Tender Loving Greed*, Knopf, New York, 1974.

Bernice L. Neugarten (ed.), *Middle Age and Aging: A Reader in Social Psychology*, Univ. of Chicago Press, 1968.

Donn Pearce, *Dying in the Sun*, Charterhouse, New York, 1974.

Eric Pfeiffer (ed.), *Alternatives to Institutional Care for Older Americans: Practice and Planning*, Duke Center for the Study of Aging and Human Development, Durham, N.C., 1973.

Bert Kruger Smith, *Aging in America*, Beacon Press, Boston, 1973.

Part Five

Social Work
Personnel, Education,
and Research

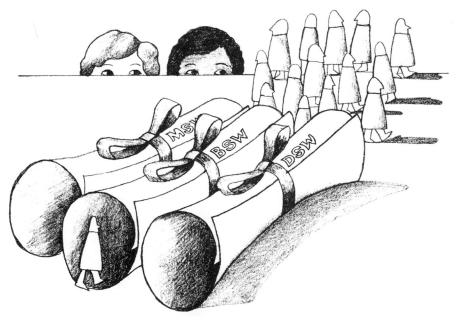

Having given the reader an acquaintance with social work methods and activities, the survey of the field will be completed with issues of interest to students considering a social work career: Who does social work, what preparation is needed, and how outcomes can be measured.

This section will present:

The roles of the volunteer and the indigenous worker that provide opportunities to test out an interest in the field

Social work education at four levels
The dilemmas of the minority practitioner
Research tools to evaluate social work activities

Do you want to become a social worker?
How do you make intelligent decisions about a social work career?

Chapter 22

Volunteers
and Paraprofessionals

What are the nonprofessional roles?
Why be a volunteer?
How are paraprofessionals used?
Are indigenous workers effective?

You probably have served as a volunteer, giving time without pay. Some of you may also have served in Action, Vista, or the Peace Corps as a full-time volunteer. If you had no special work degree but worked for pay in a social work capacity, you were a paraprofessional worker. You may also have been chosen for a job because of the common experiences that you shared with those receiving your services, living in the same neighborhood, facing the same problems, and perhaps sharing the same ethnic identity. Then you served as an indigenous worker.

Students in social welfare and other human service programs tend to have a special interest in volunteering and provide the major personnel for direct services and for organization and management of programs.

This chapter deals with the social service roles that usually involve no specialized education—the volunteer and the paraprofessional.

VOLUNTEERING DEFINED

Volunteering involves one person helping another with some task or problem too big to handle alone. If the task or problem were complex, many individuals might volunteer to help out. In an earlier day farmers helped each other bring in the crops or rebuild a barn. This self-help activity was offered and accepted on the basis of friendship among the participants. It was often taken for granted. As our country developed larger urban centers, volunteering took other forms characteristic of the environment in which people lived and required more organization.

Volunteering depends on personal awareness. Ideally, the offer to help is given with no thought of personal gain except perhaps an increase in the volunteer's own sense of self. Sometimes volunteer services are formed to offer help to those "less fortunate." When this benevolent attitude is perceived as patronizing by those whom the volunteer tries to help, the activity is less successful. A true volunteer activity is freely given and freely received because the two parties have a personal respect for each other.

In a simple agrarian society there was little need for specialists. As society became urban, industrialized, and complex, people specialized. Groups with like interests formed organizations that made possible marshaling the talents and energies of many toward a common purpose.

The Range of Volunteer Activities

Volunteers have three typical functions—giving direct service, fund raising, and policy determination. The greatest number are involved in providing services, from being Big Brothers to providing casework services that would be professional if the volunteer received pay. Fund-raising activities range from ringing doorbells to writing copy for brochures and making spot announcements on television. Policy determination is the role of board members at local, regional, or national levels.

Direct Service Roles   In all types of agencies volunteers can help raise funds, carry out clerical tasks, and furnish transportation. In hospitals they share a variety of patient care roles. They also serve as snack bar and gift shop attendants and as messengers. They often help with letter writing and personal errands. In institutions, they may serve as recreational leaders, care personnel, tutors, and confidants. Volunteers may go into homes to care for children while the mother goes to the doctor or seeks employment. In child welfare agencies, they may learn to license day care homes or serve as recruiters of foster or adoptive parents. In youth-serving programs, they volunteer as Scoutmasters or in other leadership roles. The roles are virtually unlimited depending upon the skills of the person and the imagination of the agency in using his or her talents.

The Volunteer as Board Member   You will recall from Chapter 3 that citizen volunteers also provide direction to the organization and administration of social welfare services through participation on boards. As we have seen, privately supported social agencies have a board of directors composed of people who volunteer. They set program and policy, hire staff, and provide for the general governance of the organization. Public social agencies use citizen advisory boards to help interpret policy and enable legislation. Sometimes board members are selected, at least in part, from the people receiving the services of the organization. In any case, citizen boards composed of volunteers aid in maintaining and developing policy for the agency.

Types of Programs Violet Sieder has provided a system for categorizing volunteer programs:[1] membership groups, such as American Red Cross or the Junior League of America; self-help groups, including ex-addicts and tenant councils; social action or advocacy groups such as Planned Parenthood or the American Civil Liberties Union; and radical groups, which seek to change our society. Others include general voluntary and public social welfare services, federally encouraged volunteer programs, federally sponsored volunteer programs, and private and public volunteer coordinating organizations.

Throughout these multiple roles filled by volunteers is one element— someone cares enough about someone else to contribute time and talent on his behalf.

SCOPE OF VOLUNTEER PROGRAMS

How big is the pool of volunteers? In 1969 13 percent of adult citizens in the United States served on some kind of community problem committee.[2] An estimated six of every ten adults would be interested in some form of volunteering for an average of four hours per week. If all these people volunteered at the same time, obviously it would be difficult to deploy them effectively and provide activities that would satisfy them.

The American Red Cross, the largest user of volunteers, reports that 2.3 million adults donate time. A half million volunteers participate in the various local United Way programs throughout the country. Add to this the millions of church and synagogue members plus the multitude of fraternal and social groups who regularly contribute volunteer time, and the total becomes significant. The work done by volunteers in just one year would cost billions of dollars.[3]

Problems in Using Volunteers

In social welfare, in spite of the great need, professional workers frequently do not have the skills to recruit or train volunteers. Also, they may view the use of volunteers as a threat to professionalism. The employed staff often just don't see what a volunteer could do. Sometimes a staff member is given the task of working with volunteers as an afterthought—when all the other work is completed; or the social agency may take the opposite direction and begin a volunteer program in order to save large amounts of money. Both approaches usually end in failure. Volunteer programs need to be administered well in order to use the talents available. These talents usually fall outside the professional realm. The volunteer's contribution very often is a means of extending services to enrich and supplement the social service program but rarely to supplant it.

Many volunteers contribute their time and energy for relatively short periods—from a day to a few months. Only a small proportion of volunteers stay with the same activity for years. As a result, social welfare service personnel constantly need to recruit new volunteers.

Recruitment The stereotyped volunteer was the middle-class unemployed housewife who had reared her children and needed an outlet for her free time. This group remains an important source of talent, but several other pools of people have been discovered in recent years. Older citizens have offered their services for everything from foster-grandparenting to helping the young and inexperienced businessman. The energy and talent of youth have also been recognized as a source of volunteers. Traditional volunteer roles such as hospital candy-stripers and playground assistants are still important. Also many high school and college groups have formed their own volunteer organizations, frequently taking complete responsibility for recruitment and programming. Finally, the poor and minority-group members are volunteering their special skills in increasing numbers.

Minimal Bureaucracy Unfortunately, agencies may deemphasize the element that permits volunteering to succeed. They may become so wrapped up in bureaucratic rules that the warmth of friendship and personal relationships become subordinate to policy. When the rules become more important than the people, volunteering fails. If volunteers do not get personal satisfaction, or if their unique contribution fails to be recognized, they drop out.

All volunteers need to feel a sense of satisfaction to remain in a program. In programs for permanent residents, volunteers often serve a program for many years. Some remain in the same role for a long time, but others prefer a variety of activities. In programs for college students, turnover is especially high. Not only are students temporary residents, but their course demands and work schedules often lead to uncertainty of participation. Also if the students want to sample possible future careers, they may move rapidly from one volunteer program to another. High turnover is costly. Students participate longer if their goals are met. The idealism of a college volunteer was revealed in her report to her student organization.[4]

> If a volunteer feels useful, he will exert himself to a fuller extent and be excited about his project and the possibilities for further experience it offers. Today's volunteer works with people toward the betterment of society. He is not a martyr to the relentless, paradoxical conditions of societal existence today. He is an optimist looking for direction in which to develop and display his hope for mankind.

A high proportion of those recruited through publicity campaigns will drop out after a short time because they simply did not find the satisfaction they were looking for. Those who remain find satisfaction in a specific kind of volunteering. If they feel that their contribution is important, they can carry a major share of the responsibility for additional recruitment. They will tell their friends about what they do. A candidate brought in by a volunteer has a good chance of being another good volunteer.

VOLUNTEER TRAINING

How much training do volunteers need? Professionals tend to think there is much for the volunteer to learn before the job can be done. The professional usually conceptualizes the role of the volunteer as largely a duplication of what he does.

This obviously requires lengthy training. The beginning volunteer, on the other hand, may see little or no need for training. The volunteer at this stage sees the role in terms of what he or she already knows. To attempt to provide extensive preservice training causes potentially qualified volunteers to drop out.

Preservice A carefully structured session or two of preservice training will permit the new volunteer to become oriented to the agency functions, the program, and his or her own role. If experienced volunteers train new ones, they may provide more realism than a professional trainer. Experienced volunteers can conduct informal discussions about what they do and provide observation-apprenticeship learning for the new volunteers in small groups. The style should be informal and emphasize "doing" rather than didactic learning.

In-Service On-going in-service training will have two very important functions. First, training is needed to deal with situations in which the volunteer lacks skills and wants help. In-service training needs to be paced so that problems can be addressed early enough for the volunteer to understand his role and to have resources for help. Second, in-service training is needed to reinforce the volunteer. Periodic in-service sessions can help keep the volunteer from getting in a rut. Agency personnel should offer recognition of the volunteer's efforts, and the volunteers as a group may provide reinforcement. When planning training experiences for volunteers, enough time for socializing should also be built in to help the group gain cohesion.

In addition to training, a volunteer program will need office space, meeting rooms, travel experiences, and insurance coverage—all major items that indicate the need for management skills.

MONITORING AND EVALUATING

Monitoring and evaluation fulfill several important functions. Reporting regularly helps emphasize the importance of the activity and maintains its "goal-directedness." Reporting the problems encountered reveals needs for additional training. Monitoring provides a measure of the services rendered and helps to justify the cost of the program. Without reports of what was done and measurement of its success, the program may appear to be too costly. Data from the reports also provide information for recruitment and for publicity.

STUDENT VOLUNTEERS

College and high school students carry out a wide range of activities in community service agencies. Many college volunteer programs involve large numbers of students who provide substantial campus and community service. While most operate with relatively small budgets, a few have funds for paid staff. According to a recent survey of some thirty major universities, participants in volunteer programs ranged from 100 up to 2,500.[5]

Activities in social services cover a broad field. Some were unique to a particular campus and its community. Typical volunteer projects were:

1 Tutoring, both young children and other college students.

2 Serving as classroom assistants.

3 Recreation programs for both children and adults.

4 Mental health services—hot-line telephone services, assisting with the care or education of the mentally retarded, and special recreation or friendship programs for the mentally ill and the mentally retarded.

5 Services to the offender, especially to the juvenile, as a quasi-probation officer—by being a special friend or assisting in a detention facility.

6 Services to the aged—especially those in nursing homes. College students seem to be especially successful in working with this group.

Only one of the programs reported a social action emphasis. Such activities are usually carried on outside of volunteer programs. Social action objectives in social agencies are often accomplished informally, but the primary emphasis has been on direct service.

Special Problems The problems of college and high school programs include heavy academic schedules and uneven demands on time, conflict of personal needs for independence with the needs of persons served, and impatience for rapid change. For college students, mobility is a major problem. Recruitment and training must be continuous because of the turnover. The difficulties, however, are often offset by the strong sense of commitment.

Sponsorship of Student Programs

A college or university program can usually gain some financial support from the institution. Important advantages generally result from continuity and expertise when a college or university staff person coordinates the volunteer program and takes initiative in program planning, budgeting, and training. Many programs are highly successful because university officials support the student volunteers.

Many students disagree with college or university sponsorship. They believe that the programs should be volunteer-controlled. They do not want to participate in another institutional effort. The skill and talent of the college or university staff person may also deprive student leaders of management and policy respon-

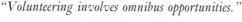

"Volunteering involves omnibus opportunities."

sibility. The students then are limited to direct service without responsibility for making the volunteer service function.

To avoid these constraints, volunteer services can be run exclusively by students, who provide their own governance, raise funds, train staff, plan programs, and recruit volunteers. Even in a completely student-run volunteer program, considerable faculty-staff-institutional support must be provided. In the college-university operated program there is also student advice and counsel and exercise of student power.

Academic Credit for Volunteering

Some students will volunteer only if they receive credit, but their motivation to serve may be low. Also, academic credit ordinarily implies faculty control of activities that should be volunteer-service-oriented rather than academic-course-oriented. Course objectives may interfere with the volunteering objectives. When the course ends, those students with marginal commitment tend to drop out even though the need for the volunteer service continues.

After students participate as volunteers, many are eager and ready to take on leadership activities. Credit may best be given for course work on how to lead a volunteer activity. Topics include recruiting volunteers, program planning, coordination and supervision, public relations, conducting in-service training, and budgeting and fund raising. Such study increases the competence of student leadership and prepares them for community volunteer activity following graduation.

Some colleges and universities have coopted the volunteer movement by academic programs requiring students to participate. This reflects a lack of understanding of the volunteer concept and negates the essential voluntary offering of self.

Financing a Student Volunteer Program

Why does a student volunteer program need money? Many people assume that since it is a *volunteer* program and the people involved contribute their time, funds have a low priority. While student volunteer programs can be operated on a shoestring budget, some funding is obviously essential. It costs money to recruit volunteers. Postage, brochures, and publicity must be paid for, and travel costs must be met. A full-time secretary is also a good investment. The amount of direct expense varies with the program. Part of it may be absorbed by the college or university budget.

Another major expense is the in-service training of volunteers. Many social welfare agencies provide training. Depending on the nature of the total volunteer program, this may suffice, but students usually wish to undertake their own training program. Then expenditures for the training of volunteers become critical to the success of the program.

Student volunteer programs frequently encounter large expenses for transportation. Expenses in getting to off-campus locations may seriously limit the program and exclude qualified and interested students. The specific location of the college or university campus determines the need for transportation. Inexpensive and convenient commercial transportation may be available in a

LOOKING FOR SOME ACTION?

ACTION, the governmental program that administers the Peace Corps, VISTA, the Service Corps of Retired Executives, and the Foster Grandparent Program recruits people of all ages. For voluntary agencies and programs, the National Center for Voluntary Action has a similar program. The two advertisements shown here are among the recruitment materials used by the agencies.

You'll never know how much good you can do until you do it.

You can help people.

In fact, there's a crying need for you. Your talents. Your training. Your concerns. They make you valuable to your business. They can make you priceless to your community.

We can put you in touch with local organizations hard at work doing things you'd be proud to be part of. Join one. Or, if you see the need, start a new one.

If you can spare even a few hours a week, call the Voluntary Action Center in your town. Or write: "Volunteer," Washington, D.C. 20013.

It'll do you good to see how much good you can do.

Volunteer.

The National Center for Voluntary Action.

 A Public Service of This Newspaper & The Advertising Council

VOLUNTEER CAMPAIGN
NEWSPAPER AD NO. V-74-272-330 LINES (3 col. x 8")

metropolitan area, but a college in a smaller city may not have a mass transit system. Then car pools, taxicabs, and even chartered buses may be needed.

Two other organizational functions may result in major expense, namely, general administration and program evaluation. General administration of the program may be accomplished by some of the volunteers themselves. Expenditures are inevitably involved in monitoring and evaluating the programs, for this provides the only means to answer basic questions, including: What are the program objectives? What kind of training is needed by the volunteers to be able to provide the services necessary to attain the objectives? Is there a way to accomplish the objectives better? More cheaply? What community/campus needs should the volunteer service address? How many volunteer hours per week are needed and how many are contributed for each program? Do volunteers stay with the program long enough to do their job? Answers require the use of informal conversation, simple surveys, and the regular reporting of data about activities.

Fund Raising   There are always more good causes than there are funds. Students contribute money, but citizens of the community where the program operates provide most of the support. While participants in student volunteer programs may believe that they operate in a financial desert, the campus and its business community can maintain a program. Develop a strong case for the importance and worth of the student volunteer program. After the case is outlined, present it persuasively. Almost everyone—individual, business firm, or foundation—receives many requests for funds. "Whatever way you communicate it, your summary . . . should first state the problem at hand. Then describe your unique approach to a solution: What needs to be done . . . why you are equipped to do it . . . what you propose to do . . . who supports or will support you . . . what the project will cost (have a specific budget ready to show) . . . and what the reader, or listener, can do to help."[6]

Involve people. Never send a letter if you can have a personal contact. Always use a friend or acquaintance to ask the potential giver rather than a stranger. Figure out ahead of time how the representation of the student volunteer organization can prevent the person from saying "no" to the request. Make it easy for him to say "yes." It helps to be able to have a plan for accomplishing the budget goal. Your group may decide that students can give x percent and faculty x percent, and the community then may support the volunteer program with x percent if the campus gives you its support.

Finally, a student volunteer program should issue press releases and human interest stories about its activities and accomplishments. If the president of XYZ corporation knows about the program, it is much harder to say "no."

WHY YOU SHOULD VOLUNTEER

Why should the college or university student volunteer? The student may feel that he or she is too busy, or that the skills are lacking for a worthwhile contribution, even though students agree that it is good to help others. At least three reasons based on self-interest make it worthwhile to participate in a student volunteer program.

Career Testing and Development   In our complex society, a short-range job experience is difficult in many occupational fields. Often the student would like to try working in a general field of interest before making the full commitment to a long course of study and apprenticeship. Volunteering provides a way to get on the inside, to find out what really goes on, and to learn at very little risk if something has promise as a career.

Citizen Development   A democracy is dependent for its existence upon informed citizens. Volunteering offers opportunities to learn about some of the major social problems and what is being done about them. As a volunteer, you can learn first-hand the needs of children without families, the problems when youngsters have nowhere to play, how it feels to be in a mental hospital, what it's like to have been in jail, and—of great importance—how people live in poverty. Experiences obtained as a college volunteer will be utilized in providing a better understanding of human problems.

Enjoyment and Social Skills   Volunteering is fun and an excellent way to meet other people with similar interests and concerns. People who volunteer find it satisfying to engage in rap sessions with others. We learn how to work with others and gain confidence through volunteering.

Daniel Thursz, Dean of the University of Maryland School of Social Work, has presented "Ten Commandments for Volunteers":[7]

1   Understand the job you undertake.
2   Accept training appreciatively and contribute your own experience.
3   Match your interests to the needs about you and the job.
4   Serve faithfully and report new insights about your work.
5   Discover its meaning to the total program of which it is a part.
6   Open yourself to opportunities for growth in skill, sympathy, self-confidence, and responsibility.
7   Value your special two-way role as community interpreter.
8   Contribute to supervision by self-evaluation and a willingness to speak.
9   Give loyalty to your institution and its program.
10   Take pride in the volunteer's career. It pays handsomely in treasures of the spirit.

PARAPROFESSIONALS

In the social welfare field the demarcation lines between volunteer, paraprofessional, and the professional have been changing and unclear. Social work as an organized activity first began with friendly visitors who were volunteers. Gradually training programs were initiated, and social work became professionalized, but professional social workers are assisted by people who carry out critical tasks in a paraprofessional capacity. Sometimes the only difference between the volunteer and the paraprofessional is that the latter is paid. At other times the paraprofessional fulfills a more complex role through experience and training.

Relationship to the Professional In considering the paraprofessional, an understanding of professionalism is important. A professional person has a combination of knowledge and skill acquired after study and practice, applied according to a value system accepted by those engaged in the specific profession. The knowledge and skill are complex and expensive to obtain. In almost every occupation some tasks or functions are less complex but still essential. These tasks and functions constitute occupational roles filled by paraprofessionals. Occasionally a paraprofessional occupation involves a high degree of knowledge and skill of its own, either through special schooling or through on-the-job training. At other times persons are sought for paraprofessional roles because they have unique cultural or personal attributes necessary for the successful delivery of the service.

Activities of Paraprofessionals

The term "paraprofessional" is usually reserved for people who participate directly in the basic activity of the agency. Clerical, fund raising, or publicity personnel would not be considered paraprofessionals. While the term indicates that the person is not qualified to be a professional social worker, competence rather than credentials should determine the individual's role in the agency.

The Case Aide The case aide is the most common paraprofessional in casework agencies. The aide performs tasks assigned by the professional staff typically involving information gathering or supportive service that involve clear routines and require little supervision once the tasks are learned. This restricted view of the aide is giving way, however, to much more individualized assignments. With professional staff shortages and budget restrictions, aides often perform more central roles in the helping process. Some agencies have much more liberal policies in the use of such manpower than do others.

Roles in Group Work Group work agencies have a larger proportion of paraprofessional staff than most casework agencies. Some are primarily responsible for recreational programs, but increasingly they are also leaders of socialization groups that deal with personality development and social skills. There is a particular need for young people who can get teenagers to identify with them. Since groups often meet in the evening and on weekends, paraprofessionals often serve in part-time jobs.

Roles in Community Work All the employees of some agencies can be considered paraprofessional in that some agencies employ no social workers. They draw people with wide varieties of education and experience. Residence in a given community and a strong commitment to it are seen as more important than credentials. The familiar roles of enabler, broker, and advocate characterize the activities.

The Team Secretary Ordinarily, clerical workers are not considered paraprofessionals, but in many team models, the team secretary has a key role in the provision of direct service. In child welfare teams, for example, she serves as the contact person for many kinds of inquiries and makes decisions about monthly payments, medical needs, clothing purchases, and visits of the natural parents, to name but a few. The extent of responsibility is a function of relative competence. These roles qualify the secretary as a paraprofessional.

The Outreach Worker Another particularly interesting paraprofessional role involves *outreach*. The antipoverty programs popularized this function. The outreach person knows a given neighborhood and serves as a "door knocker" to make residents aware of available services and expresses the desire to discuss and help solve problems. These efforts led to increased applications for welfare benefits and strengthened the development of welfare rights organizations. The outreach paraprofessional was usually indigenous in that he belonged to the group being served and had life experiences that provided the basis for acceptance by neighborhood residents.

Career Ladders One of the major goals in social work is to provide "career ladders" so that paraprofessionals can advance in responsibility and status. Community colleges fulfill an important role in providing basic courses that carry academic credit. Many people have been interested in helping paraprofessionals gain professional status through part-time study and through educational leaves of absence.

Maximizing the Contributions of Paraprofessionals

Agencies need to maximize both the contribution and the job satisfaction of personnel. As a recent monograph has indicated, "The establishment of teams appears to be the most prudent way of introducing non-professionals into an agency because the professional knowledge, values and knowhow are built into the service delivery system. Standards of service can be maintained without losing the services of those who have not been entirely socialized into the social work culture."[8]

Using a team organization, people with a variety of skills and interests work together. In casework the team can bring to bear a much wider variety of skills than can an individual worker. The team format has two advantages for the nonprofessional. He can learn from his colleagues through observation and through staff meetings. At the same time, he is a participant in a system that builds in accountability. With increasing experience, the team member is able to expand his responsibilities as he grows in competence. Also he can be encouraged to develop special interests that are not otherwise available to the team.

THE INDIGENOUS WORKER

What are indigenous workers? How do they differ from the paraprofessional or the volunteer? The indigenous worker has a marketable skill because of his or her life experience and can offer the skill to a client or client group with limited in-service training.

The indigenous worker is paid for offering services; the volunteer is not. Usually the indigenous worker is a member of the client group being served, or at least has similar social, cultural, and economic characteristics. The skill of the indigenous worker is frequently dependent upon his access to this client group through personal knowledge of the group and the ability to communicate with its members. Therefore the indigenous worker may be an excellent choice for case-finding, intake, reception, or data-gathering contacts. He is also frequently best able to carry on educational or public relations programs aimed at a special class or group of clients. Job titles of indigenous workers are frequently descriptive of the primary duties—"outreach worker" (case finding), "home visitor" (case finding or neighborhood organization), and "neighborhood aide" (program interpretation and client education).

Special Problems of the Indigenous Worker

When people learn a job reasonably well, they are usually ready to move toward a more challenging goal. Advancement has been a problem for indigenous workers. They are selected because of their intelligence, judgment, and broad experience. Some are soon socialized into the agency program and perform their assigned tasks at a high level of competence. Then they feel ready to move to more complex assignments. Usually promotion requires more formal higher education. Then, regardless of level of performance, they may find themselves in a dead-end job.

During the War on Poverty it was charged that indigenous workers were employed to both help their brothers and keep the lid on dissatisfaction and revolt. If indigenous workers fulfilled the function of maintaining calm among their particular social, cultural, or economic group, so that members of the group did not pressure for their rights under the law, this use of the indigenous worker raises moral and ethical questions. Even when the indigenous workers may not have been intentionally employed for control, they were frequently perceived by their neighbors and friends as one of "them" and now no longer one of "us." The indigenous worker seemed to identify more with the agency staff and less with the members of the client group. Since indigenous workers often fail to have the educational requirements for career advancement, the positions become frustrating and anxiety-producing. Then workers find themselves cut off both from their client groups and from identification with the professional staff—they become the victims of cooptation.

Development of paraprofessional and indigenous workers emerged from the volunteer system. Payment assures continuity of services and provides financial rewards for people who have valuable skills but can't afford to give their time free. All three roles, paraprofessional, indigenous worker, and volunteer, are invaluable to agencies and provide citizen involvement in the social services.

Richard J. Anderson

KEY TERMS

volunteer	social action groups
paraprofessional	radical groups
indigenous	monitoring
membership groups	career testing
self-help groups	cooptation

FOR DISCUSSION

1   How is volunteering related to private charity?
2   Is Seider's classification of groups applicable in your community?
3   How long should training of volunteers take?
4   Should one agency conduct volunteer training for the others?
5   What is your attitude toward official college sponsorship?
6   Volunteer programs under the federal government have been combined into a single agency called Action. Is it effective?
7   Review the discussion of informal charity at the end of Chapter 1 of this book. What problems are shared by volunteer programs?
8   Summarize the volunteer programs on your campus. What are the gaps?
9   Discuss the use of pins and other awards for volunteering.
10 Investigate the career of volunteer supervisor and the special skills needed.
11 How can role conflict between volunteers and professional workers be minimized?
12 Discuss: "An indigenous worker can't remain indigenous."
13 How does cooptation become a problem for indigenous workers?

PROJECTS

1   If there is a volunteer program on your campus, invite one of the leaders to present the objectives and describe the organization. (If this chapter is considered early in the term, students may wish to volunteer and report on their activities from time to time.)
2   If there is no volunteer organization on your campus, use the class as a pilot group to provide such service. Evaluate the experience, and consider the problems of extending it campuswide.
3   Find out from the local welfare council the organizations that make the most extensive use of volunteers. Describe the program in each of the agencies and prepare a composite report.
4   Analyze the special opportunities for volunteer activities for older people. What roles are now available to them in the community? What others can be developed? What arguments are there for paying older people for their services?
5   Explore local high schools to see whether they have service clubs or other volunteer organizations. Investigate the opportunities for college students to work with them as leaders.
6   Interview a member of the college or university administration to determine the relationship between the institution and volunteer programs. What kinds of support can the administration provide? What is its attitude about giving academic credit for volunteer efforts?
7   Organize a panel to consider the relationship between volunteer experiences and the choice of a career in social work. Pool past volunteer experiences of class members as a means to get data on social services.
8   Explore with several agencies their use of indigenous workers. Have they been employed? Are they employed now? What opportunities have been provided for advancement?

FOR FURTHER STUDY

Charles Grosser et al. (eds.), *Non-professionals in the Human Services*, Jossey-Bass, San Francisco, 1965.

Linda Millman and Catherine Schulman, *Poor People at Work*, U.S. Social and
    Rehabilitation Service, 1969. An annotated bibliography on semiprofession-
    als.
Arthur Pearl and Frank Riessman, *New Careers for The Poor*, Free Press, New
    York, 1965.
John G. Cull and Richard E. Hardy, *Volunteerism: An Emerging Profession*,
    Charles C Thomas, Springfield, Ill., 1974.
Arthur R. Pell, *Recruiting, Training and Motivating Volunteer Workers*, Pell
    Books, New York, 1972.
The following materials are from the National Center for Voluntary Action, 1785
    Massachusetts Avenue, N.W., Washington, D.C. Single copies are free:
"Planning . . . Implementing . . . Evaluating . . . A Workshop for Volunteer Di-
    rectors: A University-Community Effort in Philadelphia."
"Outreach Projects: Decentralization Experiences of Five Voluntary Action Cen-
    ters."
"Recruiting Low Income Volunteers: Experience of Five Voluntary Action Cen-
    ters."
Directory of College-University Resources in Education and Training for Volun-
    tary Action.
Portfolio   1, "Drug Education and Rehabilitation Programs and the Volunteer."
Portfolio   2, "Volunteers in Preschool, Day Care, Head Start and After School
    Programs."
Portfolio   7, "Volunteer Drivers."

Chapter 23

Social Work Education

Vocational/preprofessional goals in one program?
What is the professional bachelor's degree?
The master's degree . . . just more of the same?
Where does the doctorate lead?

The levels of social work education and questions posed by students about them are discussed in this chapter.

Social work education is offered at four levels leading to associate, bachelor's, master's, and doctor's degrees. The goal is to provide a well-articulated continuum with each successive level building on the others. The relationship among the associate, bachelor's, and master's levels has been described as three sets of steps placed close enough together that one can move with ease from the lower one to the middle one to the taller one.[1]

TWO-YEAR ASSOCIATE PROGRAMS

The past decade has seen a rapid growth of two-year community colleges with a wide variety of programs. Community colleges provide a range of options to students at a modest cost. Human services include social services, education, and nonmedical care of individuals. The programs seek to achieve two goals simultaneously—training for employment and the foundation for additional collegiate education. As a result the typical program is both vocational and preprofessional. Students who expect to go to work also seek assurances that their credits will be transferable if they decide later to pursue a bachelor's degree.

A representative selection of specific titles for which training is offered includes:

Community Services Technician/Community Service Assistant/Community Social Service
Child Care Technology/Residential Child Care
Social Service Aide/Social Service Associate/Social Service Technical
Recreation Leadership/Recreation Aide
Classroom Aide/Teacher Aide/Educational Aide
Parole Aide
Nursery School Assistant/Child Development-Preschool Education
Mental Health Aide/Mental Health Associate
Human Services Aide[2]

Four components are generally included in the curriculum—general education, specific core courses for the field of choice, courses dealing with specific skills and methods, and a field practicum.

Candidates for Associate Degrees   Associate degree programs must meet the needs of four quite different groups of students: (1) recent high school graduates who may want either vocational skills or the beginning of a longer college career. This group is the youngest and has the widest range of goals. In a restricted job market, age and lack of work experience may be a barrier to placement; (2) second careerists, including both people who want more satisfying jobs and those who have been out of the labor force usually because of childbearing and childrearing. This group often has a strong interest in general education as well as preprofessional content; (3) people already in the human service occupations who want to improve their skills and their economic capability. This group may be the most highly vocationally oriented; and (4) new careerists—residents in a poverty area sometimes with little formal education but who are recruited to provide special services to their own communities. This group may have a special interest in social action. The new careerist concept was strongly supported by the Office of Economic Opportunity.

Local Opportunities   The community college can meet local needs directly. Local opportunities help shape the program. Linkages to agencies and to senior colleges are important to assure both job placements and transferability of credits. The influence of specific community needs is illustrated in the Chicago City Colleges Human Services program where needs of state agencies for day care personnel and caretakers for the mentally retarded and training for community representatives in OEO programs helped shape the structure at the outset.³ Programs cannot be so community specific, however, that they restrict mobility. There is no assurance that a person will work in the community where he is educated or go to the senior college in his home town.

Colleges at least within the same state have developed increasingly close communication to assure more uniformity of content and standards. It is not always easy to achieve equitable standards since some community colleges seek to offer opportunities to all on the assumption that all residents are community college material.

Holders of associate degrees have faced two special problems—lack of jobs in social services when large numbers are graduated or inadequate opportunities for advancement on the job through a career ladder. Unavailability of employment often leads people to go on immediately for a bachelor's degree. An associate degree program that is heavily technical may mean that many liberal arts courses must be taken to make up prerequisites, or that some credits may not be transferable. For a useful career ladder, continuing work study opportunities are essential for additional education to help employees advance.

More standardization of associate degree programs will probably not be achieved unless the Council on Social Work Education develops a plan for accreditation. The council has already sponsored conferences and helped develop program guidelines, but there is little demand for accreditation.

THE B.S.W.—THE FIRST PROFESSIONAL DEGREE*

Bachelor's degree programs in social work have become increasingly popular in the 1970s. Improved salaries and the greater potential for advancement are attractive features. Opportunities exist particularly for social workers in corrections, community mental health, and neighborhood organizations.

Careers in human service fields have also become popular because they provide challenging opportunities in traditional social welfare and nonwelfare occupations. Education in human service skills and methods permits a broad choice of jobs and considerable geographic mobility. Even if one does not enter a human service career, the educational programs offered today are usually broad enough to provide the background for other advanced study and for active and informed participation in dealing with social problems.

For holders of bachelor's degrees, job opportunities were limited during the 1950s and early 1960s. The trend toward professionalization of human services and the relatively easy availability of training funds led to the expansion of educational requirements. Employers began to require a master's degree as the minimum qualification. Personnel with the bachelor's degree were generally unable to get responsible positions if candidates with master's degrees were available, although the tasks assigned to the two were often indistinguishable. Persons with bachelor's degrees were hired as substitutes for "qualified" staff. This attitude was reflected in the professional literature that used "subprofessional" and "untrained" to refer to the bachelor's degree holder. Member-

*As in Chapter 15, the term B.S.W. will be used here to identify any bachelor's degree involving an approved social work major with field work.

ship in the National Association of Social Workers was limited to holders of the master's degree.

Federal legislation of the 1960s brought about significant changes in manpower deployment. The "Great Society" programs increased the demand for services and staff. Under the pressure of necessity the grip of "credentialism" in social work began to loosen. Employers found it expedient to hire more personnel with bachelor's degrees. The current budget crunch in social welfare has continued the assault on credentialism. The constraints imposed on human service agency budgets have forced a reexamination of social work roles and professional responsibilities. It is now recognized that people with a bachelor's degree can perform most services competently. The bachelor's degree in social work is now considered the basic credential for entry into professional practice. For several years, NASW has admitted to membership persons with an approved bachelor's degree. Since three out of four line positions in major program areas—public assistance, child welfare, and corrections—are currently filled by persons holding bachelor's degrees, this recognition is somewhat after the fact. If student aid for graduate study continues to be scarce, social workers with bachelor's degrees will find more opportunities for employment and professional advancement.

Skills of the B.S.W.

Attempts to clarify and differentiate the appropriate educational preparation for the various levels of social work practice have often terminated in failure. Agency administrators and professional educators are often hard pressed to distinguish between the activities of a college graduate with several years of productive practice experience and those of an M.S.W.

Social workers with a bachelor's degree must be prepared to enter a variety of practice settings upon graduation. Employers expect B.S.W.'s to demonstrate certain basic skills, whether they were acquired through general life experiences, formal education, or specific work training.

Workers must be able to:

1 Communicate confidently with other people to convey accurately observations, analyses, and plans.

2 Establish and maintain purposeful, concerned relationships through which their clients' problems may be examined and effective helping strategies developed.

3 Exhibit an understanding of social work methods and skills in order to work effectively, whether the focus is on individuals, groups, or community structures.

4 Function responsibly as team members and independently within the agency structure.

5 Examine their own practice and their agency programs and work with others to improve them.

Development of Undergraduate Programs

In the mid-1950s very few undergraduate social welfare programs existed in colleges or universities. Most B.A. workers were graduated from a general liberal arts curriculum. Students who wanted to go to work after graduation prepared for practice by majoring in one of the social sciences and possibly taking one or two courses in social work. Some even had majors in agriculture, art, or philosophy. They had to rely heavily on practical experience and agency in-service training programs for specific knowledge and skill. Unfortunately, the quality of learning experiences was highly variable; some were well planned, and others were haphazard and superficial. Courses and credit hours varied widely. Field instruction was not generally included. Preparation was oriented toward preprofessional training, and graduates remained inadequately prepared to provide direct services.

Practitioners and social work educators alike recognized that fundamental changes were necessary if a bachelor's degree in social work were to lead to a professional career. A study published in 1965 recognized the need for the development of a system of manpower differentiation and utilization. Its recommendations included development of specialized undergraduate curricula that would "prepare baccalaureate students for direct entry into social work practice as well as for entry into graduate social work schools."[4] The report observed that social workers could acquire professional stature if graduates were given recognition both by the National Association of Social Workers and state licensure programs.

In 1970, the National Association of Social Workers extended regular membership privileges to graduates of bachelor's programs approved by the Council on Social Work Education. The CSWE then established new standards for educational institutions offering undergraduate programs in social work that clearly defined the bachelor's degree in social work as the first professional degree.

As a result of these developments and the profession's reexamination of personnel practices and educational preparation, the professional bachelor's degree program in social work—the B.S.W.—was developed.

B.S.W. graduates should have a common base of knowledge and competence. Approval by the CSWE is intended to assure students and employers alike that these programs meet minimal educational requirements and that graduates are prepared for beginning levels of social work practice. Two hundred fifteen undergraduate programs have been approved by the council, and over 20,000 students are enrolled in approved undergraduate social work programs across the United States.[5]

Opposition to a Bachelor's Degree

The development of a professional bachelor's degree was not always strongly supported by faculty or practicing social workers, despite the student interest in the degree. Some believe strongly that the undergraduate curriculum should provide a major in a liberal arts discipline and perhaps a major concentration of courses in social welfare, but no opportunity for direct practice. They argue that the B.S.W. provides too narrow a base for undergraduate education. A letter in the bulletin of the Chicago area chapter of NASW commented:[6]

> We leapt with vigor and spirit into anti-rational, anti-professional postures fashionable in the current scenes. N.A.S.W., in opening its doors to admit these members, did nothing to raise standards for professional practice.

Indeed, the move was hailed as honest and open, for there is something shameful about "credentials." In the name of democracy and egalitarianism and serving people, *we reduce ourselves to the lowest common denominator.*

The B.S.W. Curriculum

According to the Council on Social Work Education, a program that prepares for beginning professional practice shall demonstrate that it:[7]

1 builds on and is integrated with a liberal arts base that includes knowledge in the humanities, social, behavioral and biological sciences.

2 provides content in the areas of (a) social work practice, (b) social welfare policy and services, (c) human behavior and the social environment, and (d) social research.

3 requires educationally directed field experiences for at least 300 clock hours, for which academic credit commensurate with the time invested is given.

4 To achieve the objectives of a social work program, the educational experience must be coherent and offer the content identified above in an order that affords the student the opportunity for integrated, nonrepetitive learning. In the dissemination of knowledge and development of skills there should be, throughout the curriculum, an emphasis on diverse ethnic, racial, and cultural patterns as well as on the profession as both a science and an art.

Liberal Arts Base   What courses should be included in the broad liberal arts base? Preparation for professional roles must include theoretical and practical education.

The most appropriate undergraduate preparation is a concentration in the social and behavioral sciences—courses that will contribute to an understanding of normal and deviant behavior, of the process of social change, and of individual, group, and organizational dynamics. An introductory knowledge of government, law and regulations pertaining to welfare and family, and poverty economics will also be useful.

Courses that facilitate the development of skill in research and critical analysis are also essential today and will play an even greater role in the future.

Social workers must be able to communicate well. Courses in speech, drama, and linguistics serve to develop proficiency in verbal expression. Courses on composition, speed reading, shorthand, and typing provide valuable practical skills.

Courses with Social Work Content   We find widely different programs from one campus to another, but some fundamental similarities exist. All approved programs provide a historical perspective on social welfare services and social work practice; an understanding of current policies, programs, and issues related to social welfare services and institutions; and an introduction to social work practice theory and methods.

Field Instruction

Field instruction takes on new importance in the B.S.W. programs. Without it students would be inadequately prepared for direct practice. The introduction to social work methods and social welfare systems in the classroom is coordinated with field instruction programs that directly involve students in the process of helping people. Objectives of the field experience are no less educational than traditional classroom courses. Just as chemistry and foreign language students practice in their laboratories, social work students must reach out into the communities to develop their skills.

Field instruction should provide a range of different experiences that will be useful for entering professional practice or graduate social work programs. Schools must select field work agencies which can make this possible. Agencies which can provide a variety of services and encourage students to practice several different problem-solving methods are preferred. Direct service opportunities must be provided. Training agency volunteers, researching the effectiveness of agency delivery programs, and participating in the development of grant proposals are also important. Although the duties, learning experiences, and roles required differ from agency to agency and program to program, activities should focus on providing contacts with clients and resources most appropriate to the student's own competence and past experience.

Field Instruction Agencies   Undergraduate social work faculty have generally tried to develop field instruction programs that best utilize the educational and agency resources available and encourage outcomes most relevant to the needs of modern social service delivery systems. Typically students are placed in child and family welfare agencies, public assistance offices, rehabilitation services, and mental health programs. Students are also assigned to innovative community organization programs; special interest centers, such as halfway houses for parolees, alcoholics, or drug users and "drop-in" or telephone crisis centers; and local government programs, such as police departments, probation and parole offices, housing projects, and day care facilities.

Two Formats for Field Instruction   Concurrent and block placement plans have been described earlier in Chapter 15. The differences are important for understanding B.S.W. programs.

More than 75 percent of the accredited undergraduate programs use a *concurrent* plan, in which students divide their time between the classroom and the agency where they are placed. Optimally a concurrent plan permits classroom and field experiences to reinforce each other, with little delay between the acquisition of classroom content and its application to reality. It provides students the opportunity to get ideas from the classroom of possible immediate value in their field placements and to use examples from the practice field for classroom discussion.

Some agency administrators and staff find this plan impractical, because students cannot assume enough responsibility in the time available. Client needs and agency programs generally do not concur with students' classroom schedules. Crisis intervention, court hearings, doctors' and clinic visits, and out-of-town appointments and meetings are examples of potential schedule conflicts. Timing is another problem. Principles are often needed in the field before they are presented in the classroom. A concurrent plan may not provide sufficient opportunity for practice, particularly for those students with limited previous experience in social service settings.

In response to these criticisms and the recognition that more time must be spent in the field if undergraduates are to be prepared for direct practice, an increasing number of schools are offering block placements as either a requirement or an option.

In a *block* placement, students for one or more terms devote themselves almost full time to their field instruction program. Originally this plan developed in schools that lacked the local resources to educate their students in the field. Soon its educational value became evident, especially when it was offered with a concurrent field seminar to help students integrate their experiences with practice theory.

The block plan has three main advantages. First, students can become more intensely involved with the functioning of the agency and the community in which they are placed, resulting in a more accelerated comprehensive learning experience. Second, supervisors and program administrators are more willing to give students significant responsibility for direct and indirect service to clients. This reduces the possibility that students will be used only as observers. Finally, block placements may make possible the development of paid field placements. To the student who needs financial aid this advantage is obvious. Agency administrators find that certain positions can be adequately filled year round by a succession of student interns. This increases their willingness to invest time and money in students.

Supervision

Effective supervision is necessary for any successful field instruction program. Most supervisors are M.S.W.'s with several years of experience. Because of the rapidly expanding roles for social workers in nontraditional settings, some programs have also successfully used police and probation officers, public health nurses, community organizers, housing project directors, and other personnel as student supervisors.

Supervisors develop assignments consistent with the educational goals of the curriculum and are also responsible for providing the student with a thorough agency orientation, staff development aid, regular conference time, and other necessary support.

The particular method of supervision differs. In one placement a student may be a member of a service team and receive supervision from several persons with different areas of expertise. In another students may meet regularly with a single supervisor individually or in a group for consultation and discussion.

Evaluation

Evaluating a student's progress in the field is necessary. Psychological tests, objective forms, reviews of taped and filmed interviews, personal observation by supervisors and peers, and client reports have been used to judge a student's ability.

Common methods of evaluation use structured questionnaires and interviews with the supervisors and students, checklists of desired attitudes and behaviors, and open-ended questionnaires completed by the supervisors and students.

Student logs and self-evaluations are another way of evaluating a student's progress and experiences:[8]

I would describe my field work semester as being the most enlightening and relevant experience I've had at the University. Whereas readings, lectures, and papers are useful tools for learning, nothing can compare with actual field experience. Field instruction gave me a practical knowledge of social work.

From the logs, supervisors and instructors also observe that students learn many different things, some of which are not in the course outline:[9]

During my placement with the state child welfare agency I learned an incredible amount about bureaucracy, paperwork, staff interrelations, and bullshitting other agencies and authorities. I even learned a little about working with people.

Students placed in the same agency often perceive their experiences from a different point of view. In a children's residential center that used intensive behavior modification techniques with predelinquent teenagers, one student found the placement exciting and applied for permanent employment in the program upon graduation. The other said:[10]

After working on the learning unit as a staff member for two months or so, I began to feel like a robot. Everything I did had to be so controlled. I must not become ego-involved, must never become mad or too happy, must always maintain a calm disposition and conversational tone of voice. It drove me nuts. When I came home, I'd jump up and down, scream and yell, and act silly, just so that I could feel human again.
  Behavioral modification techniques were difficult because they were unnatural to me. I tend to be spontaneous in responding to situations. I get angry, sad, silly, and upset. Although I understand the theoretical reasons for remaining cool, calm and totally rational, I found it hard to suddenly transform myself into that kind of person, especially since I don't really want to be that kind of person.

This student found that although she still wanted a social work career, she did not want to work in a residential setting. She probably would not have reached this conclusion without the field experience.
  Students frequently profess an unqualified love for humanity when they first enter field placements, but they may have to cope with a very different personal response. They soon realize that what people say is less important than their actions:[11]

It's so easy to dislike some of the kids here, but those feelings shouldn't interfere with your work. Many times a horribly obnoxious brat needs your attention much more than the pleasant loving child. You don't have to like someone in order to work with them and help them; sometimes this is really hard to remember but it is most important.

Dealing with their own relative youth can represent problems for beginning workers in new situations:[12]

> At first I reacted very personally to everything that happened. I thought it was difficult enough for a young worker to represent authority without being asked for a date by a seventeen-year-old client. Soon I realized that this was just his way of saying that he appreciated our relationship. I was able to accept his request for what it was rather than as a proposition.

Student reports also demonstrate progress in the assumption of professional roles and responsibilities:[13]

> I had little knowledge of mental health resources initially. As time passed, I developed a working knowledge of the community agencies. My position allowed easy access to other agencies to ask questions about them and what they could do for my clients. Day-to-day contact also gives an added advantage. Most anyone could learn their community's resources from reading a directory, but you have to work in the field daily to find out the difference between what the agencies say they do and what they do in reality. It takes more than a few visits to each agency to cut through all the public relations.

Students view field instruction as a test of their interest in social work and their ability to perform appropriately:[14]

> The learning we gain from real life situations cannot be found in books. Nor can volunteer work compare with daily supervised involvement with an agency. It is much better to find out whether one is cut out for social work before going to graduate school or taking a job.

Example of a Student Placement

The Tele-Care Program Tele-Care is a countywide program to provide and coordinate services to permit older persons to maintain independent living arrangements in the community. The program is staffed by three part-time M.S.W.'s, a volunteer coordinator, and over a hundred volunteers. Counseling, friendly visiting, and transportation are provided free to clients. Clients are also assisted in locating and obtaining financial, legal, health, food, and homemaking service. Anyone over forty-five years of age is eligible for service.

Two B.S.W. students placed at Tele-Care were twenty and twenty-one years old. One had no previous work or volunteer experience in the human services area. The other had volunteered in several local social service agencies and had been employed for a summer as an activities director in a sheltered workshop program.

They were supervised by the director of social services, an experienced social worker. They had weekly supervisory conferences either individually or in a group. They also carried joint responsibility for some cases with their supervisor. Through their supervisory meetings the students were able better to understand the agency's service, the community structure, and the methods and skills necessary to carry out their field assignments. The supervisor was able to help the students identify the kind of difficulties to anticipate and to test out the ways to cope with a situation before direct intervention with their clients.

Initially the students were very dependent and asked many questions:

How do I go about obtaining public aid for Mrs. McNeil? Her retirement funds have almost dwindled away.

Dr. Bailey says that Mrs. Cowger has to have someone stay with her until her hip heals. Can we place a homemaker with her until she is well? Mrs. Brooks will stay with her if we can find sufficient funds.

Later on, as the students gained greater knowledge, the supervisory role became more difficult, and the questions more complicated:

Mr. Corcoran is going blind and he has already lost most of his hearing. He says that one of these days he is going to commit suicide so that his friends wouldn't have to worry about him any more. What can I do to help him?

Supervision should enable students to progress steadily and to evaluate their own work and progress. Changes can be seen even in a short period of time. One student reported:

I learned a great deal by working with one family over four months. I could see progress in the family and I could also see my own development. I gained a greater ease in talking with them. I began to be able to ask the "right" questions and to focus our conversations. I knew I gained confidence in myself as the family gained confidence in me. I no longer had to plot out each interview in advance. I no longer panicked when the script was not followed.

Tasks and Learning Experiences The students acted in the role of social work generalists. The intervention-required modalities placed an immediate demand on the students to acquire new skills. Supervision focused primarily on social work methodology and skills, crisis intervention techniques, and means of utilizing and developing supportive community resources. Most tasks, whether during crisis periods or in short-term casework, focused on helping clients cope with loss of income, health, mobility, or family members.

Practice skills and learning experiences were provided through individual and group discussions on aging with other staff and community resources; case assignments of elderly clients with differing needs; reading on services for the aged; observation of other social workers; and service-related contacts with community institutions and services such as nursing homes, the local Committee on Aging, the Department of Public Welfare, and other public mental health and health agencies, and community self-help groups.

Evaluation The students' progress was evaluated through structured and unstructured interviews and open-ended questionnaires completed by the students and their supervisor. Additional direct observations of the students' work were made by the university's field work seminar instructor. At the end of the semester all the reports were reviewed before completing the final evaluation.

Employment

Obviously the best academic preparation possible will not help you if social work employment commensurate with your education and training does not exist. The number of jobs available for B.S.W. social workers is affected by the tight economy, the federal government's de-escalation of domestic social programs, and competition with more experienced social work personnel. But these conditions can change rapidly, as evidenced by the huge personnel shortages of the 1960s.

Nevertheless, good employment opportunities exist in a variety of settings. Freedom to relocate and a willingness to accept less desirable positions to gain work experience will facilitate your job-hunting task. Salaries and responsibility become more competitive with those of M.S.W.'s after you have four or five years' experience. Job openings vary considerably in different localities. Rural areas of most states provide especially good employment opportunities.

Looking for initial employment experience in agencies with high turnover rates is also recommended. County public assistance offices traditionally fit this role; however, the recent action to separate services from income maintenance has reduced positions available. Other programs with high turnover are residential care centers, community organization programs, and agencies in center-city "high risk" areas.

Public Agencies   County, state, and federal social service programs have consistently provided the best employment opportunities for graduates with little or no experience. In some instances these positions include excellent training and supervision and attractive career ladders. Examples include public assistance programs at the local and state level; child welfare activities, such as protective services, foster care, and health services; residential programs for the mentally ill, retarded, handicapped, dependent, or delinquent; community centers; recreation facilities; and camping programs for all age groups. Other sources of employment are probation and parole offices, correctional institutions, community mental health programs, hospital social services, day care, Head Start programs, vocational rehabilitation and employment counseling, community organization programs, and "crisis" drop-in and telephone services for adult and youth.

Civil Service and Merit Systems   The same programs may provide additional incentives for qualified graduates through their civil service or merit rating systems. Special recognition has developed slowly, but its growth has been significant. A recent CSWE survey found that at least twenty-one states gave some kind of differential recognition to B.A.'s in social work with supervised field practice experience.[15] Other states (such as Illinois, Pennsylvania, and North Carolina) permit a social work major to be hired at a higher level than non-majors—as a Caseworker I or Social Worker I, rather than a trainee. Wisconsin and Minnesota give equal preference to undergraduate majors in social work, psychology, and sociology.

In most other states social service positions are offered to college graduates with a major in any one of the social sciences. Professional social work organizations support a distinctive role for the B.S.W. and a civil service classification that will differentiate it from other bachelor's degrees.

Private Agencies   Although public agencies provide the most opportunities, private social service agencies provide other potential job resources. Organizations such as the National Federation of Settlements and Neighborhood Centers, YMCA and YWCAs, Jewish, Catholic, and Protestant social service programs, children's homes, and family and community service agencies are willing and sometimes anxious to hire qualified B.S.W.'s.

You may also want to look into the opportunities provided by some of the social action programs. Salaries are generally low and working conditions difficult, but many are rich in learning experiences, social camaraderie, and effective social change. These programs range from Ralph Nader's prestigious Center for the Study of Responsive Law in Washington, D.C., to a store-front community council. Their potential influence, methods, and focus differ significantly, yet their goal is still the same—improving the quality of life.

Salaries   Differences in qualifications, geographical location, agency auspices, and cost of living factors make it difficult to present average data on salaries for B.A. workers. In public agencies workers with little experience can expect to earn from $5,500 to $7,500 in the less industrial, less urbanized states, and from $7,000 to $8,500 in the others. For example, a beginning B.A. child welfare caseworker in Nebraska will earn about $6,500 a year, whereas the same worker in Pennsylvania would start at about $8,500.[16] The salaries in private agencies are generally comparable to those in the public sector and vary depending on the particular location, program size, and job responsibilities. Inflation also serves to increase salaries each year.

THE MASTER'S DEGREE PROGRAM

Why spend two years beyond the bachelor's degree with a concentration in social work? The master's degree has been the standard educational preparation for professional social work practice. It makes possible a wide range of job options and constitutes the basic qualification for advanced practice and for progression into management and administration. A graduate degree qualifies a person for a higher salary, and along with professional experience it is the basis for advanced certification in the profession. While the exact degree awarded varies from school to school, the names are interchangeable. For our discussion we will use M.S.W. (Master of Social Work), the most commonly used degree designation.

With the development of the bachelor's degree in social work, most master's programs will be modified in the next few years. More advanced content will be included. The time for the degree is also being shortened by at least half of the schools of social work for those who majored in social work and had field practice as undergraduates.

Personnel Trends

Graduate education for social work is best understood in relation to personnel trends and utilization of personnel in social welfare. Why is graduate study needed now that a professional undergraduate degree in social work is available? For what kinds of roles is a graduate degree uniquely appropriate? How do the master's and doctor's degrees relate to each other? What is the content of M.S.W. study? What learning experiences are provided in the curriculum? What issues in professional social work education are still unresolved?

Since 1950, the number of social welfare jobs has increased by about 5 percent each year. In 1950, 75,000 people were employed.[17] Ten years later there were 116,000. In 1972, there were 170,000 social welfare workers. The Department of Labor estimated that during the remainder of the 1970s, 18,000 new workers would be needed to keep pace with demand.[18] Employment prospects in social welfare were rated as "very good," especially for college graduates with specialized social work training.

In 1960, two-thirds of the 116,000 workers were employed in public agencies and one-third in voluntary agencies. This group included workers both with and without professional degrees. The median salary was $5,120. Three-fifths of the people in these programs were in direct service positions (caseworkers 47 percent, group workers 5 percent, and other 9 percent), and two-fifths were administrators, supervisors, consultants, staff development specialists, or teachers. Less than 20 percent were members of the National Association of Social Workers.[19]

What are the characteristics of *professional* social workers? These are best typified by the members of the NASW, which until recently required a master's degree for membership. In 1968 there were 50,500 members. Sixty-eight percent were women, and one-tenth were members of an ethnic or racial minority group. The median age of the members was forty-three years.[20]

Members were employed in various areas:

Category	Percent
Psychiatric social work	21
Child welfare	17
Medical social work	12
Family services	12
Public assistance	8
Teaching in universities and colleges	8
School social work	6
Community organization services	6
Group work services	4
All other services	6

In this professional group, only a little more than one-third were in direct service delivery. Twenty-nine percent were in administration and management, 18 percent in supervision, 8 percent in teaching and staff development, and 5 percent in consultation and research. Three-fifths worked in public agencies, and one-half worked in urban centers of more than 500,000 population. After 1968, NASW showed a sharp membership increase in its present total to over 60,000.

NASW salary studies show a median salary of $11,329 in 1968 and $13,418 in 1970, compared with $7,000 in 1961.[21] At the time of graduation, entry salaries of workers with the bachelor's and the master's degree differ by $1,000 to $2,000,

*"I'm afraid this is my last
visit, Mrs. Segarra. There's no money in social work."*

according to public agency salary classifications. Data also indicate that the numbers employed in social welfare have been increasing steadily, and the demand has remained high.

Traditionally, as we have observed, the provision of *direct services*, chiefly casework with individuals and families, has been carried out by people with a bachelor's degree and little if any professional study in social work. People with a master's degree are involved either in *advanced practice* (psychotherapy, group therapy, family therapy, counseling of complex and difficult case situations) or in some aspect of *management* of the delivery of direct services (administration, supervision, consultation, team management, or staff development). Only since 1970, when the Council on Social Work Education and the National Association of Social Workers began to recognize undergraduate professional study in social work, have most schools of social work responded realistically to the principle of differential use of workers.

Focus of Graduate Study in Social Work

Social work education and most other professional training programs started with an apprenticeship model. Agencies employing social workers trained the new worker, the apprentice, through supervision provided by the experienced worker, the master. On-the-job instruction was supplemented in time by formal instruction in groups taught by people from outside the agencies. Ultimately these efforts developed into one-year programs of instruction that finally became schools connected with universities. Thus education for social work has been based in both the professional school and the agency. A combination of theoretical study with practical training continues to characterize social work education. Later the program was extended to cover two academic years.

In university-based social work education, the curriculum focus was on skill in practice of some one method of direct service—most commonly casework. Today over one-third of the full-time graduate students are concentrating on casework. Seven percent major in group work. Another third are in a "combined concentration"—usually casework and group work—and 8 percent are in community organization. Together the three direct service methods account for four-fifths of the total graduate students.[22]

Another early emphasis in schools was on the *fields of practice*—typically, psychiatric social work, medical social work, or child welfare. Specialized membership organizations for certain areas of practice, e.g., American Association of Medical Social Workers or American Association of Group Workers, reviewed curricula to determine whether they included the content basic to the specialized practice. Such a focus is still reflected in the nature of the field practicum in which students are placed.

Graduate students in 1973 were found in the following field placements:[23]

Category	Percentage
Psychiatric services	13
Community mental health	11
Medical public health	9
Family services	9
Child welfare	7
Combined fields	7
Community planning	6
School social work	6
Corrections & criminal justice	5
Public welfare & assistance	3
Miscellaneous	4
Other or not assigned	18

Sixty-one percent of the students were in services that traditionally have relied primarily on casework.

Traditionally, to become an administrator one first had to be a skilled caseworker, then a supervisor, a casework director, and finally the agency director. While perhaps appropriate for a small voluntary agency, this pattern did not always fit the large bureaucratic public agency. Students who are required to master a direct service skill do not have the opportunity to master administration, management, consultation, and supervision, too. Yet three-fifths of the professionally trained personnel are not in direct service. Conventional programs at the graduate level have not been congruent with the differential practice pattern of professional social work.

Current Developments

The inauguration of the Bachelor of Social Work degree as the first professional practice degree will probably lead to a more rational curriculum for the M.S.W. program. M.S.W. candidates are likely to follow one of two tracks in their graduate study—advanced practice in direct service or social service management.

Students involved in study for the undergraduate professional degree who expect to go to graduate school will need to make decisions about their future career goals earlier, since the courses they take in the B.S.W. program should be selected in terms of the track they wish to pursue as M.S.W. students. If they plan on a career in advanced practice, they will need a more extensive background in psychology, anthropology, and sociology than will management students. Students interested in management should choose such subjects as political science, economics, public finance, organizational theory and behavior, planning and personnel management. Learning theory, systems analysis, computer technology, and research methods will also have particular relevance.

Some schools of social work organize the curriculum around a generalist or integrated methods sequence to teach the common elements and techniques of all direct practice methods as well as their differences. An evaluation of use and effectiveness of the methods in relation to a range of problems and problem-solving situations is usually included in the courses. Such an integrated methods approach is particularly congruent with the "generalist" concept.

As we have already seen in Chapter 15, some schools have organized their curricula around problem areas such as poverty, child welfare, mental health, health and rehabilitation, or treatment of delinquents and adult offenders. The focus on certain practice tracks is not unlike the earlier emphasis on specialties—psychiatric social work, medical social work, or child welfare.

The M.S.W. Curriculum

To be accredited by the Council of Social Work Education, schools of social work must meet certain curriculum standards. Thus master's degree programs will be similar in many respects:[24]

> The program must be a two-academic-year curriculum except that holders of an approved undergraduate program—e.g., the B.S.W.—may receive one year of advanced standing.
> At least one year of the program must involve full-time study.
> A practicum must be part of the students' learning experiences and must involve them . . . "in engagement in service activities."
> The curriculum content should include substantive knowledge in three basic areas: social welfare policy and services, human behavior and the social environment, and social work practice.
> The curriculum must include one or more concentrations which organize learning experiences . . . "appropriate to a specific range of professional roles and functions."

The council's curriculum policy statement elaborates the objectives, policies, procedures, and legislative bases of the social services and the problems that the services are designed to alleviate or resolve. Such study of services should include "structural and administrative patterns, their service delivery systems, the populations served by the agencies, their linkages with related programs and other organizations, and their social and political environments." The issues, deficiencies, emerging trends, and alternative social policies should also be a component. Comparative analysis of international social welfare systems is an appropriate subject of study. Study of the social work role in service delivery should include helping the student become an effective change agent.

Finally, the curriculum policy statement suggests that while learning about the whole system, each student should have an opportunity to concentrate on some sector of social welfare which conforms to his or her career interests. The student interested primarily in future practice in mental health services or child welfare, for example, should be able to gain greater depth of understanding in his or her specialty.

Human Behavior and the Social Environment   To serve clients well, social workers must comprehend the dynamics of human behavior. This area should develop "the student's understanding of the individual, group, organizational, institutional, and cultural contexts within which human behavior is expressed and by which it is significantly influenced."[25] Since no one theory or discipline explains all the influences or determinants of human behavior, the approach should be pluralistic. Relevant theories and knowledge from the biological, psychological, and social sciences as well as the humanities are needed to provide a frame of reference for understanding behavior.

Social Work Practice   The curriculum policy statement requires learning experiences, including the practicum, which will help each student to:

Understand the use of knowledge, skill, and values in appraising problems and deciding interventive strategies to be used in relation to them.

Develop self-awareness and self-discipline in providing services to people.

Understand the helping roles of different professionals and the methods used in providing services to individuals, groups, organizations, and communities.

Understand the role of the social worker in providing services, preventing social problems, and helping perfect the social welfare systems.

Accept responsibility for continuing self-education through incorporation into his or her practice of emerging new knowledge in the future.

To teach social work practice, schools organize practice theory and knowledge in a variety of ways. For each concentration the school must state:

1   The objectives of the concentration and their relation to social work
2   The roles for which the concentration prepares the practitioner
3   The professional knowledge base
4   The relationship of knowledge and practice components in the concentration

5 The relationship of the concentration to the total curriculum and other concentrations

The Council's curriculum policy statement does not specifically set out *research* as a required area of the curriculum, but it does include objectives for student learning which can be attained only through study of research and quantitative methods. The curriculum should provide a basis for scientific and scholarly inquiry in advancing professional knowledge, improving standards of practice, and helping students acquire an ability for critical analysis of problems. Thus schools include courses in research and usually require a research project, thesis, or practicum.

Organization of Learning Experiences in the M.S.W.

As for the B.S.W., the concurrent model has been followed by most of the graduate schools. In 1971, sixty-four of the seventy-six accredited schools used this plan for the first year of graduate study. Typically, first-year students were in class three days each week and in the field two days. Twelve schools used *block* placements exclusively, and six used a combination of concurrent and block.[26]

A third curriculum model now under consideration involves an internship or residency. The term "intern" could denote undergraduate placements and *resident* M.S.W. placements. Such a model would more clearly differentiate the respective roles of the two worlds—theoretical knowledge versus field learning—in assuming responsibility for helping the professional student to learn what he needs to become a responsible practitioner. The academic world would clearly be responsible for teaching basic knowledge, theory, and technology of practice. The practice world through the agency would be responsible for teaching the student—a resident or intern—how to use his academic learning in practice. Such placements would generally involve payment from the agency. Several schools of social work are considering this model.

Such a differential assignment of responsibilities between the university and the agencies is more common in other professions than in social work, but it is appropriate for social work. Unless the school runs its own service-giving agency, the degree of "skill in practice" it can teach is sharply limited. Likewise the agency, under the strain of meeting service demands that can never be completely fulfilled, is not able to teach knowledge not used in its operation. A residency program also recognizes that the two areas of learning—knowledge and practice—supplement each other rather than form an integrated whole for the student. Integration requires several years of practice.

DOCTORAL PROGRAMS

In 1971, twenty-four schools of social work offered doctoral-level study to 502 students; 129 doctoral degrees were awarded. Doctoral study in social work is of recent origin. Twenty years ago only six schools had such programs, and together they awarded only eight degrees in 1951–1952. By 1974 there were 28 doctoral programs, with 156 students. More than half of the schools with doctoral programs award the Ph.D., while the remainder award the D.S.W. (Doctor of Social Work or Doctor of Social Welfare). The names of the degrees indicate no consistent differences.

Doctoral programs are intended to prepare people for one or more of four roles in social work—teaching, advanced practice, research, or social policy analysis and development. Some schools offer several of these concentrations. Study in a discipline outside social work—in a social or behavioral science or some other relevant minor area—is usually required. Doctoral programs emphasize scholarship, research, and mastery of advanced knowledge.

The Council on Social Work Education has noted that doctoral programs should not be merely "a simple gradual extension of the Master's Degree program . . ." but should have their own integrity.[27] Skill in practice, a common focus for the M.S.W. programs, has a low priority in doctoral curricula. Most advanced programs do not include field learning. When such experience is included, it has often been focused on testing and evaluating methods rather than on development of an individual's skills.

STUDENT AID FOR GRADUATE EDUCATION

In 1971–1972, 56 percent of all the full-time graduate students received some form of financial aid.[28] The remainder financed study through their own resources, help from their families, or loans. About one-half of the aid was from grants awarded by a public agency with the understanding that the student would be employed by the agency after study was completed. Stipends for a fourth of the students who were aided came from funds provided through the National Institute of Mental Health or the Social and Rehabilitation Services of the U.S. Department of Health, Education and Welfare. Awards to a fifth of the students came from the schools and universities, frequently limited to remission of tuition and fees. Some university fellowships and scholarships cover living costs as well. Less than one-tenth of the students received aid from private social agencies, and a similar proportion received support from the U.S. Veterans Administration.

The federal administration recently phased out support of professional education with a loss of 2,300 stipends from the NIMH and the SRS. In addition, support for a fourth of all full-time faculty in graduate social work education has been lost. Universities probably cannot absorb the financial obligations covered by federal grants. As a result of cuts in student aid and faculty support, we may see a reversal of enrollment trends in schools of social work.

Apparently the federal government contemplates support of students in higher education through a loan program from the Office of Education. However, the proposal does not provide support for graduate study. Thus the future of student support is uncertain. Agency sources for such costs will be even more important in the future. Students have been reluctant in the past to accept stipends which carry a work commitment to an agency, but their only other choice may be support through loans.

CHOOSING A SCHOOL

Today there are some ninety accredited schools of social work in the United States and Canada characterized by considerable variation in focus, program emphasis, and concentrations. Students therefore should assess their interests and choose a school to fit their career goals. For example, a particular school may have a stronger program in social treatment than in community work. In another, the opposite may be true.

Sources of Information Students will want to consult bulletins from the schools. Another good source of information is *Statistics on Social Work Education* published by the Council on Social Work Education. Many college libraries have this publication. Enrollment data for the number of faculty, the concentrations schools offer, the number of field placements by area of practice, tuition and fees, ethnic and racial characteristics, and age of students are included for each school.

In addition to reviewing written materials about schools, students may profit from a conference with faculty members in schools of social work, since the latter can respond to questions about the school with which they are affiliated and also may provide information about other schools.

Joint Programs Students will have increasing opportunities to enter joint programs. The George Warren Brown School of Social Work and the Washington University Law School in St. Louis have a program leading to degrees in both fields. Programs in management are developing at several universities with the help of schools of business. Other areas for joint curriculum programming include architecture, theology, and public health.

Gary Shaffer, Estie Bomzer, and Mark P. Hale

KEY TERMS

B.S.W. degree
field instruction
concurrent placement
block placement
Council on Social Work Education
M.S.W. degree
direct service

advanced practice
management
fields of practice
accreditation
intern
resident

FOR DISCUSSION

1 What is the social work education continuum?
2 What is the initial program of collegiate social work education, and how long does it take?
3 What are the specific objectives of associate programs?
4 What special problems are found in associate programs?
5 Why is the B.S.W. referred to as the entry-level *professional* program?
6 How large is the B.S.W. program? What is its goal?
7 What are the two other different general objectives of the degree program?
8 What is the outlook for employment for B.S.W.'s?
9 Why require a liberal arts base for the B.S.W.?
10 To be approved, how much field instruction does a B.S.W. program have to include?
11 What methods of student supervision are used?

12 Why are students' comments on their own progress and experiences used as examples of evaluation?
13 What is Tele-Care?
14 Do public or voluntary agencies provide more jobs for B.S.W. workers?
15 What proportion of the states give special recognition in their civil service system to professional bachelor's degrees in social work?
16 Why are schools of social work shortening the time required for the M.S.W. degree?
17 Can previous experience in social agencies be accorded advanced credit in graduate schools of social work?
18 In addition to skills for social work practice, what other emphasis do graduate programs often include?
19 What type of field placements tend to predominate in graduate programs?
20 Summarize the basic curriculum requirements for the M.S.W.
21 Discuss the main traditional reason for block field placements.
22 What career outlets are there for those with a doctoral degree in social work?

PROJECTS

1 Plan a social work career day for your college, with presentations by representatives of schools of social work and employing agencies, public and private. Include time for students to schedule individual conferences with resource people.
2 Invite a member of the state personnel agency to explain the civil service system as it applies to social work, including how to apply to take examinations.
3 Organize a panel of several social work students who have had field placements to describe and evaluate their experiences.
4 Some states are developing programs to employ "human services generalists" rather than social workers. Find out whether your state department of social services has considered this step, and ask a staff member to discuss it with your class.
5 Prepare a report on several professional social work programs for the B.S.W., using college catalogs. How do they differ?
6 Make a similar comparison of M.S.W. programs.
7 What courses would you consider most important for people who want to work in management of the social services?

FOR FURTHER STUDY

Edward Allen Brawley and Ruben Schindler, *Community and Social Service Education in the Community College*, Council on Social Work Education, New York, 1972.

Betty Lacy Jones, *Current Patterns in Field Instruction in Graduate Social Work Education*, Council on Social Work Education, New York, 1969.

Frank M. Lowenberg, *Time and Quality in Graduate Social Work Education*, Council on Social Work Education, New York, 1972.

Frank M. Lowenberg and Ralph Dolgoff, *Teaching of Practice Skills in Undergraduate Programs in Social Welfare and Other Helping Services*, Council on Social Work Education, New York, 1972.

Patricia W. Soyka, *Unlocking Human Resources—a Career in Social Work*, Public Affairs Committee, New York, 1971.

Chapter 24

The Minority Practitioner

What is the new consciousness that has united minorities?
Why must social workers recognize diversities?
How can leadership be developed?
What problems are faced in established agencies?

Twenty years ago a black college student interested in a profession would most likely have chosen social work, education, or the ministry if he planned to go to a white college. To become a doctor, dentist, or lawyer would usually have required attendance at a black college. Only a few black students could enter the physical sciences. Recently, however, Blacks have demanded and gained entry into fields that were formerly virtually closed to them. They can aspire to the higher-status professions and, if they can find the money, attend a wider choice of schools. Many colleges now make special efforts to recruit black students.

Why are students from minority groups still interested in careers in fields that deal with psychological, educational, or social problems? Some trace their interest to practitioners they have known. A young person may be favorably impressed with a social worker who has helped him. Another complains bitterly about social workers and wants to enter the field because he feels that he can do better. Students also recognize that the social sciences have the potential for answering the "I/we" questions that minorities must raise in American society—

Who am I/are we? How do I/we break out of the bonds of oppression? What can I/we do to help our cause?

DOUBLE CONSCIOUSNESS AND THE NEW CONSCIOUSNESS

The minority practitioner entering social work today has unique legacies to overcome. In the past, black professionals were locked into a "double consciousness." The black practitioner lived in two environments—one white, the other black. The consequences have been inner contradiction, frustration, and group self-criticism.[1]

Black social workers suffered the consequences of double consciousness. One alternative was to identify with the prevailing ideology of racial integration and to perform competently by white standards. Yet many agencies did not treat the workers as equals. In some agencies black workers could only work with black clients, while white workers were assigned clients of both races. Earlier we saw that in an attempt to dissociate themselves from low socioeconomic status some black professionals in public welfare agencies seemed to be harder on black recipients than white social workers were. These workers tended to accept the notion that the victims were the ones at fault.

In their attempt to imitate the white professionals, black social workers were seen as being ashamed of their race. The unquestioned acceptance of agency programs was widespread enough that black laymen still denounce black social workers along with white social workers. At the first National Conference of Black Social Workers in 1969, black professionals admonished each other to alter their behaviors and attitudes. The understanding of double consciousness is important, otherwise we may criticize traditional black social workers without understanding their motivations and their handicaps.

Society is now experiencing the "new consciousness." Perhaps a more accurate term would be *renewed* consciousness, since at an earlier time some Blacks that we now regard as heroes shared the same philosophy. Blacks with new consciousness are described by Bennet as "the advanced guard of the movement for renewal" who accept the implications and meaning of their own experiences, who accept that experience to become conscious agents of change. "The conscious Negro holds up a mirror to the Negro and the white man and reveals them to themselves as victims and creators of each other. . . . The conscious Negro takes his stand within the context of his tradition and projects himself outwardly with the full knowledge that a man is most human when he is most himself."[2]

The new consciousness offers a challenge and an opportunity to minority practitioners and to those who teach them because of its implications for roles, tasks, and attitudes.

ROLES, TASKS, AND ATTITUDES

Social Distance   "Once black professionals have made it, they forget those who haven't." So goes a familiar complaint. Black social workers imbued with the new consciousness say that they will not behave this way. Some assert that since they are from "the community" they will be able to avoid the hazard of lost obligations, but having grown up in a community does not automatically ensure that group obligations will be met.

Attitudes of Others   When a young person goes off to college, the community may be either proud or resentful. If the person faces resentment, he will have difficulty working among people in his neighborhood. A broadening of his horizons in college may make it difficult for him to relate successfully to his old friends or even to his family. Changes in interest and even in vocabulary may establish a feeling of distance.

The minority social worker must convey to those he serves a sense of their dignity and worth and the value of their participation.

Knowledge of Issues   The minority practitioner has to analyze the current issues in the minority community and developments in the larger systems as well—in politics, social welfare, education, and economic policy. Because many of the problems of minority groups stem from broad social policies, problems must be translated in terms of political, economic, and social disadvantages. Welfare reform, social security, medical care, housing, and revenue sharing are among the major current issues that require understanding.

One may also need to reorient the way causes and effects are perceived. Ryan indicates how the poor and particularly minorities are the victims of society, yet they are blamed for their condition. Guilt is added to social and economic disadvantages and may lead to pathological behavior.[3]

Misery may be overemphasized or it may be romanticized. Both tendencies are unfortunate and make social change more difficult. Films are frequently criticized for taking one extreme point of view or the other of black life.

Awareness of Diversities   Minority practitioners must recognize diversities. As black professionals have gained a more thorough understanding of social problems, generalizations have been advanced that are not valid. Even when the majority white society does not see blacks as a diverse society, the black practitioner must be able to do so.

Recognition of diversity is important for other reasons. Blacks often make sweeping generalizations about other blacks, creating a feeling of animosity. Followers of one ideology frequently depreciate those who do not do things their way. As a consequence strategies may be imposed on a community that are inappropriate and may create divisions.

Emphasis on Strengths   The best results come from looking to the strengths of individuals and groups rather than to their perceived weaknesses. Hylan Lewis is particularly concerned with the tendency to impute to a total people the most threatening characteristics of a segment.[4] Examples are: Black low-income children are nonverbal. Low-income black parents do not value education. Unwed motherhood is an acceptable norm. Black people are lazy and do not want to work. Black women dominate black men. Black low-income people have no perception of time and space. Unfortunately programs are being planned and operated on the basis of these "facts."

Robert Hill adopts the same perspective as Lewis in concentrating on strengths. He emphasizes the need for accurate interpretation of statistics and observation of lifestyles. His research on black families reports strong kinship ties, strong work orientation, adaptability of family roles, and strong achievement orientation.[5] These areas of strength have significant implications for social welfare planning.

Categorization Two analytical studies also demonstrate the dangers of categorization. Andrew Billingsley in a social systems approach discusses the structure and function of the black family. While Blacks share a sense of peoplehood, they are not a uniform group. Social class, rural or urban residence, and the region of the country in which one lives all provide important distinctions. Billingsley suggests that black families should not be contrasted with white families but with each other. He also observes that the black family cannot carry out effectively its function of meeting physical and emotional needs unless the major economic, educational, and health institutions function adequately.[6]

Leadership Stereotyped thinking sometimes prompts the comment "The problem for black people is that they have no national leader." Consider this observation by Robert Penn Warren:[7]

> Somewhere back in the mind of many people there is an image of *the* Negro leader—a glare-eyed robot propelled by a merciless mechanism to stalk forward over the smiling landscape, where good clean citizens (including well-adjusted Negroes) go happily about their constructive business. Many of us who are white—in our moments of stereotype and cartoon thinking—share that vision. In those moments we do not realize that there is, in one sense, no Negro leader. There are a number of leaders who happen to occupy positions of leadership.

The minority practitioner cannot afford to wait for a national leader or even to assume that one national leader will bring all black people together. Many Blacks who now extol Malcolm X or Martin Luther King did not agree with their ideologies, strategies, or tactics while they lived.

The minority social work practitioner can assume leadership in his own locale in combating social problems that face minority groups. He can be the group leader, the man who sets the ideals of the community where he lives, directs its thoughts, and leads its social movements.

Participation in professional social work organizations is another way in which the minority practitioner can assume leadership. In the white-dominated organizations, he can ensure minority input. He will also get many ideas from membership in the National Association of Black Social Workers.

Social workers should also work with black caucuses in other disciplines—psychology, law, medicine, politics, and education. The caucuses differ from older black organizations established primarily as the result of exclusion from the larger society's organizations. Caucuses take a much more aggressive stance. The various disciplines can reinforce each other's aims and find means for mutually beneficial interchange. Cooperation with other Blacks in the mass communications media is of particular importance to provide social issues and data as the basis for program development.

Black social workers have been particularly interested in another manifestation of leadership—building black-controlled alternative institutions to serve the needs of black people. Institution building is not easy, yet the new consciousness has led to a number of successful efforts. Among them are the activities of the Black Muslims in educational, economic, social, communications, and religious arenas. Other projects include Imamu Maraka's Spirit House in New Jersey, the Afro-American Family and Child Service in Chicago, the Nairobi Day School in Palo Alto, and the Black Child Development Institute and the Leadership Training Institute in Washington, D.C. Black-run alternative school programs across the country are examples of the importance of education to black people.

These organizations do not simply parallel white institutions. They provide conscious alternatives to the institutions in the larger society. An organization must be controlled by the minority group, but it must also offer something different to meet the needs of its constituents.

Most minority social workers who assume leadership, however, will do so within Establishment agencies. Nevertheless, their services are important. The minority practitioner can still be radical in the sense of reconstructing theories and programs as they apply to minority people.

EXPERIENCES OF BLACK STUDENTS

Minority graduate students working in white-dominated social agencies reported several problems:

1 Some were given all-black caseloads.
2 Students were expected to be authorities on Blacks and were frequently consulted by other workers.
3 Some white workers considered themselves the experts on black people and accepted no suggestions or ideas.
4 When black workers were permitted to develop their own ways of making contact and channeling services, white workers were upset by the departure from the rules.

Most students remarked that while they would prefer to work with Blacks, an all-black caseload implied that both the clients and the worker were inferior.

The students did not like to be perceived as authorities on Blacks because they recognized that individual differences made pat answers impossible. They felt some conflicts in giving advice to white practitioners, unless the practitioner had already tried several approaches before seeking advice. They felt that practitioners should work on their own cases. If they had tried several ideas already, the request was just like any other consultation. Their objection was to a nonblack social worker consulting them almost automatically. However, the black students decided that they would prefer to be consulted than to have a white worker serving the consumer ineffectively. The opposite problem arose when workers who had little experience with black clients did not know when to seek help and therefore continued to make serious mistakes.

THE MINORITY WORKER ON THE JOB

The minority worker in white agencies often asks himself: "Why have I been hired?" Several years ago a black social worker might have assumed that it was because of his competence. Now, with the civil rights pressure and the governmental affirmative action programs, black workers are uncertain whether their talent or their skin color is desired. Thus, a healthy skepticism and a certain self-isolation may accompany him to the job. The worker may meet resistance from white colleagues if he is a product of "affirmative action," seen by some white people as simply "reverse discrimination"; these Whites may be quick to say that competence is what counts. Blacks perceive this as saying that they are not competent. Considering the many ways in which Whites have acquired jobs, Blacks wonder why competence is now suggested as the only criterion for employment. For every white professional who may dislike affirmative action to compensate for past exclusions and injustices, there is a black professional who feels that it is tragic that organizations have had to be forced to hire minorities.

Hiring Blacks on a priority basis probably will not last long. Other white ethnic groups who feel left out are likely to push for recognition. Studies give the erroneous impression that Blacks have progressed so dramatically that affirmative action programs are less necessary.

Social Participation   White social work professionals sometimes wonder why some black social workers no longer seem to want to mix socially with them. The minority worker who chooses his own group probably has good reason. Dubois gave a picture of the dilemma at an earlier time. He described the professional who took every opportunity to join in the political and cultural life of Whites, "but he pays for this and pays dearly. He so often meets actual insult or more or less veiled rebuffs from the Whites that he becomes nervous and truculent through expectation of dislike, even when its manifestation does not always appear." Dubois describes another sort of black professional who withdraws from contact with Whites. "He too pays. He becomes provincial in his outlook. He attributes to Whites a dislike and racial prejudice of which many of them are unconscious and guiltless." There are a range of interracial patterns, but "in practically all cases the net result is a more or less clear and definite crystalization of the culture elements among colored people into their own groups for social and cultural contact." Dubois felt that deliberately planned social and cultural self-integration was the best course of action while black people worked on a number of problems including economic equality, but he feared that his notion would be labeled complete racial segregation.[8]

The Blacks Respond   Recently some parts of the American society went through a phase of integration. After several years Blacks came to feel that integration was one-sided. At white social affairs black people could not be natural but had to conform to white standards. Black individuals were still subject to rebuffs, although rejection was more subtle. In spite of research studies which concluded that black professionals had more in common with their white counterparts than with the black uneducated masses, the black professional found a world of difference. Why bother with conversation that one finds irrelevant, listen to music that one does not appreciate, overhear subtle individual racist remarks to which one is now sharply attuned, and wonder if one's social invitation is extended to legitimize the host's view of himself as liberal? Whether the black professional is socially acceptable to whites is no longer a concern for many Blacks.

THE BLACK "MIDDLE CLASS"

The Wattenberg and Scammon report takes liberals and black persons to task for not proclaiming black advancement. "American Blacks have been moving up into the middle class so that by now these numbers can be said to add up to a majority of black Americans—a slender majority, but a majority nevertheless."[9]

Now the black middle class refers not only to engineers and teachers but also to plasterers, painters, bus drivers, lathe operators, secretaries, bank tellers, automobile assembly-line workers: the kinds of people who, when they are white, are described as Middle Americans.

Billingsley agrees with the difficulties the concept presents:[10]

> The problems associated with the description of Negro families in social class terms are so great that a number of students of the Negro experience are beginning to question its utility. It is completely inappropriate for describing behavior or values or styles of life or child rearing patterns in the Negro community.

Why isn't this progress a source of satisfaction to Blacks? Wattenberg and Scammon answer their own question: Black family income is only 63 percent of white family income, and that is "scandalously low." Blacks have thought that the race was progressing economically before, only to find that it wasn't.

An answer to why black Americans are not "turning handsprings over their good fortune" comes from William Raspberry:[11]

> It involves . . . insecurity skepticism (some would call it paranoia), some basic judgments about the nature of white America and some mostly inarticulate conflicts over what constitutes Black progress in the first place. The most fundamental question is whether the socio-economic elevation of increasing numbers of individual Black Americans is in fact the same as Black progress. The answer implicit in the attitudes of large numbers of Blacks is that it isn't. . . .
>
> Blacks seem to have decided: We can't make it as individuals so we'll have to make it as a group. And since progress has so often been such an illusory thing, we'd better not dupe ourselves into believing that some of us have "made it" in any permanent sense.
>
> It is undeniable that more and more Blacks are entering the middle class. But an awful lot of them see themselves as strangers in that land, subject to deportation at whim.

The minority practitioner cares about those "strangers."

HOW OTHER MINORITIES COPE WITH PRACTITIONER ISSUES

Most ethnic groups have directed their concerns to the schools of social work because they feel that the educational institutions tend to control the market for social workers and particularly for social work leaders. The recruitment of students and the allocation of student aid resources have been major concerns, but once schools agree to these two objectives, the question immediately becomes the availability of minority faculty who understand the students' problems and who can interpret the situation to nonminority students.

There has been somewhat less concern about these issues from black students because the most successful effort has been achieved to recruit black faculty, and black students have received some preference for student aid. Also there are two well-established schools of social work that have had predominantly black enrollments—Howard University in Washington, D.C., and Atlanta University. Recently, San Jose State College established a school with a Chicano emphasis.

Faculty recruitment and expectations are sources of special conflict since fewer minority members have earned graduate degrees in social work, particularly at the doctoral level. Many of them are not interested in research, from which promotion is likely to come most rapidly. As a result there is a greater emphasis on community service as a substitute for research. Some universities buy these criteria better than others. Minority group members often feel that they have had little chance of attaining tenure by doing the things that seem to them to be the most important. They feel that traditional university standards are often racist. The Chicanos have developed an interesting concept of the "barrio" professor. A recent account will illustrate the main ideas involved:[12]

The Barrio Professor

The Barrio Professor does not have the standard academic credentials that attest to his knowledge and expertise in social work practice in the barrio.* However, he has received certification from the barrios that he has served adequately. He is knowledgeable in Chicano culture, language, life styles, class differences, value bases, folk curing (*curanderismo*), and the overall function of the barrio system. Such knowledge comes from having lived in the barrio from infancy and from having worked intimately with Chicanos for several years. The Barrio Professor is also familiar with many social work theories, methodologies, and terminology sets used in the social work profession. While the learning process of professional social workers is generally conducted through their socialization in the academic educational system, the Barrio Professor is also learning, but learning through action: learning actual skills, not about skills; testing hypotheses in real life situations, not through library research; and gaining a general consciousness of self as a person and as a helping agent.

An outstanding characteristic of the Barrio Professor is that he is not

---

*A *barrio* is a Chicano urban community. In some ways it parallels the term "ghetto."

constrained to function in a highly structured and institutionalized manner, but rather is adept in functioning in an informal style compatible with barrio life styles. Unlike many college graduates who have accepted or tolerated some degree of assimilation and acculturation to dominant Anglo-American values, the Barrio Professor has not been "contaminated" by social work professionalism or the mythology of academia and can still act consistently with barrio attitudes and values, enabling him to make decisions congruent with barrio values rather than decisions foreign to these values. His primary accountability is to the barrio, not to the maintenance of an institution or a profession.

Each Barrio Professor brings a variety of skills to social work education, including: fluency in both English and Spanish (formal *and* barrio Spanish), enabling him to communicate with Chicano clients as well as established human service institutions; an understanding of how to work effectively with folk-culture–oriented Chicanos; an ability to articulate his knowledge of the barrio and to instruct students, individually and in groups, in classroom and field settings; and an ability to develop effective learning opportunities that are related to barrio realities.

The Barrio Professor's role in social work education is strengthened by his capacity to function compatibly in communicating and working with faculty, students, and barrio residents. His barrio contacts and relationships enhance the information-gathering process essential to knowledge building research and facilitate barrio acceptance of the participation of social work students in barrio activities. In addition to his knowledge and skills, the Barrio Professor possesses a sensitivity to the pulse of the barrio which his life experience there has given him. His strong commitment to, and identification with, his barrio allows him to reflect the emotional impact produced by practice in the barrio. Finally, he has the capacity to act as liaison between the barrio and the school, assuring barrio participation at all levels of decision-making and in turn interpreting school policies, practices, and activities to the barrio. In essence, the Barrio Professor reflects *"el oro del barrio,"* epitomizing the spirit and wisdom of the bilingual-bicultural barrio. He possesses those humanistic values which depict society as socially and culturally pluralistic.

Although the knowledge, skills, values, and attitudes of the Barrio Professor may differ from those of other Chicano faculty with MSW degrees, there exists a degree of commonality between these two groups. Some of their common characteristics are: bilingualism and biculturalism; their relationship to the social work profession; their commitment to the barrio; and most importantly, their beliefs in *Chicanismo*.

The Indians and Puerto Ricans have the same concerns about extending opportunities for their own groups in social work education, but have not had the impact of Blacks and Chicanos. Certainly the place to begin to develop more opportunities for minority students is in the undergraduate programs to which they will be first attracted and out of which many seek a meaningful professional role.

Ione Dugger Vargus

KEY TERMS

double consciousness   black caucuses
new consciousness   alternative institutions
social distance   Association of Black Social Workers
blaming the victim   black perspective

FOR DISCUSSION

1 In white colleges, why were social work, education, and the ministry the first areas to admit Blacks?
2 Does a double consciousness still operate?
3 Why is the reduction of social distance a special problem for middle-class Blacks who would like to improve their housing?
4 Interpret the statement: "Best results may come from leaning to the strengths of individuals and groups rather than to their weaknesses."
5 Why do black people often resent research projects?
6 What problems are likely to face an agency that serves only Blacks?
7 Why do you think Blacks have emphasized the need for a strong and visible leader such as Malcolm X or Martin Luther King?
8 How must social agency personnel learn to tolerate diversities?
9 Why may black workers distrust affirmative action programs?
10 Why may relations between white and black workers be difficult?
11 Why are minority students often critical of social work approaches?

PROJECTS

1 Present this debate: "Resolved, that a minority group should form its own separate social services organization as soon as its numbers justify the action."
2 Read and compare *The Souls of Black Folk* (1903) and *Dusk of Dawn* (1940) with the current renewed consciousness. What changes have come about since 1903?
3 Invite a social worker from a minority-oriented agency and one who works in a traditional agency to discuss affirmative action, service policies, staff relations, and other topics of interest to the class.
4 Ask black student social workers who are receiving field instruction to discuss their experiences both with clients and with sponsoring agencies.
5 Choose a minority group for study, and give as many examples as you can of the diversities within the group. Why does failure to consider diversities make it harder to solve social problems?
6 Analyze developments and present your views on racial strategies for 1980. Indicate the evidence for your predictions.
7 Ask a member of the Black Social Workers Association and one from the National Association of Social Workers to present the current goals and concerns of each group. How do their goals compare concerning racism?

FOR FURTHER STUDY

James Goodman (ed.), *The Dynamics of Racism in Social Work*, National Association of Social Workers, Washington, D.C., 1973.
Elinor L. Gordon, *Racism and American Education*, Harper & Row, New York, 1970.

Terry Jones, "Institutional Racism in the United States," *Social Work*, 19, March 1974, pp. 218–225.

John Longres, "The Impact of Racism on Social Work Education," *Education for Social Work*, 8, Winter, 1972, pp. 31–41.

Carl A. Scott (ed.), *Ethnic Minorities in Social Work Education*, Council on Social Work Education, New York, 1970.

Alexander Thomas and Samuel Sillen, *Racism and Psychiatry*, Brunner/Mazel, New York, 1972.

Chapter 25

Social Work Evaluation and Research

Is evaluation necessary?
What's wrong with social work research?
Is "effectiveness" the new challenge?
Is research a major planning tool?

Do social workers accomplish what they set out to accomplish? How close do they come to their goals? The answers to these questions involve an evaluative process—some way of judging effectiveness—and the use of research.

EVALUATING SOCIAL WORK SERVICES

The research enterprise is based on certain premises: (1) The world is real; (2) the world is knowable and measurable with objective instruments; (3) properly built experimentation leads to generalization and scientific knowledge in the form of laws. These presuppositions are basic to the classical experiment in which a hypothesis about reality is stated, the terms are defined, an instrument is selected and applied, data are collected and analyzed, and a conclusion is reached that relates the research to a theory upon which generalizations can be built.

The "pure" science approach is useful for gathering basic knowledge about the world, but it is not usually possible in an applied discipline. Social work needs the kind of research that seeks to set a value on a given procedure or activity. Such research does not ask what is true, but rather: "How good is it?"

Traditionally, the question of the value of social work effort never seemed to require hard answers. Since social workers are basically humanitarian, it was assumed that what they did was good by definition. For the most part social work and social welfare efforts have been measured in terms of numbers of people served, days of care provided, and amount of money spent. Social welfare personnel themselves had few doubts about the value of their efforts, so they were content with the simple reporting of gross activity.

Now social work and social welfare have become big business. The services rendered by welfare institutions and personnel touch the lives of many people. Citizens who pay to support welfare services want to know how their money is spent, and consumers have become more vocal about their concerns for the quality of service. Social work and social welfare can no longer be accountable only for money spent for a number of hours of service. Increasingly, both public and private services are expected to show concrete evidence of efficiency to a wider and more critical public. The Ford administration is likely to continue its predecessor's evaluation.

Needed: Better Research Methods

Can social workers be expected to demonstrate results when many of the factors are intangible? The answer is yes, if social work researchers will accept more rigor in conceptualization, more precise instrumentation, and clearer definitions of payoff. The major difficulties with social work research in the past have been its "softness" in outcome definition and lack of clear procedure.

A plea for the need for better research is not new to social work. In the very first issue of *Social Work*, Preston and Mudd reported a study of previous social work research.[1] They identified seven types of studies, most dealing with highly specific and local concerns. This review raised two questions: Of 468 titles, why are 80 percent of the publications directed to specific questions of primary value only to specific agencies or programs? Why is research designed to test carefully formulated hypotheses rare in social work?

Social Work—An Art? Some say that good research cannot be done because social work is basically an art. This is a fallacious answer. N. L. Gage has replied to an analogous suggestion made by Gilbert Highet that teaching is an art, therefore not subject to scientific analysis. Gage suggests that art in any form follows rules. When these rules are identified, they constitute a theory of artistic performance.[2] Any art can still be studied and evaluated. Such study is a legitimate concern for any skill or craft interested in improving its performance or in reproducing its art in new recruits to the field.

Research Capability Most social workers are not sufficiently prepared to do more than prepare descriptive reports. In a climate that raises the question of accountability, social workers have denied themselves the tools to help provide it. If social work had developed more research capability, it would be less vulnerable.

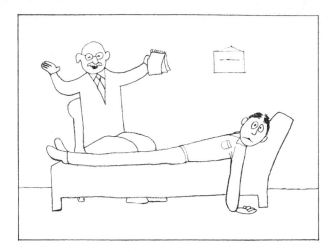

*"This is our 1,883d session; who needs research
to know that you've improved remarkably?"*

Fear of Research   Good research studies have been rare because social
workers have been afraid of research. Administrators fear that research might
point up lacks and raise embarrassing questions. It is discomfiting to give
researchers access to one's program in the belief that they are friendly allies and
then discover that their finished product is detrimental to administrative interests.

Major Problems in Evaluative Research

Social workers have trouble agreeing when they have reached a satisfactory
resolution to a problem. Recall an example from the chapter on the family.
Suppose a social worker is dealing with a married couple who have been getting
along badly for some time. The social worker will schedule a series of appointments with the couple. A process ensues involving the social worker and the
marriage partners separately or together. Eventually the couple decide to get a
divorce. Has the social worker failed? Would he have succeeded only if the
couple had remained married? Or is it enough to say that social work service was
effective when the couple had developed enough insight into their feelings and
difficulties to recognize that the marriage was irreconcilable? Actually, any of
these outcomes might be acceptable if one is willing to state the desired outcome
clearly and can reach a decision on what he will take as evidence of the outcome.
The trouble is that social work researchers have usually become lost in this
process and have tried to deal with complex outcomes that are among the hardest
to measure.

Clear Indicators and Outcomes

A Delinquency Example   Other social science researchers have learned to
deal with behaviorally oriented outcomes and clear social indicators. This is not as
hard as it sounds. For instance, suppose that the researcher wants to evaluate the

effectiveness of a program aimed at the delinquent. There is no valid reason why he cannot use the delinquency rate as an indicator of outcome. Arguments against such a simple criterion may sound learned, but they are specious. The public expects delinquency to be reduced. Since delinquency rates are impersonal, it makes no difference whether delinquency is to be reduced through heavy patrols and public horsewhipping or through a revolutionary change in the social structure and value system of the world. If the activity is effective, delinquency rates will go down. This is what the supporters of the effort want to see.

Social work research in an age of accountability has to be concerned with clear and socially desirable outcomes that have the least ambiguity. Clear objectives for the agency or program to be evaluated are essential if success is to be achieved. This is now the problem for both the researcher and the agency administrator.

Crime Statistics as Indicators   The delinquency example was chosen with the full realization that crime statistics are generally not the most perfect indicators,[3] since they tend to be more reflective of police activity than of delinquent activity. However, they have a conventional meaning. Their weaknesses are known, but they are the best criterion that exists for the purpose. Unfortunately, the needs of accountability will not wait on the development of perfect tools. If social work cannot demonstrate its effectiveness, it may not be around when more perfect measures are developed. It does social work no good to argue that the really important outcomes may be intangible and may exist even though they are not measurable. The same can be said of snake oil! To argue that there are too many variables is useless. Social workers have used the "too many uncontrolled variables" argument when it appears that research may not turn out in their favor. It seldom comes up when the results seem likely to be favorable.

Research on a Complex Problem

Busing Helped in Sacramento

Black students who have been bused to integrated schools perform better in reading and mathematics than those blacks who remain in segregated classrooms, according to a recent study conducted by the Sacramento, California, school system.

"There is something happening here that didn't happen by chance," said Edward Morrison, who conducted the research effort. Comparing the performance of 79 black pupils who were bused to integrated schools with the scores of a control group of 198 black youngsters, the integrated students were found to achieve higher ratings in nearly every situation, often scoring higher than national averages. Children in both groups were given extra attention under a federal compensatory education program.

"Research Notes," *The Phi Delta Kappan*.[4]

Clear Hypotheses and Terms

Much social work research lacks clear hypotheses and defined terms. Again, this problem can be solved if social workers are prepared to refine their terminology. A cursory glance at published reports will verify this contention. One is apt to find a statement: "Different social workers will respond differently to different clients," rather than a more tersely stated and limited hypothesis that can lend itself to objective measurement.

The remedy is clear. Social work researchers need to learn the best techniques from sociology, psychology, and education, even though the research in these fields is not perfect. The student can profitably compare the research published in *Social Work*, *Social Casework*, and the *Social Service Review* with that in the *Journal of Experimental Education*, the *Journal of Educational Psychology*, the *American Sociological Review*, or the *American Journal of Psychology*, to name a few. Social work researchers could also improve their research through use of comparison groups.[5]

Appropriate Statistics

Social work researchers often rely on percentages or on the chi-square test when they can obtain the data to use much more appropriate statistical techniques to determine whether findings are statistically significant or only a function of chance.[7] Most social workers have not had an adequate knowledge of statistics. This is partially defensible in that they conceive of themselves as practitioners. However, all social work students will not be practitioners. A specialized research major should be available for those students who have such interests. Faculties must identify potential researchers and provide the kind of preparation (including courses in other departments) that will produce at least a small supply of well-prepared researchers.

Also, researchers need to pay more attention to sound instrumentation. It is customary for social work researchers to devise new instruments and tests for any and all occasions. Well-designed tests may already exist that will do a more reliable job, but social work researchers seem to be unaware of them.

SAMPLING PROBLEMS

Social work agencies do not deal with normal samples. Normal distributions are a requirement for the valid application of the statistical procedures taught in most elementary courses. If a researcher cannot claim that the characteristics he is studying are normally distributed, he has to use statistics that do not involve assumptions of normality.

Social work researchers also frequently face the problem of very small samples. If a researcher wanted to evaluate the effectiveness of a group treatment procedure for six patients, he would have a real problem. To get satisfactory research data, he may wish that he had ten or fifteen groups of six, but they may not be available. If they are, the agency may not think it appropriate to "experiment" on them. This is a problem without a practical solution until agencies become more committed to research efforts. We must get larger samples if we want results to be capable of generalization.

EXAMPLES OF SOCIAL WORK RESEARCH

The foregoing should not be taken to mean that no worthwhile social work research has been done. Research of high quality is not common because of the lack of governmental and institutional support and lack of research personnel. Now let us look at a few examples of social work research.

Delinquency Prevention

Girls at Vocational High, by Meyer, Borgatta, and Jones,[6] is a study of the effectiveness of social work service in delinquency prevention.

> Over the course of four years girls with potential problems who entered a vocational high school in New York City were identified from information available to the school. From this pool of students a random sample of cases was referred to an agency where they were offered casework or group counseling services by professional social workers. A control group was selected at random from the same pool of potential problem cases in order that a comparison could be made between girls who received service and similar girls who did not.

The staff of Youth Consultation Service of New York had held that service for adolescent girls came too late to interrupt delinquent careers. Consequently, the staff were willing to try a new approach and have the results evaluated. This willingness allowed an experimental design that provided random assignment of subjects and the use of a control group, a rarity in social work research.

The Sample and the Method   The subjects came from a high school that served "a good general mix of students." Admission records were screened for potential problematic students. This definition was purposefully loose and inclusive. The girls selected for service were referred to YCS by Vocational High. The social workers thought that the girls were upset by the referral, but since most of them returned after the initial interview and had a median number of sixteen interviews, the social workers' beliefs were apparently not well founded. Of the 189 girls who completed the intake procedure, only 3 percent failed to have at least one further service contact with a social worker at YCS. Generally, schools only refer students who clearly need service, and agencies are customarily more selective of their clientele. However, the preventive and experimental aspect of this study justified varying usual procedure. The authors point out:[7]

> It was not the effectiveness of the agency with its usual clientele that was in question but rather the effectiveness of its special effort with a determinate clientele that was to be examined through the experimental project.

The Results   The novelty of preventive counseling could easily have affected the results. Something did, since the results failed to confirm the effectiveness of social work treatment. Outcomes were measured along two dimensions, objective and subjective. Using school completion, academic performance and school-related behavior (e.g. attendance truancy, teacher ratings), and out-of-school behavior (e.g. coming to the attention of authorities, unmarried pregnancy), there were only slight differences in favor of social work intervention. The authors gently and charitably conclude that the lack of differences . . . testifies to the difficulty of changing deviant careers.

On self-reports, attitude measures, personality scales, and sociometric data no important differences were found, but, as with the objective measures, trends favored the treated group.

Interpretation   The authors point out that social workers do not see the payoff for their efforts in specific objective outcomes nor in improved scores on personality tests. They describe their aims:[8]

> . . . to increase self-understanding, to develop more adequate psychological and social functioning, to facilitate maturation, to supplement emotional resources inadequate for the ordinary and extraordinary stresses of adolescence.

Since social workers did not have the same objectives as the researchers, it could be argued that the whole research program was invalid. It does not seem fair to measure an effort along a set of outcomes that the effort does not directly address. On the other hand, there was an indirect link between the social workers' goals and the research outcomes, and the social workers believed that ultimately their efforts would reduce drop-out rates, delinquency, and personality problems. Perhaps the real problems revealed by this research lie in social workers' unwillingness to concentrate on specific behavioral outcomes in favor of more esoteric results. If so, then a valuable by-product of *Girls at Vocational High* should be more precise statements of the outcomes expected. Two contrasting reviews of this study are provided by Schorr[9] and Macdonald.[10]

A Study of School Social Workers

Lela Costin attempted to answer two questions:[11] How do school social workers define the content of school social work and the relative importance of its roles? Does such a definition provide a promising basis for experimentation in assigning responsibilities to social work staff with different levels of education or training? Costin gathered data from 368 professional school social workers—a 25 percent sample of those active in the field. She got a return of 73 percent on a mailed questionnaire that asked respondents to rate the importance of 107 tasks expressed in behavioral terms. The respondents were also asked if each task could be performed by a person with less education and training than the respondent.

Factor analysis was used to locate major clusters of school social work tasks from the 107 behavioral statements, because it correlates variables against each other to allow one to reduce a long list of variables to meaningful clusters. Costin identified nine factors or clusters of tasks that school social workers considered important. The most important one was casework service to the child and his parents. Caseload management, interpreting social work service, and clinical treatment of children with emotional problems were the next most important.[12]

The chief emphasis was on helping the individual child accommodate himself to the school situation rather than attempting to modify patterns within a school's operations which might be generating difficulties for him and for large numbers of other children as well.

On the question of delegation of tasks:[13]

. . . School social workers are inclined to see most of their activity as quite important and are reluctant to consider the delegation of very much of it.

She concludes:[14]

. . . The definition of school social work revealed in this study reflects the school social work literature of the 1940's and 1950's and shows little or no general response to the concerns expressed in both education and social work literature of the 1960's.

The definition of school social work in workers' minds was found to be static and did not address a number of pressing modern problems; school social workers are unready to delegate tasks. This study has a large sample of the population. The statistical procedure is appropriate and technically sound. The purpose of the research is clear, and the tasks to be rated were stated in behavioral terms. The study addresses an important area of practice that needs clarification, and the results are capable of being generalized.

Service to Families Receiving Public Assistance

Applicants for AFDC and AFDC-U were selected for study by the Community Service Society in cooperation with the New York City Department of Public Welfare.[15] The project attempted to assess the effects of collaborative social work intervention by CSS and the social services division of DPW. Early sustained counseling was hypothesized to lead to higher income, more employment, better housing, better health practices, better marketing skills, improved family relationships, and better psychological functioning on the part of mothers and children.

Families were randomly assigned to experimental and contrast groups. The contrast group received services as customarily provided through DPW, in addition to any other services which they independently secured for themselves. Experimental families were given from five to nearly a hundred direct or indirect services from a total of twenty-two master's-degree practitioners in nineteen CSS centers throughout the city.

Fourteen months after application, families in the experimental and contrast groups were interviewed, using a precoded, structured questionnaire. Fighty-three variables were examined to test twenty-seven different hypotheses. Items on the questionnaire were not pretested, but where possible were based on standardized scales.

Findings showed no overall difference between experimental and contrast groups, holding education, ethnic background, and family structure constant. A slight, statistically nonsignificant difference on most outcome variables favored the experimental group.

Staff Criticisms   Although the study was carried out to extend collaborative efforts between CSS and DPW, the social work staff at CSS rejected the findings of the study and refused to consider their implications for practice. CSS practitioners claimed that there were gross inconsistencies between progress as noted in case recordings on experimental families and self-reports by the families themselves in the research interview. The social workers generally believed that clients failed to acknowledge change when it had taken place—or had unreasonable goals for themselves and therefore did not subjectively experience help even where help was given.

This study has several interesting features. The hypothesized outcomes were clearly desirable for the clientele and did not refer to cherished beliefs of practitioners. There was random assignment to experimental and contrast groups. The outcomes were operationalized in concrete terms. Scores on standardized instruments wherever possible were used in order to objectify outcomes.

Even when research is well done it is often not utilized, while the research utilized is not always well done.

Use of Knowledge

Let no one suppose that it is to be taken for granted that the demand for the ascertainment of reliable knowledge in any field automatically guarantees that such knowledge will be put to profitable use. It is one thing to discover the cure for a disease, but it is sometimes another to induce your patient to try it. For years it has been known by doctors that the dreadful Oriental scourge called beri-beri is the direct result of a diet of fish and hulled white rice. If people would only change to a diet of fish and the cheaper unhulled brown rice, beri-beri would disappear. But dietary habits are not easily or swiftly changed by argument, especially in countries with a relatively low level of public enlightenment. Even in more sophisticated circles, it is one of the melancholy reflections of all students of government that the typical resting-place of an expensive report of a fact-finding commission is a shelf in a cellar. Scientists never tire of reminding us that our knowledge in dozens of fields is miles ahead of our will and ability to apply it. Every time we pass a library, we should recall how much more knowledge men have on tap in books than they manage to utilize in action.

Harold A. Larrabee, *Reliable Knowledge*.[16]

MODELS OF EVALUATION

What models should social work use? A useful model must provide:

1   Clear description of program goals. This means a clear statement of what the agency is trying to do.
2   Adequate study design with clearly defined concepts and testable hypotheses.

3 Efficient and appropriate statistical tools. Here the computer and its technology can be used.

4 Clearly defined outcome criteria.

Social work researchers can use a number of models of evaluation. Some can be borrowed from education,[17] or the evaluator can take advantage of Herzog's model.[18] Let us apply Stake's model to social work.[19]

1 What is the agency trying to do? Often the goal is implicit or poorly stated, or not shared by all participants in the operation. Find out what significant actors involved in a given program want. What do the staff intend for the clientele? What is the intent of the board? What do the administration see as the intent of the program? What do financial supporters (taxpayers and voluntary givers) expect the program to do? What expectations do clients have when they come to the agency? Seldom do evaluative studies ask these questions in researchable terms. Therefore, these bodies do not take the research seriously.

Obviously not all of the key people involved in a given program have the same intent. Their expectations are value-laden, but they deserve answers from the evaluative process. A value statement can be articulated and made explicit, and an answer can be obtained. For instance, suppose that the board members of a family agency have as their intent lowering the divorce rate, but that the staff have a different set of intentions. They direct their efforts toward the personal growth of the clients and consider the divorce rate irrelevant. The clients have yet another set of expectations. Faced with a painful relationship, relief may mean divorce, or it may mean reconciliation. All these expectations can be collected as statements of goal or intent. They can be made explicit. The evaluation design can take them into account. Each set of key actors can be given an answer. A useful by-product of evaluation should be the recognition of differential goals.

2 What is actually going on? This question involves gathering data from the participants in the situation. The focus is on the interactions and transactions between staff and clientele, of course, but should not stop there. How much staff time does a given program take? What does it cost? What do the administrators do? What are the unanticipated consequences of the program? The evaluator is obliged to gather as much information as he can on what actually happens from many different sources. The number and complexity of the observations on which the evaluation is based should be limited only by the technology, funds, and time available.

3 What are the outcomes of activity? Too often evaluative research considers only simply defined outcomes for consumers. One should look not only at the effects of the program on clients, but at its effects on staff, administration, and the community as a whole. Good evaluation looks at unintended consequences as well as intended outcomes. It looks at costs and benefits. Again the more outcomes that can be included, the better the evaluation. Short-term as well as long-term benefits are important.

4 Is the product any good? At this point many evaluations break down. People seem to be afraid to commit themselves to a judgment. Yet someone must decide whether or not the intended outcomes and the actual outcomes are congruent. Standards for making judgments do exist. The trouble is that standards may not always be explicit nor congruent with each other. Therefore, the job of the evaluator is to gather the standards available and use them. Experts have opinions. Clients as consumers of services have opinions, as do administrators and staff, by which an agency, program, or technique may be judged. The evaluator's problem is to make these standards explicit in order to judge whether or not they have been met. Even severe critics may contribute a basis for judgments. Comparisons can often be made with absolute standards, such as those of the Child Welfare League of America. In any event, hard judgments must be made if social work is to improve its accountability and credibility.

The model is not foolproof. It obviously depends upon the ability of the evaluator to derive intents, observations, and standards from a number of sources to be used as the basis for evaluation. However, the alternative is to settle for less than is available and to continue to do incomplete evaluation of social work effort.

Another similar model is PPBS—Program Planning Budgeting System. The object is to be able to define the tasks, to organize in the most efficient way (in terms of cost benefits), and to field the most effective program.

The accent on efficiency is a direct outgrowth of the pressures placed on governmental structures to provide accountability and efficient use of limited funds. Increasingly, social work will have to prove itself in hard-headed terms to skeptical, budget-conscious people—and this goes for social work operations on both the public and private level.

Jack Bloedorn has set forth a systems analysis in social work that includes nine steps:[20]

    1 Carefully define the problem.
    2 Set objectives by carefully spelling out what you are trying to do.
    3 Determine criteria for success.
    4 Research the situation until you understand the problem and its setting completely.
    5 Find out the practical constraints in the situation which will mitigate for or against reaching the objective you have set.
    6 Develop alternatives for reaching your goal.
    7 Test the alternatives against the criteria.
    8 Select the best alternative from a cost-benefit point of view and plan for its installation.
    9 Install the alternative and monitor system for continuous feedback and change.

These models seek better cost-benefit output, clearer objectives, and more meaningful outcome criteria. However, Stake's model accents accountability to sponsors, consumers, and staff, while PPBS is mainly concerned with costs and efficiency—the financial support base.

Program budgeting and cost effectiveness systems have serious limitations:[21]

(1) The attempt to quantify things that cannot be quantified, (2) conflict between emphasis on budget and evaluation criteria vs. meeting human needs, e.g. "skimming" potentially successful clients in order to meet

efficiency and effectiveness criteria, (3) the use of measuring instruments that are too primitive to assess what is really going on in a complex world, organization, program or person, (4) the treatment of social work practice as a purely scientific endeavor, (5) the centralization of planning which makes social welfare organizations less flexible to immediate needs, (6) emphasis on efficiency at the expense of effectiveness.

INFORMATION SYSTEMS

Management information systems for social service organizations are basic to evaluation. Researchers generally think of evaluation projects as requiring considerable special information about workers and clients that would not ordinarily be gathered. Workers resent this activity and often claim that the data are gathered only for research and are obviously irrelevant. The social worker often holds that such information does not show whether he does a good job. Ironically, then, the evaluator uses one set of data criteria to judge success but the workers and administrators use others. Management information systems adapted from industry are intended to make the collection of information for judging success or failure a task.

Types of Information In order of difficulty, three kinds of information can be produced by such systems: (1) the *number* and *characteristics* of clients seeking or receiving service; (2) *units of service*, such as interviews held, group meetings attended, or hours of child care provided and the average cost of each unit; and (3) *transactions of clients in seeking and obtaining service*, the time taken, the sequence of services received, and the changes produced by the service. Few systems have been able to deal adequately with changes produced by the service.

Measuring Success

Two problems are typical. First, for example, in vocational rehabilitation job placements obtained are a typical measure of success. Two clients may meet this criterion. One may have lost two fingers in a power saw, and the other may be severely ill, have a third-grade education, and be a member of a minority group. To aid in evaluation the system provides classification of situations in terms of their comparative difficulty.

Second, counting of time spent in interviews is often used as evidence of good work because interviews are the best example of direct contact. Without valid measures of client change, such a criterion may encourage more and more interviewing whether or not it is effective.

Measurement Required While many workers will not be enthusiastic about the forms and procedures required by an information system, we can expect such systems to become mandatory. We must understand them and shape them to reflect human needs and professional values. This also suggests the need for knowledge of management techniques leading to the ability to collaborate with others who understand the systems but who may know much too little about the goals and the methods of the social service.

Standardization presents major issues. With different agencies, localities, and states, developing various systems cannot be easily combined for measuring trends or forecasting. Increased cooperation among governmental and private agencies can lead to uniform systems that make the efforts far more useful.

A consortium of twenty mental health agencies serving an area of 155,000 persons in California developed the "Human Accountability System," involving a centralized data system.[22] The system contains no clinical information. Twelve transactions constitute the basic data. Identifying data include name, address, sex, and date of birth. A single $8\frac{1}{2}''$ x 11" form is used that can be filled out in thirty seconds.

The system can generate a master list of all patients known to the system, messages to alert all agencies about their patients in the system, and transaction reports including the frequency of occurrence of each type of transaction and the movement between agencies.

The system automatically receives a history of every patient. It produces lists of active patients, those on the waiting lists, and those who have been discharged. The system indicates to other members those facilities that may be able to accept new patients. Patients in concomitant care in other agencies are also reported.

The limits of this information system for evaluation are apparent, because as yet it does not provide statements of agency objectives and patients' objectives. The system does illustrate a clear approach to fact gathering that can be expanded to provide the capability for evaluation.

SOCIAL WELFARE PLANNING

Research and information systems are tools for planning. Planning is used with a range of large and small social welfare issues. What are the types of planning and how can they be illustrated?

Incremental Planning

A Typical Example   The aim is often to continue to do the same thing, but to do it *better* or to do *more* of it, or both. At the urging of the United Fund a child welfare agency decides to increase the number of adoptions it completes. The specific question is how to place more children, preferably with fewer staff hours per child and no decrease in quality of service.

Planning requires information about past experience as well as the need to forecast future conditions. The agency reviews how many children it has placed, how much the program cost, and how many placements did and did not eventuate in adoption. Other familiar facts are also important. Fewer children are being born. Contraceptive methods are generally effective for those who do not really want to have a child. Abortion is available if contraception fails. Unmarried mothers now tend to want to keep their children, but we do not know how many ultimately place them anyhow.

The agency may conclude that the only way to increase adoptions is to change the status of children now in foster care. The major thrust then will not be outreach to unmarried mothers but to the courts—to achieve termination of parental rights for those who do not and cannot care for their children.

Implications   Incremental planning of this sort seems simple enough. In this example, the agency already has the expertise. It has legal sanction for the program. It requires no new types of personnel. But the effort will bring the agency into new relationships. To find adoptive homes, outposts may be needed in black neighborhoods. Lobbying may be required for financial subsidies for adoptive parents. What started out to be incremental planning may lead to far-reaching changes.

Incremental planning may also ignore broader implications. The program may be put into effect across several age levels whether or not adoption is the best plan. As part of an incremental strategy, to provide adoption for adolescents who already seek emancipation from adults would possibly be both unfeasible and undesirable.

Planning at the National Level   The frequent across-the-board percentage increase in social security benefits is an obvious incremental means to give people more money, even though greater increases for those who have smaller incomes would be fairer. The former plan is recommended by congressional committees because it is both simple and politically popular.

Comprehensive Planning

Systems rather than single issues are the concern of comprehensive planning. Goals are broader and lead to significant changes in organizational structure. A guaranteed income system to replace the traditional public assistance system is an example. Such a plan affects taxation, social services, and manpower policy for both the unemployed and the underemployed. It has implications for work incentives, family structure, housing, mental health services, programs for the aged, and even national economic well-being. It involves organizational changes in all fifty states and affects millions of people. Vast amounts of information and a series of demonstration experiments should be part of the comprehensive planning process on a guaranteed income.

Comprehensive planning is also illustrated by a community effort to devise an effective services system. The numbers affected are much smaller than in the preceding example, but questions of turf and money and agency power plus limitations in available resources contribute to the complexity of the task. Conflict is especially likely if existing agencies are expected to merge or to go out of business as part of the plan.

A Combination Model

Amitai Etzioni[23] emphasizes the need for a combination planning model that starts with a broad overview to identify the elements that most need change, then these elements become the focus. This approach is called *mixed scanning* because it takes a comprehensive view but concentrates on specific alterations that may or may not be largely incremental.

Barriers to Success   Planning efforts often fail because of limited finances or manpower or because of value conflicts. An adoption of a foster child may require four times the staff hours of an infant adoption. Thus the effort proposed may fail for lack of funds. Existing agencies may make it impossible to implement a comprehensive community plan. Provision of a guaranteed income may be rational but not politically salable. Planning requires not only development of facts and forecasts but the skill to make potentially effective plans feasible so they are accepted.

As this chapter has suggested, social work has become subject to evaluation and will require more evidence and fewer altruistic feelings for its acceptance. If you are interested in research, information systems, and planning, specialized courses are offered in schools of business and public administration and increasingly in schools of social work. Social workers who like to develop facts and look at present impact and future trends are needed for a partnership with their colleagues who concentrate on helping people directly.

Charles R. Atherton

KEY TERMS

hypothesis	unintended consequences
outcomes	management information systems
accountability	incremental planning
social indicators	comprehensive planning
sampling	mixed scanning
factor analysis	

FOR DISCUSSION

1   Why is social work research *applied* rather than pure?
2   Why is accountability in social work now very important?
3   Criticize studies that deal with highly specific concerns.
4   How can social work as an art still be the subject for research?
5   What are the problems with using delinquency rates as a measure of the success of a program?
6   What can social work researchers learn from such social sciences as psychology and sociology?
7   How is sampling important to choice of statistical techniques?
8   What is the major finding of the study *Girls at Vocational High*?
9   What statistical technique was used in Costin's study of school social workers?
10   What common research difficulty is illustrated in the project for AFDC recipients by the Community Services Society in New York City?
11   In Stake's model, why are goals of the agency the first concern?
12   Outcomes are usually studied in terms of effects on the clients. What other effects should be considered?
13   What does Bloedorn's model illustrate?
14   What are the purposes of an information system?
15   Why did workers find the Human Accountability System easy to use?

16   What type of planning is most common?
17   What three elements are linked together by planning?

PROJECTS

1   Organize a panel to discuss the use and misuse of statistics. *How to Lie with Statistics* will be a helpful resource.
2   Consider the members of the class as a research sample. Develop an attitude questionnaire on a topic related to social welfare. Tabulate the results and see whether the responses of the men and the women differ. Test the differences statistically. Seek faculty consultation if necessary.
3   Choose an example of social work research. Evaluate the sampling, the method, and the findings. Compare your comments with those of other class members. *Social Work Abstracts* is a source for current research.
4   Invite a faculty member who is engaged in research to discuss his project with your group. Ask him to describe the funding and sponsorship as well as the objectives and research methods.
5   Prepare a brief talk for the class illustrating the difference between *efficiency* and *effectiveness*. Indicate how research techniques may provide evidence on both.
6   Invite a staff member responsible for evaluation in a large public agency to talk to the class. What kinds of data is he expected to present? Have the demands changed? How does electronic data processing help?

FOR FURTHER STUDY

Philip Fellin et al. (eds.), *Exemplars of Social Research*, Peacock Publishers, Itasca, Ill., 1969.

Darrell Huff, *How to Lie with Statistics*, Norton, New York, 1954.

Ralph H. Kolstoe, *Introduction to Statistics for the Behavioral Sciences*, Dorsey, Homewood, Ill., 1969.

Henry S. Maas (ed.), *Research in the Social Services, A Five-Year Review*, National Association of Social Workers, New York, 1971.

Making Evaluation Research Useful, American City Corporation, Columbia Md., 1972.

Tony Tripodi et al. (eds.), *The Assessment of Social Research—Guidelines for the Use of Research on Social Work and Social Science*, Peacock Publishers, Itasca, Ill., 1969.

References
and Notes

Cited references especially useful for general knowledge are starred. Additional references are provided in the section "For Further Study," which occurs at the end of each chapter.

In cited court decisions, the name of the case is followed by the volume number, the publication, the page on which the decision begins, and the date. In Chapter 1, item 7, *Shapiro v. Thompson* is found in Volume 394 of the U.S. Supreme Court Reports beginning on page 618. The date was 1969.

CHAPTER 1   Social Work and Society

1 Daniel Schorr, *Don't Get Sick in America*, Aurora Publishers, Nashville, 1970, p. 18.
2 U.S. Bureau of the Census, *Statistical Abstract of the United States, 1973*, p. 218.
3 *Work in America: Report of a Special Task Force to the Secretary of Health, Education, and Welfare*, M.I.T. Press, Cambridge, Mass., n.d., pp. 14–15.
*4 David Caplovitz, *The Poor Pay More*, Free Press, New York, 1967, pp. 25–26.
*5 Henry J. Aaron, *Shelter and Subsidies—Who Benefits from Federal Housing Policies?*, Brookings, Washington, D.C., 1972, p. 5.
6 *A Right to a Decent Home*, U.S. Government Printing Office, 1970, pp. 17–18.
7 *Shapiro v. Thompson*, 394 U.S. 618 (1969).

8 Kenneth E. Boulding, "The Social System and the Energy Crisis," *Science*, vol. 184, April 1974, pp. 255–259.

9 Francis P. Purcell and Harry Specht, "The House on Sixth Street," *Social Work*, vol. 10, October 1965, p. 72.

CHAPTER 2   Public Social Services

1 Charles I. Schottland, "Federal Planning for Health and Welfare," *Welfare Forum*, Columbia Univ. Press, New York, 1963, pp. 97–120.

2 Peter M. Blau, *Bureaucracy in Modern Society*, Random House, New York, 1956, p. 57.

3 *Townsend v. Swank*, 404 U.S. 282 (1971).

4 Directory of State Human Services Agencies, Human Services Institute for Children & Families, Washington, D.C., 1974.

5 Philip Brown, Joseph Julius, and Judith Voelker, "The Department of Human Services, A New Model," unpublished paper, 1973.

6 The 25 jurisdictions that included unemployed fathers in their AFDC program on March 31, 1974 were: California, Colorado, Delaware, Hawaii, Illinois, Iowa, Kansas, Maryland, Massachusetts, Michigan, Minnesota, Nebraska, New York, Ohio, Oklahoma, Oregon, Pennsylvania, Rhode Island, Utah, Vermont, Washington, West Virginia, Wisconsin, the District of Columbia, and Guam. These benefits were formerly offered in several other states.

7 Malcolm X, *Autobiography*, Grove Press, New York, 1965, pp. 17–18.

CHAPTER 3   Voluntary Social Services

*1 For general discussion of voluntarism, see Herman Levin, "The Future of Voluntary Family and Children's Social Work: A Historical View," *Social Service Review*, vol. 38, 1964, pp. 163–173; "The Essential Voluntary Agency," *Social Work*, vol. 11, January 1966, pp. 98–196; and "Voluntary Organizations in Social Welfare," *Encyclopedia of Social Work*, National Association of Social Workers, New York, 1971, pp. 1518–1524.

2 Arthur Kruse, *The Future of Voluntary Welfare Services*, The Community Fund, Chicago, 1965, p. 17.

3 Arthur Kruse, *What the Community Expects of the United Fund*, The Community Fund, Chicago, 1968, pp. 8–9.

4 Donald Brieland, "Black Identity and the Helping Person," *Children*, vol. 16, 1969, pp. 171–176.

5 J. McV. Hunt and L. S. Kogan, *Measuring Results in Social Casework*, Family Service Association of America, New York, 1952.

CHAPTER 4   Social Services in Other Countries

*1 Social Security Administration, Department of Health, Education, and Welfare, *Social Security Programs throughout the World, 1971*, Office of Research and Statistics, Research Report No. 40, 1971.

2 Family Welfare Association, *Guide to the Social Services*, Macdonald and Evans, London, England, 1973. The guide is revised annually and includes data on both statutory and voluntary services.

3 Odin W. Anderson, *Health Care: Can There Be Equity?* The United States, Sweden and England, Wiley, New York, 1973, p. 217.

4 Ivor M. Jones, *Health Services Financing*, Report of British Medical Association Committee, London, England, 1970, pp. 149–156.

*5 Eveline M. Burns, *Social Security and Public Policy*, McGraw-Hill, New York, 1956, pp. 269–278.

6 *Some Data about Sweden, 1972–73*, Skandinaviska Enskilda Banken, Stockholm, Sweden, 1973. The gross national product, hereafter referred to as GNP, is the total national output of all goods and services at market prices. It includes all purchases of goods and services by consumers and government, gross private domestic investments, and net exports of goods and services.

7 Ibid.

8 Derived to compare with Swedish categories as nearly as possible from tables in Alfred M. Skolnik and Sophie R. Dales, "Social Welfare Expenditures, 1972–73," *Social Security Bulletin*, vol. 37, January 1974, pp. 5–11.

9 *Some Data about Sweden, 1972–73*, op. cit., p. 76.

10 European Economic Community, *Report on the Development of the Social Situation in the Community in 1972*, Brussels-Luxembourg, February 1973, p. 8.

CHAPTER 5   Security for the Employed

1 See Frederick L. Nussbaum, *A History of Economic Institutions of Modern Europe*, Crofts, New York, 1933; Karl De Schweinitz, *England's Road to Social Security*, Barnes, New York, 1961; George Coulton, *Medieval Scene*, Cambridge Univ. Press, 1959; and Max Weber, *General Economic History*, Macmillan, New York, 1961.

2 Ralph H. Blodgett and Donald L. Kemmerer, *Comparative Economic Development*, McGraw-Hill, New York, 1956, pp. 125–126.

3 Phyllis Deane, *The First Industrial Revolution*, Cambridge Univ. Press, England, 1965, pp. 84–133.

4 Donald L. Kemmerer and C. Clyde Jones, *American Economic History*, McGraw-Hill, New York, 1959, p. 32.

5 Deane, op. cit.; see also Weber, op. cit.

*6 Paul Samuelson, *Economics*, 8th ed., McGraw-Hill, 1970, pp. 403–405.

7 For discussion of the difference between private and social insurance, see Joseph A. Pechman, Henry J. Aaron, and Michael K. Taussig, *Social Security Perspectives for Reform*, Brookings, Washington, D.C., 1968. An opposing view is given by Robert J. Myers, "Social Security Taxes: Regressivity and Subsidies," *Tax Review*, vol. 24, December 1973, pp. 45–48.

8 "Changing Fortunes of the Small Cities," *U.S. News and World Report*, May 1, 1972, pp. 66–67; and Harry M. Caudill, *Night Comes to the Cumberlands*, Atlantic Monthly, Boston, 1963.

9 See the monthly publication by the Bureau of Labor Statistics, *Employment and Earnings*.

10 President's Commission on Income Maintenance, *Background Papers*, 1970, pp. 178–190.

11 Clair Wilcox, *Toward Social Welfare*, Irwin, Homewood, Ill., 1969, pp. 112–114.

12 Richard A. Lester, "Financing of Unemployment Compensation," *Industrial and Labor Relations Review*, vol. 16, October 1960, pp. 52–67.

*13 John G. Turnbull, C. Arthur Williams, and Earl Cheit, *Economic and Social Security*, 4th ed., Ronald, New York, 1973, p. 235.

14 Gaston V. Rimlinger, *Welfare Policy and Industrialization in Europe, America, and Russia*, Wiley, New York, 1971.

15 Paul A. Brinker, *Economic Insecurity and Social Security*, Appleton-Century-Crofts, New York, 1968, pp. 51–55.

16 For a current summary of congressional legislation and administration, see *1974 Social Security and Medicare Explained*, Commerce Clearinghouse, Inc., Chicago, 1974.
17 "Social Security in Review," *Social Security Bulletin*, vol. 36, September 1973, p. 2.
18 Commerce Clearinghouse, op. cit., p. 20.
19 Eveline M. Burns, *Social Security and Public Policy*, McGraw-Hill, New York, 1956, pp. 33–37.
20 President's Commission on Income Maintenance, op. cit., pp. 191–193.
21 National Commission on State Workmen's Compensation Laws, *A Compendium on Workmen's Compensation*, 1972, chap. 12.
22 See "Congress Readies Pension Control," *Business Week*, Mar. 18, 1972, pp. 66–67; President's Committee on Corporate Funds and Other Private Retirement and Welfare Programs, *Public Policy and Private Pension Programs—A Report to the President on Private Employee Benefit Plans*, 1965; and Special Committee on Aging, U.S. Senate, *Pension Aspects of the Economics of Aging: Present and Future Roles of Private Pensions*, Jan. 26, 1970.

CHAPTER 6   Poverty and Income Security

1 Characteristics of the low-income population were first summarized by the President's Council of Economic Advisers, *Economic Report of the President*, 1964, pp. 56–57. This basic profile has been updated regularly in the *Current Population Reports*, ser. P-60.
2 U.S. Bureau of the Census, "Characteristics of the Low-Income Population, 1971," *Current Population Reports*, ser. P-60, no. 86, 1972, p. 1; and "Money Income in 1971 of Families and Persons in the United States," *Current Population Reports*, ser. P-60, no. 83, 1972, p. 1.
3 Genevieve Carter, *Research in Public Welfare*, Univ. of Southern California School of Social Work, Regional Institute in Social Welfare, 1970, p. 8.
4 See Mollie Orshansky, "Counting the Poor: Another Look at the Poverty Profile," *Social Security Bulletin*, vol. 28, January 1965, pp. 3–29, for discussion of the administration. A criticism of this method is given by Martin Rein, "Problems in the Definition and Measurement of Poverty," in L. Kornbluh and Alan Haber (eds.), *Poverty in America*, Univ. of Michigan Press, Ann Arbor, 1968, pp. 116–131. The absolute poverty line is usually calculated on the basic cost of food for a family of four. This has been considered to require one-third of a family's income. If $1,400 is required annually for a basic diet, then $4,200 would constitute the poverty line. The poverty line rises as the cost of living increases.
5 U.S. Bureau of the Census, "Money Income in 1971 of Persons and Families in the United States," *Current Population Reports*, ser. P-60, no. 85, December 1972.
*6 For a discussion of the social costs of poverty, see President's Commission on Income Maintenance, *Background Papers*, 1970, pp. 13–15.
7 A. Emminghaus (ed.), *Das Armenwesen und die Armengesetzgebung in Europäischen Staaten*, Herbig, Berlin, 1870, pp. 2–10.
8 C. J. Ribton-Turner, *A History of Vagrants and Vagrancy and Beggars and Begging*, Chapman & Hall, London, 1887, pp. 161–182; Blanche Coll, *Perspectives on Public Welfare*, U.S. Government Printing Office, 1969, p. 6;

E. M. Hampson, *The Treatment of Poverty in Cambridgeshire, 1597–1834*, Cambridge Univ. Press, England, 1934, pp. 31–37.

9 George Coode, *Report to the Poor Law Board on the Law of Settlement and Removal of the Poor, Being a Further Report in Addition to Those Printed in 1850*, London, 1851, pp. 16–22, 27–35, 52–55.

10 See *Report from His Majesty's Commissioners for Inquiring into the Administration and Practical Operation of the Poor Laws*, B. Fellowes, London, 1834.

11 Coll, op. cit., pp. 17–18.

12 See Walter Oates, *Fiscal Federalism*, Harcourt Brace Jovanovich, New York, 1972.

13 Paul Brinker, *Economic Insecurity and Social Security*, Appleton-Century-Crofts, New York, 1968.

14 Coll, op. cit., pp. 66–67.

15 Winifred Bell, *Aid to Dependent Children*, Columbia Univ. Press, New York, 1965, pp. 60–61.

16 Gilbert Steiner, *The State of Welfare*, Brookings, Washington, D.C., 1971, pp. 88–94.

17 Joint Economic Committee, *Handbook of Public Income Transfer Programs*, Paper no. 2, Studies in Public Welfare series, October 1972, p. 9.

18 Carter, op. cit.; see also Lawrence Podell, *Families on Welfare in New York City*, Center for the Study of Urban Problems, New York, 1969; U.S. Department of Health, Education and Welfare, *Dependent Children and Their Families: Findings of the 1961 National Study*, 1963.

19 U.S. Department of Health, Education, and Welfare, *Welfare Myths v. Facts*, 1971.

20 Perry Levinson, "The Next Generation: A Study of Children in AFDC Families," *Welfare in Review*, vol. 7, March-April 1969, pp. 5–12.

21 Norman C. Weissberg, "International Welfare Dependency, A Critical Review," *Social Problems*, 1970, pp. 257–274.

22 Perry Levinson, "The Social and Economic Conditions Associated with the Rising AFDC Caseload in New York City," *The Administration of Aid to Families with Dependent Children in New York City*, Report of a Joint Review Council by the U.S. Department of Health, Education and Welfare and the New York State Department of Social Services, September 1969 (mimeographed); Harry Posman, "Poverty and Social Welfare: Research in Public Assistance," *Proceedings of a Conference on Research on Poverty*, Bureau of Social Science Research, Washington, D.C., 1968, pp. 6–9; and Brinker, op. cit., p. 92.

23 *Characteristics of Old Age Assistance Recipients: Highlights of Findings of the 1965 Study*, U.S. Department of Health, Education, and Welfare, May 1967; and Brinker, op. cit., pp. 92, 101.

24 Joel F. Handler and Ellen J. Hollingsworth, *The Administration of Social Services in AFDC: The Views of Welfare Recipients*, Institute for Research on Poverty, Univ. of Wisconsin, April 1969.

25 Merlin Taber and Wayne Epperson, "Flat Grants: A Statistical, Legal and Political Advancement," Illinois Department of Public Aid, July, 1973 (mimeographed); see also Joint Economic Committee, *Income-Tested Social Benefits in New York: Adequacy, Incentives and Equity*, Studies in Public Welfare, Series Paper no. 8, July 8, 1974, U.S. Government Printing Office, Washington, D.C., pp. 155–160.

26 Harold Feldman and Margaret Feldman, *A Study of the Effects of the Family*

Due to Employment of the Welfare Mother, Cornell Univ. Press, Ithaca, N. Y., 1972.

27 Frances Piven and Richard Cloward, *Regulating the Poor*, Pantheon, New York, 1971.

28 Sar Levitan et al., *Work and Welfare Go Together*, Johns Hopkins, Baltimore, 1972.

29 Harold Watts, "Adjusted and Extended Preliminary Results from the Urban Graduated Work Incentive Experiment," Discussion Papers, Institute for Research on Poverty, Univ. of Wisconsin, 1970.

30 Handler and Hollingsworth, ibid.; Harold Yar and Richard Pomeroy, *Studies in Public Welfare: Effects of Eligibility Investigation on Welfare Clients*, Center for the Study of Urban Problems, New York, 1969.

31 "1968 National Interview Study of the AFDC Program," Report to the Social and Rehabilitation Service, Bureau of Social Science Research, Department of Health, Education, and Welfare, 1970.

32 E. Gordon Brown, *The Multi-Problem Dilemma*, Scarecrow Press, Metuchen, N.J., 1968; Edward J. Mullen, Robert Chazin, and David Feldstein, *Preventing Chronic Dependency—An Evaluation of Public-Private Collaborative Intervention with First-Time Public Assistance Families*, Community Service Society, New York, 1969; "Social Services: Do They Help Welfare Recipients Achieve Self-Support or Reduced Dependency?", *Report to the Congress*, June 27, 1973.

33 Joint Economic Committee, *The Effectiveness of Manpower Training Programs: A Review of Research on the Impact on the Poor*, Public Welfare Studies, Series Paper no. 2, U.S. Government Printing Office, Washington, D.C., 1972.

34 Joint Economic Committee, op. cit.

35 Richard M. Nixon, "Welfare Reform: A Message from the President of the United States," House Document No. 94-146, *Congressional Record*, vol. 115, 136, 1969; several other administration proposals are summarized in Theodore Marmor, *Poverty Policy*, Aldine-Atherton, Chicago, 1971, pp. 48–54.

36 For a discussion of many of the cash transfer proposals in the past decade, see Marmor, op. cit.

CHAPTER 7   Health

1 U.S. Department of Health, Education, and Welfare, Social Security Administration, *Delivery of Health Services for the Poor, A Program Analysis*, 1969.

*2 Anne R. Somers, *Health Care in Transition: Directions for the Future*, Hospital Research and Educational Trust, Chicago, 1971, p. 23.

 3 E. Koos, *The Health of Regionsville: What the People Thought and Did About It*, Columbia Univ. Press, New York, 1954.

 4 Data from the National Education Association, Washington, D.C.

 5 U.S. Department of Health, Education and Welfare, *Delivery of Health Services for the Poor, A Program Analysis*, Office of the Secretary for Planning and Evaluation, 1967.

 6 Elaine M. Brody, "Aging," in *Encyclopedia of Social Work*, National Association of Social Workers, New York, 1971, p. 59.

 7 Harold B. Meyers, "The Medical Industrial Complex," *Fortune*, 1970, pp. 79–99 and 150.

8 *New York Times*, Jan. 15, 1973.

9 Eleanor Clark, "Nursing Homes," in *Encyclopedia of Social Work*, National Association of Social Workers, New York, 1971, pp. 886–890.

10 Claire Townsend, *Old Age, The Last Segregation: Ralph Nader's Study Group on Nursing Homes*, Grossman Publishers, New York, 1971.

11 U.S. Bureau of the Census, op. cit.

12 Somers, op. cit., p. 12.

13 Marjorie Smith Muller, *Social Security Bulletin*, vol. 35, 1972, pp. 3–19.

14 *Report of the Task Force on Medicaid and Related Programs*, U.S. Department of Health, Education and Welfare, 1970.

15 Somers, op. cit., p. 100.

16 Martin Cherkasky, "The Hospital as a Social Instrument: Recent Experiences at Montefiore Hospital," in J. H. Knowles (ed.), *Hospitals, Doctors, and the Public Interest*, Harvard Univ. Press, 1965, pp. 93–110.

17 Sidney R. Garfield, "The Delivery of Medical Care," *Scientific American*, vol. 222, 1970, pp. 15–23.

18 Herbert Notkin, "Health Care System: Ambulatory Care," in *Encyclopedia of Social Work*, National Association of Social Workers, New York, 1971, pp. 523–529.

CHAPTER 8   Population and Family Planning

*1 *Population and the American Future: The Report of the Commission on Population Growth and the American Future*, U.S. Government Printing Office, 1972.

2 Rufus E. Miles, Jr., "Man's Population Predicament," *Population Bulletin*, vol. 27, April 1971, pp. 4–39.

3 Donald J. Bogue, *Principles of Demography*, Wiley, New York, 1969, pp. 45–46.

4 Population Reference Bureau, Inc., *1972 World Population Data Sheet*, an annual publication of the Bureau.

5 U.S. Bureau of the Census, "Projections of the United States, by Age and Sex: 1970 to 2020," *Current Population Reports*, ser. P-25, no. 470, 1971.

6 Thomas Frejka, "Reflections on the Demographic Conditions Needed to Establish a United States Stationary Population Growth," *Population Studies*, vol. 22, 1968, p. 382.

7 Rufus E. Miles, Jr., Statement at the hearings of the President's Commission on Population Growth and the American Future, Apr. 15, 1971, *Population Bulletin*, vol. 27, June 1971, p. 13.

8 Harrison Brown, *The Challenge of Man's Future*, Viking, New York, 1954, pp. 145–148.

9 Paul R. Ehrlich and Anne H. Ehrlich, *Population, Resources, Environment: Issues in Human Ecology*, Freeman, San Francisco, 1970, p. 67.

10 Ibid., p. 101.

11 Ibid., p. 65.

12 Ibid., p. 61.

13 Harold Hartley, "World Energy Prospects," in Calder Nigel (ed.), *The World in 1984*, vol. 1, Penguin Books, Baltimore, 1965, p. 71.

14 Ehrlich and Ehrlich, op. cit., pp. 118–119.

15 Ibid., p. 126.

16 Ibid., p. 128.

17 Bernard Berelson, "The Present State of Family Planning Programs," *Studies in Family Planning*, vol. 57, September 1970, p. 2.

18 Ibid., p. 1.
19 "Jumping Population Curve," *The Overseas Hindustan Times*, Apr. 24, 1971, p. 1.
20 Bernard Berelson, "Beyond Family Planning," *Studies in Family Planning*, vol. 38, February 1969, p. 16.
21 Charles F. Westoff, "The Modernization of U.S. Contraceptive Practice," *Family Planning Perspectives*, vol. 4, July 1972, pp. 9–12.
22 Ibid., p. 9.
23 Frederick S. Jaffe, "Low-Income Families: Fertility Changes in the 1960's," *Family Planning Perspectives*, vol. 4, January 1972, pp. 43–47.
24 *Summary of Current Status of Education for Social Workers in Family Planning*, Council on Social Work Education n.d., pp. 13–19 (mimeographed).
25 Ketayun H. Gould, *Provision of Family Planning Services to Welfare Clients*, unpublished study, 1972.
26 Alice A. Varela, "Developing an In-Service Training Program for Social Workers on Family Planning," in Joanna F. Gorman (ed.), *The Social Worker and Family Planning*, Univ. of California Press, Berkeley, 1970.
27 National Center for Family Planning Services, Health Services and Mental Health Administration, *Family Planning Digest*, U.S. Department of Health, Education, and Welfare, March 1972, p. 1.

CHAPTER 9   Education

1 *The Times (London)*, July 23, 1970, p. 9.
2 Edgar Faure, et al., *Learning to Be: The World of Education Today and Tomorrow*, UNESCO, Paris, 1972, pp. 40–49.
3 Martin M. Frankel, *Projections of Educational Statistics to 1982–83*, U.S. Office of Education, Publication # 74-11105, 1973.
4 The President's Commission on School Finance, *Schools, People, and Money, The Need for Educational Reform* (final report), U.S. Government Printing Office, 1970, p. 11.
5 Illinois Bell Telephone Co., *Your Children and the Cost Crisis in Illinois Schools*, Chicago, 1969, p. 7.
6 U.S. Bureau of the Census, *Statistical Abstract of the United States, 1973*, p. 128.
7 The President's Commission on School Finance, op. cit., p. 11.
8 Michael J. Sniffen, *Associated Press Dispatch*, Oct. 16, 1972.
*9 John E. Coons, Stephen D. Sugarman, and William H. Clune III, *Private Wealth and Public Education*, Belknap Press, Cambridge, Mass., 1970.
10 *Serrano v. Priest*, 5 Cal. 3d 584, 96 Cal. Rept. 601 (1971).
11 *San Antonio Independent School District v. Rodriguez*, 411 U.S. 1 (1973).
*12 Norman K. Denzin, "Children and Their Caretakers," *Trans-Action*, July-August 1971, pp. 62–72.
13 Edith Abbott and Sophonisba P. Breckinridge, *Truancy and Non-Attendance in the Chicago Schools: A Study of the Social Aspects of the Compulsory Education and Child Labor Legislation of Illinois*, Univ. of Chicago Press, Chicago, 1917, p. 241.
14 *Tinker v. Des Moines Independent Community School District*, 89 U.S. 733 (1969).
15 Walter Cronkite, C.B.S. Evening News, Oct. 20, 1972.
16 *Associated Press Dispatch*, Oct. 23, 1972.

17 *Associated Press Dispatch*, Nov. 20, 1972.

18 *Brown v. Board of Education of Topeka*, 74 U.S. S. Ct. 686 (1954).

19 James B. Coleman et al., *Equality of Educational Opportunity*, U.S. Government Printing Office, 1966, pp. 22, 302.

20 Lillian D. Wald, *The House on Henry Street*, Henry Hall, New York, 1915, p. 106.

21 Lela B. Costin, "An Analysis of the Tasks in School Social Work," *Social Service Review*, vol. 43, September 1969, pp. 274–285.

22 John Alderson, "Models of School Social Work Practice," in Frank F. Maple and Rosemary Sarri (eds.), *The School in the Community*, National Association of Social Workers, Washington, D.C., 1972, pp. 57–74.

23 Sam Negrin, "Foreword," in Frank F. Maple and Rosemary Sarri (eds.), op. cit., pp. 5–6.

CHAPTER 10   Legal Rights and Protection

1 Illinois Youth Council, *Legal Age Provisions in Illinois*, 1971 (mimeographed).

*2 Homer H. Clark, Jr., *Law of Domestic Relations*, West, St. Paul, Minn., 1968, p. 58.

3 *Loving v. Commonwealth of Virginia*, 388 U.S. 1 (1967).

4 Norman H. Robbins, "Have We Found Fault in No Fault Divorce?", *Family Coordinator*, vol. 22, 1972, pp. 359–362.

5 *Skinner v. Oklahoma*, 316 U.S. 535 (1942).

6 *Griswold v. Connecticut*, 381 U.S. 479 (1965).

7 Edwin W. Tucker, *Adjudication of Social Issues*, West, St. Paul, Minn., 1971, p. 21.

8 *Jane Roe v. Henry Wade*, 410 U.S. 113 (1973).

9 U.S. Bureau of the Census, *Statistical Abstract of the United States, 1973*, p. 54.

10 Harry D. Krause, *Illegitimacy and Social Policy*, Bobbs-Merrill, Indianapolis, 1971.

11 *Uniform Parentage Act*, National Conference of Commissioners on Uniform State Laws, Chicago, 1973.

12 *Stanley v. Illinois*, 405 U.S. 645 (1972).

*13 David Gil, *Violence Against Children and Physical Child Abuse in the United States*, Harvard Univ. Press, Cambridge, Mass., 1970, p. 93.

14 Vincent DeFrancis, *Protecting the Child Victim of Sex Crimes Committed by Adults*, The American Humane Association, Denver, 1969, p. 36.

15 Arizona Revised Statutes, Art. 2, Title 8, Chap. 5, Sec. 8-531, 1974.

16 Elizabeth Elmer, "Abused Young Children Seen in Hospitals," *Social Work*, vol. 5, October 1960, pp. 98–102.

17 *In re Gault*, 387 U.S. 1 (1967).

18 *In re Kent*, 1304 U.S. App. D.C. 343 (1968).

19 *Argersinger v. Hamlin*, 407 U.S. 25 (1972).

CHAPTER 11   Racism

1 Report of the National Advisory Commission on Civil Disorders, U.S. Government Printing Office, Mar. 19, 1968.

2 Richard Hofstadter, *The American Political Tradition*, Knopf, New York, 1948, p. 116.

3 John Hope Franklin, *An Illustrated History of Black Americans*, Time-Life Books, New York, 1970, pp. 40–41.

4 Abram Kardiner and Lionel Ovesey, *The Mark of Oppression: Explorations in the Personality of the American Negro*, World, Cleveland, 1961, p. 365.

5 *Brown v. Board of Education of Topeka*, 347 U.S. 483 (1954).

6 *Plessy v. Ferguson*, 163 U.S. 537 (1896).

7 Stanford M. Lyman, *The Asian in the West*, Univ. of Nevada Press, Reno and Las Vegas, 1970.

8 *The People v. Hall*, 4 California Reports, 399 (1854).

9 Ruth McKee, *Wartime Exile: The Exclusion of the Japanese Americans from the West Coast*, U.S. Government Printing Office, 1949.

10 *Annual Reports of Commissioner of Immigration and Naturalization*, U.S. Government Printing Office, 1943–1971.

11 Bok-Lim C. Kim, "Casework with Japanese and Korean Wives of Americans," *Social Casework*, vol. 53, May 1972, pp. 273–279.

12 Vine Deloria, Jr., *Custer Died for Your Sins*, Macmillan, New York, 1969, p. 171.

13 William S. Willis, "Divide and Rule: Red, White and Black in the Southeast," in Roger L. Nichols and George R. Adams (eds.), *The American Indian: Past and Present*, Xerox College Publishing, Waltham, Mass., 1971, pp. 74–85.

14 Deloria, op. cit., p. 172.

15 Jimm G. Good Tracks, "Native American Non-Interference," *Social Work*, vol. 18, November 1973, pp. 30–35.

16 Charles E. Farris, "A White House Conference on the American Indian," *Social Work*, vol. 18, January, 1973, pp. 80–87.

17 Lydia R. Aguirre, "The Meaning of the Chicano Movement," *Social Casework*, vol. 52, May 1971, p. 259.

18 Tomas C. Atencio, "The Survival of LaRaza Despite Social Services," *Social Casework*, vol. 52, May 1971, p. 267.

19 John F. Longres, Jr., "Racism and Its Effects on Puerto Rican Continentals," *Social Casework*, vol. 55, February 1974, p. 69.

20 Ibid., p. 72.

21 J. Julian Rivera, "Growth of a Puerto Rican Awareness," *Social Casework*, vol. 55, February 1974, p. 86.

22 Ibid., p. 84.

CHAPTER 12   Services for Individuals

1 William Turner, Merlin Taber, and Frank Itzin, "Services for the Aged in Linn County," *Supplement to the Bulletin of the University of Iowa Institute of Gerontology*, vol. 11, July 1964, pp. 3–5.

*2 Carol H. Meyer, *Social Work Practice: A Response to the Urban Crisis*, Free Press, New York, 1970, pp. 103–185.

*3 Alan Keith-Lucas, *Giving and Taking Help*, Univ. of North Carolina Press, Chapel Hill, 1972, pp. 20–21.

4 Frances H. Scherz, "Theory and Practice of Family Therapy," in Robert W. Roberts and Robert H. Nee (eds.), *Theories of Social Casework,* Univ. of Chicago Press, 1970, pp. 219–264.

5 Virginia Satir, *Conjoint Family Therapy*, Science and Behavior Books, Palo Alto, Calif., 1967, pp. 36–37.

6 From a student's case summary.

7 Satir, op. cit., pp. 63-90.

8 The importance of accurate empathy, unconditional positive regard, and genuineness are reported in Charles B. Truax and Kevin M. Mitchell, "Research on Certain Therapist Interpersonal Skills in Relation to Process and Outcome," in Allen E. Bergin and Sol L. Garfield (eds.), *Handbook of Psychotherapy and Behavior Change: An Empirical Analysis,* Wiley, New York, 1971, pp. 299–344; and in Carl R. Rogers (ed.), *The Therapeutic Relationship and Its Impact,* Univ. of Wisconsin Press, Madison, 1967.

9 Alfred Kadushin, *The Social Work Interview,* Columbia Univ. Press, New York, 1972, p. 75.

10 Ibid., pp. 75–76.

11 Harriett M. Bartlett, *The Common Base of Social Work Practice,* National Association of Social Workers, New York, 1970, pp. 65–69.

12 Felix P. Biestek, *The Casework Relationship,* Loyola Univ. Press, Chicago, 1957, p. 17.

13 Truax and Mitchell, op. cit., pp. 299–344; Rogers, op. cit.

14 John E. Mayer and Noel Timms, *The Client Speaks,* Routledge, London, 1970, p. 193.

15 Several writers both within and outside social work have expressed these values. Some of the writings are: Donald F. Krill, "Existentialism: A Philosophy for Our Current Revolution," *Social Service Review,* vol. 40, 1966, pp. 289–301, and "Existential Psychotherapy and the Problem of Anomie," *Social Work,* vol. 14, April 1969, pp. 33–49; Viktor E. Frankl, *Man's Search for Meaning,* Washington Square, New York, 1963.

16 Martin Buber's "I and Thou" establishes the ideal for relationship. See Will Herberg, *The Writings of Martin Buber,* Meridian Books, New York, 1956, pp. 43–62.

17 Kathleen O'Meara, *Frederic Ozanam, His Life and Works,* Catholic Publication Society, New York, 1878, pp. 61–62.

18 Mary E. Richmond, *Social Diagnosis,* Russell Sage Foundation, New York, 1917, p. 31.

19 C. Edmund Maurice, *Life of Octavia Hill,* Macmillan, London, 1913, p. 258.

20 Richmond, op. cit., pp. 134–203.

*21 Florence Hollis, *Casework a Psychosocial Therapy,* Random House, New York, 1972, p. 9.

22 Ibid., pp. 23–24.

23 Ruth E. Smalley, "Social Casework: The Functional Approach," in Robert Morris (ed.), *Encyclopedia of Social Work,* National Association of Social Workers, New York, 1971, p. 1195.

24 The functional approach is also explained in more detail in Ruth E. Smalley, "The Functional Approach to Casework Practice," in Roberts and Nee, op. cit., pp. 77–128, and in Virginia P. Robinson, *Jessie Taft: Therapist and Social Work Educator,* Univ. of Pennsylvania Press, Philadelphia, 1962, pp. 193–342.

25 Helen H. Perlman, *Social Casework: A Problem-Solving Process,* Univ. of Chicago Press, 1957.

*26 Helen H. Perlman, "The Problem-Solving Model in Social Casework," in Roberts and Nee, op. cit., pp. 135–136; and "Social Casework: The Problem-Solving Approach," in Morris, op. cit., pp. 1207–1208.

*27 Lydia Rapaport, "Crisis Intervention As a Mode of Brief Treatment," in Roberts and Nee, op. cit., p. 277.

28 For further review of crisis intervention see Lydia Rapaport, "The State of Crisis: Some Theoretical Considerations," in Howard Parad (ed.), *Crisis Intervention,* and Morris, op. cit., pp. 196–202.

*29 William J. Reid and Laura Epstein, *Task-Centered Casework,* Columbia Univ. Press, New York, 1972.

30 William J. Reid and Ann W. Shyne, *Brief and Extended Casework*, Columbia Univ. Press, New York, 1969.

31 Reid and Epstein, op. cit., pp. 20–23.

32 Richard B. Stuart, "Applications of Behavior Theory to Social Casework," in Edwin J. Thomas (ed.), *The Socio-Behavioral Approach and Applications to Social Work*, Council on Social Work Education, New York, 1967, pp. 19–38.

33 Leonard P. Ullman and Leonard Krasner, *Case Studies in Behavior Modification*, Holt, New York, 1965, p. 1.

34 Edwin J. Thomas, "Social Casework and Social Group Work: The Behavioral Approach," in Morris, op. cit., pp. 1229–1232.

35 Ibid., pp. 1223.

*36 Scott Briar and Henry Miller, *Problems and Issues in Social Casework*, Columbia Univ. Press, New York, 1971, p. 27.

37 Joel Fischer, "Is Casework Effective? A Review," *Social Work*, vol. 18, January 1973, pp. 5–20.

38 Scott Briar, "The Casework Predicament," *Social Work*, vol. 13, January 1968, pp. 5–11.

39 Mayer and Timms, op. cit.; and John E. Mayer and Noel Timms, "Clash in Perspective Between Worker and Client," *Social Casework*, vol. 50, 1969, pp. 32–40.

40 Aaron Rosenblatt, "The Practioner's Use and Evaluation of Research," *Social Work*, vol. 13, January 1968, pp. 53–59; and Robert Foren and Malcolm J. Brown, *Planning For Service*, Charles Knight, London, 1971, pp. 79–88.

41 Richard A. Cloward and Irwin Epstein, "Private Social Welfare's Disengagement From the Poor: The Case of Family Adjustment Agencies," in Mayer N. Zald (ed.), *Social Welfare Institutions*, Wiley, New York, 1965, pp. 623–644.

42 Andrew Billingsley, *The Role of the Social Worker in a Child Protective Agency—A Comparative Analysis*, Massachusetts Society for the Prevention of Cruelty to Children, Boston, 1964; and Harry Wasserman, "The Professional Worker in a Bureaucracy," *Social Work*, vol. 16, January 1971, pp. 89–95.

43 Henry Miller, "Value Dilemmas in Social Casework," *Social Work*, vol. 13, January 1968, pp. 27–33.

44 Frank H. Itzin, "Social Work Education and the Social Work Enterprise," *Child Welfare*, vol. 52, 1973, pp. 277–286.

CHAPTER 13   Services for Groups

1 Helen Harris Perlman, "Social Work Method: A Review of the Past Decade," *Trends in Social Work Practice and Knowledge*, National Association of Social Workers, New York, 1966, p. 84.

2 John W. Drakeford, *Farewell to the Lonely Crowd*, Word Books, Waco, Tex., 1969, p. 3.

3 Arthur Fink, C. Wilson Anderson, and Merrill B. Conover, *The Field of Social Work*, Holt, New York, 1968, pp. 112–115.

*4 Sheldon D. Rose, *Treating Children in Groups*, Jossey-Bass Publishers, San Francisco, 1973, pp. 1–2.

5 John W. Bennett, "Communes: The Oldest 'New' Movement in Western Civilization," *Washington University Magazine*, vol. 41, 1971, p. 21.

6 O. Hobart Mowrer, "Peer Groups and Medication, The Best 'Therapy' For Professionals and Laymen Alike," *Psychotherapy: Theory, Research, and Practice*, vol. 8, 1971, pp. 44–54.

*7   Morton A. Lieberman, Ervin D. Yalom, and Matthew B. Miles, "Encounter: The Leader Makes the Difference," *Psychology Today*, vol. 6, 1973, p. 11.

8   Emanuel Tropp, "The Group: In Life and in Social Work," *Social Casework*, vol. 49, 1968, pp. 267–74.

*9   Robert D. Vinter (ed.), *Readings in Group Work Practice*, Campus Publishers, Ann Arbor, Mich., 1967, p. 2.

*10   William Schwartz and Serapio R. Zalba (eds.), *The Practice of Group Work*, Columbia Univ. Press, New York, 1971, p. 7.

11   Daniel Fullmer, *Counseling: Group Theory and System*, International Textbook Co., Scranton, Pa., 1971; and James K. Whittaker, *Social Treatment*, Aldine, Chicago, 1974.

12   Ruth R. Middleman, *The Non-Verbal Method in Working with Groups*, Association Press, New York, 1968.

13   Jane Addams, *Twenty Years at Hull House*, New American Library, New York, 1960, p. 98.

14   Fritz Redl, *Children Who Hate*, Free Press, Glencoe, Ill., 1951; and *Controls From Within*, Free Press, Glencoe, Ill., 1952.

15   Maxwell Jones, *The Therapeutic Community*, Basic Books, New York, 1953; and *Beyond the Therapeutic Community*, Yale Univ. Press, New Haven, 1968.

16   Gisela Konopka, *Group Work in the Institution*, Whiteside, Inc., New York, 1954.

17   Minnie M. Harlow, "Group Work in a Psychiatric Hospital: Today a Patient, Tomorrow—?", paper presented at the Annual Meeting of the National Conference on Social Welfare, 1960.

18   Werner W. Boehm, "The Nature of Social Work," *Social Work*, vol. 3, April 1958, pp. 10–18.

19   Grace Coyle, "Some Basic Assumptions about Social Group Work," in Marjorie Murphy (ed.), *The Social Group Work Method in Social Work Education*, Council on Social Work Education, New York, 1959, pp. 88–105.

20   Helen U. Phillips, *Essentials of Social Group Work Skill*, Association Press, New York, 1957, p. 97.

21   Gerald L. Euster, "Mental Health Workers: New Mental Hospital Personnel for the Seventies," *Mental Hygiene*, vol. 55, 1971, pp. 283–290.

22   Gerald L. Euster, "The Job Market for Undergraduate Social Work Majors: Implications for Social Work Education," *Social Work Education Reporter*, vol. 21, 1973, pp. 39–44.

CHAPTER 14   Services for Communities

1   Robert Morris and Martin Rein, "Emerging Patterns in Community Planning," *Social Work Practice*, Columbia Univ. Press, New York, 1963, p. 174.

2   Tom Wolfe, *Radical Chic and Mau-Mauing the Flak Catchers*, Farrar, Straus & Giroux, New York, 1970, pp. 144–147.

3   Ralph M. Kramer and Harry Specht, *Readings in Community Organization Practice*, Prentice-Hall, Englewood Cliffs, N.J., 1969, p. 13.

4   Arnold Gurin, "Social Planning and Community Organization," in Robert Morris (ed.), *Encyclopedia of Social Work*, National Association of Social Workers, New York, 1971, pp. 1324–1337.

*5   Joan Ecklein and Armand A. Lauffer, *Community Organizers and Social Planners*, Wiley, New York, 1972.

*6   Jack Rothman, "Three Models of Community Organization Practice," in

Fred M. Cox, John L. Erlich, Jack Rothman, and John E. Tropman (eds.), *Strategies of Community Organization*, Peacock Publishers, Itasca, Ill., 1974, pp. 26–27.

7 Alfred M. Stamm, *NASW Membership Characteristics, Deployment and Salaries. Personnel Information*, vol. 12, May 1969, p. 49.

CHAPTER 15   Other Approaches to Methods

1 Paul L. Schwartz, *"Curriculum for Undergraduate Social Welfare,"* in *Curriculum Building for the Continuum for Social Welfare Education*, State Univ. System of Florida, Tallahassee, 1972, pp. 39–40.

2 Harold L. McPheeters and Robert M. Ryan, *A Core of Competence for Baccalaureate Social Welfare*, Southern Regional Education Board, Atlanta, 1971, p. 13.

3 Ian Westbury, Bernece K. Simon, and John Korbelik (eds.), *Generalist Practice, Description and Evaluation*, Univ. of Chicago, 1973, pp. 24–26.

4 Howard W. Borsuk, "Agency-School Communication: The Influence of Changing Patterns of Education," in Betty Lacy Jones (ed.), *Current Patterns in Field Instruction in Graduate Social Work Education*, Council on Social Work Education, New York, 1969, pp. 51–59.

5 The Policy Institute Program at the University of Chicago is an example of the concentration in policy analysis.

6 Tulane and the University of Illinois at Urbana-Champaign are among a number of schools that have developed programs in social services management.

CHAPTER 16   Children in Need of Protection

1 White House Conference on Children, *Profiles on Children*, U.S. Government Printing Office, 1970.

2 *Child Labor in Agriculture 1970: A Special Report*, American Friends Service Committee, Philadelphia, 1971.

3 Julia Lathrop, "Child Welfare Standards: A Test for Democracy," Presidential Address, Proceedings of the National Conference of Social Work, Atlantic City, N.J., 1919, Rogers and Hall Co., Chicago, 1920.

4 Andrew Billingsley and Jeanne M. Giovannoni, *Children of the Storm: Black Children and American Child Welfare*, Harcourt Brace Jovanovich, New York, 1972.

5 Winifred Bell, *Aid to Dependent Children*, Columbia Univ. Press, New York, 1965.

6 Deborah Shapiro, "Social Distance and Illegitimacy: A Comparative Study of Attitudes and Values," Ph.D. thesis, Columbia University, 1966.

7 Ruth Reed, *The Illegitimate Family in New York City*, Columbia Univ. Press, New York, 1934.

8 Alfred J. Kahn, *Social Policy and Social Services*, Random House, New York, 1973, pp. 74–76.

9 Florence A. Ruderman, *Child Care and Working Mothers, A Study of Arrangements for Daytime Care of Children*, Child Welfare League of America, 1968, p. 127.

10 Ibid., pp. 211–213.

11 Alfred J. Kahn, "Therapy, Prevention and Developmental Provisions: A

Social Work Strategy," in *Public Health Concepts in Social Work Education*, Council on Social Work Education, New York, 1962, pp. 146–147.

12 Norman A. Polansky et al., "Child Neglect in a Rural Community," *Social Casework*, vol. 49, October 1968, p. 468.

13 Zira De Fries, Shirley Jenkins, and Ethelyn C. Williams, "Foster Family Care for Disturbed Children—A Nonsentimental View," *Child Welfare*, vol. 44, February 1965, pp. 73–84; Leon Eisenberg, "The Sins of the Fathers: Urban Decay and Social Pathology," *American Journal of Orthopsychiatry*, vol. 32, January 1962, pp. 5–17; David Fanshel, "The Role of Foster Parents in the Future of Foster Care," in Helen D. Stone (ed.), *Foster Care in Question*, Child Welfare League of America, New York, 1970, pp. 228–240; and Delores A. Taylor and Philip Starr, "Foster Parenting: An Integrative Review of the Literature," *Child Welfare*, vol. 46, July 1967, pp. 371–385.

14 Henry S. Maas and Richard E. Engler, Jr., *Children in Need of Parents*, Columbia Univ. Press, New York, 1959.

CHAPTER 17   Serving the Family

*1 Evelyn M. Duvall, "Family Development Applications: An Essay Review," *The Family Coordinator*, vol. 21, July 1972, pp. 331–333.

2 Paul C. Glick, "The Life Cycle of the Family," *Marriage and Family Living*, vol. 17, February 1944, pp. 3–6.

3 Lillian E. Troll, "The Family of Later Life: A Decade Review," *Journal of Marriage and the Family*, vol. 33, May 1971, pp. 263–290.

4 Chart from the Family Service Association of America.

5 Ellen P. Manser, Jeweldean Jones, and Selma B. Ortof, "An Overview of Project ENABLE," *Social Casework*, vol. 48, 1967, pp. 609–618.

6 Ellen Manser (ed.), *Family Advocacy: A Manual for Action*. Family Service Association of America, New York, 1973.

7 Statistics provided by Family Service Association of America.

CHAPTER 18   People with Emotional Problems

1 William C. Hill, Joseph B. Lehmann, and Elizabeth Slotkin, *Family Service Agencies and Mental Health Clinics: A Comparative Study*, Family Service Association of America, New York, 1971.

*2 Irving Goffman, *Asylums*, Anchor Books, Garden City, N.Y., 1961, p. xiii.

*3 Thomas Szasz, "The Myth of Mental Illness," *American Psychologist*, vol. 15, 1960, pp. 113–118; also see Thomas Scheff, *Being Mentally Ill*, Aldine, Chicago, 1966.

4 D. L. Rosenhan, "On Being Sane in Insane Places," *Science*, vol. 179, 1973, pp. 250–257.

5 J. S. Backhoven, *Moral Treatment in American Psychiatry*, Springer, New York, 1963.

*6 Leonard Ullman and Leonard Krasner, *A Psychological Approach to Abnormal Behavior*, Prentice-Hall, Englewood Cliffs, N.J., 1969, pp. 127–129.

*7 Calvin Hall and Gardner Lindzey, *Theories of Personality*, Wiley, New York, 1957, pp. 29–72.

8 Patrick Mullahy, *Psychoanalysis and Interpersonal Psychiatry: The Contributions of Harry Stack Sullivan*, Science House, New York, 1970.

9 Raymond Glasscote, James Sussex, Elaine Cumming, and Lauren Smith, *The Community Mental Health Center: An Interim Appraisal*, Joint Information

Service, American Psychiatric Association and the National Association for Mental Health, Washington, D.C., 1969.

10   Loren Mosher, John Sunderson, and Sherry Buchsbaum, "Special Report: Schizophrenia, 1972," *Schizophrenia Bulletin*, vol. 7, Winter 1973, National Institute of Mental Health, Washington, D.C., pp. 44–45.

11   "The Psychosocial Treatment of Schizophrenia," *Schizophrenia Bulletin*, vol. 3, Winter 1970, National Institute of Mental Health, p. 4.

12   Franklin D. Chu and Sharland Trotter, *Task Force Report on the National Institute of Mental Health, Part I: Community Mental Health Centers*, Center for Study of Responsive Law, Washington, D.C., 1972.

13   Paul Lowinger et al., "Radical Psychiatry," in Jason Aronson (ed.), *International Journal of Psychiatry*, vol. 9, 1970–71, Science House, New York.

14   O. H. Mowrer, "Integrity Groups: Basic Principles and Objectives," *The Counseling Psychologist*, vol. 3, 1972, pp. 7–30.

15   David Reiss, "Competing Hypotheses and Warring Factions: Applying Knowledge of Schizophrenia," *Schizophrenia Bulletin*, vol. 8, Spring 1974, National Institute of Mental Health, pp. 7–10; also see James C. Coleman, *Abnormal Psychology and Modern Life*, 4th ed., Scott, Foresman, Glenview, Ill., 1972, pp. 329–330.

16   *Report on the XYY Chromosomal Abnormality*, The National Institute of Mental Health Center for Studies of Crime and Delinquency, U.S. Government Printing Office, 1970.

17   U.S. Bureau of the Census, *Statistical Abstract of the United States, 1964*, p. 79; also see *Statistical Abstract, 1973*, p. 79.

18   R. D. Laing and A. Esterson, *Sanity, Madness and the Family*, Tavistock Publications, London, 1964; also see Theodore Lidz, Stephen Fleck, and Alice Cornelison, *Schizophrenia and the Family*, International University Press, New York, 1965.

19   Gregory Bateson, Don Jackson, Jay Haley, and John Weakland, "Toward a Theory of Schizophrenia," *Behavioral Science*, vol. 1, 1956, pp. 251–264.

20   Goffman, op. cit.

21   Scheff, op. cit.

22   Merlin Taber and Anthony Vattano, "Clinical and Social Orientations in Social Work: An Empirical Study," *Social Service Review*, vol. 44, March 1970, p.35.

23   Thomas A. Harris, *I'm OK–You're OK: A Practical Guide to Transactional Analysis*, Harper, New York, 1969.

24   J. B. Watson and R. Rayner, "Conditional Emotional Reactions," *Journal of Experimental Psychology*, vol. 3, 1920, pp. 1–14.

25   B. F. Skinner, *Beyond Freedom and Dignity*, Knopf, New York, 1971.

26   Joen Fagen and Irma Lee Shepherd (eds.), *Gestalt Therapy Now: Theory, Techniques, Applications*, Science and Behavior Books, Palo Alto, Calif., 1970.

27   Carl Rogers, *Carl Rogers on Encounter Groups*, Harper, New York, 1970.

28   Jane Howard, *Please Touch*, McGraw-Hill, New York, 1970.

29   Morton A. Lieberman, Irvin D. Yalom, and Matthew Miles, "Encounter: The Leader Makes the Difference," *Psychology Today*, vol. 6, March 1973, pp. 69–76.

30   Anthony J. Vattano, "Power to the People: Self-Help Groups," *Social Work*, vol. 17, July 1972, pp. 7–15.

31   *Diagnostic and Statistical Manual of Mental Disorders*, 2d ed., American Psychiatric Association, Washington, D.C., 1968.

32   Thomas Szasz, *Psychiatric Justice*, Macmillan, New York, 1965.

33   L. Srole, T. S. Langner, S. T. Michael, M. K. Opler, and T. A. Rennie, *Mental Health in the Metropolis: Midtown Manhattan Study No. 1*, McGraw-Hill, New York, 1962.

34   S. M. Miller and Elliott Mishler, "Social Class, Mental Illness, and American Psychiatry: An Expository Review," in Frank Riessman et al., *Mental Health of the Poor*, Free Press, New York, 1964, pp. 16–35.

CHAPTER 19   The Handicapped

1   H. von Hentig, *The Criminal and His Victim*, Yale Univ. Press, New Haven, 1948, p. 16.

2   *Chronic Conditions and Limitations of Activity and Mobility in the United States, July 1965–June 1967*, Vital and Health Statistics Data from the National Health Survey, ser. 10, no. 61, U.S. Department of Health, Education, and Welfare.

3   Lawrence D. Haber, *Social Security Survey of the Disabled: 1966*, Social Security Administration, U.S. Department of Health, Education, and Welfare, 1968–69.

4   Ibid.

5   National Council on Rehabilitation, *Symposium on the Process of Rehabilitation*, Cleveland, Ohio, 1944, p. 6.

*6   Beatrice A. Wright (ed.), *Psychology and Rehabilitation*, American Psychological Association, Washington, D.C., 1959, pp. 26–28.

7   Harold Russell and Victor Dosen, *Victory in My Hands*, Farrar, Straus & Cudahy, New York, 1949, pp. 4–5.

8   Marie Bell McCoy, *Journey Out of Darkness*, David McKay, New York, 1963.

*9   Christy Brown, *The Story of Christy Brown*, Pocket Books, New York, 1971, pp. 40–41.

10   M. O. Shere, "Socio-emotional Factors in the Family of Twins with Cerebral Palsy," *Exceptional Children*, vol. 22, 1956, pp. 196–199, 206–208.

11   S. Richardson, A. Hastorf, N. Goodman, and S. Dornbusch, "Cultural Uniformity in Reaction to Physical Disabilities," *American Sociological Review*, vol. 26, April 1961, pp. 241–247.

12   Katherine Butler Hathaway, *The Little Locksmith*, Curtis Books, New York, 1942, pp. 41, 46–47.

13   R. G. Barker, B. A. Wright, and H. R. Gonick, *Adjustment to Physical Handicap and Illness: A Survey of the Social Psychology of Physique and Disability*, Social Science Council Bulletin 55, 1946, pp. 55–117.

*14   Beatrice A. Wright, *Physical Disability—A Psychological Approach*, Harper, New York, 1960, p. 259.

15   T. Litman, "The Influence of Self Conception and Life Orientation Factors in the Rehabilitation of the Orthopedically Disabled," *Journal of Health and Human Behavior*, vol. 3 1962, pp. 240–256.

16   R. Kleck, H. Ono, and A. H. Hastorf, "The Effects of Physical Deviance upon Face-to-Face Interaction," *Human Relations*, vol. 19, 1966, pp. 425–436.

17   Fred Davis, "Deviance Disavowal: The Management of Strained Interaction by the Visibly Handicapped," in Howard S. Becker (ed.), *The Other Side: Perspectives on Deviance*, Free Press, New York, 1964, p. 123.

18   National Commission on Architectural Barriers to Rehabilitation of the Handicapped, *Design for All Americans*, Social and Rehabilitation Service, U.S. Department of Health, Education, and Welfare, 1967.

19 Esco C. Oberman, *A History of Vocational Rehabilitation in America*, Dennison, Minneapolis, 1965, pp. 75–77.

*20 James Garrett, "Historical Background," in Malikin, David, and Rusalem (eds.), *Vocational Rehabilitation of the Disabled: An Overview*, New York Univ. Press, New York, 1969.

21 Salvatore G. DiMichael, "The Current Scene," in Malikin, David, and Rusalem, op. cit.

22 *Presidential Documents: Richard Nixon, 1973*, vol. 9, no. 39, p. 1197.

23 *The Regulations Governing the Vocational Rehabilitation Program*, sec. 401.18, 1954.

24 *A National Effort for the Physically Handicapped*, the Report of the President's Task Force on the Physically Handicapped, July 1970, p. 2.

CHAPTER 20   The Offender

1 *Task Force Report: Corrections*, The President's Commission on Law Enforcement and the Administration of Justice, 1967, p. 27.

2 Ibid., p. 167.

3 *The Challenge of Crime in a Free Society*, President's Commission on Law Enforcement *and the* Administration of Justice, 1967, p.44.

4 U.S. Bureau of the Census, *Statistical Abstract of the United States, 1973*, p. 152.

5 Ibid., p. 151.

6 *Task Force Report: Corrections*, op. cit., p. 7.

7 W. C. Reckless and S. Dinitz, "Self Concept and Delinquency," *Journal of Criminal Law, Criminology, and Police Science*, December 1967.

8 L. T. Empey and S. G. Lubeck, *The Silverlake Experiment*, Aldine, Chicago, 1971; J. F. Short and F. L. Strodtbeck, *Group Process and Gang Delinquency*, Univ. of Chicago Press, 1965.

9 H. Treger, "Breakthrough in Preventive Corrections: A Police–Social Work Team Model," *Federal Probation*, vol. 36, December 1972, pp. 53–58.

10 Developed by the author from the National Survey of Corrections and Tabulations from the Federal Bureau of Prisons and the Administrative Office of the U.S. Courts.

11 *Challenge of Crime in a Free Society*, op. cit., p. 169.

CHAPTER 21   The Aged

1 Jessie Bernard, *Social Problems at Midcentury*, Holt, New York, 1957.

*2 Matilda W. Riley and Anne Foner, *Aging and Society, Vol. 1: An Inventory of Research Findings*, Russell Sage Foundation, New York, 1968, p. 18.

3 Ibid., pp. 15–18.

4 M. R. Greene, H. C. Pyron, U. V. Manion, and H. Winklevoss, *Early Retirement: A Survey of Company Policies and Retirees' Experiences*, Administration on Aging, U.S. Department of Health, Education, and Welfare, Administrative Paper No. 17, 1969.

5 Riley and Foner, op. cit., pp. 196–220; and U.S. Department of Health, Education, and Welfare, Social Security Administration, *The Size and Shape of the Medical Care Dollar,* 1971, p. 30.

6 Merlin Taber, *Age and Family Roles in Popular Magazine Fiction, 1900–1950*, 1962 (mimeographed).

*7 Irving Rosow, *Social Integration of the Aged*, Free Press, New York, 1967.

8 Riley and Foner, op. cit., p. 43.

9 Ibid., p. 70, and U.S. Department of Health, Education and Welfare, Social Security Administration, *Resources of People 65 and Over*, 1971.
10 Ibid.
11 Rosow, op. cit., pp. 221–240.
12 Riley and Foner, op. cit., p. 10.
13 Ibid., pp. 195–220.
14 Ibid, pp. 15–38.
15 Ibid., pp. 121–156.
*16 Claire Townsend, *Old Age: The Last Segregation*, Grossman, New York, 1971.
17 Susan Sontag, "The Double Standard of Aging," *Saturday Review: Society*, vol. 55, October 1972, pp. 29–38.
18 Townsend, op. cit., pp. xiii–xviii; see also Mary Adelaide Mendelson, *Tender Loving Greed*, Knopf, New York, 1974, and Donn Pearce, *Dying in The Sun*, Charterhouse, New York, 1974.
19 Elaine Cumming and William E. Henry, *Growing Old*, Basic Books, New York, 1961.
20 Arnold Rose, "A Current Theoretical Issue in Social Gerontology", in Arnold M. Rose and William A. Peterson (eds.), *Older People and Their Social World*, F. A. Davis, Philadelphia, 1965, pp. 359–366.
21 "President's Message on Older Americans: Proposed Strategy to Meet Their Problems," *Aging*, vol. 211, May 1972, pp. 3, 29–31.
22 Ibid.
23 *Annals of the American Academy of Political and Social Science*, vol. 279, 1952, pp. 1–10.
*24 Merlin Taber and Marilyn Flynn, "Social Policy and Social Provision for the Elderly in the 1970's," *The Gerontologist*, 1971, pp. 2, 51–54.
25 Ibid.
26 E. Shanas and others, *Old People in Three Industrial Societies*, Atherton, New York, 1968.
27 E. M. Goldberg, *Helping the Aged: A Field Experiment in Social Work*, Allen & Unwin, London, 1970.
28 U.S. Department of Labor, Bureau of Labor Statistics, 1961. *Salaries and Working Conditions of Social Welfare Manpower in 1960*, National Social Welfare Assembly, New York, 1961.
29 F. Keefer, *A Nutrition Program for Senior Citizens in Public Schools*, Nutrition Ser. 14-K, Administration on Aging, U.S. Department of Health, Education, and Welfare, 1972.
30 Eugene A. Friedmann, "The Impact of Aging on the Social Structure," in Clark Tibbitts (ed.), *Handbook of Social Gerontology*, Univ. of Chicago Press, 1960, pp. 120–244.
31 Leonard S. Cottrell, Jr., "The Adjustment of the Individual to His Age and Sex Roles," *American Sociological Review*, vol. 7, 1942, pp. 617–620 (618).
32 Marvin B. Sussman, "Family Relations and the Aged," in A. M. Hoffman (ed.), *The Daily Needs and Interests of Older People*, Charles C Thomas, Springfield, Ill., 1970, pp. 300–322.

CHAPTER 22   Volunteers and Paraprofessionals

1 Violet M. Sieder, "Volunteers," in Robert Morris (ed.), *Encyclopedia of Social Work*, National Association of Social Workers, New York, 1971, pp. 1525–1534.
2 Joseph Neum (ed.), "People Helping People, U.S. Volunteers in Action," *U.S. News and World Report*, Washington, D.C., 1971, p. 15.

3 David Horton Smith and Richard D. Reddy, "Improving Participation in Voluntary Action," The Center for a Voluntary Society (Occasional Paper No. 1), 1971; and David Horton Smith, "Voluntary Organization Activity and Poverty," *The Urban and Social Change Review*, vol. 5, Fall 1971, pp. 2–7.

4 Laura Sandrolini, unpublished report to the Student Board of Directors, Volunteer Illini Projects, University of Illinois at Urbana, May 1972.

5 Ibid.

6 "A Matter of Money," *Voluntary Action News*, vol. 3, May 1972, p. 4.

7 Daniel Thursz, "Ten Commandments for Volunteers and Professional Staff," *Shifting Scenes*, Newsletter of the Travelers' Aid Association of America, Winter 1970.

8 Donald Brieland, Thomas Briggs, and Paul Leuenberger, *The Team Model of Social Work Practice*, Syracuse Univ. Press, Syracuse, N.Y., 1973, p. 5.

CHAPTER 23   Social Work Education

1 Joan Swift, "Curriculum for Human Services Career Programs in Community Colleges," in Michael J. Austin (ed.), *Curriculum Building for the Continuum in Social Welfare Education*, State University System of Florida, Tallahassee, 1972, p. 37.

2 Joan W. Swift, *Human Services Career Programs and the Community Colleges*, American Association of Junior Colleges, Washington, D.C., 1971, p. 25.

3 Ibid., p. 36.

4 U.S. Task Force on Social Work Education and Manpower, *Closing the Gap in Social Work Manpower*, 1965.

5 "Structure and Quality in Social Work Education," Doc. No. 74-426-1, Council on Social Work Education, New York, 1974 (mimeographed).

6 *NASW Bulletin*, Chicago Chapter, vol. 11, November 1972, p. 8.

7 Council on Social Work Education, *Standards for the Accreditation of Baccalaureate Degree Programs in Social Work*, July 1, 1974.

8 through 14 Examples are from the Jane Addams School of Social Work, Urbana-Champaign.

15 *NASW News*, vol. 18, March 1973, p. 10.

16 Gary Shaffer, unpublished salary data.

17 *Social Workers in 1950*, American Association of Social Workers, New York, 1952, p. 1.

18 U.S. Department of Labor, Bureau of Labor Statistics, *Outlook for Jobs in the '70's*, Washington, D.C., 1972.

19 *Salaries and Working Conditions of Social Welfare Manpower in 1960*, National Social Welfare Assembly, New York, p. 1.

20 Alfred M. Stamm, "NASW Membership: Characteristics, Deployment, and Salaries," *Personnel Information*, National Association of Social Workers, vol. 12, May 1969, pp. 34–45.

21 Grant Loavenbruck, "NASW Manpower Survey Finds Increase in Pay for Most Members," *NASW News*, vol. 18, March 1973.

22 Lilian Ripple, *Statistics on Social Work Education in the U.S., 1973*, Council on Social Work Education, New York, 1973, p. 20.

23 Ibid., p. 22.

24 *Manual of Accrediting Standards for Graduate Professional Schools of Social Work*, Council on Social Work Education, New York, 1971.

25 Ibid., p. 58.

26 Ripple, op. cit., p. 24.

27 *Manual of Accrediting Standards . . .* , op. cit., p. 77.

28 Ibid.

CHAPTER 24 The Minority Practitioner

1 W. E. B. Dubois, *The Souls of Black Folk*, New American Library, New York, 1903, 1965.

*2 Lerone Bennet, *The Negro Mood*, Ballantine Books, New York, 1964, p. 91.

3 William Ryan, "The Social Welfare Client: Blaming the Victim," *The Social Welfare Forum*, 1971, pp. 41–54.

4 Hylan Lewis, "Culture, Class, and the Behavior of Low Income Families," paper prepared for the conference on Lower Class Culture, New York, June 1963.

5 Robert Hill, *The Strengths of Black Families*, Emerson Hall, New York, 1972.

*6 Andrew Billingsley, *Black Families in White America*, Prentice-Hall, Englewood Cliffs, N.J., 1968.

7 Robert Penn Warren, *Who Speaks for the Negro?*, Random House, New York, 1965, p. 405.

8 W. E. B. Dubois, "The Colored World Within," in *Dusk of Dawn*, Schocken Books, New York, 1968.

9 Ben Wattenberg and Richard Scammon, "Black Progress and Liberal Rhetoric," in *Commentary*, April 1973, pp. 35–44.

10 Billingsley, op. cit.

11 William Raspberry, "Black Progress Defined," *Washington Post*, Apr. 16, 1973, p. A-23.

12 Ernesto Gomez, "The Barrio Professor, An Emerging Concept in Social Work Education," in D. J. Curren (ed.), *The Chicano Faculty Development Program: A Report*, Council on Social Work Education, New York, 1973, pp. 101–103.

CHAPTER 25 Social Work Evaluation and Research

1 Malcolm G. Preston and Emily H. Mudd, "Research and Service in Social Work: Conditions for a Stable Union," *Social Work*, vol. 1, January 1956.

2 N. L. Gage, "Theories in Teaching," in E. R. Hilgard (ed.), *Theories of Learning and Instruction*, The National Society for the Study of Education, Chicago, 1964, p. 270.

3 Donald R. Cressey, "Crime," in Robert K. Merton and Robert A. Nisbet (eds.), *Contemporary Social Problems*, Harcourt, New York, 1966, pp. 141–160.

4 The Phi Delta Kappan, *Research Notes*, vol. 53, 1972, p. 327.

5 See Donald T. Campbell and Julian C. Stanley, *Experimental and Quasi-Experimental Designs for Research*, Rand McNally, Chicago, 1963.

6 Henry J. Meyer, Edgar F. Borgatta, and Wyatt C. Jones, *Girls at Vocational High*, Russell Sage Foundation, New York, 1965.

7 Ibid., p. 15.

8 Ibid., p. 8.

9 Alvin L. Schorr, "Mirror on the Wall," *Social Work*, vol. 10, July 1965, pp. 112–113.

10 Mary E. Macdonald, "Reunion at Vocational High," *Social Service Review*, vol. 40, 1966, pp. 175–189.

11 Lela B. Costin, "An Analysis of the Tasks in School Social Work," *Social Service Review*, vol. 43, 1969, pp. 274–285.

12 Ibid., p. 278.

13 Ibid., p. 279.

14 Ibid., p. 280.

15 Edward J. Mullen, Robert M. Chazin, and David M. Feldstein, *Preventing Chronic Dependency—An Evaluation of Public-Private Collaborative Intervention with First-Time Public Assistance Families*, Institute of Welfare Research, Community Service Society of New York, New York, December 1970.

16 Harold A. Larrabee, *Reliable Knowledge*, Houghton Mifflin, Boston, 1945, p. 74.

17 Michael Scriven, "The Methodology of Evaluation," in Ralph W. Tyler, Robert M. Gagne, and Michael Scriven (eds.), *Perspectives of Curriculum Evaluation*, No. 1 in the AERA Monograph Series on Curriculum Evaluation, Rand McNally, Chicago, 1967.

18 Elizabeth Herzog, "Some Guidelines for Evaluative Research," U.S. Government Printing Office, 1959.

19 Robert E. Stake, "The Countenance of Educational Evaluation," *Teacher's College Record*, vol. 68, April 1967, pp. 523–540.

20 Jack C. Bloedorn, "Application of the Systems Analysis Approach to Social Welfare Problems and Organizations," *Public Welfare*, vol. 28, July 1970, pp. 280–290.

21 Charles D. Cowger, "Organizational Theory in Social Welfare: The Budgeting and Cost Effectiveness Example," unpublished paper, 1974.

22 Bernard Bloom, "Human Accountability in a Community Mental Health Center," *Community Mental Health Journal,* vol. 8, 1972, pp. 252–253.

23 Amitai Etzioni, "Mixed-Scanning: A 'Third' Approach to Decision Making," *Public Administration Review*, vol. 27, 1967, pp. 385–392.

Name Index

Name Index

Subject Index

Subject Index

Page references in **boldface** indicate basic discussion.